INTERNATIONAL STUDIES

The End of the Post-War Era

INTERNATIONAL STUDIES

The End of the Post-War Era

Documents on Great-Power Relations 1968-1975

EDITED BY JAMES MAYALL
Senior Lecturer in International Relations,
London School of Economics and Political Science

AND CORNELIA NAVARI
Lecturer in Political Science, University of Birmingham

CAMBRIDGE UNIVERSITY PRESS

Cambridge
London   New York   New Rochelle
Melbourne   Sydney

Published by the Press Syndicate of the University of Cambridge
The Pitt Building, Trumpington Street, Cambridge CB2 1RP
32 East 57th Street, New York, NY 10022, USA
296 Beaconsfield Parade, Middle Park, Melbourne 3206, Australia

© Cambridge University Press 1980

First published 1980

Printed in Great Britain at the University Press, Cambridge

Library of Congress Cataloguing in Publication Data
Main entry under title:
The end of the post-war era.
(International studies)
1. Treaties. 2. International relations — Sources.
3. World politics — 1965—1975 — Sources.
4. International economic relations — Sources.
I. Mayall, James. II. Navari, Cornelia, 1941—
JX68.E5   327'.09'046   79-50512
ISBN 0 521 22698 8

Contents

B. Independent initiatives of the Western Powers

a. France

b. Great Britain

c. Japan

C. Negotiations on Security in Europe

III CHANGES IN THE WESTERN ALLIANCE

A. The North Atlantic Treaty Organization

B. The Eurogroup

Members are: Belgium, Denmark, the Federal Republic of Germany, Greece, Italy, Luxembourg, the Netherlands, Norway, Turkey and the United Kingdom

C. The European Community

IV   THE WARSAW TREATY ORGANISATION

V   THE GREAT POWERS AND THE MIDDLE EAST WAR OF OCTOBER 1973

VI   THE CRISIS OF THE INTERNATIONAL ECONOMIC ORDER

A. The International Monetary System

B. The Framework of International Trade

C. The Question of Energy and Raw Materials

Preface

This collection of documents covers the relations of the great powers between 1968 and 1975, the dates being fixed by the Soviet invasion of Czechoslovakia and the signing of the Helsinki Agreement on European security respectively. In selecting from the very wide range of printed sources available we have kept purely illustrative material to a minimum and printed only those documents which either indicated a change in the policy of a particular country from its established position or recorded a substantive and agreed change in the structure of great-power relations. The coverage in the various sections of the volume is not in all cases, therefore, bound by the period covered by the collection as a whole: if there was no major structural change after, say, 1973 the continuing diplomacy on that subject will not be documented. Even using these criteria we have had to keep the scope of our selection in line with the realities of publishing costs. Where we have been forced to exclude supporting documents to major agreements or material which might have helped to complete the picture, we have cited the appropriate references in the Introduction or in Editor's Notes which are printed following the documents to which they refer. Otherwise we have attempted to keep footnoting to a minimum: as a general rule, cross-references have been confined to documents which fall within the 1968–75 period and which appear in *other* sections of the volume. We have defined the great powers as the five major wartime allies: Britain, China, France, the Soviet Union and the United States, together with their major opponents, Germany and Japan.

We should like to thank John Montagu for his help in preparing the EEC material, David Stafford for his help on the French documents and Margaret Duff for general editorial assistance. In coping with the problems of selection, and of cutting, we have benefited from the expertise of Professor Geoffrey Goodwin, Professor Donald Watt and Dr Michael Leifer. We should also like to thank the staff of the Library and Press Library of the Royal Institute of International Affairs for their assistance and the International Studies Research Division at the LSE for financial support.

Cornelia Navari
James Mayall

Source Abbreviations

Bull. EC	*Bulletin of the European Communities* (Brussels, Secretariat of the Commission)
Bulletin	*The Bulletin* (Federal Republic of Germany, Press and Information Office)
Cmnd.	Command Papers (London, HMSO)
DSB	*The Department of State Bulletin* (Washington, DC, USA Government Printing Office)
Europe Documents	*Europe, Documents, Bulletins quotidiens et*
Europe, Bulletins	*Suppléments* (Brussels, Agence Internationale d'Information pour la Presse)
HC Deb.	House of Commons Debates (Hansard)
OJ	*Official Journal of the European Communities* (Luxembourg, Office for official publications of the European Communities)
SWB	*Summary of World Broadcasts* (British Broadcasting Monitoring Service)
USIS	*United States Information Service* (London, United States Embassy)
WEU *Political Year in Europe*	*A Retrospective View of the Political Year in Europe* (Brussels, Western European Union, General Affairs Committee)

Note on the texts of the documents
Except in a few cases where an unofficial translation has been used, the documents are reproduced in the form in which they were originally published in English, without corrections either of syntax or of sense.

Introduction

For more than thirty years we have grown accustomed to thinking of the history of our times as 'post-war', the war itself standing for most people as a great barrier reef between an international order still dominated by the European great powers and the modern world of nuclear technology and super-power rivalry. In international relations some periods are demarcated by events of such momentous significance that their contours are obvious even to contemporaries. But there are other times when a combination of developments will alter decisively the major relationships involved in international politics, without any such obvious or cathartic break with the past. It is our belief that the period documented in this volume is of this kind. Between 1968 and 1975 a series of developments in the relations of the major world powers transformed the arrangements by which they had been governed since the end of the Second World War. The assumption on which the documents have been drawn together is that these years marked a definitive transition in the history of the contemporary states-system, after which it could no longer be described, except in a purely literal sense, as 'post-war'. It was during this time that the great powers of the wartime alliance against the Axis finally evolved a kind of peace agreement, whose absence had shaped the basic pattern of their relations since 1945. The cold war finally came to an end and in consequence the framework of great-power relations was changed.

The centre-piece of the final Second World War 'peace agreement' involved the settlement of that most intractable of post-war problems — the future shape and political configuration of Germany. The *de facto* division of the former Reich into two states, each welded into and managed by a complex web of alliance relations, was finally confirmed *de jure* at the end of 1971. As a consequence of the German settlement both NATO and the Warsaw Pact were accorded an institutional permanence and, more important, since they were after all familiar features of the post-war scene, an institutional legitimacy. In the period covered by this volume the focus of great-power relations shifted from the confrontation of blocs to an agreement on spheres of influence, an agreement which was to underpin a super-power detente and an extended freedom of super-power action. At the same time, it was to limit and circumscribe the freedom of action of the super-powers' respective allies. If up to 1968 the hope had persisted that the structure of the two blocs might be overcome, and that each ally might find a way to act in a convincing

1

manner outside the framework of the alliances, after 1973 that was no longer the case. The two alliances became, and were recognised as becoming, the long-term living-space of the European states.

The end of the cold war

The turning-point for the settlement of the German question was the Soviet invasion of Czechoslovakia in August 1968, a show of both weakness and strength which demonstrated to the Western powers that there could be no formal territorial revision of the post-war European settlement. Consequently, in a political sense, it also demonstrated that in the future no German leader would be able to use, however vaguely, an appeal to German unification as an obstacle to any East—West detente. Ironically, this was what the Soviet Union had always claimed, namely that a detente could not be achieved without some attention to the anomalous situation created by an unrecognised second Germany with its disputed borders. Until 1968, the detente policies pursued by the governments of France, the Federal Republic of Germany and the United States had all attempted to circumvent what the Soviet government called 'political facts', by which it meant the explicit international recognition of East Germany and its new borders with Poland. Now, in the months that followed the invasion of Czechoslovakia, one after another the Western powers reversed their previous policies which had attempted to by-pass the German problem in favour of a more general relaxation of East—West relations, both politically and economically. Now, although their policies varied, they all focussed explicitly on legal status, borders, and above all on the German question. To these changes in Western attitudes and policy the Soviet Union also responded.

  The first moves were essentially stabs in the dark. The United States attempted to open the question of Berlin (1)[1] while the Soviet Union offered to drop its campaign of vilification against the Federal Republic and to enter into some kind of long-term relationship.[2] But while the invasion appears to have shocked the Western powers into action, the critical event, which was subsequently to act as the linchpin between the various sets of East-West negotiations, had occurred the previous March. This was the speech of the then Federal German Foreign Minister, Willy Brandt, at an SPD party conference on 16 March 1968 in which he signalled a possible willingness to legitimise the Oder—Neisse frontier between East Germany and Poland, an offer which was seized upon by the Polish leader, Mr Gomulka, as a possible basis for the normalisation of relations between his own country and the Federal Republic (2). The significance of this speech was not only to lie in its implications for a real breakthrough in Polish—West German relations. It also signalled the beginning of a process in which the Federal Republic redefined its own position on the question of German reunification. This process was overseen

  1 All bracketed numerals in the Introduction refer to the numbered documents in the collection.
  2 See the speech by Mr Gromyko, the Soviet Foreign Minister, to the UN General Assembly, 3 October 1968: *Soviet News*, 8 October 1968.

by Willy Brandt, when he succeeded to the Chancellorship after the victory of his Socialist Party in the elections of August 1969. The formal redefinition of German reunification, the issue which had been the single greatest obstacle to any recognition of the European *status quo* by NATO, was finally accomplished by Chancellor Brandt's statement of 28 October 1969 (5).

Between 1966 and 1968 there had been a virtual free-for-all in Western policies towards the Soviet bloc. The new West German and American initiatives were still separate and uncoordinated responses to a new situation, but during the summer of 1969 a certain coordination began to emerge. At a meeting in Washington between Chancellor Kiesinger and President Nixon, each agreed to 'pace' his policy towards the Soviet Union against the progress of the others (4). In specific terms, the conclusion of any German—Soviet treaty was to be made dependent on the 'successful' conclusion of the Berlin talks, an agreement which not only meant that the Soviet Union's relations with the Federal Republic were made subject to Soviet behaviour as one of the four occupying powers, but gave the Federal Republic a virtual veto over Four-Power provisions touching on Berlin, whose status it wished to preserve.

Despite being subjected to this exercise in 'pacing', the Soviet Union went ahead. The Soviet leaders agreed to talks on Berlin, which opened on 26 March 1970 (10) allowing the Federal Republic to announce its guidelines for a Soviet—German Treaty in July (13). A text was signed on 11 August, but its final ratification by the West German government awaited a Berlin settlement. What the American—West German agreement had done was to reciprocate, in a context of their own choice, the Soviet insistence on preconditions for detente. If it had to be conceded that no great-power detente was possible which did not include an explicit recognition of the post-war European settlement, nor was it now to be possible to resolve the German problem without preserving the special status of Berlin.

With the evidence of the success of their version of 'linkage' provided by the actual text of a treaty, an overall Western strategy on detente began to emerge. On one level this involved widening the link. Not only was the Soviet—German treaty to be made dependent on a successful outcome to the Berlin negotiations, but Berlin was made the testing ground of Soviet intentions over the whole range of East—West security questions. In the first instance this strategy required the forging of a further link between progress over Berlin and Western agreement to the proposed European Security Conference. This link was established by the NATO communiqué of 4 June 1971 (101). But more generally it also implied a policy of linkage between all East—West issues which were under negotiation, a policy managed through the NATO Council, which emerged after the June meeting as the central coordinating agency for the Western moves towards detente (e.g. 102).

By the summer of 1971 the Soviet Union was subjected to a series of multiple pressures: first, the prospective success of its own normalisation of relations with the Federal Republic; second, pressure applied by its own ally Poland; and third, the prospect of an overall East—West settlement which was being held out as a possibility through the proposed European Security Conference. But the consummation of all these successes depended on the Soviet government in turn legitimising the *status quo* of a divided Berlin. In effect, the tables had been turned. The Soviet leaders rejected any notion of 'links' but acted increasingly as if they accepted their existence.

First the Berlin problem was settled. After difficult negotiations turning essentially on the legal status of the city and the rights of Britain, France and the United States to hold on to their positions in the Western sectors, an agreement was reached in September which publicly acknowledged the legitimacy of the *status quo* and regularised contact between the western part of the city and the Federal Republic (20).

Next, the Soviet leaders tacitly backed the Western strategy against their own East German allies. As part of the Quadripartite Agreements certain measures regarding transit traffic from West Berlin to West Germany were delegated by the Four Powers to be worked out between the Federal Republic and the East German government. Through these provisions, which had to be completed before the Berlin Agreements themselves were complete, full ratification of the Soviet and Polish treaties was linked to the willingness of East Germany to negotiate directly on these matters with the government in Bonn and the West Berlin Senate.

At his meeting with Chancellor Brandt at Erfurt in March 1970, the East German Prime Minister, Mr Stoph, rejected the 'one nation, two states' formula (8). In the context of West German politics this reformulation of the West German position on unification had represented a major policy change, but for the East German regime its implications for the future were too ambiguous, particularly when linked, as it quite deliberately was, to the continuation of a Western presence in Berlin. (For Brandt, of course, the anomalous status of Berlin was the single point of reality in the 'one nation, two states' formula which is no doubt why he fought so hard to have it accepted.) Hence up to the point of the Quadripartite Agreements no progress had been made in the normalisation of political relations between the two Germanies. However, with their accomplishment in September 1971, the context changed dramatically; for the Berlin agreements and the Soviet and Polish treaties all now hung on what was in a sense a continuation of the Erfurt talks, and the Soviet Union had by implication accepted the responsibility for pushing its East German ally into normalising its relations with the Federal Republic. In this way the Western policy of linkage was assuming a dynamic of its own. The transit treaties were agreed on 17 December 1971;[1] the Bundestag ratified the treaties with the Soviet Union and Poland the following May (22), and within two weeks the final protocol of the Berlin Agreements was signed by the Four Powers, bringing them into force (23).

The final phase of the Federal Republic's *Ostpolitik*, as it had become, turned on completing the process of political normalisation, begun by these specific agreements, on the basis of the 'one nation, two states' formula, which despite Stoph's resistance, remained in West Germany the declared policy on which the whole exercise depended. Once again success at the centre was, in a practical sense, to be the precondition of detente further afield. On the normalisation of relations between the two Germanies depended the furtherance of any long-term relations between

1 Not published here; for texts, see *Texte zur Deutschland politike*, Band 9 (German Federal Republic, Bundministerium für innerdeutsche Beziehungen, Bonn, February 1972).

the Federal Republic and Czechoslovakia, Hungary and Bulgaria. Brandt's policy, which emerged during his meeting with Brezhnev at Oreanda in the Crimea in September 1971, was to offer the Soviet Union the prospect of a deepened relationship with West Germany on condition that the Soviet leaders continued to bring pressure to bear on East Germany (21).

For a second time the Western strategy was successful. The treaty between the two Germanies, leaving unresolved the 'national question', was concluded in November 1972 (24). Soviet–West German relations expanded in response (27); a treaty normalising relations between West Germany and Czechoslovakia was signed in December 1973, as were also more limited agreements to enter diplomatic relations with Hungary and Bulgaria (30–32).

By the end of 1973 the Federal Republic's *Ostpolitik* was complete. What remained was the implementation of Brandt's promise to the West Germans, that is, the actual creation of better relations with East Germany, but that was no longer an 'international' question. With the official recognition by the Western powers of the post-war *status quo*, and with the decision by the Federal Republic to recognise East Germany and the borders surrounding it, and to leave West Berlin a protected enclave in the centre of East Germany, the territorial situation in the centre of Europe had been stabilised. Indeed there was probably no more stable set of borders in all of Europe. Given that stability, and so long as they remained independent states, the relationship between the two Germanies was no longer a question with wide ramifications. At least for the time being, the German question had been converted by the *Ostpolitik* into a question for the two German states alone.

Although it had taken two years to formalise this settlement, and although the Western use of linkage had presumably implied the possibility of setbacks, the prospect of a new stability in European relations was already, by the end of 1971, affecting great-power diplomacy. Indeed, the implications of intra-European stability for a super-power detente were recognised almost at once. It is unlikely, for example, that the United States government would have felt free to elaborate such a wide-ranging policy of 'engagement' during the Moscow summit meeting in June 1972, without the stability implied by the Berlin agreements and the Federal Republic's ongoing *Ostpolitik*. Once a European, or at least a German, settlement was in sight, certain benefits, particularly of strategic superiority, could be safely foregone. By the time a treaty between the two German states had actually been achieved at the end of 1972, both sides could agree, as they did during Brezhnev's visit to the United States in the following June, to do their utmost to prevent nuclear war (65).

Throughout the post-war period, Europe had always been the theatre where a nuclear war was most likely. In a sense, it was precisely the super-power freedom to threaten a nuclear exchange over Europe which had imparted, through the mechanism of deterrence, a paradoxical and precarious stability to the unresolved and hence intrinsically unstable European settlement. But with the international acceptance of the two Germanies, the ability of the United States and the Soviet Union to threaten, which had so long held this European instability in place, no longer *had* to be maintained at the cost of their mutual antagonism. There were of course other reasons

besides Europe for Soviet–American tension, but with their traditional battleground
neutralised, there was for the first time the prospect of a super-power condominium;
the outstanding question to be settled concerned the rules of the game between them,
and for the first time the opportunity existed to establish such rules on an essentially
bilateral basis.

In a characteristically American fashion, the Nixon administration opened the
bidding on this issue with a policy of 'positive engagement', which aimed at providing
an overall 'structure of peace'. The Grand Design has been a recurrent theme of
American diplomacy ever since the United States self-consciously accepted the
responsibility of international management after 1945. Whether this latest version
was more than presentation, or rather a way of making political capital out of the
dubious inheritance of some of the policies of the previous administration, is an
open question. In any event, no 'structure of peace' could in fact be built merely
on the basis of a German settlement. The cold war had always centred on Germany
but never been confined there. Thus before there could be any wider normalisation
of international relations, two other legacies of the cold-war period had to be dealt
with. These were respectively the international status of the People's Republic of
China and the Vietnam war.

Although in its new strategy the Nixon administration claimed a link between
the China and Vietnam questions, and indeed was right to do so in the sense that
from 1949 onwards American policy-makers had consistently regarded the spread
of communism as *the* major problem in Asian politics, their implications for great-
power relations were nonetheless quite different. While American hostility to the
Chinese communist regime has its own domestic history which goes a long way
towards explaining the annual veto of Chinese membership of the United Nations,
it is nonetheless possible to argue that during the cold war, China had also been a
victim of a genuine Western confusion between Soviet actions in Europe and the
effects of a worldwide confrontation between 'communism' and the 'free world'.
After all the Sino-Soviet dispute only finally emerged into full public view in the
early 1960s while in the formative years of the cold war the two communist
powers had seemed to follow parallel and indeed concerted policies.

This kind of argument cannot be advanced so easily in the case of Vietnam,
particularly after 1963 when not only was the administration fully aware of the
depth of Sino-Soviet differences, but elsewhere in the third world United States
policy had been modified to accommodate both neutrality in the cold war and,
within limits, anti-Western nationalism. But although in 1960 President Kennedy
had broken, at least so far as his public utterances were concerned, with the moral
fundamentalism of the Dulles era, in Vietnam his administration both accepted the
anachronistic legacy of Dulles' 'undifferentiated globalism' and fatally escalated
American involvement. In doing so they not only committed the country to a long
and debilitating war, which as it turned out the United States could not win, but
also seriously limited their capacity to pursue any wider East–West disengagement,
including any normalisation of relations with Peking. Originally, therefore, Presi-

dent Nixon's proposed 'structure of peace' was not so much a structure of mutually dependent parts, as he claimed, as an umbrella hastily erected in order to rationalise and make coherent what had previously been incoherent and misconceived policies.

It became a genuine structure, however, as the administration pursued two separate but related goals. The first involved ending 'with honour' the war in Vietnam, a goal which was dictated both by an increasingly insistent domestic opposition and by the virtually complete absence of any support from the United States' European allies. Its purpose was to free American policy from the quagmire of subtle dependencies into which an unjustifiable war had thrust it, and so allow the United States a freedom of movement on a global scale which secure borders in Europe were to provide across the European divide. The second, a continuation of the first, lay in reviving America's 'Chinese connection'.

Ending the war in Vietnam appeared to American policy-makers to require a normalisation of Sino-American relations, initially with the limited aim of persuading Peking to put pressure on Hanoi. In this it singularly failed. But by the time it became clear that this limited objective would not be achieved, the admission of the People's Republic into the respectable comity of nations had achieved an importance far outweighing the specific issue of Vietnam. In the new post-cold-war context the Nixon administration conceived a role for China, in which Chinese policy would constitute an opposite pillar to America along the Pacific basin, thus supporting the 'structure of peace' in a parallel manner to the constructive opposition of Soviet and American policies 'over' Europe. In the event, the outcome of Nixon's Chinese diplomacy was considerably more modest than suggested by this somewhat grandiose conception or the disproportionate effort that the American administration expended on its relations with Peking. Indeed, from one point of view, the initiative by the United States could be said to have backfired; little more was accomplished than to place its ally, Japan, in a difficult position *vis-à-vis* detente (see II.B(c)).

But on one point at least, the Chinese action probably did have a bearing on the super-power detente. Ironically, the People's Republic was converted into the foremost supporter of the NATO alliance, the opening to the West reflecting the continued deterioration of Sino-Soviet relations in the East.

Although in retrospect it may seem that the conclusions which the Chinese leaders drew from the Soviet invasion of Czechoslovakia marked a turning-point in the development of Chinese foreign policy, from the public record it is not clear that any fundamental change occurred in the structure of Sino-Soviet relations between 1968 and 1975, and for this reason the exchanges between two states have not been documented in this volume. On the other hand there is no doubt that the gulf between them was further deepened, and Chinese fears confirmed, by the border fighting along the River Ussuri in March 1969. In this case the two sides eventually agreed to hold ministerial negotiations on the boundary; but these were inconclusive and the issue remained unresolved since the Chinese continued to insist that the boundary with the Soviet Union had been imposed on China by Tsarist Russia in a series of unequal treaties during the nineteenth century, and therefore required wholesale negotiation, and more generally that the Soviet leadership had embarked upon expansionist policies in Asia as well as Europe.[1]

Against this background the American initiatives were bound to be viewed with suspicion by the Soviet Union. In the summer of 1972 it was rumoured that the Soviet government came close to cancelling the summit meeting planned for June in protest against the American mining of Haiphong Harbour the previous month.[2] It may reasonably be inferred that their eventual decision to go ahead with the meeting was influenced by the prospect of the United States and China elaborating a special relationship on the basis of the communiqué issued at the end of President Nixon's visit to China in February (39), before the basis of an understanding between the super-powers themselves had been achieved. Within this limited context, then, there appeared to be a genuine dependency between the various elements of the American policy. The United States played off its Far East policy, more by luck than by design, against its relations with the Soviet Union, to assure that the modalities of ending the 'phoney war' did not in fact impede the super-power dialogue. With the ending of the American involvement in the Vietnam war (37) the last vestige of the extended cold war was disposed of. Whether, in the more fluid diplomatic setting that now existed, the emerging detente between all the major powers could be made to yield a new international order – the declared aim of the American design – remained to be seen.

The diplomacy of detente

If the German settlement, the American withdrawal from Vietnam, and a new United States relationship with China underpinned, in varying degrees, the opportunities for super-power engagement, the preparatory debates leading to this engagement were in turn to set the stage for the process of European detente which was to follow it. Although the ending of the cold war freed the super-powers from the need to channel their own bilateral relations through Europe, it neither divested them of European interests nor provided the European powers with a similar freedom in East–West relations. In other words, a new concept of purely European security did not follow automatically from the stabilisation of the *status quo* in the centre of Europe. Not only might the European dialogue never have occurred, but the fact that it did occur owed more to specific concerns of the super-powers in their relationship to one another, than to any new freedom of action in Europe.

1 On the development of the Sino-Soviet dispute, see John Gittings (ed.) *The Sino-Soviet Dispute 1956–63* (London, 1964), and *Survey of the Sino-Soviet Dispute: a commentary and extracts from the recent polemics* (London, 1968). For the exchanges on the Ussuri border incident, see statements by the Soviet government, 29 March, 13 June 1969 (*Soviet News* 1 April, 17 June 1969), and statements by the Government of the People's Republic of China, 24 May, 7, 8, October 1969 (*Peking Review* 30 May, 10 October 1969).
2 For the text of President Nixon's address on American radio and television on 8 May 1972 in which he announced this decision, see *DSB*, 29 May 1972 pp. 747–50.

It was super-power concerns which not only made a dialogue including the Europeans necessary but which determined the framework and ultimately the outcome of that dialogue.

In a fundamental sense this interweaving of the two detente exercises reflected the fact that unlike the United States, the Soviet Union was, after all, a European as well as a super-power. The Soviet Union and its allies had renewed and indeed intensified pressure for a generalised European security conference (91) aimed both at legitimising the existence of an Eastern bloc and at achieving an agreed set of guidelines on relations between the blocs. These proposals were rejected by the NATO alliance which put forward a counter-proposal aimed at silencing them (95). The Western proposal was for specific security guarantees which would result from negotiations between the two blocs on force reductions, a proposal which in turn the Soviet Union would not accept (96). The two levels of negotiations (i.e. those on Mutual Balanced Force Reductions — MBFR — and the proposed European Security Conference — ESC) into which the issue of European security was to be channelled at the end of 1972, were initially counter-proposals, contrary and mutually exclusive. It became clear that any specifically European detente was likely to be checked by a dispute between the Soviet Union and the Western powers concerning the precise subject-matter of any negotiations which might take place between them.

The break in the ensuing deadlock was foreshadowed in the winter of 1970—1 during the preliminary manoeuvring over the question of talks between the two super-powers on strategic arms limitation (SALT). Since the United States had first proposed some form of limitation talks in the late 1960s, negotiations had been impeded — indeed the negotiations scarcely got off the ground — by the Soviet refusal to consider anything less than the total strategic deployment against it, and in particular the existence of forward-based missiles in Europe. Then, in late March 1971, without any apparent warning, the Soviet Union changed its policy on MBFR (99) and the United States responded by announcing, in two statements on 17 and 20 May, what amounted to a compromise (100 and 49). It now appeared that the Soviet Union would agree to some form of MBFR nego- tiations, and by implication treatment of forward-based missile systems within that context, while SALT would concentrate on anti-ballistic-missile (ABM) systems and some form of strategic arms limitation. In other words, the Soviet Union com- mitted itself to discussing force reductions in Europe as the means of achieving what it could not achieve in SALT, while the United States, if it had not been entirely serious up to that point in proposing the MBFR talks, now accepted their necessity as the means of ensuring that SALT might proceed without sacrifice to the interests of Alliance defence. The results of this compromise were SALT I, the first-stage strategic arms limitation agreements, which were signed at the Moscow summit in May 1972 (55) and a long-term and less specific understanding that the two sides would enter into negotiations for some form of mutual force reductions in Europe (58).

If the dialogue with the United States had forced the Soviet government to a commitment to negotiate on force reductions in Europe, the contrary commitment by NATO to a security conference was slower to evolve. Having implicitly abandoned force reductions as a precondition of their participation in a security conference (since these talks were now to occur anyway) the alliance insisted on a successful conclusion to the Berlin negotiations as a further and explicit precondition, thus again postponing their final decision. The Western powers also pressed the Soviet government for an early start to the force reduction talks by announcing their intention to appoint a NATO ambassador to them and making it clear that they wished to see them under way before they committed themselves finally on the ESC (101). But the grounds on which the postponement was justified also implied that once the Berlin agreements had been concluded, the alliance would have to adopt a more positive attitude towards the conference, as was recognised, for example, by United States Secretary of State Rogers in his speech to the Overseas Writers' Conference at the beginning of December 1971.[1] The final NATO agreement appeared in a ministerial meeting communiqué the following May (102).

Having finally accepted that the question of European security should be handled in two separate sets of negotiations, the Western allies appeared anxious to establish a direct link between them, the tactic they had already employed successfully over Germany. On the same day that the American government accepted the Finnish invitation to participate in the ESC,[2] the alliance issued an invitation to the Warsaw Pact countries to begin the MBFR talks (103). By implication it made the beginning of each set of negotiations, and subsequently perhaps their progress, dependent on the other. But although, in December 1972, the NATO Council 'reaffirmed their view that progress in each set of the different negotiations would have a favourable effect on the other',[3] and it was rumoured that a link would be made explicit, none appeared. Indeed a Security Conference document was to be completed and implemented before any substantive progress was recorded in the MBFR talks (cf. 104 and 107).

The first reason for this lay in the implication of the super-power detente for the European balance of forces. As the prospect of nuclear war in Europe receded, the European balance came increasingly to depend on conventional armaments and the number of troops deployed by each side.[4] Secondly, during 1973, i.e. even before the changed status of the European balance had been generally acknowledged, a subtle reversal of positions occurred. This reversal cannot be directly documented but it was reflected in the increasing attention which the NATO allies paid to the ESC and the Soviet Union to the MBFR talks. On the one hand NATO came to regard the ESC, rather than force reductions, about the prospects of which they were increasingly dubious, as the best mode for overcoming the rigidity of interbloc relations. On the other, the Soviet government increasingly came to regard

1 For text, see *DSB*, 20 December 1971, pp. 694–5.

2 For the text of the American note to the Finnish Ministry of Foreign Affairs of 16 Novembe 1972, see *DSB*, 4 December 1972, p. 660.

3 Communiqué of the NATO Council, Brussels, 8 December 1972. For text, see *DSB*, 1 January 1973, pp. 1–4.

4 See below, pp. 12–14.

the MBFR talks as the context within which the future relations of the blocs might be determined.

Since, on the Soviet side, their primary objective, the legitimation of the existing bloc structure, was being accomplished in any case by the legitimation of the *status quo* in the centre of Europe, the ESC was no longer strictly necessary. Nothing that occurred between mid-1973 and the signing of the Final Act of the Security Conference on 1 August 1975 (107) suggests that this assessment was mistaken. With the constant pressure of the Western powers to open up East–West relations at other than the official level, the Soviet leadership evidently regarded the MBFR negotiations, and the bloc-to-bloc form which these took, as less dangerous and as offering more possibilities to improve the position of the Warsaw Pact. As for the Western powers, their growing opposition to MBFR, signalled, as so often was the case, by the French earlier than the others, and their increasing enthusiasm for political conferences, were reflections of the profound changes which detente was working upon the Western alliance, changes which were already making them politically insecure and which, in the end, were to make them more insecure militarily as well.

The Western alliance in the era of detente

The first change in the alliance could be summed up as stabilisation. The invasion of Czechoslovakia called an immediate halt to the fissiparous tendencies which had marked the alliance during the previous two years. The immediate reaction to the invasion within the alliance had been a renewal of political commitments (108) and a widening of its political – as opposed to its military – base (109, 110).

As a result of this development, the independent great-power initiatives tended to fade away. After 1968, the powers used the NATO Council as the channel through which they articulated their policies on East–West relations. In the Council these were generally amalgamated into single positions to which the alliance as a whole was committed. Although the nine members of the European Community put forward the Western negotiating position at the ESC,[1] this largely reflected the United States' determination to adopt a 'low profile' towards the conference, and the position still had to be cleared through NATO. The Nine were merely acting as the authorised agency of the NATO Council. Detente and security were both essentially bloc-to-bloc.

France, while still a member of the alliance, had left the integrated military organisation in 1966. But French activity in the years under review – for example the agreement of principles of cooperation with the Soviet Union in October 1971 (75) – was not, despite appearances, in contradiction to the stabilisation of the alliance. French successes were posited on NATO successes; the environment which made them feasible was one in which everyone recognised that security was essentially an inter-bloc question. The French government's Eastern initiatives were no longer regarded, even by the French themselves, as competitive with those of the other

1 See footnote 1, p. 276; Document No. 102.

Western powers. After the invasion of Czechoslovakia, and the May riots in France itself, which had revealed the illusory nature of French 'independence' from the Western system, there was no attempt to return to the 'free rider' policies which had been the hallmark of de Gaulle's later presidency. The continued development of the opening to the East, which he had pioneered, was now regarded by his successors as complementary to the coordinated Western approach, or at most as a way of keeping open the option of a renewed independence against an uncertain future.

In a sense, of course, even this echo of Gaullist policy continued to mark the French government as the 'odd man out' in the alliance. But the gap between France and her allies had nonetheless narrowed. Rather than continuing an independent French '*Ostpolitik*', for which there was no longer any political room, the French Presidents returned to the traditional Gaullism of the early 1960s and challenged Western orthodoxies from within. The old frustration with American leadership and suspicion of Anglo-Saxon intellectual and political assumptions remained, but French dissidence was now dissidence *within* Atlantic councils, aimed, for example, at dispelling the monetary power of the United States (179), setting up a separate European dialogue with the Arab oil producers (203, 204) and reforming the enlarged EEC.[1] French policy now appeared to take the long-term existence of the NATO framework granted.

The second, and perhaps more significant, change in the Western Alliance after 1968 was the tightening and improvement of its defence planning and structure. The period under review was marked not only by the increasingly frequent meetings of the Nuclear Planning Group and the Defence Planning Committee (DPC), but by the use of these forums, especially the latter, for increasingly important decision-making (116, 119). Indeed, the full Council meetings often merely rubber-stamped DPC decisions.

The shock of the invasion of Czechoslovakia was not the only or even the primary, reason for defence improvements. Paradoxically, these were also part of the fabric of the renewed detente itself. The tightening of the NATO defence structure was necessary both because an East—West detente was posited on the basis of an ongoing alliance structure, and more to the point, perhaps, because some improvement in Western defences was required by the specific agreements emerging from it. The more restrained the super-powers became in their nuclear relationship, the more *both* alliances were forced into a more realistic assessment of their *conventional* capabilities *vis-à-vis* one another, and of the military requirements for actually fighting a ground war. In other words the deterrent was becoming conventionalised, and the balance of power was entering a new, and not entirely foreseen, phase.

The greater importance of the alliance, politically and militarily, contributed to a resurgent Europeanism throughout Western Europe. In the post-war history of Western Europe there has often been an apparently dialectical opposition between the rival conceptions of Western political organisation represented by Europeanism and Atlanticism respectively. In reality, however, this dialectic has always been

1 See below, pp. 13—15.

strictly contextual. Deep as the opposition has undoubtedly been, it was always on the question of how to organise relations within the alliance, that is within the Atlantic framework, not on whether it should be abandoned altogether. In this sense Europeanism always presupposed Atlanticism. Indeed, European experimentation had always been at its strongest when strategic and political considerations required the strengthening of alliance bonds, as in the period between 1958 and 1963, when confrontation over Berlin forced upon the alliance the need for strict coordination, and at its weakest when the powers were free to act independently, as appeared to be the case increasingly between 1964 and 1968. This complementarity between the alliance and Europe was displayed to the full in the renewed interest in Europeanism following the invasion of Czechoslovakia. Implying as it did that East would remain East and West would remain West, the invasion triggered off an immediate effort on the part of the Western Europeans to repair the damaged Europeanism which their previous squabbles had left behind. If the alliance was henceforth to be their allotted living-space, it behoved them finally to decide on the arrangement of the political furniture.

Their shared desire to give a renewed impetus to the political reorganisation of Western Europe did not prevent the powers from returning to their historic quarrels about *how* to reorganise it, and, more specifically, on which institutional base. The European Economic Community had always had the strongest claim to be considered as the home of the European idea, but President de Gaulle's vetoes of British entry to the EEC in 1963 and 1967 ruled this out at the start; it was, therefore, to the WEU that the other five EEC states first turned under the initial leadership of the Italian and Belgian governments.[1] De Gaulle refused to consider such a use of the WEU, boycotted the organisation and proposed instead a plan of his own. The French plan, which was mooted privately to the British ambassador in Paris, was in a sense a revival of the plan the British had themselves proposed in the mid 1950s as an alternative to the EEC, and envisaged the creation of a new free-trade area embracing the four major European powers, France, Germany, Italy and Britain. In de Gaulle's version, however, the new organisation would be underwritten by a special Anglo-French entente.[2] President de Gaulle, it seemed, was prepared to countenance British 'entry', albeit in a different institutional form. With their eyes still firmly fixed on the Community, the British government refused to consider the plan and made it public.[3] As a result, the attempt to establish a new European dispensation remained in stalemate until President de Gaulle's retirement several months later, when his successor, President Pompidou, broke the deadlock by agreeing to reopen negotiations on British entry into the EEC.[4] Europeanism was now to be firmly rooted in the Community.

1 See the Italian Government proposals submitted to the Council of the WEU, 6 February 1969 (WEU, *Political Union, 1963–73*, pp. 76–7).

2 See the communiqué issued by the French Ministry of Foreign Affairs, 14 February 1969 (WEU, *Political Union, 1963–73*, p. 78).

3 See the statement to the House of Commons by Mr Stewart, British Secretary of State for Foreign and Commonwealth Affairs, 24 February 1969 (HC Deb., vol. 778 cc. 1088–9).

4 See press conference by President Pompidou, Paris, 10 July 1969 (WEU, *Political Year in Europe, 1969*, pp. 109–10).

Parallel with the decision to enlarge the European Community there was also a
new initiative for identifying and asserting a specifically European interest in the
defence field, an area from which Europeanism had been excluded since the collapse of the European Defence Community (EDC) in 1954, and in which the
powers had therefore had to make do with the existing 'Atlantic' machinery of
NATO, and with political coordination within the WEU. In March 1969, the
British Defence Minister, Mr Healey, proposed an *ad hoc* meeting of European
Defence Ministers which became known as the Eurogroup, an informal European
defence organisation statutorily separate from NATO, but with the task of coordinating and improving the West European military contribution to NATO
defences (121). Initially, the aims were not entirely clear, but the function which
the Group was to perform became obvious as the alliance stabilised in response
to the new fluidity in intra-European and East–West relations. It was to set the
terms for the increasingly European conventional base of the deterrent.

The establishment of the Eurogroup provides a striking illustration of the way
in which, during the period covered by this volume, the Western powers openly
acknowledged the symbiosis rather than opposition between the European and
Atlantic ideas of political organisation. For while the proposed enlargement of
the EEC reflected the search both for a 'European' stance in international diplomacy
and for the means of making it felt, and so made the Eurogroup a logical development, the West's European defences did not always run together with Community
boundaries even after enlargement. Thus, while in some contexts (for example,
as we have seen, in proposing their agenda for the ESC) the nine EEC member
countries could speak for the alliance, the Eurogroup included three NATO countries,
Greece, Norway and Turkey, which were not members of the Community, while
it still excluded one of the major EEC states, France, as well as Iceland and Portugal.
As on previous occasions when the alliance had been under pressure, the renewed
debate about European unification between 1969 and 1971 complemented, over-
lapped with and was made possible by an equally energetic development of the
alliance and rationalisation of its structure. Over these years, indeed, NATO evolved
an increasingly complex division of labour. There was the Nuclear Planning Group
for the discussion of overall nuclear strategy, an activity which essentially involved
the allies in listening to American strategic revisions; the Defence Planning Committee which became increasingly important for planning NATO's overall conventional
strategy; and the Eurogroup where the Europeans registered their particular concerns
within the strategy set by the Defence Planning Committee.

When the European Heads of State met at the Hague in December 1969 (128),
the final seal was set on the European settlements with the formal agreement to
embark on British entry to the EEC. Implying as this did a break in the long deadlock over the political management of the Community, itself the result of the dispute
between France and the other five original member states over British entry, the
effect of these agreements in turn was to clear the malaise which had settled on the
institutional structure of the Community after the original French veto six years
previously. Agreements now came thick and fast. The following April (1970), final

agreement was reached on providing the Community with its own resources, thus completing the outline of the Common Agricultural Policy (CAP) (130); a budgetary compromise was reached which referred back to the 1965 crisis (when the French had first boycotted the Council of Ministers over the issue of majority voting) (131), and the first report on political union was agreed (132), providing for the co-ordination of members' foreign policies. By the following September an agreement had been reached in principle on the establishment of an Economic and Monetary Union. Finally, in October 1972, the new Community spirit was given its fullest expression – indeed reached its high point at the Paris summit meeting of the Heads of State of the englarged EEC. The Summit took the Community into some thirty-five new policy areas and crowned this achievement by dedicating the EEC, in somewhat cavalier and utopian fashion, it must be admitted, to full economic and monetary union by 1980 (134 and 135).

But if, by the end of 1972, Europe was finally poised for 'take-off', the political and economic setting within which the machinery had been designed had also changed. This situation was paradoxical: the coordination of European defence policies depended on *changes* in the overall strategic environment and in particular on the resolution of differences across the European divide, but the implementation of the Western European commitment to economic, monetary and political union depended on the maintenance of the *status quo* in the Western international economy, or at least on the orderly handling of its various long-standing problems within the existing structure. Unfortunately for the Europeans, the shocks to which all the major powers – and indeed the world as a whole – were subjected between 1971 and 1974 were administered in areas which were covered by Community agreement but where the Europeans were to prove extremely vulnerable, and where the Community proved not complete enough and the member states not self-sufficient enough to adapt their policies. The effect of these shocks, therefore, was to halt the Community itself at the moment when ironically the institutional questions had finally been settled.

The first shock came with the increasing disruption of Western monetary relations. The problem had been maturing for more than a decade, indeed ever since 1958 when the post-war recovery of the West European states had allowed them to establish – on the basis of fixed exchange rates – the system of convertibility between the world's major currencies which had been originally planned at Bretton Woods, New Hampshire, in 1944. When the crisis broke in August 1971 it revolved around two features of this Bretton Woods settlement. The first, which was central to the operating philosophy of the whole system, concerned the separation of functions between the three institutions, the International Monetary Fund (IMF), the International Bank for Reconstruction and Development (IBRD), and the General Agreement on Tariffs and Trade (GATT), which were set up to manage the international economy. In other words, while the basic objective of all three institutions was the same, namely the support of an open liberal international economy, there was to be no direct linkage between their activities. The progressive liberalisation of trade through the GATT was thus not to be made dependent on agreeing specific international monetary reforms within the IMF, or vice versa. Even less were trading or monetary concessions to be exchanged for political concessions within the Atlantic Alliance. Stalin had regarded the Bretton Woods system as nothing more than the economic infrastructure of the Western Alliance, and on these grounds prevented East European participation, but in conception it was a universal, not an Atlantic, arrangement.

The second feature of the Bretton Woods system involved in the 1971 crisis concerned the role of the United States. The alleged universality of the system had never concealed its dependence on United States leadership. Under the gold exchange standard which developed after 1945 there was a sense in which, in the absence of an international central bank, the United States occupied that role. In practical terms what this meant — or rather had always been assumed to mean — was that the United States could not devalue the dollar, in terms of which all other currencies were ultimately denominated, and which remained pegged to gold at thirty-five dollars an ounce, thus providing foreign governments with the guarantee that their reserve dollar holdings were 'as good as gold'. This system had evolved during the period of acute dollar shortage so that any potential political difficulty arising from the dollar's twin roles — as a major trading and a reserve currency — had at first been masked. But throughout the 1960s the United States had run a large and persistent balance-of-payments deficit which duly exposed the tension between these two functions and provoked the European powers, and particularly France, to demand its reversal as a prior condition of international monetary reform.

At the heart of the long debate over monetary reform was a dispute over liquidity, the volume and source of new assets required to finance the continued expansion of world trade. Although the rival positions in this debate cut across national boundaries, in broad terms there had always been a division of both interest and philosophy between the reserve currency states, the United States and Britain, and the continental Europeans. While it was generally agreed that the persistence of the United States deficit undermined confidence in the system, there was no agreement on the effects of its early removal. Successive American administrations favoured moving the system away from its dependence on gold, and creating, by international agreement, a new reserve asset to replace gradually the dollars which, so long as the American balance of payments was in deficit, provided the major new source of international liquidity. Against this position was ranged a contrary view, namely that the creation of new assets would fuel inflation and merely provide an excuse for the United States and Britain to delay necessary domestic reforms. As on other issues of intra-alliance relations, the French government carried the argument for monetary discipline even further than the other European states by advocating a return to the gold standard and the abandonment of the reserve currency system altogether.

The fact that the United States had committed itself to the elimination of its deficit as long ago as 1963 did not solve the the continental European dilemma: how to ensure that world trade, in which after all the European states had an interest, would continue to expand if and when the supply of new dollars dried up? The French might continue to argue that the problem could be handled when the time came by a simple increase in the gold price (a measure which it was believed would both favour France and limit the freedom of action of the United States) but for the other major powers, and particularly for the Federal German Republic with its traditional sensitivity to American policy and opinion, this was never a serious option. Thus it was that negotiations were eventually started which led in 1967 to the decision to create Special Drawing Rights (SDRs), a new asset for use in both international settlements and official reserves,[1] and in 1968 to the first cautious moves to demonetise gold (175).

But if these measures represented a victory for the American view of monetary reform in the long run, the immediate problem, that is, the persistence of the United States deficit, proved much more intractable. Despite repeated assurances from Washington that the government was determined to eliminate it, by 1970 the deficit was larger than ever. More alarming still, in that year there was a change in its character: for the first time the deficit was not merely on capital account (that, after all, could reasonably be regarded as evidence of the strength of the United States' economy), but there was now also a deficit in visible trade, evidence, in the administration's view, that the dollar was over-valued as a trading currency. But if as banker to the whole system the United States government was prevented from taking the final corrective step, namely to devalue the dollar, it followed, in their view, that America's Western allies should share the burden of management by realigning the exchange rates of their own currencies to achieve the same effect. Indeed, it was a recurrent theme in American thinking that this kind of 'burden-sharing' should feature more prominently in the activities of the alliance (see, for example, 111); in other words, despite the official doctrine of functional separatism which had kept the Bretton Woods system out of alliance politics, the Americans implicitly argued as though it was a responsibility of the alliance to maintain this essentially fictitious separation.

The West Germans acted as though they accepted this proposition, at least partially, although in revaluing the mark in 1969 and then allowing it to float in May 1971, they were acting as much to check the massive and unwanted inflow of hot money (itself a reflection of the rapidly declining confidence in the dollar) and to curb domestic inflation, as from a desire to help the United States out of its difficulties. Moreover, now that the dispute concerned trade as well as money, the Germans were not in a position to offer any more than the EEC could concede

1 The decision to create a 'Facility Based on Special Drawing Rights in the International Monetary Fund' was taken during the annual meeting of the Fund in Rio de Janeiro in September 1967. The Executive Directors submitted detailed proposals to the Governors for amendments to the Articles of Agreement on 17 April 1968. These were approved on 31 May 1968 and entered into force on 28 July 1969. The first allocation ($3.5 billion) of SDRs was made in 1970. For the text of the 1967 resolution, and of the Report by the Executive Directors to the Governors of the Fund and the Amendments to the Articles of Agreement, see J. K. Horsefield (ed.) *The International Monetary Fund, 1945—65* (IMF, Washington, 1969), pp. 497—541.

collectively. The trouble here was the American tendency to argue that its trade deficit was partly the result of EEC protectionism and of the CAP in particular. This charge was repeatedly repudiated, although in an attempt to turn the tide of American criticism the Community did make a unilateral offer on agricultural trade in June 1971 (188).

If this move was intended to signal the Community's acceptance of 'burden-sharing', at a time when the American commitment to Western Europe was no longer as automatic as in the past, from the American point of view it probably seemed too little too late. Moreover, it was not merely a bilateral Atlantic problem but involved the triangular relationship between the United States, Japan and Western Europe. In recent years the Japanese had made heavy inroads into the American market, a development which the administration regarded both as a problem in its own right and as at least partly the fault of the Europeans, who they believed had not taken their fair share of low-cost Japanese imports. In any event the Community offer failed to deter the administration from forcing the economic crisis into the open. When, on 15 August 1971, President Nixon suspended the convertibility of the dollar and imposed a ten per cent surcharge on all imports pending a realignment of the major currencies and a fundamental overhaul of the whole monetary system (177) he not only broke with the Bretton Woods system in its original form but also extended 'linkage' politics, which had hitherto been as taboo in Western economic relations as the idea of dollar revaluation, to the Western Alliance itself.

The Community's reaction was predictably hostile but not exclusively so (178). The truth was, as the European states were all aware, that neither individually nor collectively could they afford to ignore the American challenge. Indeed, between August and December, when a settlement of sorts was reached at the Smithsonian Institute in Washington (182), the crisis was enacted in the ritual fashion typical of such intra-alliance disputes: each side was careful to publicise its own position in a way that made it clear that they expected a compromise to emerge.[1]

For the EEC, critical as it was of the Nixon administration's use of strong-arm methods, the crisis none the less offered opportunities as well as dangers. The main danger was that with fluctuating exchange rates between the dollar and the various European currencies, the CAP (which had been designed on the assumption of fixed exchange rates) would collapse and with it the hope of any significant progress towards economic and monetary union. By the same token, however, the need to preserve the CAP, as also the common negotiating position on trade with the United States, put a premium on some positive measures to concert European monetary policies (178). Thus a year later, in October 1972, the Paris summit conference confirmed an earlier Community decision to create a monetary cooperation fund

1 See, for example, the exchanges in the GATT. The American position was defended before the Council on 24 August by Mr Samuels, Deputy Under-Secretary of State for Economic Affairs, and an EEC position paper was presented at the same meeting. The Council also set up a Working Party on the United States surcharge which reported on 16 September 1971. For the text of this report, see GATT press release of the same date, and for the United States and EEC statements, see WEU, *Political Year in Europe, 1971*, pp. 231–4.

as the first phase of economic and monetary union (134–136) and to support the European 'snake in the tunnel', i.e. the narrowing of the permitted fluctuation margins of the Community currencies.[1]

By this time, however, it was becoming clear both that there would be no quick end to the reserve currency status of the dollar, providing the basis for a return to a revamped system of fixed exchange rates, as the French evidently hoped (179), and that within Europe most of the fundamental problems involved in economic and monetary union were as far away from solution as ever. While the new practice (it could hardly be called a system) of relatively free exchange rates quickly assumed a permanence that few would have suspected prior to August 1971, the crisis none the less had the effect of slowing down the momentum of reform and innovation at both global and regional levels.

In global terms the commitment to long-term monetary reform receded into the background as the major powers found that they could live with the new fluidity in monetary relations and the United States found it positively to its advantage. The official pretext which the United States administration gave for its second devaluation in February 1973 – that progress with fundamental reform had been too slow – was hardly convincing, but nor did it provoke a crisis. On this occasion, in any event, the administration was careful to prepare the grouns and to emphasise, by linking the announcement of the devaluation with a reaffirmation of its commitment to seek enabling legislation for a new round of trade negotiations within the GATT (cf. 183 and 189–191), that the rift between America and her allies had been repaired.

In regional terms, the return to the GATT could in a sense be regarded as a victory for the Europeans, since for the time being it left their policies intact, formally put trade relations once more outside the context of alliance politics, and might provide the Community with a stimulus for collective policy-making as the Kennedy Round of trade negotiations had done a few years previously. But, although the so-called Tokyo Round of GATT negotiations was scheduled to end in 1975, by that time no significant results had been achieved and the date was postponed. In the meantime the quadrupling of the oil price in the wake of the Middle East war of October 1973 provided the occasion for some further defensive concerting of European policies, and indeed was to lead fairly rapidly to the establishment of the Political Coordination Committee and the regular summit meetings of the Heads of State of the Nine within the European Council (137, 140, 144, 148 and 149). But while the economic crisis persuaded the member states of the importance of political cooperation, this was at least partly because, in substantive matters of economic and monetary unification, it also left the Community in a state of near-paralysis.

American policies during the monetary crisis were part of a more general shock which the Western powers had to absorb over the period covered by this volume.

1 For a detailed analysis of the attempt to establish economic and monetary union during this period, see Loukas Tsoukalis, *The Politics and Economics of European Monetary Integration* (London, 1977).

This sprang from the unforeseen effects of detente on the alliance as a whole. Detente resulted, somewhat paradoxically, in the loosening of the link between alliance politics and world politics. By the stabilisation of European borders, the link between Berlin, Germany, alliance confrontation in Europe and global confrontation across the whole front of the cold war, the link which had characterised the post-war era, was broken. Europe could no longer conceivably come under the threat of blackmail as the result of super- or great-power activity in *other* parts of the world, and activity in Europe no longer threatened to constrain the super-powers in their behaviour either towards one another or in third-world areas.

This shift caused a revolutionary change in the position of the NATO Alliance. Whereas until the early 1970s, the alliance had represented *the* base of American power, an extension of its armed forces and its political bargaining potential over the whole area of world affairs, the process of detachment meant that this was no longer so. The alliance was crucial for underlining detente in Europe and for European stability, but it was no longer the base from which the United States acted outside, either at the super-power level or in third-world areas; and it was no longer necessary in consequence for the United States to take the political temperature in Europe before acting. With the stabilisation of European borders and the ending of the Vietnam war, the United States could bring the whole weight of its political and economic strength to bear in any part of the world directly, without having first to filter its policies through a mesh of European concerns and interests.

What this meant was the 'regionalisation' of Europe, a phrase actually coined by Secretary of State Kissinger in his speech to the Associated Press Writers in April 1973 in which he called for a new 'Atlantic Charter' (114). For the Europeans, their 'regionalisation' meant a gradual but definite loss of bargaining power with the United States, a process which, as we have seen, had already been brought home to them during the 1971 monetary crisis. The purpose of the proposed Atlantic Charter was first an ordering of relations between the partners of the alliance without reference to the world outside. Secondly, it threatened to legitimise the practice of 'linkage' within the alliance over troop levels and offset agreements, and of issues formerly held to be outside of alliance concerns, namely monetary relations and trade, to which the European powers had taken such exception in 1971. Thirdly, had 'linkage' been conceded, it held open to the Europeans the prospect that on any 'agenda item' which arose in their relations with the United States, the Americans could bring pressure to bear along multifarious fronts. It seemed that just when the alliance had been detached from world politics as a whole, and the United States freed from alliance constraints, the Nixon administration was threatening to turn the entire 'free world' into a form of alliance, to be governed by a set of rules elaborated for and previously confined to alliance relations with the Soviet Union and its allies.

The European panic which followed the famous 'Year of Europe' speech cannot be directly documented. In practical terms, the Europeans refused to treat monetary and trade issues as part of an Atlantic package. They continued to insist that trade be treated within the framework of the GATT and that specific trade problems between the United States and the Community be dealt with in a second charter unconnected with the affairs of the alliance. The process of negotiating an Atlantic Charter was thus broken down into two different processes covering trade and political relations, the first of which was never achieved while the second finally took the form of an anodyne Community declaration of good intentions.[1] In general terms, political relations between the United States and its European allies were extremely bad.

The overall effect of these political and economic shocks on the alliance was cumulative. The increasing functionalisation of the alliance, its increasingly specific task orientation, combined with the unchaining of American power both within and outside it, caused a loss of what had been an underlying sense of political community. The alliance did not become any less necessary. Indeed, in some ways, it was more necessary. But it became less generally loved.

The Soviet bloc

The attempt on the part of the United States to establish a new framework for political consultations among the NATO allies, the increased pressure for cohesion in the alliance and the strengthening of the alliance's internal structure were paralleled by similar pressures and an equivalent strengthening among the countries of the Warsaw Pact. Like the United States, the Soviet Union apparently lost the battle to get any agreement on a political framework; the Brezhnev doctrine (150) was not translated into a fundamental tenet of pact relations. The meeting of the World Conference of Communist Parties in Moscow in June 1969 passed a final report which, while it acknowledged the need to protect the socialist camp, kept alive the doctrine of the 'national roads' (151). It agreed only to the importance of the role of communist parties in the transition to socialism. But Soviet tank strength was substantially increased during 1974.[2] More significantly, the Soviet Union won a major battle for increased joint planning within the framework of the Council for Mutual Economic Assistance. The Warsaw Pact countries had by 1971 filled out the framework of the so-called Complex Plan, agreed to in principle at the CMEA meeting in 1969, a document of 198 pages which provided for the implementation of a socialist division of labour (152). It was notable for the adherence of Romania, long an opponent of any economic division of labour among the countries of Eastern Europe.

The great powers and the Middle East war of 1973

The full impact of this conjunction of 'post-cold-war' changes, both in relations

1 See the Draft Declaration on the Principles of Relations between the United States and th the European Economic Community, proposed by the EEC, Copenhagen, 10 September 1973 (*New York Times*, 24 September 1973).

2 Soviet tank strength increased from 17,000 to 20,000 in 1974. Not documented; see ISS, *The Military Balance, 1974–75*.

between the two super-powers and within the Western Alliance, was nowhere more clearly displayed than during the Middle East war of October 1973 and the world-wide energy crisis that followed it. The crisis was marked throughout by an unparalleled level of super-power freedom of action combined with an unparalleled level of alliance disaffection.

At the level of super-power relations, the Soviet Union apparently grasped the opportunity provided by European stabilisation to spur on its Middle Eastern allies (153) without any real concern either for its specific undertaking to the United States of the previous June (66) or for the overall course of detente, which, in the event, was scarcely affected by Soviet policies in the Middle East (68 and 70). It was to be only the first of a series of displays of Soviet strength, notably in southern Africa, which fall outside the scope of this volume. If the United States had won freedom of action through European stabilisation, so had the Soviet Union.

At the level of the alliance, the Europeans refused to allow an extension of NATO arrangements to the Middle East. This was reflected in their refusal to allow over-flights or the transfer of NATO material to aid the Israelis.[1] The Middle East was not, of course, and had never been a NATO responsibility; nevertheless, implicit in their reaction was a denial of that sense of political community within the alliance which had previously existed, and without which they were now unwilling to see it used as a flexible support system for a purely American defence of Israel. Instead there was an attempt, albeit contested amongst the Nine themselves, to deal with the aftermath of the Middle East war and Arab oil embargo which accompanied it, on a purely European basis.

The oil embargo, together with the subsequent dramatic rise in the oil price, provided the Nixon administration with an opportunity to press that part of Henry Kissinger's Atlantic strategy which called for concerting alliance positions beyond their traditional limits, in this instance with scant regard for existing European ties and interests. The proposal for a concerted 'consumer' response to OPEC and OAPEC militancy and the subsequent Washington Energy Conference in February 1974 (197) which led to the establishment of the International Energy Agency (200) were the results of this pressure. But the point which impressed the Europeans was that while the United States had no doubt been the ultimate target of the embargo, it had in fact had its main impact upon the European states with their much greater dependence on Middle East oil. Consequently, while they were no more able than during the monetary crisis to ignore American initiatives, there was a distinct reluctance to have Western European interests in the area determined from Washington. The French government, whose Middle East policy had in any case been at odds with the other European powers since 1967, was particularly critical of the American approach. But in this situation, which had already produced a somewhat hopeful EEC declaration on a 'European identity' (139), French dis-

---

1 See the press conference by Mr McCloskey, spokesman of the United States Department of State, Washington, 26 October 1973 (WEU, *Political Year in Europe, 1973*, pp. 249–50); also Document No. 155.

sidence within the Alliance for once struck a responsive chord amongst the other European members.

The stage was thus set, primarily in response to French diplomatic efforts, first for the establishment of the Euro-Arab dialogue (203–204) and subsequently for the Paris Conference on International Economic Cooperation (CIEC). The progress of CIEC – in duration rather than achievement – demonstrated the constraints operating on an independent European diplomacy.[1] In the course of the negotiations it became clear that the divisions within Europe on energy and raw material power were deeper than their common commitment to the Paris talks might have suggested, and that West Germany and Japan in particular were closer to the United States' approach to North–South relations than to that of the other European powers.

The irony was that the changed situation of the alliance, its removal from a privileged position at the centre of world politics, undercut precisely that freedom of action on the part of the European states which it simultaneously permitted to the super-powers. It is true that in some areas, particularly in relations with the developing countries, the United States was not able to exploit its new freedom. Indeed, in the aftermath of the Middle East crisis, the United States was finally persuaded to endorse the European conception of a North–South dialogue. The American agreement to take part in this exercise was the price which they had to pay to secure the agreement of the other industrial countries to the setting up of the International Energy Agency as an instrument of policy coordination – the core of the Kissinger approach – for the industrial world as a whole. But although, in the attempt to repair the damage to the Western economy, the Americans were not always insensitive to European initiatives, the Europeans themselves could do relatively little on their own account. The Euro-Arab dialogue, for example, scarcely got off the ground. In other words it became increasingly clear that, as a basis for an independent diplomacy, a largely cosmetic dialogue with the third world was not an adequate substitute for a dissolving sense of political community within the Atlantic Alliance itself.

More generally, in the context of detente, the European powers discovered that they could not harness or control the process of change between the two halves of Europe on their own behalf. While their influence with the United States declined, the growing *need* for a European defence made them anxious about the extent of a continuing American commitment to Europe (117 and 121 on the issue of United States troop reductions). They were forced to rely solely on United States initiatives to bring the Middle East war to an end, and even on the question of their own monetary relations they were forced back into relying on the Group of Ten, and beyond that on the smaller group of the six leading OECD countries, both essentially Atlantic frameworks, when the European 'snake' finally left the tunnel in March 1973 with the defection of Britain, Iceland and Italy (185–186).

This failure of Europeanism did not produce a new political commitment to a revived Atlanticism. The 'Atlantic Charter' which was finally signed in Ottawa in June 1974 was anodyne and avoided all contentious issues (118). But it did indicate

1 See, for example, footnote 1, p. 520; Document No. 149.

that such Atlanticist organisation as already and necessarily existed, set limits to the scope and impact of the Europeanist revival. The contrary document to the Atlantic Charter was the 'European Charter' and it is as feeble as its Atlantic counterpart (139).

The failure of the 'Year of Europe', on the European as well as the Atlantic level, inspired a new round of institutional innovations in Europe. In August 1974 the French President, M. Giscard d'Estaing, suggested the need for periodic European summit meetings on an institutionalised basis.[1] At the first such meeting in December the nine EEC countries agreed to establish the 'European Council' (144) thus adding yet another level of decision-making, *de facto* if not *de jure*, to the Community structure (148–149). A second innovation designed to shift the Community's malaise was the decision taken at the Rome meeting of the European Council in December 1975 on direct elections to the European Parliament. The Heads of State were scarcely united in enthusiasm for this project; in particular the British government refused to commit itself to the proposed date, May or June 1978, for the first Pan-European elections. But the decision to change the status of the European Parliament was in any case perhaps a reflection of the degree to which the member states of the EEC were committed to giving Europe the appearance of a reality, while the substance of elaborated common policies in the crucial areas of economic and monetary union continued to elude them.

It was in an atmosphere of fading hope and institutional disarray that the long-awaited agreement between the thirty-five participants in the European Security Conference was finalised. In August 1975 the powers went to Helsinki to sign the document that was to have provided the framework for a process of change in relations between European states. By the time they did so, however, the changes that they had hoped it might institute had already occurred, and they had taken directions other than those which the Western European powers had expected when the reformed detente was begun in 1968.

The Bloc structures had been strengthened, instead of fading away as the powers had hoped, and in the case of NATO rendered more, not less, inclusive. Nor could such strengthening be justified by an increase in the 'threat'. NATO had been strengthened as the price of removing the threat, at least in central Europe. What this meant for the European powers, particularly in the case of the Federal Republic's abortive attempt to establish normal relations with East Germany, was that it was not the Helsinki conference which was to provide the framework for the future, but a reformed structure of alliances. Helsinki had been converted, by the modalities of detente, from a framework of freer relations between Eastern and Western Europe to a particular agreement on the form of relations between the two alliances. It became yet another East–West agreement.

The United States was not much more enthusiastic than the Europeans about the outcome of its detente policies. By the end of 1975 its own negotiations with

1 For the text of President Giscard d'Estaing's speech on French television, in which he made the suggestion, see *Bull. EC* 7/8–1974, p. 123.

the Soviet Union were getting bogged down, a situation which, when combined with Soviet behaviour during the Middle East war, was to bring the administration under the charge that detente was earning the United States no 'pay-off'.

The real problem lay in the ambiguous nature of the pay-off. Detente had, after all, created a concrete reality — an agreed settlement in central Europe and, in effect, a peace treaty with Germany. That it had not changed the Soviet Union, indeed that it had rather freed the Soviet government from its habitual preoccupation with 'escalation' and the arms race, and from the caution which had previously been induced by post-war instability in central Europe, was the price which the United States paid for that agreed peace.

Thus, although in a real sense detente had finally ended the post-war period, it had not given rise to a new international order. Rather it had created an entirely new and uncomfortable context of relations for all the great powers, a context which was to require an entirely new set of rules; and detente itself could not provide those rules. It had been a process by which, largely through the use of 'linkage', a series of contexts had been decoupled. That was in effect all that had occurred. To provide new rules for great-power relations, a new framework altogether would have to be created. This in turn would no doubt require the discipline of events as yet unforeseen. In any event, at the end of 1975 no such exercise was in prospect.

I.   The end of the Cold War

A. Germany

1. Remarks by President Nixon at the Siemens Factory, West Berlin, 27 February 1969[1]

I first apologize for the fact that we have kept you waiting. But as we came through the city, the crowds were so large that we were unable to keep on our schedule.

So the reason we are here is a demonstration of the truth of what the Mayor has just said: that the people of Berlin are free and that, despite a wall, this is one city and one people and one nation.

I saw many signs as we came through the streets of the city — some were in English, most were in German. The ones in German, of course, I could not understand. But there was one sign that was a combination that made me feel very much at home.

I first came to this city 22 years ago. At that time most of those that I see here — or many of those — were not yet born; and to many who came here then, Berlin seemed to be city without hope and without a future. But the pessimists at that period, over 20 years ago, did not know the people of Berlin.

There is no more remarkable story in human history than the creation of this island of freedom and prosperity, of courage and determination, in the center of postwar Europe.

And it is you who have done it.

It is you who have rebuilt this great city; it is you who have stood the shock of crises; it is you who have kept the faith in yourselves and in your allies.

Berlin may look lonely on the map. But it is a vital part of the world that believes in the capacity of man to govern himself with responsibility and to shape his destiny in dignity.

If this is an age of symbols, one of the great symbols of the age is this city. And what you do here is done for free men everywhere throughout the world. You stand for a cause much bigger than yourself, and this is the greatest destiny that a man or woman can have — because your will to remain free strengthens the will to freedom of all men; your courage in the face of deliberate and constant challenge fortifies the courage of all those who love liberty.

The presence of an American President in Berlin, following a recent visit by a

1 *DSB*, 24 March 1969, pp. 260–2.

British Prime Minister, is another kind of symbol. It is a way of demonstrating unmistakably our longstanding commitment to the people of West Berlin.

Let there be no miscalculation: No unilateral move, no illegal act, no form of pressure from any source will shake the resolve of the Western nations to defend their rightful status as protectors of the people of free Berlin.

All the world admires bravery. But there are different kinds of bravery. Bravery in crisis is expected of those who love freedom; what is much more difficult, much more rare, is bravery day by day — the steady fortitude that resists remorseless pressures and refuses to permit the slow erosion of liberties. That is the remarkable bravery of the Berliner, and it stands as a shining example for everyone throughout the world.

The partnership between our two peoples was forged back in the dark days of the blockade, when men like Lucius Clay and Ernst Reuter personified our determination to survive as free men. It is appropriate, 20 years after the end of that blockade, that we pay tribute to all who suffered for the ideal of freedom in those days of physical privation and spiritual triumph. As I viewed the progress of this vital city today, I knew that that sacrifice was not in vain.

And to all the people of Berlin today, I bring this message from the heart of America: You have justified the support and the commitment of your friends, and as a result, no city in the world has more friends, more devoted friends, than has the city of Berlin.

The American responsibility here is derived from the most solemn international agreements. But what we have gone through together in those 24 years has given those agreements a special meaning. Four Presidents before me have held to this principle, and I tell you at this time and in this place that I, too, hold fast to this principle: Berlin must be free.

I do not say this in any spirit of bravado or belligerence. I am simply stating an irrevocable fact of international life.

Our commitment to the freedom of Berlin has never been more steady, never more firm, than it is today. For more than a generation we have pledged American lives to an ideal and a reality; that Berlin shall be free and that Berlin shall live. For its part, Berlin has remained steadfast. So have we; and steadfast we shall stay.

No one should doubt the determination of the United States to live up to its obligations. The question before the world is not whether we shall rise to the challenge of defending Berlin — we have already demonstrated that we shall. The question now is how best to end the challenge and clear the way for a peaceful solution to the problem of a divided Germany.

When we say that we reject any unilateral alteration of the status quo in Berlin, we do not mean that we consider the status quo to be satisfactory. Nobody benefits in a stalemate, least of all the people of Berlin.

Let us set behind us the stereotype of Berlin as a 'provocation'. Let us, all of us, view the situation in Berlin as an invocation, a call to end the tension of the past age here and everywhere.

Our common attitude can best be expressed in a motto of Goethe: Without haste, but without rest. That is, step by step we shall strive together to construct a durable peace.

There were times in the past when Berlin had to stand its ground in defiance of horrible forces that threatened to overwhelm it. Your determination in those times of danger demonstrated beyond a shadow of a doubt that threats of force would never succeed. Your determination in those times of danger demonstrated beyond a shadow of a doubt that the threats and coercion could never succeed. By your fortitude you have created conditions which may in time permit another kind of determination — a determination that we shall, by negotiation among governments and reconciliation among men, bring an end to the division of this city, this nation, and this continent, and this planet.

By your faith in the future you have inspired renewed faith in the hearts of all men. The men of the past thought in terms of blockades and walls; the men of the future will think in terms of open channels. The men of the past were trapped in the gray overcast of cold war; the men of the future — a future toward which we will all work — if only they remember the tragedy and triumph of Berlin, will be free to walk in the warm sunlight of a just peace.

And now one final message from the hearts of the people of America to the people of Berlin: Sometimes you must feel that you are very much alone. But always remember we are with you, and always remember that people who are free and who want to be free around the world are with you. In the sense that the people of Berlin stand for freedom and peace, all the people of the world are truly Berliners.

2. Speech by Mr Gomulka, First Secretary of the Central Committee of the Polish Communist Party, Warsaw, 17 May 1969[1] (extracts)

For some time trends have been appearing in definite circles in the German Federal Republic which seem to indicate a slightly different line of Bonn's eastern policy. In the present state of affairs it is hard to judge how much these trends reflect tactics and a political manoeuvre and how much they are an expression of an attempt to evaluate realistically the reality of Germany and Europe. I have in mind first of all certain statements by the leaders of the West German Social—Democratic Party at its congresses in Nuremberg and Bad Godesberg as well as other public declarations made especially by the GFR Vice-Chancellor, Mr. Brandt.

The chief measure of GFR policy has been, is and will be the West German government's attitude towards the recognition of the borders existing in Europe, including the Odra and Lusatian Nysa line, as final and the recognition of the existence of the German Democratic Republic as a sovereign and fully legal German state . . .

As is known, Chancellor Kiesinger's government is a coalition government. In

1 *On the German Problem: Articles and Speeches by Wladyslaw Gomulka* (Warsaw, 1969), pp. 398—404.

addition to representatives of the two Christian–Democratic parties it includes representatives of the Social–Democratic Party with its chairman Mr Brandt at the head, who performs in this government the functions of Vice-Chancellor and, at the same time, Minister of Foreign Affairs. As follows from many publications, representatives of the Social–Democratic Party in this government take their own position on certain important matters of Bonn politics, which does not fully correspond to the position of their coalition partners. This applies especially to the attitude towards the Budapest Appeal and the question of the GFR's signing the non-proliferation treaty, and there are also signs of differences of view on the question of the GFR's attitude towards the GDR and on the problem of Bonn's eastern policy.

Let us consider the last-named subject.

In a speech at the SPD congress in Nuremberg, on 16 March, 1968, Willy Brandt declared:

'. . . outside the debate I have been asked by many comrades what I had in mind by my remark on the Odra–Nysa line. I repeated the relevant sentence: Hence there follows – so I said – (the necessity) to recognize or respect the Odra–Nysa line until settlement by a peace treaty. This means that we wish for violence to be given up and for reconciliation with Poland. We wish to have this also before a peace treaty, if this is possible. We do not want and cannot change by violence the frontiers that exist in Europe. This applies also to inner German frontiers. This applies also to the Odra–Nysa line, which incidentally, is not a frontier of the German Federal Republic.'

The essence of Brandt's attitude towards the Odra–Nysa frontier was also repeated in a document of the Nuremberg congress which says:

'This policy will bring the greater advantages the more clearly we express our readiness to respect and recognize the existing frontiers in Europe, particularly the present Western frontier of Poland, until the time the boundaries of Germany are finally determined by a settlement under a peace treaty which all those concerned will be able to recognize as just and lasting.'

After the Nuremberg SPD congress, statements to a similar effect by Vice-Chancellor Brandt and other SPD leaders were reiterated many times. Chancellor Kiesinger did not confirm the formula of the Minister of Foreign Affairs and Vice-Chancellor of his government on the recognition of the existing boundaries in Europe. This formula is actually repeated only by SPD members of the coalition government.

We cannot underrate the fact that from a political point of view the Nuremberg SPD formula on the GFR recognition of the Odra–Nysa frontier represents a step forward in comparison with the position expressed on this subject by all GFR governments. At the same time we have to fully appreciate the fact that every inter-state agreement between Poland and the GFR on the basis of this formula, even with its most favourable interpretation for us, could not contain more than a de facto recognition of the Odra–Nysa frontier by the GFR and only a temporary one, e.g. until the moment a peace treaty with Germany is concluded. So even assuming that the Bonn government would adopt the Nuremberg formula of Vice-Chancellor Brandt it would actually change nothing in the present state of affairs. A change can only occur if the GFR government recognizes the existing frontier of Poland on the Odra–Nysa as final and inviolable without any reservations.

In his book 'A Peaceful Policy in Europe' Mr Brandt says:

'The Western frontier of the Polish state is included in our offer of renunciation of violence toward everybody. Good relations with Poland are particularly important for us. This is a cornerstone of our policy directed eastwards . . . This reconciliation includes not only the rejection of any thought of force from our aspirations but also a consciousness that no germ for future disputes must be left.'

This is precisely what we mean: that the GFR recognition of the existing Western frontier of Poland should be unequivocal and, as Mr Brandt says, should leave 'no germ for future disputes'. Only such a form of recognition of this frontier could give credibility to assurances by Mr Brandt and the GFR government about their desire to reconcile with Poland and the other socialist countries.

Contrary to Mr Brandt's assurances the SPD Nuremberg formula on the recognition of European frontiers carries a mark of potential revisionism by assuming a priori that final settlement of these frontiers remains open and is postponed to the time of a peace conference. With the help of this Nuremberg formula the GFR attempts to avoid any accusation in the eyes of public opinion that it is questioning the Odra–Nysa frontier. In fact it is simultaneously trying to avoid recognition of this frontier as final maintaining that it is unable to do so in view of the letter of the Potsdam Agreements which state that the final delineation of Poland's western frontiers must be left until the peace conference.

No obstacles of a legal nature exist to prevent the GFR recognizing Poland's existing Western frontier as final . . . We are prepared to conclude such an international treaty with the GFR at any time just as 19 years ago we concluded a treaty on this subject with the GDR. If however, the GFR government insists that conclusion of such a treaty with Poland prior to the conclusion of a peace treaty with Germany would not be in agreement with the Potsdam Agreements, we must propose to them that they approach the Soviet Union, France, Great Britain and the United States with the following question: does the GFR possess the sovereign right to conclude a treaty with Poland which would recognize the existing Polish frontier on the Odra–Nysa as final? Every reply will be illuminating for the whole of Europe.

Poland will never conclude a treaty with the GFR which did not conform with the Zgorzelec Treaty concluded with the German Democratic Republic. Such an action would constitute a step backwards, a blow aimed against ourselves and all our friends and allies and against those countries and political forces in the West which share our opinion on the final nature of this frontier.

The SPD in its resolution on the German question says that: 'It would be contrary to reality were we to deny the existence of a state in the other part of Germany or were we to refuse taking cognisance of it'. This might be understood as a desire to recognize the de facto existence of a second German state – the German Democratic Republic. Hence also from this point of view Bonn cannot consider the Zgorzelec Treaty as non-existent or not binding . . .

3. Statement by Mr Gromyko to the Supreme Soviet, 10 July 1969[1] (extract)

In the very centre of Europe there is a point which demands very close attention in Soviet external policy. It is West Berlin. During the post-war years complications have arisen over this city on more than one occasion. West Berlin has an international status unique in the world. It is situated in the centre of a sovereign State, the German Democratic Republic, and can maintain contact with the rest of the world only by using that State's communications. The social and administrative system in West Berlin, the economic and monetary systems and other conditions obtaining there, differ from the system and conditions in the GDR. But that is not the source of the friction. The friction is brought about by unlawful encroachments by the German Federal Republic on West Berlin and attempts to use the city's territory for purposes hostile to the GDR, the Soviet Union and other socialist States. The USSR's policy on West Berlin, like that of the GDR, is clear. We believe that the people and authorities of the city should be able to engage in all activities necessary to ensure normal existence of West Berlin as an independent political entity. However, we cannot allow anything to impinge on our interests or the legitimate interests of our ally the GDR, or to violate the special status of West Berlin. If the other Powers who were our allies in the war and share the responsibility for the situation in West Berlin would take into account the interests of European security in their approach to this question, they would find the USSR ready for an exchange of opinions on how to prevent complications over West Berlin now and in the future. We will not agree to any steps, of course, which harm the legitimate interests of the GDR or affect the special status of West Berlin . . .

4. Joint statement issued by President Nixon and Chancellor Kiesinger, Washington, 8 August 1969[2]

President Nixon and Chancellor Kiesinger issued the following joint statement at the conclusion of their meeting at the White House on August 8:

The President and Chancellor Kiesinger are very pleased to have had the opportunity to meet together during the past two days and to continue their personal consultations on important issues which they had begun during President Nixon's visit to Germany in February. They agreed that the meetings just concluded were extremely useful. They were characterized by an atmosphere of warm friendship

1 *SWB*, SU/3123, 12 July 1969, C/7.
2 *DSB*, 8 September 1969, pp. 213–14.

and mutual confidence which is an important element in relations between the United States of America and the Federal Republic of Germany.

During their meetings President Nixon and Chancellor Kiesinger agreed on the importance of staying in close communication with one another. In order to assure that they will be able to communicate rapidly in case of emergency, the President and the Chancellor have agreed to the establishment of a 'hot line' between the White House and the Chancellor's office. The line will be installed as soon as technical arrangements are completed.

The Chancellor and the President exchanged views on the international situation. In particular, they discussed the full range of issues affecting relations between East and West including prospects for strategic arms limitation talks and broadening discussions on European security. They agreed on the desirability of continuing efforts to bring existing international conflicts to a just end, to achieve progress toward disarmament and to seek to eliminate the causes of tensions in Europe. The President and the Chancellor agreed that negotiations to this end are desirable. The Chancellor welcomed the opportunity for full consultation in NATO on the strategic arms limitation talks and on issues affecting European security. The President assured the Chancellor that the United States would take full account of the interests of its Allies in the strategic arms limitation talks. They were of the opinion that progress in strategic arms limitation is interrelated with a climate favorable for dealing with long-existing European problems.

President Nixon took the opportunity during the meetings to give Chancellor Kiesinger a detailed account of the impressions he gained during his recent trip to Asia and Romania.

Chancellor Kiesinger reported on developments in Berlin and Germany which have occurred since the last meeting between the Chancellor and the President. Chancellor Kiesinger and President Nixon share the hope that the Soviet Union will respond in a constructive manner to the tripartite initiative aimed at improving the situation in and around Berlin and between the two parts of Germany.[1] President Nixon expressed his strong support of the efforts of the Federal Republic of Germany to alleviate the hardships that result from the division of Germany.

The Chancellor and President reaffirmed their conviction that the North Atlantic Alliance is an essential instrument in the maintenance of peace and stability in the North Atlantic area. They agreed that the proposed NATO committee on the challenges of modern society would add a new dimension to the Alliance and give a direct part in the challenging task of marshalling resources of member nations to improve the quality of life for all people.

1 On 6 and 7 August, during Chancellor Kiesinger's visit to Washington, the heads of the missions of the three powers in Berlin sent separate démarches to the Soviet Foreign Ministry in which they announced the Federal Government's readiness to engage in discussions with the German Democratic Republic on traffic problems, expressed the wish for an improvement in the Berlin situation, particularly with regard to access, and indicated, concerning Soviet complaints about certain activities on the part of the Federal Republic, the Federal Republic's readiness to reach a compromise. The Soviet Government replied on 12 September indicating its readiness for discussions. Unpublished documents. (Federal Republic Press and Information Office, *The Berlin Settlement* (1972), pp. 155–6.)

The President and the Chancellor welcomed the recently-concluded offset agreement between the United States and the Federal Republic which they regarded as symbolic of the determination of the two governments to cooperate in the maintenance of a sound defense posture within the necessary framework of economic stability.

The Chancellor and the President expressed satisfaction over the agreement envisioned on Special Drawing Rights which is one important step to an orderly development of the international monetary system. The President and the Chancellor are confident that agreement on SDRs will facilitate the continued advance of world trade and investment. President Nixon outlined his Government's resolve to bring inflation under control and to strengthen the position of the dollar as a world currency. In the interest of international trade and monetary developments, the Chancellor and the President agreed on the continued necessity of maintaining closest cooperation between the United States and Germany. Both opposed additional barriers to international trade.

Chancellor Kiesinger reported to the President on recent developments in the European Community and on prospects for future development. The President affirmed that the United States has consistently supported European unity, and expressed his conviction that European nations will move forward in a way which will meet their interests and at the same time contribute to an international climate of cooperation and prosperity.

On the subject of bilateral technological cooperation, the President and the Chancellor welcomed the progress made, especially in the field of space research, where the joint Project Helios is of great importance. They agreed to continue and to widen this cooperation.

The Chancellor extended the invitation to the astronauts of Apollo 11 to visit Germany as his guests in the near future.

At the conclusion of their talks the President and the Chancellor expressed their renewed conviction that the close understanding and harmony of interests between the United States and the Federal Republic provide a sound basis for continuing constructive cooperation between the two countries and, beyond that, constitute a very important element of strength in the search for the resolution of international problems and the achievement of a just and lasting peace to which both countries are dedicated.

5. Statement by Chancellor Brandt in the Bundestag, 28 October 1969[1] (extracts)

This Government works on the assumption that the questions which have arisen for the German people out of the Second World War and from the national treachery committed by the Hitler regime can find their ultimate answers only in a European

1 WEU, *Political Year in Europe, 1969*, pp. 127–31.

peace arrangement. However, no one can dissuade us from our conviction that the Germans have a right to self-determination just as has any other nation.

The object of our practical political work in the years immediately ahead is to preserve the unity of the nation by decontracting the relationship between the two parts of Germany.

The Germans are one not only by reason of their language and their history with all its splendour and its misery: we are all at home in Germany. And we still have common tasks and a common responsibility: to ensure peace among us and in Europe.

Twenty years after the establishment of the Federal Republic of Germany and of the GDR we must prevent any further alienation of the two parts of the German nation, that is, arrive at a regular *modus vivendi* and from there proceed to cooperation.

This is not just a German interest, for it is of importance also for peace in Europe and for East—West relations. Our own attitude and that of our friends towards the international relations of the GDR depend not least on the attitude of East Berlin itself. It is, by the way, not our intention to curtail the benefits derived by our compatriots from international trade and cultural exchanges.

The Federal Government will continue the policy initiated in December 1966 and again offers the Council of Ministers of the GDR negotiations at government level without discrimination on either side, which should lead to contractually agreed cooperation. International recognition of the GDR by the Federal Republic is out of the question. Even if there exist two States in Germany, they are not foreign countries to each other: their relations with each other can only be of a special nature.

Following up the policy of its predecessor, the Federal Government declares that its readiness for binding agreements on the reciprocal renunciation of the use or threat of force applies equally with regard to the GDR.

The Federal Government will advise the United States, Britain, and France to continue energetically the talks begun with the Soviet Union on easing and improving the situation of Berlin. The status of the city of Berlin under the special responsibility of the four powers must remain untouched. This must not be a hindrance to seeking facilities for traffic within and to Berlin.

We shall continue to ensure the viability of Berlin. West Berlin must be placed in a position to assist in improving the political, economic and cultural relations between the two parts of Germany.

We welcome the renewed increase of intra-German trade. This has partly been due to the facilities provided by the agreement of 6 December 1968. The Federal Government considers a further expansion of these neighbourly trade relations desirable.

In conformity with its functions and responsibilities, we have changed the name of the former Ministry for All-German Questions to Ministry for Inner-German Relations. Our German policy as a whole cannot be a matter for one department alone. It is a permanent responsibility for the entire government and embraces aspects of foreign policy, of security and European policies, as much as the efforts to maintain the coherence of our people and the relations within divided Germany . . .

The German people needs peace in the full sense of that word also with the peoples of the Soviet Union and all peoples of the European East. We are prepared to make an honest attempt at understanding, in order to help overcome the aftermath of the disaster brought on Europe by a criminal clique.

We do not harbour false hopes: interests, power constellations and social differences can neither be dissolved dialectically nor must they be obscured. And yet our partners for talks must also realise: the right to self-determination embodied in the United Nations Charter applies also to the German nation. This right and the will to defend it are not negotiable.

We are not deluding ourselves to believe that reconciliation will be easy or quick to achieve. It is a process; but it is time now to push ahead that process.

In continuation of its predecessor's policy the Federal Government aims at equally binding agreements on the mutual renunciation of the use or threat of the use of force. Let me repeat: this readiness also applies as far as the GDR is concerned. And I wish to make as unmistakably clear that we are prepared to arrive with Czechoslovakia — our immediate neighbour — at arrangements which bridge the gulf of the past.

It is the Federal Government's firm conviction that the policy of renunciation of the use of force which respects the territorial integrity of the respective partner constitutes an essential contribution towards a relaxation of tensions in Europe. Renunciation of the use of force would create an atmosphere which makes further steps possible.

The joint efforts, too, to promote trade, technical cooperation and cultural exchanges are serving this purpose.

Today the Federal Government deliberately abstains from committing itself to statements or formulae going beyond the framework of this statement, which might complicate the negotiations it desires. It is well aware that there will be no progress unless the governments in the capitals of the Warsaw Pact countries adopt a cooperative attitude.

The Federal Government will make a number of short-term decisions which will highlight its will to continue the hitherto prevailing policy in a steady and consistent manner:

1. At the conference in The Hague[1] the Federal Government will use its influence to to ensure that effective measures for intensifying and enlarging the Community and for strengthening political cooperation will be initiated.
2. It will take up the offer by the United States of America to let German industrial potential participate in limited areas of space research.
3. It will take an active part in the work of the Committee set up by the Council of the North Atlantic Treaty Organization for the challenges of modern society.
4. It will shortly answer the Soviet aide-mémoire on the subject of renunciation

1 Document No. 128.

of the use of force, and propose a date for negotiations in Moscow which have
been suggested by the Soviet Union.
5. It will transmit to the Government of the People's Republic of Poland a proposal concerning the beginning of talks, thereby responding to the comments
made by Vladislav Gomulka on 17 May 1969.
6. It will sign the treaty on the non-proliferation of nuclear weapons as soon as
the clarifications requested by the last Federal Government have been obtained. . . .

6. Chancellor Brandt to the Prime Minister of the German Democratic Republic, Mr Stoph, 22 January 1970[1]

Dear Mr Chairman,
On behalf of the Federal Government, I suggest that our Governments open
negotiations on the exchange of declarations on the renunciation of force. These
negotiations, which should take place according to the principle of non-discrimination,
should provide an opportunity for a wide-ranging exchange of views on the settlement of all outstanding questions between our two States, among them questions
of equality in relations.
Each side must be free to bring forward all those considerations, proposals,
principles and drafts that in its view appear proper. Discussions and negotiations on
these should be possible without any pressure of time. For your information, I
enclose what I said in this connection in my statement to the German Bundestag
on 14 January 1970.
It is my government's wish to reach settlements that will make life easier for
people in divided Germany through negotiations on practical questions.
The Federal Government is ready to begin negotiations at any time. Minister
Egon Franke is available for initial talks in which the course and progress of negotiations can be agreed.

7. Mr Stoph to Chancellor Brandt, 11 February 1970[2]

I acknowledge the receipt of your letter of 22nd January 1970 which has been
examined by the Council of Ministers of the German Democratic Republic together
with your statements to the Bundestag in Bonn on 28 October 1969 and 14 January
1970.
The Government of the German Democratic Republic takes note of your readiness,
expressed in the letter of 22 January 1970, to start negotiations between the German
Democratic Republic and the Federal Republic of Germany which should be conducted on a basis of equality and non-discrimination. The principles of equality and

1 *Bulletin*, 27 January 1970.
2 *Bulletin*, 19 February 1970.

non-discrimination obviously require that the German Democratic Republic and the Federal Republic of Germany recognise and respect each other for what they are, namely equal, sovereign subjects of international law.

To my regret I note that you do not reply in your letter to the proposal of the President of the State Council of the German Democratic Republic, Mr Walter Ulbricht, for the conclusion of a treaty establishing equal relations between the German Democratic Republic and the Federal Republic of Germany. This proposal, together with the corresponding draft treaty, was communicated to the President of the Federal Republic of Germany, Dr Gustav Heinemann, on 18 December 1969.

In his reply to the letter of the President of the State Council of the German Democratic Republic, Dr Heinemann declared that the Federal Government would examine these proposals and define its position with all necessary speed. The Federal Government has now had the draft treaty of the German Democratic Republic for almost two months, but the Federal Government's views on the proposals made by the German Democratic Republic, promised by the Federal President, have still not been received.

The Federal Government has even taken steps which run counter to the *de jure* rights of the German Democratic Republic. Negotiations on the establishment of equal relations and on the renunciation of force can achieve positive results only on the basis of mutual recognition under international law.

The draft treaty of the German Democratic Republic provides, as is known, that the German Democratic Republic and the Federal Republic of Germany agree on the establishment of normal equal relations, free from discrimination, on the basis of the generally-recognised principles and standards of international law. These relations must be based, *inter alia*, on the principles of sovereign equality, respect of territorial integrity, inviolability of the State frontiers, non-interference in internal matters and mutual benefits. That would be an effective contribution to maintaining peace in Europe, achieving organised-coexistence and relations of good neighbourliness as sovereign States.

All the provisions of the draft treaty of the German Democratic Republic – be it recognition of the frontiers in Europe resulting from the Second World War, including the frontiers between the German Democratic Republic and the Federal Republic of Germany, or the request for the admission of the German Democratic Republic and the Federal Republic of Germany to the United Nations Organisation – are in the interests of the German Democratic Republic and the Federal Republic as well as of European security.

I draw the attention of the Government of the Federal Republic of Germany to the fact that the draft treaty is based on full equality and non-discrimination, equal rights and obligations for both German States and contains no provisions which might be to the advantage of the German Democratic Republic or to the detriment of the Federal Republic of Germany.

To bring about peaceful coexistence and contractual regulation of normal relations between the German Democratic Republic and the Federal Republic of Germany on the basis of the generally recognised standards of international law, I consider it necessary for the Chairman of the Council of Ministers of the German Democratic Republic and the Chancellor of the Federal Republic of Germany to meet for direct negotiations. After all, problems of peace or war and guaranteed security for the creative work of the citizens of the German Democratic Republic and the Federal Republic of Germany are at stake.

Considering its urgency and fundamental importance, our meeting should take place as early as possible. I therefore suggest to the Federal Chancellor that it be held at the seat of the Council of Ministers in Berlin, capital of the German Democratic Republic, on 19 or 26 February 1970 at 11 a.m. We can reach agreement directly on the time and place by telephone or telex.

For the German Democratic Republic, the Minister for Foreign Affairs, Mr Otto Winzer, will also take part in the meeting.

8. Statement by Mr Stoph, Erfurt, 19 March 1970[1] (extracts)

The Government of the German Democratic Republic holds it is necessary that . . . we . . . address ourselves to the following basic questions:

1. Creation of normal, equal relations between the GDR and the FRG on the basis of international law and free of any discrimination. Renunciation of the claim of the Government of the FRG to be the lone representative [of the German people].

2. Non-intervention in the foreign relations of the other State. Final, clear rejection of the Hallstein doctrine.

3. In accordance with Article 2, paragraph 4, of the United Nations Charter, renunciation of the use of force between the German Democratic Republic and the Federal Republic of Germany under full, equal recognition of legal subjectivity, territorial integrity and inviolability of borders.

4. Application for membership by the GDR and FRG in the Organisation of the United Nations.

5. Renunciation of the demand for and possession of nuclear weapons in any form. Renunciation of the production, use and storage of B (biological) and C (chemical) weapons and reduction of defence spending by 50%.

6. Discussion of questions that are connected with the necessary burial of all vestiges of the second world war.

7. Settlement of all debts the FRG owes the GDR and regulation of the reparations responsibility of the FRG . . .

9. Statement by Chancellor Brandt, Erfurt, 19 March 1970[2] (extract)

1. Both States have the duty to preserve the unity of the German nation. They are not foreign to one another.

1 *Bulletin*, 24 March 1970.
2 *Bulletin*, 24 March 1970.

2. Additionally, the generally-acknowledged principles of international law must apply, particularly the exclusion of all forms of discrimination, respect of territorial integrity, the commitment to peaceful solution of all disputes, and respect of mutual borders.

3. This embodies the commitment not to wish to change by force the social structure in the territory of contractual partners.

4. The two governments should strive for neighbourly cooperation, particularly for settlement on specialist-technical cooperation, in which joint facilitation can be laid down in governmental agreements.

5. The existing rights and responsibilities of the four powers in respect to Germany as a whole and to Berlin must be respected.

6. The efforts of the four powers to reach agreements on improvement of the situation in and around Berlin must be supported. . .

10. Statement by the NATO Council on the occasion of the meeting between the Ambassadors of France, Great Britain, the United States and the Soviet Union, Berlin, 26 March 1970[1]

The North Atlantic Council welcomes the opening, today, of quadripartite negotiations on Berlin by the Governments of France, the United Kingdom and the United States with the Government of the Soviet Union. It is the common hope of the Alliance members that these talks will have a fruitful outcome.

They have noted that, following consultation in the North Atlantic Council, the three powers responsible for the Allied Travel Office have announced the suspension of the system of issuance of Temporary Travel Documents to East Germans who wish to travel in member countries of the Alliance.

With immediate effect, allied governments have decided not to require prior possession of a TTD by East German travellers applying for visas.

All members of the Alliance regard this decision as a step to improve the atmosphere. They express the hope that the Soviet Union will seriously consider reciprocating with measures which might be taken to improve the situation concerning Berlin and free access to the city.

11. Statement by Chancellor Brandt, Kassel, 21 May 1970[2]

I am pleased to welcome you, Mr Chairman, and the members of your delegation here in Kassel for our second meeting. And I hope that in spite of all our differences of opinion we shall be able to achieve progress both in matters of principle and on practical questions.

Our meeting in Erfurt was without doubt an event of political significance, as

1 NATO Press Service.
2 *Bulletin*, 26 May 1970.

you, Mr Chairman, said in your first statement at the time. It was keenly followed by our population, and caught lively attention among all those countries who take a special interest in what happens in and with Germany. This places a great duty and responsibility on us. We can only meet it if, as I said in Erfurt, we continue to search for areas where it will be possible to achieve progress for peace and for the people in Germany.

I consider it an encouraging sign that it was possible, since our Erfurt meeting, to conclude partial agreements in the field of posts and telecommunications. Yet judging by the tasks we face and the possibilities we have, that is but a modest beginning.

We both know that the way to a settlement of our relations is long and stony. We should not render it even more difficult by unfounded reproaches and accusations being made — as has frequently been the case since Erfurt. The fact that we are meeting here today — something we have both equally helped to bring about — should be proof enough that on both sides the will to reduce tensions is not lacking.

I do not think it would be right to burden our meeting with polemical statements. I therefore confine myself to assuring you that the insinuations and imputations cast on my government almost every day will neither be helpful nor make us abandon our conviction. Nor are they apt to influence public opinion on our side favourably.

This also holds true for the charges made in connection with the Federal Government's position at the meeting of the World Health Organisation in Geneva. My Government has never concealed the fact that its attitude to the GDR's international relations is conditional upon the development of relations between the two parts of Germany. Thus it is quite out of place to say that we have broken our word.

I also find it hard to understand how your side can present as a discrimination the offer of practical cooperation of the GDR in the work of the United Nations Economic Commission for Europe (ECE). The Federal Republic of Germany cannot be held responsible for the fact that in this way the GDR has excluded itself from these activities.

Our attitude implies neither tutelage nor presumption. Our attitude reflects our efforts to improve the relationship between the two States in Germany step by step. Certainly, it would have been useful if in Erfurt we had agreed to appoint representatives and come to initial arrangements. But it is not too late to do that now.

I have repeatedly proposed to you, Mr Chairman, that we open negotiations for a contractual settlement of relations between our two States on a basis of equality. And I have also said that any mutual discrimination should be excluded by such arrangements. I formally underline this readiness.

But if there is so much talk about discrimination, one should not pass over in silence the advantages that have accrued, and are accruing, to the GDR in a number of fields — such as trade — through the attitude of the Federal Republic of Germany. On the other hand, it must be mentioned that the GDR has constantly tried to thwart the Federal Government's efforts to improve its relations with the countries of Eastern Europe.

As I pointed out in Erfurt, the constitutions of the two German States are based on the unity of the nation. Neither of them envisages division as a permanent state. I feel that we cannot achieve a meaningful arrangement of relations with each other without making allowance for these constitutional principles. This brings me to our actual task.

I see no point in telling each other than one cannot take the second step before the first, and in arguing what the second or third should be before having taken the first one. To me it is in each case the next possible step that matters. As things are standing at present that next step can only be negotiations between our two governments on practical and also political problems — and that in itself would be a great deal.

The purpose of such negotiations ought to be to place relations between the two States in Germany on a contractual basis both in the interest of the people and of peace, and for the sake of the future of the nation. The Federal Government is prepared to do so.

Naturally, such a treaty, or several of them, can only be concluded on the basis of equality and non-discrimination. But it is also natural that contractual relations must have substance that really will mean progress in our mutual relations and for the conditions of life in Germany. Agreements must not consist of mere formalities.

In Erfurt I expounded on the matters which we feel should be settled. I left no doubt that contractual arrangements must be consistent with the special situation prevailing between our two States, but legally they must be as binding as similar agreements which each party concludes with third States. I also made it clear that we neither intend to by-pass the rights of the four powers, which continue to have effect, nor to recognise the division of Germany under international law.

However, I cannot believe that the demand for formal recognition is all that the Government of the GDR can contribute to our negotiations, especially as it to this day has failed to indicate more specifically how it visualises these relations. If the GDR had nothing to offer other than charges and accusations, demands and conditions, then we would not be living up to the significance of this meeting, to the expectations of our people, and to our far-reaching task.

In the hope and the assumption that this is not the case, I suggest that we today reach agreement on the opening of negotiations and on details of procedure. The arrangements I have in mind should include a treaty forming the basis for the relationship between our two States. The Federal Government has elaborated a number of principles and ideas for such a treaty and thereby stated its position regarding the draft which the Chairman of the Council of State of the GDR sent to the Federal President on 18 December 1969. I communicated those principles to you, Mr. Chairman, on 22 January 1970, and drew attention to some of them in Erfurt.

I feel we should use what little time we have to get proper negotiations going.

This we shall not be able to do alone, of course. Our job is to delegate the work and take decisions. Our colleagues and officials will have to prepare such decisions. It should not be hard to establish the level of preparatory negotiations if we can agree that this should be done. Of course, this presupposes that the conditions are right for effective cooperation. You will remember that in Erfurt I proposed that permanent working possibilities should be established for our representatives at our respective seats of government.

The Federal Government developed its concept of the elements of an agreement between our two States, which I would now like to enlarge upon.

The Federal Government considers that the contractual settlement governing our relations is inseparably linked with the substance of the contractual and other relations between our two States. This is how, in spite of all other differences, we have also understood the draft agreement proposed by the GDR.

Our concept of the principles and elements of a treaty regulating relations between the Federal Republic of Germany and the German Democratic Republic on a basis of equality are as follows:

1. The Federal Republic of Germany and the German Democratic Republic, whose constitutions are oriented to the unity of the nation, conclude, in the interest of peace and the future and coherence of the nation, a treaty regulating relations between the two States in Germany, improving contacts between the populations of the two States, and helping to eliminate existing disadvantages.

2. The agreement should be submitted to the respective legislative bodies of both sides for approval, in the form prescribed by their constitutions.

3. Both sides should proclaim their desire to regulate their relations on the basis of human rights, equality, peaceful coexistence and non-discrimination as the generally valid rules of law governing relations between States.

4. Both sides undertake not to use or threaten to use force against each other, and to resolve all existing mutual problems by peaceful means. This includes respect for each other's territorial integrity and frontiers.

5. Both sides respect the independence and autonomy of each of the two States in matters relating to their inner sovereignty.

6. Neither of the two German States can act on behalf of or represent the other.

7. The two contracting parties declare that war must never again originate in Germany.

8. They undertake to refrain from any actions likely to disturb the peaceful coexistence of nations.

9. The two sides reaffirm their intention to support all efforts to achieve disarmament and arms control that will enhance European security.

10. The treaty must proceed from the consequences of the Second World War and the particular situation of Germany and the Germans, who live in two States yet regard themselves as belonging to one nation.

11. Their respective responsibilities towards the French Republic, the United Kingdom of Great Britain and Northern Ireland, the United States of America, and the Union of Soviet Socialist Republics, which are based on the special rights and

agreements of those powers with respect to Berlin and Germany as a whole, shall remain unaffected.

12. The four-power agreements on Berlin and Germany will be respected. The same applies to the links that have grown between West Berlin and the Federal Republic of Germany. Both sides undertake to support the four powers in their efforts to bring about a normalisation of the situation in and around Berlin.

13. The two sides will examine the areas where the legislation of the two States collides. They will endeavour to eliminate such collision so as to avoid creating disadvantages for the citizens of the two States in Germany. In doing so they will start from the principle that the sovereign authority of both sides is limited to their respective territories.

14. The treaty should provide for measures to increase the possibilities for travel between the two States and seek to achieve freedom of movement.

15. A solution should be found for the problems ensuing from the separation of families.

16. The district and municipal authorities in the border areas should be enabled to solve existing problems on a good-neighbourly basis.

17. Both sides should reaffirm their readiness to intensify and extend their cooperation in various fields, such as transport and travel, postal relations and telecommunications, the exchange of information, science, education, culture, environmental problems and sport, to their mutual advantage, and to open negotiations on the details.

18. As regards mutual trade, the existing agreements, commissions, and arrangements will continue to apply. Trade relations should be further developed.

19. The two governments will appoint plenipotentiaries with the rank of Minister and establish offices for the permanent representatives of the plenipotentiaries. The duties of the plenipotentiaries and their representatives will be specified. They will be given working possibilities at the seat of the respective government and be afforded the necessary facilities and privileges.

20. On the basis of the treaty to be concluded between them, the Federal Republic of Germany and the German Democratic Republic will make the necessary arrangements for their membership of and participation in international organisations.

This Mr Chairman, is the text of the principles and elements which I now hand over to you. These proposals, together with the draft treaty proposed by the GDR and other statements and suggestions that we have both put forward or intend to put forward, should be the subject of our further exchanges of views. We should at the same time consider which questions can be immediately tackled and solved in practice, and which can only be dealt with as part of a fundamental regulation of relations between our two States. We shall be making specific proposals in this respect in the course of further negotiations.

In Erfurt I also made some specific remarks about Berlin. I now merely wish to add that the Federal Government welcomes the commencement of four-power talks. It is convinced that progress towards a normalisation of the situation in and around Berlin will also be consequential for the further course of negotiations between our two governments.

12. Statement by Mr Stoph, Kassel, 21 May 1970[1] (extracts)

On behalf of the Council of Ministers of the German Democratic Republic I declare that we are ready immediately to prepare and to sign a treaty on relations that are based on international law. That would be the practicable way to make possible such relations between our countries as can lead to a relationship of peaceful coexistence between the German Democratic Republic and the Federal Republic of Germany.

I must tell you, Mr Chancellor, that our delegation possesses the clear and binding mandate of the People's Chamber of the German Democratic Republic 'to contrive on the basis of international law relations of peaceful coexistence contractually regularised and characterised by equality of status between the German Democratic Republic and the Federal Republic of Germany such as are customary between sovereign States and are indispensable for the guaranteeing of peace'. Thus reads the relevant resolution of the People's Chamber of the German Democratic Republic of 21st March last.

Everyone knows that we regard the attitude of the Government of the Federal Republic of Germany towards the draft treaty of the German Democratic Republic as a criterion as to whether statements made on your side on a normalisation of relations, a reduction of tension and peace are intended seriously. It is difficult to believe that your government has left the draft treaty of the German Democratic Republic, which has been in your hands for months, not only officially unanswered but has persisted in its 'No' to international relations between our two countries, and thus to the treaty's fundamental concerns. If now on your side there is talk of discussions about the treaty, though from the very outset you dismiss this goal, it can only mean beating about the bush and deluding the public.

It contradicts the elementary interests of peace in Europe when a State at the heart of our continent refuses to recognise a neighbouring State internationally and sets its status of sovereign equality at naught, when it calls its frontiers in question and seeks to change the territorial *status quo*. Anyone who wishes to leave the fundamental issues of peace or war open on the line of demarcation between the great military groupings constantly evokes the danger of a serious hostile situation which does not reduce tensions but renders them more bitter. The international recognition by the Federal Republic of Germany of the German Democratic Republic and the territorial *status quo* in Europe is — I would like to place the greatest emphasis on this — not only a juristic question or, for example, a matter of the prestige of the German Democratic Republic or of another State, but a fundamental requirement for peace and security in Europe. As the government of a socialist State, we allow ourselves, in all our actions, to be ruled by human interests . . .

1 Federal Republic, Press and Information Office, *Kassel, 21st May 1970 – A Documentation*.

What is to be understood by 'equality of status' under international law? The principle of sovereign equality, laid down in Article 2 of the Charter of the United Nations, is the first of all the principles to which all States have to adhere. In this sense, the principle of the sovereign equality of States includes, in particular, the following norms:

 — States are equal in law.
 — Every State enjoys the rights inherent in full sovereignty.
 — Every State has the obligation to respect the sovereignty of other States.
 — The territorial integrity and political independence of a State are inviolable.
 — Every State has the right freely to choose and to develop its political, social, economic and cultural systems.
 — Every State has the obligation strictly and honourably to fulfil its international commitments and to live in peace with other nations.

All these elements of the principle of the sovereign equality of States, confirmed by the United Nations, must also be fully applied in the relations between the German Democratic Republic and the Federal Republic of Germany. Thus, equality of status signifies that what the Federal Republic of Germany claims for herself in international relations, the German Democratic Republic can, and must, also demand in line with international law.

I should like to take this opportunity of making a remark about the foreign trade relations between the German Democratic Republic and the Federal Republic of Germany. Recently, in all too obvious a manner, representatives of the Federal Republic of Germany and other quarters have been spreading rumours about alleged advantages for the German Democratic Republic in foreign trade with the Federal Republic of Germany. What exactly is the purpose of this distortion of the facts? I do not wish to go into details here, but I say as a general principle that it was the Federal Republic of Germany which instituted a whole system of trade regimentation with licensing procedures, quotas, limitations on value and a great many special regulations in respect of the German Democratic Republic. If the foreign trade between the German Democratic Republic and the Federal Republic of Germany over the last twenty years is analysed — and this we have done — it is seen that it is precisely the Federal Republic of Germany that has had considerable advantages, in addition to which there is the demonstrable harm done to the German Democratic Republic through the Federal Republic of Germany's interference in the German Democratic Republic's economic relations with third countries. Those are the actual facts.

Mr Chancellor, since you have not yet replied to my question as to the actual aim of your policy, what strategic goal you are pursuing, I would like to revert yet again to this fundamental question. We are greatly interested in receiving a conclusive answer from your lips. Perhaps it will help if I enlarge upon my question somewhat.

Are you ready, in the interest of peace in Europe, to countenance the preparation for a European security peace conference in which all the countries of our continent participate actively on terms of equality?

Are you ready, without reservation and at last, to recognise the European *status quo*, the European frontiers, and in your foreign policy aims to let yourself be guided by the principle of non-interference?

Are you ready to abandon, clearly and in every form, the claim to sole representation, obviously imbued with aggressive aims, as a means of the Federal Government and, instead, to set in its place the principle of equality of status and to act according to this principle?

Are you ready to promote peace and security in Europe through concerted steps to disarmament?

Are you, above all, ready to conclude a treaty on the establishment of international relations between the German Democratic Republic and the Federal Republic of Germany on terms of equality?

Allow me to emphasise: a 'No' to the validity of international law in the relations between the German Democratic Republic and the Federal Republic of Germany, a 'No' to a treaty as already proposed by the German Democratic Republic in December 1969 is directed against a reduction of tensions and against constructive steps towards European security, against the normalisation of the relations between our two States, against the very interest of the people in a secured and peaceful future.

The German Democratic Republic continues to maintain her constructive position. Our proposals are on the table, and — backed up by the mandate of the People's Chamber and on behalf of the Government of the German Democratic Republic — I would like to state that we are prepared immediately to conclude the treaty on the establishment of international relations between our two States on a basis of equality. As I mentioned already at the beginning, we are ready to enter into negotiations about the draft treaty.

As things are, to set up any sort of commissions or representatives, in order to start with the deliberation of questions ranking second or third before an agreement in principle has been reached between the Heads of Government on the establishment of international relations on a basis of equality would make little sense and would avoid the nub of the matter.

We seek genuine solutions creating a solid foundation for normal relations between our States.

The German Democratic Republic looks upon the Charter of the United Nations as a Basic Law for relations between sovereign States on a basis of equality. Ever since the first day of her existence the German Democratic Republic has framed her policy in the spirit of the Charter of the United Nations. The German Democratic Republic's Application for membership in the world organisation, made already a long time ago, is in conformity with this. In the interest of peace and security, in the interest of the peoples of our States, is it not time that the German Democratic Republic and the Federal Republic of Germany are admitted to the United Nations in order, as members, to act in accordance with UNO's principles and aims, to help to secure peace and harmony among nations?

Thereby it can, of course, only mean that the German Democratic Republic and the Federal Republic of Germany are admitted on terms of complete equality and not burdened by any reservations or conditions whatever on the part of the Federal Republic of Germany. The Federal Republic of Germany's arrogant attitude to wish to decide whether or not the German Democratic Republic may become a member of the United Nations Organisation conflicts with the UNO Charter and the principles of the universality of the world organisation. In the view of the Government of the German Democratic Republic, the admission of the German Democratic Republic and the Federal Republic of Germany stands on the agenda. It would be welcomed if you Mr Chancellor, were, here today, to intimate a corresponding readiness on the part of your government.

The German Democratic Republic confirms her firm determination to do everything necessary for peace and security in Europe. She would regard it as regrettable in the highest degree if an unchanged 'No' of the Federal Government were then to make it impossible to arrive at international relations between the German Democratic Republic and the Federal Republic of Germany. Nor, certainly, would the peoples of Europe be able to understand this. We appeal to you, Mr Chancellor, to take into account, on your side too, the exigencies of our times and to cooperate so that firm guarantees for peace are created in the heart of Europe.

13. Guidelines for negotiations on a renunciation of force treaty with the Soviet Union, issued by the Federal Government, 23 July 1970[1] (extract)

1. Relations between the Federal Republic of Germany and the Soviet Union should in future be based just as much on the principle of the renunciation of the threat of force or the use of it as has been the case up to now between the Federal Republic of Germany and the three western powers. This also applies to the inviolability of the territorial integrity of all States and their frontiers. . .

2. The Federal Government's attitude on the Berlin question remains unaffected. We are proceeding on the assumption that the four-power negotiations will lead to a securing of the close ties between the Federal Republic and West Berlin, as well as of unhindered access to West Berlin. Without such a guarantee, the renunciation-of-force pact could not come into effect.

3. The validity of existing treaties and agreements with third States will remain unaffected by the treaty to be concluded. This also includes the Germany treaty.

4. The right of the Germans to self-determination will not be affected by the treaty to be concluded. The Basic Law, including its preamble, is not open to negotiation.

5. The Federal Government is proceeding on the assumption that the treaties sought with the Soviet Union, Poland and other States of the Warsaw Pact, especially the settlement of relations with the German Democratic Republic on the basis of the Federal Government's 20 points put forward at Kassel, will lead to the establish-

1 *Bulletin*, 28 July 1970.

ment and development of normal relations. It regards this policy for better co-existence among peoples and to secure peace in Europe as a single entity.

6. The Federal Government notes with satisfaction that this policy is being given the full approval and support of the three western powers, and the member States of Western European Union and the Atlantic Alliance.

14. The Government of the Federal Republic of Germany to the Governments of France, Great Britain and the United States, 7 August 1970[1]

The Embassy of the Federal Republic of Germany presents its compliments to the ... Embassy and has the honour, on the instructions of its Government, to transmit the following Note with the request that its contents be communicated to the Government of ... as expeditiously as possible:

The Government of the Federal Republic of Germany has the honour, in connection with the imminent signing of a Treaty between the Federal Republic of Germany and the Union of Soviet Socialist Republics, to inform it of the following:

The Federal Minister for Foreign Affairs has, in the context of the negotiations, set forth the Federal Government's position as regards the rights and responsibilities of the Four Powers with regard to Germany as a whole and Berlin.

Since a peace settlement is still outstanding, both sides proceeded on the understanding that the proposed Treaty does not affect the rights and responsibilities of the French Republic, the United Kingdom of Great Britain and Northern Ireland, the Union of Soviet Socialist Republics and the United States of America.

The Federal Minister for Foreign Affairs has in this connection declared to the Soviet Foreign Minister on 6 August 1970:

'The question of the rights of the Four Powers is in no way connected with the Treaty which the Federal Republic of Germany and the Union of Soviet Socialist Republics intend to conclude, and will not be affected by it.'

The Foreign Minister of the Union of Soviet Socialist Republics thereupon made the following declaration:

'The question of the rights of the Four Powers was not the subject of negotiations with the Federal Republic of Germany.

The Soviet Government proceeded on the understanding that this question should not be discussed.

Nor will the question of the rights of the Four Powers be affected by the Treaty which the USSR and the Federal Republic of Germany intend to conclude. This is the position of the Soviet Government regarding this question.'

---

1 *Bulletin*, 13 August 1970. This note was sent by the Federal German Embassy in Moscow to the Moscow Embassies of France, Britain and the United States.

The Embassy of the Federal Republic of Germany avails itself of this opportunity to renew to the . . . Embassy the assurance of its high consideration.

15. The Government of the United States to the Government of the Federal Republic of Germany, 11 August 1970[1] (extracts)

The Government of the United States of America has the honour of informing the Government of the Federal Republic of Germany that it has received the note transmitted by the Government of the Federal Republic of Germany on 7th August 1970. . .

The Government of the United States takes full cognizance of this note, including the declarations made by the Foreign Minister of the Federal Republic of Germany and the Foreign Minister of the Union of Soviet Socialist Republics as part of the negotiations prior to the initiating of the treaty which is to be concluded between the Federal Republic of Germany and the Soviet Union.

For its part, the Government of the United States also considers that the rights and responsibilities of the four powers for Berlin and Germany as a whole which derive from the outcome of the second world war and which are reflected in the London Agreement of 14th November 1944, and in the Quadripartite Declaration of 5th June 1945, and in other wartime and post-war agreements, are not and cannot be affected by a bilateral treaty between the Federal Republic of Germany and the Union of Soviet Socialist Republics, including the present treaty. . .

16. Treaty between the Federal Republic of Germany and the Soviet Union, Moscow, 12 August 1970[2]

The High Contracting Parties

ANXIOUS to contribute to strengthening peace and security in Europe and the world.

CONVINCED that peaceful cooperation among States on the basis of the purposes and principles of the Charter of the United Nations complies with the ardent desire of nations and the general interests of international peace.

APPRECIATING the fact that the agreed measures previously implemented by them, in particular the conclusion of the Agreement of 13 September 1955 on the Establishment of Diplomatic Relations have created favourable conditions for new important steps destined to develop further and to strengthen their mutual relations.

DESIRING to lend expression, in the form of a treaty, to their determination to improve and extend cooperation between them, including economic relations as well as scientific, technological and cultural contacts, in the interest of both States

HAVE AGREED as follows:

1 *Bulletin*, 13 August 1970.
2 *Bulletin*, 13 August 1970.

Article 1

The Federal Republic of Germany and the Union of Soviet Socialist Republics consider it an important objective of their policies to maintain international peace and achieve detente.

They affirm their endeavour to further the normalization of the situation in Europe and the development of peaceful relations among all European States, and in so doing proceed from the actual situation existing in this region.

Article 2

The Federal Republic of Germany and the Union of Soviet Socialist Republics shall in their mutual relations as well as in matters of ensuring European and international security be guided by the purposes and principles embodied in the Charter of the United Nations. Accordingly they shall settle their disputes exclusively by peaceful means and undertake to refrain from the threat or use of force, pursuant to Article 2 of the Charter of the United Nations, in any matters affecting security in Europe or international security, as well as in their mutual relations.

Article 3

In accordance with the foregoing purposes and principles the Federal Republic of Germany and the Union of Soviet Socialist Republics share the realization that peace can only be maintained in Europe if nobody disturbs the present frontiers.
- They undertake to respect without restriction the territorial integrity of all States in Europe within their present frontiers;
- They declare that they have no territorial claims against anybody nor will assert such claims in the future;
- They regard today and shall in future regard the frontiers of all States in Europe as inviolable such as they are on the date of signature of the present Treaty, including the Oder-Neisse line which forms the western frontier of the People's Republic of Poland and the frontier between the Federal Republic of Germany and the German Democratic Republic.

Article 4

The present Treaty between the Federal Republic of Germany and the Union of Soviet Socialist Republics shall not affect any bilateral or multilateral treaties or arrangements previously concluded by them.

Article 5

The present Treaty is subject to ratification and shall enter into force on the date of exchange of the instruments of ratification which shall take place in Bonn.

17. The Government of the Federal Republic of Germany to the Government of the Soviet Union, 12 August 1970[1]

In connection with today's signature of the Treaty between the Federal Republic of Germany and the Union of Soviet Socialist Republics the Government of the Federal Republic of Germany has the honour to state that this Treaty does not conflict with the political objective of the Federal Republic of Germany to work for a state of peace in Europe in which the German nation will recover its unity in free self-determination.

18. Treaty between the Federal Republic of Germany and the People's Republic of Poland, Warsaw, 18 November 1970[2]

The Governments of the Federal Republic of Germany and the People's Republic of Poland,

1. Considering the fact that more than 25 years have passed since the end of the Second World War in which Poland was the first victim and which brought great misfortune upon the people of Europe:

2. Bearing in mind that, in the meantime, a new generation has grown up in both countries for whom a peaceful future should be assured:

3. Wishing to create a durable basis for a peaceful coexistence and the development of good and normal relations between them:

4. In the endeavour to fortify peace and security in Europe:

5. Conscious that the inviolability of frontiers and respect for territorial integrity and the sovereignty of all states in Europe, within their present frontiers, is a fundamental condition for peace, have agreed as follows:—

Article One

(i) The Federal Republic of Germany and the People's Republic of Poland declare in agreement that the existing border line, the course of which was determined in Chapter IX of the decisions of the Potsdam conference of 2 August 1945 as from the Baltic Sea immediately west of Swinemunde, thence along the Oder to the confluence of the Lausitzer Neisse, and along the Lausitzer Neisse to the frontier with Czechoslovakia, forms the western state frontier of the People's Republic of Poland.

(ii) They affirm the inviolability of their existing frontiers, now and in the future, and mutually commit themselves to unrestricted respect for their territorial integrity

---

1 *Bulletin*, 13 August 1970.
2 *The Times*, 21 November 1970. The Treaty was initialled on 18 November and signed on 7 December.

(iii) They declare that they have no territorial claims against one another, and will not raise such claims in the future.

Article Two

(i) The Federal Republic of Germany and the People's Republic of Poland will be guided in their mutual relations, as well as in questions concerning the safeguarding of security in Europe and in the world, by the purposes and principles laid down in the Charter of the United Nations.

(ii) Therefore they will, in accordance with Articles 1 and 2 of the Charter of the United Nations, settle all their disputes exclusively by peaceful means and will refrain from the threat of force or use of force in questions which affect European and international security, as well as in their mutual relations.

Article Three

(i) The Federal Republic of Germany and the People's Republic of Poland will undertake further steps towards full normalization and comprehensive development of their mutual relations of which this treaty forms the firm foundation.

(ii) They are agreed that an expansion of their cooperation in the area of economic, scientific, scientific-technical, cultural and other relations lies in their common interest.[1]

Article Four

This treaty does not affect bilateral or multilateral international agreements previously concluded by, or affecting the parties.

Article Five

This treaty requires ratification. It will come into force on the day the instruments of ratification are exchanged. This shall be done in Bonn.

19. The Government of the Federal Republic of Germany to the Government of the United Kingdom, 19 November 1970[2]

The German Federal Foreign Office presents its compliments to Her Britannic Majesty's Embassy and has the honour to communicate to the Embassy the following

---

1 See the Joint Communiqué issued following the visit of the Federal German Foreign Minister, Mr Genscher, to Poland, 10 October 1975: *Bulletin*, 15 October 1975.
2 *Bulletin*, 24 November 1970. Identical notes were sent simultaneously to the Governments of the United States and France.

text of a note of today's date of the Government of the Federal Republic of German
to the Government of the United Kingdom of Great Britain and Northern Ireland:
'The Government of the Federal Republic of Germany has the honour to inform
the Government of the United Kingdom of Great Britain and Northern Ireland
of the attached text of a treaty between the Federal Republic of Germany and
the People's Republic of Poland concerning the basis for normalising their
mutual relations, which was initialled on 18 November 1970 in Warsaw.

In the course of the negotiations which took place between the Government
of the Federal Republic of Germany and the Government of the People's Republi
of Poland concerning this treaty, it was made clear by the Federal Government
that the treaty between the Federal Republic of Germany and the People's
Republic of Poland does not and cannot affect the rights and responsibilities of
the French Republic, the United Kingdom of Great Britain and Northern Ireland,
the Union of Soviet Socialist Republics, and the United States of America as
reflected in the known treaties and agreements. The Federal Government further
pointed out that it could only act on behalf of the Federal Republic of Germany.

The Government of the French Republic and the Government of the United
States of America have received identical notes.'

The Federal Foreign Office avails itself of this opportunity to renew to Her
Britannic Majesty's Embassy the assurances of its highest consideration.

20. Agreement on Berlin by the Governments of France, Great Britain, the United States and the Soviet Union, 3 September 1971, with Annexes and Related Documents[1]

The Governments of the United States of America, the French Republic, the Union
of Soviet Socialist Republics and the United Kingdom of Great Britain and Northern
Ireland.

Represented by their Ambassadors, who held a series of meetings in the building
formerly occupied by the Allied Control Council in the American Sector of Berlin.

Acting on the basis of their quadripartite rights and responsibilities, and of the
corresponding wartime and postwar agreements and decisions of the Four Powers,
which are not affected.

Taking into account the existing situation in the relevant area,

Guided by the desire to contribute to practical improvements of the situation,

Without prejudice to their legal positions,

Have agreed on the following:

Part I
General Provisions

1. The four Governments will strive to promote the elimination of tension and the
prevention of complications in the relevant area.

1 *DSB*, 27 September 1971, pp. 318–25.

2. The four Governments, taking into account their obligations under the Charter of the United Nations, agree that there shall be no use or threat of force in the area and that disputes shall be settled solely by peaceful means.

3. The four Governments will mutually respect their individual and joint rights and responsibilities, which remain unchanged.

4. The four Governments agree that, irrespective of the differences in legal views, the situation which has developed in the area, and as it is defined in this Agreement as well as in the other agreements referred to in this Agreement, shall not be changed unilaterally.

Part II
Provisions Relating to the Western Sectors of Berlin

A. The Government of the Union of Soviet Socialist Republics declares that transit traffic by road, rail and waterways through the territory of the German Democratic Republic of civilian persons and goods between the Western Sectors of Berlin and the Federal Republic of Germany will be unimpeded; that such traffic will be facilitated so as to take place in the most simple and expeditious manner; and that it will receive preferential treatment.

Detailed arrangements concerning this civilian traffic, as set forth in Annex I, will be agreed by the competent German authorities.

B. The Governments of the French Republic, the United Kingdom and the United States of America declare that the ties between the Western Sectors of Berlin and the Federal Republic of Germany will be maintained and developed, taking into account that these Sectors continue not to be a constituent part of the Federal Republic of Germany and not to be governed by it.

Detailed arrangements concerning the relationship between the Western Sectors of Berlin and the Federal Republic of Germany are set forth in Annex II.

C. The Government of the Union of Soviet Socialist Republics declares that communications between the Western Sectors of Berlin and areas bordering on these Sectors and those areas of the German Democratic Republic which do not border on these Sectors will be improved. Permanent residents of the Western Sectors of Berlin will be able to travel to and visit such areas for compassionate, family, religious, cultural or commercial reasons, or as tourists, under conditions comparable to those applying to other persons entering these areas.

The problems of small enclaves, including Steinstuecken, and of other small areas may be solved by exchange of territory.

Detailed arrangements concerning travel, communications and the exchange of territory, as set forth in Annex III, will be agreed by the competent German authorities.

D. Representation abroad of the interests of the Western Sectors of Berlin and consular activities of the Union of Soviet Socialist Republics in the Western Sectors of Berlin can be exercised as set forth in Annex IV.

Part III
Final Provisions

This Quadripartite Agreement will enter into force on the date specified in a Final Quadripartite Protocol to be concluded when the measures envisaged in Part II of this Quadripartite Agreement and in its Annexes have been agreed.

ANNEX I
Communication From the Government of the Union of Soviet Socialist Republics to the Governments of the French Republic, the United Kingdom and the United States of America

The Government of the Union of Soviet Socialist Republics, with reference to Part II(A) of the Quadripartite Agreement of this date and after consultation and agreement with the Government of the German Democratic Republic, has the honor to inform the Governments of the French Republic, the United Kingdom and the United States of America that:

1. Transit traffic by road, rail and waterways through the territory of the German Democratic Republic of civilian persons and goods between the Western Sectors of Berlin and the Federal Republic of Germany will be facilitated and unimpeded. It will receive the most simple, expeditious and preferential treatment provided by international practice.

2. Accordingly,

(*a*) Conveyances sealed before departure may be used for the transport of civilian goods by road, rail and waterways between the Western Sectors of Berlin and the Federal Republic of Germany. Inspection procedures will be limited to the inspection of seals and accompanying documents.

(*b*) With regard to conveyances which cannot be sealed, such as open trucks, inspection procedures will be limited to the inspection of accompanying documents. In special cases where there is sufficient reason to suspect that unsealed conveyances contain either material intended for dissemination along the designated routes or persons or material put on board along these routes, the content of unsealed conveyances may be inspected. Procedures for dealing with such cases will be agreed by the competent German authorities.

(*c*) Through trains and buses may be used for travel between the Western Sectors of Berlin and the Federal Republic of Germany. Inspection procedures will not include any formalities other than identification of persons.

(*d*) Persons identified as through travellers using individual vehicles between the Western Sectors of Berlin and the Federal Republic of Germany on routes designated for through traffic will be able to proceed to their destinations without paying individual tolls and the fees for the use of the transit routes. Procedures applied for such travellers shall not involve delay. The travellers, their vehicles and personal baggage will not be subject to search, detention or exclusion from use of the designated routes, except in special cases, as may be agreed by the competent German authorities, where there is sufficient reason to suspect that misuse of the transit routes is intended for purposes not related to direct travel to and from the Western Sectors of Berlin and is contrary to generally applicable regulations concerning public order.

(*e*) Appropriate compensation for fees and tolls and for other costs related to traffic on the communication routes between the Western Sectors of Berlin and the Federal Republic of Germany, including the maintenance of adequate routes, facilities and installations used for such traffic, may be made in the form of an annual lump sum paid to the German Democratic Republic by the Federal Republic of Germany.

3. Arrangements implementing and supplementing the provisi ns of paragraphs 1 and 2 above will be agreed by the competent German authorities.

ANNEX II
Communication From the Governments of the French Republic, the United Kingdom and the United States of America to the Government of the Union of Soviet Socialist Republics

The Governments of the French Republic, the United Kingdom and the United States of America, with reference to Part II(B) of the Quadripartite Agreement of this date and after consultation with the Government of the Federal Republic of Germany, have the honor to inform the Government of the Union of Soviet Socialist Republics that:

1. They declare, in the exercise of their rights and responsibilities, that the ties between the Western Sectors of Berlin and the Federal Republic of Germany will be maintained and developed, taking into account that these Sectors continue not to be a constituent part of the Federal Republic of Germany and not to be governed by it. The provisions of the Basic Law of the Federal Republic of Germany and of the Constitution operative in the Western Sectors of Berlin which contradict the above have been suspended and continue not to be in effect.

2. The Federal President, the Federal Government, the Bundesversammlung, the Bundesrat and the Bundestag, including their Committees and Fraktionen, as well as other state bodies of the Federal Republic of Germany will not perform in the Western Sectors of Berlin constitutional or official acts which contradict the provisions of paragraph 1.

3. The Government of the Federal Republic of Germany will be represented in the Western Sectors of Berlin to the authorities of the three Governments and to the Senat by a permanent liaison agency.

ANNEX III
Communication From the Government of the Union of Soviet Socialist Republics to the Governments of the French Republic, the United Kingdom and the United States of America

The Government of the Union of Soviet Socialist Republics, with reference to

Part II(C) of the Quadripartite Agreement of this date and after consultation and agreement with the Government of the German Democratic Republic, has the honor to inform the Governments of the French Republic, the United Kingdom and the United States of America that:

1. Communications between the Western Sectors of Berlin and areas bordering on these Sectors and those areas of the German Democratic Republic which do not border on these Sectors will be improved.

2. Permanent residents of the Western Sectors of Berlin will be able to travel to and visit such areas for compassionate, family, religious, cultural or commercial reasons, or as tourists, under conditions comparable to those applying to other persons entering these areas. In order to facilitate visits and travel, as described above by permanent residents of the Western Sectors of Berlin, additional crossing points will be opened.

3. The problems of the small enclaves, including Steinstuecken, and of other small areas may be solved by exchange of territory.

4. Telephonic, telegraphic, transport and other external communications of the Western Sectors of Berlin will be expanded.

5. Arrangements implementing and supplementing the provisions of paragraphs 1 to 4 above will be agreed by the competent German authorities.

ANNEX IV

A. Communication From the Governments of the French Republic, the United Kingdom and the United States of America to the Government of the Union of Soviet Socialist Republics

The Governments of the French Republic, the United Kingdom and the United States of America, with reference to Part II(D) of the Quadripartite Agreement of this date and after consultation with the Government of the Federal Republic of Germany, have the honor to inform the Government of the Union of Soviet Socialist Republics that:

1. The Governments of the French Republic, the United Kingdom and the United States of America maintain their rights and responsibilities relating to the representation abroad of the interests of the Western Sectors of Berlin and their permanent residents, including those rights and responsibilities concerning matters of security and status, both in international organizations and in relations with other countries.

2. Without prejudice to the above and provided that matters of security and status are not affected, they have agreed that:

(*a*) The Federal Republic of Germany may perform consular services for permanent residents of the Western Sectors of Berlin.

(*b*) In accordance with established procedures, international agreements and arrangements entered into by the Federal Republic of Germany may be extended to the Western Sectors of Berlin provided that the extension of such agreements and arrangements is specified in each case.

(*c*) The Federal Republic of Germany may represent the interests of the Western Sectors of Berlin in international organizations and international conferences.

(*d*) Permanent residents of the Western Sectors of Berlin may participate jointly with participants from the Federal Republic of Germany in international exchanges and exhibitions. Meetings of international organizations and international conferences as well as exhibitions with international participation may be held in the Western Sectors of Berlin. Invitations will be issued by the Senat or jointly by the Federal Republic of Germany and the Senat.

3. The three Governments authorize the establishment of a Consulate General of the USSR in the Western Sectors of Berlin accredited to the appropriate authorities of the three Governments in accordance with the usual procedures applied in those Sectors, for the purpose of performing consular services, subject to provisions set forth in a separate document of this date.

B. Communication From the Government of the Union of Soviet Socialist Republics to the Governments of the French Republic, the United Kingdom and the United States of America

The Government of the Union of Soviet Socialist Republics, with reference to Part II(D) of the Quadripartite Agreement of this date and to the communication of the Governments of the French Republic, the United Kingdom and the United States of America with regard to the representation abroad of the interests of the Western Sectors of Berlin and their permanent residents, has the honor to inform the Governments of the French Republic, the United Kingdom and the United States of America that:

1. The Government of the Union of Soviet Socialist Republics takes note of the fact that the three Governments maintain their rights and responsibilities relating to the representation abroad of the interests of the Western Sectors of Berlin and their permanent residents, including those rights and responsibilities concerning matters of security and status, both in international organizations and in relations with other countries.

2. Provided that matters of security and status are not affected, for its part it will raise no objection to:

(*a*) the performance by the Federal Republic of Germany of consular services for permanent residents of the Western Sectors of Berlin;

(*b*) in accordance with established procedures, the extension to the Western Sectors of Berlin of international agreements and arrangements entered into by the Federal Republic of Germany provided that the extension of such agreements and arrangements is specified in each case;

(*c*) the representation of the interests of the Western Sectors of Berlin by the Federal Republic of Germany in international organizations and international conferences;

(*d*) the participation jointly with participants from the Federal Republic of Germany of permanent residents of the Western Sectors of Berlin in international exchanges and exhibitions, or the holding in those Sectors of meetings of international organizations and international conferences as well as exhibitions with international participation, taking into account that invitations will be issued by the Senat or jointly by the Federal Republic of Germany and the Senat.

3. The Government of the Union of Soviet Socialist Republics takes note of the fact that the three Governments have given their consent to the establishment of a Consulate General of the USSR in the Western Sectors of Berlin. It will be accredited to the appropriate authorities of the three Governments, for purposes and subject to provisions described in their communication and as set forth in a separate document of this date.

RELATED DOCUMENTS
Agreed Minute I

It is understood that permanent residents of the Western Sectors of Berlin shall, in order to receive at appropriate Soviet offices visas for entry into the Union of Soviet Socialist Republics, present:

(*a*) a passport stamped 'Issued in accordance with the Quadripartite Agreement of September 3, 1971';

(*b*) an identity card or other appropriately drawn up document confirming that the person requesting the visa is a permanent resident of the Western Sectors of Berlin and containing the bearer's full address and a personal photograph.

During his stay in the Union of Soviet Socialist Republics, a permanent resident of the Western Sectors of Berlin who has received a visa in this way may carry both documents or either of them, as he chooses. The visa issued by a Soviet office will serve as the basis for entry into the Union of Soviet Socialist Republics, and the passport or identity card will serve as the basis for consular services in accordance with the Quadripartite Agreement during the stay of that person in the territory of the Union of Soviet Socialist Republics.

The above-mentioned stamp will appear in all passports used by permanent residents of the Western Sectors of Berlin for journeys to such countries as may require it.

Agreed Minute II

Provision is hereby made for the establishment of a Consulate General of the USSR in the Western Sectors of Berlin. It is understood that the details concerning this Consulate General will include the following. The Consulate General will be accredited to the appropriate authorities of the three Governments in accordance with the usual procedures applying in those Sectors. Applicable Allied and German legislation and regulations will apply to the Consulate General. The activities of the Consulate General will be of a consular character and will not include political functions or any matters related to quadripartite rights or responsibilities.

The three Governments are willing to authorize an increase in Soviet commercial activities in the Western Sectors of Berlin as described below. It is understood that pertinent Allied and German legislation and regulations will apply to these activities. This authorization will be extended indefinitely, subject to compliance with the provisions outlined herein. Adequate provision for consultation will be made. This increase will include establishment of an 'Office of Soviet Foreign Trade Associations in the Western Sectors of Berlin', with commercial status, authorized to buy and sell on behalf of foreign trade associations of the Union of Soviet Socialist Republics. Soyuzpushnina, Prodintorg and Novoexport may each establish a bonded warehouse in the Western Sectors of Berlin to provide storage and display for their goods. The activities of the Intourist office in the British Sector of Berlin may be expanded to include the sale of tickets and vouchers for travel and tours in the Union of Soviet Socialist Republics and other countries. An office of Aeroflot may be established for the sale of passenger tickets and air freight services.

The assignment of personnel to the Consulate General and to permitted Soviet commercial organizations will be subject to agreement with the appropriate authorities of the three Governments. The number of such personnel will not exceed twenty Soviet nationals in the Consulate General; twenty in the office of the Soviet Foreign Trade Associations: one each in the bonded warehouses; six in the Intourist office; and five in the Aeroflot office. The personnel of the Consulate General and of permitted Soviet commercial organizations and their dependents may reside in the Western Sectors of Berlin upon individual authorization.

The property of the Union of Soviet Socialist Republics at Lietzenburgerstrasse 11 and at Am Sandwerder 1 may be used for purposes to be agreed between appropriate representatives of the three Governments and of the Government of the Union of Soviet Socialist Republics.

Details of implementation of the measures above and a time schedule for carrying them out will be agreed between the four Ambassadors in the period between the signature of the Quadripartite Agreement and the signature of the Final Quadripartite Protocol envisaged in that Agreement.

The Ambassadors of France, Great Britain and the United States to the Ambassador of the Soviet Union

The Ambassadors of the French Republic, the United Kingdom of Great Britain and Northern Ireland and the United States of America have the honor, with reference to the statements contained in Annex II of the Quadripartite Agreement to be signed on this date concerning the relationship between the Federal Republic of Germany and the Western Sectors of Berlin, to inform the Ambassador of the Union of Soviet Socialist Republics of their intention to send to the Chancellor of the Federal Republic of Germany immediately following signature of the Quadripartite Agreement a letter containing clarifications and interpretations which represent the understanding of their Governments of the statements contained in Annex II of the Quadripartite Agreement. A copy of the letter to be sent to the Chancellor of the Federal Republic of Germany is attached to this Note.

The Ambassadors avail themselves of this opportunity to renew to the Ambassador of the Union of Soviet Socialist Republics the assurances of their highest consideration.

The Governments of France, Great Britain and the United States to the Federal German Chancellor

With reference to the Quadripartite Agreement signed on 3 September 1971, our Governments wish by this letter to inform the Government of the Federal Republic of Germany of the following clarifications and interpretations of the statements contained in Annex II, which was the subject of consultation with the Government of the Federal Republic of Germany during the quadripartite negotiations.

These clarifications and interpretations represent the understanding of our Governments of this part of the Quadripartite Agreement, as follows:

a. The phrase in Paragraph 2 of Annex II of the Quadripartite Agreement which reads '. . . will not perform in the Western Sectors of Berlin constitutional or official acts which contradict the provisions of Paragraph 1' shall be interpreted to mean acts in exercise of direct state authority over the Western Sectors of Berlin.

b. Meetings of the Bundesversammlung will not take place and plenary sessions of the Bundesrat and the Bundestag will continue not to take place in the Western Sectors of Berlin. Single committees of the Bundesrat and the Bundestag may meet in the Western Sectors of Berlin in connection with maintaining and developing the ties between those Sectors and the Federal Republic of Germany. In the case of Fraktionen, meetings will not be held simultaneously.

c. The liaison agency of the Federal Government in the Western Sectors of Berlin includes departments charged with liaison functions in their respective fields.

d. Established procedures concerning the applicability to the Western Sectors of Berlin of legislation of the Federal Republic of Germany shall remain unchanged.

e. The term 'state bodies' in Paragraph 2 of Annex II shall be interpreted to mean: the Federal President, the Federal Chancellor, the Federal Cabinet, the Federal Ministers and Ministries, and the branch offices of those Ministries, the Bundesrat and the Bundestag, and all Federal courts.

Accept, Excellency, the renewed assurance of our highest esteem.

The Governments of France, Great Britain and the United States to the Federal German Chancellor

We have the honor by means of this letter to convey to the Government of the Federal Republic of Germany the text of the Quadripartite Agreement signed this day in Berlin. The Quadripartite Agreement was concluded by the Four Powers in the exercise of their rights and responsibilities with respect to Berlin.

We note that, pursuant to the terms of the Agreement and of the Final Quadripartite Protocol which ultimately will bring it into force, the text of which has been agreed, these rights and responsibilities are not affected and remain unchanged. Our Governments will continue, as heretofore, to exercise supreme authority in the Western Sectors of Berlin, within the framework of the Four Power responsibility which we share for Berlin as a whole.

In accordance with Part II(A) of the Quadripartite Agreement, arrangements implementing and supplementing the provisions relating to civilian traffic will be agreed by the competent German authorities. Part III of the Quadripartite Agreement provides that the Agreement will enter into force on a date to be specified in a Final Quadripartite Protocol which will be concluded when the arrangements envisaged between the competent German authorities have been agreed. It is the request of our Governments that the envisaged negotiations now take place between authorities of the Federal Republic of Germany, also acting on behalf of the Senat, and authorities of the German Democratic Republic.

Part II(B) and (D) and Annexes II and IV of the Quadripartite Agreement relate to the relationship between the Western Sectors of Berlin and the Federal Republic. In this connection, the following are recalled inter alia:

— the communications of the three Western Military Governors to the Parliamentary Council of 2 March, 22 April and 12 May 1949.
— the letter of the three High Commissioners to the Federal Chancellor concerning the exercise of the reserved Allied rights relating to Berlin of 26 May 1952 in the version of the letter X of 23 October 1954.
— the Aide Memoire of the three Governments of 18 April 1967 concerning the decision of the Federal Constitutional Court of 20 January 1966 in the Niekisch case.

Our Governments take this occasion to state, in exercise of the rights and responsibilities relating to Berlin, which they retained in Article 2 of the Convention on Relations between the Three Powers and the Federal Republic of Germany of 26 May 1952 as amended October 23 1954, that Part II(B) and (D) and Annexes II and IV of the Quadripartite Agreement concerning the relationship between the Federal Republic of Germany and the Western Sectors of Berlin accord with the position in the above mentioned documents, which remains unchanged.

With regard to the existing ties between the Federal Republic and the Western Sectors of Berlin, it is the firm intention of our Governments that, as stated in Part II(B)(1) of the Quadripartite Agreement, these ties will be maintained and developed in accordance with the letter from the three High Commissioners to the Federal Chancellor on the exercise of the reserved rights relating to Berlin of 26 May 1952, in the version of letter X of October 23 1954, and with pertinent decisions of the Allied Kommandatura of Berlin.

Accept, Excellency, the renewed assurance of our highest esteem.

Communication from Allied Kommandatura to the Governing Mayor of Berlin

The Allied Kommandatura refers to the Quadripartite Agreement signed on September 3 in Berlin.

Part II(C) and Annex III, Paragraph 5, of the Quadripartite Agreement provide that arrangements implementing and supplementing the provisions relating to travel, communications and the exchange of territory will be agreed by the competent German authorities. Part IV of the Quadripartite Agreement provides that the Agreement will enter into force on a date to be specified in a Final Quadripartite Protocol which will be concluded when the arrangements envisaged between the competent German authorities have been agreed.

The Senat of Berlin is hereby authorized and requested to conduct appropriate negotiations on the subjects covered in Paragraphs 1, 2 and 3 in Annex III.

21. Communiqué issued following the talks between Chancellor Brandt and Mr Brezhnev, Oreanda, Crimea, 18 September 1971[1]

The Federal Chancellor of the Federal Republic of Germany Willy Brandt paid a visit to the Soviet Union from 16 to 18 September 1971, in accordance with an agreement reached during his stay in Moscow in August 1970.

A number of conversations between the general secretary of the CPSU central committee Leonid Brezhnev and Federal Chancellor Willy Brandt took place in the Crimea during the visit. The talks were of a businesslike and frank nature, and were held in an atmosphere of mutual understanding.

Taking part in the meeting were: from the Soviet side – senior officials of the secretariat of the general secretary of the CPSU central committee and the USSR Ministry of Foreign Affairs; and from the FRG side – senior officials of the Federal Chancellor's office and the Ministry of Foreign Affairs of the Federal Republic of Germany.

In a spirit of complete loyalty to their allies, the two sides discussed a wide range of international problems of interest to both parties, devoting the main attention to the development of the situation in Europe. They exchanged views on questions concerning the state of relations between the USSR and the Federal Republic of Germany and the possibilities of their development.

The prime importance of the treaty signed by the Soviet Union and the Federal Republic on 12 August 1970 for the present and future of the relations between the two States was stressed. Already at the present time, this treaty facilitates an improvement of the political climate between the two States and is exerting a favourable influence on the entire course of European affairs.

Leonid Brezhnev and Willy Brandt discussed questions concerning the ratification of the treaty by the USSR Supreme Soviet and the Bundestag of the FRG, and expressed the firm conviction that the entry into force in the very near future of the treaty between the USSR and the Federal Republic of Germany, and of the treaty between the Polish People's Republic and the FRG will make it possible to ensure a resolute turn in relations between the abovementioned countries in the

1 *Soviet News*, 21 September 1971.

direction of extensive, firm and lasting cooperation to the great benefit of present and future generations of the peoples of these countries and their neighbours, and of the strengthening of peace in Europe.

The two sides unanimously stated that development in this direction accorded with their aims and intentions, and that they would tirelessly work to overcome the vestiges of the grim past and to enhance thereby the implementation of the ideas of peaceful cooperation, both in inter-State relations and in contacts between public organisations and citizens of the two States.

In this connection considerable attention was paid in the talks to questions connected with the signing by the USSR, the United Kingdom, the United States and France on 3 September this year of the quadripartite agreement, which is a major step along the road of easing European and international tensions. The two sides agree that the reaching of this agreement creates good prerequisites for further practical steps aimed at improving the situation in the centre of Europe and at consolidating security and developing cooperation on the continent.

Questions concerning the preparation of a conference on questions of security and cooperation in Europe held an important place in the talks. It was found that the situation which is now taking shape in Europe facilitates the convocation of an all-European conference with the participation of the United States and Canada. The Soviet Union and the Federal Republic intend to hold consultations shortly with each other and with their allies and other European States in order to speed up the holding of the conference.

The two sides outlined their views on the reduction of armed forces and armaments in Europe without detriment to the participating States and found that common elements existed in their positions. They are convinced that a solution to this complex problem would seriously strengthen the mainstays of European and international peace. The future of the European continent, just as of other areas of the world, should be based, not on a military confrontation of States but on equal cooperation and on ensuring security for each State individually and all States together.

The normalisation of relations between the German Democratic Republic and the Federal Republic of Germany on the basis of complete equality, non-discrimination and mutual respect for the independence of both States in matters concerning their internal competence, within their appropriate borders, today appears to be possible and of much importance. The joining by both these States, in the process of detente in Europe, of the United Nations and specialised international institutions will be one of the important steps in this direction. In accordance with an earlier agreement, the Soviet Union and the Federal Republic will duly assist such a solution of the question.

Questions concerning the development of bilateral relations between the USSR and the Federal Republic of Germany were thoroughly discussed during the conversations between the general secretary of the CPSU central committee and the Federal Chancellor. The two sides have come to the conclusion that extensive possibilities exist for organising and constantly building up mutually beneficial cooperation between the two countries in the most diverse fields, which would accord with the letter and spirit of the treaty of 12 August 1970.

In accordance with this, the two sides declared themselves in favour of an expansion of trade relations and scientific, technical, cultural and sports ties, as well as exchanges between youth organisations, and affirmed their readiness to achieve the speedy conclusion of appropriate agreements. A mixed commission will be set up to develop economic cooperation.

Leonid Brezhnev and Willy Brandt believe that the practice of exchanging views and of consultations at various levels, now taking shape between the USSR and the FRG both on questions of bilateral relations and on international problems, is useful and should be continued.

It was noted with satisfaction in this connection that the Ministers of Foreign Affairs of both States are to meet this autumn in New York and later in the Soviet Union.

22. Resolution adopted by the Bundestag on the Ratification of the Treaties with the Soviet Union and Poland, 17 May 1972[1]

In connection with the voting on the treaty of 12 August 1970 between the Federal Republic of Germany and the Union of Soviet Socialist Republics, and on the treaty of 7 December 1970 between the Federal Republic of Germany and the Polish People's Republic concerning the basis for normalising their mutual relations, the German Bundestag declares:

1. One of the determining aims of our foreign policy is to preserve peace in Europe and the security of the Federal Republic of Germany. The treaties with Moscow and Warsaw, in which the contracting parties solemnly and wholly renounce the use and threat of the use of force, are designed to serve those aims. They constitute important elements of the *modus vivendi* which the Federal Republic of Germany seeks to establish with its eastern neighbours.

2. The Federal Republic of Germany has assumed on its own behalf the obligations it undertook in the treaties. The treaties proceed from the frontiers as actually existing today, the unilateral alteration of which they exclude. The treaties do not anticipate a peace settlement for Germany by treaty and do not create any legal foundation for the frontiers existing today.

3. The inalienable right to self-determination is not affected by the treaties. The policy of the Federal Republic of Germany aiming at the peaceful restoration of national unity within the European framework is not in contradiction to the treaties which do not prejudice the solution of the German question. By demanding the implementation of the right of self-determination, the Federal Republic of Germany does not make any territorial claims nor does it claim any alteration of frontiers.

4. The German Bundestag states that the continued and unrestricted validity of the Bonn conventions and of the related arrangements and declarations of 1954

1 *Bulletin*, 23 May 1972.

as well as the continued validity of the agreement concluded on 13 September 1955 between the Federal Republic of Germany and the Union of Soviet Socialist Republics are not affected by the treaties.

5. The rights and responsibilities of the four powers relating to Germany as a whole and to Berlin are not affected by the treaties. In view of the fact that the final settlement of the German question as a whole is still outstanding, the German Bundestag considers as essential the continuance of those rights and responsibilities.

6. As regards the significance of the treaties, the German Bundestag furthermore refers to the memoranda which the Federal Government has submitted to the legislative bodies together with the bills for the ratification of the treaties of Moscow and Warsaw.

7. The Federal Republic of Germany is firmly embedded in the Atlantic Alliance, which continues to form the basis of its security and freedom.

8. The Federal Republic of Germany will, together with its partners in the Community, unwaveringly pursue the policy of European unification with the aim of developing the Community progressively into a political union.

In this connection the Federal Republic of Germany proceeds on the understanding that the Soviet Union and other socialist countries will enter into cooperation with the EEC.

9. The Federal Republic of Germany reasserts its firm resolve to maintain and develop the ties between Berlin (West) and the Federal Republic of Germany in accordance with the quadripartite agreement and the German supplementary arrangements thereto. It will also in the future ensure the city's viability and the well-being of its people.

10. The Federal Republic of Germany advocates the normalisation of the relationship between the Federal Republic of Germany and the GDR. It proceeds on the understanding that the principles of detente and good neighbourliness will be fully applied to the relationship between people and institutions in both parts of Germany.

23. Final Protocol bringing into force the Quadripartite Agreement on Berlin of 3 September 1971, 3 June 1972[1]

The Governments of the United States of America, the French Republic, the Union of Soviet Socialist Republics and the United Kingdom of Great Britain and Northern Ireland,

Having in mind Part III of the quadripartite agreement of 3 September 1971 and taking note with satisfaction of the fact that the agreements and arrangements mentioned below have been concluded,

Have agreed on the following:

1 Foreign Office, Bonn.

1. The four governments, by virtue of this protocol, bring into force the quadripartite agreement, which, like this protocol, does not affect quadripartite agreements or decisions previously concluded or reached.

2. The four governments proceed on the basis that the agreements and arrangements concluded between the competent German authorities:

'Agreement between the Government of the Federal Republic of Germany and the Government of the German Democratic Republic on the transit traffic of civilian persons and goods between the Federal Republic of Germany and Berlin (West)' dated 17 December 1971;

'Arrangement between the Senate and the Government of the German Democratic Republic on facilitations and improvements in travel and visitor traffic' dated 20 December 1971;

'Arrangement between the Senate and the Government of the German Democratic Republic on the resolution of the problem of enclaves by exchange of territory' dated 20 December 1971;

Points 6 and 7 of the 'Protocol on negotiations between a delegation of the Federal Ministry for Post and Telecommunications of the Federal Republic of Germany and a delegation of the Ministry for Post and Telecommunications of the German Democratic Republic' dated 30 September 1971;[1]

shall enter into force simultaneously with the quadripartite agreement.

3. The quadripartite agreement and the consequent agreements and arrangements of the competent German authorities referred to in this protocol settle important issues examined in the course of the negotiations and shall remain in force together.

4. In the event of a difficulty in the application of the quadripartite agreement or any of the abovementioned agreements or arrangements which any of the four governments considers serious, or in the event of non-implementation of any part thereof, that government will have the right to draw the attention of the other three governments to the provisions of the quadripartite agreement and this protocol and to conduct the requisite quadripartite consultations in order to ensure the observance of the commitments undertaken and to bring the situation into conformity with the quadripartite agreement and this protocol.

5. This protocol enters into force on the date of signature.

24. Treaty on the Basis of Relations between the Federal Republic of Germany and the German Democratic Republic, Bonn, 8 November 1972, with Protocol, statements and letters[2]

The High Contracting Parties,

Conscious of their responsibility for the preservation of peace,

Anxious to render a contribution to detente and security in Europe.

1 Not published here; for texts see *Texte zur Deutschland politike*, Band 9 (German Federal Republic, Bundesministerium für innerdeutsche Beziehungen, Bonn, February 1972).

2 *Bulletin*, 14 November 1972.

Aware that the inviolability of frontiers and respect for the territorial integrity and sovereignty of all States in Europe within their present frontiers are a basic condition for peace,

Recognizing that therefore the two German States have to refrain from the threat or use of force in their relations,

Proceeding from the historical facts and without prejudice to the different views of the Federal Republic of Germany and the German Democratic Republic on fundamental questions, including the national question,

Desirous to create the conditions for cooperation between the Federal Republic of Germany and the German Democratic Republic for the benefit of the people in the two German States,

Have agreed as follows:

Article 1

The Federal Republic of Germany and the German Democratic Republic shall develop normal, good-neighbourly relations with each other on the basis of equal rights.

Article 2

The Federal Republic of Germany and the German Democratic Republic will be guided by the aims and principles laid down in the United Nations Charter, especially those of the sovereign equality of all States, respect for their independence, autonomy and territorial integrity, the right of self-determination, the protection of human rights, and non-discrimination.

Article 3

In conformity with the United Nations Charter the Federal Republic of Germany and the German Democratic Republic shall settle any disputes between them exclusively by peaceful means and refrain from the threat or use of force.

They reaffirm the inviolability now and in the future of the frontier existing between them and undertake fully to respect each other's territorial integrity.

Article 4

The Federal Republic of Germany and the German Democratic Republic proceed on the assumption that neither of the two States can represent the other in the international sphere or act on its behalf.

Article 5

The Federal Republic of Germany and the German Democratic Republic shall promote peaceful relations between the European States and contribute to security and cooperation in Europe.

They shall support efforts to reduce forces and arms in Europe without allowing disadvantages to arise for the security of those concerned.

The Federal Republic of Germany and the German Democratic Republic shall support, with the aim of general and complete disarmament under effective international control, efforts serving international security to achieve armaments limitation and disarmament, especially with regard to nuclear weapons and other weapons of mass destruction.

Article 6

The Federal Republic of Germany and the German Democratic Republic proceed on the principle that the sovereign jurisdiction of each of the two States is confined to its own territory. They respect each other's independence and autonomy in their internal and external affairs.

Article 7

The Federal Republic of Germany and the German Democratic Republic declare their readiness to regulate practical and humanitarian questions in the process of the normalization of their relations. They shall conclude agreements with a view to developing and promoting on the basis of the present Treaty and for their mutual benefit cooperation in the fields of economics, science and technology, transport, judicial relations, posts and telecommunications, health, culture, sport, environmental protection, and in other fields. The details have been agreed in the Supplementary Protocol.

Article 8

The Federal Republic of Germany and the German Democratic Republic shall exchange Permanent Missions. They shall be established at the respective Government's seat.

Practical questions relating to the establishment of the Missions shall be dealt with separately.

Article 9

The Federal Republic of Germany and the German Democratic Republic agree that the present Treaty shall not affect the bilateral and multilateral international treaties and Agreements already concluded by them or relating to them.

Article 10

The present Treaty shall be subject to ratification and shall enter into force on the day after the exchange of notes to that effect.

SUPPLEMENTARY PROTOCOL

Re Article 3
The Federal Republic of Germany and the German Democratic Republic have agreed to form a Commission composed of agents of the Governments of the two States. They will review and, where necessary, renew or supplement the marking of the frontier existing between the two States and draw up the necessary documentation on the course of the frontier. In the same way the Commission will contribute to regulating other problems connected with the course of the frontier, e.g. water management, energy supply and the prevention of damage.

The Commission shall commence its work after the signing of the Treaty.

Re Article 7
1. Trade between the Federal Republic of Germany and the German Democratic Republic shall be developed on the basis of the existing agreements.

The Federal Republic of Germany and the German Democratic Republic shall conclude long-term agreements with a view to promoting the continued development of their economic relations, adapting outdated arrangements, and improving the structure of trade.

2. The Federal Republic of Germany and the German Democratic Republic proclaim their intention to develop cooperation in the fields of science and technology for their mutual benefit and to conclude the necessary treaties for this purpose.

3. The cooperation in the field of traffic which began with the Treaty of 26 May 1972 shall be widened and intensified.

4. The Federal Republic of Germany and the German Democratic Republic declare their readiness to regulate their judicial relations as simply and expediently as possible by treaty in the interests of those seeking justice, especially in the fields of civil and criminal law.

5. The Federal Republic of Germany and the German Democratic Republic agree to conclude an agreement on posts and telecommunications on the basis of the Constitution of the Universal Postal Union and the International Telecommunication Convention. They will notify the Universal Postal Union (UPU) and the International Telecommunication Union (ITU) of the conclusion of that agreement.

The existing agreements and the procedures beneficial to both sides will be incorporated in that agreement.

6. The Federal Republic of Germany and the German Democratic Republic declare their interest in cooperation in the field of health. They agree that the appropriate treaty shall also regulate the exchange of medicaments as well as the treatment of patients in special clinics and sanatoria as far as practicable.

7. The Federal Republic of Germany and the German Democratic Republic intend to develop their cultural cooperation. To this end they shall enter into negotiations on the conclusion of intergovernmental agreements.

8. The Federal Republic of Germany and the German Democratic Republic reaffirm their preparedness to assist the appropriate sports organizations, after the Treaty has been signed, in bringing about arrangements for the promotion of relations in the field of sport.

9. Agreements are to be concluded between the Federal Republic of Germany and the German Democratic Republic in the field of environmental protection in order to help prevent hazards and harm to each other.

10. The Federal Republic of Germany and the German Democratic Republic will conduct negotiations with a view to enhancing the acquisition of each other's books, periodicals, radio and television productions.

11. The Federal Republic of Germany and the German Democratic Republic shall, in the interest of the people concerned, enter into negotiations to regulate non-commercial payment and clearing procedures. In this connexion they shall, in their mutual interest, give priority to the early conclusion of agreements on social grounds.

PROTOCOL NOTE

Owing to the different legal positions with regard to questions of property and assets these matters could not be regulated by the Treaty.

JOINT STATEMENT ON THE EXTENSION OF AGREEMENTS AND ARRANGEMENTS TO BERLIN (WEST); REPRESENTATION OF THE INTERESTS OF BERLIN(WEST)

It is agreed that the extension to Berlin (West) of agreements and arrangements envisaged in the Supplementary Protocol to Article 7 may be agreed in each individual case in conformity with the Quadripartite Agreement of 3 September 1971.

The Permanent Mission of the Federal Republic of Germany in the German Democratic Republic shall, in conformity with the Quadripartite Agreement of 3 September 1971, represent the interests of Berlin (West).

Arrangements between the German Democratic Republic and the Senate shall remain unaffected.

JOINT STATEMENT ON POLITICAL CONSULTATION

The two Governments have agreed to consult each other in the process of the normalization of relations between the Federal Republic of Germany and the German Democratic Republic on questions of mutual interest, in particular on those important for the safeguarding of peace in Europe.

MR BAHR, STATE SECRETARY OF THE FEDERAL CHANCELLERY, TO MR KOHL, STATE SECRETARY TO THE COUNCIL OF MINISTERS OF THE GERMAN DEMOCRATIC REPUBLIC CONCERNING AN APPLICATION FOR MEMBERSHIP IN THE UNITED NATIONS

I have the honour to inform you of the following:

The Government of the Federal Republic of Germany has noted that the Government of the German Democratic Republic initiates the necessary steps in conformity with domestic legislation to acquire membership of the United Nations Organization.

The two Governments will inform each other of the date on which the application will be made.

MR BAHR TO MR KOHL CONCERNING ARTICLE 9 OF THE TREATY

I have the honour to inform you that the German Federal Foreign Office will today transmit in notes to the Ambassadors of the French Republic, the United Kingdom of Great Britain and Northern Ireland, and the United States of America to the Federal Republic of Germany the following text:

'The Federal Republic of Germany and the German Democratic Republic, with reference to Article 9 of the the Treaty on the basis of relations, dated . . . . . ., affirm that the rights and responsibilities of the Four Powers and the corresponding, related Quadripartite agreements, decisions and practices cannot be affected by this Treaty.'

MR BAHR TO MR KOHL CONCERNING THE REUNIFICATION OF FAMILIES, FACILITATION OF TRAVEL, AND IMPROVEMENTS IN NON-COMMERCIAL GOODS TRAFFIC

On the occasion of the signing today of the Treaty on the Basis of Relations between the Federal Republic of Germany and the German Democratic Republic, I have the honour to inform you of the following:

The Government of the Federal Republic of Germany will in the process of the normalization of relations and after the entry into force of the Treaty take steps to regulate matters in the following fields:

1. The solution of problems resulting from the separation of families.

2. Further to the exchange of letters of 26 May 1972, measures for the further improvement of border-crossing travel and visitor traffic, including tourism.

3. Improvement of non-commercial goods traffic between the Federal Republic of Germany and the German Democratic Republic:

— further measures to facilitate border-crossing traffic in gift parcels and packages;
— further facilities for travellers to carry non-commercial goods in border-crossing travel and visitor traffic;
— corresponding review of existing import and export regulations;
— simplification of procedures to obtain permits for the removal of personal and household effects and for hereditaments.[1]

25. Declaration by the Governments of France, Great Britain, the United States and the Soviet Union, 9 November 1972[2]

The Governments of the United States of America, the French Republic, the Union of Soviet Socialist Republics, and the United Kingdom of Great Britain and Northe. Ireland, having been represented by their Ambassadors, who held a series of meetin; in the building formerly occupied by the Allied Control Council, are in agreement that they will support the applications for membership in the United Nations when submitted by the Federal Republic of Germany and the German Democratic Republic, and affirm in this connection that this membership shall in no way affect the rights and responsibilities of the Four Powers and the corresponding related Quadripartite agreements, decisions, and practices.

26. Agreement between the Soviet Union and the Federal Republic of Germany on the Development of Economic, Industrial and Technical Cooperation, Bonn, 19 May 1973[3]

The government of the Union of Soviet Socialist Republics and the government of the Federal Republic of Germany,

Desiring, in accordance with the Treaty between the Union of Soviet Socialist Republics and the Federal Republic of Germany of 12 August 1970, to deepen economic, industrial and technical cooperation,

Mindful of the Agreement on General Questions of Trade and Navigation betwee the Union of Soviet Socialist Republics and the Federal Republic of Germany of 25 April 1958, and the long-term agreement between the government of the Union of Soviet Socialist Republics and the government of the Federal Republic of Germany on trade and economic cooperation of 5 July 1972.

Desiring to promote the development of cooperation in Europe.

Recognising the feasibility of ensuring and extending cooperation through the conclusion of agreements for a longer period, have agreed as follows:

1 Not published here are three letters in identical terms from Mr Kohl to Mr Bahr.
2 *DSB*, 27 November 1972, p. 623.
3 *Soviet News*, 22 May 1973.

Article 1

The contracting parties will strive to expand and deepen economic, industrial and technical cooperation between their competent bodies and enterprises on the basis of mutual benefit and will promote such cooperation within the framework of their possibilities.

Article 2

The contracting parties will, through the commission mentioned in Article 7, determine the branches in which expansion of cooperation for longer terms is desirable. In doing so the contracting parties will first of all take into consideration mutual requirements and resources of raw materials, different kinds of energy, technology, equipment and consumer goods.

Article 3

Cooperation within the present agreement will, in particular, cover:

Establishment of industrial complexes meeting mutual economic interests and also expansion and modernisation of individual industrial enterprises,

Cooperation in the production of individual items of equipment and other commodities,

Cooperation in the production of individual kinds of raw materials,

Exchange of patents, licences, know-how and technical information, application and improvement of existing, or the development of new, technology, and also the dispatch of specialists to give technical services or for training.

Article 4

The contracting parties will promote the conclusion and implementation of contracts for projects of economic, industrial and technical cooperation and will do all in their power to create the necessary facilities for this.

Article 5

Terms of individual projects of economic, industrial and technical cooperation shall be coordinated by appropriate interested organisations and enterprises of both sides in accordance with the laws and regulations existing in each state.

Article 6

The contracting parties will assist the cooperation of their competent bodies and enterprises in third countries.

Article 7

Guidance of work for the practical implementation of this agreement shall be vested in the commission of the Union of Soviet Socialist Republics and the Federal Republic of Germany for economic, scientific and technical cooperation. To that end it shall draft proposals for long-term development of mutual economic industria and technical cooperation.[1]

Article 8

In accordance with the quadripartite agreement of 3 September 1971, this agreemen shall apply to Berlin (West) in conformity with established procedures.

Article 9

This agreement does not affect the bilateral and multilateral treaties and agreements concluded earlier by the Union of Soviet Socialist Republics and the Federal Repub of Germany.

In this connection, if required, the contracting parties, on the proposal of one of them, will hold consultations, provided that these consultations do not affect the main aims of this agreement.

Article 10

This agreement shall enter into force upon signature and shall remain in force for 10 years.

Not later than six months prior to the expiry of the given period the two parties shall agree on measures needed for the further development of economic, industrial and technical cooperation.

27. Joint statement by Mr Brezhnev and Chancellor Brandt on the occasion of Mr Brezhnev's visit to the Federal Republic, Koenigswinter-Petersburg, 21 May 1973[2]

General Secretary of the Central Committee of the Communist Party of the Soviet Union and member of the Presidium of the Supreme Soviet of the Union of Soviet Socialist Republics L. I. Brezhnev paid a visit to the Federal Republic of Germany from 18 to 22 May at the invitation of the Federal Chancellor of the Federal Republic of Germany W. Brandt.

1 See the Agreement between the Soviet Union and the Federal Republic of Germany on the Further Development of Economic Cooperation, signed at Moscow, 30 October 1974: *Soviet News*, 12 November 1974.
2 *Soviet News*, 29 May 1973.

The following agreements, called upon to contribute towards a further expansion and deepening of bilateral relations, were signed during the visit:

An Agreement on the Development of Economic, Industrial and Technical Cooperation;

An Agreement on Cultural Cooperation;

An additional protocol to the Agreement of Air Travel of 11 November 1971.

The General Secretary of the CPSU Central Committee and the Federal Chancellor discussed major questions concerning relations between the Union of Soviet Socialist Republics and the Federal Republic of Germany. Much attention was also paid to urgent international problems and, in the first place, to the prospects of ensuring peace in Europe and throughout the world. The talks took place in a frank and businesslike atmosphere and in a spirit of mutual understanding, in keeping with the character of the relations between the two countries.

Both sides regard the treaty of 12 August 1970 as a historic milestone in the relations between the Union of Soviet Socialist Republics and the Federal Republic of Germany and in European development in general. They unanimously note that the treaty is a reliable basis for overcoming the grim past and for rebuilding and improving relations between the two countries. Tangible results in many spheres of cooperation have been achieved in the short time since the treaty was signed.

The two sides expressed their determination to translate the treaty into life and, proceeding from it, to work consistently to improve and develop relations between the Soviet Union and the Federal Republic of Germany. The joint efforts in this direction which both sides will continue to make in the future as well, give rise to mutual understanding and trust between them. A special role in this is played by meetings and exchanges between leading personalities. It was agreed to hold such meetings in the future, too.

It was stated with satisfaction that the practice of exchanging views and holding consultations at other levels as well has become a permanent element in the co-operation between the two states. This practice has proved its worth. It will be continued and expanded. Both international problems of mutual interest and questions concerning bilateral relations will be the subject of consultations.

The General Secretary of the CPSU Central Committee and the Federal Chancellor noted with satisfaction that in the period since the treaty of 12 August 1970, was concluded, trade between the Soviet Union and the Federal Republic of Germany has grown substantially. An agreement has been signed on trade and economic cooperation, and also an agreement on air travel. Relations between organisations and firms of the two sides in the field of industry have become much more active. Scientific and technical exchanges are expanding. A number of agreements have been signed on cooperation in the fields of science and technology. Consulates-general have been opened in Hamburg and Leningrad. It has been confirmed during the talks that the development of economic and industrial ties is an important goal in the policy of the two countries, for developments of this kind bring great benefits to the people and create a reliable material foundation for peace. In this connection there was expressed a readiness actively to make use of the opportunities of the commissions of the USSR and the FRG on economic, scientific and technical cooperation.

The two sides expressed the desire to expand their relations and, in addition to the agreements signed during the visit to sign new ones, particularly on scientific and technical cooperation, on road transport, on seagoing shipping and on co-operation in the field of the environment, and also agreements in other fields. An exchange of exhibitions will take place in 1974 with the aim of giving an idea of the achievements of the two countries in the fields of the national economy and culture.

The General Secretary of the CPSU Central Committee and the Federal Chan-cellor welcomed the negotiations now under way on a number of major industrial projects, including the project for the construction of a steel complex in the Soviet Union with the participation of firms of the Federal Republic of Germany, based on the direct reduction of iron.

It was agreed to encourage cooperation in developing up-to-date methods of production and in creating new industrial capacities, particularly in making machine tools, in instrument making and in the manufacture of engines on the territory of the USSR.

There is also a mutual interest in further developing cooperation in the chemical industry, in the use of atomic energy for peaceful purposes, in the generation of electricity and in the joint development of particular kinds of mineral deposits on the territory of the USSR. The Federal Government expressed an interest in the expansion of oil deliveries from the Soviet Union.

The two sides expressed their readiness to assist in every way in the implemen-tation of the agreements already reached in principle.

The General Secretary of the CPSU Central Committee and the Federal Chancello believe that the new stage that has been opened up in the relations between the two states provides opportunities for improving and strengthening ties in other fields as well. The two sides will encourage wider relations between parliamentarians, the development of exchanges in the fields of culture, education, sport and tourism, and contacts between trade union, youth and other organisations and also between citizens of the two states, and they will facilitate the settlement of questions of a humanitarian nature. Attention was drawn to the benefit to be derived from establishing ties between towns of the Soviet Union and the Federal Republic of Germany. The development of such contacts and exchanges on a collective or individual basis is called upon to assist the growth of mutual trust and understanding the mutual spiritual enrichment of people and stronger peace and good-neighbourline

It has been found desirable to undertake the necessary steps towards organising cooperation in the field of public health, on both a multilateral and a bilateral basis, and in the first place by pooling efforts for developing methods of treating cancerous and cardio-vascular diseases.

When discussing international problems, the General Secretary of the CPSU Centra Committee and the Federal Chancellor noted with satisfaction that since their last meeting in September 1971 further substantial progress had been achieved in the process of easing tension in Europe. The treaties of the Union of Soviet Socialist Republics, of the Polish People's Republic and of the German Democratic Republic with the Federal Republic of Germany, and the four-power agreement of 3 September 1971, which proceed from the actual situation as it exists in Europe and serve to ensure peaceful development, have facilitated this favourable process.

L. I. Brezhnev and W. Brandt emphasised the importance of the Treaty on the Basic Principles of Relations between the Federal Republic of Germany and the German Democratic Republic for easing tension in Europe. They welcome the forthcoming entry of the two German states into the United Nations organisation.

A detailed exchange of views was held on questions relating to the four-power agreement of 3 September 1971. L. I. Brezhnev and W. Brandt are fully agreed that the strict observance and complete implementation of this agreement are essential prerequisites for a firm detente in Central Europe and for improving relations between the states concerned, and particularly between the Soviet Union and the Federal Republic of Germany.

The Federal Chancellor informed the Soviet side of the position with regard to the Federal Government's negotiations with the government of the Czechoslovak Socialist Republic to normalise bilateral relations on a basis mutually acceptable to the two states and of the Federal Government's efforts in this connection to draw a final line under the question of the Munich agreement. L. I. Brezhnev and W. Brandt were fully agreed that the successful completion of the talks between the government of the Federal Republic of Germany and the government of the Czechoslovak Socialist Republic would be of great importance for the further easing of tension in Europe. The Federal Chancellor emphasised the readiness of the Federal Government to establish diplomatic relations also with those states in the east of Europe with which such relations have not as yet been established.

Questions concerning the preparations for, and the holding of, an all-European conference on security and cooperation, which is now in the forefront of European politics, were discussed in detail. The hope was expressed that the multilateral preparatory consultations in Helsinki would be concluded shortly and that the conference would be convened at an early date and would be held at a level corresponding to the international importance of this measure. The two sides are fully resolved to help towards the success of the conference with the aim of creating a firm foundation for peace, security and cooperation in Europe.

An exchange of views was held on questions concerning mutual reductions of armed forces and armaments in Central Europe. The two sides were unanimous in considering that agreed settlements, in keeping with the principle of not jeopardising the security of the states taking part, would serve the purpose of strengthening peace in Europe. They declared their readiness to assist through multilateral negotiations in agreeing on an approach to the solution of these problems acceptable to all the participants. The two sides welcome the multilateral consultations which are being conducted in a constructive spirit in Vienna in order to prepare such negotiations, and they express the hope that these consultations will soon be successfully concluded.

It was noted with satisfaction that the treaty of 1 July 1968, on the non-proliferation of nuclear weapons had been signed and ratified by a large number of states. Taking into account the agreement between Euratom and the International Atomic Energy Agency, signed on 5 April of this year, the Federal Government will submit the treaty to the legislative bodies for approval. The two sides believe that the implementation of this treaty will be a step towards disarmament and will help to reduce the danger of nuclear war and further strengthen international security.

L. I. Brezhnev and W. Brandt welcome the agreement signed in Paris on 27 January 1973, on ending the war and restoring peace in Vietnam,[1] which was an important contribution towards the improvement of the entire international situation. They believe that observance of the Paris Agreement by all the parties that are signatories to this document is a major prerequisite for ensuring lasting peace in that part of the globe.

The two sides noted with concern the dangerous tension which is continuing in the Middle East and emphasised the need for the related problems to be settled in accordance with the United Nations Security Council's resolution of 22 November 1967. They stated that they would support all efforts aimed at achieving a just and lasting peace in the Middle East.

The General Secretary of the CPSU Central Committee and the Federal Chancellor were fully agreed that the talks which had been held had facilitated the further expansion of spheres of cooperation between the two states, including cooperation on international questions, and had opened up prospects for the active development of ties between the Soviet Union and the Federal Republic of Germany in the political, economic, scientific, technical and cultural fields in the interests of both states. The results achieved give grounds for both countries to look confidently towards the future.

L. I. Brezhnev expressed gratitude for the hospitality accorded him during his stay in the Federal Republic of Germany. Invitations were extended to Federal President Dr G. Heinemann and Federal Chancellor W. Brandt to pay official visits to the Soviet Union. The invitations were accepted with gratitude.

28. Resolution adopted by the UN General Assembly, 18 September 1973[2]

The General Assembly,

Having received the recommendation of the Security Council of 22 June 1973 that the German Democratic Republic and the Federal Republic of Germany should be admitted to membership in the United Nations,

Having considered separately the application for membership of the German

1 Document No. 37.
2 GA Res. No. 3050 (XXVIII).

Democratic Republic and the application for membership of the Federal Republic of Germany,

1. Decides to admit the German Democratic Republic to membership in the United Nations;

2. Decides to admit the Federal Republic of Germany to membership in the United Nations.

29. France, Great Britain and the United States to Mr Waldheim, Secretary-General of the United Nations, 7 December 1973[1]

In the name of our three governments we have the honour, in connection with the entry of the Federal Republic of Germany into the United Nations, to direct your attention to the representation abroad of the interests of the western sectors of Berlin.

On the basis of the supreme authority that they maintain and exercise in the western sectors of Berlin, the Governments of France, the United Kingdom and the United States have long authorised the Federal Republic of Germany to assure, with certain limitations, the representation outside Berlin of the interests of the western sectors of Berlin and of their permanent residents. This authorisation was reaffirmed in a communication to the Government of the Union of Soviet Socialist Republics which is an integral part (Annex IV A) of the quadripartite agreement of 3 September 1971, registered with the Secretariat of the United Nations on 14 June 1973.

In that communication, the three powers recalled that they maintain their rights and responsibilities relating to the representation abroad of the interests of the western sectors of Berlin and their permanent residents, including those rights and responsibilities concerning matters of security and status, both in international organisations and in relations with other countries.

The three powers also recalled their agreement in particular that, without prejudice to the above and provided that matters of security and status were not affected, the Federal Republic of Germany may represent the interests of the western sectors in international organisations and international conferences.

For its part, the Government of the Union of Soviet Socialist Republics, in a communication to the governments of the three powers, which is similarly an integral part (Annex IV B) of the quadripartite agreement of 3 September 1971, affirmed that it would raise no objection to the representation of the interests of the western sectors of Berlin by the Federal Republic of Germany in international organisations and international conferences, provided that matters of security and status were not affected.

In accordance with the above, the three powers have agreed, pursuant to their rights and responsibilities relating to Berlin, to the assumption by the Federal Republic of Germany of the rights and obligations of the Charter of the United

1 UN Doc. A/9431.

Nations also with respect to the western sectors of Berlin and have approved the representation of the interests of the western sectors of Berlin by the Federal Republic of Germany in the United Nations and in its subsidiary organs.

We have the honour to request that this letter be circulated as an official document of the General Assembly, under item 27, and of the Security Council.

30. Treaty on Mutual Relations between the Federal Republic of Germany and Czechoslovakia, Prague, 11 December 1973[1]

The Federal Republic of Germany and the Czechoslovak Socialist Republic,

In the historic awareness that the harmonious coexistence of the nations in Europe is a necessity for peace:

Determined to put an end once and for all to the disastrous past in their relations, especially in connection with the Second World War which has inflicted immeasurable suffering on the peoples of Europe;

Recognising that the Munich agreement of 29 September 1938 was imposed on the Czechoslovak Republic by the National Socialist régime under the threat of force;

Considering the fact that a new generation has grown up in both countries which has a right to a secure and peaceful future;

Intending to create lasting foundations for the development of good-neighbourly relations;

Anxious to strengthen peace and security in Europe;

Convinced that peaceful cooperation on the basis of the purposes and principles of the United Nations Charter complies with the wishes of nations and the interests of peace in the world,

Have agreed as follows:

Article I

The Federal Republic of Germany and the Czechoslovak Socialist Republic, under the present treaty, deem the Munich agreement of 29 September 1938 void with regard to their mutual relations.

Article II

1. The present treaty shall not affect the legal effects on natural or legal persons of the law as applied in the period between 30 September 1938 and 9 May 1945.

This provision shall exclude the effects of measures which both contracting partie deem to be void owing to their incompatibility with the fundamental principles of justice.

1 WEU, *Political Year in Europe, 1973*, pp. 308–9.

2. The present treaty shall not affect the nationality of living or deceased persons ensuing from the legal system of either of the two contracting parties.

3. The present treaty, together with its declarations on the Munich agreement, shall not constitute any legal basis for material claims by the Czechoslovak Socialist Republic and its natural and legal persons.

Article III

1. The Federal Republic of Germany and the Czechoslovak Socialist Republic shall in their mutual relations as well as in matters of ensuring European and international security be guided by the purposes and principles embodied in the United Nations Charter.

2. Accordingly they shall, pursuant to Articles 1 and 2 of the United Nations Charter, settle all their disputes exclusively by peaceful means and shall refrain from any threat or use of force in matters affecting European and international security, and in their mutual relations.

Article IV

1. In conformity with the said purposes and principles, the Federal Republic of Germany and the Czechoslovak Socialist Republic reaffirm the inviolability of their common frontier now and in the future and undertake to respect each other's territorial integrity without restriction.

2. They declare that they have no territorial claims whatsoever against each other and that they will not assert any such claims in the future.

Article V

1. The Federal Republic of Germany and the Czechoslovak Socialist Republic will undertake further steps for the comprehensive development of their mutual relations.

2. They agree that an extension of their neighbourly cooperation in the economic and scientific fields, in their scientific and technological relations, and in the fields of culture, environmental protection, sport, transport and in other sectors of their relations, is in their mutual interest.[1]

Article VI

The present treaty shall be subject to ratification and enter into force on the date of the exchange of instruments of ratification which shall take place in Bonn.

In witness whereof the plenipotentiaries of the contracting parties have signed this treaty.

1 See the Joint Communiqué issued following the visit of the Federal German Foreign Minister to Prague, 25 March 1975: *Bulletin*, 2 April 1975.

31. Communiqué issued by the Federal German Foreign Office on the establishment of diplomatic relations with Bulgaria, 21 December 1973[1]

The Governments of the Federal Republic of Germany and of the People's Republic of Bulgaria, guided by the wish further to develop relations between their two countries, have decided to establish diplomatic relations as from today and to open embassies in Bonn and in Sofia.

They will shortly nominate their representatives with the rank of ambassador extraordinary and plenipotentiary.

32. Communiqué issued by the Federal German Foreign Office on the establishment of diplomatic relations with Hungary, 21 December 1973[2]

The Governments of the Federal Republic of Germany and of the People's Republic of Hungary, guided by the wish further to develop relations between their countries in their mutual interest, have decided to establish diplomatic relations between their countries as from today and to open embassies.

Both sides will shortly nominate their ambassadors.

33. Treaty of Friendship, Cooperation and Mutual Assistance between the Soviet Union and the German Democratic Republic, Moscow, 7 October 1975[3]

The Union of Soviet Socialist Republics and the German Democratic Republic;

Basing themselves on the fact that between the Union of Soviet Socialist Republi and the German Democratic Republic a close fraternal alliance has taken shape, which rests on the foundation of Marxism—Leninism and socialist internationalism;

Firmly convinced that the utmost strengthening of unity and friendship between the Union of Soviet Socialist Republics and the German Democratic Republic is in the fundamental interests of the peoples of both countries and of the entire community of socialist states, and serves the cause of the further drawing together of the socialist countries;

Guided by the desire, in conformity with the principles and purposes of socialist foreign policy, to ensure the most favourable international conditions for the building of socialism and communism;

1 *Bulletin*, 21 December 1973.
2 *Bulletin*, 21 December 1973.
3 *Soviet News*, 14 October 1975.

Attaching paramount significance to the cause of guarding the territorial integrity and sovereignty of both states against any encroachments;

Being resolved to abide strictly by the commitments stemming from the Warsaw Treaty of Friendship, Cooperation and Mutual Assistance of 14 May 1955;

Declaring themselves consistently and unswervingly for the consolidation of the unity of all the countries of the socialist community, based on the identity of their social system and ultimate goals;

Reaffirming the fact that the support, strengthening and safeguarding of the socialist gains, achieved at the cost of heroic efforts and selfless labour of the peoples, is the common international duty of the socialist countries;

Attaching great importance to the further improvement of political and ideological cooperation, and to the development and deepening of socialist economic integration;

Expressing firm determination to contribute to the further strengthening of peace and security in Europe and throughout the world, and to make their contribution to the implementation of collectively worked out principles of relations among states with different social systems and to the development, on this basis, of fruitful and mutually beneficial cooperation on the European continent;

Mindful that the German Democratic Republic, which has carried out the principles of the Potsdam agreement, and, as a sovereign independent socialist state, has become a full-fledged member of the United Nations organisation;

Attaching great importance to the further development and improvement of the juridical basis of their relations, and taking into account the changes which have taken place in Europe and throughout the world;

Guided by the purposes and principles of the Charter of the United Nations organisation,

Have adopted the following:

Article 1

The High Contracting Parties will, in accordance with the principles of socialist internationalism, continue to strengthen their relations of eternal and indestructible friendship and fraternal mutual assistance in all spheres. They will systematically and consistently develop and deepen comprehensive cooperation and render each other every assistance and support, based on mutual respect of national sovereignty and independence, equality and non-interference in each other's internal affairs.

Article 2

The High Contracting Parties will combine their efforts for the effective use of the material and spiritual potentials of their peoples and states in building socialist and communist society and consolidating the socialist community. In conformity with the principles and aims of socialist economic integration and in the interests of the better satisfaction of the material and cultural requirements of their peoples, they will strengthen and expand mutually beneficial bilateral and multilateral economic, scientific and technical cooperation, including cooperation within the framework of the Council for Mutual Economic Assistance.

The Parties will continue to coordinate their national long-term economic plans, expand specialisation and cooperation in the fields of production and research, coordinate long-term measures to develop major branches of the economy, science and technology, exchange the knowledge and experience amassed in the course of building socialism and communism and ensure ever closer cooperation of the nation economies of the two states in the interests of raising the efficiency of social production.

Article 3

The High Contracting Parties will facilitate cooperation between the organs of state power and voluntary organisations and promote broad contacts in the fields of scien culture, education, art, literature, the press, radio, cinema, television, public health, environmental protection, tourism, physical culture and sports, and in other spheres They will also encourage the development of contacts between the working people of the two countries.

Article 4

The High Contracting Parties will help in every way the further development of fraternal relations between all the states of the socialist community and constantly act in the spirit of strengthening their unity and cohesion. They declare their preparedness to take the necessary measures to protect and defend the historic achievements of socialism and the security and independence of both countries.

Article 5

The High Contracting Parties will continue to take all possible measures for the consistent implementation of the principles of peaceful coexistence between states with different social systems, for the expansion and deepening of the process of detente in international relations and will work for the final exclusion of war from the life of all nations. They will also exert every effort for the defence of international peace and the security of peoples from the encroachments of the aggressive forces of imperialism and reaction, for the end of the arms race and the promotion of universal and complete disarmament, for the final abolition of colonialism in all its forms and manifestations, and the rendering, to states which have freed themselves from colonial oppression, of support in strengthening their national independence and sovereignty.

Article 6

The High Contracting Parties regard the inviolability of the state borders in Europe as the most important prerequisite for ensuring European security and express the firm resolution, jointly and in alliance with other member-states of the Warsaw Treaty of Friendship, Cooperation and Mutual Assistance of 14 May 1955, to ensure, in accordance with it, the inviolability of the borders between the German Democratic Republic and the Federal Republic of Germany, as they emerged as a result of the Second World War and post-war development.

The Parties will exert joint efforts to counteract any manifestations of revanchism and militarism, and will work for the undeviating fulfilment of the treaties concluded with the aim of consolidating European security.

Article 7

In accordance with the quadripartite agreement of 3 September 1971, the High Contracting Parties will maintain and develop their ties with West Berlin, on the basis that it is not part of the Federal Republic of Germany and shall also not be controlled by it in the future.

Article 8

Should one of the High Contracting Parties become the object of armed attack by any state or group of states, the other High Contracting Party will view this as an attack also upon itself, and will render without delay all kinds of assistance, including military assistance, and will also give support with all the means available by way of exercising the right to individual or collective self-defence in line with Article 51 of the United Nations Charter.

The High Contracting Parties will inform the UN Security Council without delay of the measures taken on the basis of the present Article and will act in line with the provisions of the UN Charter.

Article 9

The High Contracting Parties will keep each other informed, consult each other and act in all important international matters, proceeding from the common stand agreed upon in line with the interests of both states.

Article 10

The present Treaty does not affect the rights and commitments of the High Contracting Parties under already effective bilateral and multilateral agreements.

Article 11

The present Treaty is to be ratified and will come into force from the day of the exchange of the instruments of ratification which will take place in Berlin at the earliest possible date.

Article 12

The present Treaty shall be operative for 25 years and will be automatically prolonged subsequently for 10-year periods, unless either of the High Contracting Parties declares 12 months before the expiry of the current term its desire to terminate the Treaty.

34. Statement by the Governments of France, Great Britain and the United States, 14 October 1975[1]

The governments of France, the United Kingdom and the United States wish to state that no treaty concluded by any of the Four Powers with a third state can in any way effect the rights and responsibilities of the Four Powers and the corresponding, related quadripartite agreements, decisions, and practices.

Therefore, the rights and responsibilities of the Four Powers for Berlin and Germany as a whole remain unaffected by the treaty of friendship, cooperation and mutual assistance concluded by the USSR and GDR on the 7 October 1975.

1 *Bulletin*, 21 October 1975.

B. Indochina

35. Address by President Johnson on American radio and television, 31 March 1968[1] (extract)

Good evening, my fellow Americans. Tonight I want to speak to you of peace in Vietnam and Southeast Asia.

No other question so preoccupies our people. No other dream so absorbs the 250 million human beings who live in that part of the world. No other goal motivates American policy in Southeast Asia.

For years, representatives of our Government and others have traveled the world seeking to find a basis for peace talks.

Since last September, they have carried the offer that I made public at San Antonio.[2]

That offer was this: that the United States would stop its bombardment of North Vietnam when that would lead promptly to productive discussions – and that we would assume that North Vietnam would not take military advantage of our restraint.

Hanoi denounced this offer, both privately and publicly. Even while the search for peace was going on, North Vietnam rushed their preparations for a savage assault on the people, the Government, and the allies of South Vietnam.

Their attack – during the Tet holidays – failed to achieve its principal objectives.

It did not collapse the elected government of South Vietnam or shatter its army, as the Communists had hoped.

It did not produce a 'general uprising' among the people of the cities, as they had predicted.

The Communists were unable to maintain control of any of the more than 30 cities that they attacked. And they took very heavy casualties.

But they did compel the South Vietnamese and their allies to move certain forces from the countryside into the cities. They caused widespread disruption and suffering. Their attacks, and the battles that followed, made refugees of half a million human beings.

The Communists may renew their attack any day. They are, it appears, trying to

1 *DSB*, 15 April 1968, pp. 481–6.
2 See *DSB*, 23 October 1967, p. 519.

make 1968 the year of decision in South Vietnam – the year that brings, if not final victory or defeat, at least a turning point in the struggle.

This much is clear: If they do mount another round of heavy attacks, they will not succeed in destroying the fighting power of South Vietnam and its allies.

But tragically, this is also clear: Many men – on both sides of the struggle – will be lost. A nation that has already suffered 20 years of warfare will suffer once again. Armies on both sides will take new casualties. And the war will go on.

There is no need for this to be so.

There is no need to delay the talks that could bring an end to this long and this bloody war.

Tonight I renew the offer I made last August – to stop the bombardment of North Vietnam. We ask that talks begin promptly, that they be serious talks on the substance of peace. We assume that during those talks Hanoi will not take advantage of our restraint.

We are prepared to move immediately toward peace through negotiations.

So tonight, in the hope that this action will lead to early talks, I am taking the first step to deescalate the conflict. We are reducing – substantially reducing – the present level of hostilities. And we are doing so unilaterally and at once.

Tonight I have ordered our aircraft and our naval vessels to make no attacks on North Vietnam, except in the area north of the demilitarized zone where the continuing enemy buildup directly threatens Allied forward positions and where the movements of their troops and supplies are clearly related to that threat.

The area in which we are stopping our attacks includes almost 90 percent of North Vietnam's population and most of its territory. Thus there will be no attacks around the principal populated areas or in the food-producing areas of North Vietnam.

Even this very limited bombing of the North could come to an early end if our restraint is matched by restraint in Hanoi. But I cannot in good conscience stop all bombing so long as to do so would immediately and directly endanger the lives of our men and our allies. Whether a complete bombing halt becomes possible in the future will be determined by events.

Our purpose in this action is to bring about a reduction in the level of violence that now exists.

It is to save the lives of brave men and to save the lives of innocent women and children. It is to permit the contending forces to move closer to a political settlement.

And tonight I call upon the United Kingdom and I call upon the Soviet Union, as cochairmen of the Geneva conferences and as permanent members of the United Nations Security Council, to do all they can to move from the unilateral act of deescalation that I have just announced toward genuine peace in Southeast Asia.

Now, as in the past, the United States is ready to send its representatives to any forum, at any time to discuss the means of bringing this ugly war to an end.

I am designating one of our most distinguished Americans, Ambassador Averell Harriman, as my personal representative for such talks. In addition, I have asked

Ambassador Llewellyn Thompson, who returned from Moscow for consultation, to
be available to join Ambassador Harriman at Geneva or any other suitable place
just as soon as Hanoi agrees to a conference.

I call upon President Ho Chi Minh to respond positively and favorably to this
new step toward peace.

But if peace does not come now through negotiations, it will come when Hanoi
understands that our common resolve is unshakable and our common strength is
invincible. . .

36. Address by President Nixon on American radio and television, the 'Guam Doctrine', 3 November 1969[1] (extract)

At the time we launched our search for peace, I recognized we might not succeed
in bringing an end to the war through negotiation.

I therefore put into effect another plan to bring peace — a plan which will bring
the war to an end regardless of what happens on the negotiating front. It is in line
with a major shift in US foreign policy which I described in my press conference at
Guam on 25 July.[2]

Let me briefly explain what has been described as the Nixon doctrine — a policy
which not only will help end the war in Vietnam but which is an essential element
of our program to prevent future Vietnams.

We Americans are a do-it-yourself people. We are an impatient people. Instead
of teaching someone else to do a job, we like to do it ourselves. And this trait has
been carried over into our foreign policy.

In Korea and again in Vietnam, the United States furnished most of the money,
most of the arms, and most of the men to help the people of those countries defend
their freedom against Communist aggression.

Before any American troops were committed to Vietnam, a leader of another
Asian country expressed this opinion to me when I was travelling in Asia as a private
citizen. He said: 'When you are trying to assist another nation defend its freedom,
US policy should be to help them fight the war, but not to fight the war for them.'

Well, in accordance with this wise counsel, I laid down in Guam three principles
as guidelines for future American policy toward Asia:
— First, the United States will keep all of its treaty commitments.
— Second, we shall provide a shield if a nuclear power threatens the freedom of a
   nation allied with us or of a nation whose survival we consider vital to our
   security.
— Third, in cases involving other types of aggression, we shall furnish military
   and economic assistance when requested in accordance with our treaty com-

1 *DSB*, 24 November 1969, pp. 437–43.
2 By the President's request, no official text of this press conference was issued; for the fullest
unofficial account, see *New York Times*, 26 July 1969.

mitments. But we shall look to the nation directly threatened to assume the primary responsibility of providing the manpower for its defense.

After I announced this policy, I found that the leaders of the Philippines, Thailand Vietnam, South Korea, and other nations which might be threatened by Communist aggression welcomed this new direction in American foreign policy.

The defense of freedom is everybody's business — not just America's business. And it is particularly the responsibility of the people whose freedom is threatened. In the previous administration we Americanized the war in Vietnam. In this administration we are Vietnamizing the search for peace.

The policy of the previous administration not only resulted in our assuming the primary responsibility for fighting the war but, even more significantly, did not adequately stress the goal of strengthening the South Vietnamese so that they could defend themselves when we left.

The Vietnamization plan was launched following Secretary [of Defense Melvin R Laird's visit to Vietnam in March. Under the plan, I ordered first a substantial increase in the training and equipment of South Vietnamese forces.

In July, on my visit to Vietnam, I changed General Abrams' orders so that they were consistent with the objectives of our new policies. Under the new orders, the primary mission of our troops is to enable the South Vietnamese forces to assume the full responsibility for the security of South Vietnam.

Our air operations have been reduced by over 20 percent.

And now we have begun to see the results of this long-overdue change in America policy in Vietnam:

- After 5 years of Americans going into Vietnam, we are finally bringing America men home. By December 15, over 60,000 men will have been withdrawn from South Vietnam, including 20 percent of all our combat forces.
- The South Vietnamese have continued to gain in strength. As a result, they have been able to take over combat responsibilities from our American troops.

EDITOR'S NOTE: THE PEACE INITIATIVES OF 1971–2

The Agreement on ending the war in Vietnam (Documents Nos. 37–39 below) followed a series of peace initiatives by the Democratic Republic of Vietnam, the South Vietnamese Provisional Revolutionary Government and the Government of the United States. For the texts of these initiatives, see:

Peace initiative issued by the delegation of the Democratic Republic of Vietnam, Paris, 26 June 1971 (Communiqué issued by the delegation of the Democratic Republic of Vietnam).

Peace initiative issued by the delegation of the South Vietnamese Provisional Revolutionary Government, Paris, 1 July 1971 (*Keesing's Contemporary Archives*, 5–12 February 1972, p. 25079).

Peace initiative issued by the Governments of the United States and the Republic of Vietnam, Washington, 25 January 1972 (*DSB*, 14 February 1972, pp. 185–6).

Statement by the Government of the People's Republic of Vietnam, 26 October 1972 (New York Times, 27 October 1972).

37. Agreement on Ending the War and Restoring Peace in Vietnam, Paris, 23 January 1973[1]

The parties participating in the Paris conference on Vietnam, with a view to ending the war and restoring peace in Vietnam on the basis of respect for the Vietnamese people's fundamental national rights and the South Vietnamese people's right to self-determination, and to contributing to the consolidation of peace in Asia and the world, have agreed on the following provisions and undertake to respect and to implement them:

Chapter I The Vietnamese people's fundamental national rights

Article 1

The United States and all other countries respect the independence, sovereignty, unity, and territorial integrity of Vietnam as recognized by the 1954 Geneva agreements on Vietnam.

Chapter II Cessation of Hostilities — Withdrawal of troops

Article 2

A cease-fire shall be observed throughout South Vietnam as of 2400 hours G.M.T., on 27 January 1973. At the same hour, the United States will stop all its military activities against the territory of the Democratic Republic of Vietnam by ground, air and naval forces, wherever they may be based, and end the mining of the territorial waters, ports, harbours, and waterways of the Democratic Republic of Vietnam. The United States will remove, permanently deactivate or destroy all the mines in the territorial waters, ports, harbours, and waterways of North Vietnam as soon as this agreement goes into effect. The complete cessation of hostilities mentioned in this Article shall be durable and without limit of time.

Article 3

The parties undertake to maintain the cease-fire and to ensure a lasting and stable peace. As soon as the cease-fire goes into effect:

(a) The United States forces and those of the other foreign countries allied with the United States and the Republic of Vietnam shall remain in-place pending the

1 *USIS*, 25 January 1973.

implementation of the plan of troop withdrawal. The four-party joint military commission described in Article 16 shall determine the modalities.

(b) The armed forces of the two South Vietnamese parties shall remain in-place. The two-party joint military commission described in Article 17 shall determine the areas controlled by each party and the modalities of stationing.

(c) The regular forces of all services and arms and the irregular forces of the parties in South Vietnam shall stop all offensive activities against each other and shall strictly abide by the following stipulations:

– All acts of force on the ground, in the air, and on the sea shall be prohibited;
– All hostile acts, terrorism and reprisals by both sides will be banned.

Article 4

The United States will not continue its military involvement or intervene in the internal affairs of South Vietnam.

Article 5

Within sixty days of the signing of this agreement, there will be a total withdrawal from South Vietnam of troops, military advisers, and military personnel, including technical military personnel and military personnel associated with the pacification programme, armaments, munitions, and war material of the United States and those of the other foreign countries mentioned in Article (a). Advisers from the above mentioned countries to all paramilitary organizations and the police force will also be withdrawn within the same period of time.

Article 6

The dismantlement of all military bases in South Vietnam of the United States and of the other foreign countries mentioned in Article 3(a) shall be completed within sixty days of the signing of this agreement.

Article 7

From the enforcement of the cease-fire to the formation of the government provided for in Articles 9 (b) and 14 of this agreement, the two South Vietnamese parties shall not accept the introduction of troops, military advisers, and military personnel including technical military personnel, armaments, munitions and war material into South Vietnam.

The two South Vietnamese parties shall be permitted to make periodic replacement of armaments, munitions and war material which have been destroyed, damaged worn out or used up after the cease-fire, on the basis of piece-for-piece, of the same characteristics and properties, under the supervision of the joint military commission of the two South Vietnamese parties and of the International Commission of Control and Supervision.

Chapter III The return of captured military personnel and foreign civilians, and captured and detained Vietnamese civilian personnel

Article 8

(*a*) The return of captured military personnel and foreign civilians of the parties shall be carried out simultaneously with and completed not later than the same day as the troop withdrawal mentioned in Article 5. The parties shall exchange complete lists of the above-mentioned captured military personnel and foreign civilians on the day of the signing of this agreement.

(*b*) The parties shall help each other to get information about those military personnel and foreign civilians of the parties missing in action, to determine the location and take care of the graves of the dead so as to facilitate the exhumation and repatriation of the remains, and to take any such other measures as may be required to get information about those still considered missing in action.

(*c*) The question of the return of Vietnamese civilian personnel captured and detained in South Vietnam will be resolved by the two South Vietnamese parties on the basis of the principles of Article 21(b) of the agreement on the cessation of hostilities in Vietnam of 20 July 1954. The two South Vietnamese parties will do so in a spirit of national reconciliation and concord, with a view to ending hatred and enmity, in order to ease suffering and to reunite families. The two South Vietnamese parties will do their utmost to resolve this question within ninety days after the cease-fire comes into effect.

Chapter IV The exercise of the South Vietnamese people's right to self-determination

Article 9

The Government of the United States of America and the Government of the Democratic Republic of Vietnam undertake to respect the following principles for the exercise of the South Vietnamese people's right to self-determination:

(*a*) The South Vietnamese people's right to self-determination is sacred, in-alienable, and shall be respected by all countries.

(*b*) The South Vietnamese people shall decide themselves the political future of South Vietnam through genuinely free and democratic general elections under international supervision.

(*c*) Foreign countries shall not impose any political tendency or personality on the South Vietnamese people.

Article 10

The two South Vietnamese parties undertake to respect the cease-fire and maintain peace in South Vietnam, settle all matters of contention through negotiations, and avoid all armed conflict.

Article 11

Immediately after the cease-fire, the two South Vietnamese parties will:
- Achieve national reconciliation and concord, end hatred and enmity, prohibit all acts of reprisal and discrimination against individuals or organizations that have collaborated with one side or the other;
- Ensure the democratic liberties of the people: personal freedom, freedom of speech, freedom of the press, freedom of meeting, freedom of organization, freedom of political activities, freedom of belief, freedom of movement, freedom of residence, freedom of work, right to property ownership, and right to free enterprise.

Article 12

(*a*) Immediately after the cease-fire, the two South Vietnamese parties shall hold consultations in a spirit of national reconciliation and concord, mutual respect, and mutual non-elimination to set up a National Council of National Reconciliation and Concord of three equal segments. The Council shall operate on the principle of unanimity. After the National Council of National Reconciliation and Concord has assumed its functions, the two South Vietnamese parties will consult about the formation of councils at lower levels. The two South Vietnamese parties shall sign an agreement on the internal matters of South Vietnam as soon as possible and do their utmost to accomplish this within ninety days after the cease-fire comes into effect, in keeping with the South Vietnamese people's aspirations for peace, independence and democracy.

(*b*) The National Council of National Reconciliation and Concord shall have the task of promoting the two South Vietnamese parties' implementation of this agreement, achievement of national reconciliation and concord and ensurance of democratic liberties. The National Council of National Reconciliation and Concord will organize the free and democratic general elections provided for in Article 9 (b) and decide the procedures and modalities of these general elections. The institutions for which the general elections are to be held will be agreed upon through consultations between the two South Vietnamese parties. The National Council of National Reconciliation and Concord will also decide the procedures and modalities of such local elections as the two South Vietnamese parties agree upon.

Article 13

The question of Vietnamese armed forces in South Vietnam shall be settled by the two South Vietnamese parties in a spirit of national reconciliation and concord, equality and mutual respect, without foreign interference, in accordance with the postwar situation. Among the questions to be discussed by the two South Vietnamese parties are steps to reduce their military effectives and to demobilize the troops being reduced. The two South Vietnamese parties will accomplish this as soon as possible.

Article 14

South Vietnam will pursue a foreign policy of peace and independence. It will be prepared to establish relations with all countries irrespective of their political and social systems on the basis of mutual respect for independence and sovereignty and accept economic and technical aid from any country with no political conditions attached. The acceptance of military aid by South Vietnam in the future shall come under the authority of the government set up after the general elections in South Vietnam provided for in Article 9 (b).

Chapter V The reunification of Vietnam and the relationship between North and South Vietnam

Article 15

The reunification of Vietnam shall be carried out step by step through peaceful means on the basis of discussions and agreements between North and South Vietnam, without coercion or annexation by either party, and without foreign interference. The time for reunification will be agreed upon by North and South Vietnam. Pending reunification:

(*a*) The military demarcation line between the two zones at the 17th parallel is only provisional and not a political or territorial boundary, as provided for in paragraph 6 of the final declaration of the 1954 Geneva conference.

(*b*) North and South Vietnam shall respect the demilitarized zone on either side of the provisional military demarcation line.

(*c*) North and South Vietnam shall promptly start negotiations with a view to reestablishing normal relations in various fields. Among the questions to be negotiated are the modalities of civilian movement across the provisional military demarcation line.

(*d*) North and South Vietnam shall not join any military alliance or military bloc and shall not allow foreign powers to maintain military bases, troops, military advisers, and military personnel on their respective territories, as stipulated in the 1954 Geneva agreements on Vietnam.

Chapter VI The Joint Military Commissions, The International Commission of Control and Supervision, The International Conference

Article 16

(*a*) The parties participating in the Paris conference on Vietnam shall immediately designate representatives to form a four-party joint military commission with the task of ensuring joint action by the parties in implementing the following provisions of this agreement:

- The first paragraph of Article 2, regarding the enforcement of the cease-fire throughout South Vietnam;
- Article 3 (a), regarding the cease-fire by US forces and those of the other foreign countries referred to in that Article;
- Article 3 (c), regarding the cease-fire between all parties in South Vietnam;
- Article 5, regarding the withdrawal from South Vietnam of US troops and those of other foreign countries mentioned in Article 3 (a);
- Article 6, regarding the dismantlement of military bases in South Vietnam of the United States and those of the other foreign countries mentioned in Article 3 (a);
- Article 8 (a), regarding the return of captured military personnel and foreign civilians of the parties;
- Article 8 (b), regarding the mutual assistance of the parties in getting information about those military personnel and foreign civilians of the parties missing in action.

(*b*) The four-party joint military commission shall operate in accordance with the principle of consultations and unanimity. Disagreements shall be referred to the International Commission of Control and Supervision.

(*c*) The four-party joint military commission shall begin operating immediately after the signing of this agreement and end its activities in sixty days, after the completion of the withdrawal of US troops and those of the other foreign countries mentioned in Article 3 (a) and the completion of the return of captured military personnel and foreign civilians of the parties.

(*d*) The four parties shall agree immediately on the organization, the working procedure, means of activity, and expenditures of the four-party joint military commission.

Article 17

(*a*) The two South Vietnamese parties shall immediately designate representatives to form a two-party joint military commission with the task of ensuring joint action by the two South Vietnamese parties in implementing the following provisions of this agreement;
- The first paragraph of Article 2, regarding the enforcement of the cease-fire throughout South Vietnam, when the four-party joint military commission has ended its activities;
- Article 3 (*b*), regarding the cease-fire between the two South Vietnamese parties;
- Article 3 (*c*), regarding the cease-fire between all parties in South Vietnam, when the four-party joint military commission has ended its activities;
- Article 7, regarding the prohibition of the introduction of troops into South Vietnam and all other provisions of this Article;

– Article 8 (*c*), regarding the question of the return of Vietnamese civilian personnel captured and detained in South Vietnam;
– Article 13, regarding the reduction of the military effectives of the two South Vietnamese parties and the demobilization of the troops being reduced.

(*b*) Disagreements shall be referred to the International Commission of Control and Supervision.

(*c*) After the signing of this agreement, the two-party joint military commission shall agree immediately on the measures and organization aimed at enforcing the cease-fire and preserving peace in South Vietnam.

Article 18

(*a*) After the signing of this agreement, an International Commission of Control and Supervision shall be established immediately.

(*b*) Until the international conference provided for in Article 19 makes definitive arrangements, the International Commission of Control and Supervision will report to the four parties on matters concerning the control and supervision of the implementation of the following provisions of this agreement:
– The first paragraph of Article 2, regarding the enforcement of the cease-fire throughout South Vietnam;
– Article 3 (*a*), regarding the cease-fire by US forces and those of the other foreign countries referred to in that Article;
– Article 3 (*c*) regarding the cease-fire between all the parties in South Vietnam;
– Article 5, regarding the withdrawal from South Vietnam of US troops and those of the other foreign countries mentioned in Article 3 (*a*);
– Article 6, regarding the dismantlement of military bases in South Vietnam of the United States and those of the other foreign countries mentioned in Article 3 (*a*);
– Article 8 (*a*), regarding the return of captured military personnel and foreign civilians of the parties. The International Commission of Control and Supervision shall form control teams for carrying out its tasks. The four parties shall agree immediately on the location and operation of these teams. The parties will facilitate their operation.

(*c*) Until the international conference makes definitive arrangements, the International Commission of Control and Supervision will report to the two South Vietnamese parties on matters concerning the control and supervision of the implementation of the following provisions of this agreement:
– The first paragraph of Article 2, regarding the enforcement of the cease-fire throughout South Vietnam, when the four-party joint military commission has ended its activities;
– Article 3 (*b*), regarding the cease-fire between the two South Vietnamese parties;
– Article 3 (*c*), regarding the cease-fire between all parties in South Vietnam, when the four-party joint military commission has ended its activities;

— Article 7, regarding the prohibition of the introduction of troops into South Vietnam and all other provisions of this Article;
— Article 8 (*c*), regarding the question of the return of Vietnamese civilian personnel captured and detained in South Vietnam;
— Article 9 (*b*), regarding the free and democratic general elections in South Vietnam;
— Article 13, regarding the reduction of the military effectives of the two South Vietnamese parties and the demobilization of the troops being reduced. The International Commission of Control and Supervision shall form control teams for carrying out its tasks. The two South Vietnamese parties shall agree immediately on the location and operation of these teams. The two South Vietnamese parties will facilitate their operation.

(*d*) The International Commission of Control and Supervision shall be composed of representatives of four countries: Canada, Hungary, Indonesia and Poland. The chairmanship of this Commission will rotate among the members for specific periods to be determined by the Commission.

(*e*) The International Commission of Control and Supervision shall carry out its tasks in accordance with the principle of respect for the sovereignty of South Vietnam.

(*f*) The International Commission of Control and Supervision shall operate in accordance with the principle of consultations and unanimity.

(*g*) The International Commission of Control and Supervision shall begin operating when a cease-fire comes into force in Vietnam. As regards the provisions in Article 18 (*b*) concerning the four parties, the International Commission of Control and Supervision shall end its activities when the Commission's tasks of control and supervision regarding these provisions have been fulfilled. As regards the provisions in Article 18 (*c*) concerning the two South Vietnamese parties, the International Commission of Control and Supervision shall end its activities on the request of the government formed after the general election in South Vietnam provided for in Article 9 (*b*).

(*h*) The four parties shall agree immediately on the organization, means of activity and expenditures of the International Commission of Control and Supervision. The relationship between the International Commission and the international conference will be agreed upon by the International Commission and the international conference

Article 19

The parties agree on the convening of an international conference within thirty days of the signing of this agreement to acknowledge the signed agreements; to guarantee the ending of the war, the maintenance of peace in Vietnam, the respect of the Vietnamese people's fundamental national rights, and the South Vietnamese people's right to self-determination; and to contribute to and guarantee peace in Indochina. The United States and the Democratic Republic of Vietnam, on behalf of the parties participating in the Paris conference on Vietnam, will propose to the following parties that they participate in this international conference: the People's Republic of China, the Republic of France, the Union of Soviet Socialist Republics, the United Kingdom, the four countries of the International Commission of Control and Supervision, and the Secretary-General of the United Nations, together with the parties participating in the Paris conference on Vietnam.

Chapter VII Regarding Cambodia and Laos

Article 20

(*a*) The parties participating in the Paris conference on Vietnam shall strictly respect the 1954 Geneva agreements on Cambodia and the 1962 Geneva agreements on Laos, which recognized the Cambodian and the Lao peoples' fundamental national rights, i.e., the independence, sovereignty, unity, and territorial integrity of these countries. The parties shall respect the neutrality of Cambodia and Laos.

The parties participating in the Paris conference on Vietnam undertake to refrain from using the territory of Cambodia and the territory of Laos to encroach on the sovereignty and security of one another and of other countries.

(*b*) Foreign countries shall put an end to all military activities in Cambodia and Laos, totally withdraw from and refrain from reintroducing into these two countries troops, military advisers and military personnel, armaments, munitions and war material.

(*c*) The internal affairs of Cambodia and Laos shall be settled by the people of each of these countries without foreign interference.

(*d*) The problems existing between the Indochinese countries shall be settled by the Indochinese parties on the basis of respect for each other's independence, sovereignty, and territorial integrity, and non-interference in each other's internal affairs.[1]

Chapter VIII The relationship between the United States and The Democratic Republic of Vietnam

Article 21

The United States anticipates that this agreement will usher in an era of reconciliation with the Democratic Republic of Vietnam as with all the peoples of Indochina. In pursuance of its traditional policy, the United States will contribute to healing the wounds of war and to postwar reconstruction of the Democratic Republic of Vietnam and throughout Indochina.

1 Pursuant to Article 20, an Agreement on Restoring Peace and Achieving National Concord in Laos was signed on 21 February 1973 by the Vientiane Government and the Party of the Patriotic Forces; for text, see International Institute of Strategic Studies, *Survival*, XV, 3, May/June 1973, pp. 138–40.

Article 22

The ending of the war, the restoration of peace in Vietnam, and the strict implementation of this agreement will create conditions for establishing a new, equal and mutually beneficial relationship between the United States and the Democratic Republic of Vietnam on the basis of respect for each other's independence and sovereignty, and non-interference in each other's internal affairs. At the same time this will ensure stable peace in Vietnam and contribute to the preservation of lasting peace in Indochina and Southeast Asia.

Chapter IX Other provisions

Article 23

This agreement shall enter into force upon signature by plenipotentiary representatives of the parties participating in the Paris conference on Vietnam. All the parties concerned shall strictly implement this agreement and its protocols. Done in Paris this twenty-seventh day of January, one thousand nine hundred and seventy-three, in Vietnamese and English. The Vietnamese and English texts are official and equally authentic.[1]

Agreement on ending the war and restoring peace in Vietnam

The Government of the United States of America, with the concurrence of the Government of the Democratic Republic of Vietnam, with the concurrence of the Provisional Revolutionary Government of the Republic of South Vietnam, with a view to ending the war and restoring peace in Vietnam on the basis of respect for the Vietnamese people's fundamental national rights and the South Vietnamese people's right to self-determination, and to contributing to the consolidation of peace in Asia and the world, have agreed on the following provisions and undertake to respect and to implement them:

(Text of agreement chapters I–VIII same as above)

Chapter IX Other provisions

Article 23

The Paris agreement on ending the war and restoring peace in Vietnam shall enter into force upon signature of this document by the Secretary of State of the Government of the United States of America and the Minister for Foreign Affairs of the

1 The signatures to this text of the agreement were placed on two separate pages. On the first page appear the signatures of the plenipotentiaries for the United States and the Republic of Vietnam; on the second page appear those of the plenipotentiaries for the Democratic Republic of Vietnam and the Provisional Revolutionary Government of the Republic of South Vietnam.

Government of the Democratic Republic of Vietnam, and upon signature of a document in the same terms by the Secretary of State of the Government of the United States of America, the Minister for Foreign Affairs of the Government of the Republic of Vietnam, the Minister for Foreign Affairs of the Government of the Democratic Republic of Vietnam, and the Minister for Foreign Affairs of the Provisional Revolutionary Government of the Republic of South Vietnam. The agreement and the protocols to it shall be strictly implemented by all the parties concerned. Done in Paris this twenty-seventh day of January, one thousand nine hundred and seventy-three, in Vietnamese and English. The Vietnamese and English texts are official and equally authentic.[1]

EDITOR'S NOTE: PROTOCOLS TO THE AGREEMENT ON ENDING THE WAR AND RESTORING PEACE IN VIETNAM

The following protocols were also signed. The texts were published by USIS on 26 January 1973.
    Protocol concerning Supervisory Commission
    Protocol concerning Prisoners of War
    Protocol concerning Ceasefire, Military Commissions
    Protocol concerning Removal of Mines.

38. Act of the International Conference on Vietnam, Paris, 2 March 1973[2]

The Government of the United States of America;
The Government of the French Republic;
The Provisional Revolutionary Government of the Republic of South Vietnam;
The Government of the Hungarian People's Republic;
The Government of the Republic of Indonesia;
The Government of the Polish People's Republic;
The Government of the Democratic Republic of Vietnam;
The Government of the United Kingdom of Great Britain and Northern Ireland;
The Government of the Union of Soviet Socialist Republics;
The Government of Canada; and
The Government of the People's Republic of China;
In the presence of the Secretary-General of the United Nations;
With a view to acknowledging the signed Agreements; guaranteeing the ending of the war, the maintenance of peace in Vietnam, the respect of the Vietnamese people's fundamental national rights, and the South Vietnamese people's right to self-determination; and contributing to and guaranteeing peace in Indochina;

1 This text of the agreement was signed by the plenipotentiaries for the United States and the Democratic Republic of Vietnam only.
2 *DSB*, 26 March 1973, pp. 345–6.

Have agreed on the following provisions, and undertake to respect and implement them;

Article 1

The Parties to this Act solemnly acknowledge, express their approval of, and support the Paris Agreement on Ending the War and Restoring Peace in Vietnam signed in Paris on 27 January 1973, and the four Protocols to the Agreement signed on the same date (hereinafter referred to respectively as the Agreement and the Protocols).

Article 2

The Agreement responds to the aspirations and fundamental national rights of the Vietnamese people, i.e. the independence, sovereignty, unity, and territorial integrity of Vietnam, to the right of the South Vietnamese people to self-determination, and to the earnest desire for peace shared by all countries in the world. The Agreement constitutes a major contribution to peace, self-determination, national independence and the improvement of relations among countries. The Agreement and the Protocols should be strictly respected and scrupulously implemented.

Article 3

The Parties to this Act solemnly acknowledge the commitments by the parties to the Agreement and the Protocols to strictly respect and scrupulously implement the Agreement and the Protocols.

Article 4

The Parties to this Act solemnly recognize and strictly respect the fundamental national rights of the Vietnamese people, i.e. the independence, sovereignty, unity, and territorial integrity of Vietnam, as well as the right of the South Vietnamese people to self-determination. The Parties to this Act shall strictly respect the Agreement and the Protocols by refraining from any action at variance with their provisions.

Article 5

For the sake of a durable peace in Vietnam, the Parties to this Act call on all countries to strictly respect the fundamental national rights of the Vietnamese people, i.e., the independence, sovereignty, unity, and territorial integrity of Vietnam and the right of the South Vietnamese people to self-determination and to strictly respect the Agreement and the Protocols by refraining from any action at variance with their provisions.

Article 6

(a) The four parties to the Agreement or the two South Vietnamese parties may, either individually or through joint action, inform the other Parties to this Act about the implementation of the Agreement and the Protocols. Since the reports and views submitted by the International Commission of Control and Supervision concerning the control and supervision of the implementation of those provisions of the Agreement and the Protocols which are within the tasks of the Commission will be sent to either the four parties signatory to the Agreement or to the two South Vietnamese parties, those parties shall be responsible, either individually or through joint action, for forwarding them promptly to the other Parties to this Act.

(b) The four parties to the Agreement or the two South Vietnamese parties shall also, either individually or through joint action, forward this information and these reports and views to the other participant in the International Conference on Vietnam for his information.

Article 7

(a) In the event of a violation of the Agreement or the Protocols which threatens the peace, the independence, sovereignty, unity, or territorial integrity of Vietnam, or the right of the South Vietnamese people to self-determination, the parties signatory to the Agreement and the Protocols shall, either individually or jointly, consult with the other Parties to this Act with a view to determining necessary remedial measures.

(b) The International Conference on Vietnam shall be reconvened upon a joint request by the Government of the United States of America and the Government of the Democratic Republic of Vietnam on behalf of the parties signatory to the Agreement or upon a request by six or more of the Parties to this Act.

Article 8

With a view to contributing to and guaranteeing peace in Indochina, the Parties to this Act acknowledge the commitment of the parties to the Agreement to respect the independence, sovereignty, unity, territorial integrity, and neutrality of Cambodia and Laos as stipulated in the Agreement, agree also to respect them and to refrain from any action at variance with them, and call on other countries to do the same.

Article 9

This Act shall enter into force upon signature by plenipotentiary representatives of all twelve Parties and shall be strictly implemented by all the Parties. Signature of this Act does not constitute recognition of any Party in any case in which it has not previously been accorded.

39. Joint communiqué issued by the Governments of the United States, the Democratic Republic of Vietnam and the Republic of Vietnam, and by the Provisional Revolutionary Government of the Republic of South Vietnam, Paris, 13 June 1973[1]

The Parties signatory to the Paris Agreement on ending the war and restoring peace in Vietnam, signed on 27th January 1973,

Considering that strict respect and scrupulous implementation of all provisions of the Agreement and its Protocols by all the parties signatory to them are necessary to ensure the peace in Vietnam and contribute to the cause of peace in Indochina and South-East Asia.

Have agreed on the following points (in the sequence of the relevant articles in the Agreement):

1. In conformity with Article 2 of the Agreement, the United States shall cease immediately, completely, and indefinitely aerial reconnaissance over the territory of the Democratic Republic of Vietnam.

2. In conformity with Article 2 of the Agreement and with the Protocol on mine clearance:

(*a*) The United States shall resume mine clearance operations within five days from the date of signature of this joint communiqué and shall successfully complete those operations within thirty days thereafter.

(*b*) The United States shall supply to the Democratic Republic of Vietnam mean which we are agreed to be adequate and sufficient for sweeping mines in rivers.

(*c*) The United States shall announce when the mine clearance in each main channel is completed and issue a final announcement when all the operations are completed.

3. In implementation of Article 2 of the Agreement, at 1200 hours GMT, 14 June 1973, the High Commands of the two South Vietnamese parties shall issue identical orders to all regular and irregular armed forces and the armed police under their command, to strictly observe the cease-fire throughout South Vietnam beginning at 0400 hours, GMT, 15 June 1973, and scrupulously implement the Agreement and its Protocols.

4. The two South Vietnamese parties shall strictly implement Articles 2 and 3 of the Protocol on the cease-fire in South Vietnam which read as follows:

'*Article 2*

(*a*) As soon as the cease-fire comes into force and until regulations are issued by the joint Military Commissions, all ground, river, sea and air combat forces of the partie in South Vietnam shall remain in place; that is, in order to ensure a stable cease-fire, there shall be no major redeployments or movements that would extend each party'

1 *DSB*, 9 July 1973, pp. 50–2.

rea of control or would result in contact between opposing armed forces and clashes
which might take place.

(b) All regular and irregular armed forces and the armed policy of the parties
a South Vietnam shall observe the prohibition of the following acts:

(1) armed patrols into areas controlled by opposing armed forces and flights by
bomber and fighter aircraft of all types, except for unarmed flights for
proficiency training and maintenance;

(2) armed attacks against any person either military or civilian, by any means
whatsoever, including the use of small arms, mortars, artillery, bombing
and strafing by airplanes and any other type of weapon or explosive device;

(3) all combat operations on the ground, on rivers, on the sea and in the air;

(4) all hostile acts, terrorism or reprisals; and

(5) all acts endangering lives or public or private property.

rticle 3

z) The above-mentioned prohibitions shall not hamper or restrict:

(1) civilian supply, freedom of movement, freedom to work, and freedom of the
people to engage in trade, and civilian communication and transportation
between and among all areas in South Vietnam;

(2) the use by each party in areas under its control of military support elements,
such as engineer and transportation units, in repair and construction of
public facilities and the transportation and supplying of the population;

(3) normal military proficiency training conducted by the parties in the areas
under their respective control with due regard for public safety.

b) The joint Military Commissions shall immediately agree on corridors, routes
nd other regulations governing the movement of military transport aircraft, military
·ansport vehicles, and military transport vessels of all types of one party going
irough areas under the control of other parties.

5. The two-party joint Military Commission shall immediately carry out its task
ursuant to Article 3 (b) of the Agreement to determine the areas controlled by
ach of the two South Vietnamese parties and the modalities of stationing. This
*sk shall be completed as soon as possible. The Commission shall also immediately
iscuss the movements necessary to accomplish a return of the armed forces of the
wo South Vietnamese parties to the positions they occupied at the time the cease-
re entered into force on 28 January 1973.

6. Twenty-four hours after the cease-fire referred to in paragraph 3 enters into
orce, the commanders of the opposing armed forces at those places of direct contact
iall meet to carry out the provisions of Article 4 of the Protocol on the cease-fire
a South Vietnam with a view to reaching an agreement on temporary measures to
vert conflict and to ensure supply and medical care for these armed forces.

7. In conformity with Article 7 of the Agreement:

(a) The two South Vietnamese parties shall not accept the introduction of troops, military advisers, and military personnel, including technical military personnel, into South Vietnam.

(*b*) The two South Vietnamese parties shall not accept the introduction of armaments, munitions, and war material into South Vietnam. However, the two South Vietnamese parties are permitted to make periodic replacement of armament munitions, and war material, as authorised by Article 7 of the Agreement, through designated points of entry and subject to supervision by the two-party joint Military Commission and the International Commission of Control and Supervision.

In conformity with Article 15 (*b*) of the Agreement regarding the respect of the demilitarised zone, military equipment may transit the demilitarised zone only if introduced into South Vietnam as replacements pursuant to Article 7 of the Agreement and through a designated point of entry.

(*c*) Twenty-four hours after the entry into force of the cease-fire referred to in paragraph 3, the two-party joint Military Commission shall discuss the modalities for the supervision of the replacements of armaments, munitions, and war material permitted by Article 7 of the Agreement at the three points of entry already agreed upon for each party. Within fifteen days of the entry into force of the cease-fire referred to in paragraph 3, the two South Vietnamese parties shall also designate by agreement the additional points of entry for each party in the area controlled by that party.

8. In conformity with Article 8 of the Agreement:

(*a*) Any captured personnel covered by Article 8 (*a*) of the Agreement who have not yet been returned shall be returned without delay, and in any event within no more than thirty days from the date of signature of this joint communiqué.

(*b*) All the provisions of the Agreement and the Protocol on the return of captured personnel shall be scrupulously implemented. All Vietnamese civilian personn covered by Article 8 (*c*) of the Agreement and Article 7 of the Protocol on the return of captured personnel shall be returned as soon as possible. The two South Vietnamese parties shall do their utmost to accomplish this within forty-five days from the date of signature of this joint communiqué.

(*c*) In conformity with Article 8 of the Protocol on the return of captured perso nel, all captured and detained personnel covered by that Protocol shall be treated humanely at all times. The two South Vietnamese parties shall immediately implem Article 9 of that Protocol and, within fifteen days from the date of signature of thi joint communiqué, allow national Red Cross societies they have agreed upon to visit all places where these personnel are held.

(*d*) The two South Vietnamese parties shall cooperate in obtaining information about missing persons and in determining the location of and in taking care of the graves of the dead.

(*e*) In conformity with Article 8 (*b*) of the Agreement, the parties shall help eac other to get information about those military personnel and foreign civilians of the parties missing in action, to determine the location and take care of the graves of the dead so as to facilitate the exhumation and repatriation of the remains, and to

ake any such other measures as may be required to get information about those
till considered missing in action. For this purpose, frequent and regular liaison
lights shall be made between Saigon and Hanoi.

9. The two South Vietnamese parties shall implement Article 11 of the Agreement, which reads as follows:

'Immediately after the cease-fire, the two South Vietnamese parties will:

— achieve national reconciliation and concord, end hatred and enmity, prohibit
all acts of reprisal and discrimination against individuals or organisations that
have collaborated with one side or the other;

— ensure the democratic liberties of the people: personal freedom, freedom of
speech, freedom of the press, freedom of meeting, freedom of organisation,
freedom of political activities, freedom of belief, freedom of movement, freedom of residence, freedom of work, right to property ownership and right
to free enterprise.'

10. Consistent with the principles for the exercise of the South Vietnamese
people's right to self-determination stated in Chapter IV of the Agreement:

(*a*) The South Vietnamese people shall decide themselves the political future of
South Vietnam through genuinely free and democratic general elections under
international supervision.

(*b*) The National Council of National Reconciliation and Concord consisting of
three equal segments shall be formed as soon as possible, in conformity with Article
12 of the Agreement.

The two South Vietnamese parties shall sign an agreement on the internal matters
of South Vietnam as soon as possible, and shall do their utmost to accomplish this
within forty-five days from the date of signature of this joint communiqué.

(*c*) The two South Vietnamese parties shall agree through consultations on the
institutions for which the free and democratic general elections provided for in
Article 9 (*b*) of the Agreement will be held.

(*d*) The two South Vietnamese parties shall implement Article 13 of the Agreement, which reads as follows:

'The question of Vietnamese armed forces in South Vietnam shall be settled by
the two South Vietnamese parties in a spirit of national reconciliation and concord,
equality and mutual respect, without foreign interference, in accordance with the
postwar situation. Among the questions to be discussed by the two South Vietnamese parties are steps to reduce their military effectives and to demobilise the
troops being reduced. The two South Vietnamese parties will accomplish this as
soon as possible.'

11. In implementation of Article 17 of the Agreement:

(*a*) All the provisions of Articles 16 and 17 of the Protocol on the cease-fire in
South Vietnam shall immediately be implemented with respect to the two-party
joint Military Commission. That Commission shall also immediately be accorded the
eleven points of privileges and immunities agreed upon by the four-party joint
Military Commission. Frequent and regular liaison flights shall be made between

Saigon and the headquarters of the regional two-party joint Military Commissions and other places in South Vietnam as required for the operations of the two-party joint Military Commission. Frequent and regular liaison flights shall also be made between Saigon and Loc Ninh.

(b) The headquarters of the central two-party joint Military Commission shall be located in Saigon proper or at a place agreed upon by the two South Vietnamese parties where an area controlled by one of them adjoins an area controlled by the other. The locations of the headquarters of the regional two-party joint Military Commissions and of the teams of the two-party joint Military Commission shall be determined by that Commission within fifteen days after the entry into force of the cease-fire referred to in paragraph 3. These locations may be changed at any time as determined by the Commission. The locations, except for teams at the poin of entry, shall be selected from among those towns specified in Article 11 (b) and (c) of the Protocol on the cease-fire in South Vietnam and those places where an area controlled by one South Vietnamese party adjoins an area controlled by the other, or at any other place agreed upon by the Commission.

(c) Once the privileges and immunities mentioned in paragraph 11 (a) are accord by both South Vietnamese parties, the two-party joint Military Commission shall be fully staffed and its regional commissions and teams fully deployed within fifteen days after their locations have been determined.

(d) The two-party joint Military Commission and the International Commission of Control and Supervision shall closely cooperate with and assist each other in carrying out their respective functions.

12. In conformity with Article 18 of the Agreement and Article 10 of the Proto on the International Commission of Control and Supervision, the International Con mission, including its teams, is allowed such movements for observation as is reason required for the proper exercise of its functions as stipulated in the Agreement. In carrying out these functions, the International Commission, including its teams, shall enjoy all necessary assistance and cooperation from the parties concerned. The two South Vietnamese parties shall issue the necessary instructions to their personnel and take all other necessary measures to ensure the safety of such movement.

13. Article 20 of the Agreement, regarding Cambodia and Laos, shall be scrupulc implemented.

14. In conformity with Article 21 of the Agreement, the United States—Democr Republic of Vietnam Joint Economic Commission shall resume its meetings four da from the date of signature of this joint communiqué and shall complete the first phase of its work within fifteen days thereafter.

Affirming that the parties concerned shall strictly respect and scrupulously implement all the provisions of the Paris Agreement, its Protocols, and this joint communiqué, the undersigned representatives of the parties signatory to the Paris Agree ment have decided to issue this joint communiqué to record and publish the points which they have agreed.

C. China

40. Albania, Algeria and sixteen Member Countries to the Secretary-General of the United Nations, 15 July 1971, with Explanatory Memorandum[1]

On the instructions of our governments, we have the honour to request you to include an item entitled 'Restoration of the Lawful Rights of the People's Republic of China in the United Nations' in the agenda of the 26th Session of the General Assembly, as being a question of an urgent character.

In accordance with Rule 20 of the Rules of Procedure of the General Assembly, an explanatory memorandum and the text of a draft resolution are attached to this letter.

Explanatory Memorandum

1. The Governments of Albania, Algeria, Cuba, Guinea, Iraq, Mali, Mauritania, the People's Democratic Republic of Yemen, the People's Republic of the Congo, Romania, Somalia, Sudan, Syria, the United Republic of Tanzania, Yemen, Yugoslavia and Zambia consider that the question of the restoration of the lawful rights of the People's Republic of China in the United Nations is more vital than ever, especially for the future of the organization. They remain firmly convinced of the justice of the position which they have defended and which has been proved once again by the support which the majority of member states have given to the restoration of the lawful rights of the People's Republic of China in the United Nations at the 25th Session of the General Assembly.

2. For years these governments have unceasingly decried and protested against the hostile and discriminatory policy followed by several governments with regard to the lawful government of China, the sole genuine representative of the remarkable Chinese people, which is heir to an ancient civilization and has irresistibly embarked on the path of progress. The persistent refusal to restore to the People's Republic of China the seat in the United Nations which belongs to it by right is obviously not only an extremely grave denial of justice but is, above all, inconsistent with one of the essential principles of our organization, namely that of universality. This

1 GAOR, 26th Session, *Annexes*, Agenda item 93, Doc. A/8392.

refusal, which is based on entirely political considerations, is contrary to the spirit which guided the creation of our organization.

3. This great power, the most densely populated on earth, with more than 700 million inhabitants, or one quarter of all mankind, a founding member of the United Nations and a permanent member of the Security Council, has since 1949 been refused by systematic manoeuvres the right to occupy the seat to which it is entitled ipso jure. Entrusting the representation of the Chinese people to the Chiang Kai-shek clique is nothing more than an obstinate, deliberate, absurd and dangerous refusal to recognize realities.

4. Moreover, there is no need to reiterate that in the field of international relations the Government of the People's Republic of China has always followed a policy aimed at settling by peaceful means all disputes which may exist or arise between independent states. The best possible example of this policy is furnished by its scrupulous observance of the Geneva Agreements of 1954 on Indochina and those of 1962 on Laos, to which it is a signatory.

5. The facts have amply demonstrated and continue to demonstrate that China sincerely desires peace and peaceful coexistence with all countries on the basis of the principles of respect for independence and territorial integrity, non-interference in domestic affairs, equality, mutual respect and the right of each people to decide its own destiny. The international relations of the People's Republic of China are steadily developing and an ever-growing number of countries are one by one establishing diplomatic and other relations with it. China has always expressed support for the peoples struggling against colonialism in all its forms in order to exercise their right to self-determination and independence in conformity with the principles of the United Nations Charter.

6. By opposing the restoration to the People's Republic of China of its lawful rights in the United Nations, on fallacious pretexts and accusations concerning the international conduct of that country, the United States is ipso facto violating the principles and purposes of the Charter. Our governments are in a position to contradict these assertions. By maintaining friendly relations with China, like most states of the international community, and by doing so despite the differences in their political, economic and social systems, our states daily prove the baselessness of these accusations. In this connexion, it should be noted that the People's Republic of China has always displayed full respect for the independence and dignity of other countries.

7. The 'quarantine' policy which certain powers have pursued for many years with regard to the People's Republic of China is unrealistic and dangerous, because it is recognized that no important international problem can be solved without the participation of that country. It has been amply demonstrated that it is impossible to exclude China, a great nuclear and space power, from major decisions while at the same time requiring it to subscribe to the obligations imposed by agreements which it had no part in concluding. It is impossible simultaneously to recognize on the one hand, the international role of the People's Republic of China and to dispute on the other hand, its lawful place in the United Nations, whose main purpose is

, common search for solutions to the problems which arise in the world. This position is logically and practically untenable.

8. The reality of the existence of the People's Republic of China cannot, of course, be changed to suit the myth of a so-called 'Republic of China', fabricated out of a portion of Chinese territory. It is well known that the unlawful authorities installed n the island of Taiwan, who claim to represent China, remain there only because of the permanent presence of the armed forces of the United States of America.

9. It is in the fundamental interest of the United Nations promptly to put an nd to this unacceptable and dangerous situation which some continue to seek to mpose on the international community, in defiance of all principles, in order to ulfil and implement a policy which is being increasingly repudiated. Furthermore, his attitude, through the unhappy precedent which it creates, cannot but give rise o uncertainty regarding the future of the national and territorial unity of many member states.

10. Consequently, our governments are convinced that the restoration to the People's Republic of China of its lawful rights in the United Nations and in all its subsidiary and affiliated bodies, and the recognition of the representatives of the Government of the People's Republic of China as the sole legitimate representatives of China to the United Nations is absolutely and urgently necessary in order to strengthen the authority and prestige of the organization. This implies the immediate expulsion of the representatives of Chiang Kai-shek's clique from the seat which hey unjustly occupy in the United Nations and in all the bodies affiliated to it. Our governments consider that to delay this inevitable move would only help to weaken further the authority of the United Nations in the eyes of the international community at a time in its history when it is in such need of this authority in order o achieve its principal objectives.

11. We are attaching hereto for consideration by member states, a draft resolution[1] calling for the restoration to the People's Republic of China of all its rights, the recognition of the representatives of its Government as the sole legitimate representatives of China to the United Nations and the recognition of the People's Republic of China as one of the five permanent members of the Security Council, as also the immediate expulsion of the representatives of Chiang Kai-shek from the seat which hey unlawfully occupy in the United Nations and in all the bodies affiliated to it. Following consultations, the Government of Pakistan supports this proposal and has oined in sponsoring the draft resolution.

41. Resolution of the United Nations General Assembly, adopted 25 October 1971[2]

The General Assembly,
Recalling the principles of the Charter of the United Nations,

1 The draft resolution was adopted unchanged on 25 October; for text, see next document.
2 GA Res. No. 2758 (XXVI).

Considering that the restoration of the lawful rights of the People's Republic of China is essential both for the protection of the Charter of the United Nations and for the cause that the United Nations must serve under the Charter,

Recognizing that the representatives of the Government of the People's Republic of China are the only lawful representatives of China to the United Nations and that the People's Republic of China is one of the five permanent members of the Security Council,

Decides to restore all its rights to the People's Republic of China and to recognize the representatives of its Government as the only legitimate representatives of China to the United Nations, and to expel forthwith the representatives of Chiang Kai-shek from the place which they unlawfully occupy at the United Nations and in all the organizations related to it.

42. Joint communiqué issued by the People's Republic of China and the United States, following President Nixon's visit to China, Shanghai, 27 February 1972[1]

President Richard Nixon of the United States of America visited the People's Republic of China at the invitation of Premier Chou En-Lai of the People's Republic of China from February 21 to February 28, 1972. Accompanying the president were Mrs Nixon, US Secretary of State William Rogers, Assistant to the President Dr Henry Kissinger, and other American officials.

President Nixon met with Chairman Mao Tsetung of the Communist Party of China on February 21. The two leaders had a serious and frank exchange of views on Sino-US Relations and world affairs.

During the visit, extensive, earnest and frank discussions were held between President Nixon and Premier Chou En-Lai on the normalization of relations between the United States of America and the People's Republic of China, as well as on other matters of interest to both sides. In addition, Secretary of State William Rogers and Foreign Minister Chi Pen-Fei held talks in the same spirit.

President Nixon and his party visited Peking and viewed cultural, industrial and agricultural sites, and they also toured Hangchow and Shanghai where, continuing discussions with Chinese leaders, they viewed similar places of interest.

The leaders of the People's Republic of China and the United States of America found it beneficial to have this opportunity, after so many years without contact, to present candidly to one another their views on a variety of issues. They reviewed the international situation in which important changes and great upheavals are taking place and expounded their respective positions and attitudes.

The US side stated: peace in Asia and peace in the world requires efforts both to reduce immediate tensions and to eliminate the basic causes of conflict. The United States will work for a just and secure peace: just, because it fulfills the aspirations of peoples and nations for freedom and progress; secure, because it removes the

1 *USIS*, 28 February 1972, pp. 1–4.

anger of foreign aggression. The United States supports individual freedom and
ocial progress for all the peoples of the world, free of outside pressure or inter-
ention. The United States believes that the effort to reduce tensions is served by
mproving communication between countries that have different ideologies so as
o lessen the risks of confrontation through accident, miscalculation or misunder-
tanding. Countries should treat each other with mutual respect and be willing to
ompete peacefully, letting performance be the ultimate judge. No country should
laim infallibility and each country should be prepared to reexamine its own atti-
udes for the common good. The United States stressed that the peoples of Indo-
hina should be allowed to determine their destiny without outside intervention;
ts constant primary objective has been a negotiated solution. The eight-point
roposal put forward by the Republic of Vietnam and the United States on
7 January 1972[1] represents a basis for the attainment of that objective; in the
bsence of a negotiated settlement the United States envisages the ultimate with-
rawal of all US forces from the region consistent with the aim of self-determination
or each country of Indochina. The United States will maintain its close ties with and
upport for the Republic of Korea; the United States will support efforts of the
Republic of Korea to seek a relaxation of tension and increased communication
n the Korean Peninsula. The United States places the highest value on its friendly
elations with Japan; it will continue to develop the existing close bonds. Consistent
with the United Nations Security Council Resolution of 21 December 1971, the
United States favors the continuation of the cease-fire between India and Pakistan
nd the withdrawal of all military forces to within their own territories and to their
wn sides of the cease-fire line in Jammu and Kashmir; the United States supports
he right of the peoples of South Asia to shape their own future in peace, free of
nilitary threat, and without having the area become the subject of great-power
ivalry.

The Chinese side stated: wherever there is oppression, there is resistance. Countries
want independence, nations want liberation and the people want revolution — this
as become the irresistible trend of history. All nations, big or small, should be equal;
ig nations should not bully the small and strong nations should not bully the weak.
China will never be a superpower and it opposes hegemony and power politics of
ny kind. The Chinese side stated that it firmly supports the struggles of all the
ppressed people and nations for freedom and liberation and that the people of all
ountries have the right to choose their social systems according to their own wishes
nd the right to safeguard the independence, sovereignty and territorial integrity of
heir own countries and oppose foreign aggression, interference, control and subversion.
All foreign troops should be withdrawn to their own countries.

The Chinese side expressed its firm support to the peoples of Vietnam, Laos
nd Cambodia in their efforts for the attainment of their goal and its firm support
o the seven-point proposal of the Provisional Revolutionary Government of the

1 The correct date is 25 January 1972. See Editor's Note: The Peace Initiatives of 1971–2,
p. 92 above. For text, see *DSB*, 14 February 1972, pp. 185–6.

Republic of South Vietnam[1] and the elaboration of February this year on the two
key problems in the proposal, and to the joint declaration of the summit conference
of the Indochinese peoples. It firmly supports the eight-point program for the peace
unification of Korea put forward by the Government of the Democratic People's
Republic of Korea on 12 April 1971, and the stand for the abolition of the 'UN Com
mission for the Unification and Rehabilitation of Korea'.[2] It firmly opposes the
revival and outward expansion of Japanese militarism and firmly supports the Japan
people's desire to build an independent, democratic, peaceful and neutral Japan. It
firmly maintains that India and Pakistan should, in accordance with the United Nati
resolutions on the India—Pakistan question, immediately withdraw all their forces
to their respective territories and to their own sides of the cease-fire line in Jammu
and Kashmir and firmly supports the Pakistan Government and people in their
struggle to preserve their independence and sovereignty and the people of Jammu
and Kashmir in their struggle for the right of self-determination.

Both sides are of the view that it would be against the interests of the peoples
of the world for any major country to collude with another against other countries,
or for major countries to divide up the world into spheres of interest.

The two sides reviewed the long-standing serious disputes between China and the
United States. The Chinese side reaffirmed its position: the Taiwan question is the
crucial question obstructing the normalization of relations between China and the
United States; the Government of the People's Republic of China is the sole legal
government of China; Taiwan is a province of China which has long been returned
to the motherland; the liberation of Taiwan is China's internal affair in which no
other country has the right to interfere; and all US forces and military installations
must be withdrawn from Taiwan. The Chinese Government firmly opposes any
activities which aim at the creation of 'one China, one Taiwan', 'one China, two
Governments', 'two Chinas', and 'independent Taiwan' or advocate that 'the status
of Taiwan remains to be determined'.

There are essential differences between China and the United States in their
social systems and foreign policies. However, the two sides agreed that countries,
regardless of their social systems, should conduct their relations on the principles
of respect for the sovereignty and territorial integrity of all states, non-aggression
against other states, non-interference in the internal affairs of other states, equality
and mutual benefit, and peaceful coexistence. International disputes should be
settled on this basis, without resorting to the use or threat of force. The United
States and the People's Republic of China are prepared to apply these principles
to their mutual relations.

With these principles of international relations in mind the two sides stated
that:
  — progress toward the normalization of relations between China and the United
    States is in the interests of all countries;

1 For text, see *Keesing's Contemporary Archives*, 5—12 February 1972, p. 25079.
2 Document No. 44.

— both wish to reduce the danger of international military conflict;
— neither should seek hegemony in the Asia—Pacific region and each is opposed
   to efforts by any other country or group of countries to establish such hegemony;
   and
— neither is prepared to negotiate on behalf of any third party or to enter into
   agreements or understandings with the other directed at other states.

he US side declared: the United States acknowledges that all Chinese on either side
f the Taiwan Strait maintain there is but one China and that Taiwan is a part of
hina. The United States Government does not challenge that position. It reaffirms
s interest in a peaceful settlement of the Taiwan question by the Chinese them-
elves. With this prospect in mind, it affirms the ultimate objective of the with-
rawal of all US forces and military installations from Taiwan. In the meantime, it
ill progressively reduce its forces and military installations on Taiwan as the
ension in the area diminishes.

The two sides agreed that it is desirable to broaden the understanding between
he two peoples. To this end, they discussed specific areas in such fields as science,
echnology, culture, sports and journalism, in which people-to-people contacts and
xchanges would be mutually beneficial. Each side undertakes to facilitate the further
evelopment of such contacts and exchanges.

Both sides view bilateral trade as another area from which mutual benefit can
e derived, and agreed that economic relations based on equality and mutual benefit
re in the interest of the peoples of the two countries. They agree to facilitate the
rogressive development of trade between their two countries.

The two sides agreed that they will stay in contact through various channels,
cluding the sending of a senior US representative to Peking from time to time for
oncrete consultations to further the normalization of relations between the two
ountries and continue to exchange views on issues of common interest.

The two sides expressed the hope that the gains achieved during this visit would
pen up new prospects for the relations between the two countries. They believe
hat the normalization of relations between the two countries is not only in the
nterest of the Chinese and American peoples but also contributes to the relaxation
f tension in Asia and the world.

President Nixon, Mrs Nixon and the American party expressed their appreciation
or the gracious hospitality shown them by the Government and people of the
eople's Republic of China.

EDITOR'S NOTE: UNITED STATES—CHINESE RELATIONS 1973—4

ollowing President Nixon's visit, Dr Kissinger made three further visits to Peking
n February and November 1973 and November 1974. After the first of these
isits, liaison offices were established in Peking and Washington. For texts of com-
uniqués issued following these visits, see *DSB*, 19 March 1973, p. 313; 10 December
973, p. 716; 23 December 1974, p. 907.

43. Address by President Ford to the East—West Center, University of Hawaii, the 'Pacific doctrine', 7 December 1975[1] (extract)

America, a nation of the Pacific Basin, has a very vital stake in Asia and a responsibility to take a leading part in lessening tensions, preventing hostilities, and preservir peace. World stability and our own security depend upon our Asian commitments.

In 1941, 34 years ago today, we were militarily unprepared. Our trade in the Pacific was very limited. We exercised jurisdiction over the Philippines. We were preoccupied with Western Europe.

Our instincts were isolationist. We have transcended that age. We are now the world's strongest nation. Our great commercial involvement in Asia is expanding. W(led the way in conferring independence upon the Philippines. Now we are working out new associations and arrangements with the trust territories of the Pacific.

The center of political power in the United States has shifted westward. Our Pacific interests and concerns have increased. We have exchanged the freedom of action of an isolationist state for the responsibilities of a great global power.

As I return from this trip to three major Asian countries, I am even more aware of our interests in this part of the world. The security concerns of great world powers intersect in Asia. The United States, the Soviet Union, China, and Japan are all Pacific powers.

Western Europe has historic and economic ties with Asia. Equilibrium in the Pacific is absolutely essential to the United States and to the other countries in the Pacific.

The first premise of a new Pacific doctrine is that American strength is basic to any stable balance of power in the Pacific. We must reach beyond our concern for security; but without security, there can be neither peace nor progress.

The preservation of the sovereignty and the independence of our Asian friends and allies remains a paramount objective of American policy. We recognize that force alone is insufficient to assure security. Popular legitimacy and social justice are vital prerequisites of resistance against subversion or aggression. Nevertheless, we owe it to ourselves and to those whose independence depends upon our continue support to preserve a flexible and balanced position of strength throughout the Pacific.

The second basic premise of a new Pacific doctrine is that partnership with Japan is a pillar of our strategy. There is no relationship to which I have devoted more attention, nor is there any greater success story in the history of American efforts to relate to distant cultures and to people.

The Japanese—American relationship can be a source of great, great pride to every American and to every Japanese. Our bilateral relations have never been better. The recent exchange of visits symbolized a basic political partnership. We have begun to

1 *DSB*, 24 December 1975, pp. 913–16.

evelop with the Japanese and other advanced industrial democracies better means
f harmonizing our economic policy.

We are joining with Japan, our European friends, and representatives of the
eveloping nations this month to begin shaping a more efficient and more equitable
attern of North—South economic relations.

The premise of a new Pacific doctrine is the normalization of relations with the
eople's Republic of China, the strengthening of our new ties with this great nation
epresenting nearly one-quarter of mankind. This is another recent achievement of
.merican foreign policy. It transcends 25 years of hostility.

I visited China[1] to build on the dialogue started nearly four years ago. My wide-
inging exchanges with the leaders of the People's Republic of China — with Chair-
ian Mao Tse-tung and Vice Premier Teng Hsiao-p'ing — enhanced our understanding
f each other's views and each other's policies.

There were, as expected, differences of perspective. Our societies, our philosophies,
ur varying positions in the world, give us differing perceptions of our respective
ational interests.

But we did find a common ground. We reaffirmed that we share very important
reas of concern and agreement. They say, and we say, that the countries of Asia
iould be free to develop a world where there is mutual respect for the sovereignty
nd territorial integrity of all states; where people are free from the threat of foreign
ggression; where there is non-interference in the internal affairs of others; and where
ie principles of equality, mutual benefit, and coexistence shape the development
f peaceful international order.

We share opposition to any form of hegemony in Asia or in any other part of
he world.

I reaffirmed the determination of the United States to complete the normalization
f relations with the People's Republic of China on the basis of the Shanghai com-
iuniqué. Both sides regarded our discussions as significant, useful, and constructive.

Our relationship is becoming a permanent feature of the international political
indscape. It benefits not only our two peoples but all peoples of the region and the
ntire world.

A fourth principle of our Pacific policy is our continuing stake in stability and
ecurity in Southeast Asia.

After leaving China, I visited Indonesia and the Philippines. Indonesia is a nation
f 140 million people, the fifth largest population in the world today. It is one of
ur important new friends and a major country in that area of the world.

The Republic of the Philippines is one of our oldest and dearest allies. Our friend-
hip demonstrates America's longstanding interest in Asia.

I spent three days in Jakarta and Manila. I would have liked to have had time to
isit our friends in Thailand, Singapore, and Malaysia. We share important political
nd economic concerns with these five nations who make up the Association of
outheast Asian Nations.

1 No communiqué was issued after President Ford's visit to China, 1—5 December 1975.

I can assure you that Americans will be hearing much more about the ASEAN organization. All of its members are friends of the United States. Their total population equals our own. While they are developing countries, they possess many, many assets: vital peoples, abundant natural resources, and well-managed agricultures. They have skilled leaders and the determination to develop themselves and to solve their own problems. Each of these countries protects its independence by relying on its own national resilience and diplomacy. We must continue to assist them.

I learned during my visit that our friends want us to remain actively engaged in the affairs of the region. We intend to do so.

We retain close and valuable ties with our old friends and allies in the southwest Pacific, Australia on the one hand and New Zealand on the other.

A fifth tenet of our new Pacific policy is our belief that peace in Asia depends upon a resolution of outstanding political conflicts. In Korea tension persists. We have close ties with the Republic of Korea; and we remain committed to peace and security on the Korean Peninsula, as the presence of our forces there attests.

Responding to the heightened tension last spring, we reaffirmed our support of the Republic of Korea. Today, the United States is ready to consider constructive ways of easing tensions on the peninsula, but we will continue to resist any moves which attempt to exclude the Republic of Korea from discussion of its own future.

In Indochina, the healing effects of time are required. Our policies toward the new regimes of the peninsula will be determined by their conduct toward us. We are prepared to reciprocate gestures of good will, particularly the return of remains of Americans killed or missing in action or information about them. If they exhibit restraint toward their neighbors and constructive approaches to international problems, we will look to the future rather than to the past.

The sixth point of our new policy in the Pacific is that peace in Asia requires a structure of economic cooperation reflecting the aspirations of all the peoples in the region.

The Asian–Pacific economy has recently achieved more rapid growth than any other region in the world. Our trade with East Asia now exceeds our transactions with the European Community. America's jobs, currency, and raw materials depend upon economic ties with the Pacific Basin. Our trade with the region is now increasing by more than 30 percent annually, reaching some $46 billion last year. Our economies are increasingly interdependent as cooperation grows between developed and developing nations.

Our relations with the five ASEAN countries are marked by growing maturity and by more modest and more realistic expectations on both sides. We no longer approach them as donor to dependent. These proud people look to us less for outright aid than for new trading opportunities and more equitable arrangements for the transfer of science and technology.

There is one common theme which was expressed to me by the leaders of every Asian country that I visited. They all advocate the continuity of steady and responsi

American leadership. They seek self-reliance in their own future and in their own relations with us.

Our military assistance to allies and friends is a modest responsibility, but its political significance far surpasses the small cost involved. We serve our highest national interests by strengthening their self-reliance, their relations with us, their solidarity with each other, and their regional security.

I emphasized to every leader I met that the United States is a Pacific nation. I pledged, as President, I will continue America's active concern for Asia and our presence in the Asian–Pacific region.

Asia is entering a new era. We can contribute to a new structure of stability founded on a balance among the major powers, strong ties to our allies in the region, an easing of tension between adversaries, the self-reliance and regional solidarity of smaller nations, and expanding economic ties and cultural exchanges. . .

D. Korea

44. Appeal of the Supreme People's Assembly of the Democratic People's Republic of Korea, the 'eight-point proposal', Pyongyang, 13 April 1971[1] (extract)

Overthrow the Pak Jung Hi puppet clique, the contemptible lackey of the US imperialists and the Japanese militarists and the most wicked traitor to the nation.

All patriotic and democratic forces of South Korea, unite close as one and shatter to pieces the long-term office scheme of the Pak Jung Hi puppet clique.

Overthrow through a powerful mass struggle the Pak Jung Hi military fascist 'regime' fanning antagonism and split between the North and South and establish a patriotic, democratic regime aspiring to national unity and peaceful unification.

It is our invariable line to sweep away all the foreign aggressor forces and traitor from South Korea and solve the question of the country's unification by the efforts of the Korean people themselves in a peaceful way, without interference of any outside forces.

We are fully ready to settle the issue of the unification of the country in a peace ful way through North—South negotiation when a genuine power of the people is established or patriotic democratic personages come to power in South Korea after the Pak Jung Hi puppet clique are overthrown.

In this connection the Supreme People's Assembly of the Democratic People's Republic of Korea, in accordance with the proposals we made long ago on the basis of the basic line of the national unification advanced by Respected and Beloved Premier Kim Il Sung, solemnly puts forth here the following eight-point programme of national salvation:

1. To make the US imperialist aggressor troops withdraw from South Korea and solve the national question by the efforts of the Korean people themselves on the principles of national self-determination;

2. To reduce the armed forces in North and South Korea to 100,000 or less each and lighten heavy burdens of military expenses to relax the tension and guarantee a durable peace in our country and jointly counter the aggression by the US imperialists and the Japanese militarists:

3. To abolish and declare invalid the 'South Korea—US mutual defence pact',

1 *Egyptian Gazette*, 26 April 1971.

the 'South Korea–Japan treaty' and all other treacherous and enslaving treaties and agreements concluded with foreign countries against the interests of the nation and oppose all forms of interference in the domestic affairs by foreign aggressor forces and attain national sovereignty;

4. To hold free North–South general elections on the principles of universal, equal and direct suffrage by secret ballot in a completely democratic atmosphere in which the freedom of the expression of the will by the people is fully guaranteed, without interference by any outside force, and establish a unified democratic central government representing the general will of the entire Korean people.

5. To ensure people of all walks of life in South Korea freedom of speech, the press, assembly, association, demonstration and to strike and all other democratic rights, release all the political prisoners who have been arrested and imprisoned on charges of having called for the peaceful unification of the fatherland and guarantee all the political parties, public organisations and individual personages of North and South Korea the conditions for freely conducting political activities in any area of the country;

6. To establish a confederation of North and South Korea as a transitional step for solving the urgent problems of common concern of the nation and hastening the national unification, leaving the present differing socio-political system in the North and South intact. If need be, prior to complete unification.

7. To promote economic intercourse and mutual cooperation in the spheres of science, culture, arts and sports between the North and South and make possible travel and correspondence to alleviate the sufferings of the people resulting from the split and restore the severed ties of the nation;

8. To hold a political consultative meeting of the North and South for discussing the immediate tasks of the nation and solving the question of the country's unification. . .

45. Joint communiqué issued by the Democratic People's Republic of Korea and the Republic of Korea, Pyongyang and Seoul, 4 July 1972[1]

Recently there were talks held both in Pyongyang and Seoul to discuss problems of improving South–North relations and unifying the divided Fatherland.

Director Lee Hu-rak of the Central Intelligence Agency of Seoul visited Pyongyang from 2 to 5 May 1972 to hold talks with Director Kim Young-joo of the Organization and Guidance Department [of the Korea Workers Party] of Pyongyang. Second Vice Premier Park Sung-chul, acting on behalf of Director Kim Young-joo, also visited Seoul from 29 May to 1 June 1972 to hold further talks with Director Lee Hu-rak.

With the common desire to achieve peaceful unification of the Fatherland as

1 *Korea Times*, 5 July 1972.

early as possible, the two sides in these talks had frank and open-hearted exchanges of views, and made great progress in promoting mutual understanding.

In the course of the talks, the two sides, in an effort to remove the misunder-standings and mistrust and mitigate increased tensions that have arisen between the South and the North as a result of long separation, and further to expedite unificati of the Fatherland have reached full agreement on the following points:

1. The two sides have agreed to the following principles for unification of the Fatherland:

First, unification shall be achieved through independent Korean efforts without being subject to external imposition or interference.

Second, unification shall be achieved through peaceful means, and not through the use of force against each other.

Third, as a homogeneous people, a great national unity shall be sought above all, transcending differences in ideas, ideologies, and systems.

2. In order to ease tensions and foster an atmosphere of mutual trust between the South and the North, the two sides have agreed not to slander or defame each other, not to undertake armed provocations whether on a large or small scale, and to take positive measures to prevent inadvertent military incidents.

3. The two sides, in order to restore severed national ties, promote mutual under standing and to expedite independent peaceful unification, have agreed to carry out various exchanges in many fields.

4. The two sides have agreed to cooperate positively with each other to seek early success of the South—North Red Cross talks, which are underway with the fervent expectations of the entire people.

5. The two sides, in order to prevent the outbreak of unexpected military inciden and to deal directly, promptly and accurately with problems arising between the South and the North, have agreed to install a direct telephone line between Seoul and Pyongyang.

6. The two sides, in order to implement the aforementioned agreed items, solve various problems existing between the South and the North and to settle the unifi-cation problem on the basis of the agreed principles for unification of the Father-land, have agreed to establish and operate a South—North Coordinating Committee co-chaired by Director Lee Hu-rak and Director Kim Young-joo.

7. The two sides, firmly convinced that the aforementioned agreed items corresp with the common aspirations of the entire people, who are anxious to see an early unification of the Fatherland, hereby solemnly pledge before the entire Korean peo that they will faithfully carry out these agreed items.

46. Joint announcement issued by the Democratic People's Republic of Korea and the Republic of Korea, Pyongyang, 4 November 1972, with Agreed Minutes[1]

1. The second meeting of the co-chairmen of the South—North Coordinating Com-mittee was held in Pyongyang from 2 to 4 Nov. 1972.

1 *Korea Times*, 5 November 1972.

2. Director Lee Hu-rak of the Central Intelligence Agency, co-chairman of the South–North Coordinating Committee of Seoul, and his party visited, and had a discussion with, Premier Kim Il-sung on 3 Nov. 1972.

3. The second meeting of the co-chairmen of the South–North Coordinating Committee had two sessions on 2 Nov. and 3 Nov.

This meeting was attended by, from Seoul, co-chairman Lee Hu-rak; former deputy premier Chang Key-young; Choi Kyu-hah, special advisor to the President; Kang In-dok, ninth bureau director of the CIA; and Chung Hong-jin, consultation and coordination bureau director of the CIA; and, from Pyongyang, second vice premier Park Sung-chul acting on behalf of co-chairman Kim Young-joo; Yu Chang-sik, deputy director of the organization and guidance department and concurrently director of the overseas affairs department of the Workers' Party; Lee Kyong-sok, counsellor to the cabinet; Han Ung-sik, senior guidance official under the direct command of the political council of the central committee of the Workers' Party; and Kim Tok-hyon, senior guidance official under the direct command of the political council of the central committee of the Workers' Party.

4. The meeting proceeded in a sincere, patriotic atmosphere with the aspiration of improving south–north relations and realizing the independent and peaceful unification of the fatherland as soon as possible, and made progress toward deepening mutual understanding and solving a series of problems.

5. The two sides reached agreement on jointly undertaking programs with mutual efforts in various fields between the south and north in compliance with the spirit of the South–North Joint Communiqué (of 4 July).

6. The two sides agreed in the meeting on the following problems:

(A) The two sides held identical opinions on formation and operation of the South–North Coordinating Committee and accordingly signed and exchanged the 'Agreed Minutes on Organization and Operation of the South-North Coordinating Committee'.

(B) The two sides in accordance with a provision of the South–North Joint Communiqué calling for not slandering or defaming each other, decided to discontinue, effective 00:00 hours 11 Nov. 1972 (their respective) broadcasting against the south and north, loudspeaker broadcasting against the south and north, across the Military Demarcation Line and scattering leaflets in each other's territory.

Agreed Minutes

The two sides agreed on organization and operation of the South–North Coordinating Committee as follows:

1. The South–North Coordinating Committee makes it its objective to settle national unification problems on the basis of the agreed-upon principles for unification of the fatherland, including (the problems) of carrying out matters agreed upon in the South–North Joint Communiqué of 4 July 1972, of improving and developing relations between the south and north, and of undertaking programs with joint efforts in various fields.

2. The functions of the South–North Coordinating Committee are as follows:

(A) Consults and decides on problems of realizing independent and peaceful unification of the country on the basis of the agreed-upon principles of unification of the fatherland and assures implementation of decisions on them.

(B) Consults and decides on problems of realizing wide range of political exchanges between parties, social organizations and individuals in the south and north, and assures implementation of decisions on them.

(C) Consults and decides on problems of economic, cultural and social exchanges and on undertaking programs with joint efforts and assures implementation of decisions on them.

(D) Consults and decides on problems of easing tension between the south and north, preventing military clashes and dissolving the situation of military confrontation and assures implementation of decisions on them.

(E) Consults and decides on problems of taking joint steps in overseas activities between the south and north and enhancing the national prestige as a homogeneous people and assures implementation of decisions on them.

3. The South–North Coordinating Committee shall be organized as follows:

(A) The South–North Coordinating Committee shall be composed of one co-chairman, one vice chairman, one executive member and two members from each side.

The number of members can be increased as necessary.

The co-chairmen are Director Lee Hu-rak of the Central Intelligence Agency and Director Kim Young-joo of the Organization and Guidance Department (of the Workers' Party).

The vice chairmen, executive members and members shall be of minister or vice-minister level, and be appointed by the co-chairmen of each side through previous consultations.

(B) The South–North Coordinating Committee shall have Executive Conference (Kansa Hweui).

The Executive Conference consults and decides on various problems which arise during the recess of the South–North Coordinating Committee at the instruction of the co-chairmen and assures implementation of decisions on them.

The Executive Conference shall be composed of executive members of the two sides and two secretaries from each side.

(C) The South–North Coordinating Committee shall have Sub-committees on Political Affairs, Military, Foreign Affairs, Economy and Culture.

The Sub-committees shall be established as programs of the South–North Coordinating Committee progress and their organizations and functions shall be determined through mutual agreement.

(D) The South–North Coordinating Committee shall establish Joint Secretariat in Panmunjom.

Each side shall appoint its co-director of the Joint Secretariat and the necessary number of staff members under the co-director.

4. The South—North Coordinating Committee shall be operated as follows:

(A) The South—North Coordinating Committee, in principle, holds meetings in Seoul and Pyongyang alternately and may hold meetings in Panmunjom as required.

(B) The South—North Coordinating Committee meetings shall be held once every two or three months and Executive Conference once a month. Besides, extraordinary meetings may be held in accordance with mutual agreement.

(C) Meetings of the South—North Coordinating Committee shall be held either publicly or behind closed doors.

(D) The South—North Coordinating Committee meetings and Executive Conference may be participated in by the necessary number of specialists and staff members of Joint Secretariat.

(E) The final agreement in the South—North Coordinating Committee shall be completed with the signature of the co-chairmen of the two sides and the agreed-upon minutes shall be announced through the Joint Secretariat in accordance with mutual agreement.

(F) Detailed rules on the operation of the South—North Coordinating Committee shall be determined separately.

5. This Agreed Minutes shall be effective when the two sides have signed and exchanged them.

47. Consensus adopted by the United Nations General Assembly, 28 November 1973[1]

It is noted with satisfaction that a joint communiqué was issued by the North and the South of Korea on 4 July 1972, which provides for the following three principles on the reunification of Korea:

(*a*) The reunification of the country should be achieved independently, without reliance upon outside force or its interference;

(*b*) The reunification of the country should be achieved by peaceful means, without recourse to the use of arms against the other side;

(*c*) Great national unity should be promoted.

It is the general hope that the South and the North of Korea will be urged to continue their dialogue and widen their many-sided exchanges and cooperation in the above spirit so as to expedite the independent peaceful reunification of the country.

The General Assembly decides to dissolve immediately the United Nations Commission for the Unification and Rehabilitation of Korea.

1 UN Doc. A/9341, par. 21.

II.   The Diplomacy of Detente

A. Relations between the United States and the Soviet Union

48. Treaty on the Non-proliferation of Nuclear Weapons, signed by the United States, the Soviet Union and Fifty-five other States, Washington, 1 July 1968[1]

The States concluding this Treaty, hereinafter referred to as the 'Parties to the Treaty',

Considering the devastation that would be visited upon all mankind by a nuclear war and the consequent need to make every effort to avert the danger of such a war and to take measures to safeguard the security of peoples,

Believing that the proliferation of nuclear weapons would seriously enhance the danger of nuclear war,

In conformity with resolutions of the United Nations General Assembly calling for the conclusion of an agreement on the prevention of wider dissemination of nuclear weapons,

Undertaking to cooperate in facilitating the application of International Atomic Energy Agency safeguards on peaceful nuclear activities,

Expressing their support for research, development and other efforts to further the application, within the framework of the International Atomic Energy Agency safeguards system, of the principle of safeguarding effectively the flow of source and special fissionable materials by use of instruments and other techniques at certain strategic points,

Affirming the principle that the benefits of peaceful applications of nuclear technology, including any technological by-products which may be derived by nuclear-weapon States from the development of nuclear explosive devices, should be available for peaceful purposes to all Parties to the Treaty, whether nuclear-weapon or non-nuclear-weapon States,

Convinced that, in furtherance of this principle, all Parties to the Treaty are entitled to participate in the fullest possible exchange of scientific information for, and to contribute alone or in cooperation with other States to, the further development of the applications of atomic energy for peaceful purposes,

Declaring their intention to achieve at the earliest possible date the cessation of the

1 *DSB*, 1 July 1968, pp. 9–11.

nuclear arms race and to undertake effective measures in the direction of nuclear disarmament,

Urging the cooperation of all States in the attainment of this objective,

Recalling the determination expressed by the Parties to the 1963 Treaty banning nuclear weapon tests in the atmosphere, in outer space and under water in its preamble to seek to achieve the discontinuance of all test explosions of nuclear weapons for all time and to continue negotiations to this end,

Desiring to further the easing of international tension and the strengthening of trust between States in order to facilitate the cessation of the manufacture of nuclear weapons, the liquidation of all their existing stockpiles, and the elimination from national arsenals of nuclear weapons and the means of their delivery pursuant to a Treaty on general and complete disarmament under strict and effective international control,

Recalling that, in accordance with the Charter of the United Nations, States must refrain in their international relations from the threat or use of force against the territorial integrity or political independence of any State, or in any other manner inconsistent with the Purposes of the United Nations, and that the establishment and maintenance of international peace and security are to be promoted with the least diversion for armaments of the world's human and economic resources,

Have agreed as follows:

Article I

Each nuclear-weapon State Party to the Treaty undertakes not to transfer to any recipient whatsoever nuclear weapons or other nuclear explosive devices or control over such weapons or explosive devices directly, or indirectly; and not in any way to assist, encourage, or induce any non-nuclear-weapon State to manufacture or otherwise acquire nuclear weapons or other nuclear explosive devices, or control over such weapons or explosive devices.

Article II

Each non-nuclear-weapon State Party to the Treaty undertakes not to receive the transfer from any transferor whatsoever of nuclear weapons or other nuclear explosive devices or of control over such weapons or explosive devices directly, or indirectly; not to manufacture or otherwise acquire nuclear weapons or other nuclear explosive devices; and not to seek or receive any assistance in the manufacture of nuclear weapons or other nuclear explosive devices.

Article III

1. Each non-nuclear-weapon State Party to the Treaty undertakes to accept safeguards, as set forth in an agreement to be negotiated and concluded with the International Atomic Energy Agency in accordance with the Statute of the International

Atomic Energy Agency and the Agency's safeguards system, for the exclusive purpose of verification of the fulfilment of its obligations assumed under this Treaty with a view to preventing diversion of nuclear energy from peaceful uses to nuclear weapons or other nuclear explosive devices. Procedures for the safeguards required by this article shall be followed with respect to source or special fissionable material whether it is being produced, processed or used in any principal nuclear facility or is outside any such facility. The safeguards required by this article shall be applied on all source or special fissionable material in all peaceful nuclear activities within the territory of such State, under its jurisdiction, or carried out under its control anywhere.

2. Each State Party to the Treaty undertakes not to provide: (a) source or special fissionable material, or (b) equipment or material especially designed or prepared for the processing, use or production of special fissionable material, to any non-nuclear-weapon State for peaceful purposes, unless the source or special fissionable material shall be subject to the safeguards required by this article.

3. The safeguards required by this article shall be implemented in a manner designed to comply with article IV of this Treaty, and to avoid hampering the economic or technological development of the parties or international cooperation in the field of peaceful nuclear activities, including the international exchange of nuclear material and equipment for the processing, use or production of nuclear material for peaceful purposes in accordance with the provisions of this article and the principle of safeguarding set forth in the preamble.

4. Non-nuclear-weapon States Party to the Treaty shall conclude agreements with the International Atomic Energy Agency to meet the requirements of this article either individually or together with other States in accordance with the Statute of the International Atomic Energy Agency. Negotiation of such agreements shall commence within 180 days from the original entry into force of this Treaty. For States depositing their instruments of ratification or accession after the 180-day period, negotiation of such agreements shall commence not later than the date of such deposit. Such agreements shall enter into force not later than eighteen months after the date of initiation of negotiations.

Article IV

1. Nothing in this Treaty shall be interpreted as affecting the inalienable right of all the Parties to the Treaty to develop research, production and use of nuclear energy for peaceful purposes without discrimination and in conformity with articles I and II of this Treaty.

2. All the Parties to the Treaty undertake to facilitate, and have the right to participate in, the fullest possible exchange of equipment, materials and scientific and technological information for the peaceful uses of nuclear energy. Parties to the Treaty in a position to do so shall also cooperate in contributing alone or together with other States or international organizations to the further development of the applications of nuclear energy for peaceful purposes, especially in the territories

of non-nuclear-weapon States Party to the Treaty, with due consideration for the needs of the developing areas of the world.

Article V

Each Party to the Treaty undertakes to take appropriate measures to ensure that, in accordance with this Treaty, under appropriate international observation and through appropriate international procedures, potential benefits from any peaceful application of nuclear explosions will be made available to non-nuclear-weapon States Party to the Treaty on a non-discriminatory basis and that the charge to such Parties for the explosive devices used will be as low as possible and exclude any charge for research and development. Non-nuclear-weapon States Party to the Treaty shall be able to obtain such benefits, pursuant to a special international agreement or agreements, through an appropriate international body with adequate representation of non-nuclear-weapon States. Negotiations on this subject shall commence as soon as possible after the Treaty enters into force. Non-nuclear-weapon States Party to the Treaty so desiring may also obtain such benefits pursuant to bilateral agreements.

Article VI

Each of the Parties to the Treaty undertakes to pursue negotiations in good faith on effective measures relating to cessation of the nuclear arms race at an early date and to nuclear disarmament, and on a Treaty on general and complete disarmament under strict and effective international control.

Article VII

Nothing in this Treaty affects the right of any group of States to conclude regional treaties in order to assure the total absence of nuclear weapons in their respective territories.

Article VIII

1. Any Party to the Treaty may propose amendments to this Treaty. The text of any proposed amendment shall be submitted to the Depositary Governments which shall circulate it to all Parties to the Treaty. Thereupon, if requested to do so by one third or more of the Parties to the Treaty, the Depositary Governments shall convene a conference, to which they shall invite all the Parties to the Treaty, to consider such an amendment.

2. Any amendment to this Treaty must be approved by a majority of the votes of all the Parties to the Treaty, including the votes of all nuclear-weapon States Party to the Treaty and all other Parties which, on the date the amendment is circulated, are members of the Board of Governors of the International Atomic Energy Agency. The amendment shall enter into force for each Party that deposits

its instrument of ratification of the amendment upon the deposit of such instruments of ratification by a majority of all the Parties, including the instruments of ratification of all nuclear-weapon States Party to the Treaty and all other Parties which, on the date the amendment is circulated, are members of the Board of Governors of the International Atomic Energy Agency. Thereafter, it shall enter into force for any other Party upon the deposit of its instrument of ratification of the amendment.

3. Five years after the entry into force of this Treaty, a conference of Parties to the Treaty shall be held in Geneva, Switzerland, in order to review the operation of this Treaty with a view to assuring that the purposes of the Preamble and the provisions of the Treaty are being realized. At intervals of five years thereafter, a majority of the Parties to the Treaty may obtain, by submitting a proposal to this effect to the Depositary Governments, the convening of further conferences with the same objective of reviewing the operation of the Treaty.

Article IX

1. This Treaty shall be open to all States for signature. Any State which does not sign the Treaty before its entry into force in accordance with paragraph 3 of this article may accede to it at any time.

2. This Treaty shall be subject to ratification by signatory States. Instruments of ratification and instruments of accession shall be deposited with the Governments of the Union of Soviet Socialist Republics, the United Kingdom of Great Britain and Northern Ireland and the United States of America, which are hereby designated the Depositary Governments.

3. This Treaty shall enter into force after its ratification by the States, the Governments of which are designated Depositaries of the Treaty, and forty other States signatory to this Treaty and the deposit of their instruments of ratification. For the purposes of this Treaty, a nuclear-weapon State is one which has manufactured and exploded a nuclear weapon or other nuclear explosive device prior to 1 January 1967.

4. For States whose instruments of ratification or accession are deposited subsequent to the entry into force of this Treaty, it shall enter into force on the date of the deposit of their instruments of ratification or accession.

5. The Depositary Governments shall promptly inform all signatory and acceding States of the date of each signature, the date of deposit of each instrument of ratification or of accession, the date of the entry into force of this Treaty, and the date of receipt of any requests for convening a conference or other notices.

6. This Treaty shall be registered by the Depositary Governments pursuant to Article 102 of the Charter of the United Nations.

Article X

1. Each Party shall in exercising its national sovereignty have the right to withdraw

from the Treaty if it decides that extraordinary events, related to the subject matter of this Treaty, have jeopardized the supreme interests of its country. It shall give notice of such withdrawal to all other Parties to the Treaty and to the United Nations Security Council three months in advance. Such notice shall include a statement of the extraordinary events it regards as having jeopardized its supreme interests.

2. Twenty-five years after the entry into force of the Treaty, a Conference shall be convened to decide whether the Treaty shall continue in force indefinitely, or shall be extended for an additional fixed period or periods. This decision shall be taken by a majority of the Parties to the Treaty.

Article XI

This Treaty, the English, Russian, French, Spanish and Chinese texts of which are equally authentic, shall be deposited in the archives of the Depositary Governments. Duly certified copies of this Treaty shall be transmitted by the Depositary Governments to the Governments of the signatory and acceding States.

49. Statement by President Nixon on American radio and television, 20 May 1971[1]

Good afternoon, ladies and gentlemen. As you know, the Soviet–American talks on limiting nuclear arms have been deadlocked for over a year. As a result of negotiation involving the highest level of both Governments, I am announcing today a significant development in breaking the deadlock.

The statement that I shall now read is being issued simultaneously in Moscow and Washington – Washington, 12 o'clock, and Moscow, 7 p.m.

The Governments of the United States and the Soviet Union, after reviewing the course of their talks on the limitation of strategic armaments, have agreed to concentrate this year on working out an agreement for the limitation of the deployment of anti-ballistic missile systems (ABMs). They have also agreed that, together with concluding an agreement to limit ABMs, they will agree on certain measures with respect to the limitation of offensive strategic weapons.

The two sides are taking this course in the conviction that it will create more favorable conditions for further negotiations to limit all strategic arms. These negotiations will be actively pursued.

This agreement is a major step in breaking the stalemate on nuclear arms talks. Intensive negotiations, however, will be required to translate this understanding into a concrete agreement.

This statement that I have just read expresses the commitment of the Soviet and American Governments at the highest levels to achieve that goal. If we succeed,

1 *DSB*, 7 June 1971, pp. 741–2.

his joint statement that has been issued today may well be remembered as the
beginning of a new era in which all nations will devote more of their energies
nd their resources not to the weapons of war, but to the works of peace.

50. Agreement on Measures to Reduce the Risk of Outbreak of Nuclear War, Washington, 30 September 1971[1]

The United States of America and the Union of Soviet Socialist Republics, herein-
fter referred to as the Parties:

Taking into account the devastating consequences that nuclear war would have
or all mankind, and recognizing the need to exert every effort to avert the risk of
utbreak of such a war, including measures to guard against accident or unauth-
rized use of nuclear weapons,

Believing that agreement on measures for reducing the risk of outbreak of nuclear
var serves the interests of strengthening international peace and security, and is in
o way contrary to the interests of any other country,

Bearing in mind that continued efforts are also needed in the future to seek ways
f reducing the risk of outbreak of nuclear war,

Have agreed as follows:

Article 1

ach Party undertakes to maintain and to improve, as it deems necessary, its existing
rganizational and technical arrangements to guard against the accidental or un-
uthorized use of nuclear weapons under its control.

Article 2

The Parties undertake to notify each other immediately in the event of an accidental,
nauthorized or any other unexplained incident involving a possible detonation of
nuclear weapon which could create a risk of outbreak of nuclear war. In the event
f such an incident, the Party whose nuclear weapon is involved will immediately
nake every effort to take necessary measures to render harmless or destroy such
veapon without its causing damage.

Article 3

The Parties undertake to notify each other immediately in the event of detection by
nissile warning systems of unidentified objects, or in the event of signs of inter-
erence with these systems or with related communications facilities, if such occurrences
ould create a risk of outbreak of nuclear war between the two countries.

1 *DSB*, 18 October 1971, pp. 400–1.

Article 4

Each Party undertakes to notify the other Party in advance of any planned missile launches if such launches will extend beyond its national territory in the direction of the other Party.

Article 5

Each Party, in other situations involving unexplained nuclear incidents, undertakes to act in such a manner as to reduce the possibility of its actions being misinterprete by the other Party. In any such situation, each Party may inform the other Party or request information when, in its view, this is warranted by the interests of avertir the risk of outbreak of nuclear war.

Article 6

For transmission of urgent information, notifications and requests for information in situations requiring prompt clarification, the Parties shall make primary use of the Direct Communications Link between the Governments of the United States of America and the Union of Soviet Socialist Republics.

    For transmission of other information, notifications and requests for informatio the Parties, at their own discretion, may use any communications facilities, includin diplomatic channels, depending on the degree of urgency.

Article 7

The Parties undertake to hold consultations, as mutually agreed, to consider questio relating to implementation of the provisions of this Agreement, as well as to discuss possible amendments thereto aimed at further implementation of the purposes of this Agreement.

Article 8

This Agreement shall be of unlimited duration.

Article 9

This Agreement shall enter into force upon signature.

51. Agreement on Measures to Improve the USA—USSR Direct Communications Link, Washington, 30 September 1971[1] with Annex

The United States of America and the Union of Soviet Socialist Republics, hereinafter referred to as the Parties,

1 *DSB*, 18 October 1971, pp. 401–3.

Noting the positive experience gained in the process of operating the existing Direct Communications Link between the United States of America and the Union of Soviet Socialist Republics, which was established for use in time of emergency pursuant to the Memorandum of Understanding Regarding the Establishment of a Direct Communications Link, signed on 20 June 1963,

Having examined, in a spirit of mutual understanding, matters relating to the improvement and modernization of the Direct Communications Link,

Have agreed as follows:

Article 1

1. For the purpose of increasing the reliability of the Direct Communications Link, there shall be established and put into operation the following:

(*a*) two additional circuits between the United States of America and the Union of Soviet Socialist Republics each using a satellite communications system, with each Party selecting a satellite communications system of its own choice.

(*b*) a system of terminals (more than one) in the territory of each Party for the Direct Communications Link, with the locations and number of terminals in the United States of America to be determined by the United States side, and the locations and number of terminals in the Union of Soviet Socialist Republics to be determined by the Soviet side.

2. Matters relating to the implementation of the aforementioned improvements of the Direct Communications Link are set forth in the Annex which is attached hereto and forms an integral part hereof.

Article 2

Each Party confirms its intention to take all possible measures to assure the continuous and reliable operation of the communications circuits and the system of terminals of the Direct Communications Link for which it is responsible in accordance with this Agreement and the Annex hereto, as well as to communicate to the head of its Government any messages received via the Direct Communications Link from the head of Government of the other Party.

Article 3

The Memorandum of Understanding Between the United States of America and the Union of Soviet Socialist Republics Regarding the Establishment of a Direct Communications Link, signed on 20 June 1963, with the Annex thereto, shall remain in force, except to the extent that its provisions are modified by this Agreement and Annex hereto.

Article 4

The undertakings of the Parties hereunder shall be carried out in accordance with their respective Constitutional processes.

Article 5

This Agreement, including the Annex hereto, shall enter into force upon signature.

Annex

Improvements to the USA—USSR Direct Communications Link shall be implement in accordance with the provisions set forth in this Annex.

I. Circuits

(*a*) Each of the original circuits established pursuant to paragraph 1 of the Annex to the Memorandum of Understanding, dated June 20 1963, shall continue to be maintained and operated as part of the Direct Communications Link until such time, after the satellite communications circuits provided for herein become operational, as the agencies designated pursuant to paragraph III (hereinafter referred to as the 'designated agencies') mutually agree that such original circuit is no longer necessary. The provisions of paragraph 7 of the Annex to the Memorandum of Und standing, dated 20 June 1963, shall continue to govern the allocation of the costs of maintaining and operating such original circuits.

(*b*) Two additional circuits shall be established using two satellite communicatio systems. Taking into account paragraph I(c) below, the United States side shall provide one circuit via the Intelsat system and the Soviet side shall provide one circuit via the Molniya II system. The two circuits shall be duplex telephone bandwidth circuits conforming to CCITT [International Telephone and Telegraph Consultative Committee] standards, equipped for secondary telegraphic multiplexi Transmission and reception of messages over the Direct Communications Link shall be effected in accordance with applicable recommendations of international communications regulations, as well as with mutually agreed instructions.

(*c*) When the reliability of both additional circuits has been established to the mutual satisfaction of the designated agencies, they shall be used as the primary circuits of the Direct Communications Link for transmission and reception of teleprinter messages between the United States and the Soviet Union.

(*d*) Each satellite communications circuit shall utilize an earth station in the territory of the United States, a communications satellite transponder, and an earth station in the territory of the Soviet Union. Each Party shall be responsible for linking the earth stations in its territory to its own terminals of the Direct Communications Link.

(*e*) For the circuits specified in paragraph I(b):
— The Soviet side will provide and operate at least one earth station in its territory for the satellite communications circuit in the Intelsat system, and will also arrange for the use of suitable earth station facilities in its territory for the satellite communications circuit in the Molniya II system. The United States side, throug a governmental agency or other United States legal entity, will make appropriate

arrangements with Intelsat with regard to access for the Soviet Intelsat earth station to the Intelsat space segment, as well as for the use of the applicable portion of the Intelsat space segment.

– The United States side will provide and operate at least one earth station in its territory for the satellite communications circuit in the Molniya II system, and will also arrange for the use of suitable earth station facilities in its territory for the satellite communications circuit in the Intelsat system.

(*f*) Each earth station shall conform to the performance specifications and operating procedures of the corresponding satellite communications system and the ratio of antenna gain to the equivalent noise temperature should be no less than 31 decibels. Any deviation from these specifications and procedures which may be required in any unusual situation shall be worked out and mutually agreed upon by the designated agencies of both Parties after consultation.

(*g*) The operational commissioning dates for the satellite communications circuits based on the Intelsat and Molniya II systems shall be as agreed upon by the designated agencies of the Parties through consultations.

(*h*) The United States side shall bear the costs of (1) providing and operating the Molniya II earth station in its territory; (2) the use of the Intelsat earth station in its territory; and (3) the transmission of messages via the Intelsat system. The Soviet side shall bear the costs of: (1) providing and operating the Intelsat earth station in its territory; (2) the use of the Molniya II earth station in its territory; and (3) the transmission of messages via the Molniya II system. Payment of the costs of the satellite communications circuits shall be effected without any transfer of payments between the Parties.

(*i*) Each Party shall be responsible for providing to the other Party notification of any proposed modification or replacement of the communications satellite system containing the circuit provided by it that might require accommodation by earth stations using that system or otherwise affect the maintenance or operation of the Direct Communications Link. Such notification should be given sufficiently in advance to enable the designated agencies to consult and to make, before the modification, or replacement is effected, such preparation as may be agreed upon for accommodation by the affected earth stations.

I. Terminals

(*a*) Each Party shall establish a system of terminals in its territory for the exchange of messages with the other Party, and shall determine the locations and number of terminals in such a system. Terminals of the Direct Communications Link shall be designated 'USA' and 'USSR'.

(*b*) Each Party shall take necessary measures to provide for rapidly switching circuits among terminal points in such a manner that only one terminal location is connected to the circuits at any one time.

(*c*) Each Party shall use teleprinter equipment from its own sources to equip the additional terminals for the transmission and reception of messages from the United

States to the Soviet Union in the English language and from the Soviet Union to the United States in the Russian language.

(*d*) The terminals of the Direct Communications Link shall be provided with encoding equipment. One-time tape encoding equipment shall be used for transmissions via the Direct Communications Link. A mutually agreed quantity of encoding equipment of a modern and reliable type selected by the United States side, with spares, test equipment, technical literature and operating supplies, shall be furnished by the United States side to the Soviet side against payment of the cost thereof by the Soviet side; additional spares for the encoding equipment supplied will be furnished as necessary.

(*e*) Keying tapes shall be supplied in accordance with the provisions set forth in paragraph 4 of the Annex to the Memorandum of Understanding, dated 20 June 1963. Each Party shall be responsible for reproducing and distributing additional keying tapes for its system of terminals and for implementing procedures which ensure that the required synchronization of encoding equipment can be effected from any one terminal at any time.

III. Other Matters

Each Party shall designate the agencies responsible for arrangements regarding the establishment of the additional circuits and the systems of terminals provided for in this Agreement and Annex, for their operation and for their continuity and reliability. These agencies shall, on the basis of direct contacts:

(*a*) arrange for the exchange of required performance specifications and operating procedures for the earth stations of the communications systems using Intelsat and Molniya II satellites;

(*b*) arrange for testing, acceptance and commissioning of the satellite circuits and for operation of these circuits after commissioning; and,

(*c*) decide matters and develop instructions relating to the operation of the secondary teleprinter multiplex system used on the satellite circuits.

Agreements reached at the summit meeting between President Nixon and Mr Brezhnev, Moscow, 22–30 May 1972:

52. Agreement concerning Cooperation in the Exploration and Use of Outer Space for Peaceful Purposes, 24 May 1972[1]

The Union of Soviet Socialist Republics and the United States of America;

Considering the role which the USSR and the USA play in the exploration and use of outer space for peaceful purposes;

Striving for a further expansion of cooperation between the USSR and the USA in the exploration and use of outer space for peaceful purposes;

1 *Soviet News*, 13 June 1972

Noting the positive cooperation which the Parties have already experienced in this area;

Desiring to make the results of scientific research gained from the exploration and use of outer space for peaceful purposes available for the benefit of the peoples of the two countries and of all peoples of the world;

Taking into consideration the provisions of the Treaty on Principles Governing the Activities of States in the Exploration and Use of Outer Space, Including the Moon and Other Celestial Bodies, as well as the Agreement on the Rescue of Astronauts, the Return of Astronauts, and the Return of Objects Launched in Outer Space;

In accordance with the Agreement between the Union of Soviet Socialist Republics and the United States of America on Exchanges and Cooperation in Scientific, Technical, Educational, Cultural, and Other Fields, signed 11 April 1972, and in order to develop further the principles of mutually beneficial cooperation between the two countries;

Have agreed as follows:

Article 1

The Parties will develop cooperation in the fields of space meteorology; study of the natural environment; exploration of near earth space, the moon and the planets; and space biology and medicine; and, in particular, will cooperate to take all appropriate measures to encourage and achieve the fulfilment of the Summary of Results of Discussion on Space Cooperation Between the Academy of Sciences of the USSR and the US National Aeronautics and Space Administration dated 21 January 1971.

Article 2

The Parties will carry out such cooperation by means of mutual exchanges of scientific information and delegations, through meetings of scientists and specialists of both countries, and also in such other ways as may be mutually agreed. Joint working groups may be created for the development and implementation of appropriate programmes of cooperation.

Article 3

The Parties have agreed to carry out projects for developing compatible rendezvous and docking systems of Soviet and United States manned spacecraft and stations in order to enhance the safety of manned flights in space and to provide the opportunity for conducting joint scientific experiments in the future. It is planned that the first experimental flight to test these systems be conducted during 1975, envisaging the docking of a Soviet *Soyuz*-type spacecraft and a United States *Apollo*-type spacecraft with visits of astronauts in each other's spacecraft. The implementation of these projects will be carried out on the basis of principles and procedures which will be developed in accordance with the Summary of Results of the Meeting Between Representatives of the USSR Academy of Sciences and the US National Aeronautics and Space Administration on the Question of Developing Compatible Syste* for Rendezvous and Docking of Manned Spacecraft and Space Stations of the USSF and the USA dated 6 April 1972.

Article 4

The Parties will encourage international efforts to resolve problems of international law in the exploration and use of outer space for peaceful purposes with the aim of strengthening the legal order in space and further developing international space law and will cooperate in this field.

Article 5

The Parties may by mutual agreement determine other areas of cooperation in the exploration and use of outer space for peaceful purposes.

Article 6

This Agreement shall enter into force upon signature and shall remain in force for five years. It may be modified or extended by mutual agreement of the Parties.

53. Agreement on the Prevention of Incidents on or over the Sea, 25 May 1972[1]

The Government of the Union of Soviet Socialist Republics and the Government of the United States of America,
    Desiring to assure the safety of navigation of the ships of their respective Armed Forces on the high seas and flight of their military aircraft over the high seas, and
    Guided by the principles and rules of international law,
    Have decided to conclude this Agreement and have agreed as follows:

Article 1

For the purposes of this Agreement the following definitions shall apply:
    1. 'Ship' means:
    (A) A warship belonging to the naval forces of the Parties bearing the external marks distinguishing warships of its nationality, under the command of an officer duly commissioned by the government and whose name appears in the navy list, and manned by a crew who are under regular naval discipline;

1 *Soviet News*, 13 June 1972.

(B) Naval auxiliaries of the Parties, which include all naval ships authorised to ly the naval auxiliary flag where such a flag has been established by either Party.

2. 'Aircraft' means all military manned heavier-than-air and lighter-than-air raft, excluding space craft.

3. 'Formation' means an ordered arrangement of two or more ships proceeding ogether and normally manoeuvred together.

Article 2

'he Parties shall take measures to instruct the commanding officers of their re-pective ships to observe strictly the letter and spirit of the International Regulations or Preventing Collisions at Sea, hereinafter referred to as the Rules of the Road. 'he Parties recognise that their freedom to conduct operations on the high seas is ased on the principles established under recognised international law and codified n the 1953 Geneva Convention on the High Seas.

Article 3

. In all cases ships operating in proximity to each other, except when required to naintain course and speed under the Rules of the Road, shall remain well clear to void risk of collision.

2. Ships meeting or operating in the vicinity of a formation of the other Party hall, while conforming to the Rules of the Road, avoid manoeuvring in a manner vhich would hinder the evolutions of the formation.

3. Formations shall not conduct manoeuvres through areas of heavy traffic where nternationally recognised traffic separation schemes are in effect.

4. Ships engaged in surveillance of other ships shall stay at a distance which voids the risk of collision and also shall avoid executing manoeuvres embarrassing r endangering the ships under surveillance. Except when required to maintain ourse and speed under the Rules of the Road, a surveillant shall take positive arly action so as, in the exercise of good seamanship, not to embarrass or endanger hips under surveillance.

5. When ships of both Parties manoeuvre in sight of one another, such signals flag, sound, and light) as are prescribed by the Rules of the Road, the International ̦ode of Signals, or other mutually agreed signals, shall be adhered to for signalling perations and intentions.

6. Ships of the Parties shall not simulate attacks by aiming guns, missile launchers, orpedo tubes, and other weapons in the direction of a passing ship of the other 'arty, not launch any object in the direction of passing ships of the other Party, and ot use searchlights or other powerful illumination devices to illuminate the navigation ridges of passing ships of the other Party.

7. When conducting exercises with submerged submarines, exercising ships shall how the appropriate signals prescribed by the International Code of Signals to warn hips of the presence of submarines in the area.

8. Ships of one Party when approaching ships of the other Party conducting operations as set forth in rule 4 (C) of the Rules of the Road, and particularly ships engaged in launching or landing aircraft as well as ships engaged in replenishment underway, shall take appropriate measures not to hinder manoeuvres of such ships and shall remain well clear.

Article 4

Commanders of aircraft of the Parties shall use the greatest caution and prudence in approaching aircraft and ships of the other Party operating on and over the high seas, in particular, ships engaged in launching or landing aircraft, and in the interest of mutual safety shall not permit: simulated attacks by the simulated use of weapon against aircraft and ships or performance of various aerobatics over ships, or droppi various objects near them in such a manner as to be hazardous to ships or to constit a hazard to navigation.

Article 5

1. Ships of the Parties operating in sight of one another shall raise proper signals concerning their intent to begin launching or landing aircraft.
2. Aircraft of the Parties flying over the high seas in darkness or under instrumer conditions shall, whenever feasible, display navigation lights.

Article 6

Both Parties shall:
1. Provide through the established system of radio broadcasts of information and warning to mariners, not less than 3 to 5 days in advance as a rule, notification of actions on the high seas which represent a danger to navigation or to aircraft in fligh
2. Make increased use of the informative signals contained in the International Code of Signals to signify the intentions of their respective ships when manoeuvring in proximity to one another. At night or in conditions of reduced visibility, or unde conditions of lighting and such distances when signal flags are not distinct, flashing light should be used to inform ships of manoeuvres which may hinder the movemer of others or involve a risk of collision.
3. Utilise on a trial basis signals additional to those in the International Code of Signals, submitting such signals to the Intergovernmental Maritime Consultative Organisation for its consideration and for the information of other States.

Article 7

The Parties shall exchange appropriate information concerning instances of collision incidents which result in damage, or other incidents at sea between ships and aircraft of the Parties. The United States Navy shall provide such information throu ιe Soviet Naval Attaché in Washington and the Soviet Navy shall provide such ιformation through the United States Naval Attaché in Moscow.

rticle 8

his agreement shall enter into force on the date of its signature and shall remain in ϱrce for a period of three years. It will thereafter be renewed without further ϲtion by the Parties for successive periods of three years each.

This Agreement may be terminated by either Party upon six months written ϱtice to the other Party.

rticle 9

'he Parties shall meet within one year after the date of the signing of this Agreeιent to review the implementation of its terms. Similar consultations shall be held ιereafter annually, or more frequently as the Parties may decide.

rticle 10

'he Parties shall designate members to form a committee which will consider specific ιeasures in conformity with this Agreement. The committee will, as a particular ιart of its work, consider the practical workability of concrete fixed distances to ιe observed in encounters between ships, aircraft, and ships and aircraft. The comιittee will meet within six months of the date of signature of this Agreement and ιbmit its recommendations for decision by the Parties during the consultations ιescribed in Article IX.

4. Treaty on the Limitation of Anti-Ballistic Missile Systems, '6 May 1972[1]

'he United States of America and the Union of Soviet Socialist Republics, hereinafter ϱferred to as the parties, proceeding from the premise that nuclear war would have ιevastating consequences for all mankind,

Considering that effective measures to limit anti-ballistic missile systems would ιe a substantial factor in curbing the race in strategic offensive arms and would lead ϱ a decrease in the risk of outbreak of war involving nuclear weapons,

Proceeding from the premise that the limitation of anti-ballistic missile systems, ιs well as certain agreement measures with respect to the limitation of strategic ϝffensive arms, would contribute to the creation of more favourable conditions for ιrther negotiations on limiting strategic arms,

Mindful of their obligations under Article VI of the treaty on the non-proliferation ϝf nuclear weapons,

1 *DSB*, 26 June 1972, pp. 918–20.

Declaring their intention to achieve at the earliest possible date the cessation of the nuclear arms race and to take effective measures toward reductions in strategic arms, nuclear disarmament, and general and complete disarmament.

Desiring to contribute to the relaxation of international tension and the strength ening of trust between states,

Have agreed as follows:

Article 1

1. Each party undertakes to limit anti-ballistic missile (ABM) systems and to adopt other measures in accordance with the provisions of this treaty.

2. Each party undertakes not to deploy ABM systems for a defence of the territory of its country and not to provide a base for such a defence, and not to deploy ABM systems for defence of an individual region except as provided for in Article 3 of this treaty.

Article 2

1. For the purpose of this treaty an ABM system is a system to counter strategic ballistic missiles or their elements in flight trajectory, currently consisting of:

(*a*) ABM interceptor missiles, which are interceptor missiles constructed and deployed for an ABM role, or of a type tested in an ABM mode:

(*b*) ABM launchers, which are launchers constructed and deployed for launching ABM interceptor missiles, and

(*c*) ABM radars, which are radars constructed and deployed for an ABM role, or of a type tested in ABM mode.

2. The ABM system components listed in paragraph I of this article include those which are:

(*a*) Operational,

(*b*) Under construction,

(*c*) Undergoing testing,

(*d*) Undergoing overhaul, repair or conversion, or

(*e*) Mothballed.

Article 3

Each party undertakes not to deploy ABM systems or their components except that

(*a*) Within one ABM system deployment area having a radius of one hundred and fifty kilometres and centred on the party's national capital, a party may deploy (1) No more than one hundred ABM launchers and no more than one hundred ABM interceptor missiles at launch sites, and (2) ABM radars within no more than six ABM radar complexes, the area of each complex being circular and having a diameter of no more than three kilometres, and

(*b*) Within one ABM system deployment area having a radius of one hundred and ifty kilometres and containing ICBM silo launchers, a party may deploy: (1) No more than one hundred ABM launchers and no more than one hundred ABM interceptor missiles at launch sites, (2) Two large phased-array ABM radars comparable in potential to corresponding ABM radars operational or under construction on the date of signature of the treaty in an ABM system deployment area containing ICBM silo launchers, and (3) No more than eighteen ABM radars each having a potential less than the potential of the smaller of the above-mentioned two large phased-array ABM radars.

Article 4

The limitations provided for in Article 3 shall not apply to ABM systems or their components used for development or testing, and located within current or additionally agreed test ranges. Each party may have no more than a total of fifteen ABM launchers at test ranges.

Article 5

1. Each party undertakes not to develop, test, or deploy ABM systems or components which are sea-based, air-based, space-based, or mobile land-based.
2. Each party undertakes not to develop, test, or deploy ABM launchers for launching more than one ABM interceptor missile at a time from each launcher, nor to modify deployed launchers to provide them with such a capability, nor to develop, test, or deploy automatic or semi-automatic or other similar systems for rapid reload of ABM launchers.

Article 6

To enhance assurance of the effectiveness of the limitations on ABM systems and their components provided by this treaty, each party undertakes:

(*a*) Not to give missiles, launchers, or radars, other than ABM interceptor missiles, ABM launchers, or ABM radars, capabilities to counter strategic ballistic missiles or their elements in flight trajectory, and not to test them in an ABM mode, and

(*b*) Not to deploy in the future radars for early warning of strategic ballistic missile attack except at locations along the periphery of its national territory and oriented outward.

Article 7

Subject to the provisions of this treaty, modernization and replacement of ABM systems or their components may be carried out.

Article 8

ABM systems or their components in excess of the numbers or outside the areas specified in this treaty, as well as ABM systems or their components prohibited by this treaty, shall be destroyed or dismantled under agreed procedures within the shortest possible agreed period of time.

Article 9

To assure the viability and effectiveness of this treaty, each party undertakes not to transfer to other states, and not to deploy outside its national territory, ABM systems or their components limited by this treaty.

Article 10

Each party undertakes not to assume any international obligations which would conflict with this treaty.

Article 11

The parties undertake to continue active negotiations for limitations on strategic offensive arms.

Article 12

1. For the purpose of providing assurance of compliance with the provisions of this treaty, each party shall use national technical means of verification at its disposal in a manner consistent with generally recognized principles of international law.

2. Each party undertakes not to use deliberate concealment measures which impede verification by national technical means of compliance with the provisions of this treaty. This obligation shall not require changes in current construction, assembly, conversion, or overhaul practices.

Article 13

1. To promote the objectives and implementation of the provisions of this treaty, the parties shall establish promptly a standing consultative commission, within the framework of which they will:

(*a*) consider questions concerning compliance with the obligations assumed and related situations which may be considered ambiguous,

(*b*) provide on a voluntary basis such information as either party considers necessary to assure confidence in compliance with the obligations assumed,

(*c*) consider questions involving unintended interference with national technical means of verification,

(*d*) consider possible changes in the strategic situation which have a bearing on the provisions of this treaty,

(*e*) agree upon procedures and dates for destruction or dismantling of ABM stems or their components in cases provided for by the provisions of this treaty,

(f) consider, as appropriate, possible proposals for further increasing the vi-
ility of this treaty, including proposals for amendments in accordance with the
ovisions of this treaty,

(g) consider, as appropriate, proposals for further measures aimed at limiting
rategic arms.

2. The parties through consultation shall establish, and may amend as appropriate,
gulations for the standing consultative commission governing procedures, com-
sition and other relevant matters.

rticle 14

Each party may propose amendments to this treaty. Agreed amendments shall
ter into force in accordance with the procedures governing the entry into force
 this treaty.

2. Five years after entry into force of this treaty, and at five-year intervals there-
ter, the parties shall together conduct a review of this treaty.

rticle 15

This treaty shall be of unlimited duration.

2. Each party shall, in exercising its national sovereignty, have the right to with-
aw from this treaty if it decides that extraordinary events related to the subject
atter of this treaty have jeopardized its supreme interests. It shall give notice of its
cision to the other party six months prior to withdrawal from the treaty. Such
tice shall include a statement of the extraordinary events the notifying party
gards as having jeopardized its supreme interests.

rticle 16

. This treaty shall be subject to ratification in accordance with constitutional
ocedures of each party. The treaty shall enter into force on the day of the exchange
 instruments of ratification.

2. This treaty shall be registered pursuant to Article 102 of the Charter of the
nited Nations.

5. Interim Agreement on Certain Measures with Respect to the imitation of Strategic Offensive Arms, 26 May 1972,[1] with rotocol

he Union of Soviet Socialist Republics and the United States of America, herein-
ter referred to as the parties, convinced that the Treaty on the Limitation of Anti-

1 *DSB*, 26 June 1972, pp. 920–1.

Ballistic Missile Systems and this Interim Agreement on certain measures with respect to the limitation of strategic offensive arms, will contribute to the creation of more favourable conditions for active negotiations on limiting strategic arms as well as to the relaxation of international tension and the strengthening of trust between states, taking into account the relationship between strategic offensive and defensive arms, mindful of their obligations under Article VI of the Treaty on the Nonproliferation of Nuclear Weapons, have agreed as follows:

Article 1

The parties undertake not to start construction of additional fixed land-based inter continental ballistic missile (ICBM) launchers after 1 July 1972.

Article 2

The parties undertake not to convert land-based launchers for light ICBMs, or for ICBMs of older types deployed prior to 1964, into land-based launchers for heavy ICBMs of types deployed after that time.

Article 3

The parties undertake to limit submarine-launched ballistic missile (SLBM) launcher and modern ballistic missile submarines to the numbers operational and under construction on the date of signature of this Interim Agreement, and in addition launchers and submarines constructed under procedures established by the parties as replacements for an equal number of ICBM launchers of older types deployed pr to 1964 or for launchers on older submarines.

Article 4

Subject to the provisions of this Interim Agreement, modernisation and replacemen of strategic offensive ballistic missiles and launchers covered by this Interim Agreement may be undertaken.

Article 5

1. For the purpose of providing assurance of compliance with the provisions of this Interim Agreement, each party shall use national technical means of verification at its disposal in a manner consistent with generally recognized principles of international law.

2. Each party undertakes not to interfere with the national technical means of verification of the other party operating in accordance with paragraph I of this Article.

3. Each party undertakes not to use deliberate concealment measures which

npede verification by national technical means, of compliance with the provisions
f this Interim Agreement. This obligation shall not require changes in current
onstruction, assembly, conversion, or overhaul practices.

Article 6

'o promote the objectives and implementation of the provisions of this Interim
Agreement, the parties shall use the standing consultative commission established
nder Article XIII of the Treaty on the Limitation of Anti-Ballistic Missile Systems
1 accordance with the provisions of that Article.

Article 7

'he parties undertake to continue active negotiations for limitations on strategic
ffensive arms. The obligations provided for in this Interim Agreement shall not
rejudice the scope or terms of the limitations on strategic offensive arms which
nay be worked out in the course of further negotiations.

Article 8

. This Interim Agreement shall enter into force upon exchange of written notices
f acceptance by each party, which exchange shall take place simultaneously with
he exchange of instruments of ratification of the Treaty on the Limitation of Anti-
Ballistic Missile Systems.

2. This Interim Agreement shall remain in force for a period of five years unless
eplaced earlier by an agreement on more complete measures limiting strategic
ffensive arms. It is the objective of the parties to conduct active follow-on nego-
iations with the aim of concluding such an agreement as soon as possible.

3. Each party shall, in exercising its national sovereignty, have the right to with-
Iraw from this Interim Agreement if it decides that extraordinary events related to
he subject matter of this Interim Agreement have jeopardized its supreme interests.
t shall give notice of its decision to the other party six months prior to withdrawal
rom this Interim Agreement. Such notices shall include a statement of the extra-
rdinary events the notifying party regards as having jeopardised its supreme interests.

Protocol

The United States of America and the Union of Soviet Socialist Republics, herein-
fter referred to as the parties, having agreed on certain limitations relating to sub-
narine-launched ballistic missile launchers and modern ballistic missile submarines,
nd to replacement procedures, in the Interim Agreement, have agreed as follows:

The parties understand that, under Article III of the Interim Agreement, for the
eriod during which that agreement remains in force:

The US may have no more than 710 ballistic missile launchers on submarines

(SLBMs) and no more than 44 modern ballistic missile submarines. The Soviet Union may have no more than 950 ballistic missile launchers on submarines and no more than 62 modern ballistic missile submarines.

Additional ballistic missile launchers on submarines up to the above-mentioned levels – in the US over 656 ballistic missile launchers on nuclear-powered submarines, and in the USSR over 740 ballistic missile launchers on nuclear-powered submarines, operational and under construction – may become operational as replacements for equal numbers of ballistic missile launchers of older types deployed prior to 1964 or of ballistic missile launchers on older submarines.

The deployment of modern SLBMs on any submarine, regardless of type, will be counted against the total level of SLBMs permitted for the US and the USSR.

This Protocol shall be considered an integral part of the Interim Agreement.

56. Agreed interpretations and unilateral statements concerning the Agreement on Certain Measures with Respect to the Limitation of Strategic Offensive Arms, 26 May 1972[1]

1. AGREED INTERPRETATIONS
(a) Initialed Statements

The texts of the statements set out below were agreed upon and initialed by the Heads of the Delegations on 26 May 1972.

ABM Treaty

(A) The Parties understand that, in addition to the ABM radars which may be deployed in accordance with subparagraph (1) of Article III of the Treaty, those non-phased-array ABM radars operational on the date of signature of the Treaty within the ABM system deployment area for defense of the national capital may be retained.

(B) The Parties understand that the potential (the produce of mean emitted power in watts and antenna area in square meters) of the smaller of the two large phased-array ABM radars referred to in subparagraph (b) of Article III of the Treaty is considered for purposes of the Treaty to be three million.

(C) The Parties understand that the center of the ABM system deployment area centered on the national capital and the center of the ABM system deployment area containing ICBM silo launchers for each Party shall be separated by no less than thirteen hundred kilometers.

(D) The Parties agree not to deploy phased-array radars having a potential (the product of mean emitted power in watts and antenna area in square meters) exceeding three million, except as provided for in Articles III, IV and VI of the Treaty, or

1 *DSB*, 3 July 1972, pp. 11–14.

except for the purposes of tracking objects in outer space or for use as national technical means of verification.

(E) In order to insure fulfillment of the obligation not to deploy ABM systems and their components except as provided in Article III of the Treaty, the Parties agree that in the event ABM systems based on other physical principles and including components capable of substituting for ABM interceptor missiles, ABM launchers, or ABM radars are created in the future, specific limitations on such systems and their components would be subject to discussion in accordance with Article XIII and agreement in accordance with Article XIV of the Treaty.

(F) The Parties understand that Article V of the Treaty includes obligations not to develop, test or deploy ABM interceptor missiles for the delivery by each ABM interceptor missile of more than one independently guided warhead.

(G) The Parties understand that Article IX of the Treaty includes the obligation of the US and the USSR not to provide to other States technical descriptions or blueprints specially worked out for the construction of ABM systems and their components limited by the Treaty.

Interim Agreement

H) The Parties understand that land-based ICBM launchers referred to in the Interim Agreement are understood to be launchers for strategic ballistic missiles capable of ranges in excess of the shortest distance between the northeastern border of the continental US and the northwestern border of the continental USSR.

(I) The Parties understand that fixed land-based ICBM launchers under active construction as of the date of signature of the Interim Agreement may be completed.

(J) The parties understand that in the process of modernization and replacement the dimensions of land-based ICBM silo launchers will not be significantly increased.

(K) The Parties understand that dismantling or destruction of ICBM launchers of older types deployed prior to 1964 and ballistic missile launchers on older submarines being replaced by new SLBM launchers on modern submarines will be initiated at the time of the beginning of sea trials of a replacement submarine, and will be completed in the shortest possible agreed period of time. Such dismantling or destruction, and timely notification thereof, will be accomplished under procedures to be agreed in the Standing Consultative Commission.

(L) The Parties understand that during the period of the Interim Agreement there shall be no significant increase in the number of ICBM or SLBM test and training launchers, or in the number of such launchers for modern land-based heavy ICBMs. The Parties further understand that construction or conversion of ICBM launchers at test ranges shall be undertaken only for purposes of testing and training.

b) Common Understandings

Common understanding of the Parties on the following matters was reached during the negotiations:

A. Increase in ICBM Silo Dimensions

Ambassador Smith made the following statement on 26 May 1972: 'The Parties agree that the term "significantly increased" means that an increase will not be greater than 10–15 percent of the present dimensions of land-based ICBM silo launchers.'

Minister Semenov replied that this statement corresponded to the Soviet understanding.

B. Location of ICBM Defenses

The US Delegation made the following statement on 26 May 1972:'Article III of the ABM Treaty provides for each side one ABM system deployment area centered on its national capital and one ABM system deployment area containing ICBM silo launchers. The two sides have registered agreement on the following statement: "Th Parties understand that the center of the ABM system deployment area centered on the national capital and the center of the ABM system deployment area containing ICBM silo launchers for each Party shall be separated by no less than thirteen hundi kilometers."In this connection, the US side notes that its ABM system deployment area for defense of ICBM silo launchers, located west of the Mississippi River, will be centered in the Grand Forks ICBM silo launcher deployment area.' (See Initialed Statement (C).)

C. ABM Test Ranges

The US Delegation made the following statement on 26 April 1972: 'Article IV of the ABM Treaty provides that "the limitations provided for in Article III shall no apply to ABM systems or their components used for development or testing, and located within current or additionally agreed test ranges". We believe it would be useful to assure that there is no misunderstanding as to current ABM test ranges. It is our understanding that ABM test ranges encompass the area within which ABM components are located for test purposes. The current US ABM test ranges are at White Sands, New Mexico, and at Kwajalein Atoll, and the current Soviet ABM test range is near Sary Shagan in Kazakhstan. We consider that non-phased-array radars of types used for range safety or instrumentation purposes may be located outside of ABM test ranges. We interpret the reference in Article IV to "additionall' agreed test ranges" to mean that ABM components will not be located at any other test ranges without prior agreement between our Governments that there will be such additional ABM test ranges.'

On 5 May 1972, the Soviet Delegation stated that there was a common understanding on what ABM test ranges were, that the use of the types of non-ABM radars for range safety or instrumentation was not limited under the Treaty, that the reference in Article IV to 'additionally agreed' test ranges was sufficiently clear, and that national means permitted identifying current test ranges.

. Mobile ABM Systems

n January 28, 1972, the US Delegation made the following statement: 'Article V (1)
f the Joint Draft Text of the ABM Treaty includes an undertaking not to develop,
st, or deploy mobile land-based ABM systems and their components. On May 5,
971, the US side indicated that, in its view, a prohibition on deployment of mobile
.BM systems and components would rule out the deployment of ABM launchers
.d radars which were not permanent fixed types. At that time, we asked for the
oviet view of this interpretation. Does the Soviet side agree with the US side's
.terpretation put forward on May 5, 1971?'

On April 13, 1972, the Soviet Delegation said there is a general common under-
anding on this matter.

. Standing Consultative Commission

.mbassador Smith made the following statement on May 24, 1972: 'The United
.tates proposes that the sides agree that, with regard to initial implementation of
.e ABM Treaty's Article XIII on the Standing Consultative Commission (SCC)
.d of the consultation Articles to the Interim Agreement on offensive arms and
.e Accidents Agreement,[1] agreement establishing the SCC will be worked out early
. the follow-on SALT negotiations; until that is completed, the following arrange-
.ents will prevail: when SALT is in session, any consultation desired by either side
.der these Articles can be carried out by the two SALT Delegations; when SALT
. not in session, *ad hoc* arrangements for any desired consultations under these
.rticles may be made through diplomatic channels.'

Minister Semenov replied that, on an *ad referendum* basis, he could agree that the
.S statement corresponded to the Soviet understanding.

. Standstill

.n May 6, 1972, Minister Semenov made the following statement: 'In an effort
. accommodate the wishes of the US side, the Soviet Delegation is prepared to
.oceed on the basis that the two sides will in fact observe the obligations of both
.e Interim Agreement and the ABM Treaty beginning from the date of signature
. these two documents.'

In reply, the US Delegation made the following statement on May 20, 1972:
'he US agrees in principle with the Soviet statement made on May 6 concerning
.servance of obligations beginning from date of signature but we would like to
.ake clear our understanding that this means that, pending ratification and ac-
.ptance, neither side would take any action prohibited by the agreements after
.ey had entered into force. This understanding would continue to apply in the

1 See Article 7 of Agreement to Reduce the Risk of Outbreak of Nuclear War Between the
.nited States of America and the Union of Soviet Socialist Republics, signed September 20,
.71. [Footnote in original.]

absence of notification by either signatory of its intention not to proceed with ratification or approval.'

The Soviet Delegation indicated agreement with the US statement.

2. Unilateral Statements

(a) The following noteworthy unilateral statements were made during the negotiations by the United States Delegation:

A. Withdrawal from the ABM Treaty

On May 9, 1972, Ambassador Smith made the following statement: 'The US delegation has stressed the importance the US Government attaches to achieving agreement on more complete limitations on strategic offensive arms, following agreement on an ABM Treaty and on an Interim Agreement on certain measures with respect to the limitation of strategic offensive arms. The US Delegation believes that an objective of the follow-on negotiations should be to constrain and reduce on a long-term basis threats to the survivability of our respective strategic retaliato forces. The USSR Delegation has also indicated that the objectives of SALT would remain unfulfilled without the achievement of an agreement providing for more complete limitations on strategic offensive arms. Both sides recognize that the initial agreements would be steps toward the achievement of more complete limitations on strategic arms. If an agreement providing for more complete strategic offensive arms limitations were not achieved within five years, US supreme interest could be jeopardized. Should that occur, it would constitute a basis for withdrawa from the ABM Treaty. The US does not wish to see such a situation occur, nor do we believe that the USSR does. It is because we wish to prevent such a situation th we emphasize the importance the US Government attaches to achievement of mor complete limitations on strategic offensive arms. The US Executive will inform the Congress, in connection with Congressional consideration of the ABM Treaty and the Interim Agreement of this statement of the US position.'

B. Land-Mobile ICBM Launchers

The US Delegation made the following statement on May 20, 1972: 'In connectio with the important subject of land-mobile ICBM launchers, in the interest of concluding the Interim Agreement the US Delegation now withdraws its proposal that Article I or an agreed statement explicitly prohibit the deployment of mobile land based ICBM launchers. I have been instructed to inform you that, while agreeing to defer the question of limitation of operational land-mobile ICBM launchers to the subsequent negotiations on more complete limitations on strategic offensive arms, the US would consider the deployment of operational land-mobile ICBM launchers during the period of the Interim Agreement as inconsistent with the objectives of that Agreement.'

C. Covered Facilities

The US Delegation made the following statement on May 20, 1972: 'I wish to emphasize the importance that the United States attaches to the provisions of Article V, including in particular their application to fitting out or berthing submarines.'

D. 'Heavy' ICBMs

The US Delegation made the following statement on May 26, 1972: 'The US Delegation regrets that the Soviet Delegation has not been willing to agree on a common definition of a heavy missile. Under these circumstances, the US Delegation believes it necessary to state the following: The United States would consider any ICBM having a volume significantly greater than that of the largest light ICBM now operational on either side to be a heavy ICBM. The US proceeds on the premise that the Soviet side will give due account to this consideration.'

E. Tested in ABM Mode

On April 7, 1972, the US Delegation made the following statement: 'Article II of the Joint Draft Text uses the term "tested in an ABM mode", in defining ABM components, and Article VI includes certain obligations concerning such testing. We believe that the sides should have a common understanding of this phrase. First, we would note that the testing provisions of the ABM Treaty are intended to apply to testing which occurs after the date of signature of the Treaty, and not to any testing which may have occurred in the past. Next, we would amplify the remarks we have made on this subject during the previous Helsinki phase by setting forth the objectives which govern the US view on the subject, namely, while prohibiting testing of non-ABM components for ABM purposes: not to prevent testing of ABM components, and not to prevent testing of non-ABM components for non-ABM purposes. To clarify our interpretation of "tested in an ABM mode", we note that we would consider a launcher, missile or radar to be "tested in an ABM mode" if, for example, any of the following events occur: (1) a launcher is used to launch an ABM interceptor missile, (2) an interceptor missile is flight tested against a target vehicle which has a flight trajectory with characteristics of a strategic ballistic missile flight trajectory, or is flight tested in conjunction with the test of an ABM interceptor missile or an ABM radar at the same test range, or is flight tested to an altitude inconsistent with interception of targets against which air defenses are deployed, (3) a radar makes measurements on a cooperative target vehicle of the kind referred to in item (2) above during the reentry portion of its trajectory or makes measurements in conjunction with the test of an ABM interceptor missile or an ABM radar at the same test range. Radars used for purposes such as range safety or instrumentation would be exempt from application of these criteria.'

F. No-Transfer Article of ABM Treaty

On April 18, 1972, the US Delegation made the following statement: 'In regard to this Article [IX], I have a brief and I believe self-explanatory statement to make. The US side wishes to make clear that the provisions of this Article do not set a precedent for whatever provision may be considered for a Treaty on Limiting Strategic Offensive Arms. The question of transfer of strategic offensive arms is a far more complex issue, which may require a different solution.'

G. No Increase in Defense of Early Warning Radars

On July 28, 1970, the US Delegation made the following statement: 'Since Hen House radars [Soviet ballistic missile early warning radars] can detect and track ballistic missile warheads at great distances, they have a significant ABM potential. Accordingly, the US would regard any increase in the defenses of such radars by surface-to-air missiles as inconsistent with an agreement.'

(*b*) The following noteworthy unilateral statement was made by the Delegation of the USSR and is shown here with the US reply:

On May 17, 1972, Minister Semenov made the following unilateral 'Statement of the Soviet Side': 'Taking into account that modern ballistic missile submarines are presently in the possession of not only the US, but also of its NATO allies, the Soviet Union agrees that for the period of effectiveness of the Interim "Freeze" Agreement the US and its NATO allies have up to 50 such submarines with a total of up to 800 ballistic missile launchers thereon (including 41 US submarines with 656 ballistic missile launchers). However, if during the period of effectiveness of the Agreement US allies in NATO should increase the number of their modern submarines to exceed the numbers of submarines they would have operational or under construction on the date of signature of the Agreement, the Soviet Union will have the right to a corresponding increase in the number of its submarines. In the opinion of the Soviet side, the solution of the question of modern ballistic missile submarines provided for in the Interim Agreement only partially compensates for the strategic imbalance in the deployment of the nuclear-powered missile submarines of the USSR and the US. Therefore, the Soviet side believes that this whole question, and above all the question of liquidating the American missile submarine bases outside the US will be appropriately resolved in the course of follow-on negotiations.'

On May 24, Ambassador Smith made the following reply to Minister Semenov: 'The United States side has studied the "statement made by the Soviet side" of May 17 concerning compensation for submarine basing and SLBM submarines belonging to third countries. The United States does not accept the validity of the considerations in that statement.'

On May 26 Minister Semenov repeated the unilateral statement made on May 17. Ambassador Smith also repeated the US rejection on May 26.

57. Basic Principles of Relations between the United States and the Soviet Union, 29 May 1972[1]

The United States of America and the Union of Soviet Socialist Republics:
Guided by their obligations under the Charter of the United Nations and by a desire to strengthen peaceful relations with each other and to place these relations on the firmest possible basis,
Aware of the need to make every effort to remove the threat of war and to create conditions which promote the reduction of tensions in the world and the strengthening of universal security and international cooperation,
Believing that the improvement of US–Soviet relations and their mutually advantageous development in such areas as economics, science and culture will meet these objectives and contribute to better mutual understanding and business-like cooperation, without in any way prejudicing the interests of third countries,
Conscious that these objectives reflect the interests of the peoples of both countries,
Have agreed as follows:
First: They will proceed from the common determination that in the nuclear age there is no alternative to conducting their mutual relations on the basis of peaceful coexistence. Differences in ideology and in the social systems of the USA and the USSR are not obstacles to the bilateral development of normal relations based on the principles of sovereignty, equality, non-interference in internal affairs and mutual advantage.
Second: The USA and the USSR attach major importance to preventing the development of situations capable of causing a dangerous exacerbation of their relations. Therefore, they will do their utmost to avoid military confrontations and to prevent the outbreak of nuclear war. They will always exercise restraint in their mutual relations, and will be prepared to negotiate and settle differences by peaceful means. Discussions and negotiations on outstanding issues will be conducted in a spirit of reciprocity, mutual accommodation and mutual benefit.
Both sides recognize that efforts to obtain unilateral advantages at the expense of the other, directly or indirectly, are inconsistent with these objectives. The prerequisites for maintaining and strengthening peaceful relations between the USA and the USSR are the recognition of the security interests of the parties based on the principle of equality and the renunciation of the use or threat of force.
Third: The USA and the USSR have a special responsibility, as do other countries which are permanent members of the United Nations Security Council, to do everything in their power so that conflicts or situations will not arise which would serve to increase international tensions. Accordingly, they will seek to promote conditions in which all countries will live in peace and security and will not be subject to outside interference in their internal affairs.
Fourth: The USA and the USSR intend to widen the juridical basis of their mutual

1 *DSB*, 26 June 1972, pp. 898–9.

relations and to exert the necessary efforts so that bilateral agreements which they have concluded and multilateral treaties and agreements to which they are jointly parties are faithfully implemented.

Fifth: The USA and the USSR reaffirm their readiness to continue the practice of exchanging views on problems of mutual interest and, when necessary, to conduct such exchanges at the highest level, including meetings between leaders of the two countries.

The two governments welcome and will facilitate an increase in productive contacts between representatives of the legislative bodies of the two countries.

Sixth: The parties will continue their efforts to limit armaments on a bilateral as well as on a multilateral basis. They will continue to make special efforts to limit strategic armaments. Whenever possible, they will conclude concrete agreements aimed at achieving these purposes.

The USA and the USSR regard as the ultimate objective of their efforts the achievement of general and complete disarmament and the establishment of an effective system of international security in accordance with the purposes and principles of the United Nations.

Seventh: The USA and the USSR regard commercial and economic ties as an important and necessary element in the strengthening of their bilateral relations and thus will actively promote the growth of such ties. They will facilitate cooperation between the relevant organizations and enterprises of the two countries and the conclusion of appropriate agreements and contracts, including long-term ones.

The two countries will contribute to the improvement of maritime and air communications between them.

Eighth: The two sides consider it timely and useful to develop mutual contacts and cooperation in the fields of science and technology. Where suitable, the USA and the USSR will conclude appropriate agreements dealing with concrete cooperation in these fields.

Ninth: The two sides reaffirm their intention to deepen cultural ties with one another and to encourage fuller familiarization with each other's cultural values. They will promote improved conditions for cultural exchanges and tourism.

Tenth: The USA and the USSR will seek to ensure that their ties and cooperation in all the above-mentioned fields and in any others in their mutual interest are built on a firm and long-term basis. To give a permanent character to these efforts, they will establish in all fields where this is feasible joint commissions or other joint bodies.

Eleventh: The USA and the USSR make no claim for themselves and would not recognize the claims of anyone else to any special rights or advantages in world affairs. They recognize the sovereign equality of all States.

The development of US—Soviet relations is not directed against third countries and their interests.

Twelfth: The basic principles set forth in this document do not affect any obligations with respect to other countries earlier assumed by the USA and the USSR.

58. Joint communiqué issued by the United States and the Soviet Union, 29 May 1972[1]

By mutual agreement between the United States of America and the Union of Soviet Socialist Republics, the President of the United States and Mrs Richard Nixon paid an official visit to the Soviet Union from May 22 to May 30, 1972.

The President was accompanied by Secretary of State William P. Rogers, Assistant to the President Dr Henry A. Kissinger, and other American officials. During his stay in the USSR President Nixon visited, in addition to Moscow, the cities of Leningrad and Kiev.

President Nixon and L. T. Brezhnev, General Secretary of the Central Committee of the Communist Party of the Soviet Union, N. V. Podgorny, Chairman of the Presidium of the Supreme Soviet of the USSR, and A. N. Kosygin, Chairman of the Council of Ministers of the USSR, conducted talks on fundamental problems of American–Soviet relations and the current international situation.

Also taking part in the conversations were:

On the American side: William P. Rogers, Secretary of State; Jacob D. Beam, American Ambassador to the USSR; Dr Henry A. Kissinger, Assistant to the President for National Security Affairs; Peter M. Flanigan, Assistant to the President; and Martin J. Hillenbrand, Assistant Secretary of State for European Affairs.

On the Soviet side: A. A. Gromyko, Minister of Foreign Affairs of the USSR; N. S. Patolichev, Minister of Foreign Trade; V. V. Kuznetsov, Deputy Minister of Foreign Affairs of the USSR; A. F. Dobrynin, Soviet Ambassador to the USA; A. M. Aleksandrov, Assistant to the General Secretary of the Central Committee, CPSU; G. M. Korniyenko, member of the Collegium of the Ministry of Foreign Affairs of the USSR.

The discussions covered a wide range of questions of mutual interest and were frank and thorough. They defined more precisely those areas where there are prospects for developing greater cooperation between the two countries, as well as those areas where the positions of the two sides are different.

Bilateral Relations

Guided by the desire to place US–Soviet relations on a more stable and constructive foundation, and mindful of their responsibilities for maintaining world peace and for facilitating the relaxation of international tension, the two sides adopted a document entitled: 'Basic Principles of Mutual Relations Between the United States of America and the Union of Soviet Socialist Republics', signed on behalf of the US by President Nixon and on behalf of the USSR by General Secretary Brezhnev.

Both sides are convinced that the provisions of that document open new possibilities for the development of peaceful relations and mutually beneficial cooperation between the USA and the USSR.

1 *DSB*, 26 June 1972, pp. 899–902.

Having considered various areas of bilateral US–Soviet relations, the two sides agreed that an improvement of relations is possible and desirable. They expressed their firm intention to act in accordance with the provisions set forth in the above-mentioned document.

As a result of progress made in negotiations which preceded the summit meeting, and in the course of the meeting itself, a number of significant agreements were reached. This will intensify bilateral cooperation in areas of common concern as well as in areas relevant to the cause of peace and international cooperation.

Limitation of Strategic Armaments

The two sides gave primary attention to the problem of reducing the danger of nucle war. They believe that curbing the competition in strategic arms will make a significant and tangible contribution to this cause.

The two sides attach great importance to the treaty on the limitation of anti-ballistic missile systems and the interim agreement on certain measures with respect to the limitation of strategic offensive arms concluded between them.

These agreements, which were concluded as a result of the negotiations in Moscov constitute a major step towards curbing and ultimately ending the arms race.

They are a concrete expression of the intention of the two sides to contribute to the relaxation of international tension and the strengthening of confidence between States, as well as to carry out the obligations assumed by them in the Treaty on the Non-Proliferation of Nuclear Weapons (Article VI). Both sides are convinced that the achievement of the above agreements is a practical step towards saving mankind from the threat of the outbreak of nuclear war. Accordingly, it corresponds to the vital interests of the American and Soviet peoples as well as to the vital interests of all other peoples.

The two sides intend to continue active negotiations for the limitation of strategi offensive arms and to conduct them in a spirit of goodwill, respect for each other's legitimate interests and observance of the principle of equal security.

Both sides are also convinced that the agreement on measures to reduce the risk of outbreak of nuclear war between the USA and the USSR, signed in Washington on September 30, 1971, serves the interests not only of the Soviet and American peoples, but of all mankind.

Commercial and Economic Relations

Both sides agreed on measures designed to establish more favourable conditions for developing commercial and other economic ties between the USA and the USSR. The two sides agree that realistic conditions exist for increasing economic ties. These ties should develop on the basis of mutual benefit and in accordance with generally accepted international practice.

Believing that these aims would be served by conclusion of a trade agreement between the USA and the USSR, the two sides decided to complete in the near future the work necessary to conclude such an agreement. They agreed on the desirability of credit arrangements to develop mutual trade and of early efforts to resolve other financial and economic issues. It was agreed that a lend-lease settlement will be negotiated concurrently with a trade agreement.

In the interests of broadening and facilitating commercial ties between the two countries, and to work out specific arrangements, the two sides decided to create a US–Soviet joint commercial commission. Its first meeting will be held in Moscow in the summer of 1972.

Each side will help promote the establishment of effective working arrangements between organizations and firms of both countries and encourage the conclusion of long-term contracts.

Maritime Matters – Incidents at Sea

The two sides agreed to continue the negotiations aimed at reaching an agreement on maritime and related matters. They believe that such an agreement would mark a positive step in facilitating the expansion of commerce between the United States and the Soviet Union.

An agreement was concluded between the two sides on measures to prevent incidents at sea and in air space over it between vessels and aircraft of the US and Soviet navies. By providing agreed procedures for ships and aircraft of the two navies operating in close proximity, this agreement will diminish the chances of dangerous accidents.

Cooperation in Science and Technology

It was recognized that the cooperation now under way in areas such as atomic energy research, space research, health and other fields, benefits both nations and has contributed positively to their overall relations. It was agreed that increased scientific and technical cooperation on the basis of mutual benefit and shared effort for common goals is in the interest of both nations and would contribute to a further improvement in their bilateral relations. For these purposes the two sides signed an agreement for cooperation in the fields of science and technology. A US–Soviet joint commission on scientific and technical cooperation will be created for identifying and establishing cooperative programmes.

Cooperation in Space

Having in mind the role played by the US and the USSR in the peaceful exploration of outer space, both sides emphasized the importance of further bilateral cooperation in this sphere. In order to increase the safety of man's flights in outer space and the future prospects of joint scientific experiments, the two sides agreed to make suitable arrangements to permit the docking of American and Soviet spacecraft and stations. The first joint docking experiment of the two countries' piloted spacecraft, with visits by astronauts and cosmonauts to each other's spacecraft, is contemplated for 1975. The planning and implementation of this flight will be carried out by the US National Aeronautics and Space Administration and the USSR Academy of Sciences, according to principles and procedures developed through mutual consultations.

Cooperation in the Field of Health

The two sides concluded an agreement on health cooperation which marks a fruitful beginning of sharing knowledge about, and collaborative attacks on, the common enemies, disease and disability. The initial research efforts of the programme will concentrate on health problems important to the whole world — cancer, heart diseases, and the environmental health sciences.

This cooperation subsequently will be broadened to include other health problems of mutual interest. The two sides pledged their full support for the health cooperation programme and agreed to continue the active participation of the two governments in the work of international organizations in the health field.

Environmental Cooperation

The two sides agreed to initiate a programme of cooperation in the protection and enhancement of man's environment. Through joint research and joint measures, the United States and the USSR hope to contribute to the preservation of a healthful environment in their countries and throughout the world.

Under the new agreement on environmental cooperation there will be consultation in the near future in Moscow on specific cooperative projects.

Exchanges in the Fields of Science, Technology, Education and Culture

Both sides note the importance of the agreement on exchanges and cooperation in scientific, technical, educational, cultural, and other fields in 1972–3, signed in Moscow on April 11, 1972. Continuation and expansion of bilateral exchanges in these fields will lead to better understanding and help improve the general state of relations between the two countries. Within the broad framework provided by this agreement the two sides have agreed to expand the areas of cooperation, as reflected in new agreements concerning space, health, the environment and science and technology.

The US side, noting the existence of an extensive programme of English language instruction in the Soviet Union, indicated its intention to encourage Russian language programmes in the United States.

International Issues
Europe

In the course of the discussions on the international situation, both sides took note of favourable developments in the relaxation of tensions in Europe.

Recognizing the importance to world peace of developments in Europe, where both World Wars originated, and mindful of the responsibilities and commitments which they share with other powers under appropriate agreements, the USA and the USSR intend to make further efforts to ensure a peaceful future for Europe, free of tensions, crises and conflict.

They agree that the territorial integrity of all States in Europe should be repected.

Both sides view the September 3, 1971, quadripartite agreement relating to the Western sectors of Berlin as a good example of fruitful cooperation between the States concerned, including the USA and the USSR.[1] The two sides believe that the implementation of that agreement in the near future, along with other steps, will further improve the European situation and contribute to the necessary trust among States.

Both sides welcomed the treaty between the USSR and the Federal Republic of Germany signed on August 12, 1970.[2] They noted the significance of the provisions of this treaty as well as of other recent agreements in contributing to confidence and cooperation among the European States.

The USA and the USSR are prepared to make appropriate contributions to the positive trends on the European continent toward a genuine detente and the development of relations of peaceful cooperation among States in Europe on the basis of the principles of territorial integrity and inviolability of frontiers, non-interference in internal affairs, sovereign equality, independence and renunciation of the use or threat of force.

The US and the USSR are in accord that multilateral consultations looking toward a conference on security and cooperation in Europe could begin after the signature of the final quadripartite protocol of the agreement of September 3, 1971. The two governments agree that the conference should be carefully prepared in order that it may concretely consider specific problems of security and cooperation and thus contribute to the progressive reduction of the underlying causes of tension in Europe. This conference should be convened at a time to be agreed by the countries concerned, but without undue delay.

Both sides believe that the goal of ensuring stability and security in Europe would be served by a reciprocal reduction of armed forces and armaments, first of all in Central Europe. Any agreement on this question should not diminish the security of any of the sides. Appropriate agreement should be reached as soon as practicable between the States concerned on the procedures for negotiations on this subject in a special forum.

The Middle East

The two sides set out their positions on this question. They reaffirm their support for a peaceful settlement in the Middle East in accordance with Security Council Resolution 242.

1 Document No. 20.
2 Document No. 16.

Noting the significance of constructive cooperation of the parties concerned with the special representative of the UN Secretary General, Ambassador Jarring, the US and the USSR confirm their desire to contribute to his mission's success and also declare their readiness to play their part in bringing about a peaceful settlement in the Middle East. In the view of the US and the USSR, the achievement of such a settlement would open prospects for the normalization of the Middle East situation and would permit, in particular, consideration of further steps to bring about a military relaxation in that area.

Indochina

Each side set forth its respective standpoint with regard to the continuing war in Vietnam and the situation in the area of Indochina as a whole.

The US side emphasized the need to bring an end to the military conflict as soon as possible and reaffirmed its commitment to the principle that the future of South Vietnam should be left for the South Vietnamese people to decide for themselves, free from outside interference.

The US side explained its view that the quickest and most effective way to attain the above-mentioned objective is through negotiations leading to the return of all Americans held captive in the region, the implementation of an internationally supervised Indochina-wide ceasefire and the subsequent withdrawal of all American forces stationed in South Vietnam within four months, leaving the political question to be resolved by the Indochinese peoples themselves.

The United States reiterated its willingness to enter into serious negotiations with the North Vietnamese side to settle the war in Indochina on a basis just to all.

The Soviet side stressed its solidarity with the just struggle of the peoples of Vietnam, Laos and Cambodia for their freedom, independence and social progress. Firmly supporting the proposals of the DRV and the Republic of South Vietnam, which provide a realistic and constructive basis for settling the Vietnam problem, the Soviet Union stands for a cessation of bombings of the DRV, for a complete and unequivocal withdrawal of the troops of the USA and its allies from South Vietnam, so that the peoples of Indochina would have the possibility to determine for themselves their fate without any outside interference.

Disarmament Issues

The two sides expressed their positions on arms limitation and disarmament issues.

The two sides note that in recent years their joint and parallel actions have facilitated the working out and conclusion of treaties which curb the arms race or ban some of the most dangerous types of weapons. They note further that these treaties were welcomed by a large majority of the States in the world, which became parties to them.

Both sides regard the convention on the prohibition of the development, product and stockpiling of bacteriological (biological) and toxic weapons and on their destruction as an essential disarmament measure. Along with Great Britain, they are the depositories for the convention which was recently opened for signature by all States. The USA and the USSR will continue their efforts to reach an international agreement regarding chemical weapons.

The USA and the USSR, proceeding from the need to take into account the security interests of both countries on the basis of the principle of equality, and without prejudice to the security interests of third countries, will actively participate in negotiations aimed at working out new measures designed to curb and end the arms race. The ultimate purpose is general and complete disarmament, including nuclear disarmament, under strict international control. A world disarmament conference could play a role in this process at an appropriate time.

Strengthening the United Nations

Both sides will strive to strengthen the effectiveness of the United Nations on the basis of strict observance of the UN Charter. They regard the United Nations as an instrument for maintaining world peace and security, discouraging conflicts, and developing international cooperation. Accordingly, they will do their best to support United Nations efforts in the interests of international peace.

Both sides emphasized that agreements and understandings reached in the negotiations in Moscow, as well as the contents and nature of these negotiations, are not in any way directed against any other country. Both sides proceed from the recognition of the role, the responsibility and the prerogatives of their interested States, existing international obligations and agreements, and the principles and purposes of the UN Charter.

Both sides believe that positive results were accomplished in the course of the talks at the highest level. These results indicate that despite the differences between the USA and the USSR in social systems, ideologies, and policy principles, it is possible to develop mutually advantageous cooperation between the peoples of both countries, in the interests of strengthening peace and international security.

Both sides expressed the desire to continue close contact on a number of issues that were under discussion. They agreed that regular consultations on questions of mutual interest, including meetings at the highest level, would be useful.

In expressing his appreciation for the hospitality accorded him in the Soviet Union, President Nixon invited General Secretary L. I. Brezhnev, Chairman N. V. Podgorny, and Chairman A. N. Kosygin to visit the United States at a mutually convenient time.

This invitation was accepted.

EDITOR'S NOTE: AGREEMENTS ON ENVIRONMENTAL PROTECTION, AND COOPERATION IN MEDICAL SCIENCE AND PUBLIC HEALTH, AND IN SCIENCE AND TECHNOLOGY

Three other agreements were signed at the Moscow summit. These were:

Agreement on Environmental Protection
Agreement on Cooperation in Medical Science and Public Health
Agreement on Cooperation in the Fields of Science and Technology
For texts, see *DSB*, 26 June 1972, pp. 921–7.

59. Agreement regarding Certain Maritime Matters, Washington, 14 October 1972[1]

The Government of the United States of America and the Government of the
Union of Soviet Socialist Republics;

Being desirous of improving maritime relations between the United States and
the Soviet Union, particularly through arrangements regarding port access and
cargo carriage by sea; and

Acting in accordance with Article Seven of the Basic Principles of Relations
Between the United States of America and the Union of Soviet Socialist Republics,
signed in Moscow on May 29, 1972,

Have agreed as follows:

Article 1

For purposes of this Agreement:

a. 'Vessel' means a vessel sailing under the flag of a Party, registered in the territor
of that Party, or which is an unregistered vessel belonging to the Government of
such Party, and which is used for:

(i) Commercial maritime shipping, or

(ii) Merchant marine training purposes, or

(iii) Hydrographic, oceanographic, meteorological, or terrestrial magnetic field
research for civil application.

b. 'Vessel' does not include:

(i) Warships as defined in the 1958 Geneva Convention on the High Seas;

(ii) Vessels carrying out any form of state function except for those mentioned
under paragraph a of this Article.

Article 2

This Agreement does not apply to or affect the rights of fishing vessels, fishery
research vessels, or fishery support vessels. This Agreement does not affect existing
arrangements with respect to such vessels.

Article 3

The ports on the attached list of ports of each Party (Annexes I and II, which are a
part of this Agreement) are open to access by all vessels of the other Party.[2]

1 *DSB*, 4 December 1972, pp. 664–5.
2 The annexes are not printed here.

Article 4

Entry of all vessels of one Party into such ports of the other Party shall be permitted subject to four days' advance notice of the planned entry to the appropriate authority.

Article 5

Entry of all vessels referred to in subparagraphs a(ii) and a(iii) of Article 1 into the ports referred to in Article 3 will be to replenish ships' stores or fresh water, obtain bunkers, provide rest for or make changes in the personnel of such vessels, and obtain minor repairs and other services normally provided in such ports, all in accordance with applicable rules and regulations.

Article 6

Each Party undertakes to ensure that tonnage duties upon vessels of the other Party will not exceed the charges imposed in like situations with respect to vessels of any other country.

Article 7

While recognizing the policy of each Party concerning participation of third flags in its trade, each Party also recognizes the interest of the other in carrying a substantial part of its foreign trade in vessels of its own registry, and thus both Parties intend that their national flag vessels will each carry equal and substantial shares of the trade between the two nations in accordance with Annex III which is a part of this Agreement.

Article 8

Each Party agrees that, where it controls the selection of the carrier of its export and import cargoes, it will provide to vessels under the flag of the other Party participation equal to that of vessels under its own flag in accordance with the agreement in Annex III.[1]

Article 9

The Parties shall enter into consultations within fourteen days from the date a request for consultation is received from either Party regarding any matter involving the application, interpretation, implementation, amendment, or renewal of this Agreement.

Article 10

This Agreement shall enter into force on January 1, 1973; provided that this date

1 The annexes are not printed here.

may be accelerated by mutual agreement of the Parties. The Agreement will remain in force for the period ending December 31, 1975, provided that the Agreement may be terminated by either Party. The termination shall be effective ninety days after the date on which written notice of termination has been received.

60. Agreement regarding Trade, Washington, 18 October 1972[1]

The Government of the United States of America and the Government of the Union of Soviet Socialist Republics,

Considering that the peoples of the United States of America and of the Union of Soviet Socialist Republics seek a new era of commercial friendship, an era in which the resources of both countries will contribute to the well-being of the people of each and an era in which common commercial interest can point the way to better and lasting understanding,

Having agreed at the Moscow Summit that commercial and economic ties are an important and necessary element in the strengthening of their bilateral relations,

Noting that favorable conditions exist for the development of trade and economic relations between the two countries to their mutual advantage,

Desiring to make the maximum progress for the benefit of both countries in accordance with the tenets of the Basic Principles of Relations Between the United States of America and the Union of Soviet Socialist Republics signed in Moscow on May 29, 1972,

Believing that agreement on basic questions of economic trade relations between the two countries will best serve the interests of both their peoples,

Have agreed as follows:

Article 1

1. Each Government shall accord unconditionally to products originating in or exported to the other country treatment no less favorable than that accorded to like products originating in or exported to any third country in all matters relating to:

(*a*) customs duties and charges of any kind imposed on or in connection with importation or exportation including the method of levying such duties and charges;

(*b*) internal taxation, sale, distribution, storage and use;

(*c*) charges imposed upon the international transfer of payments for importation or exportation; and

(*d*) rules and formalities in connection with importation or exportation.

2. In the event either Government applies quantitative restrictions to products originating in or exported to third countries, it shall afford to like products originating in or exported to the other country equitable treatment vis-à-vis that applied in respect of such third countries.

3. Paragraphs 1 and 2 of this Article 1 shall not apply to (i) any privileges which

1 *DSB*, 20 November 1972, pp. 595–7.

re granted by either Government to neighboring countries with a view toward acilitating frontier traffic, or (ii) any preferences granted by either Government n recognition of Resolution 21 (II) adopted on March 26, 1968 at the Second JNCTAD [United Nations Conference on Trade and Development], or (iii) any ction by either Government which is permitted under any multilateral trade agreement to which such Government is a party on the date of signature of this Agreement, if such agreement would permit such action in similar circumstances with espect to like products originating in or exported to a country which is a signatory hereof, or (iv) the exercise by either Government of its rights under Articles 3 r 8 of this Agreement.

Article 2

. Both Governments will take appropriate measures, in accordance with the laws nd regulations then current in each country, to encourage and facilitate the exhange of goods and services between the two countries on the basis of mutual dvantage and in accordance with the provisions of this Agreement. In expectation f such joint efforts, both Governments envision that total bilateral trade in comarison with the period 1969–1971 will at least triple over the three-year period ontemplated by this Agreement.

2. Commercial transactions between the United States of America and the Union f Soviet Socialist Republics shall be effected in accordance with the laws and egulations then current in each country with respect to import and export control nd financing, as well as on the basis of contracts to be concluded between natural nd legal persons of the United States of America and foreign trade organizations f the Union of Soviet Socialist Republics. Both Governments shall facilitate, in ccordance with the laws and regulations then current in each country, the conlusion of such contracts, including those on a long-term basis, between natural and egal persons of the United States of America and foreign trade organizations of the Jnion of Soviet Socialist Republics. It is understood that such contracts will enerally be concluded on terms customary in international commercial practice.

3. Both Governments, by mutual agreement, will examine various fields, in which he expansion of commercial and industrial cooperation is desirable, with regard or, in particular, the long-term requirements and resources of each country in raw naterials, equipment and technology and, on the basis of such examination, will romote cooperation between interested organizations and enterprises of the two ountries with a view toward the realization of projects for the development of atural resources and projects in the manufacturing industries.

4. The Government of the Union of Soviet Socialist Republics expects that, uring the period of effectiveness of this Agreement, foreign trade organizations of he Union of Soviet Socialist Republics will place substantial orders in the United tates of America for machinery, plant and equipment, agricultural products, ndustrial products and consumer goods produced in the United States of America.

Article 3

Each Government may take such measures as it deems appropriate to ensure that the importation of products originating in the other country does not take place in such quantities or under such conditions as to cause, threaten or contribute to disruption of its domestic market. The procedures under which both Governments shall cooperate in carrying out the objectives of this Article are set forth in Annex which constitutes an integral part of this Agreement.[1]

Article 4

All currency payments between natural and legal persons of the United States of America and foreign trade and other appropriate organizations of the Union of Soviet Socialist Republics shall be made in United States dollars or any other freely convertible currency mutually agreed upon by such persons and organizations.

Article 5

1. The Government of the United States of America may establish in Moscow a Commercial Office of the United States of America and the Government of the Un of Soviet Socialist Republics may establish in Washington a Trade Representation of the Union of Soviet Socialist Republics. The Commercial Office and the Trade Representation shall be opened simultaneously on a date and at locations to be agreed upon.

2. The status concerning the functions, privileges, immunities and organization of the Commercial Office and the Trade Representation is set forth in Annexes 2 and 3, respectively, attached to this Agreement, of which they constitute an integra part.[1]

3. The establishment of the Commercial Office and the Trade Representation shall in no way affect the rights of natural or legal persons of the United States of America and of foreign trade organizations of the Union of Soviet Socialist Repub either in the United States of America or in the Union of Soviet Socialist Republics to maintain direct relations with each other with a view to the negotiation, executi and fulfilment of trade transactions. To facilitate the maintenance of such direct relations the Commercial Office may provide office facilities at its location to employees or representatives of natural and legal persons of the United States of America, and the Trade Representation may provide office facilities at its location employees or representatives of foreign trade organizations of the Union of Soviet Socialist Republics, which employees and representatives shall not be officers or members of the administrative, technical or service staff of the Commercial Office or the Trade Representation. Accordingly, the Commercial Office and the Trade Representation, and their respective officers and staff members, shall not participat directly in the negotiation, execution or fulfillment of trade transactions or otherw carry on trade.

1 The annexes are not printed here.

Article 6

. In accordance with the laws and regulations then current in each country, natural
nd legal persons of the United States of America and foreign trade organizations
f the Union of Soviet Socialist Republics may open their representations in the
nion of Soviet Socialist Republics and the United States of America, respectively.
formation concerning the opening of such representations and provision of
cilities in connection therewith shall be provided by each Government upon the
quest of the other Government.

2. Foreign trade organizations of the Union of Soviet Socialist Republics shall
ot claim or enjoy in the United States of America, and private natural and legal
ersons of the United States of America shall not claim or enjoy in the Union of
oviet Socialist Republics, immunities from suit or execution of judgment or other
ability with respect to commercial transactions.

3. Corporations, stock companies and other industrial or financial commercial
rganizations, including foreign trade organizations, domiciled and regularly organized
 conformity to the laws in force in one of the two countries shall be recognized
s having a legal existence in the other country.

Article 7

. Both Governments encourage the adoption of arbitration for the settlement of
isputes arising out of international commercial transactions concluded between
atural and legal persons of the United States of America and foreign trade organ-
zations of the Union of Soviet Socialist Republics, such arbitration to be provided
or by agreements in contracts between such persons and organizations, or, if it
as not been so provided, to be provided for in separate agreements between them
 writing executed in the form required for the contract itself, such agreements:

(*a*) to provide for arbitration under the Arbitration Rules of the Economic Commission for Europe of January 20, 1966, in which case such agreement should also
esignate an Appointing Authority in a country other than the United States of
America or the Union of Soviet Socialist Republics for the appointment of an
rbitrator or arbitrators in accordance with those Rules; and

(*b*) to specify as the place of arbitration a place in a country other than the United
States of America or the Union of Soviet Socialist Republics that is a party to the
958 Convention on the Recognition and Enforcement of Foreign Arbitral Awards.
uch persons and organizations, however, may decide upon any other form of arbi-
ration which they mutually prefer and agree best suits their particular needs.

2. Each Government shall ensure that corporations, stock companies, and other
ndustrial or financial commercial organizations, including foreign trade organizations,
omiciled and regularly organized in conformity to the laws in force in the other
ountry shall have the right to appear before the courts of the former, whether for
he purpose of bringing an action or of defending themselves against one, including
ut not limited to, cases arising out of or relating to transactions contemplated by
his Agreement. In all such cases the said corporations, companies and organizations

shall enjoy in the other country the same rights which are or may be granted to similar companies of any third country.

Article 8

The provisions of this Agreement shall not limit the right of either Government to take any action for the protection of its security interests.

Article 9

1. This Agreement shall enter into force upon the exchange of written notices of acceptance.[1] This Agreement shall remain in force for three years, unless extended by mutual agreement.

2. Both Governments will work through the Joint US—USSR Commercial Commission established in accordance with the Communiqué issued in Moscow on May 26, 1972, in overseeing and facilitating the implementation of this Agreement in accordance with the terms of reference and rules of procedure of the Commission

3. Prior to the expiration of this Agreement, the Joint US—USSR Commercial Commission shall begin consultations regarding extension of this Agreement or preparation of a new agreement to replace this Agreement.

61. Agreement regarding Settlement of Lend Lease, Reciprocal Aid and Claims, Washington, 18 October 1972[2]

The Government of the United States of America and the Government of the Union of Soviet Socialist Republics,

Considering the need to settle obligations arising out of prosecution of the war against aggression in order to foster mutual confidence and the development of trade and economic relations between the two countries,

Desiring to further the spirit of friendship and mutual understanding achieved by the leaders of both countries at the Moscow Summit,

Recognizing the benefits of cooperation already received by them in the defeat of their common enemies, and of the aid furnished by each Government to the other in the course of the war, and

Desiring to settle all rights and obligations of either Government from or to the other arising out of lend lease and reciprocal aid or otherwise arising out of the prosecution of the war against aggression,

Have agreed as follows:

1. This Agreement represents a full and final settlement of all rights, claims, benefits and obligations of either Government from or to the other arising out of or relating to:

1 See Document No. 71.
2 *DSB*, 20 November 1972, pp. 603—4.

(a) the Agreement of June 11, 1942, between the Governments of the United tates of America and the Union of Soviet Socialist Republics on principles applying) mutual aid in the prosecution of the war against aggression, including the ar ngements between the two Governments preliminary to and replaced by said greement,

(b) the Agreement of October 15, 1945, between the Governments of the United tates of America and the Union of Soviet Socialist Republics concerning the isposition of lend-lease supplies in inventory or procurement in the United States f America, and

(c) any other matter in respect of the conduct of the war against aggression uring the period June 22, 1941 through September 2, 1945.

2. In making this Agreement both Governments have taken full cognizance of he benefits and payments already received by them under the arrangements referred o in Paragraph 1 above. Accordingly, both Governments have agreed that no further enefits will be sought by either Government for any obligation to it arising out of r relating to any matter referred to in said Paragraph 1.

3. (a) The Government of the Union of Soviet Socialist Republics hereby acquires, nd shall be deemed to have acquired on September 20, 1945, all such right, title nd interest as the Government of the United States of America may have in all nd-lease materials transferred by the Government of the United States of America o the Government of the Union of Soviet Socialist Republics, including any rticle (i) transferred under the Agreement of June 11, 1942, referred to above, ii) transferred to the Government of the Union of Soviet Socialist Republics nder Public Law 11 of the United States of America of March 11, 1941, or trans erred under that Public Law to any other government and re-transferred prior to eptember 20, 1945 to the Government of the Union of Soviet Socialist Republics, iii) transferred under the Agreement of October 15, 1945, referred to above, or iv) otherwise transferred during the period June 22, 1941 through September 20, 945 in connection with the conduct of the war against aggression.

(b) The Government of the United States of America hereby acquires, and shall e deemed to have acquired on September 20, 1945, all such right, title and interest s the Government of the Union of Soviet Socialist Republics may have in all eciprocal aid materials transferred by the Government of the Union of Soviet iocialist Republics to the Government of the United States of America during the eriod June 22, 1941 through September 20, 1945.

4. (a) The total net sum due from the Government of the Union of Soviet Socialist Republics to the Government of the United States of America for the settlement of ll matters set forth in Paragraph 1 of this Agreement shall be US $722,000,000 ayable as provided in subparagraphs (b), (c), and (d) of this Paragraph 4.

(b) (i) Three installments shall be due and payable as follows: $12,000,000 on)ctober 18, 1972, $24,000,000 on July 1, 1973, and $12,000,000 on July 1, 1975. ii) Subject to subparagraph (c) of this Paragraph 4, after the date ('Notice Date') n which a note from the Government of the United States of America is delivered o the Government of the Union of Soviet Socialist Republics stating that the

Government of the United States of America has made available most-favored-nation treatment for the Union of Soviet Socialist Republics no less favorable than that provided in an Agreement Between the Government of the United States of America and the Union of Soviet Socialist Republics Regarding Trade signed on the date hereof, the balance of $674,000,000 in payment of lend lease accounts shall be paid in equal installments ('Regular Installments') as follows:

(1) If the Notice Date falls on or before May 31, 1974, the first Regular Installm shall be due and payable on July 1, 1974, and subsequent Regular Installments sha be due and payable annually on July 1 of each year thereafter through July 1, 2001, or

(2) If the Notice Date falls on or after June 1, 1974, and (A) If the Notice Date occurs in the period of June 1 through December 1 of any year, the first Regular Installment shall be due and payable not more than 30 days following the Notice Date and subsequent Regular Installments shall be due and payable annually on July 1 of each year thereafter through July 1, 2001; or (B) If the Notice Date occu in the period of December 2 of any year through May 31 of the following year, the first Regular Installment shall be due and payable on the July 1 next following the Notice Date and subsequent Regular Installments shall be due and payable annually on July 1 of each year thereafter through July 1, 2001.

(c) In any year, upon written notice to the Government of the United States of America that a deferment of a Regular Installment (except the first and last Regula Installment) next due is necessary in view of its then current and prospective economic conditions, the Government of the Union of Soviet Socialist Republics shall have the right to defer payment of such Regular Installment ('Deferred Regula Installment'). Such right of deferment may be exercised on no more than four occasions. On each such occasion, without regard to whether the Government of the Union of Soviet Socialist Republics defers any subsequent Regular Installments the Deferred Regular Installment shall be due and payable in equal annual installme on July 1 of each year commencing on the July 1 next following the date the Deferred Regular Installment would have been paid if the Government of the Union of Soviet Socialist Republics had not exercised its right of deferment as to such Regular Installment with the final payment on the Deferred Regular Installment on July 1, 2001, together with interest on the unpaid amount of the Deferred Regular Installment from time to time outstanding at three percent per annum, payable at the same time as the Deferred Regular Installment is due and payable.

(d) The Government of the Union of Soviet Socialist Republics shall have the right to prepay at any time all or any part of its total settlement obligation, provide that no such prepayment may be made at any time when any payment required to be made under this Paragraph 4 has not been paid as of the date on which it became due and payable.

5. Both Governments have agreed that this Agreement covers only rights, claims, benefits and obligations of the two Governments. Further, nothing in this Agreement shall be deemed to terminate the provisions of Article III of the Agreement of June 11, 1942, referred to above.

2. Memorandum of Understanding regarding the Establishment of a Standing Consultative Committee, Geneva, 21 December 1972[1]

The Government of the United States of America and the Government of the Union of Soviet Socialist Republics hereby establish a Standing Consultative Commission.

I

The Standing Consultative Commission shall promote the objectives and implementation of the provisions of the Treaty between the USA and the USSR on the Limitation of Anti-Ballistic Missile Systems of May 26, 1972, the Interim Agreement between the USA and the USSR on Certain Measures with Respect to the Limitation of Strategic Offensive Arms of May 26, 1972, and the Agreement on Measures to Reduce the Risk of Outbreak of Nuclear War between the USA and the USSR of September 30, 1971, and shall exercise its competence in accordance with the provisions of Article XIII of said Treaty, Article VI of said Interim Agreement, and Article 7 of said Agreement on Measures.

II

Each Government shall be represented on the Standing Consultative Commission by a Commissioner and a Deputy Commissioner, assisted by such staff as it deems necessary.

IV

The Standing Consultative Commission shall hold periodic sessions on dates mutually agreed by the Commissioners but no less than two times per year. Sessions shall also be convened as soon as possible, following reasonable notice, at the request of either Commissioner.

V

The Standing Consultative Commission shall establish and approve Regulations governing procedures and other relevant matters and may amend them as it deems appropriate.

VI

The Standing Consultative Commission will meet in Geneva. It may also meet at such other places as may be agreed.

1 *DSB*, 15 January 1973, pp. 60–1.

Agreements reached at the summit meeting between President Nixon and Mr Brezhnev, Washington, 18–25 June 1973:

63. Basic Principles of Negotiations on the Further Limitation of Strategic Arms, 21 June 1973[1]

The President of the United States of America, Richard Nixon, and the General Secretary of the Central Committee of the CPSU, L. I. Brezhnev,

Having thoroughly considered the question of the further limitation of strategic arms, and the progress already achieved in the current negotiations,

Reaffirming their conviction that the earliest adoption of further limitations of strategic arms would be a major contribution in reducing the danger of an outbreak of nuclear war and in strengthening international peace and security,

Have agreed as follows:

First. The two Sides will continue active negotiations in order to work out a permanent agreement on more complete measures on the limitation of strategic offensive arms, as well as their subsequent reduction, proceeding from the Basic Principles of Relations between the United States of America and the Union of Soviet Socialist Republics signed in Moscow on May 29, 1972, and from the Interim Agreement between the United States of America and the Union of Soviet Socialist Republics of May 26, 1972 on Certain Measures with Respect to the Limitation of Strategic Offensive Arms.

Over the course of the next year the two Sides will make serious efforts to work out the provisions of the permanent agreement on more complete measures on the limitation of strategic offensive arms with the objective of signing it in 1974.

Second. New agreements on the limitation of strategic offensive armaments will be based on the principles of the American–Soviet documents adopted in Moscow in May 1972 and the agreements reached in Washington in June 1973; and in particular, both Sides will be guided by the recognition of each other's equal security interests and by the recognition that efforts to obtain unilateral advantage directly or indirectly, would be inconsistent with the strengthening of peaceful relations between the United States of America and the Union of Soviet Socialist Republics.

Third. The limitations placed on strategic offensive weapons can apply both to their quantitative aspects as well as to their qualitative improvement.

Fourth. Limitations on strategic offensive arms must be subject to adequate verification by national technical means.

Fifth. The modernization and replacement of strategic offensive arms would be permitted under conditions which will be formulated in the agreements to be concluded.

Sixth. Pending the completion of a permanent agreement on more complete measures of strategic offensive arms limitation, both Sides are prepared to reach agreements on separate measures to supplement the existing Interim Agreement of May 26, 1972.

1 *DSB*, 23 July 1973, p. 158.

Seventh. Each Side will continue to take necessary organizational and technical measures for preventing accidental or unauthorized use of nuclear weapons under its control in accordance with the Agreement of September 30, 1971 between the United States of America and the Union of Soviet Socialist Republics.

4. Agreement on Scientific Cooperation in the Peaceful Uses of Atomic Energy, 21 June 1973[1]

The United States of America and the Union of Soviet Socialist Republics;

Attaching great importance to the problem of satisfying the rapidly growing energy demands in both countries as well as in other countries of the world;

Desiring to combine the efforts of both countries toward the solution of this problem through the development of highly efficient energy sources;

Recognizing that solutions to this problem may be found in more rapid development of certain nuclear technologies already under study, such as controlled thermonuclear fusion and fast breeder reactors, as well as in additional basic research on the fundamental properties of matter;

Noting with satisfaction the successful results of previous cooperation between the parties in the field of peaceful uses of atomic energy;

Wishing to establish a more stable and long-term basis for cooperation in this field for the benefit of both their peoples and of all mankind;

In accordance with and in further development of the agreement between the Government of the United States of America and the Government of the Union of Soviet Socialist Republics on cooperation in the fields of science and technology of May 24, 1972; the memorandum on cooperation in the peaceful uses of atomic energy of September 28, 1972 between the US Atomic Energy Commission and the USSR State Committee for the Utilization of Atomic Energy; and the general agreement between the United States of America and the Union of Soviet Socialist Republics on contacts, exchanges and cooperation of June 19, 1973;

Have agreed as follows:

Article 1

The parties will expand and strengthen their cooperation in research, development and utilization of nuclear energy, having as a primary objective the development of new energy sources. This cooperation will be carried out on the basis of mutual benefit, equality and reciprocity.

Article 2

1. Cooperation will be concentrated in the following three areas:
a. Controlled thermonuclear fusion.
The aim of cooperation in this area is the eventual development of prototype and

1 *DSB*, 23 July 1973, pp. 159–60.

demonstration-scale thermonuclear reactors. Cooperation may include theoretical, calculational, experimental and design-construction studies at all stages up to industrial-scale operations.

b. Fast breeder reactors.

Cooperation in this area will be directed toward finding solutions to mutually agreed basic and applied problems connected with the design, development, construction and operation of nuclear power plants utilizing fast breeder reactors.

c. Research on the fundamental properties of matter.

Cooperation in this area will include joint theoretical and experimental studies on mutually agreed subjects, and particularly in high, medium and low energy physics, through utilization of accelerators, data processing equipment and other facilities of the two countries. Cooperation may also be undertaken on the design, planning and construction of joint facilities to be used in this area of research.

2. Further details of cooperation in each of these three areas will be arranged through individual implementing protocols.

3. Other areas of cooperation may be added by mutual agreement.

4. Cooperation under this agreement shall be in accordance with the laws of the respective countries.

Article 3

1. Cooperation provided for in the preceding Articles may take the following forms

a. Establishment of working groups of scientists and engineers for design and execution of joint projects;

b. Joint development and construction of experiments, pilot installations and equipment;

c. Joint work by theoretical and experimental scientists in appropriate research centres of the two countries;

d. Organization of joint consultations, seminars and panels;

e. Exchanges of appropriate instrumentation, equipment and construction mater

f. Exchanges of scientists and specialists; and

g. Exchanges of scientific and technical information, documentation and results of research.

2. Other forms of cooperation may be added by mutual agreement.

Article 4

In furtherance of the aims of this agreement, the parties will, as appropriate, encour facilitate and monitor the development of cooperation and direct contacts between organizations and institutions of the two countries, including the conclusion, as appropriate, of implementing protocols and contracts for carrying out cooperative activities under this agreement.

Article 5

1. For the implementation of this agreement, there shall be established a US–USSR

oint committee on cooperation in the peaceful uses of atomic energy. Meetings will be convened once a year in the United States and the Soviet Union alternately, unless otherwise mutually agreed.

2. The joint committee shall take such action as is necessary for effective implementation of this agreement including, but not limited to, approval of specific projects and programmes of cooperation; designation of appropriate participating organizations and institutions responsible for carrying out cooperative activities; and making recommendations, as appropriate, to the two governments.

3. The executive agents of this agreement shall be, for the United States of America, the US Atomic Energy Commission, and for the Union of Soviet Socialist Republics, the USSR State Committee for the Utilization of Atomic Energy. The executive agents, on their respective sides, shall be responsible for the operation of the joint committee and shall coordinate and supervise the development and implementation of cooperative activities conducted under this agreement.

Article 6

Nothing in this agreement shall be interpreted to prejudice other agreements concluded between the parties.

Article 7

1. This agreement shall enter into force upon signature and shall remain in force for ten years. It may be modified or extended by mutual agreement of the parties.

2. The termination of this agreement shall not affect the validity of implementing protocols and contracts concluded under this agreement between interested organizations and institutions of the two countries.

65. Agreement on the Prevention of Nuclear War, 22 June 1973[1]

The United States of America and the Union of Soviet Socialist Republics, hereinafter referred to as the Parties,

Guided by the objectives of strengthening world peace and international security,

Conscious that nuclear war would have devastating consequences for mankind,

Proceeding from the desire to bring about conditions in which the danger of an outbreak of nuclear war anywhere in the world would be reduced and ultimately eliminated,

Proceeding from their obligations under the Charter of the United Nations regarding the maintenance of peace, refraining from the threat or use of force, and the avoidance of war, and in conformity with the agreements to which either Party has subscribed,

Proceeding from the Basic Principles of Relations between the United States of

1 *DSB*, 23 July 1973, pp. 160–1.

America and the Union of Soviet Socialist Republics signed in Moscow on May 29, 1972,

Reaffirming that the development of relations between the United States of America and the Union of Soviet Socialist Republics is not directed against other countries and their interests,

Have agreed as follows:

Article 1

The United States and the Soviet Union agree that an objective of their policies is to remove the danger of nuclear war and of the use of nuclear weapons.

Accordingly, the Parties agree that they will act in such a manner as to prevent the development of situations capable of causing a dangerous exacerbation of their relations, as to avoid military confrontations, and as to exclude the outbreak of nuclear war between them and between either of the Parties and other countries.

Article II

The Parties agree, in accordance with Article I and to realize the objective stated in that Article, to proceed from the premise that each Party will refrain from the threat or use of force against the other Party, against the allies of the other Party and against other countries, in circumstances which may endanger international peace and security. The Parties agree that they will be guided by these consideration in the formulation of their foreign policies and in their actions in the field of international relations.

Article III

The Parties undertake to develop their relations with each other and with other countries in a way consistent with the purposes of this Agreement.

Article IV

If at any time relations between the Parties or between either Party and other countries appear to involve the risk of a nuclear conflict, or if relations between countries not parties to this Agreement appear to involve the risk of nuclear war between the United States of America and the Union of Soviet Socialist Republics or between either Party and other countries, the United States and the Soviet Union acting in accordance with the provisions of this Agreement, shall immediately enter into urgent consultations with each other and make every effort to avert this risk.

Article V

Each Party shall be free to inform the Security Council of the United Nations, the

Secretary General of the United Nations and the Governments of allied or other countries of the progress and outcome of consultations initiated in accordance with Article IV of this Agreement.

Article VI

Nothing in this Agreement shall affect or impair:

(a) the inherent right of individual or collective self-defense as envisaged by Article 51 of the Charter of the United Nations,

(b) the provisions of the Charter of the United Nations, including those relating to the maintenance or restoration of international peace and security, and

(c) the obligations undertaken by either Party towards its allies or other countries in treaties, agreements, and other appropriate documents.

Article VII

This Agreement shall be of unlimited duration.

Article VIII

This Agreement shall enter into force upon signature.

66. Communiqué issued at the conclusion of Mr Brezhnev's visit to the United States, 25 June 1973[1]

I. THE GENERAL STATE OF US–SOVIET RELATIONS

Both sides expressed their mutual satisfaction with the fact that the American–Soviet summit meeting in Moscow in May, 1972 and the joint decisions taken there have resulted in a substantial advance in the strengthening of peaceful relations between the USA and the USSR and have created the basis for the further development of broad and mutually beneficial cooperation in various fields of mutual interest to the peoples of both countries and in the interests of all mankind.

They noted their satisfaction with the mutual effort to implement strictly and fully the treaties and agreements concluded between the USA and the USSR, and to expand areas of cooperation.

They agreed that the process of reshaping relations between the USA and the USSR on the basis of peaceful coexistence and equal security as set forth in the basic principles of relations between the USA and the USSR signed in Moscow on May 29, 1972 is progressing in an encouraging manner. They emphasized the great importance that each side attaches to these basic principles.

They reaffirmed their commitment to the continued scrupulous implementation

1 *DSB*, 23 July 1973, pp. 130–4.

and to the enhancement of the effectiveness of each of the provisions of that document.

Both sides noted with satisfaction that the outcome of the US–Soviet meeting in Moscow in May, 1972 was welcomed by other states and by world opinion as an important contribution to strengthening peace and international security, to curbing the arms race and to developing businesslike cooperation among states with different social systems.

Both sides viewed the return visit to the USA of the General Secretary of the Central Committee of CPSU, L. I. Brezhnev, and the talks held during the visit as an expression of their mutual determination to continue the course toward a major improvement in US–Soviet relations.

Both sides are convinced that the discussions they have just held represent a further milestone in the constructive development of their relations.

Convinced that such a development of American–Soviet relations serves the interests of both of their peoples and all of mankind, it was decided to take further major steps to give these relations maximum stability and to turn the development of friendship and cooperation between their peoples into a permanent factor for worldwide peace.

II. THE PREVENTION OF NUCLEAR WAR AND THE LIMITATION OF STRATEGIC ARMAMENTS

Issues related to the maintenance and strengthening of international peace were a central point of the talks between President Nixon and General Secretary Brezhnev.

Conscious of the exceptional importance for all mankind of taking effective measures to that end, they discussed ways in which both sides could work toward removing the danger of war, and especially nuclear war, between the USA and the USSR and between either party and other countries.

Consequently, in accordance with the charter of the United Nations and the basic principles of relations of May 29, 1972, it was decided to conclude an agreement between the USA and the USSR on the prevention of nuclear war. That agreement was signed by the President and the General Secretary on June 22, 1973. The text has been published separately.

The President and the General Secretary, in appraising this agreement, believe that it constitutes a historical landmark in Soviet–American relations and substantially strengthens the foundations of international security as a whole.

The United States and the Soviet Union state their readiness to consider additional ways of strengthening peace and removing forever the danger of war, and particularl nuclear war.

In the course of the meetings, intensive discussions were held on questions of strategic arms limitation. In this connection both sides emphasized the fundamental importance of the treaty on the limitation of anti-ballistic missile systems and the interim agreement on certain measures with respect to the limitation of strategic offensive arms signed between the USA and the USSR in May, 1972 which, for the first time in history, place actual limits on the most modern and most formidable types of armaments.

Having exchanged views on the progress in the implementation of these agreements, both sides reaffirmed their intention to carry them out and their readiness to move ahead jointly toward an agreement on the further limitation of strategic arms.

Both sides noted that progress has been made in the negotiations that resumed in November 1972, and that the prospects for reaching a permanent agreement on more complete measures limiting strategic offensive armaments are favourable.

Both sides agreed that the progress made in the limitation of strategic armaments is an exceedingly important contribution to the strengthening of US–Soviet relations and to world peace.

On the basis of their discussions, the President and the General Secretary signed on June 21, 1973, basic principles of negotiations on the further limitation of strategic offensive arms. The text has been published separately.

The USA and the USSR attach great importance to joining with all states in the cause of the strengthening of peace, reducing the burden of armaments, and reaching agreements on arms limitation and disarmament measures.

Considering the important role which an effective international agreement with respect to chemical weapons would play, the two sides agreed to continue their efforts to conclude such an agreement in cooperation with other countries.

The two sides agree to make every effort to facilitate the work of the Committee on Disarmament which has been meeting in Geneva. They will actively participate in negotiations aimed at working out new measures to curb and end the arms race. They reaffirm that the ultimate objective is general and complete disarmament, including nuclear disarmament, under strict international control. A world disarmament conference could play a role in this process at an appropriate time.

III. INTERNATIONAL QUESTIONS: THE REDUCTION OF TENSIONS AND STRENGTHENING OF INTERNATIONAL SECURITY

President Nixon and General Secretary Brezhnev reviewed major questions of the current international situation. They gave special attention to the developments which have occurred since the time of the US–Soviet summit meeting in Moscow. It was noted with satisfaction that positive trends are developing in international relations toward the further relaxation of tensions and the strengthening of cooperative relations in the interests of peace.

In the opinion of both sides, the current process of improvement in the international situation creates new and favourable opportunities for reducing tensions, settling outstanding international issues, and creating a permanent structure of peace.

Indochina

The two sides expressed their deep satisfaction at the conclusion of the agreement on ending the war and restoring peace in Vietnam, and also at the results of the international conference on Vietnam which approved and supported that agreement.

The two sides are convinced that the conclusion of the agreement on ending the war and restoring peace in Vietnam,[1] and the subsequent signing of the agreement on restoring peace and achieving national concord in Laos, meet the fundamental interests and aspirations of the peoples of Vietnam and Laos and open up a possibility for establishing a lasting peace in Indochina, based on respect for the independence, sovereignty, unity and territorial integrity of the countries of that area. Both sides emphasized that these agreements must be strictly implemented.

They further stressed the need to bring an early end to the military conflict in Cambodia in order to bring peace to the entire area of Indochina. They also reaffirmed their stand that the political futures of Vietnam, Laos, and Cambodia should be left to the respective peoples to determine, free from outside interference.

Europe

In the course of the talks both sides noted with satisfaction that in Europe the proce of relaxing tensions and developing cooperation is actively continuing and thereby contributing to international stability.

The two sides expressed satisfaction with the further normalization of relations among European countries resulting from treaties and agreements signed in recent years, particularly between the USSR and the FRG. They also welcome the coming into force of the quadripartite agreement of September 3, 1971.[2] They share the conviction that strict observance of the treaties and agreements that have been concluded will contribute to the security and well-being of all parties concerned.

They also welcome the prospect of United Nations membership this year for the FRG and the GDR and recall, in this connection, that the USA, USSR, UK and France have signed the quadripartite declaration of November 9, 1972, on this subject.[3]

The USA and the USSR reaffirm their desire, guided by the appropriate provision of the joint US–USSR communiqué adopted in Moscow in May 1972, to continue their separate and joint contributions to strengthening peaceful relations in Europe. Both sides affirm that ensuring a lasting peace in Europe is a paramount goal of their policies.

In this connection satisfaction was expressed with the fact that as a result of common efforts by many states, including the USA and the USSR, the preparatory work has been successfully completed for the Conference on Security and Cooperation in Europe, which will be convened on July 3, 1973.[4]

The USA and the USSR hold the view that the conference will enhance the

1 Document No. 37.
2 Document No. 20.
3 Document No. 25.
4 Document No. 105.

possibilities for strengthening European security and developing cooperation among the participating states. The USA and the USSR will conduct their policies so as to realize the goals of the conference and bring about a new era of good relations in this part of the world.

Reflecting their continued positive attitude toward the conference, both sides will make efforts to bring the conference to a successful conclusion at the earliest possible time. Both sides proceed from the assumption that progress in the work of the conference will produce possibilities for completing it at the highest level.

The USA and the USSR believe that the goal of strengthening stability and security in Europe would be further advanced if the relaxation of political tensions were accompanied by a reduction of military tensions in central Europe.

In this respect they attach great importance to the negotiations on the mutual reduction of forces and armaments and associated measures in central Europe which will begin on October 30, 1973.

Both sides state their readiness to make, along with other states, their contribution to the achievement of mutually acceptable decisions on the substance of this problem, based on the strict observance of the principle of the undiminished security of any of the parties.

Middle East

The parties expressed their deep concern with the situation in the Middle East and exchanged opinions regarding ways of reaching a Middle East settlement.

Each of the parties set forth its position on this problem.

Both parties agreed to continue to exert their efforts to promote the quickest possible settlement in the Middle East. This settlement should be in accordance with the interests of all states in the area, be consistent with their independence and sovereignty and should take into due account the legitimate interests of the Palestinian peoples.

IV. COMMERCIAL AND ECONOMIC RELATIONS

The President and the General Secretary thoroughly reviewed the status of and prospects for commercial and economic ties between the USA and the USSR. Both sides noted with satisfaction the progress achieved in the past year in the normalization and development of commercial and economic relations between them.

They agreed that mutually advantageous cooperation and peaceful relations would be strengthened by the creation of a permanent foundation of economic relationships.

They recall with satisfaction the various agreements on trade and commercial relations signed in the past year. Both sides note that American–Soviet trade has shown a substantial increase, and that there are favourable prospects for a continued rise in the exchange of goods over the coming years.

They believe that the two countries should aim at a total of 2–3 billion dollars of trade over the next three years. The joint US–USSR commercial commission continues to provide a valuable mechanism to promote the broad-scale growth of economic relations. The two sides noted with satisfaction that contacts between American firms and their Soviet counterparts are continuing to expand.

Both sides confirmed their firm intention to proceed from their earlier understanding on measures directed at creating more favourable conditions for expanding commercial and other economic ties between the USA and the USSR.

It was noted that as a result of the agreement regarding certain maritime matters signed in October, 1972, Soviet and American commercial ships have been calling more frequently at ports of the United States and the USSR, respectively, and since late May of this year a new regular passenger line has started operating between New York and Leningrad.

In the course of the current meeting, the two sides signed a protocol augmenting existing civil air relations between the USA and the USSR providing for direct air services between Washington and Moscow and New York and Leningrad, increasing the frequency of flights and resolving other questions in the field of civil aviation.

In the context of reviewing prospects for further and more permanent economic cooperation, both sides expressed themselves in favour of mutually advantageous long term projects. They discussed a number of specific projects involving the participation of American companies, including the delivery of Siberian natural gas to the United States. The President indicated that the USA encourages American firms to work out concrete proposals on these projects and will give serious and sympathetic consideration to proposals that are in the interest of both sides.

To contribute to expanded commercial, cultural and technical relations between the USA and the USSR, the two sides signed a tax convention to avoid double taxation on income and eliminate, as much as possible, the need for citizens of one country to become involved in the tax system of the other.

A protocol was also signed on the opening by the end of October, 1973 of a trade representation of the USSR in Washington and a commercial office of the United States in Moscow. In addition, a protocol was signed on questions related to establishing a US—Soviet Chamber of Commerce. These agreements will facilitate the further development of commercial and economic ties between the USA and the USSR.

V. FURTHER PROGRESS IN OTHER FIELDS OF BILATERAL COOPERATION

The two sides reviewed the areas of bilateral cooperation in such fields as environme protection, public health and medicine, exploration of outer space, and science and technology, established by the agreements signed in May 1972 and subsequently the noted that these agreements are being satisfactorily carried out in practice in accord with the programmes as adopted.

In particular, a joint effort is under way to develop effective means to combat those diseases which are most widespread and dangerous for mankind: cancer, cardi vascular or infectious diseases and arthritis. The medical aspects of the environment problems are also subjects of cooperative research.

Preparations for the joint space flight of the Apollo and Soyuz spacecraft are proceeding according to an agreed timetable.

The joint flight of these spaceships for a rendezvous and docking mission, and mutual visits of American and Soviet astronauts in each other's spacecraft, are scheduled for July, 1975.

Building on the foundation created in previous agreements, and recognizing the potential of both the USA and the USSR to undertake cooperative measures in current scientific and technological areas, new projects for fruitful joint efforts were identified and appropriate agreements were concluded.

Peaceful uses of Atomic Energy

Bearing in mind the great importance of satisfying the growing energy demands in both countries and throughout the world, and recognizing that the development of highly efficient energy sources could contribute to the solution of this problem, the President and the General Secretary signed an agreement to expand and strengthen cooperation in the fields of controlled nuclear fusion, fast breeder reactors, and research on the fundamental properties of matter. A joint committee on cooperation in the peaceful uses of atomic energy will be established to implement this agreement, which has a duration of ten years.

Agriculture

Recognizing the importance of agriculture in meeting mankind's requirement for food products and the role of science in modern agricultural production, the two sides concluded an agreement providing for a broad exchange of scientific experience in agricultural research and development, and of information on agricultural economics. A US–USSR joint committee on agricultural cooperation will be established to oversee joint programmes to be carried out under the agreement.

World Ocean Studies

Considering the unique capabilities and the major interest of both nations in the field of world ocean studies, and noting the extensive experience of US–USSR oceanographic cooperation, the two sides have agreed to broaden their cooperation and have signed an agreement to this effect. In so doing, they are convinced that the benefits from further development of cooperation in the field of oceanography will accrue not only bilaterally but also to all peoples of the world. A US–USSR joint committee on cooperation in world ocean studies will be established to coordinate the implementation of cooperative programmes.

Transportation

The two sides agreed that there are opportunities for cooperation between the USA and the USSR in the solution of problems in the field of transportation. To permit expanded, mutually beneficial cooperation in this field, the two sides concluded an agreement on this subject. The USA and the USSR further agreed that a joint committee on cooperation in transportation would be established.

Contacts, Exchanges and Cooperation

Recognizing the general expansion of US–USSR bilateral relations and, in particular the growing number of exchanges in the fields of science, technology, education and culture, and in other fields of mutual interest, the two sides agreed to broaden the scope of these activities under a new general agreement on contacts, exchanges, and cooperation, with a duration of six years. The two sides agreed to this in the mutual belief that it will further promote better understanding between the peoples of the United States and the Soviet Union and will help to improve the general state of relations between the two countries.

Both sides believe that the talks at the highest level, which were held in a frank and constructive spirit, were very valuable and made an important contribution to developing mutually advantageous relations between the USA and the USSR. In the view of both sides, these talks will have a favourable impact on international relations.

They noted that the success of the discussions in the United States was facilitated by the continuing consultation and contacts as agreed in May, 1972. They reaffirmed that the practice of consultation should continue. They agreed that further meetings at the highest level should be held regularly.

Having expressed his appreciation to President Nixon for the hospitality extended during the visit to the United States, General Secretary Brezhnev invited the President to visit the USSR in 1974. The invitation was accepted.

EDITOR'S NOTE: OTHER AGREEMENTS, CONVENTIONS AND PROTOCOLS OF THE WASHINGTON SUMMIT MEETING

The following agreements were also signed at the Washington summit:
Agreement on Cooperation in Agriculture
Agreement on Cooperation in Transportation
Agreement on Cooperation in Studies of the World Ocean
General Agreement on Contacts, Exchanges and Cooperation
Convention on Matters of Taxation
Protocol on a US–USSR Chamber of Commerce
Protocol on Commercial Facilities
Protocol on the Expansion of Air Services
For texts, see *DSB*, 23 July 1973, pp. 161–75.

Agreements reached following President Nixon's visit to the Soviet Union, 27 June–3 July 1974:

57. Joint statement on the Dangers of the Military Use of Environmental Modification, Moscow, 3 July 1974[1]

The United States of America and the Union of Soviet Socialist Republics:

Desiring to limit the potential danger to mankind from possible new means of warfare;

Taking into consideration that scientific and technical advances in environmental fields, including climate modification, may open possibilities for using environmental modification techniques for military purposes;

Recognizing that such use could have widespread, longlasting, and severe effects harmful to human welfare;

Recognizing also that proper utilization of scientific and technical advances could improve the inter-relationship of man and nature;

1. Advocate the most effective measures possible to overcome the dangers of the use of environmental modification techniques for military purposes.

2. Have decided to hold a meeting of United States and Soviet representatives this year for the purpose of exploring this problem.

3. Have decided to discuss also what steps might be taken to bring about the measures referred to in paragraph 1.

58. Joint communiqué signed by President Nixon and Mr Brezhnev, Moscow, 3 July 1974[2]

In accordance with the agreement to hold regular US–Soviet meetings at the highest level and at the invitation, extended during the visit of General Secretary of the Central Committee of the Communist Party of the Soviet Union L. I. Brezhnev to the USA in June 1973, the President of the United States of America and Mrs Richard Nixon paid an official visit to the Soviet Union from June 27 to July 3, 1974.

During his stay President Nixon visited, in addition to Moscow, Minsk and the Southern Coast of the Crimea.

The President of the United States and the Soviet leaders held a thorough and useful exchange of views on major aspects of relations between the USA and the USSR and on the present international situation.

On the Soviet side the talks were conducted by L. I. Brezhnev, General Secretary of the Central Committee of the Communist Party of the Soviet Union; N. V. Podgorny,

1 *DSB*, 29 July 1974, p. 185.
2 *DSB*, 29 July 1974, pp. 185–91.

Chairman of the Presidium of the USSR Supreme Soviet; A. N. Kosygin, Chairman of the USSR Council of Ministers; and A. A. Gromyko, Minister of Foreign Affairs of the USSR.

Accompanying the President of the USA and participating in the talks was Dr Henry A. Kissinger, US Secretary of State and Assistant to the President for National Security Affairs.

Also taking part in the talks were:

On the American Side: Walter J. Stoessel, Jr, American Ambassador to the USSR; General Alexander M. Haig, Jr, Assistant to the President; Mr Ronald L. Ziegler, Assistant to the President and Press Secretary; Major General Brent Scowcroft, Deputy Assistant to the President for National Security Affairs; Mr Helmut Sonnenfeldt, Counselor of the Department of State; and Mr Arthur A. Hartman, Assistant Secretary of State for European Affairs.

On the Soviet Side: A. F. Dobrynin, Soviet Ambassador to the USA; A. M. Aleksandrov, Assistant to the General Secretary of the Central Committee, CPSU; L. M. Zamyatin, Director General of TASS; and G. M. Korniyenko, Member of the Collegium of the Ministry of Foreign Affairs of the USSR.

The talks were held in a most businesslike and constructive atmosphere and were marked by a mutual desire of both Sides to continue to strengthen understanding, confidence and peaceful cooperation between them and to contribute to the strengthening of international security and world peace.

I. PROGRESS IN IMPROVING US–SOVIET RELATIONS

Having considered in detail the development of relations between the USA and the USSR since the US–Soviet summit meeting in May, 1972, both Sides noted with satisfaction that through their vigorous joint efforts they have brought about over this short period a fundamental turn toward peaceful relations and broad, mutually beneficial cooperation in the interests of the peoples of both countries and of all mankind.

They emphasized the special importance for the favorable development of relations between the USA and the USSR of meetings of their leaders at the highest level, which are becoming established practice. These meetings provide opportunities for effective and responsible discussion, for the solution of fundamental and important bilateral questions, and for mutual contributions to the settlement of international problems affecting the interests of both countries.

Both Sides welcome the establishment of official contacts between the Congress of the US and the Supreme Soviet of the USSR. They will encourage a further development of such contacts, believing that they can play an important role.

Both Sides confirmed their mutual determination to continue actively to reshape US–Soviet relations on the basis of peaceful coexistence and equal security, in strict conformity with the spirit and the letter of the agreements achieved between the two countries and their obligations under those agreements. In this connection they noted once again the fundamental importance of the joint documents adopted as a result of the summit meetings in 1972 and 1973, especially of the Basic Principles of Relations Between the USA and the USSR, the Agreement on the Prevention of Nuclear War, the Treaty on the Limitation of Anti-Ballistic Missile Systems and the Interim Agreement on Certain Measures with Respect to the Limitation of Strategic Offensive Arms.

Both Sides are deeply convinced of the imperative necessity of making the process of improving US–Soviet relations irreversible. They believe that, as a result of their efforts, a real possibility has been created to achieve this goal. This will open new vistas for broad mutually beneficial cooperation, and for strengthening friendship between the American and Soviet peoples, and will thus contribute to the solution of many urgent problems facing the world.

Guided by these worthy goals, both Sides decided to continue steadfastly to apply their joint efforts — in cooperation with other countries concerned, as appropriate — first of all in such important fields as:

— removing the danger of war, including particularly war involving nuclear and other mass-destruction weapons;
— limiting and eventually ending the arms race especially in strategic weapons, having in mind as the ultimate objective the achievement of general and complete disarmament under appropriate international control;
— contributing to the elimination of sources of international tension and military conflict;
— strengthening and extending the process of relaxation of tensions throughout the world;
— developing broad, mutually beneficial cooperation in commercial and economic, scientific-technical and cultural fields on the basis of the principles of sovereignty, equality and non-interference in internal affairs with a view to promoting increased understanding and confidence between the peoples of both countries.

Accordingly, in the course of this summit meeting both Sides considered it possible to take new constructive steps which, they believe, will not only advance further the development of US–Soviet relations but will also make a substantial contribution to strengthening world peace and expanding international cooperation.

II. FURTHER LIMITATION OF STRATEGIC ARMS AND OTHER DISARMAMENT ISSUES

Both Sides again carefully analyzed the entire range of their mutual relations connected with the prevention of nuclear war and limitation of strategic armaments. They arrived at the common view that the fundamental agreements concluded between them in this sphere continue to be effective instruments of the general improvement of US–Soviet relations and the international situation as a whole. The USA and the USSR will continue strictly to fulfill the obligations undertaken in those agreements.

In the course of the talks, the two Sides had a thorough review of all aspects of the problem of limitation of strategic arms. They concluded that the Interim Agreement on offensive strategic weapons should be followed by a new agreement betwee the United States and the Soviet Union on the limitation of strategic arms. They agreed that such an agreement should cover the period until 1985 and deal with both quantitative and qualitative limitations. They agreed that such an agreement should be completed at the earliest possible date, before the expiration of the Interim Agreement.

They hold the common view that such a new agreement would serve not only the interests of the United States and the Soviet Union but also those of a further relaxation of international tensions and of world peace.

Their delegations will reconvene in Geneva in the immediate future on the basis of instructions growing out of the summit.

Taking into consideration the interrelationship between the development of offensive and defensive types of strategic arms and noting the successful implementati of the Treaty on the Limitation of Anti-Ballistic Missile Systems concluded betweer them in May, 1972, both Sides considered it desirable to adopt additional limitatior on the deployment of such systems. To that end they concluded a protocol providir for the limitation of each Side to a single deployment area for ABM Systems instead of two such areas as permitted to each Side by the Treaty.

At the same time, two protocols were signed entitled 'Procedures Governing Replacement, Dismantling or Destruction and Notification Thereof, for Strategic Offensive Arms' and 'Procedures Governing Replacement, Dismantling or Destructic and Notification Thereof for ABM Systems and Their Components'. These protoco were worked out by the Standing Consultative Commission which was established to promote the objectives and implementation of the provisions of the Treaty and the Interim Agreement signed on May 26, 1972.

The two Sides emphasized the serious importance which the US and USSR also attach to the realization of other possible measures – both on a bilateral and on a multilateral basis – in the field of arms limitation and disarmament.

Having noted the historical significance of the Treaty Banning Nuclear Weapon Tests in the Atmosphere, in Outer Space and Under Water, concluded in Moscow in 1963, to which the United States and the Soviet Union are parties, both Sides expressed themselves in favor of making the cessation of nuclear weapon tests comprehensive. Desiring to contribute to the achievement of this goal the USA and the USSR concluded, as an important step in this direction, the Treaty on the Limitatio of Underground Nuclear Weapon Tests providing for the complete cessation, startin from March 31, 1976, of the tests of such weapons above an appropriate yield threshold, and for confining other underground tests to a minimum.

The Parties emphasized the fundamental importance of the Treaty on the Non-Proliferation of Nuclear Weapons. Having reaffirmed their mutual intention to observe the obligations assumed by them under that Treaty, including Article VI thereof, they expressed themselves in favor of increasing its effectiveness.

A joint statement was also signed in which the US and USSR advocate the most effective measures possible to overcome the dangers of the use of environmental modification techniques for military purposes.

Both Sides reaffirmed their interest in an effective international agreement which would exclude from the arsenals of States such dangerous instruments of mass destruction as chemical weapons. Desiring to contribute to early progress in this direction, the USA and the USSR agreed to consider a joint initiative in the Conference of the Committee on Disarmament with respect to the conclusion, as a first step, of an international Convention dealing with the most dangerous, lethal means of chemical warfare.

Both Sides are convinced that the new important steps which they have taken and intend to take in the field of arms limitation as well as further efforts toward disarmament will facilitate the relaxation of international tensions and constitute a tangible contribution to the fulfillment of the historic task of excluding war from the life of human society and thereby of ensuring world peace. The US and the USSR reaffirmed that a world disarmament conference at an appropriate time can play a positive role in this process.

III. PROGRESS IN THE SETTLEMENT OF INTERNATIONAL PROBLEMS

In the course of the meeting detailed discussions were held on major international problems.

Both Sides expressed satisfaction that relaxation of tensions, consolidation of peace, and development of mutually beneficial cooperation are becoming increasingly distinct characteristics of the development of the international situation. They proceed from the assumption that progress in improving the international situation does not occur spontaneously but requires active and purposeful efforts to overcome obstacles and resolve difficulties that remain from the past.

The paramount objectives of all states and peoples should be to ensure, individually and collectively, lasting security in all parts of the world, the early and complete removal of existing international conflicts and sources of tension and the prevention of new ones from arising.

The United States and the Soviet Union are in favor of the broad and fruitful economic cooperation among all states, large and small, on the basis of full equality and mutual benefit.

The United States and the Soviet Union reaffirm their determination to contribute separately and jointly to the achievement of all these tasks.

Europe

Having discussed the development of the situation in Europe since the last American–Soviet summit meeting, both Sides noted with profound satisfaction the further appreciable advances toward establishing dependable relations of peace, good-neighborliness and cooperation on the European continent.

Both Sides welcome the major contribution which the Conference on Security and Cooperation in Europe is making to this beneficial process. They consider that substantial progress has already been achieved at the Conference on many significant questions. They believe that this progress indicates that the present stage of the Conference will produce agreed documents of great international significance expressing the determination of the participating states to build their mutual relations on a solid jointly elaborated basis. The US and USSR will make every effort, in cooperation with the other participants, to find solutions acceptable to all for the remaining problems.

Both Sides expressed their conviction that successful completion of the Conference on Security and Cooperation in Europe would be an outstanding event in the interests of establishing a lasting peace. Proceeding from this assumption the USA and the USSR expressed themselves in favor of the final stage of the Conference taking place at an early date. Both Sides also proceed from the assumption that the results of the negotiations will permit the Conference to be concluded at the highest level, which would correspond to the historic significance of the Conference for the future of Europe and lend greater authority to the importance of the Conference's decisions.

Both Sides reaffirmed the lasting significance for a favorable development of the situation in Europe of the treaties and agreements concluded in recent years between European states with different social systems.

They expressed satisfaction with the admission to the United Nations of the Federal Republic of Germany and the German Democratic Republic.

Both Sides also stressed that the Quadripartite Agreement of September 3, 1971, must continue to play a key role in ensuring stability and detente in Europe. The US and USSR consider that the strict and consistent implementation of this Agreement by all parties concerned is an essential condition for the maintenance and strengthening of mutual confidence and stability in the center of Europe.

The USA and the USSR believe that, in order to strengthen stability and security in Europe, the relaxation of political tension on this continent should be accompanied by measures to reduce military tensions.

They therefore attach great importance to the current negotiations on the mutual reduction of forces and armaments and associated measures in Central Europe, in which they are participating. The two Sides expressed the hope that these negotiations will result in concrete decisions ensuring the undiminished security of any of the parties and preventing unilateral military advantages.

Middle East

Both Sides believe that the removal of the danger of war and tension in the Middle East is a task of paramount importance and urgency, and therefore, the only alternative is the achievement, on the basis of UN Security Council Resolution 338,[1] of a just and lasting peace settlement in which should be taken into account the legitimate interests of all peoples in the Middle East, including the Palestinian people, and the right to existence of all states in the area.

As Co-Chairmen of the Geneva Peace Conference on the Middle East, the USA and

1 Document No. 157.

the USSR consider it important the Conference resume its work as soon as possible, with the question of other participants from the Middle East area to be discussed at the Conference. Both Sides see the main purpose of the Geneva Peace Conference, the achievement of which they will promote in every way, as the establishment of just and stable peace in the Middle East.

They agreed that the USA and the USSR will continue to remain in close touch with a view to coordinating the efforts of both countries toward a peaceful settlement in the Middle East.

Indochina

Both Sides noted certain further improvements in the situation in Indochina. In the course of the exchange of views on the situation in Vietnam both Sides emphasized that peace and stability in the region can be preserved and strengthened only on the basis of strict observance by all parties concerned of the provisions of the Paris Agreement of January 27, 1973, and the Act of the International Conference on Vietnam of March 2, 1973.[1]

As regards Laos, they noted progress in the normalization of the situation as a result of the formation there of coalition governmental bodies. Both Sides also pronounced themselves in favor of strict fulfillment of the pertinent agreements.

Both Sides also stressed the need for an early and just settlement of the problem of Cambodia based on respect for the sovereign rights of the Cambodian people to a free and independent development without any outside interference.

Strengthening the Role of the United Nations

The United States of America and the Soviet Union attach great importance to the United Nations as an instrument for maintaining peace and security and the expansion of international cooperation. They reiterate their intention to continue their efforts toward increasing the effectiveness of the United Nations in every possible way, including in regard to peacekeeping, on the basis of strict observance of the United Nations Charter.

IV. COMMERCIAL AND ECONOMIC RELATIONS

In the course of the meeting great attention was devoted to a review of the status of and prospects for relations between the USA and the USSR in the commercial and economic field.

Both Sides reaffirmed that they regard the broadening and deepening of mutually advantageous ties in this field on the basis of equality and non-discrimination as an important part of the foundation on which the entire structure of US—Soviet relations is built. An increase in the scale of commercial and economic ties corresponding to

---

1 Documents Nos. 37 and 38.

the potentials of both countries will cement this foundation and benefit the America and Soviet peoples.

The two Sides noted with satisfaction that since the previous summit meeting US–Soviet commercial and economic relations have on the whole shown an upward trend. This was expressed, in particular, in a substantial growth of the exchange of goods between the two countries which approximated $1.5 billion in 1973. It was noted that prospects were favorable for surpassing the goal announced in the joint US–USSR communiqué of June 24, 1973, of achieving a total bilateral trade turn-over of $2–3 billion during the three-year period 1973–1975. The Joint US–USSR Commercial Commission continues to provide an effective mechanism to promote the broad-scale growth of economic relations.

The two Sides noted certain progress in the development of long-term cooperatio. between American firms and Soviet organizations in carrying out large-scale projects including those on a compensation basis. They are convinced that such cooperation is an important element in the development of commercial and economic ties between the two countries. The two Sides agreed to encourage the conclusion and implementation of appropriate agreements between American and Soviet organizations and firms. Taking into account the progress made in a number of specific projects, such as those concerning truck manufacture, the trade center, and chemical fertilizers, the Sides noted the possibility of concluding appropriate contracts in other areas of mutual interest, such as pulp and paper, timber, ferrous and non-ferrous metallurgy, natural gas, the engineering industry, and the extraction and processing of high energy-consuming minerals.

Both Sides noted further development of productive contacts and ties between business circles of the two countries in which a positive role was played by the decisions taken during the previous summit meeting on the opening of a United States commercial office in Moscow and a USSR trade representation in Washington as well as the establishment of a US–Soviet Commercial and Economic Council. They expressed their desire to continue to bring about favorable conditions for the successful development of commercial and economic relations between the USA and the USSR.

Both Sides confirmed their interest in bringing into force at the earliest possible time the US–Soviet trade agreement of October, 1972.

Desirous of promoting the further expansion of economic relations between the two countries, the two Sides signed a Long-Term Agreement to Facilitate Economic, Industrial and Technical Cooperation between the USA and the USSR. They believe that a consistent implementation of the cooperation embodied in the Agreement over the ten-year period will be an important factor in strengthening bilateral relations in general and will benefit the peoples of both countries.

Having reviewed the progress in carrying out the Agreement Regarding Certain Maritime Matters concluded in October, 1972, for a period of three years, and based on the experience accumulated thus far, the two Sides expressed themselves in favor of concluding before its expiration a new agreement in this field. Negotiations concerning such an agreement will commence this year.

V. PROGRESS IN OTHER FIELDS OF BILATERAL RELATIONS

Having reviewed the progress in the implementation of the cooperative agreements concluded in 1972—3, both Sides noted the useful work done by joint American—Soviet committees and working groups established under those agreements in developing regular contacts and cooperation between scientific and technical organizations, scientists, specialists and cultural personnel of both countries.

The two Sides note with satisfaction that joint efforts by the USA and the USSR in such fields of cooperation as medical science and public health, protection and improvement of man's environment, science and technology, exploration of outer space and the world ocean, peaceful uses of atomic energy, agriculture and transportation create conditions for an accelerated solution of some urgent and complicated problems facing mankind.

Such cooperation makes a substantial contribution to the development of the structure of American—Soviet relations, giving it a more concrete positive content.

Both Sides will strive to broaden and deepen their cooperation in science and technology as well as cultural exchanges on the basis of agreements concluded between them.

On the basis of positive experience accumulated in their scientific and technological cooperation and guided by the desire to ensure further progress in this important sphere of their mutual relations, the two Sides decided to extend such cooperation to the following new areas.

Energy

Taking into consideration the growing energy needs of industry, transportation and other branches of the economies of both countries and the consequent need to intensify scientific and technical cooperation in the development of optimal methods of utilizing traditional and new sources of energy, and to improve the understanding of the energy programs and problems of both countries, the two Sides concluded an agreement on cooperation in the field of energy. Responsibility for the implementation of the Agreement is entrusted to a US—USSR Joint Committee on Cooperation in Energy, which will be established for that purpose.

Housing and Other Construction

The two Sides signed an agreement on cooperation in the field of housing and other construction. The aim of this Agreement is to promote the solution by joint effort of problems related to modern techniques of housing and other construction along such lines as the improvement of the reliability and quality of buildings and building materials, the planning and construction of new towns, construction in seismic areas and areas of extreme climate conditions. For the implementation of this Agreement there will be established a Joint US—USSR Committee on Cooperation in Housing and other Construction which will determine specific working programs.

For the purpose of enhancing the safety of their peoples living in earthquake-prone areas, the two Sides agreed to undertake on a priority basis a joint research project to increase the safety of buildings and other structures in these areas and, in particular, to study the behavior of pre-fabricated residential structures during earthquakes.

Artificial Heart Research

In the course of the implementation of joint programs in the field of medical science and public health scientists and specialists of both countries concluded that there is a need to concentrate their efforts on the solution of one of the most important and humane problems of modern medical science, development of an artificial heart.

In view of the great theoretical and technical complexity of the work involved, the two Sides concluded a special agreement on the subject. The US–USSR Joint Committee for Health Cooperation will assume responsibility for this project.

Cooperation in Space

The two Sides expressed their satisfaction with the successful preparations for the first joint manned flight of the American and Soviet spacecraft, Apollo and Soyuz, which is scheduled for 1975 and envisages their docking and mutual visits of the astronauts in each other's spacecraft. In accordance with existing agreements fruitful cooperation is being carried out in a number of other fields related to the exploration of outer space.

Attaching great importance to further American-Soviet cooperation in the exploration and use of outer space for peaceful purposes, including the development of safety systems for manned flights in space, and considering the desirability of consolidating experience in this field, the two Sides agreed to continue to explore possibilities for further joint space projects following the US–USSR space flight now scheduled for July 1975.

Transport of the Future

Aware of the importance of developing advanced modes of transportation, both Sides agreed that high-speed ground systems of the future, including a magnetically levitated train, which can provide economical, efficient, and reliable forms of transportation, would be a desirable and innovative area for joint activity. A working group to develop a joint research cooperation program in this area under the 1973 Agreement on Cooperation in the Field of Transportation will be established at the Fall meeting of the Joint US–USSR Transportation Committee.

Environmental Protection

Desiring to expand cooperation in the field of environmental protection, which is being successfully carried out under the US–USSR Agreement signed on May 23, 1972, and to contribute to the implementation of the 'Man and the Biosphere' international program conducted on the initiative of the United Nations Educational, Scientific and Cultural Organization (UNESCO), both Sides agreed to designate in the territories of their respective countries certain natural areas as biosphere reserves for protecting valuable plant and animal genetic strains and ecosystems, and for conducting scientific research needed for more effective actions concerned with global environmental protection. Appropriate work for the implementation of this undertaking will be conducted in conformity with the goals of the UNESCO program and under the auspices of the previously established US–USSR Joint Committee on Cooperation in the Field of Environmental Protection.

Cultural Exchanges

The two Parties, aware of the importance of cultural exchanges as a means of promoting mutual understanding, express satisfaction with the agreement between the Metropolitan Museum of Art of New York City and the Ministry of Culture of the USSR leading to a major exchange of works of art. Such an exchange would be in accordance with the General Agreement on Contacts, Exchanges and Cooperation signed June 19, 1973, under which the parties agree to render assistance for the exchange of exhibitions between the museums of the two countries.

Establishment of New Consulates

Taking into consideration the intensive development of ties between the US and the USSR and the importance of further expanding consular relations on the basis of the US–USSR Consular Convention, and desiring to promote trade, tourism and cooperation between them in various areas, both Sides agreed to open additional Consulates General in two or three cities of each country.

As a first step they agreed in principle to the simultaneous establishment of a United States Consulate General in Kiev and a USSR Consulate General in New York. Negotiations for implementation of this agreement will take place at an early date.

Both Sides highly appreciate the frank and constructive atmosphere and fruitful results of the talks held between them in the course of the present meeting. They are convinced that the results represent a new and important milestone along the road of improving relations between the USA and the USSR to the benefit of the peoples of both countries, and a significant contribution to their efforts aimed at strengthening world peace and security.

Having again noted in this connection the exceptional importance and great practical usefulness of US–Soviet summit meetings, both Sides reaffirmed their agreement to hold such meetings regularly and when considered necessary for the discussion and solution of urgent questions. Both Sides also expressed their readiness to continue their active and close contacts and consultations.

The President extended an invitation to General Secretary of the Central Committee of the CPSU, L. I. Brezhnev, to pay an official visit to the United States in 1975. This invitation was accepted with pleasure.

Agreements reached at the summit meeting between President Ford and Mr Brezhnev, Vladivostock, 23—24 November 1974:

69. Joint Statement on Strategic Offensive Arms, 24 November 1974[1]

During their working meeting in the area of Vladivostok on November 23—24, 1974, the President of the USA Gerald R. Ford and General Secretary of the Central Committee of the CPSU L. I. Brezhnev discussed in detail the question of further limitations of strategic offensive arms.

They reaffirmed the great significance that both the United States and the USSR attach to the limitation of strategic offensive arms. They are convinced that a long-term agreement on this question would be a significant contribution to improving relations between the US and the USSR, to reducing the danger of war and to enhancing world peace. Having noted the value of previous agreements on this question, including the Interim Agreement of May 26, 1972, they reaffirm the intention to conclude a new agreement on the limitation of strategic offensive arms, to last through 1985.

As a result of the exchange of views on the substance of such a new agreement, the President of the United States of America and the General Secretary of the Central Committee of the CPSU concluded that favorable prospects exist for completing the work on this agreement in 1975.

Agreement was reached that further negotiations will be based on the following provisions.

1. The new agreement will incorporate the relevant provisions of the Interim Agreement of May 26, 1972, which will remain in force until October 1977.

2. The new agreement will cover the period from October 1977 through December 31, 1985.

3. Based on the principle of equality and equal security, the new agreement will include the following limitations:

a. Both sides will be entitled to have a certain agreed aggregate number of strategic delivery vehicles;

b. Both sides will be entitled to have a certain agreed aggregate number of ICBMs and SLBMs [Intercontinental ballistic missiles; submarine-launched ballistic missiles] equipped with multiple independently targetable warheads (MIRVs).[2]

1 *DSB*, 23 December 1974, p. 879.
2 At his press conference in Washington on 2 December 1974, President Ford announced the agreed numbers as follows: a ceiling of 2,400 each on the total number of intercontinental ballistic missiles, submarine-launched missiles, and heavy bombers; and of that number a ceiling of 1,320 to be armed with multiple independently targetable warheads. [*DSB*, 23 December 1974, p. 861.]

4. The new agreement will include a provision for further neogiations beginning no later than 1980–1981 on the question of further limitations and possible reductions of strategic arms in the period after 1985.

5. Negotiations between the delegations of the US and USSR to work out the new agreement incorporating the foregoing points will resume in Geneva in January 1975.

70. Joint Communiqué issued by the United States and the Soviet Union, 24 November 1974[1]

In accordance with the previously announced agreement, a working meeting between the President of the United States of America Gerald R. Ford and the General Secretary of the Central Committee of the Communist Party of the Soviet Union L. I. Brezhnev took place in the area of Vladivostok on November 23 and 24, 1974. Taking part in the talks were the Secretary of State of the United States of America and Assistant to the President for National Security Affairs, Henry A. Kissinger and Member of the Politburo of the Central Committee of the CPSU, Minister of Foreign Affairs of the USSR, A. A. Gromyko.

They discussed a broad range of questions dealing with American–Soviet relations and the current international situation.

Also taking part in the talks were:

On the American side Walter J. Stoessel, Jr, Ambassador of the USA to the USSR; Helmut Sonnenfeldt, Counselor of the Department of State; Arthur A. Hartman, Assistant Secretary of State for European Affairs; Lieutenant General Brent Scowcroft, Deputy Assistant to the President for National Security Affairs; and William Hyland, official of the Department of State.

On the Soviet side A. F. Dobrynin, Ambassador of the USSR to the USA; A. M. Aleksandrov, Assistant to the General Secretary of the Central Committee of the CPSU; and G. M. Korniyenko, Member of the Collegium of the Ministry of Foreign Affairs of the USSR.

The United States of America and the Soviet Union reaffirmed their determination to develop further their relations in the direction defined by the fundamental joint decisions and basic treaties and agreements concluded between the two States in recent years.

They are convinced that the course of American–Soviet relations, directed towards strengthening world peace, deepening the relaxation of international tensions and expanding mutually beneficial cooperation of states with different social systems meets the vital interests of the peoples of both States and other peoples.

Both Sides consider that based on the agreements reached between them important results have been achieved in fundamentally reshaping American–Soviet relations

1 *DSB*, 23 December 1974, pp. 879–81.

on the basis of peaceful coexistence and equal security. These results are a solid foundation for progress in reshaping Soviet—American relations.

Accordingly, they intend to continue, without a loss in momentum, to expand the scale and intensity of their cooperative efforts in all spheres as set forth in the agreements they have signed so that the process of improving relations between the US and the USSR will continue without interruption and will become irreversible.

Mutual determination was expressed to carry out strictly and fully the mutual obligations undertaken by the US and the USSR in accordance with the treaties and agreements concluded between them.

II

Special consideration was given in the course of the talks to a pivotal aspect of Soviet—American relations: measures to eliminate the threat of war and to halt the arms race.

Both sides reaffirm that the Agreements reached between the US and the USSR on the prevention of nuclear war and the limitation of strategic arms are a good beginning in the process of creating guarantees against the outbreak of nuclear conflict and war in general. They expressed their deep belief in the necessity of promoting this process and expressed their hope that other states would contribute to it as well. For their part the US and the USSR will continue to exert vigorous efforts to achieve this historic task.

A joint statement on the question of limiting strategic offensive arms is being released separately.

Both sides stressed once again the importance and necessity of a serious effort aimed at preventing the dangers connected with the spread of nuclear weapons in the world. In this connection they stressed the importance of increasing the effectiveness of the Treaty on the Non-Proliferation of Nuclear Weapons.

It was noted that, in accordance with previous agreements, initial contacts were established between representatives of the US and of the USSR on questions related to underground nuclear explosions for peaceful purposes, to measures to overcome the dangers of the use of environmental modification techniques for military purpos as well as measures dealing with the most dangerous lethal means of chemical warfa. It was agreed to continue an active search for mutually acceptable solutions of thes questions.

III

In the course of the meeting an exchange of views was held on a number of international issues: special attention was given to negotiations already in progress in which the two Sides are participants and which are designed to remove existing sources of tension and to bring about the strengthening of international security and world peace.

Having reviewed the situation at the Conference on Security and Cooperation in Europe, both Sides concluded that there is a possibility for its early successful conclusion. They proceed from the assumption that the results achieved in the course of the Conference will permit its conclusion at the highest level and thus be commensurate with its importance in ensuring the peaceful future of Europe.

The USA and the USSR also attach high importance to the negotiations on mutual reduction of forces and armaments and associated measures in Central Europe. They agree to contribute actively to the search for mutually acceptable solutions on the basis of the principle of undiminished security for any of the parties and the prevention of unilateral military advantages.

Having discussed the situation existing in the Eastern Mediterranean, both Sides state their firm support for the independence, sovereignty and territorial integrity of Cyprus and will make every effort in this direction. They consider that a just settlement of the Cyprus question must be based on the strict implementation of the resolutions adopted by the Security Council and the General Assembly of the United Nations regarding Cyprus.

In the course of the exchange of views on the Middle East both Sides expressed their concern with regard to the dangerous situation in that region. They reaffirmed their intention to make every effort to promote a solution of the key issues of a just and lasting peace in that area on the basis of the United Nations resolution 338, taking into account the legitimate interests of all the peoples of the area, including the Palestinian people, and respect for the right to independent existence of all States in the area.

The Sides believe that the Geneva Conference should play an important part in the establishment of a just and lasting peace in the Middle East, and should resume its work as soon as possible.

IV

The state of relations was reviewed in the field of commercial, economic, scientific and technical ties between the USA and the USSR. Both Sides confirmed the great importance which further progress in these fields would have for Soviet—American relations, and expressed their firm intention to continue the broadening and deepening of mutually advantageous cooperation.

The two Sides emphasized the special importance accorded by them to the development on a long term basis of commercial and economic cooperation, including mutually beneficial large-scale projects. They believe that such commercial and economic cooperation will serve the cause of increasing the stability of Soviet—American relations.

Both Sides noted with satisfaction the progress in the implementation of agreements and in the development of ties and cooperation between the US and the USSR in the fields of science, technology and culture. They are convinced that the continued expansion of such cooperation will benefit the peoples of both countries and will be an important contribution to the solution of world-wide scientific and technical problems.

The talks were held in an atmosphere of frankness and mutual understanding, reflecting the constructive desire of both Sides to strengthen and develop further the peaceful cooperative relationship between the USA and the USSR and to ensure progress in the solution of outstanding international problems in the interests of preserving and strengthening peace.

The results of the talks provided a convincing demonstration of the practical value of Soviet–American summit meetings and their exceptional importance in the shaping of a new relationship between the United States of America and the Soviet Union.

President Ford reaffirmed the invitation to L. I. Brezhnev to pay an official visit to the United States in 1975. The exact date of the visit will be agreed upon later.

71. Statement by Dr Kissinger to the press, Washington, 14 January 1975[1]

Since the President signed the Trade Act on January 3, we have been in touch with the Soviet Government concerning the steps necessary to bring the 1972 US–Soviet Trade Agreement into force.

Article 9 of that agreement provides for an exchange of written notices of acceptance, following which the agreement, including reciprocal extension of non-discriminatory tariff treatment (MFN) [most-favored-nation] would enter into force. In accordance with the recently enacted Trade Act, prior to this exchange of written notices, the President would transmit to the Congress a number of documen including the 1972 agreement, the proposed written notices, a formal proclamation extending MFN to the USSR and a statement of reasons for the 1972 agreement. Either House of Congress would then have had 90 legislative days to veto the agreement.

In addition to these procedures, the President would also take certain steps, pursuant to the Trade Act, to waive the applicability of the Jackson–Vanik amendment. These steps would include a report to the Congress stating that the waiver will substantially promote the objectives of the amendment and that the President has received assurances that the emigration practices of the USSR will henceforth lead substantially to the achievement of the objectives of the amendment.

It was our intention to include in the required exchange of written notices with the Soviet Government language, required by the provisions of the Trade Act, that would have made clear that the duration of three years referred to in the 1972 Trade Agreement with the USSR was subject to continued legal authority to carry out our obligations. This caveat was necessitated by the fact that the waiver of the Jackson–Vanik amendment would be applicable only for an initial period of 18 months, with provision for renewal thereafter.

The Soviet Government has now informed us that it cannot accept a trading

1 *DSB*, 3 February 1975, pp. 139–40.

lationship based on the legislation recently enacted in this country.[1] It considers
is legislation as contravening both the 1972 Trade Agreement, which had called
or an unconditional elimination of discriminatory trade restrictions, and the principle
f noninterference in domestic affairs. The Soviet Government states that it does
ot intend to accept a trade status that is discriminatory and subject to political
onditions and, accordingly, that it will not put into force the 1972 Trade Agree-
ent. Finally, the Soviet Government informed us that if statements were made
y the United States, in the terms required by the Trade Act, concerning assurances
y the Soviet Government regarding matters it considers within its domestic juris-
iction, such statements would be repudiated by the Soviet Government.

In view of these developments, we have concluded that the 1972 Trade Agree-
ent cannot be brought into force at this time and that the President will therefore
ot take the steps required for this purpose by the Trade Act. The President does
ot plan at this time to exercise the waiver authority.

The administration regrets this turn of events. It has regarded and continues to
egard an orderly and mutually beneficial trade relationship with the Soviet Union
s an important element in the overall improvement of relations. It will, of course,
ontinue to pursue all available avenues for such an improvement, including efforts
o obtain legislation that will permit normal trading relationships.

2. Agreement on the Supply of Grain, Moscow, 20 October 1975[2]

he Government of the United States of America ('USA') and the Government of
he Union of Soviet Socialist Republics ('USSR');
    Recalling the 'Basic Principles of Relations Between the United States of America
nd the Union of Soviet Socialist Republics' of May 29, 1972;
    Desiring to strengthen long-term cooperation between the two countries on the
asis of mutual benefit and equality;
    Mindful of the importance which the production of food, particularly grain, has
or the peoples of both countries;
    Recognizing the need to stabilize trade in grain between the two countries;
    Affirming their conviction that cooperation in the field of trade will contribute
o overall improvement of relations between the two countries;
    Have agreed as follows:

Article I

he Government of the USA and the Government of the USSR hereby enter into
n Agreement for the purchase and sale of wheat and corn for supply to the USSR.
o this end, during the period that this Agreement is in force, except as otherwise
greed by the parties, (i) the foreign trade organizations of the USSR shall purchase

1 In a letter of 10 January 1975; unpublished.
2 *DSB*, 10 November 1975, pp. 663–4.

from private commercial sources, for shipment in each twelve month period beginni
October 1, 1976, six million metric tons of wheat and corn, in approximately equal
proportions, grown in the USA; and (ii) the Government of the USA shall employ it
good offices to facilitate and encourage such sales by private commercial sources.

The foreign trade organizations of the USSR may increase this quantity without
consultations by up to two million metric tons in any twelve month period, beginni
October 1, 1976 unless the Government of the USA determines that the USA has
a grain supply of less than 225 million metric tons as defined in Article V.

Purchases/sales of wheat and corn under this Agreement will be made at the
market price prevailing for these products at the time of purchase/sale and in accordance with normal commercial terms.

Article II

During the term of this Agreement, except as otherwise agreed by the Parties, the
Government of the USA shall not exercise any discretionary authority available to
it under United States law to control exports of wheat and corn purchased for suppl
to the USSR in accordance with Article I.

Article III

In carrying out their obligations under this Agreement, the foreign trade organizatio
of the USSR shall endeavor to space their purchases in the USA and shipments to
the USSR as evenly as possible over each 12-month period.

Article IV

The Government of the USSR shall assure that, except as the Parties may otherwise
agree, all wheat and corn grown in the USA and purchased by foreign trade organizations of the USSR shall be supplied for consumption in the USSR.

Article V

In any year this Agreement is in force when the total grain supply in the USA, defin
as the official United States Department of Agriculture estimates of the carry-in
stocks of grain plus the official United States Department of Agriculture forward
crop estimates for the coming crop year, falls below 225 million metric tons of all
grains, the Government of the USA may reduce the quantity of wheat and corn
available for purchase by foreign trade organizations of the USSR under Article I(i).

Article VI

Whenever the Government of the USSR wishes the foreign trade organizations of th

USSR to be able to purchase more wheat or corn grown in the USA than the amounts specified in Article I, it shall immediately notify the Government of the USA.

Whenever the Government of the USA wishes private commercial sources to be able to sell more wheat or corn grown in the USA than the amounts specified in Article I, it shall immediately notify the Government of the USSR.

In both instances, the Parties will consult as soon as possible in order to reach agreement on possible quantities of grain to be supplied to the USSR prior to purchase/sale or conclusion of contracts for the purchase/sale of grain in amounts above those specified in Article I.

Article VII

It is understood that the shipment of wheat and corn from the USA to the USSR under this Agreement shall be in accord with the provisions of the American— Soviet Agreement on Maritime Matters which is in force during the period of shipments hereunder.

Article VIII

The Parties shall hold consultations concerning the implementation of this Agreement and related matters at intervals of six months beginning six months after the date of entry into force of this Agreement, and at any other time at the request of either Party.

Article IX

This Agreement shall enter into force on execution and shall remain in force until September 30, 1981 unless extended for a mutually agreed period.

B. Independent initiatives of the Western Powers

A. FRANCE

73. Protocol on Political Consultations signed by the Governments of France and the Soviet Union, Moscow, 13 October 1970[1]

The Presidium of the Supreme Soviet of the Union of Soviet Socialist Republics and the President of the French Republic,

Confirming the provisions and spirit of the Declaration of 30 June 1966, signed jointly by the President of the Presidium of the USSR Supreme Soviet and the President of the French Republic during the visit of General de Gaulle to the Soviet Union,

Inspired by a common desire to contribute towards the maintenance of peace in all parts of the world and conscious of the responsibilities which are borne, in this connection, by the Soviet Union and France as permanent members of the United Nations Security Council.

True to the responsibilities which the two states have assumed in Europe as a result of the Second World War,

Striving in keeping with the traditional friendship existing between the two countries and peoples, to extend the special ties established between them since 1966 in the economic, scientific, technological and cultural fields.

And being firmly resolved to give fresh impetus to their political cooperation, Have agreed on the following:

1. Should situations arise which, in the opinion of the two sides, create a threat to peace or a violation of peace, or which cause international tension, the governments of the USSR and France shall immediately contact each other with the object of concerting their positions on all aspects of those situations and on steps which would make it possible to cope with those situations.

2. The Soviet Union and France shall extend and deepen their political consultations on major international problems of mutual interest.

Such consultations shall cover:

1 *Soviet News*, 20 October 1970.

The development of the situation in Europe and the promotion of a détente, cooperation and the consolidation of security on the continent;

The situation in all parts of the world where international security is threatened;

Problems of mutual interest which are the subject of multilateral international negotiations, including those under consideration at the United Nations;

Any other questions concerning which the two sides may find it useful to have an exchange of views.

3. The provisions set out above in no way affect commitments assumed earlier by the signatories with regard to third states and are not directed against any of those states.

4. The political consultations shall be held regularly.

The Ministers of Foreign Affairs or representatives specially appointed for these purposes will meet whenever necessary and, in principle, twice a year.

74. Joint declaration issued by the Governments of France and the Soviet Union, Moscow, 13 October 1970[1]

The President of the French Republic and Mme Pompidou were the guests of the Soviet Union at the invitation of the Presidium of the Supreme Soviet and the government of the Soviet Union from 6 to 13 October 1970. The President of the French Republic was accompanied by Foreign Minister Maurice Schumann.

The President of the French Republic and the members of his party visited a number of regions of the Soviet Union and acquainted themselves with various aspects of the industrial, scientific, technical and cultural achievements of the Soviet people.

Everywhere President Georges Pompidou and the French delegation were accorded a warm welcome, which reflected the long-standing sentiments of friendship uniting the peoples of the two countries.

The President of the French Republic had talks and conversations with Leonid Brezhnev, Alexei Kosygin and Nikolai Podgorny. . .

The Soviet leaders and the President of the French Republic set out the main ideas which underlie the policy of their governments. The aim of their governments is the development of peaceful relations and cooperation among all states, irrespective of their ideology and system, and also the utmost strengthening of international security.

In this spirit, the Soviet statesmen and President Pompidou examined the situation in Europe. They noted with satisfaction a tendency impelling the countries of the east and west of the continent to enlarge and deepen exchanges, contacts and relations of various kinds. They have noted as one of the most favourable factors that the evolution of relations between European states is distinguished now, not only by the development of economic, scientific, technical and cultural relations, but also by efforts aimed at normalizing and improving political relations, ensuring recognition

1 *Soviet News*, 20 October 1970, pp. 33–5.

of the inviolability of the present frontiers of all European states and respect for these frontiers by all, and excluding the threat or use of force, since only joint efforts in this direction can create the conditions for a solution to the existing problems which affect European security and make it possible to put an end to the division of Europe into military—political groupings and to safeguard peace on the continent of Europe.

In this connection, as powers sharing responsibilities under well-known quadripartite agreements, they note with satisfaction the signing of the treaty between the Soviet Union and the Federal Republic of Germany on August 12, 1970[1] and regard it as an important contribution to the development of a detente in Europe and the strengthening of European security.

They express the hope that other negotiations which are now taking place and, in particular, the quadripartite talks to promote a further improvement of the situation in Europe, will reach a favourable conclusion.

The two sides consider that a detente in Europe would be furthered by the convocation of a properly-prepared all-European conference, the purpose of which would be to promote the development of relations and the establishment of constant cooperation between all interested states, outside the framework of a policy of blocs. They consider that the aim of such a conference must be to strengthen European security by establishing a system of undertakings which would provide for renunciation of the use or threat of force in mutual relations between the states in Europe and would ensure respect for the principles of the territorial integrity of states, non-interference in their internal affairs, equality, and the independence of all states.

The two sides declare that their attitude towards the proposal for an all-European conference is favourable, and they regard it as necessary, with a view to ensuring the successful holding of such a conference, to begin active and all-round preparatory work both by bilateral contacts and — as soon as possible — within the framework of multilateral contacts. As for themselves, they are ready to make their contribution to efforts for the preparation of such a conference.

The Soviet leaders and President Pompidou are convinced that the Soviet Union and France can make a decisive contribution to a successful evolution of the situation in Europe, both through appropriate initiatives on their part and through their mutual cooperation. Realising the usefulness of Soviet—French consultations on European problems, they have agreed on the development and deepening of these consultations.

The two sides note with satisfaction the efforts made for a cease-fire in the Middle East. They express the hope that, already in the very near future, discussions will be started in a constructive spirit through Ambassador Jarring, the special envoy of the United Nations secretary-general, which will lead to an agreement on the establishment of a just and lasting peace based on the Security Council's resolution of November 22, 1967, and including provisions both for Israel's withdrawal from all the occupied territories and for recognition by each of the countries concerned of the sovereignty, political independence and territorial integrity of all the countries of this region.

1 Document No. 16.

The two sides are of the opinion that the four permanent members of the UN Security Council should step up their consultations in order to work out appropriate recommendations for Dr Jarring so as to promote the success of his mission.

The two sides note with regret that while in other parts of the world there has recently been noticeable progress towards peace and the easing of tension, the war and foreign intervention are continuing in Indochina. The exchange of views has confirmed that their positions as regards a settlement capable of restoring peace there are very close together. They have agreed to continue their efforts to promote talks between all the parties concerned in order to ensure for the peoples of this area the possibility, on the basis of the Geneva Agreements of 1954 and 1962, of being masters of their own destiny, without any foreign interference.

The two sides have stressed the great importance which the USSR and France attach to the problem of disarmament. Being conscious of the special significance of nuclear disarmament, they have reaffirmed their joint conviction that the great powers with nuclear weapons at their disposal should get together to discuss the question of disarmament in this field. They have noted the similarity of their views on the prohibition of chemical and bacteriological weapons and also on the danger which the use of the sea bed and the ocean floor for military purposes would constitute for mankind.

In connection with the 25th anniversary of the establishment of the United Nations, the Soviet Union and France reaffirm their adherence to the aims and principles of the United Nations Charter and are fully resolved to do everything in their power, and also to make use of the possibilities of the United Nations, in order to deliver present and future generations from the scourge of war.

The Soviet Union and France proclaim their desire actively to increase the effectiveness of the United Nations as an instrument of international peace and security on the basis of strict observance of its Charter, of ensuring its universality and of the active cooperation of the two sides in UN activities for the benefit of economic and social development and the defence of human rights and fundamental liberties.

While considering various aspects of relations between the USSR and France, the Soviet leaders and President Pompidou stressed the great significance which the governments of both countries attach to the strengthening of their mutual relations.

They recalled the great significance of the visit paid to the Soviet Union by General de Gaulle in 1966 and the joint decision taken on that occasion to develop cooperation and concord between the Soviet Union and France. They have noted the effectiveness of the decision taken, as the USSR and France have, since 1966, expanded contacts between the leaders of both countries and political consultations, have considerably developed exchanges and stepped up mutual cooperation in the economic, technological and scientific fields, by setting up, with these aims in view, mixed permanent bodies, the usefulness of which has been fully confirmed in practice, have exchanged visits of military representatives, and have developed cultural links on a wide scale.

Recalling the fact that by giving their cooperation an organisational framework the governments of the two countries have shown their intention of steadily improving their relations, the Soviet leaders and President Pompidou have proclaimed their determination to continue in the future the policy of *rapprochement* which accords with the aspirations of the Soviet and French peoples, and with the permanent interests of both countries.

Being fully resolved to strengthen confidence between the two countries and combine their efforts for peace and international security, the Soviet leaders and President Pompidou have pointed out that they attach great importance to consultations between the two governments on basic international issues. Expressing satisfaction with the results which have already been achieved in recent years in accordance with the Soviet–French Declaration of June 30, 1966, and with other Soviet–French documents signed subsequently, they have decided to make these consultations even more consistent and comprehensive.

Bilateral Soviet–French relations in the field of trade and economic cooperation were examined in the light of the results achieved and of the possibilities opening up in the future. The two sides have noted with satisfaction that a steady development, meeting the vital interests and aspirations of both countries, is characteristic of these relations.

The exchange of views has made it possible to sum up the results already achieved. Following the signing of the long-term trade agreement of October 30, 1964 and the signing of the Soviet–French Declaration of June 30, 1966 the goods turnover between the USSR and France increased two and a half times over in the period from 1965 to 1969. Contracts between the Soviet and French Ministries of Foreign Trade, and also between businessmen and experts, have increased, which has made it possible for responsible personalities of both countries in the economic sphere to get to know each other better and to carry out cooperation in a more effective way. Particularly noticeable results have been achieved in many industries, such as, for example, the motor, chemical, oil and gas industries, the manufacture of machine tools, and shipbuilding. The two sides have also noted with satisfaction the further progress in cooperation in the field of colour television on the basis of the joint SECAM system.

The exchange of views has also made it possible to reaffirm the aims mapped out in the new long-term trade agreement of May 26, 1969 for the period from 1970 to 1974, which expresses the desire of the two governments to double the goods turnover between the USSR and France in this period. The two sides have stressed the need to develop still further the efforts already made, aimed at stimulating an interest in larger reciprocal deliveries, and notably, at increasing France's imports of Soviet commodities, especially machinery, equipment and other industrial products, as well as raw materials.

The two sides have decided to seek to conclude long-term contracts relating to large-scale deliveries, particularly in connection with the development of new mineral deposits; some of these contracts could provide a basis for preferential cooperation between the two countries.

The signing of agreements and also contracts on the implementation of a number of major industrial projects in cooperation between the USSR and France has been noted with satisfaction and the hope has been expressed that talks on new projects of this kind and, in particular, on the participation of Soviet organisations in the construction of a metallurgical complex in France, will reach a favourable conclusion.

The two sides have agreed to promote the implementation of other major industrial projects, the scale of which will call, in some cases, for cooperation among a number of European countries, in particular, in the field of the motor industry, in which Soviet–French cooperation within the framework of the programme for increasing the output of lorries in the USSR, including the construction of a new works, should be further developed in the future on a mutually beneficial basis. The two sides have also agreed to contribute towards the conclusion of long-term contracts on reciprocal deliveries of goods by firms and associations of the two countries.

The desire for cooperation displayed by both sides, as well as the Soviet–French mixed standing commission set up in 1966 for the further development and organisation of these joint efforts have contributed to a considerable extent to the achievement of positive results. Both sides have expressed satisfaction with this successful experience acquired in the economic, technological and scientific fields. The fifth session of the Soviet–French mixed standing commission held in Paris from September 3 to 11 this year, provided fresh proof of the mutual desire to develop trade, economic, scientific and technical cooperation and was marked by new successes in these fields.

Conscious of the fact that the well-being of the population in the world today, an improvement in the conditions for its existence and the development of society and mankind in general cannot be ensured without continuously-developing and ever more complicated scientific and technical knowledge, the two sides have stressed the vital significance of international cooperation in the field of science and technology, on a multilateral as well as a bilateral basis.

Indeed, many problems which call for an urgent solution, such as, for example, the protection of the environment, go beyond the confines of individual states and, because of their large scale, call for coordinated action based on the joint use of technology and knowledge, and also for a division of labour among research workers and scientific groups.

In this connection the machinery established in accordance with the decisions of June 30, 1966, the usefulness of which has already been stressed above, has made it possible to start and carry out bilateral cooperation in the field of science and technology, which is of great interest and which is continuing and will be developed, both between responsible institutions, and in particular, through mixed bodies set up under this agreement, and also between scientific organisations and scientists within the framework of the programmes adopted by the two governments and special agreements endorsed by them. Exchanges covering an ever-increasing number of fields of knowledge have already made it possible to achieve considerable successes in some fields. A good example of this is the cooperation in high energy physics, which has resulted in the implementation at the present time of a broad programme of work with the accelerator at Serpukhov, with use being made of a French bubble chamber.

Noting the scope of the cooperation started in this way, both sides have reaffirm their mutual desire to continue the work already undertaken, constantly directing it along the lines of development that are most useful, making it increasingly effecti and encouraging exchanges in the major fields of fundamental and applied research. In this connection the two sides have noted with satisfaction the conclusions reache at the session of the Soviet–French mixed commission recently held in Paris. They have expressed their readiness to give every support to the programmes mapped out by the commission and also to programmes which provide for the practical impleme tation of international scientific and technical cooperation on a multilateral basis.

The two sides have also expressed their great readiness to develop cultural relatio between the Soviet Union and France. Noting with satisfaction the results already achieved in this field, the two sides have agreed to look for opportunities to deepen cooperation in the fields of education, art, radio, television, the cinema, sports and other forms of exchange, and to pay particular attention to the study of Russian in France and of French in the Soviet Union.

The two sides have agreed to open in the near future a consulate general of the USSR in Marseilles and a consulate general of France in Leningrad.

President Georges Pompidou gave a reminder of the invitation to L. I. Brezhnev, A. N. Kosygin and N. V. Podgorny to pay an official visit to France. It has been agreed that the Soviet visit to France will take place in 1971.

The warmth of the hospitality accorded to President Pompidou in the Soviet Union and the cordial and thorough nature of the negotiations and talks constitute fresh proof of the traditional friendship between the Soviet and French peoples and the mutual desire of their governments to direct their efforts towards the consistent development of relations between the two countries. Thus, the visit of the President of the French Republic to the USSR marks a new and important stage on the road already charted by the two governments and along which they are firmly resolved to advance in the future, with the intention of consolidating in a proper way the high level of friendly relations between the Soviet Union and France In confirming this common determination, the two sides have stated that the develo ment of concord and cooperation between the USSR and France corresponds to the interests of all European states and is a useful contribution towards strengthenin peace throughout the world.

75. Principles of Cooperation between France and the Soviet Union, adopted by M. Pompidou and Mr Brezhnev, Paris, 30 October 1971[1]

Mr Georges Pompidou, President of the French Republic, and Mr L. I. Brezhnev,

1 WEU, *Political Year in Europe, 1971*, pp. 271–6.

General Secretary of the Central Committee of the Communist Party of the Soviet Union, Member of the Presidium of the Supreme Soviet of the USSR,

Inspired by the long tradition of friendship between the two countries,

Resolved to give a new impulse to the fruitful cooperation which has become established between France and the Soviet Union since the visit to the USSR by General de Gaulle in 1966,

Prompted by the desire to strengthen the contribution of the two countries to the cause of peace in Europe and in the world and to assist the development of cooperation between all States.

Have on the occasion of the visit to France by Mr L. I. Brezhnev, adopted the following principles on which rests political cooperation between the two countries:

1. Cooperation between France and the USSR corresponds to the common aspirations and the mutual interest of the two peoples and must be based on reciprocal benefits and obligations on the part of the two countries.

2. This cooperation is not directed against the interests of any people and in no way affects the commitments made by the two countries with regard to other States.

3. The policy of entente and cooperation between France and the USSR will be continued. It is destined to become a constant in their relations and a permanent factor in international life.

4. Political cooperation between the two countries will continue to be based on respect for the principles and stipulations of the Charter of the United Nations. Its objective is to contribute to a return to peace in the zones of conflict, to the reduction of international tension, to the settlement of differences by peaceful means as well as to economic development and to the betterment of the standard of living in the world.

5. With a view to actively cooperating on the strengthening of security in Europe and in the world and on the development of peaceful cooperation of States, independent of their social systems, political consultations between the two governments will be expanded both through the usual diplomatic channels and through special meetings of their representatives, based on the French–Soviet protocol of 13 October 1970, which marks an important step in the organisation of this cooperation. Such consultations should especially enable the two countries to seek possibilities for concerted action, including concerted action within international organisations or conferences in cases where, in the opinion of the two parties, the cause of peace could benefit.

6. Duly taking into account the rights and prerogatives of the other powers concerned, this political cooperation will be particularly applicable in the exercise of the responsibilities that the two countries assume in the world as permanent members of the Security Council of the United Nations, and in Europe following the second world war.

In the event that situations should emerge creating, in the opinion of the two parties, a threat to peace, a violation of peace, or provoking international tension, France and the Soviet Union will act in compliance with the protocol of 13 October, 1970.

7. Great importance is attached to close cooperation between France and the USSR in Europe in concert with the States involved in the maintenance of peace and the pursuit of detente, in the improvement of security as well as in strengthening peaceful relations and cooperation among all the European States in the rigorous respect of the following principles:

— inviolability of present frontiers,

— non-interference in internal affairs,

— equality,

— independence,

— non-recourse to force or threat.

8. France and the USSR are convinced that the cooperation of all European peoples regarding the development of their industrial potential, the exchange of experiments and knowledge and the protection of the environment will enable Europe to increase the rate of economic, scientific and technical progress.

9. France and the USSR will strive, in the regions where peace is disturbed, to obtain as soon as possible a political settlement in the interest of overall peace.

10. The two parties will contribute as far as possible to solving the problems of general and complete disarmament and above all of nuclear disarmament, to overcoming the division of the world in blocs and to increasing the role of the United Nations in accordance with the provisions of its Charter.

11. France and the USSR will build their bilateral relations in all areas in such a way that they may serve as a good example of cooperation as equals between States with different social systems.

12. The development of economic and commercial exchanges on the basis of the agreements in force which are supplemented by the agreement of 27 October 1971,[1] cooperation for utilising natural resources and exchange of experiments in the industrial and technical area are of essential interest in order to tighten the bonds which exist between the two countries.

13. Everything which can contribute to mutual enrichment in the intellectual area and to the development of means to constantly improve the knowledge of the French and Soviet peoples of their respective cultures and activities will be encouraged taking into account their age-old relations in this area, their traditions and their friendship. The continued enlargement of university, scientific and artistic exchanges of circulation of information, of contacts between the organisations of the two countries and especially of youth organisations will help attain these goals. They will also be applied to contacts between men, including meetings between young people in a collective or individual, official or private capacity. The initiatives taken in this direction will receive the support of the competent authorities.

76. Joint communiqué issued following M. Pompidou's visit to the People's Republic of China, Peking, 14 September 1973[2]

At the invitation of Mr Tung Pi-wu, Acting Chairman of the People's Republic of

1 Not published here.

2 *SWB*, FE/4401, 18 September 1973, A1/1−2.

China, and Mr Chou En-lai, Premier of the State Council, President of the Republic of France Georges Pompidou paid an official visit to the People's Republic of China from 11th to 17th September 1973. President Pompidou was accompanied by Minister of Foreign Affairs Michel Jobert and other personalities.

The President of the Republic of France and the personalities who accompanied him visited Peking, Tatung, Hangchow and Shanghai; they thus made contacts with the Chinese people and obtained first-hand knowledge of the economic, social and cultural development of China. Wherever they went, they received a warm welcome and friendly hospitality from the Chinese Government and people.

Chairman Mao Tsetung met the President of the Republic of France. The two leaders had a long friendly conversation.

The President of the Republic of France held talks with the Premier of the State Council of the People's Republic of China. They exchanged views in a friendly and deep-going way on principal international problems and Sino-French relations.

This visit was the first official visit of a French Head of State to China. As such, it marks a new and important stage in the relations between the two countries.

The Premier of the State Council of the People's Republic of China and the President of the Republic of France note with satisfaction that the relations established in 1964 on the initiative of Chairman Mao Tsetung and General de Gaulle have undergone a continuous favourable development. They affirm their conviction that this development is in the mutual interest of the two countries and that it constitutes a positive contribution to the cause of peace and the improvement of international relations.

The talks have confirmed that the Governments of the two countries are moved by a common desire to reinforce the friendship between the two peoples and develop the relations between the two countries. Although the People's Republic of China and France have different social systems, their relations are based on a good foundation, notably because of their common adherence to the following principles: equality of all countries, big or small and irrespective of their social systems, and mutual respect for sovereignty and territorial integrity. The affairs of a country and its people should be settled by themselves free from foreign interference and in conformity with the principle of the independence of nations. For the improvement of the international situation, the two sides declare themselves against all hegemony.

Reviewing principal international questions, the two sides note that they are in extensive accord on a number of problems.

The two sides examined the situation in Asia, especially in Indochina. They express their satisfaction at the Agreement on ending the War and Restoring Peace in Vietnam, signed in Paris on 27th January 1973[1] and also at the Agreement on Restoring Peace and Realizing National Concord in Laos of 21st February 1973 and the Protocol to this Agreement, signed on 14th September 1973.[2] They hold that all the provisions of the agreements should be implemented scrupulously. They are of the opinion that the Cambodian question should be settled by the Cambodian people themselves

1 Document No. 37.
2 See footnote 1, p. 101, above.

free from foreign interference. The Chinese side reaffirms that the Royal Government of National Union of Cambodia under the leadership of Samdech Norodom Sihanouk, Head of State of Cambodia, is the sole legal Government of Cambodia, China firmly supports the five-point declaration of Samdech Norodom Sihanouk. The two sides express their support for the Joint Statement of North and South Korea issued on 4th July 1972.[1]

The two sides examined the situation in Europe. China supports the efforts made by the European peoples to safeguard the independence, sovereignty and security of their respective countries and, on this basis, to unite themselves for the preservati of their common security. With loyalty to her alliances, France pursues a policy aimed at detente, understanding and cooperation among all the peoples of the continents as well as the building of a true European union among the nine member countries of the EEC.

The two sides proceeded in addition to an extensive exchange of views on variou problems relating to the Third World, disarmament and international trade, and considered that such an exchange of views was in their mutual interest.

The various aspects of economic relations between the two countries were also examined. The two sides are gratified with the progress achieved in the field of economic exchanges and industrial and technical contacts, thanks particularly to a number of visits paid by delegations and to exhibitions and technical displays organ in the two countries. They are equally gratified with the favourable prospects which have appeared in this regard. They have also agreed to study further the practical possibilities of developing economic relations and the problem of increasing the exchanges in the field of technology as well as in that of industry, especially in the developed sectors of petro-chemistry, aeronautics and mechanical and electrical industries.

The two sides have further decided to conclude a maritime agreement and to strengthen their cooperation in the field of air transport.

The two sides express satisfaction with the progress of contacts between their two countries in the fields of culture, language teaching, science, public health and sports and are gratified with the favourable prospects promising a new development of these contacts.

The leaders of the two countries have agreed to remain in personal contact.

The two sides state with satisfaction that the official visit of the President of the Republic of France to the People's Republic of China has contributed happily to th strengthening of the ties between the two countries and the friendship between the two peoples.

77. Joint declaration on the Further Development of Friendship and Cooperation, issued by the Governments of France and the Soviet Union, Moscow, 17 October 1975[2]

The Soviet Union and France,

1 Document No. 45.
2 *Soviet News*, 28 October 1975.

Convinced that the policy of detente and cooperation is the only rational basis for relations between states with different social systems and facilitates the strengthening of peace,

Basing themselves on the historically developed traditions of friendship between the peoples of the two countries, which was strikingly manifested in the joint struggle for freedom and independence during the years of the Second World War,

Stressing the fundamental role played by the Soviet–French Declaration of 1966, the Protocol on Political Consultations of 1970 and the Principles of Cooperation between the USSR and France of 1971 in bringing the countries closer together and activating their joint efforts in the strengthening of European and world security,

Positively assessing the results achieved by Soviet–French cooperation in the last decade,

Expressing satisfaction at the improvement in relations between European states,

Welcoming the results of the Conference on Security and Cooperation in Europe which has opened a new stage in detente on the European continent, and the whole significance of the Final Act signed by the leaders of the states taking part at Helsinki,[1]

Being supporters of the consistent application in practice, as envisaged in the Final Act, of all its principles and points of agreement,

Declare the following:

The Soviet Union and France are fully resolved to follow the course of accord and cooperation steadfastly and to do all in their power to ensure the establishment of detente in international relations, and to give it a concrete material content, particularly by strengthening their joint contribution to the solution of fundamental international issues and to averting crisis situations. They favour the broadening of the dialogue and consultations between states towards this end.

The Sides consider that the atmosphere of relaxation will help to strengthen security in Europe and throughout the world and will give every state confidence in its peaceful independent development.

1

The USSR and France regard the European Conference as an event of enormous importance. They note that the provisions of the conference's Final Act create new opportunities for strengthening security in Europe and for developing cooperation between the participating states.

They declare their resolve to observe strictly and implement in every sphere of their relationships the principles of relations between states in the form proclaimed by the conference. They believe that strict observance of these principles by all the participating states should lead to stronger peace in Europe.

They also express their intention to carry out in full all the provisions of the Final Act relating to security in Europe, cooperation in the economic sphere (commercial and industrial cooperation) in science and technology, environmental protection,

1 Document No. 107.

and in humanitarian spheres (contact between people, information, cooperation and exchange in the areas of culture and education).

The Soviet Union and France see the results of the European Conference as a long-term action-programme covering broad fields of relationships between states and answering the interests of the peoples, and confirm their intention to put the provisions of the Final Act into concrete effect. They express their willingness to cooperate, among other means, by way of bilateral agreements and understandings, in the implementation of the Conference decisions.

The Sides once again stress the great importance for the favourable development of the situation in Europe of the quadripartite agreement of September 3, 1971.

2

The Sides note with satisfaction that in the past few years there have been notable advances towards a healthier international climate.

The Soviet Union and France declare their resolve to redouble their efforts to deepen detente and extend it to international relations as a whole.

Great attention was paid to the situation in the Middle East, which continues to be a cause for serious concern to the Soviet Union and France. The Sides are convinced that a just and lasting peace in that area can be ensured only if Israeli troops are withdrawn from all Arab territories occupied in 1967, if the legitimate rights of the Palestinian people are safeguarded, including their right to a national home, and if firm guarantees are given in respect to the rights of all states and peoples of that area to independent existence and development with secure and recognised borders.

The Soviet Union and France will continue to maintain constant contact on matters concerning a Middle East settlement and to hold appropriate consultations.

The Soviet Union and France expressed satisfaction over the restoration of peace in Indochina. They pointed out the need to respect the desire of the peoples of Indochina for free, independent development, without any foreign interference what soever.

The Sides declared themselves in favour of the admission of the Democratic Republic of Vietnam and the Republic of South Vietnam to membership of the United Nations.

The Sides note the coincidence of their views on the need to settle the Cyprus problem on the basis of complete respect for the independence, sovereignty and territorial integrity of the Republic of Cyprus. Such a just and lasting settlement must be found through negotiations. They stand for the early withdrawal from the Republic of Cyprus of all foreign troops and the implementation of the UN resolutio on Cyprus in their entirety.

The Sides emphasised that the efforts to lessen military confrontation and facilita disarmament, which would lead to the spread of detente to new spheres, were of considerable interest. They noted that measures taken in this direction must not infringe upon the security and independence of states.

The Sides stress the resolve of the Soviet Union and France to facilitate the mplementation of general and complete disarmament, including nuclear disarmament, nder strict and effective international control.

They are in favour of the convocation of a world disarmament conference with ll nuclear powers taking part in the preparations and work of such a conference, hich should make a substantial contribution to the advance to general and complete isarmament and the removal of the burden of armaments from mankind.

There was an exchange of views on the proposal to ban the development and pro- uction of new types of weapons of mass destruction and new systems of such eapons, which was put forward by the Soviet Union for discussion at the 30th ession of the UN General Assembly. The French side stated that it was continuing o examine this proposal with interest.

The Soviet Union and France intend to extend exchanges of views and con- ultations on these questions.

The USSR and France are convinced of the need to prevent the dissemination of uclear weapons and are fully resolved to bear the responsibility which falls on them s nuclear powers in this connection. Using appropriate means they will display oncern to ensure that the nuclear material and equipment which they supply to on-nuclear states are used exclusively for peaceful purposes, taking the view that t is on these conditions that the expectations of those for whom access to nuclear echnology is a key factor of economic development must be satisfied.

True to the aims and principles of the Charter of the United Nations, to which hey are founder-members, the USSR and France emphasise the importance of the ole vested in the UN in connection with the maintenance of peace and international ecurity, and also with the development of agreement and cooperation between tates.

They also declare their adherence to the UN Charter and consider that the harter's provisions, based as they are on generally accepted principles, continue o accord with the aspirations of the international community. They are against ttempts to revise the UN Charter and believe that a heightening of the prestige and ffectiveness of this organisation in the interests of all member-countries should be ttained by making fuller use of the great opportunities inherent in its Charter.

The Sides agreed to recognise the need to restructure international economic elations taking into account the developing countries' right to join in the world's conomic progress, to enjoy its fruits on a more equitable basis and also to influence he choice of the ways of achieving such progress. They stressed that this would be reatly facilitated by a constructive dialogue and the broad development of inter- ational economic cooperation on an equal basis.

he Soviet Union and France pointed out with satisfaction that Soviet–French co- peration, which above all takes in fundamental problems of international security, as in recent years become an integral part of international political life and has made constructive contribution to improving the situation in Europe and other parts of he world.

The Sides consider that the practice of Soviet–French political consultations has fully justified itself. They have decided to develop these consultations at every level, striving to impart a more systematic and deeper character to them, and paying particular attention to the fact that such consultations facilitate the task of carrying out concerted measures to strengthen international security.

Noting in this connection the special significance of summit meetings, which have had a decisive effect in the progress of Soviet–French relations, the Sides decided that further meetings of the top political leaders of the Soviet Union and France will be held in the future on a regular basis.

The Soviet Union and France will steadfastly continue their efforts to enrich and raise the level of their relations.

Having examined the conditions of and prospects for bilateral contacts in trade-and-economic and scientific-and-technical spheres, the Sides note with satisfaction that in recent times, including the period since the meeting in Rambouillet in December, 1974, such contacts continued to develop in a favourable direction.

They once again referred to the significance they attach to the widening and deepening of economic and industrial cooperation, which is an essential principle of Soviet–French relations.

The Sides note the advantages to progress of the exchanges of economic information carried out within the framework of existing forms of Soviet–French cooperation.

They note with satisfaction the significant growth in trade this year. Such a rate of growth must mean that it is possible to achieve the target planned for the period 1975–9 (to double or, if possible, treble the 1975 trade figure).

They have also decided to make efforts to seek means of ensuring a more balanced trade exchange. In this connection the French side has announced its readiness to increase purchases of traditional raw materials and Soviet industrial goods in 1976.

The Sides attach special significance to the carrying out of long-term, large-scale projects, including those envisaged on a reciprocal basis in the programme for deepening cooperation in the economic and industrial spheres over a 10-year period and others in addition to that. They consider that the completion of negotiations in progress between interested organisations and enterprises of both countries on the construction of large industrial complexes, in particular linked with the product of alumina and aluminium, oil and gas, and the chemical and petrochemical industri and the supply of equipment for engineering, telecommunications, electronics and computer techniques and also for the electronics, light and food industries, will represent a substantial contribution to the development of the cooperation. In this connection they have expressed satisfaction with the two major contracts recently concluded for deliveries of equipment for the third section of the Orienburg gas industry complex, and also at the conclusion during the visit of contracts for the supply of complete sets of equipment for plants producing fatty alcohols and radio-electronic components, and for the supply of equipment for the construction of an ammonia pipeline, and an agreement on the building of a hotel complex in Moscow

The Sides are fully resolved to continue work to develop mutually advantageous orms of cooperation in the extraction of minerals, in particular oil and gas; they will facilitate the further continuation of talks between the relevant organisations and enterprises of both countries on the prospecting and development of oil and gas deposits.

The Sides will aim at a further broadening and deepening of scientific and technical cooperation, drawing upon the positive experience accumulated and motivated by the desire to make their contacts in this important area of bilateral relations even more effective and well balanced. They have agreed to continue their efforts to ensure that scientific and technical cooperation is increasingly linked with industrial and economic cooperation in all fields where this is possible. Particular attention will be paid to power-engineering problems, the use of atomic energy for peaceful purposes, space research, the use of computer techniques, oceanology, environmental protection, medicine, building, town planning, architecture, scientific instrument-making, and the technology of coal extraction, and also a number of important aspects of fundamental research.

The Sides declared their resolve to ensure a significant increase, quantitatively and qualitatively, in exchange and cooperation between the two countries in the fields of art, education, culture and science.

They express their readiness to examine the question of concluding a cultural agreement serving these purposes.

The Sides state that they are prepared to look at the question of increasing meetings between young people, including student youth.

The Sides will make additional efforts to ensure an increase in the teaching of the Russian language in France and the French language in the USSR, both in secondary and higher educational institutions, and also within the framework of adult education.

The Sides will seek opportunities for creating working and living conditions, corresponding in the USSR and France, that will make for the most effective contribution by Soviet and French specialists in economic, scientific, technical and cultural cooperation.

The Sides noted the usefulness of the contacts so far made in the military sphere and expressed themselves in favour of continuing such exchanges, which strengthen the feelings of mutual respect for the armed forces of both countries.

The Sides express their satisfaction at the signing of the Agreement on Cooperation in Energy, the Agreement on Cooperation in Civil Aviation and the Aircraft Industry, and also the Agreement on Cooperation in Tourism. In their view, these important agreements open up new prospects for the development of Soviet–French relations in appropriate spheres in the spirit of the decisions of the Conference on European Security and Cooperation.

The Sides attach great significance to the development of feelings of friendship between the peoples of the Soviet Union and France. They consider that the further strengthening of those feelings will make for the creation of a favourable atmosphere for carrying out those great tasks which the USSR and France jointly set themselves in the strengthening of bilateral relations and the reinforcement of peace and security in Europe and throughout the world. The friendship between the Soviet and French peoples makes it possible to look with confidence to the future of cooperati between the two countries.

Both Sides believe that the visit of Valery Giscard D'Estaing to the USSR and the Soviet—French negotiations held during this visit were fruitful. They expressed the conviction that the results of the visit will serve further to promote relations between the USSR and France and will contribute to an improvement of the situation in Europe and on the international scene as a whole.

EDITOR'S NOTE: FRENCH INITIATIVES IN EASTERN EUROPE

In addition to the development of Franco-Soviet relations, the following Agreement and Joint Statements and Declarations were made between France and the countrie of Eastern Europe:

Joint Statement by the Governments of France and Romania, Paris, 22 June 197 (*Romania, Documents, Articles and Information*, Agerpress, Bucharest, Supplement No. 21, 22 June 1970).

Joint Declaration issued by the Governments of France and Poland, Warsaw, 27 November 1970 (*SWB* EE/3548, 1 December 1970, A1/3—4).

Declaration on Friendship and Cooperation issued by the Governments of France and Poland, Paris, 6 October 1972 (*Information Bulletin, Documents of the Communist and Workers' Parties, Articles and Speeches*, Peace and Socialism International Publishers, Prague, Nos. 18—19, 1972).

Charter of the Principles of Friendly Cooperation between the French Republic and the Polish People's Republic, Warsaw, 20 June 1975 (French Embassy release, London).

B. GREAT BRITAIN

78. Communiqué issued following the visit by Mr Gromyko to Great Britain, London, 29 October 1970[1]

The Minister of Foreign Affairs of the USSR, Mr A. A. Gromyko, made an official visit to the United Kingdom at the invitation of the British Government from 26 to 29 October, 1970. During the visit, Mr Gromyko had meetings and talks with the Prime Minister, Mr Heath, and the Foreign and Commonwealth Secretary, Sir Alec Douglas-Home, and the Minister of Trade, Mr M. Noble. In the course of the talks, a useful and frank exchange of views took place on certain important international problems and questions of Anglo—Soviet relations.

1 London Press Service.

The USSR Ambassador in London, Mr M. N. Smirnovsky, and the British Ambassador in Moscow, Sir D. Wilson, and other senior officials on both sides participated in the talks.

Agreement was reached to intensify contacts and to hold consultations on matters of common interest with a view to achieving mutual understanding.

In their review of international affairs, the Ministers started from the premise of the necessity of cooperation among all states, whatever their social systems, for the purpose of maintaining and strengthening peace and international security.

In an exchange of views on the limitation of the arms race and on disarmament, they agreed to urge all states to accede to the treaty on the non-proliferation of nuclear weapons and expressed the hope that the 25th session of the United Nations General Assembly would approve the draft of the 'Treaty to ban the placing of nuclear and other mass destruction weapons on the sea-bed and ocean floor and in the sub-soil thereof', after which this treaty should be open for signature.

The Secretary of State for Foreign and Commonwealth Affairs welcomed the Strategic Arms Limitation Talks between the Soviet Union and the United States of America, and expressed the hope of the British Government that these talks would result in an agreement which would contribute to further progress in a field of disarmament crucially important for the cause of peace.

It was agreed that both governments would persevere in their efforts to achieve early progress in the elaboration of measures for the prohibition and destruction of chemical and bacteriological (biological) means of warfare.

The importance was stressed of achieving real improvements concerning the main issues of European security.

It was agreed that the treaty recently signed between the Soviet Union and the Federal Republic of Germany[1] constituted a significant contribution to the relaxation of tension in Europe. In further discussion of the situation in Europe, the hope was expressed that before long a similar assessment could be made of the outcome of the quadripartite talks currently in progress, in which both countries are actively participating, together with the United States and France.

There was an exchange of views on the proposal for an all-European conference in which all the European states as well as the United States and Canada could participate. It was recognised that such a conference, properly prepared, which would discuss matters of common interest, and the possible establishment of permanent machinery for further consideration of these matters, could contribute to the favourable development of the situation in Europe. Consultation with a view to progress on these questions would continue.

Particular attention was devoted to the situation in the Middle East. Concern was expressed at the continuing tension in the area and the importance was emphasised of achieving a peaceful political settlement in accordance with Security Council Resolution 242/22 November 1967. There was agreement on the urgent need for progress towards such a settlement and for the resumption of Ambassador Jarring's mission at the earliest possible date: and also for the exertion of utmost efforts to

1 Document No. 16.

search for possibilities through the agreement of the parties directly concerned to extend the observance of the cease-fire for a period to be determined. The two governments would continue to work for agreement in the New York Consultations of the representatives of the Four Powers.

In a discussion of South East Asia, the views of both governments were expressed

In discussion of bilateral relations, it was noted that in recent years the Soviet Union and the United Kingdom had concluded intergovernmental treaties and agreements which were contributing to the growth of mutually advantageous ties, contac and exchanges between the two countries in trade and in the fields of economic, scientific, technological and cultural cooperation. The importance of expanding economic cooperation, as part of the general development of bilateral relations was recognised. Importance was also attached to the further development of close Anglo—Soviet cooperation in all these spheres.

It was agreed that both governments would work, in all possible ways, to develop relations between the United Kingdom and the USSR, in the confidence that this would be to the benefit of the peoples of both countries and that it would be a valuable contribution to the cause of peace.

The Minister of Foreign Affairs of the USSR, Mr A. A. Gromyko, on behalf of the Soviet Government, extended an invitation to the Prime Minister, Mr Edward Heath, to make an official visit to the Soviet Union. This invitation was accepted with pleasure. The date for the visit will be arranged later.

The Minister of Foreign Affairs of the USSR, Mr A. A. Gromyko, also invited the Secretary of State for Foreign and Commonwealth Affairs of the United Kingdo Sir Alec Douglas-Home, to make an official visit to the Soviet Union. The invitation was accepted with pleasure. The date for the visit will be arranged later.

79. Communiqué issued by Great Britain and the People's Republic of China, Peking, 13 March 1972[1]

Both confirming the principles of mutual respect for sovereignty and territorial integrity, non-interference in each other's internal affairs and equality and mutual benefit, the Government of the People's Republic of China and the Government of the United Kingdom have decided to raise the level of their respective Diplomati Representatives in each other's capitals from Chargés d'Affaires to Ambassadors as from 13 March 1972.

The Government of the United Kingdom, acknowledging the position of the Chinese Government that Taiwan is a province of the People's Republic of China, have decided to remove their official representation in Taiwan on 13 March 1972.

The Government of the United Kingdom recognise the Government of the People's Republic of China as the sole legal Government of China.

The Government of the People's Republic of China appreciates the above stand of the Government of the United Kingdom.

1 *Survey of Current Affairs* (London Central Office of Information), 2, 4 April 1972, p. 146

80. Protocol on Consultations issued by Great Britain and the Soviet Union, Moscow, 17 February 1975[1]

The Union of Soviet Socialist Republics and the United Kingdom of Great Britain and Northern Ireland, desiring to strengthen mutual confidence and understanding between their two countries and being convinced that the consolidation of peaceful and cooperative relations between the Soviet Union and the United Kingdom meets the interests of the peoples of both countries,

Conscious of the value of cooperation between their two countries and of consultations between them in the interests of maintaining international peace and security in accordance with the Charter of the United Nations, and conscious of the special responsibilities of the Soviet Union and the United Kingdom as permanent members of the United Nations Security Council,

Believing that the development of stable friendly relations between them will help to strengthen relations of peaceful coexistence, which means long-term, fruitful and mutually beneficial cooperation between states, irrespective of their political, economic and social systems, on the basis of full equality and mutual respect,

Believing that the development of such relations between them will become a permanent factor in consolidating peace and security in Europe and in the whole world,

Confirming the responsibility which both states bear in Europe as a result of the Second World War,

Determined to contribute to making the process of international detente deeper and irreversible and believing that it is in the interests of both sides to raise to a higher level their cooperation in the political, trade and economic, scientific, technological and cultural fields,

Have reached the following understanding:

1. The Soviet Union and the United Kingdom will enlarge and deepen political consultations on important international problems of mutual interest and on questions of bilateral relations.

2. The consultations will embrace:

International questions causing tension in various parts of the world;

Measures to strengthen peace and security in Europe and to develop cooperation among the countries of the European continent;

Problems of arms limitation and disarmament, including measures for the complete implementation of the Treaty on the Non-Proliferation of Nuclear Weapons;

Problems of mutual interest which are the subject of discussion in international forums, including the United Nations;

Questions of a political, economic and cultural nature, environmental questions and other subjects, concerning relations between the two countries;

Any other subjects, in respect of which the sides may find it useful to have an exchange of views.

1 *Soviet News*, 25 February 1975.

3. In the event of a situation arising which, in the opinion of the two sides, endangers peace, involves a breach of the peace or causes international tension, the governments of the Union of Soviet Socialist Republics and of the United Kingdom will make contact without delay in order to exchange views on what might be done to improve the situation.

4. The provisions set forth in Paragraphs 1, 2 and 3 above do not affect obligation previously assumed by the sides under international agreements to which they are party, and are not directed against any third state.

5. The conduct of such consultations between the Soviet Union and the United Kingdom is designed not only to promote the welfare of their peoples and to develo relations between them, but also to contribute to better relations between all countries.

6. The consultations will be carried out on a basis of reciprocity at all appropriate levels and will have a regular character.

Either side is free to recommend the holding of such consultations, including the time and level at which they should be held. The Ministers of Foreign Affairs or thei representatives will meet whenever the need arises and in principle at least once a year.

81. Declaration on the Non-proliferation of Nuclear Weapons, issued by Great Britain and the Soviet Union, Moscow, 17 February 1975[1]

The Union of Soviet Socialist Republics and the United Kingdom of Great Britain and Northern Ireland will do all in their power to strengthen international peace and security, to avert the danger of war, including nuclear war, to end the arms race and to attain general and complete disarmament under strict and effective international control. Both sides emphasise the importance and necessity of serious and urgent efforts directed at preventing the spread of nuclear weapons. They are convinced that this is in the interests of all mankind.

In this connection, the Soviet Union and the United Kingdom reaffirm the great importance of the Treaty on the Non-Proliferation of Nuclear Weapons. The two sides are resolutely in favour of the strict observance of the treaty to which the majority of states are already parties. They are also in favour of the widest possible adherence to the treaty.

The two sides, considering that the Non-Proliferation Treaty has created a favour able framework for broadening international cooperation in the peaceful uses of atomic energy, will continue to work together for such cooperation in accordance with the treaty. They are convinced that further measures could be undertaken to provide nuclear materials, equipment and information for peaceful uses in non-nucle weapon states. However, such measures should be under effective safeguards by the International Atomic Energy Agency and should not in any way contribute to the

1 *Soviet News*, 25 February 1975.

spread of nuclear weapons. It is their hope that all suppliers of nuclear material and equipment will observe the safeguards applied by the IAEA to meet Article III of the Non-Proliferation Treaty.

The two sides, conscious of the obligation to ensure that potential benefits from any peaceful applications of nuclear explosions will be made available through appropriate international procedures, will continue to cooperate within the framework of the IAEA in this field.

The Soviet Union and the United Kingdom welcome the progress achieved in recent years in limiting strategic arms and nuclear weapon tests. The two sides aim at the discontinuance of all test explosions of nuclear weapons for all time. In the meantime, till the conclusion of an appropriate international agreement for this purpose, they will work for agreements limiting the number of underground nuclear weapon tests to a minimum.

The two sides share a common concern that nuclear materials should be carefully protected at all times and that adequate safety measures should be applied by all countries to radioactive waste.

The two sides attach real importance to the conference which is to meet in Geneva in May 1975 in order to review the operation of the Non-Proliferation Treaty. They believe that this review should strengthen the effective implementation of the treaty, and it will be their joint purpose to make a success of the conference.

The Soviet Union and the United Kingdom declare their common intention to work out means of giving effect to the objectives expressed above. They will continue to strive with a sense of urgency to further the cause of disarmament at appropriate international forums, including the United Nations and the conference of the Committee on Disarmament.

32. Joint statement issued by Mr Wilson and Mr Brezhnev, Moscow, 17 February 1975[1]

At the invitation of the Soviet Government, the Prime Minister of the United Kingdom of Great Britain and Northern Ireland, the Right Honourable Harold Wilson, MP, accompanied by the Secretary of State for Foreign and Commonwealth Affairs, the Right Honourable James Callaghan, MP, paid an official visit to the Soviet Union from 13 to 17 February 1975.

During their stay in the Soviet Union the Right Honourable Harold Wilson and his party, in addition to Moscow, also visited Leningrad.

The Prime Minister laid wreaths at the Tomb of the Unknown Soldier in Moscow and at the Piskarevskoye Memorial Cemetery in Leningrad.

The Prime Minister and his party were everywhere accorded a warm welcome and cordial hospitality.

The Prime Minister and the Foreign and Commonwealth Secretary held a series of talks with L. I. Brezhnev, the General Secretary of the Central Committee of the

1 London Press Service.

Communist Party of the Soviet Union; A. N. Kosygin, member of the Politburo of the Central Committee of the CPSU and Chairman of the Council of Ministers of the USSR; and A. A. Gromyko, member of the Politburo of the Central Committe of the CPSU and Minister for Foreign Affairs of the USSR.

During the talks, which were held in a businesslike and friendly atmosphere and in a spirit of mutual respect, questions of Anglo–Soviet relations and the prospects for their expansion in the political, trade, economic, cultural and other fields were discussed in detail. There was also a wide-ranging exchange of views on current inter national issues of mutual interest.

The United Kingdom and the Soviet Union took note of the important and positive changes in Europe and in international relations as a whole in recent years. They agreed that these developments had significantly improved the prospects for deepening detente in Europe. In these circumstances they resolved upon the system expansion of relations between the United Kingdom and the Soviet Union in all fields.

The talks reflected the mutual desire of the two sides to strengthen understandin trust and cooperation between them. They agreed that the talks and negotiations which took place during the visit have marked the opening of a new phase in Anglo-Soviet relations and would make a positive contribution towards consolidating inter national peace and security, especially in Europe.

The two sides emphasised the importance which they attach to the development of bilateral relations between Britain and the USSR. They noted with satisfaction the improvements achieved in recent times in relations between their two countries and agreed on practical steps to be taken with a view to promoting their further fruitful development.

They declared their adherence to the principles of peaceful coexistence, which means long-term, fruitful and mutually beneficial cooperation between states, irrespective of their political, economic and social systems, on the basis of full equality and mutual respect.

In the interests of deepening cooperation in the political field between the Unite Kingdom and the USSR, and conscious of their special responsibilities as permanent members of the United Nations Security Council, the two sides reaffirmed their resolve to hold regular exchanges of views at various levels on important issues of international and bilateral relations.

Guided by the desire to lay a stable and constructive foundation for Anglo– Soviet relations and acknowledging the responsibility of the United Kingdom and the Soviet Union for furthering the process of detente, the Right Honourable Harol Wilson, Prime Minister of the United Kingdom, and L. I. Brezhnev, General Secreta of the Central Committee of the CPSU, signed a protocol on consultations. The two sides expressed their conviction that the implementation of this protocol would give a new impetus to the development of Anglo–Soviet cooperation in the politica field. In this context, they stressed the special significance of meetings between the leaders which thoroughly reviewed economic questions. The two sides agreed that mutually beneficial commercial links are an important element in relations between he two countries. In this connexion they noted the role of the temporary commercial greement of 16 February 1974 in the development of Anglo–Soviet relations and eaffirmed the importance of the agreement on the development of economic, cientific, technological and industrial cooperation signed in London on 6 May 974. Two long-term programmes giving practical effect to the agreement of 1974, n economic and industrial cooperation and on scientific and technological cooperation espectively, were signed during the visit by the Right Honourable Harold Wilson, 'rime Minister of the United Kingdom and A. N. Kosygin, Chairman of the Council f Ministers of the USSR. The two sides reaffirmed the importance f exchanging ppropriate information on cooperation within the framework of the above-mentioned rogrammes.

The two sides commended the work done by the permanent Anglo–Soviet Inter-overnmental Commission for Cooperation in the fields of applied science, tech-ology, trade and economic relations which first met in London in January 1971. hey expressed their hope that the fourth meeting of the joint commission to be eld in Moscow in May of this year would promote further progress in the field of conomic cooperation.

The two sides expressed their intention to make further efforts to increase the olume of trade in both directions on the basis of mutual benefit. They agreed to im at achieving a substantial increase in the level of trade and a better balance nd structure of trade over the next five years. In this connexion they noted with atisfaction the expected increase in contracts for British machinery and equipment.

The two sides noted with satisfaction the recent conclusion of contracts for the upply by British firms of the latest technology and equipment for the chemical, etrochemical, automobile and light industries. A contract for the enrichment in he Soviet Union of uranium supplied by British customers was likewise welcomed.

The two sides agreed that there were good prospects for the early conclusion of number of large-scale contracts between the organisations concerned on a mutually dvantageous basis. Particular note was taken of the promising proposals for co-peration involving Soviet organisations and enterprises and British companies in he development of natural resources including oil, the aviation industry, nuclear ower, timber and woodworking, pulp and paper, ferrous and non-ferrous metallurgy, hemicals and petrochemicals, the transportation of natural gas and of ethylene, ontainerised transportation and textile and other light industries. At the same time raditional trade with smaller and medium firms would continue to expand.

The two sides agreed to examine the possibilities for the improvement of conditions or the work of the commercial representatives, organisations and companies con-erned in London and Moscow.

Agreement was reached on credits for a 5-year period in recognition of the im-ortance of finance in commercial and economic relations and of the need for both ides to extend to each other credits on the most favourable possible terms, subject ɔ the laws and regulations in force in each country.

The special importance attached by both sides to the further development of cientific and technological cooperation was reaffirmed. The two sides resolved to continue to promote this cooperation through, in particular, the agreement on the development of economic, scientific, technological and industrial cooperation: the Anglo—Soviet Inter-Governmental Commission for cooperation in the fields of science, education and culture. The two sides recognised that the long-term program on scientific and technological collaboration would make an important contribution in this respect.

The two sides noted with satisfaction the extent of cooperation between Britain and the USSR in the field of nuclear energy, notably in contacts between the United Kingdom Atomic Energy Authority and the USSR State Committee for the Utilisat of Atomic Energy and in the framework of the Anglo—Soviet working group on problems of electricity supply and transmission. The two sides also undertook to examine the possibilities for mutually profitable cooperation in the production of equipment for nuclear power stations.

The Prime Minister of the United Kingdom, the Right Honourable Harold Wilson and the Chairman of the Council of Ministers of the USSR, A. N. Kosygin, signed an agreement on cooperation in the field of medicine and public health. The sides spoke also in favour of the further development of Anglo—Soviet cooperation in the fields of agriculture and protection of the environment.

The two sides emphasised the important role of cultural links between the peopl of the two countries as a means of promoting fuller mutual knowledge of achievements in literature, art and other fields of cultural activity. They noted in this conte the exhibitions of paintings and other important cultural events which are to take place in Britain and the USSR and also the forthcoming signature of the next in the series of Anglo—Soviet cultural agreements covering the period 1975—1977.

Guided by a desire to promote greater mutual understanding and trust, the two sides resolved to set up an Anglo—Soviet Round Table whose members would be distinguished representatives of public life, science, culture, commerce, the press, and other fields. The Royal Institute for International Affairs in Britain and the Institute for World Economy and International Affairs of the Academy of Sciences of the USSR have agreed to undertake the task of organising the meetings of the Round Table. The first meeting will be held in Britain in 1975.

The two sides confirmed the importance which they attach to the development of contacts between the British Parliament and the Supreme Soviet of the USSR, and noted with satisfaction that a delegation of the Supreme Soviet of the USSR will visit the United Kingdom later this year.

The two sides reviewed the possibilities of extending their contacts into other fields. In this connexion they reached agreement on an exchange of visits between representatives of the armed forces.

The United Kingdom and the Soviet Union noted with satisfaction the progress made in recent years in developing detente and peaceful cooperation between states irrespective of their political, economic and social systems. They agreed on the need to establish detente on a firm basis throughout the world, and pledged the efforts of their two governments to this end.

The two sides are convinced that further progress in the improvement of the inte

tional situation demands active and purposeful efforts of all states. They emphasized eir determination to ensure that favourable changes in the international situation come irreversible and that detente is extended to all areas of the world.

The two sides recognised the importance for the strengthening of universal peace the agreements and understandings achieved between the USSR and the USA, cluding the agreements on the prevention of nuclear war and on the limitation of rategic arms.[1]

The two sides noted with satisfaction the positive trends towards the establishment relations of stable peace, good neighbourliness and cooperation in Europe. They nphasised the important role which the conference on security and cooperation Europe was called upon to play in this process. The two sides stated that much ogress had been made at the conference. They are convinced that premises exist r completing the work of the conference and for holding its third stage at the ghest level in the near future.

Attaching great importance to the further strengthening of stability and security Europe, the United Kingdom and the Soviet Union expressed themselves in favour complementing measures of political detente with those of military detente. In is connexion the two sides exchanged views concerning the negotiations on the utual reduction of forces and armaments and associated measures in central rope. They recalled the agreed general objective to contribute to a more stable lationship and reaffirmed that the specific arrangements to be worked out should nform to the principle of undiminished security for each party.

In the course of an exchange of views on the Middle East the two sides expressed eir deep concern at the dangerous situation in the area, and emphasised the necessity achieving as soon as possible a just and lasting settlement, based on the implemen-tion of the resolutions of the United Nations Security Council. They confirmed eir intention to make every effort to promote a solution of the cardinal questions volved in a just and lasting peace in this region, on the basis of Security Council solution No. 338.[2] Taking due account of the legitimate interests of all states d peoples of the region including the Arab people of Palestine, and with respect the right of all states in the area to independent existence, the two sides con-lered that the Geneva Conference should play an important role in the establish-ent of a just and lasting peace in the Middle East and should resume its work at ery early date.

In connexion with recent events in Cyprus, Britain and the Soviet Union reaffirmed eir support for the principle of preserving the sovereignty, independence and rritorial integrity of the Republic of Cyprus. They support the implementation the relevant resolutions of the Security Council and the General Assembly of the ited Nations on Cyprus. Britain and the Soviet Union recognise the one lawful vernment of Cyprus headed by President Makarios.

The two sides stated the necessity of strict observance by all its parties of the

1 Documents Nos. 65 and 69
2 Document No. 157.

Paris Agreement on Ending the War and Restoring Peace in Vietnam.[1] They welcor
the concrete measures to implement the agreement on restoring peace and achievin
national accord in Laos and expressed themselves in favour of a just settlement of
the Cambodian problem with full consideration for the national interests and legiti.
rights of the people of Cambodia, without any outside interference.

The two sides consider that there are certain international economic problems
in the solution of which they are both interested. They reached a mutual understanding on holding further exchanges of views on these questions at the appropria
level within the framework of the protocol on consultations.

In order to reaffirm the great importance which the two sides attach to the
treaty on the non-proliferation of nuclear weapons and to effective measures to
control the spread of nuclear weapons and the means to make them, the Prime
Minister of the United Kingdom, the Right Honourable Harold Wilson, and the
General Secretary of the Central Committee of the CPSU, L. I. Brezhnev, signed a
declaration on the non-proliferation of nuclear weapons.

The United Kingdom and the Soviet Union are convinced that effective measure
should be taken to end the arms race and to achieve general and complete disarmament embracing both nuclear and conventional weapons under strict and
effective international control. The two sides believe that the convocation of a wor
disarmament conference may contribute to the solution for the pressing problems
of disarmament. They confirmed their intention of continuing their cooperation
with the United Nations ad hoc Committee on the world disarmament conference.

The two sides expressed confidence that the exchange of instruments of ratifica
of the convention on the prohibition of the development, production and stockpiling of bacteriological (biological) and toxic weapons and on their destruction
would take place very soon and that as a result the convention would enter into
force. The two sides are in favour of the earliest possible achievement of an international agreement on the prohibition of chemical weapons.

The two sides expressed themselves in favour of giving effect to the United
Nations General Assembly Resolution on the prohibition of action to influence the
environment and climate for military and other purposes incompatible with the
maintenance of international security, human well-being and health.

Attaching great importance to the Conference on the Law of the Sea, the two
sides pronounced themselves in favour of adopting constructive decisions in that
field on an international basis with due regard for the interests of all states. They
will continue to work to this end. They acknowledged the value of the consultatio:
held in the past between representatives of their two countries, and expressed the
intention of continuing those consultations also in the future.

The two sides declared their determination to work for the strengthening of the
United Nations and for promoting its effectiveness in the maintenance of universal
peace and security on the basis of strict observance of the purposes and principles
of the United Nations Charter. They support the work of the United Nations in

1 Document No. 37.

»romoting the consolidation of international detente, in strengthening international
»eace and security and in developing peaceful and fruitful cooperation.

The two sides shared the view that the meetings and talks held during the Prime
Minister's visit have made an important contribution to the further development of
elations between the United Kingdom and the Soviet Union and to the cause of
international detente.

The Prime Minister of the United Kingdom, the Right Honourable Harold Wilson,
invited L. I. Brezhnev, General Secretary of the Central Committee of the CPSU,
A. N. Kosygin, Chairman of the Council of Ministers of the USSR, and A. A. Gromyko,
Minister for Foreign Affairs of the USSR, to pay official visits to the United Kingdom.
The invitations were accepted with gratitude.

EDITOR'S NOTE: BRITISH INITIATIVES IN EASTERN EUROPE

In addition to the development of Anglo-Soviet relations, Declarations were signed
with the Governments of Poland and Romania:

Declaration on the Development of Friendly Relations between Great Britain
and the Polish People's Republic, Warsaw, 15 July 1975 (Cmnd. 6260).

Joint Declaration between Great Britain and Romania, Bucharest, 18 September
1975 (Romanian Embassy release, London).

C. JAPAN

33. Agreement between Japan and the United States of America concerning the Ryukyu Islands and the Daito Islands, the 'Okinawa Reversion Agreement', signed by Mr Rogers and the Japanese Foreign Minister, Mr Aichi, Tokyo and Washington, 17 June 1971[1]

Japan and the United States of America,

Noting that the Prime Minister of Japan and the President of the United States
of America reviewed together on November 19, 20 and 21, 1969, the status of the
Ryukyu Islands and the Daito Islands, referred to as 'Okinawa' in the Joint Communiqué between the Prime Minister and the President issued on November 21,
1969, and agreed that the Government of Japan and the Government of the United
States of America should enter immediately into consultations regarding the
specific arrangements for accomplishing the early reversion of these islands to Japan;

Noting that the two Governments have conducted such consultations and have

1 *DSB*, 12 July 1971, pp. 35–7.

reaffirmed that the reversion of these islands to Japan be carried out on the basis of the said Joint Communiqué;

Considering that the United States of America desires, with respect to the Ryukyu Islands and the Daito Islands, to relinquish in favor of Japan all rights and interests under Article 3 of the Treaty of Peace with Japan signed at the city of San Francisco on September 8, 1951, and thereby to have relinquished all its rights and interests in all territories under the said Article; and

Considering further that Japan is willing to assume full responsibility and authori for the exercise of all powers of administration, legislation and jurisdiction over the territory and inhabitants of the Ryukyu Islands and the Daito Islands;

Therefore, have agreed as follows:

Article I

1. With respect to the Ryukyu Islands and the Daito Islands, as defined in paragraph 2 below, the United States of America relinquishes in favor of Japan all rights and interests under Article 3 of the Treaty of Peace with Japan signed at the city of San Francisco on September 8, 1951, effective as of the date of entry into force of this Agreement. Japan, as of such date, assumes full responsibility and authority for the exercise of all and any powers of administration, legislation and jurisdiction over the territory and inhabitants of the said islands.

2. For the purpose of this Agreement, the term 'the Ryukyu Islands and the Dait Islands' mean all the territories and their territorial waters with respect to which the right to exercise all and any powers of administration, legislation and jurisdictio was accorded to the United States of America under Article 3 of the Treaty of Peace with Japan other than those with respect to which such right has already been returned to Japan in accordance with the Agreement concerning the Amami Islands and the Agreement concerning Nanpo Shoto and other islands signed between Japan and the United States of America respectively on December 24, 1953 and April 5, 1968.

Article II

It is confirmed that treaties, conventions and other agreements concluded between Japan and the United States of America, including, but without limitation, the Treaty of Mutual Cooperation and Security between Japan and the United States of America signed at Washington on January 19, 1960, and its related arrangements and the Treaty of Friendship, Commerce and Navigation between Japan and the United States of America signed at Tokyo on April 2, 1953, become applicable to th Ryukyu Islands and the Daito Islands as of the date of entry into force of this Agreement.

Article III

1. Japan will grant the United States of America on the date of entry into force of

his Agreement the use of facilities and areas in the Ryukyu Islands and the Daito
slands in accordance with the Treaty of Mutual Cooperation and Security between
apan and the United States of America signed at Washington on January 19,
960 and its related arrangements.

2. In the application of Article IV of the Agreement under Article VI of the
Treaty of Mutual Cooperation and Security between Japan and the United States
of America, regarding Facilities and Areas and the Status of United States Armed
Forces in Japan signed on January 19, 1960 to the facilities and areas the use of
which will be granted in accordance with paragraph 1 above to the United States
of America on the date of entry into force of this Agreement, it is understood that
he phrase 'the condition in which they were at the time they became available to
he United States armed forces' in paragraph 1 of the said Article refers to the con-
lition in which the facilities and areas first came into the use of the United States
rmed forces, and that the term 'improvements' in paragraph 2 of the said Article
ncludes those made prior to the date of entry into force of this Agreement.

Article IV

1. Japan waives all claims of Japan and its nationals against the United States of
America and its nationals and against the local authorities of the Ryukyu Islands and
he Daito Islands, arising from the presence, operations or actions of forces or
authorities of the United States of America in these islands, or from the presence,
operations or actions of forces or authorities of the United States of America having
ad any effect upon these islands, prior to the date of entry into force of this Agreement.

2. The waiver in paragraph 1 above does not, however, include claims of Japanese
nationals specifically recognized in the laws of the United States of America or the
ocal laws of these islands applicable during the period of United States adminis-
ration of these islands. The Government of the United States of America is authorized
o maintain its duly empowered officials in the Ryukyu Islands and the Daito Islands
n order to deal with and settle such claims on and after the date of entry into force
of this Agreement in accordance with the procedures to be established in consultation
with the Government of Japan.

3. The Government of the United States of America will make ex gratia contri-
outions for restoration of lands to the nationals of Japan whose lands in the Ryukyu
Islands and the Daito Islands were damaged prior to July 1, 1950, while placed under
he use of United States authorities, and were released from their use after June 30,
1961 and before the date of entry into force of this Agreement. Such contributions
will be made in an equitable manner in relation to the payments made under High
Commissioner's Ordinance Number 60 of 1967 to claims for damages done prior
o July 1, 1950 to the lands released prior to July 1, 1961.

4. Japan recognizes the validity of all acts and omissions done during the period
of United States administration of the Ryukyu Islands and the Daito Islands under
or in consequence of directives of the United States or local authorities, or authorized

by existing law during that period, and will take no action subjecting United States nationals or the residents of these Islands to civil or criminal liability arising out of such acts or omissions.

Article V

1. Japan recognizes the validity of, and will continue in full force and effect, final judgments in civil cases rendered by any court in the Ryukyu Islands and the Daito Islands prior to the date of entry into force of this Agreement, provided that such recognition or continuation would not be contrary to public policy.

2. Without in any way adversely affecting the substantive rights and positions of the litigants concerned, Japan will assume jurisdiction over and continue to judgment and execution any civil cases pending as of the date of entry into force of this Agreement in any court in the Ryukyu Islands and the Daito Islands.

3. Without in any way adversely affecting the substantive rights of the accused or suspect concerned, Japan will assume jurisdiction over, and may continue or institute proceedings with respect to, any criminal cases with which any court in the Ryukyu Islands and the Daito Islands is seized as of the date of entry into force of this Agreement or would have been seized had the proceedings been instituted prior to such date.

4. Japan may continue the execution of any final judgments rendered in criminal cases by any court in the Ryukyu Islands and the Daito Islands.

Article VI

1. The properties of the Ryukyu Electric Power Corporation, the Ryukyu Domestic Water Corporation and the Ryukyu Development Loan Corporation shall be transferred to the Government of Japan on the date of entry into force of this Agreement, and the rights and obligations of the said Corporations shall be assumed by the Government of Japan on that date in conformity with the laws and regulations of Japan.

2. All other properties of the Government of the United States of America, existing in the Ryukyu Islands and the Daito Islands as of the date of entry into for of this Agreement and located outside the facilities and areas provided on that date in accordance with Article III of the Agreement, shall be transferred to the Government of Japan on this date, except for those that are located on the lands returned to the landowners concerned before the date of entry into force of this Agreement and for those the title to which will be retained by the Government of the United States of America after that date with the consent of the Government of Japan.

3. Such lands in the Ryukyu Islands and the Daito Islands reclaimed by the Gove ment of the United States of America and such other reclaimed lands acquired by it in these islands as are held by the Government of the United States of America as of the date of entry into force of this Agreement become the property of the Gover ment of Japan on that date.

4. The United States of America is not obliged to compensate Japan or its ationals for any alteration made prior to the date of entry into force of this Agreeient to the lands upon which the properties transferred to the Government of Japan nder paragraphs 1 and 2 above are located.

rticle VII

'onsidering, inter alia, that United States assets are being transferred to the Governient of Japan under Article VI of this Agreement, that the Government of the Jnited States of America is carrying out the return of the Ryukyu Islands and the)aito Islands to Japan in a manner consistent with the policy of the Government of apan as specified in paragraph 8 of the Joint Communiqué of November 21, 1969, nd that the Government of the United States of America will bear extra costs, articularly in the area of employment after reversion, the Government of Japan rill pay to the Government of the United States of America in United States dollars total amount of three hundred and twenty million United States dollars (US 320,000,000) over a period of five years from the date of entry into force of this greement. Of the said amount, the Government of Japan will pay one hundred iillion United States dollars (US $100,000,000) within one week after the date of ntry into force of this Agreement and the remainder in four equal annual installients in June of each calendar year subsequent to the year in which this Agreement iters into force.

rticle VIII

'he Government of Japan consents to the continued operation by the Government f the United States of America of the Voice of America relay station in Okinawa sland for a period of five years from the date of entry into force of this Agreement 1 accordance with the arrangements to be concluded between the two Govern- ients. The two Governments shall enter into consultation two years after the date f entry into force of this Agreement on future operation of the Voice of America 1 Okinawa Island.

rticle IX

'his Agreement shall be ratified and the instruments of ratification shall be exchanged t Tokyo. This Agreement shall enter into force two months after the date of ex- hange of the instruments of ratification.

4. Communiqué issued following Mr Gromyko's visit to Japan, ˉokyo, 27 January 1972[1]

lt the invitation of the Japanese Government, Soviet Foreign Minister Andrei

1 *SWB*, FE/3901, 29 January 1972, A2/1–2.

Gromyko was staying in Japan on an official visit from 23 January to 28 January 1972. Soviet Foreign Minister Andrei Gromyko visited Tokyo, Nagoya and Toba. During his stay in Japan, USSR Foreign Minister Andrei Gromyko was received by the Emperor of Japan.

The Soviet Foreign Minister had a conversation with Japan's Prime Minister, Eisaku Sato. He also had meetings with Minister of Foreign Trade and Industry Kakuei Tanaka; Minister of Agriculture and Forestry Munenori Akagi; and State Minister, Chief of the Department for Environmental Control, Buichi Oishi. In the framework of the Soviet–Japanese consultative meeting, the Soviet Foreign Ministe had talks with the Foreign Minister of Japan, Takeo Fukuda.

During the conversations that were held in the spirit of openness and good neigh bourly relations, questions of Soviet–Japanese relations, and also some topical international problems of interest to both countries, were discussed. The sides pointed out with satisfaction that the personal contacts, exchange in trade, econom science and culture and other fields have developed between the Soviet Union and Japan and that consultations on different international problems have been widenin of late. The sides expressed a unanimous view in favour of further development of relations between the Soviet Union and Japan in all the fields, on the basis of the principles of equality, non-interference in each other's affairs and mutual advantage

The sides are convinced that such a development of relations of friendship and cooperation between the Soviet Union and Japan will be a great contribution to the cause of consolidation of peace in Asia and throughout the world. The sides expect that the visits of State leaders of both countries, on which agreement was achieved earlier, will take place.

Realising the importance of the conclusion of a peace treaty for further develop ment of Soviet–Japanese relations on a steadier basis, the sides declared in favour of holding talks on the question of concluding a Peace Treaty already this year, at a time convenient for both sides.

The sides expressed satisfaction with the development of trade and economic relations between the two countries. Highly assessing the activity of the Soviet– Japanese Committee for Business Cooperation, and expressing satisfaction with coordination and implementation of the economic projects, the sides agreed to con tinue making efforts towards the development of economic cooperation between the Soviet Union and Japan, with prospects for many years ahead.

Wishing to widen cultural relations, the Foreign Ministers exchanged on 27 January 1972 letters on cultural contacts between the Soviet Union and Japan. Both sides pointed to the fruitfulness of the spread of the relations between the Soviet Union and Japan in science and technology, and expressed readiness to hold talks on the conclusion of an agreement on scientific and technical cooperation between the two countries.

The sides pointed to the usefulness of constant cooperation between the two States in fisheries. They believe that the successful holding of the coming Soviet– Japanese talks on fisheries would be in the interests of both countries. The Foreign Ministers exchanged opinions on a wide range of international questions, from the iewpoint of consolidating peace. Both sides expressed concern with the continued conflict in Indochina. They expressed the unanimous view that firm peace in the area must be established on the basis of respect for the right of the peoples of Indochina to decide their future by themselves.

Both sides expressed concern with the situation in the Middle East and declared for the need to exert efforts to establish lasting peace in the area on the basis of the resolution of the Security Council of 22 November 1967, and with the assistance of the mission of Ambassador Jarring stemming from this resolution. Both sides, attaching a great importance to the activity of the United Nations, agreed to cooperate in enhancing its effectivity.

Both sides set out the positions of their Governments on the question of disarmament, including nuclear disarmament, and stressed the importance of the implementation of general and complete disarmament, concerning both nuclear and conventional weapons, under effective international control.

Being in favour of a regular exchange of opinions on the questions of Soviet—Japanese relations and on international problems of interest to both sides, they confirmed their agreement on holding further regular consultations at the level of Foreign Ministers of both countries at least once a year.

35. Joint statement by President Nixon and the Japanese Prime Minister, Mr Tanaka, Hawaii, 1 September 1972[1]

. Prime Minister Tanaka and President Nixon met in Hawaii August 31—September 1 for wide ranging discussions on a number of topics of mutual interest. The talks were held in an atmosphere of warmth and mutual trust reflecting the long history of friendship between Japan and the United States. Both leaders expressed the hope that their meeting would mark the beginning of a new chapter in the course of developing ever closer bonds between the two countries.

2. The Prime Minister and the President reviewed the current international situation and the prospects for the relaxation of tension and peaceful solutions to current problems in the world, with particular reference to Asia. It was stressed that the maintenance and strengthening of the close ties of friendship and cooperation between the two countries would continue to be an important factor for peace and stability in the evolving world situation. Both leaders reaffirmed the intention of the two governments to maintain the Treaty of Mutual Cooperation and Security between the two countries, and agreed that the two governments would continue to cooperate through close consultations with a view to ensuring smooth and effective implementation of the Treaty.

3. In discussing the increasing indications for peace and stability in Asia, the Prime Minister and the President welcomed the recent opening of dialogue in the Korean Peninsula, and the increasingly active efforts of Asian countries for self-reliance and regional cooperation, and shared the hope for an early realization of

1 *DSB*, 25 September 1975, pp. 331–2.

peace in Indochina. The Prime Minister and the President recognized that the President's recent visits to the People's Republic of China and the USSR were a significant step forward in this context, they shared the hope that the forthcoming visit of the Prime Minister to the People's Republic of China would also serve to further the trend for the relaxation of tension in Asia.

4. The Prime Minister and the President discussed the recent agreements reached by the United States and the USSR on the limitation of ballistic missile defenses and the interim arrangement on the limitation of strategic offensive missiles, and they agreed that such measures represented an important step forward in limiting strategic arms and contributing to world peace. They agreed to consult on the need for further steps to control strategic arms.

5. The Prime Minister and the President exchanged views in a broad perspective on issues related to economic, trade and financial matters. The Prime Minister and the President emphasized the great importance of economic relations between Japa and the United States. Both leaders expressed their conviction that their talks woul contribute to closer cooperation between the two countries in dealing with econom issues of a bilateral and global nature.

6. The Prime Minister and the President shared the view that fundamental reforn of the international monetary system is essential. They committed their governmen to work rapidly to achieve such reform. In trade, they reaffirmed the February 197 commitments of both countries to initiate and actively support multilateral trade negotiations covering both industry and agriculture in 1973. In this connection the noted the need in the forthcoming trade negotiations to lay the basis for further trade expansion through reduction of tariff and non-tariff barriers as well as for-mulations of a multilateral non-discriminatory safeguard mechanism.

7. The Prime Minister and the President agreed that both countries would endea to move towards a better equilibrium in their balance of payments and trade positi In this regard, the President explained the measures undertaken by the United States to improve its trade and payments position and stated that the Government of the United States was urging US firms to expand the volume of exports through increased productivity and improved market research, particularly to Japan. The Prime Minister indicated that the Government of Japan would also try to promote imports from the United States and that it was the intention of the Government of Japan to reduce the imbalance to a more manageable size within a reasonable perio of time. The Prime Minister and the President agreed that it would be most valuabl to hold future meetings at a high level to review evolving economic relationships, ar that they intend to hold a meeting of the Joint United States—Japan Committee on Trade and Economic Affairs as early in 1973 as feasible.

8. The Prime Minister and the President noted the endeavors of the two countrie in cooperation with other developed countries, to help bring stability and prosperit to the developing countries in Asia and other regions of the world. They acknowled the need for adequate levels of official development assistance on appropriate term They also reaffirmed that the two governments intend to continue to help strength

ae international financial institutions for the purpose of economic development
f the developing countries.

9. The Prime Minister and the President reaffirmed the need to promote efforts
ɔ improve the mutual understanding of the cultural, social and other backgrounds
etween the peoples of the two countries. They agreed further that new and improved
rograms of cultural and educational exchange are an important means to this end.
ı this connection the President underlined his high hopes for the successful activities
f the Japan Foundation to be inaugurated in October this year.

10. The Prime Minister and the President noted with satisfaction the growing
ıomentum of cooperation between the two countries in increasingly diverse fields
ınder the common aims of maintaining and promoting peace and prosperity of the
ʼorld and the well-being of their countrymen. They agreed to strengthen and expand
ıe already close cooperation between the two countries in controlling the illegal
ʼaffic in narcotics and other dangerous drugs, and they also agreed on the need
ɔr further bilateral and multilateral cooperation concerning the development and
etter utilization of energy and mineral resources and on the pressing problems of
ɪvironmental protection and pollution control. They pledged to continue appropriate
ssistance through the UN and its specialized agencies for the solution of problems
aused by too rapid population growth.

11. The Prime Minister and the President discussed cooperation in space exploration
ıcluding Japan's goal of launching geo-stationary communications and other ap-
ʾlications satellites. The President welcomed Japan's active interest in and study on
he launching of a meteorological satellite in support of the global atmospheric
esearch program.

12. The Prime Minister and the President expressed satisfaction with their talks
ınd agreed to continue to maintain close personal contact.

¦6. Joint statement issued following Mr Tanaka's visit to Peking, ¦9 September 1972[1] (extract)

. The abnormal state of affairs which has hitherto existed between the People's
ʾepublic of China and Japan is declared terminated on the date of publication of
his statement.

2. The Government of Japan recognises the Government of the People's Republic
ɪf China as the sole legal Government of China.

3. The Government of the People's Republic of China reaffirms that Taiwan is
ın inalienable part of the territory of the People's Republic of China. The Govern-
ıent of Japan fully understands and respects this stand of the Government of China
ɪnd adheres to its stand of complying with Article 8 of the Potsdam proclamation.

4. The Government of the People's Republic of China and the Government of
ʾapan have decided upon the establishment of diplomatic relations as from 29

1 *The Times*, 30 September 1972.

September 1972. The two governments have decided to adopt all necessary measur for the establishment and the performance of functions of embassies in each other' capitals in accordance with international law and practice and exchange ambassado as speedily as possible.

5. The Government of the People's Republic of China declares that in the intere of the friendship between the peoples of China and Japan, it renounces its demand for war indemnities from Japan.

6. The Government of the People's Republic of China and the Government of Japan agree to establish durable relations of peace and friendship between the two countries on the basis of the principles of mutual respect for sovereignty and territo integrity, mutual non-aggression, non-interference in each other's internal affairs, equality and mutual benefit and peaceful coexistence.

In keeping with the foregoing principles and the principles of the United Nation Charter, the Governments of the two countries affirm that in their mutual relations all disputes shall be settled by peaceful means without resorting to the use or threa of force.

7. The normalisation of relations between China and Japan is not directed again third countries. Neither of the two countries should seek hegemony in the Asia— Pacific region and each country is opposed to efforts by any other country or grou of countries to establish such hegemony.

8. To consolidate and develop the peaceful and friendly relations between the two countries, the Government of the People's Republic of China and the Govern-ment of Japan agree to hold negotiations aimed at the conclusion of a treaty of peace and friendship.

9. In order to further develop the relations between the two countries and broad the exchange of visits, the Government of the People's Republic of China and the Government of Japan agree to hold negotiations aimed at the conclusion of agree-ments on trade, navigation, aviation, fishery, etc., in accordance with the needs and taking into consideration the existing non-governmental agreements.

87. Joint statement issued following Mr Tanaka's visit to the Soviet Union, Moscow, 10 October 1973[1]

Japanese Prime Minister Kakuei Tanaka paid an official visit to the Soviet Union from October 7 to 10, 1973, at the invitation of the government of the Soviet Unio Prime Minister Tanaka was accompanied by Foreign Minister Masayoshi Ohira and other officials.

Talks on questions concerning Soviet—Japanese relations, including the question of talks on signing a peace treaty and also on very important international problems of mutual interest, were held between L. I. Brezhnev, general secretary of the CPSU central committee, A. N. Kosygin, member of the political bureau of the CPSU cen committee and Chairman of the Council of Ministers of the USSR, A. A. Gromyko,

1 *Soviet News*, 16 October 1973.

member of the political bureau of the CPSU central committee and Foreign Minister of the USSR, and Japanese Prime Minister K. Tanaka and Foreign Minister M. Ohira.

Prime Minister K. Tanaka and Foreign Minister M. Ohira were received by N. V. Podgorny, member of the political bureau of the CPSU central committee and President of the Presidium of the USSR Supreme Soviet.

A regular consultative meeting was held between Foreign Ministers A. A. Gromyko and M. Ohira.

During the meetings, which were held in a friendly atmosphere, both sides expressed satisfaction with the fact that since the time of the restoration of diplomatic relations on the basis of the 1956 joint declaration of the USSR and Japan, Soviet–Japanese relations have developed favourably and, specifically, have made considerable headway in the political, economic and cultural spheres. The two sides recognised that the strengthening of good-neighbourly and friendly relations between the USSR and Japan on the basis of the principles of non-interference in internal affairs, mutual benefit and equality, is not only in accord with the common interests of the peoples of both countries but is also a big contribution to peace and stability in the Far East and throughout the world. In this connection the two sides expressed their determination to exert efforts to develop relations between the USSR and Japan further.

1

Realising that the settlement of outstanding questions which have been left over since the time of the Second World War and the signing of a peace treaty would make a contribution to the establishment of genuinely good-neighbourly and friendly relations between the two countries, the sides held talks on questions concerning the content of a peace treaty. The two sides agreed to continue the talks on signing a peace treaty between both countries at an appropriate time in 1974.

2

The two sides exchanged views concerning ways of expanding economic cooperation between the USSR and Japan. They recognised the desirability of implementing economic cooperation between the two countries in possibly wider spheres on the basis of the principles of mutual benefit and equality. Both sides were agreed on the need to step up economic cooperation, including cooperation in connection with the development of Siberia's natural resources and also the development of trade and cooperation in agriculture, transportation and other spheres.

Both sides expressed high appreciation of the work of the Soviet–Japanese and the Japanese–Soviet committees for economic cooperation. An understanding was reached by which the governments of the two countries will help the implementation of such economic cooperation, will encourage the signing of contracts between Japanese firms — or associations being formed by these firms — and appropriate Soviet organisations, and will promote normal and timely implementation of these contracts. With this aim they agreed to practise inter-government consultations.

Both sides reaffirmed that Soviet—Japanese economic cooperation in these spheres, particularly in connection with the development of the natural resources of Siberia, does not rule out the participation of third countries.

The two sides had an exchange of views on ways of solving problems concerning Soviet and Japanese fishing. As a result of the exchange and with a view to ensuring long-lasting and stable fishing in the Northern Pacific, the two sides agreed to take appropriate measures, including measures to determine catch quotas. It was agreed that consultations should be held on this matter as soon as possible between the respective ministers of the two countries.

The two sides exchanged views on the talks which started earlier on Japanese fishing in areas on which the two sides are to hold separate negotiations.

The two sides recognised the desirability of expanding ties between the two governments in the scientific and technical field and attached great value to the signature by Foreign Minister Andrei Gromyko, on the Soviet side, and by Foreign Minister Masayoshi Ohira, on the Japanese side, on October 10, 1973, of the agreement between the government of the USSR and the government of Japan on scientif and technical cooperation.

Noting with satisfaction the favourable development of ties in the field of cultur the two sides highly assessed the importance of the signing of agreements on exchanges of scientists and postgraduates, official printed publications and the dissemination of new material, on October 10, 1973, by Foreign Minister Andrei Gromyko, on the Soviet side, and Foreign Minister Masayoshi Ohira, on the Japanes side.

The two sides recognised the need to give greater scope in future to contacts between the USSR and Japan in the field of nature and environmental protection, and attached great value to the signing of a convention between the USSR and Japan on the protection of migratory birds and birds which are under the threat of extinction and on the protection of their habitat, as the first step in this cooperation on October 10, 1973, by Foreign Minister Andrei Gromyko, on the Soviet side, and by Foreign Minister Masayoshi Ohira, on the Japanese side.

Being aware that the mastering of highly effective sources of energy can promote a solution to world energy problems, the two sides recognised the need to expand cooperation in the area of the peaceful use of atomic energy and, as the first step in such cooperation, emphasised the importance of the exchanges of scientists and technical specialists of the two countries, as well as the exchange of information

The two sides were agreed on the need to encourage broader contacts between representatives of the public of the two countries.

The two sides went on record for periodic consultations between the Ministers of Foreign Affairs of the two countries, on which an understanding was reached by the Ministers of Foreign Affairs of the USSR and Japan in 1966.

In connection with a request by Japanese Prime Minister K. Tanaka for the departure of former Japanese citizens resident in the USSR for Japan, and for visits by the Japanese to places where their relatives are buried, the Soviet side, guided by humanitarian feelings, reaffirmed its readiness to consider such matters with due attention in the future also.

The two sides had an exchange of views on major problems of mutual interest of the present-day international situation. The two sides expressed satisfaction with the fact that the international situation in recent years has, on the whole developed in the direction of detente and the normalisation of relations between states with different social systems. At the same time the two sides displayed concern over the continuation of conflicts in a number of areas of the world at present and emphasised that it was necessary that, in accord with the UN Charter, in relations with one another all states should adhere to the principles of settling conflicts by negotiations and of refraining from the threat of force or its use.

Both sides believe that the continued development of detente and the establishment of a lasting and universal peace is a fundamental problem today which affects the interests of all peoples. At the same time, in view of this, the two sides recognised that the United Nations Organisation was making an important contribution to the preservation of universal cooperation, and both declared their intention to continue their efforts to strengthen the efficiency of the UN organisation.

Realising that in order to establish a lasting peace throughout the world, it is important to achieve disarmament under effective international control, and particularly nuclear disarmament, as soon as possible, the two sides have declared their intention to exert efforts towards attaining these goals.

The two sides expressed satisfaction with the progress reached in the sphere of control over armaments and avoiding conflicts and with the appropriate understanding reached at the Strategic Arms Limitation Talks and the Soviet—US agreement on the prevention of nuclear war.

During the exchange of views on the situation in Asia, the two sides expressed satisfaction with the signing of the peace agreement in Vietnam and also the peace agreement in Laos and the protocol on the implementation of the agreement. Both sides expressed the view that these agreements, provided they are strictly complied with by all parties, open up the possibility of establishing a lasting peace in Indochina, and also that the problems of Vietnam, Laos and Cambodia should be settled by the peoples of those countries without any interference whatsoever from outside.

The two sides welcomed the fact that the way had been opened for a dialogue between the South and the North in the Korean Peninsula.

They expressed satisfaction over the efforts of the states concerned in the interests of relaxing tension on the sub-continent of Southern Asia.

They also stressed that active assistance to the individual efforts of Asian countries on the basis of respect for their sovereignty in itself was a great contribution to the cause of peace and stability in Asia.

The two sides expressed their great concern at the renewal of hostilities in the Middle East and expressed the hope that the present situation would be settled as soon as possible. They expressed their desire for the earliest possible establishment of a just and lasting peace in the Middle East.

The two sides stated the readiness of both the countries to make a constructive contribution to the cause of further strengthening a lasting peace and the security of all peoples.

The sides noted with satisfaction that the direct dialogue between the leaders of both countries, which had been held in a frank and constructive spirit, had been very useful and had made a big contribution to the development of relations between the two countries. The two sides underlined the need to continue this dialogue between the leaders of the two countries.

Having expressed gratitude for the reception accorded him during his stay in the Soviet Union, Prime Minister K. Tanaka, on behalf of the government of Japan, extended an invitation to L. I. Brezhnev, general secretary of the CPSU central committee, to N. V. Podgorny, President of the Presidium of the USSR Supreme Soviet, and to A. N. Kosygin, Chairman of the USSR Council of Ministers to visit Japan at a date to be agreed upon later. The invitations were accepted with gratitude.

88. Joint announcement issued following the meeting of President Ford and the Japanese Prime Minister, Mr Miki, Washington, 6 August 1975[1]

1. Prime Minister Miki and President Ford met in Washington August 5 and 6 for a comprehensive review of various subjects of mutual interest. The discussions between the two leaders, in which Minister for Foreign Affairs Miyazawa and Secretary of State Kissinger participated, were conducted in an informal and cordial atmosphere. Their meetings were productive and reflected the strength and breadth of the existing friendship between Japan and the United States.

2. The Prime Minister and the President reaffirmed the basic principles and common purposes underlying relations between Japan and the United States as set forth in the Joint Communiqué of November 20, 1974 on the occasion of the President's visit to Japan.[2] In so doing, the Prime Minister and the President noted that Japan and the United States, while sharing basic values and ideals, differ in their national characteristics and the circumstances in which they are placed; and yet the two nations, acting together, have drawn upon the strengths inherent in such diversity to build a mature, mutually beneficial and complementary relationship.

They emphasized the fundamental importance in that relationship of constructive and creative cooperation between the two countries toward the shared goals of world peace and prosperity. Expressing satisfaction with the open and frank dialogue

1 *DSB*, 8 September 1975, pp. 382–4.
2 Not published here.

hich has developed between the two Governments, they pledged to maintain and
rengthen this consultation. To this end, the Minister for Foreign Affairs and
ne Secretary of State will review twice a year bilateral and global matters of common
oncern.

3. The Prime Minister and the President discussed developments in Asia following
ne end of armed conflict in Indochina. The President, recognizing the importance
f Asia for world peace and progress, reaffirmed that the United States would con-
nue to play an active and positive role in that region and would continue to
phold its treaty commitments there. The Prime Minister and the President welcomed
ne efforts being made by many nations in Asia to strengthen their political, economic
nd social bases. They stated that Japan and the United States were prepared to
ontinue to extend assistance and cooperation in support of these efforts. They
greed that the security of the Republic of Korea is essential to the maintenance of
eace on the Korean peninsula, which in turn is necessary for peace and security
n East Asia, including Japan. They noted the importance of the existing security
rrangements for maintaining and preserving that peace. At the same time they
trongly expressed the hope that the dialogue between the South and North would
roceed in order to ease tensions and eventually to achieve peaceful unification. In
onnection with the Korean question in the United Nations, the Prime Minister
nd the President expressed the hope that all concerned would recognize the
mportance of maintaining a structure which would preserve the armistice now in
ffect.

4. The Prime Minister and the President expressed their conviction that the Treaty
f Mutual Cooperation and Security between Japan and the United States has
reatly contributed to the maintenance of peace and security in the Far East and
s an indispensable element of the basic international political structure in Asia,
nd that the continued maintenance of the Treaty serves the long-term interests of
oth countries. Further, they recognized that the United States nuclear deterrent
s an important contributor to the security of Japan. In this connection, the President
eassured the Prime Minister that the United States would continue to abide by its
efense commitment to Japan under the Treaty of Mutual Cooperation and Security
n the event of armed attack against Japan, whether by nuclear or conventional
orces. The Prime Minister stated that Japan would continue to carry out its obli-
ations under the Treaty. The Prime Minister and the President recognized the
esirability of still closer consultations for the smooth and effective implementation
f the Treaty. They agreed that the authorities concerned of the two countries
ould conduct consultations within the framework of the Security Consultative
ommittee on measures to be taken in cooperation by the two countries.

5. The Prime Minister and the President discussed various international issues of
ommon concern. The President noted that the United States would continue to
eek an early conclusion to negotiations of the second agreement between the United
tates and the Soviet Union on the limitation of strategic arms. The Prime Minister
nd the President expressed their strong hope that prompt progress be made through
urrent efforts toward a peaceful settlement in the Middle East.

6. The Prime Minister and the President expressed their concern over the recent trend toward nuclear proliferation in the world, and agreed that Japan and the United States should participate positively in international efforts for the preventio of nuclear proliferation and the development of adequate safeguards. They emphasi that all nuclear-weapon states should contribute constructively in the areas of nucle arms limitation, the security of non-nuclear-weapon states, and the uses of nuclear energy for peaceful purposes. The Prime Minister expressed his intention to procee with the necessary steps to bring about Japan's ratification of the nuclear non-proliferation treaty at the earliest possible opportunity.

7. In light of the increasing economic interdependence of the nations of the world, the Prime Minister and the President agreed that Japan and the United State share a special responsibility toward the development of a stable and balanced worl economy. They agreed that the two countries would work in close consultation toward the resolution in a manner beneficial to all nations of problems relating to the general condition of the world economy, international finance, trade, energy, and cooperation between developed and developing nations. They noted with satisfaction that trade and investment relations between the two countries are expanding in a steady and mutually beneficial manner.

8. Observing the importance of free and expanding trade to the world economy, the Prime Minister and the President emphasized the need for an open internationa trading system, and affirmed that Japan and the United States would continue to play a positive and constructive role in the Tokyo Round of multilateral trade negotiations currently underway in Geneva within the framework of the General Agreement on Tariffs and Trade.

9. Recognizing that there remain elements of instability in the world energy situation, the Prime Minister and the President expressed their satisfaction with the progress thus far achieved in cooperation among consumer nations.

They agreed to maintain and strengthen cooperation between Japan and the United States in this field and in the development of their respective national energ efforts. Agreeing that mutual understanding and cooperation among all nations is fundamental to the solution of the international energy problem, they noted the urgent need for the development of harmonious relations between oil producin and consuming nations. In this connection, they welcomed steps now being taken to resume the dialogue between oil producer and consumer nations and expressed their determination that the two countries should further strengthen and coordinat their cooperative efforts for that purpose.

10. Noting the desirability of establishing adequate supply and distribution to meet the world's growing demand for food, the Prime Minister and the President agreed upon the importance of cooperation in agricultural development assistance to promote the food production capabilities of developing countries. The President further noted the need for the early establishment of an internationally coordinated system of nationally held grain reserves. The Prime Minister stressed the need for a steady expansion of trade in agricultural products through cooperation between exporting and importing countries to their mutual benefit. The Prime Minister

and the President reaffirmed the interest of the two countries in maintaining and strengthening the mutually beneficial agricultural trade between them.

11. Noting the need to assist the efforts of the developing countries to promote their own economic development and to meet the human aspirations of their peoples, the Prime Minister and the President agreed upon the importance of increased co-operation, both between Japan and the United States and with the developing countries, in such areas as development assistance and trade, including that of primary commodities.

12. The Prime Minister and the President expressed appreciation for the achievements recorded during the past decade by existing bilateral cooperative programs in the fields of medicine, science, and technology, and for the work underway in the panel for the review of Japan—US Scientific and Technological Cooperation. They declared their satisfaction at the signing on August 5 by the Minister for Foreign Affairs and the Secretary of State of a new agreement between the two countries for cooperation in environmental protection. They recognized further that the promotion of mutual understanding through cultural and educational exchange is of basic importance to the strengthening of friendly relations between the Japanese and American peoples. In this regard, the Prime Minister expressed his intention of continuing to expand such exchange in addition to the promotion of Japanese studies in the United States and other projects thus far carried out by Japan, notably through the Japan Foundation. Welcoming the Prime Minister's statement, the President expressed his intention to continue his efforts to make expanded resources available for further promoting cultural and educational exchange with Japan.

13. The Prime Minister conveyed on behalf of the people of Japan sincere congratulations to the people of the United States as they celebrate the 200th anniversary of their independence in the coming year. The President thanked the Prime Minister for these sentiments and expressed the deepest appreciation of the American people.

89. Joint statement by President Ford and Mr Miki, Washington, 6 August 1975[1]

The Prime Minister of Japan and the President of the United States, recognizing that the Japanese and American peoples share fundamental democratic values and are joined together by ties of mutual trust and cooperation, affirm that their two nations will continue to work together to build a more open and free international community, and state as follows:

— A more stable and peaceful world order requires the acceptance by all nations of certain principles of international conduct, and the establishment of a creative international dialogue — transcending differences of ideology, tradition or stages of development.

— Those principles must include respect for the sovereignty of all nations,

1 *DSB*, 8 September 1975, pp. 384—5.

recognition of the legitimate interests of others, attitudes of mutual respect in international dealings, determination to seek the peaceful resolution of differences among nations, and firm commitment to social justice and economic progress around the globe.

— Japan and the United States pledge to support these principles, and to nurture a dialogue among nations which reflects them. They will expand and strengthen their cooperation in many fields of joint endeavor. Recognizing that equitable and durable peace in Asia is essential to that of the entire world, Japan and the United States will extend every support to efforts of the countries of the region to consolidate such a peace.

— International economic and social relations should promote the prosperity of all peoples and aspirations and creativity of individuals and nations. The interests of developed as well as developing countries, and of consumers as well as producers of raw materials, must be accommodated in a manner which advances the well-being of all and brings closer the goal of social and economic justice.

— In a world made small by science and technology, as well as by trade and communications, interdependence among nations has become a reality affecting the lives and welfare of all peoples. International economic institutions and systems must function in a manner reflecting that interdependence and promoting a cooperative rather than a confrontational approach to economic issues.

— The suffering caused by disease and hunger is a most serious and poignant impediment to a humane international economic and social order. The financial educational and technological resources of developed countries give them a special responsibility for the alleviation of these conditions. It is imperative that there be an increasingly effective sharing of knowledge, resources and organizational skill among all countries to hasten the day when these scourges will be eliminated from the earth. In these endeavors also, Japan and the United States will contribute fully.

C. Negotiations on security in Europe

10. Declaration of the NATO Council on Mutual and Balanced Force Reductions, Reykjavik, 25 June 1968[1]

Declaration Adopted by Foreign Ministers and Representatives of Countries Participating in the NATO Defence Programme.[2]

1. Meeting at Reykjavik on 24 and 25 June 1968, the Ministers recalled the frequently expressed and strong desire of their countries to make progress in the field of disarmament and arms control.

2. Ministers recognised that the unresolved issues which still divide the European Continent must be settled by peaceful means, and are convinced that the ultimate goal of a lasting, peaceful order in Europe requires an atmosphere of trust and confidence and can only be reached by a step-by-step process. Mindful of the obvious and considerable interest of all European states in this goal, Ministers expressed their belief that measures in this field including balanced and mutual force reductions can contribute significantly to the lessening of tension and to further reducing the danger of war.

3. Ministers noted the important work undertaken within the North Atlantic Council by member governments in examining possible proposals for such reductions pursuant to Paragraph 13 of the 'Report on the Future Tasks of the Alliance', approved by the Ministers in December 1967. In particular, they have taken note of the work being done in the committee of Political Advisers to establish bases of comparison and to analyze alternative ways of achieving a balanced reduction of forces, particularly in the central part of Europe.

4. Ministers affirmed the need for the Alliance to maintain an effective military capability and to assure a balance of forces between NATO and the Warsaw Pact. Since the security of the NATO countries and the prospects for mutual force reductions would be weakened by NATO reductions alone, Ministers affirmed the proposition that the overall military capability of NATO should not be reduced except as part of a pattern of mutual force reductions balanced in scope and timing.

5. Accordingly, Ministers directed Permanent Representatives to continue and intensify their work in accordance with the following agreed principles:

1 *DSB*, 15 July 1968, p. 77.
2 All member states except France.

55

(A) Mutual force reductions should be reciprocal and balanced in scope and timing.

(B) Mutual reductions should represent a substantial and significant step, which will serve to maintain the present degree of security at reduced cost, but should not be such as to risk destabilizing the situation in Europe.

(C) Mutual reductions should be consonant with the aim of creating confidence in Europe generally and in the case of each party concerned.

(D) To this end, any new arrangement regarding forces should be consistent with the vital security interests of all parties and capable of being carried out effectively.

6. Ministers affirmed the readiness of their Governments to explore with other interested states specific and practical steps in the arms control field.

7. In particular, Ministers agreed that it was desirable that a process leading to mutual force reductions should be initiated. To that end they decided to make all necessary preparations for discussions on this subject with the Soviet Union and oth countries of Eastern Europe as they call on them to join in this search for progress towards peace.

8. Ministers directed their Permanent Representatives to follow up on this declaration.

91. Appeal to All European Countries, adopted by the Political Consultative Committee of the Warsaw Pact countries, Budapest, 17 March 1969[1]

The People's Republic of Bulgaria, the Hungarian People's Republic, the German Democratic Republic, the Polish People's Republic, the Socialist Republic of Rumania, the Union of Soviet Socialist Republics and the Czechoslovak Socialist Republic – the States members of the Warsaw Pact – participants in the Conferenc of the Political Consultative Committee, expressing the aspirations of their peoples to live in peace and good-neighbourliness with the rest of the European peoples, as well as their firm resolve to assist in establishing an atmosphere of security and co-operation on our continent, address to all European States the following appeal for the redoubling of efforts aimed at strengthening peace and security in Europe.

The present and future of the peoples of Europe are indissolubly linked with the maintenance and consolidation of peace on our continent. Genuine security and reliable peace can be ensured, if the thoughts, pursuits and energy of the European States are directed towards the aim of relaxing tension, solving with due regard to realities international problems that are ripe for solution and arranging for all-round cooperation on an all-European basis.

The way to good-neighbourliness, confidence and mutual understanding depends on the will and efforts of the peoples and governments of all European countries. The Europe of today, as it came out of the second world war, is made up of more than thirty States, large and small, differing according to their social system, locatio

1 WEU, *Political Year in Europe, 1969*, pp. 79–80.

and interests. By the will of history they are destined to live side by side, and no one can change this fact.

More and more governments, parliaments, parties, political and social leaders are imbued with understanding of the responsibility that lies upon them before present and future generations for the prevention of a new military conflict in Europe. However, there are still active in Europe forces which put on the credit side of European development, not the settlement of disputes and peaceful agreements, but additional divisions and missiles, and new military programmes calculated for decades in advance. Also active together with them are those who have not drawn the proper lessons from the outcome of the Second World War, as a result of which German militarism and nazism were crushed. Their intrigues are a source of tension and bring complications into international relations.

The States participating in the Conference consider it their duty, in future also, to do all that lies in their power to shield Europe from the danger of new military conflicts, to clear the way for the development of cooperation among all European countries irrespective of their social system, on the basis of the principles of peaceful coexistence.

However complex unsolved problems may be, their solution must be achieved by peaceful means through negotiation and not through the use, or threat of the use, of force.

In analysing the situation in Europe, the States members of the Warsaw Pact consider that there is a real possibility of ensuring European security through common efforts, taking into account the interests of all European States and peoples.

Almost three years ago States members of the Warsaw Pact put forward at Bucharest a proposal to convoke a general European conference to consider questions of European security and peaceful cooperation. The contacts which have taken place since then have shown that not a single European government expressed opposition to the idea of a general European conference and that there are real possibilities of holding one. Not once since the Second World War have all the States of Europe come together, although there are numerous questions which await consideration at the conference table. From the standpoint of the interests of consolidating peace, there are no serious reasons for putting off the convening of a general European conference.

Such a conference would meet the interests of all European States. It would make it possible together to find ways and means of doing away with the division of Europe into military groupings and achieving peaceful cooperation among European States and peoples.

However, there are forces in the world which, because they seek to maintain the division of our continent, conduct a policy of fomenting tension, and refuse to facilitate peaceful cooperation among States and peoples, openly oppose the holding of such a conference and other measures to strengthen European security.

The States participating in the present Conference are convinced that the development of general European cooperation has been and continues to be the only real alternative to dangerous military confrontation, the armaments race and the dissensions which aggressive forces, seeking to undo the results of the Second World War and remake the map of Europe, are trying and will continue to try to impose on Europe.

The States members of the Warsaw Pact confirm their proposals against the division of the world into military blocs, against the armaments race and the resultant threat to the cause of international peace and security, and the other measures and proposals contained in the Declaration on the strengthening of peace and security in Europe adopted at Bucharest in 1966.

It is a vital necessity, for the European peoples, to avert new military conflicts, and to strengthen the political, economic and cultural links between all States on the basis of equal rights and respect for the independence and sovereignty of States. A durable system of European security will create the objective possibility and necessity of carrying out, by combined efforts, large-scale projects in the fields of power production, of transport, of the hydrospheric and atmospheric environment and of health, which have a direct bearing on the well-being of the population of the entire continent. It is precisely this common interest which can and should become the foundation for European cooperation.

One of the basic preconditions for safeguarding the security of Europe is the inviolability of the existing European frontiers, including the Oder-Neisse frontiers and those between the German Democratic Republic and the Federal Republic of Germany, recognition of the fact of the existence of those two countries, renunciation by the latter of its claims to represent the whole of the German people, and renunciation of possession in any form of nuclear weapons. West Berlin has a special status and does not belong to Western Germany.

A practical step towards strengthening European security would be a meeting in the immediate future between representatives of all the European States concerned in order to establish by mutual agreement the procedure for convening the Conference and to determine the items on its agenda. We are prepared to consider at the same time any other proposal regarding the method for preparing and convening the Conference.

The States participating in the Conference of the Political Consultative Committee address to all the countries of Europe an appeal for cooperation in convening a general European conference and in creating the necessary preconditions for ensuring that the Conference is successful and that it justifies the hopes which the people connect with it.

In order to bring about this important action, which would constitute an historic moment in the life of the continent, the States participating in the Conference make a solemn appeal to all European countries to strengthen the climate of confidence, and to that end to refrain from any action liable to poison the atmosphere in relations between States. They call upon them to go beyond general statements about peace to concrete acts and measures for the relaxation of tension and disarmament, for the development of cooperation and peace between the peoples. They appeal to all European governments to unite their efforts so that Europe may become a continent of fruitful collaboration between nations possessing equal rights and a factor for stability, peace and mutual understanding throughout the world.

2. Memorandum from the Finnish Government on the Convening of a European Security Conference, 5 May 1969[1] (extracts)

The Government of the Soviet Union approached recently the governments of European countries in the matter of the arrangement of a European security conference and of its preparations. This proposal concerning a special preparatory meeting was extended to the Government of Finland on 8 April 1969.

The Government of Finland has on several occasions stated that Finland considers a well prepared conference on European security problems useful. The Government of Finland considers well-founded the view of the Soviet Union that such a conference should be convened without any preliminary conditions. The participants should have the right to present their views and to make their proposals on European questions...

At the Foreign Ministers' meeting of Finland, Denmark, Iceland, Norway and Sweden, held in Copenhagen on 23 and 24 April 1969, a joint position was defined according to which 'preconditions for conferences on security problems are that they should be well prepared, that they should be timed so as to offer prospects of positive results, and that all States, whose participation is necessary for achieving a solution to European security problems, should be given opportunities to take part in the discussions'...

The Government of Finland considers that the preparations for the conference should begin through consultations between the governments concerned and, after the necessary conditions exist, a preparatory meeting for consideration of the questions connected with the arrangement of the conference could be convened...

The Government of Finland is willing to act as the host for the security conference as well as for the preparatory meeting provided that the governments concerned consider this as appropriate.

The Government of Finland will send this memorandum to the Governments of all European States, to those of East and West Germany and to the Governments of the United States of America and Canada...

3. Communiqué of the Conference of Foreign Ministers of the Warsaw Pact countries, Prague, 31 October 1969, with Annexes[2] (extracts)

On behalf of their governments, the Foreign Ministers of the Warsaw Pact States propose that the following questions be placed on the agenda of the all-European conference:

1. The creation of security in Europe, renunciation of the use of force and the threat of force in relations between European States;

1 WEU, *Political Year in Europe, 1969*, p. 94.
2 WEU, *Political Year in Europe, 1969*, pp. 133–6.

2. Widening commercial, economic, technical, and scientific relations between European States, serving the development of political cooperation, based on the equality of rights. . .

ANNEXES
Draft document on the expansion of trade, economic, scientific and technical relations based on the principles of equality, aimed at a promotion of political cooperation among the States of Europe

The States participants of the all-European Conference (enumeration of States follows), being convinced that the development of relations on an equal footing among States without any discrimination in the field of trade, economic, scientific and technical relations facilitates the attainment of a relaxation of tensions, normalisation of relations among all European States and the consolidation of peace and security in Europe,

Proceeding from the fact that the differences in economic and social systems are no obstacle for an expansion of trade, economic, scientific and technical international relations, relying on full equality of rights and mutual benefits,

Realising that important changes in the economic relations among European countries and the current scientific and technical revolution, which affects all spheres of social life, necessitate promotion and perfection of the trade, economic, scientific and technical cooperation among European States on which the growth of prosperity of the population of the European continent as well as the preservation of the role of Europe as one of the most important centres of world civilisation depend in considerable measure,

Sharing the views that expansion of trade, economic, scientific and technical relations among European States would be beneficial for all participants and would likewise facilitate the advance of economies and raising the living standards of the peoples of these countries,

Taking into account that the state of trade, economic, scientific and technical relations among European countries considerably affects the economic situation in the other parts of the world, and

Taking into account decisions taken by the United Nations General Assembly, the United Nations Conference on Trade and Development and by the Economic Commission for Europe, urging the governments of European States to pursue constructive efforts aimed at an improvement of their mutual relations and a further development of mutually beneficial cooperation on the basis of the renunciation of discrimination in their trade policies,

Declare that they are resolved to exert further efforts aimed at a promotion of a broader economic, trade, scientific and technical cooperation among all European States and to take all necessary measures so that the existing obstacles standing in the way of translating such a cooperation into practice be eliminated, which will facilitate the strengthening of mutual confidence and the development of good neighbourly relations among all States of Europe.

Draft document on the renunciation of force or the threat of its use in mutual relations among the States of Europe

The States (enumeration of participating States follows) that met at the all-European Conference on questions of the security and cooperation in Europe held in Helsinki,

Submitted in the course of a free discussion their views on the ways leading towards relaxation of tensions, the strengthening of peace and security and the promotion of cooperation in Europe.

The participants of the Conference,

Being resolved to eliminate forever war from the life of peoples of the continent of Europe, bearing in mind that the situation in Europe is of primary importance or the fate of world peace as well,

Being deeply aware that in any field of peaceful cooperation European States might find possibilities for new bilaterally beneficial steps, that nations are confronted by the objective to strengthen mutual peaceful and friendly relations, continually to develop all-round cooperation and understanding among all European States, irrespective of the differences in their socio-political systems and in their approaches to the existing international problems,

Proceeding from the respect for the principles of sovereignty, territorial integrity and independence of all States and also the principle of non-interference in their internal matters,

Pursuing the principles of the United Nations Charter, particularly the provisions of Article 2 and Chapter VIII,

Solemnly declare on behalf of their States and nations that in their mutual relations they shall renounce the use of force or the threat of its use; that in the settlement of any dispute and disagreement among them exclusively peaceful means shall be used,

Declare that they shall recognise and unconditionally respect the territorial integrity of all European States within their existing borders.

In no case shall this apply to the obligations that the States — participants of the all European Conference — had undertaken in virtue of valid bilateral and multilateral treaties and agreements.

94. Declaration of the NATO Council, Brussels, 5 December 1969[1]

1. Meeting at Brussels on 4 and 5 December 1969, the Ministers of the North Atlantic Alliance reaffirmed the commitment of their nations to pursue effective policies directed towards a greater relaxation of tensions in their continuing search for a just and durable peace.

2. Peace and security in Europe must rest upon universal respect for the principles of sovereign equality, political independence and the territorial integrity of each European state; the right of its peoples to shape their own destinies; the peaceful

1 *DSB*, 29 December 1969, pp. 628–30.

settlement of disputes; non-intervention in the internal affairs of any state by any other state, whatever their political or social system; and the renunciation of the use of the threat of force against any state. Past experience has shown that there is, as yet, no common interpretation of these principles. The fundamental problems in Europe can be solved only on the basis of these principles and any real and lasting improvement of East—West relations presupposes respect for them without any conditions or reservations.

3. At their meeting in Washington in April 1969, Ministers had expressed the intention of their governments to explore with the Soviet Union and other countrie of Eastern Europe which concrete issues best lend themselves to fruitful negotiation and an early resolution. To this end, the Council has been engaged in a detailed stud of various issues for exploration and possible negotiation. Ministers recognized that procedure merited closer examination, and accordingly, requested the Council in Permanent Session to report to the next Ministerial Meeting.

4. Ministers considered that, in an era of negotiation, it should be possible, by means of discussion of specific and well-defined subjects, progressively to reduce tensions. This would in itself facilitate discussion of the more fundamental questions

Arms Control and Disarmament

5. Ministers again expressed the interest of the Alliance in arms control and disarmament and recalled the Declaration on mutual and balanced force reductions adopted at Reykjavik in 1968 and reaffirmed in Washington in 1969. The Members of the Alliance have noted that up to now this suggestion has led to no result. The Allies, nevertheless, have continued, and will continue, their studies in order to prepare a realistic basis for active exploration at an early date and thereby establish whether it could serve as a starting point for fruitful negotiations. They requested that a report of the Council in Permanent Session on the preparation of models for mutual and balanced force reductions be submitted as soon as possible.

6. Ministers of countries participating in NATO's integrated defence programme consider that the studies on mutual and balanced force reductions have progressed sufficiently to permit the establishment of certain criteria which, in their view, such reductions should meet. Significant reductions under adequate verification and control would be envisaged under any agreement on mutual and balanced force reductions, which should also be consistent with the vital security interests of all parties. This would be another concrete step in advancing 'along the road of ending the arms race and of general and complete disarmament, including nuclear disarman

7. These Ministers directed that further studies should be given to measures which could accompany or follow agreement on mutual and balanced force reductions. Such measures could include advance notification of military movements and manoeuvres, exchange of observers at military manoeuvres and possibly the establishment of observation posts. Examination of the techniques and methods of inspection should also be further developed.

Germany and Berlin

8. The Ministers welcome the efforts of the governments of the United States, Great Britain, and France, in the framework of their special responsibility for Berlin and Germany as a whole, to gain the cooperation of the Soviet Union in improving the situation with respect to Berlin and free access to the city. The elimination of difficulties created in the past with respect to Berlin, especially with regard to access, would increase the prospects for serious discussions on the other concrete issues which continue to divide East and West. Furthermore, Berlin could play a constructive role in the expansion of East–West economic relations if the city's trade with the East could be facilitated.

9. A just and lasting peace settlement for Germany must be based on the free decision of the German people and on the interests of European security. The Ministers are convinced that, pending such a settlement, the proposals of the Federal Republic for a modus vivendi between the two parts of Germany and for a bilateral exchange of declarations on the non-use of force or the threat of force would, if they receive a positive response, substantially facilitate cooperation between East and West on other problems. They consider that these efforts by the Federal Republic represent constructive steps toward relaxation of tension in Europe and express the hope that the governments will therefore take them into account in forming their own attitude toward the German question.

10. The Ministers would regard concrete progress in both these fields as an important contribution to peace in Europe. They are bound to attach great weight to the responses to these proposals in evaluating the prospects for negotiations looking toward improved relations and cooperation in Europe.

Economic, technical and cultural exchanges

11. Allied governments consider that not only economic and technical but also cultural exchanges between interested countries can bring mutual benefit and understanding. In these fields more could be achieved by freer movement of people, ideas and information between the countries of East and West.

12. The benefit of the Alliance's work in the field of human environment would be enhanced if it were to become the basis of broader cooperation. This could, and should, be an early objective, being one in which the Warsaw Pact governments have indicated an interest. Further cooperation could also be undertaken, for example, in the more specialized field of oceanography. More intensive efforts in such fields should be pursued either bilaterally, multilaterally or in the framework of existing international bodies comprising interested countries.

Perspectives for negotiations

13. The Ministers considered that the concrete issues concerning European security

and cooperation mentioned in this Declaration are subjects lending themselves to possible discussions or negotiations with the Soviet Union and the other countries of Eastern Europe. The Allied governments will continue and intensify their contac discussions or negotiations through all appropriate channels, bilateral or multi-lateral, believing that progress is most likely to be achieved by choosing in each instance the means most suitable for the subject. Ministers therefore expressed thei support for bilateral initiatives undertaken by the German Federal Government wit the Soviet Union and other countries of Eastern Europe, looking toward agreement on the renunciation of force and the threat of force. Ministers expressed the hope that existing contacts will be developed so as to enable all countries concerned to participate in discussions and negotiations on substantial problems of cooperation and security in Europe with real prospects of success.

14. The Members of the Alliance remain receptive to signs of willingness on the part of the Soviet Union and other Eastern European countries to discuss measures to reduce tension and promote cooperation in Europe and to take constructive actions to this end. They have noted in this connection references made by these countries to the possibility of holding an early conference on European security. Ministers agreed that careful advance preparation and prospects of concrete results would in any case be essential. Ministers consider that, as part of a comprehensive approach, progress in the bilateral and multilateral discussions and negotiations which have already begun, or could begin shortly, and which relate to fundamental problems of European security, would make a major contribution to improving the political atmosphere in Europe. Progress in these discussions and negotiations woul help to ensure the success of any eventual conference in which, of course, the Nort American members of the Alliance would participate, to discuss and negotiate substantial problems of cooperation and security in Europe.

15. The Ministers affirmed that, in considering all constructive possibilities, including a general conference or conferences they will wish to assure that any such meeting should not serve to ratify the present division of Europe and should be the result of a common effort among all interested countries to tackle the problems which separate them.

95. Declaration on Mutual and Balanced Force Reductions issued by the NATO Council, Rome 27 May 1970[1]

1. Meeting at Rome on 26 and 27 May 1970, the Ministers representing countries participating in NATO's Integrated Defence Programme recall and reaffirm the com mitment of their nations to pursue effective policies directed towards a greater relaxation of tensions in their continuing search for a just and durable peace. They recall, in particular, the invitations they have previously addressed to the Soviet Union and other countries of Eastern Europe to join them in discussing the possibil of mutual and balanced force reductions.

1 *DSB*, 22 June 1970, p. 775.

2. The objective of the work on which their representatives have been engaged
as been to prepare a realistic basis for active explorations between the interested
arties at an early date and thereby to establish whether it could serve as a starting
oint for fruitful negotiation. Such exploratory talks would assist those concerned
a developing in detail criteria and objectives for substantive negotiations to follow
t the appropriate stage in a forum to be determined. They would also provide
angible evidence of the readiness to build confidence between East and West.

3. Ministers invite interested states to hold exploratory talks on mutual and
alanced force reductions in Europe, with special reference to the Central Region.
hey agree that in such talks the Allies would put forward the following con-
.derations:

(*a*) Mutual force reductions should be compatible with the vital security interests
f the Alliance and should not operate to the military disadvantage of either side
aving regard for the differences arising from geographical and other considerations.

(*b*) Reductions should be on a basis of reciprocity, and phased and balanced as
ɔ their scope and timing.

(*c*) Reductions should include stationed and indigenous forces and their weapons
ystems in the area concerned.

(*d*) There must be adequate verification and controls to ensure the observance of
greements on mutual and balanced force reductions.

4. As a first step Ministers requested the Foreign Minister of Italy to transmit
his Declaration on their behalf through diplomatic channels to all other interested
arties, including neutral and non-aligned governments. They further agreed that in
he course of their normal bilateral and other contacts member governments would
ɛek to obtain the responses and reactions of other governments. Members of the
.lliance will consult further regarding the outcome of their soundings with a view
ɔ enabling the Alliance to determine what further individual or joint exploration
aight be useful.

6. Memorandum issued by the Conference of Foreign Ministers f the Member States of the Warsaw Treaty, Budapest, 6 June 1970[1] (extracts)

. . The question of the composition of the conference has been clarified. All
.uropean States including the GDR and the German Federal Republic, can take
art on equal terms and on a footing of equality with other European States; so
an the United States and Canada. . .

Discussion of questions concerning the content of the work of the All-European
'onference, and its agenda, is continuing. The two items of the agenda proposed in
rague corresponding with the interests of ensuring security and developing co-
peration in Europe and are questions on which extensive accord can be reached.

1 *SWB*, EE/3417, 30 June 1970, A1/1–2.

These proposals do not evoke objections on grounds of principle. At the same time, a number of States favour an expansion of the conference agenda.

Prompted by the desire to reach accord on the agenda of the All-European conference which would be acceptable to all interested States, the Governments of the People's Republic of Bulgaria, the Hungarian People's Republic, the German Democratic Republic, the Polish People's Republic, the Socialist Republic of Rumania, the Union of Soviet Socialist Republics and the Czechoslovak Socialist Republic suggest that the creation at the All-European Conference of a body on questions of security and cooperation in Europe should be included in it.

The Governments which adopted the present Memorandum believe that a study of the question of reducing foreign armed forces on the territory of European State would serve the interests of a detente and security in Europe. In order to create as quickly as possible the most favourable conditions for the discussion of these questions at the All-European Conference, and in the interests of studying the question of the reduction of foreign armed forces in the most favourable conditions this question could be discussed in the body it is proposed to set up at the All-European Conference, or in some other manner acceptable to the States interested. They believe, moreover that questions of the environment could be discussed within the framework of the second item of the agenda suggested in Prague, and that this item could be expanded by including the development of cultural ties.

Thus the following questions could be submitted for consideration by the All-European Conference:

- Ensuring European Security and the renunciation of the use or threat of force in relations between States in Europe,
- The expansion of trade, economic, scientific—technical and cultural ties on an equitable basis, directed at the development of political cooperation between European States;
- The creation at the All-European Conference of a body on questions of security and cooperation in Europe. . .

97. Memorandum of the Austrian Government on Mutual and Balanced Force Reductions, 27 July 1970[1]

The Republic of Austria as a permanently neutral state lying between the two great military blocs, has a natural interest in all efforts directed towards a genuine detent. The proposal for a summoning of a conference, which should concern itself with questions of security and cooperation in Europe, is therefore welcome from its beginning.

In accordance with this interest, Austria has given a positive answer to the suggestion of the Finnish government that such a conference should be held in Helsink. Austria has also gone beyond this in conducting conversations with a number of interested states on all problems connected with this complex of questions.

1 *Wiener Zeitung*, 28 July 1970; unofficial translation.

This general exchange of opinion between the interested states has already borne uit insofar as in the course of this exchange of opinions bilateral questions have so been discussed. The solution of these questions should lead to cooperation in urope.

Austria is also following with attention the concrete efforts undertaken in recent onths, which have as their purpose the removal or at least the diminution in tensity of existing sources of major tension in Europe. A successful outcome of ese efforts would lead to a further diminution of the mistrust and tension in urope. With this the prospects for success for a general conference would be rengthened and a positive and dynamic influence would be exercised upon the reparations for a conference.

Austria is, therefore, of the view that these bilateral attempts at reduction of nsion and the summoning together of the conference on European security are t mutually exclusive, rather that they can be enlarged upon with great advantage.

An important task of the preparation for the conference — in which each state ould have the possibility of representing its point of view itself — lies in the aching of an agreement on the question of an agenda and on the most important ocedural principles. On the more far-reaching and important question of the embership of the conference it seems that agreement has already been reached.

In the latest declarations of the member states of the North Atlantic Treaty d also of the Warsaw Pact it is clear that a rapprochement of the points of view on e agenda has to come to show itself. The widening of the agenda proposed by the embers of the Warsaw Pact in the Prague Declaration, by the inclusion of questions f cultural cooperation and of the environment is very much welcomed by Austria.

By reason of its own geographical and military situation and on the basis of the ilitary conditions now existing in Europe, Austria believes that it can expect a ccessful outcome of the process of detente in a longer view only if the conference hich is to concern itself with security in Europe, also leads to a discussion and a lution of the question of mutual and balanced force reduction in Europe which essential for the whole question of security. Such a reduction of the military tential would also be a concrete measure which would follow naturally from the int on the agenda, 'protection of the European security and denunciation of e use of force or the threat of the use of force in mutual relations between the ropean states', and an agreement directed towards this. Any other touching upon e or more points of principle which are already established in the Charter of the N could not alone bring the European states closer to detente and security, quite art from the point that such conversation has been going on within the scope of e Legal Commission of the General Assembly of the UN for many years on a iversal basis, on the agenda point 'Principles of International Law concerning the iendly relations and cooperation between states'.

It is clear that measures of detente in the military field should not lead to any teration in the relationship between the strengths of the forces of the various ocs in Europe. This would lead only to new mistrust and an increase in tension. the Austrian view the reduction of striking forces should not be limited purely to the question of foreign troops stationed on the territories of the European states.

With these considerations in mind, Austria therefore suggests that in addition to the question of the protection of European security and the renunciation of the use of force or the threat of the use of force in the mutual relations between the European states, and the question of the 'expansion of relations on a basic equality in the field of trade, economics, science, technology and culture with the aim of the development of political cooperation between the European states', a third point should be inserted in the agenda which deals with a basic discussion of the question of mutual and balanced force reductions in Europe. The discussions on this theme could be continued and made more concrete in a special organ to be created in this conference or in a similar kind of working group.

The solution of this difficult problem would demand that the interested states should agree from the beginning not to summon together a single conference but rather a succession of them. This would have the further consequence that difficulties which might arise at the first conference should not lead to an increase in the atmosphere of mistrust and the strengthening of the existing tensions. Attempts must be made to clear up such difficulties in the time between the conference by the meeting of working parties or other organs whose establishment is to be agreed.

Austria will also cooperate in further bilateral contacts in the preparation of the conference. She believes that the time is already very near in which one can go over to multilateral conversations. On the question of preparations on a multilateral level, Austria has no objection to make against the entrusting of the representatives of the interested countries accredited to Helsinki with informal contacts, but she would rather incline to the view that those functionaries in the interested countries who are permanently concerned with these questions should be entrusted with the carrying through of these conversations. Should, however, the majority of the interested states decide for informal ambassadorial conversations in Helsinki, then Austria would naturally be prepared to accept this and to take part in them. Austria would in addition be willing, should the interested states wish this, to offer to place Vienna at the disposal of the powers for preparatory talks at a higher level of expert or to take part in such formal preliminary conversations in any other country that might seem desirable.

98. Aide-mémoire from the Finnish Government to thirty-five states, 24 November 1970[1]

In the Finnish memorandum of May 5, 1969, relating to a conference on European security, it was considered essential that all Governments concerned would particip in such a conference and that the success of the conference should be guaranteed in advance to the greatest degree possible through careful preparations. At the same

1 Finnish Embassy, London.

time, the Finnish Government declared its readiness to act as host for such a conference.

Subsequently the Finnish Government has emphasized that the participation of Governments in various stages of the present process of consultation and negotiation does not imply recognition, under international law, of existing political circumstances in Europe.

It is to be noted with satisfaction that in their reactions to the Finnish initiative the Governments responsible for security in Europe have in principle taken a positive attitude to these views of the Finnish Government.

During the present process of negotiations the Finnish Government, pursuing its policy of neutrality, has explored the possibilities for common understanding, essential in questions pertaining to security in Europe. This necessity of common understanding has been underlined in our bilateral contacts as well as in Nordic meetings. The reception of the Finnish memorandum, the talks conducted so far by Ambassador Enckell as well as other information available on the present status of the process of negotiations and consultations between the Governments concerned, indicate that, while there exists a basic political will to advance the cause of European security, further efforts are still needed in order to find such a consensus of substance as would enable the Governments responsible for the security of Europe eventually to carry out a common action designed to strengthen security in Europe.

During the current year the Finnish Government has been exploring ways and means to make use of multilateral contacts in addition to bilateral ones in order to proceed towards a common understanding. In our view the discussions relating to a conference on European security have reached a phase where it might be appropriate that the Governments concerned, as part of their endeavours to promote European security, would instruct the Heads of their Missions in Helsinki or other representatives to have consultations on the arrangement of the security conference with the Finnish Ministry for Foreign Affairs, and if agreed, to do so in multilateral gatherings in Helsinki.

The purpose of these consultations would be to intensify without commitment the exchange of relevant information. The participation in these consultations would not as such constitute a stand on the issue of holding a conference on European security. These consultations might enable the Governments concerned to obtain necessary information permitting them eventually to define their position on the possibilities of convening such a conference.

99. Peace programme submitted by Mr Brezhnev to the 24th Soviet Communist Party Congress, Moscow, 30 March 1971[1]

1. To eliminate the hotbeds of war in South-East Asia and in the Middle East and to promote a political settlement in these areas on the basis of respect for the legitimate rights of States and peoples subjected to aggression. So as to give immediate

1 *Soviet News*, 31 March 1971.

and firm rebuff to any acts of aggression and international arbitrariness, full use must also be made of the possibilities of the United Nations. Repudiation of the threat or use of force in settling outstanding issues must become a law of international life. For its part, the Soviet Union invites the countries which accept this approach to conclude appropriate bilateral or regional treaties.

2. To proceed on the basis of the definitive recognition of the territorial changes that have taken place in Europe as a result of the Second World War. To bring about a radical turn towards a detente and peace on this continent. To ensure the convocation and success of an all-European conference. To do everything to ensure collective security in Europe. We reaffirm the readiness expressed jointly by the parties to the defensive Warsaw Treaty to have a simultaneous annulment of this treaty and of the North Atlantic Alliance — or as a first step — the dismantling of their military organisations.

3. To conclude treaties banning nuclear, chemical and bacteriological weapons. To work for an end to the testing of nuclear weapons, including underground tests, by everyone everywhere. To promote the establishment of nuclear-free zones in various parts of the world. We stand for the nuclear disarmament of all States possessing nuclear weapons and for the convocation for these purposes, of a conference of the five nuclear powers — the USSR, the United States, the People's Republic of China, France and Britain.

4. To intensify the struggle to halt the race in all types of weapons. We favour the convocation of a world conference to consider questions of disarmament to their full extent. We stand for the dismantling of foreign military bases. We stand for a reduction of armed forces and armaments in areas where the military confrontation is especially dangerous, and above all in Central Europe. The Soviet Union is prepared to negotiate agreements on reducing military expenditure, above all by the major powers.

5. The United Nations decisions on the abolition of the remaining colonial regimes must be fully carried out. Manifestations of racialism and apartheid must be universally condemned and boycotted.

100. Statement by Mr Bray, the Director, Office of Press Relations, United States Department of State, 17 May 1971[1]

Since 1968 the United States and its NATO allies have called for the mutual and balanced reduction of force in Europe. Also, in 1970, the NATO alliance agreed on certain principles which might provide a framework for discussions on such force reductions. At that time, the alliance also invited interested states to begin exploratory talks. As stated in the President's report on US foreign policy (February 25, 1971), the US Government undertook to reinforce the preliminary work done in NATO with an intensive analysis of the issues in an agreement to reduce NATO and Warsaw Pact forces.

1 *DSB*, 7 June 1971, p. 741.

On Sunday, May 16, the Secretary of State indicated that he had instructed
ur Ambassador in Moscow to discuss with the Foreign Minister of the Soviet
nion Mr Brezhnev's most recent statement on the question of force reductions
Europe.

On May 17, Ambassador Beam saw Foreign Minister Gromyko. Mr Gromyko
en confirmed that the Soviet Government was prepared to discuss force reductions
d expressed interest in further exchanges on this matter.

Our Ambassador stated that the United States would now consult further with
ur allies in light of the Soviet response and US and NATO studies referred to above.

Our US Representative to the North Atlantic Treaty Organization, Ambassador
llsworth, has been instructed to consult with our allies on the basis of the Soviet
sponse.

The Secretary of State will continue these consultations with his foreign minister
olleagues in the alliance at the ministerial meeting of NATO taking place in Lisbon
n June 3–4.

01. Communiqué of the NATO Council, Lisbon, 4 June 1971[1]

he North Atlantic Council met in Ministerial Session in Lisbon on 3rd and 4th
une, 1971.

2. The continuing political aim of the Atlantic Alliance is to seek peace through
itiatives designed to relax tensions and to establish a just and durable peace order
Europe, accompanied by effective security guarantees. The Alliance remains
dispensable to peace and stability in Europe and to the security of all its members.

3. Ministers reviewed the international situation, concentrating their attention
n Europe and the Mediterranean.

4. They assessed the state of progress of the several initiatives which allied
ountries had undertaken within the framework of the established policy of the
lliance to intensify contacts, explorations and negotiations with members of the
arsaw Pact and other European states. The purpose of all these initiatives is to
ek just solutions to the fundamental problems of European security and thus to
chieve a genuine improvement of East–West relations. They noted with satisfaction
e results obtained and expressed the hope that the continuation of these efforts
ould lead to further progress helping the development of detente. The allies have
onsulted and will continue to consult closely on these diplomatic activities.

5. Ministers welcomed the continued negotiations between the US and the
SSR with the aim of placing limitations on offensive and defensive strategic arms.
hey noted the useful discussions held in the North Atlantic Council on this subject.
inisters also welcomed the agreement between the US and the USSR announced
n 20th May, regarding the framework for further negotiations,[2] and expressed the
ncere hope that it would facilitate discussions leading to the early achievement

1 *DSB*, 28 June 1971, pp. 819–21.
2 Document No. 49.

of concrete results enhancing the common security interests of the North Atlantic Alliance and stability in the world.

6. In reviewing the Berlin question, Ministers underlined the necessity of alleviating the causes of insecurity in and around the city. During the past quarter of a century, much of the tension which has characterized East—West relations in Europe has stemmed from the situation in and around Berlin. Thus, the Ministers would regard the successful outcome of the Berlin talks as an encouraging indication of the willingness of the Soviet Union to join in the efforts of the Alliance to achieve a meaningful and lasting improvement of East—West relations in Europe.

7. Ministers therefore reaffirmed their full support for the efforts of the Governments of France, the United Kingdom and the United States to reach an agreement on Berlin. They shared the view of the three Governments that the aim of the negotiations should be to achieve specific improvements based on firm commitments without prejudice to the status of Berlin. In this context, they emphasized the importance of reaching agreement on unhindered movement of persons and goods between the Federal Republic of Germany and Western sectors of Berlin, on improved opportunities for movement by residents of the Western sectors, and on respect for the relationship between the Western sectors and the Federal Republi as it has developed with the approval of the three Governments.

8. Ministers were of the view that progress in the talks between German Authorities on a modus vivendi, taking into account the special situation in Germany, would be an important contribution to a relaxation of tension in Europe.

9. Ministers, having reviewed the prospects for the establishment of multilateral contacts relating to the essential problems of security and cooperation in Europe, again emphasized the importance they attach to the successful conclusion of the negotiations on Berlin. They noted with satisfaction that these negotiations have entered into a more active phase and have enabled progress to be registered in recen weeks. They hope that before their next meeting the negotiations on Berlin will have reached a successful conclusion and that multilateral conversations intended to lead to a conference on security and cooperation in Europe may then be undertaken. In this spirit they invited the Council in Permanent Session to continue, in the framework of its normal consultations on the international situation, its periodi review of the results achieved in all contacts and talks relative to security and cooperation in Europe so that it could without delay take a position on the opening of multilateral talks.

10. In anticipation of these multilateral contacts, the Council in Permanent Session actively pursued preparations for discussions on the substance and procedur of possible East—West negotiations, and submitted a report to this effect to Ministe The report stressed that the successful outcome of such negotiations would have to be founded on universal respect for the principles governing relations between states as cited by Ministers in previous Communiqués and Declarations. The various prospects for developing cooperation between East and West in the economic, technical, scientific, cultural and environmental fields were closely examined. The report also reviewed in detail the essential elements on which agreement would be

esirable in order to promote the freer movement of people, ideas and information
ɔ necessary to the development of international cooperation in all fields.

11. Ministers noted these studies and instructed the Council in Permanent Session
ɔ continue them pending the initiation of multilateral contacts between East and
Vest. Ministers stressed that they would press on with their bilateral exploratory
onversations with all interested states.

12. Ministers took note of the report on the situation in the Mediterranean
repared by the Council in Permanent Session. While welcoming the efforts currently
ndertaken to reestablish peace in the Eastern Mediterranean, they observed that
evelopments in the area as a whole continue to give cause for concern. In the
ght of the conclusions of this report, they instructed the Council in Permanent
ession to continue consultations on this situation and to report thereon at their
ext meeting.

13. The allied Governments which issued the declarations at Reykjavik in 1968
nd Rome in 1970 and which subscribed to paragraphs 15 and 16 of the Brussels
ommuniqué of 1970[1] have consistently urged the Soviet Union and other European
ountries to discuss mutual and balanced force reductions (MBFR). They reaffirmed
hat the reduction of the military confrontation in Europe — at which MBFR is
iming — is essential for increased security and stability.

14. Against this background, Ministers representing these Governments welcomed
he response of Soviet leaders indicating possible readiness to consider reductions
f armed forces and armaments in Central Europe. These Soviet reactions, which
equire further clarification, are, together with those states, receiving the closest
ttention of the Alliance.

15. In an effort to determine whether common ground exists on which to base
egotiations on mutual and balanced force reductions, these Ministers expressed
he agreement of their Governments to continue and intensify explorations with
he Soviet Union and also with other interested Governments on the basis of the
onsiderations outlined in paragraph 3 of the Rome Declaration. They expressed
heir intention to move as soon as may be practical to negotiations. To this end these
Ministers agreed that Deputy Foreign Ministers or High Officials should meet in
Brussels at an early date to review the results of the exploratory contacts and
ɔ consult on substantive and procedural approaches to mutual and balanced force
eductions.

16. These Ministers further announced their willingness to appoint, at the ap-
ropriate time, a representative or representatives, who would be responsible to the
ouncil for conducting further exploratory talks with the Soviet Government and
he other interested Governments and eventually to work out the time, place, ar-
angements and agenda for negotiations on mutual and balanced force reductions.

17. Reviewing other developments in the field of arms control and disarmament,
hese Ministers noted as a significant step forward the conclusion of a treaty banning
he emplacement of weapons of mass destruction on the seabed and ocean floor.
Allied Ministers noted with satisfaction the work done by the Conference of the

1 Document No. 112.

Committee on Disarmament with a view to reaching an agreement eliminating bacteriological weapons and toxins. They reaffirmed the importance they attach to effective and adequately verified arms limitation and disarmament measures consistent with the security of all states and invited the Council in Permanent Session to continue to pursue the Alliance efforts and studies in all fields related to arms control and disarmament.

18. Ministers expressed satisfaction at the impressive progress achieved by the Committee on the Challenges of Modern Society as reported by the Secretary General. They noted particularly the important contribution made by the Allies to combat the pollution of the seas by oil and to the development of road safety. They welcomed the fact that intensive work was underway on problems relating to coastal and inland water pollution and disaster assistance. They further welcome the contribution the Committee had made to alerting Governments and public opinion to the problems of modern technology, as well as to the dangers for moder society arising from the deterioration of the environment. They observed that many countries of the Alliance have equipped themselves with new Government structure to cope with such problems. Ministers took special note of the fact that the benefits of allied efforts had not been confined to the countries of the Alliance but were being felt in other countries as well as in broader-based international organizations.

19. Ministers expressed their regret at the impending departure of Mr Manlio Brosio who had informed them of his intention to resign as Secretary General of the Organization. In their tributes to Mr Brosio, Ministers dwelt on his outstanding stewardship in often difficult circumstances and stressed the patience and perseverance which have marked his untiring work for both defence and detente. They expressed to him their deep appreciation for the distinguished service he has rendere to the Alliance and to peace in the past seven years.

20. The Council invited Mr Joseph Luns, Foreign Minister of the Netherlands, to become Secretary General of the Organization as from 1st October, 1971. Mr Luns informed the Council of his acceptance of this invitation.

21. The next Ministerial Session of the North Atlantic Council will be held in Brussels in December 1971.

22. Ministers requested the Foreign Minister of Italy, as President of Council, to transmit this Communiqué on their behalf through diplomatic channels to all other interested parties including neutral and non-aligned Governments.

102. Communiqué of the NATO Council, Bonn, 31 May 1972[1]

The North Atlantic Council met in ministerial session in Bonn on 30th and 31st May, 1972.

2. Ministers reaffirmed that the purpose of the alliance is to preserve the freedom and security of all its members. Defence and the relaxation of tension are inseparabl linked. The solidarity of the alliance is indispensable in this respect. Allied govern-

1 *DSB*, 3 July 1972, pp. 21–2.

ments seek an improvement in their relations with the countries of Eastern Europe and aim at a just and durable peace which would overcome the division of Germany and foster security in Europe.

3. Ministers noted progress in relations between Western and Eastern countries, increasing contacts between the leaders of these countries, and the conclusion of important agreements and arrangements. They welcomed these developments flowing from major initiatives undertaken by their governments, which had full and timely consultations on these subjects. Such consultations will continue.

4. Ministers welcomed the signing by the United States and the USSR of the treaty on the limitation of anti-ballistic missile systems and the interim agreement on certain measures with respect to the limitation of strategic offensive arms. They believe these two agreements limiting the strategic arms of the United States and the USSR will contribute to strategic stability, significantly strengthen international confidence, and reduce the danger of nuclear war. Ministers also welcomed the commitment by the United States and the USSR actively to continue negotiations on limiting strategic arms. They expressed the hope that these two agreements will be the beginning of a new and promising era of negotiations in the arms control field.

5. Ministers noted with satisfaction that the treaty of 12th August, 1970, between the Federal Republic of Germany and the Soviet Union and the treaty of December 7th, 1970, between the Federal Republic of Germany and the Polish People's Republic are to enter into force in the near future. They reaffirmed their opinion that these treaties are important, both as contributions towards the relaxation of tension in Europe and as elements of the modus vivendi which the Federal Republic of Germany wishes to establish with its eastern neighbours. Ministers welcomed the declaration of 17th May, 1972, in which the Federal Republic of Germany confirmed its policy to this end and reaffirmed its loyalty to the Atlantic alliance as the basis of its security and freedom. They noted that it remains the policy of the Federal Republic of Germany to work for circumstances of peace in Europe in which the German people, in free self-determination, can recover their unity, and that the existing treaties and agreements to which the Federal Republic of Germany is a party and the rights and responsibilities of the four powers relating to Berlin and Germany as a whole remain unaffected.

6. Ministers also welcomed the progress made since their last meeting in the talks between the Federal Republic of Germany and the GDR. They regard the conclusion of the agreements and arrangements between the competent German authorities, which supplement the quadripartite agreement on Berlin of 3rd September, 1971, as well as the signature of a treaty on questions of traffic between the Federal Republic of Germany and the GDR, as important steps in the effort to improve the situation in Germany. They thus feel encouraged in the hope that, in further negotiations between the Federal Republic of Germany and the GDR, agreement might be reached on more comprehensive arrangements which would take into account the special situation in Germany.

7. Ministers noted with satisfaction that the Governments of France, the United Kingdom, the United States and the Soviet Union have arranged to sign the final protocol to the quadripartite agreement. The entry into force of the entire Berlin agreement being thus assured, the Ministers hope that a new era can begin for Berlin, free of the tension that has marked its history for the past quarter century.

8. In the light of these favourable developments, Ministers agreed to enter into multilateral conversations concerned with preparations for a conference on security and cooperation in Europe. They accepted with gratitude the proposal of the Finnish Government to act as host for such talks in Helsinki at the level of Heads of Mission under the conditions set out in its aide-mémoire of 24th November, 1970. Accordingly they decided to work out with other interested governments the necessary arrangements for beginning the multilateral preparatory talks.

9. Ministers stated that the aim of allied governments at the multilateral preparatory talks would be to ensure that their proposals were fully considered at a conference and to establish that enough common ground existed among the participants to warrant reasonable expectations that a conference would produce satisfactory results

10. Prepared in this way, a conference on security and cooperation in Europe should constitute an important factor in the process of reducing tension. It should help to eliminate obstacles to closer relations and cooperation among the participant while maintaining the security of all. Allied governments look forward to a serious examination of the real problems at issue and to a conference which would yield practical results.

11. Ministers considered that, in the interest of security, the examination at a CSCE of appropriate measures, including certain military measures, aimed at strengthening confidence and increasing stability would contribute to the process of reducing the dangers of military confrontation.

12. Ministers noted the report of the Council in permanent session concerning a conference on security and cooperation in Europe. The report examined the issues which might be included on the agenda of a conference as set forth in paragraph 13 of the Brussels communiqué of 10th December, 1971, as well as the procedural questions relating to the convening of a conference. Ministers directed the Council in permanent session to develop further its substantive and procedural studies in preparation for a conference.[1]

13. Ministers representing countries which participate in NATO's integrated defence programme recalled the offer to discuss mutual and balanced force reduction which they had made at Reykjavik in 1968, at Rome in 1970, and subsequently reaffirmed.

14. These Ministers continue to aim at negotiations on mutual and balanced force reductions and related measures. They believe that these negotiations should be conducted on a multilateral basis and be preceded by suitable explorations. They regretted that the Soviet Government has failed to respond to the allied offer of

1 See the Draft Agenda submitted by the member states of the European Community to the Preparatory Talks on the CSCE at Helsinki, 15 January 1973, in *Europe, Bulletins*, No. 1201, 15–16 January 1973.

ctober 1971 to enter into exploratory talks. They therefore now propose that multilateral explorations on mutual and balanced force reductions be undertaken soon as practicable, either before or in parallel with multilateral preparatory talks a conference on security and cooperation in Europe.

15. These Ministers noted the studies conducted since their last meeting on political, military and technical aspects of mutual and balanced force reductions. hey instructed the permanent representatives to continue this work in preparation r eventual negotiations.

16. These Ministers stated that the present military balance of forces in Europe es not allow a unilateral relaxation of the defence efforts of the allies. Unilateral rce reductions would detract from the alliance's efforts to achieve greater stability d detente and would jeopardize the prospects for mutual and balanced force ductions.

17. Ministers took note of a report by the Council in permanent session on the tuation in the Mediterranean. They expressed their concern regarding the factors instability in the area which could endanger the security of the members of the liance. They instructed the Council in permanent session to follow closely the olution of the situation and to report to them at their next meeting.

18. The next ministerial session of the North Atlantic Council will be held in russels in December 1972.

19. Ministers requested the Foreign Minister of the Grand Duchy of Luxembourg transmit this communiqué on their behalf through diplomatic channels to all her interested parties, including neutral and non-aligned governments.

03. Statement issued by the North Atlantic Treaty Organization, russels, 16 November 1972[1]

ecognizing the importance of the question of mutual and balanced force reductions Central Europe, governments of allied countries which issued the Declaration of eykjavik agreed to propose that exploratory talks on this matter should be held ginning on 31 January 1973 in a place still to be agreed through diplomatic annels. The Governments of Belgium, Canada, the Federal Republic of Germany, uxembourg, the Netherlands, the United Kingdom and the United States are communicating this proposal to the Governments of Czechoslovakia, Poland, Hungary d the USSR. The Government of the Federal Republic of Germany is communicating this proposal to the Government of the German Democratic Republic also.

The Governments of Denmark, Greece, Italy, Norway and Turkey will confirm eir intention to be represented at the exploratory talks.

1 *DSB*, 11 December 1972, pp. 680–1.

104. Communiqué issued at the conclusion of the Preparatory Talks on Mutual and Balanced Force Reductions, Vienna, 28 June 1973[1]

1. Preparatory consultations relating to Central Europe took place in Vienna from January 31, 1973 to June 28, 1973. Participation in and procedures for these consultations were as set forth in the Record of the plenary meeting of May 14, 1973.

2. In the course of these consultations, it was decided to hold negotiations on mutual reduction of forces and armaments and associated measures in Central Eur€ The negotiations will take place in Vienna, and will begin on October 30, 1973. It was also agreed that participation in and procedures for the negotiations will be as set forth in the Record of the plenary meeting of May 14, 1973.

3. The participants in the consultations had a useful and constructive exchange of views on an agenda for the forthcoming negotiations. They agreed that during the negotiations, mutual reduction of forces and armaments and associated measur in Central Europe would be considered. It was agreed that the general objective of the negotiations will be to contribute to a more stable relationship and to the strengthening of peace and security in Europe. They agreed that, in the negotiatior an understanding should be reached to conduct them in such a way as to ensure the most effective and thorough approach to the consideration of the subject matter, with due regard to its complexity. They also agreed that specific arrangements will have to be carefully worked out in scope and timing in such a way that they will in all respects and at every point conform to the principle of undiminishe security for each party. It was decided that in the course of the negotiations, any topic relevant to the subject matter may be introduced for negotiation by any of those states which will take the necessary decisions, without prejudice to the rig of all participants to speak and to circulate papers on the subject matter. This exchange of views on an agenda will greatly facilitate the work of the forthcoming negotiations. During the negotiations, the question of establishing working bodies or working groups will be considered.

4. The participants expressed their gratitude to the Government of the Republic of Austria for the considerate assistance and facilities it provided during the consultations and for its agreement that the forthcoming negotiations can take place in Vienna.

105. Final Recommendations on the Question of the Conference on Security and Cooperation in Europe, adopted by the Preparatory Conference, Helsinki, 3 July 1973[2]

(1) The participants in the Helsinki Consultations on the question of the Conferen€

---

1 *DSB*. 26 November 1973, p. 659. The nineteen countries represented were: Belgium, Bulgaria, Canada, Czechoslovakia, Denmark, the Federal Republic of Germany, the German Democratic Republic, Greece, Hungary, Italy, Luxembourg, the Netherlands, Norway, Poland, Romania, Turkey, the USSR, the United Kingdom and the United States.
2 *DSB*, 30 July 1973, pp. 181–8; the Recommendations were agreed to by the participant at the Preparatory Talks in Helsinki on 8 June 1973.

n Security and Cooperation in Europe, representing the Governments of States
sted in the annex, recommend to their Governments that this Conference should
e convened under the conditions specified below, concerning its organization,
genda and the related instructions, participation, date, place, rules of procedure
d financial arrangements.

(2) The participants expressed their collective agreement to these Recommendations
n 8 June, 1973.

(3) Each State entitled to participate in the Conference will inform the Govern-
ent of Finland, within the time limits laid down in Chapter 3, of its decision to
ke part in this Conference, thereby indicating its intention to do so on the basis
f the Final Recommendations of the Helsinki Consultations. The Government of
inland will inform all States entitled to participate of the communications received
this respect.

(4) The Government of Finland will take the necessary measures, in accordance
ith the arrangements provided for in the Final Recommendations, to organize
e first stage of the Conference.

) Index of Recommendations

Organization of the Conference
Agenda and the Related Instructions
Participation, Contributions, Guests
Date
Place
Rules of Procedure
Financial Arrangements
Annex: List of Participating Countries

ORGANIZATION OF THE CONFERENCE ON SECURITY AND OOPERATION IN EUROPE

) The Conference on Security and Cooperation in Europe will take place in three
ages:

) *Stage I*

) The first stage will consist of a meeting of the Ministers for Foreign Affairs of
e participating States. In accordance with the recommendations of the Helsinki
onsultations, the Ministers will adopt the roles of procedure, the agenda and the
structions of the working bodies of the Conference, together with the other ar-
ngements relating to the conduct of the Conference. The Ministers will state the
ews of their Governments on the problems relating to security and cooperation
Europe. Should they so wish they will put forward, for consideration in the
urse of the second stage, proposals relating to the various topics on the agenda.

(b) Stage II

(8) The second stage will comprise the work of the specialized committees and sub-committees whose instructions are defined in Chapter 2 of these recommendations (points I, II and III of the agenda). Within this framework and on the basis of the proposals submitted either by the Ministers for Foreign Affairs, or subsequently by the delegations of the participating States, the committees and sub-committees will prepare drafts of declarations, recommendations, resolutions or any other final documents. The participating States will be represented in these bodies by such delegates and experts as they shall designate for the purpose.

(9) A coordinating committee, composed of representatives appointed by the Ministers for Foreign Affairs, will meet periodically during the second stage of the Conference. It will coordinate the activities of the committees and assemble the results of their work with a view to the final stage of the Conference. The Co-ordinating Committee shall also be entrusted with the execution of the tasks define in point IV of the agenda, as stated in Chapter 2 of the present recommendations. It will, furthermore, submit to the participating Governments such recommendatio as it may consider useful regarding the conduct of the Conference, especially the organization of its third stage.

(c) Stage III

(10) In the light of the recommendations drawn up by the Coordinating Committe the Conference will meet for its third stage.

(11) The level of representation at the third stage will be decided by the partici States during the Conference before the end of the second stage.

(12) The Conference will adopt its final documents, in formal session, at the close of this third stage.

2. AGENDA AND THE RELATED INSTRUCTIONS
I. Questions Relating to Security in Europe

(13) In carrying out the instructions set out below, the Committee will bear in min the wider objective of promoting better relations among participating States and ensuring conditions in which their people can live in peace free from any threat to or attempt against their security.

(14) In its work the Committee will proceed from the premise that the strength of security in Europe is not directed against any State or continent and should constitute an important contribution to world peace and security.

(15) In considering questions relating to security in Europe, the Committee will bear in mind the broader context of world security and in particular the relationshi which exists between security in Europe and in the Mediterranean area.

(16) The Committee will be assisted in its tasks by the appropriate Sub-Commit

17) (*a*) The Committee/Sub-Committee is charged with the task of considering and stating in conformity with the purposes and principles of the United Nations those basic principles which each participating State is to respect and apply in its relations with all other participating States, irrespective of their political, economic or social systems, in order to ensure the peace and security of all participating States.

(18) The principles to be stated shall be included in a document of appropriate form to be submitted by the Committee for adoption by the Conference. It shall express the determination of the participating States to respect and apply the principles equally and unreservedly in all aspects to their mutual relations and co-operation, in order to ensure to all participating States the benefits resulting from the application of these principles by all.

(19) The reaffirmation with such clarifications and additions as may be deemed desirable, and the precise statement, in conformity with the purposes and principles of the United Nations, of the following principles of primary significance guiding the mutual relations of the participating States, are deemed to be of particular importance:

— sovereign equality, respect for the rights inherent in sovereignty;
— refraining from the threat or use of force;
— inviolability of frontiers;
— territorial integrity of States;
— peaceful settlement of disputes;
— non-intervention in internal affairs;
— respect for human rights and fundamental freedoms, including the freedom of thought, conscience, religion or belief;
— equal rights and self-determination of peoples;
— cooperation among States;
— fulfilment in good faith of obligations under international law.

(20) In discharging itself of these tasks, the Committee/Sub-Committee shall take into account in particular the Declaration on Principles of International Law concerning Friendly Relations and Cooperation among States in accordance with the Charter of the United Nations.

(21) (*b*) The Committee/Sub-Committee shall give expression to the idea that respect for the above-listed principles will encourage the development of normal and friendly relations among the participating States as well as of their political contacts which in turn would contribute to the furthering of their cooperation. It shall also consider proposals designed to give effect to refraining from the threat or use of force. In this context, it shall study proposals for and undertake the elaboration of a method for the peaceful settlement of disputes among participating States.

2

(22) The Committee/Sub-Committee shall have regard to the fact that the participating States are desirous of eliminating any causes of tension that may exist among them and of contributing to the strengthening of peace and security in the world, bearing in mind the fact that efforts aimed at disarmament complement political detente and are essential elements in a process in which all participating States have a vital interest.

(23) In order to strengthen confidence and to increase stability and security, the Committee/Sub-Committee shall submit to the Conference appropriate proposals on confidence-building measures such as the prior notification of major military manoeuvres on a basis to be specified by the Conference, and the exchange of observers by invitation at military manoeuvres under mutually acceptable conditions. The Committee/Sub-Committee will also study the question of prior notification of major military movements and submit its conclusions.

(24) The Committee/Sub-Committee shall pay due attention to the views expressed by participating States on the various subjects mentioned in the preceding paragraphs, on the particular interest they attach thereto, especially from the point of view of their own security and of their desire to be informed about the relevant developments.

II. Cooperation in the Fields of Economics, of Sciences and Technology and of the Environment

(25) The Committee shall be responsible for drawing up a draft final document/ documents containing guidelines and concrete recommendations which could stimulate common efforts for increased cooperation in the fields of economics, science and technology and environment, which might guide the participating States in their mutual relations in these areas and which they might utilize in the conclusion of bilateral or multilateral agreements, as well as recommendations on specific measures for the development of cooperation which could be agreed by participating States.

(26) The Committee will bear in mind the contribution which such cooperation could make to the reinforcement of peace and security in Europe. It will also bear in mind the interests of developing countries and regions and the positive effects which the broadening of cooperation among participating States could have on world economic relations.

(27) The Committee, having in mind the foregoing, shall study ways and means that would make it possible, by mutual agreement among participating States, to facilitate, with due regard for the diversity of economic and social systems and under conditions of reciprocity of advantages and obligations, the development of trade and cooperation in the various fields of economic activity, science, technology and in the field of the environment. In this regard, it will in particular take account of the work of the United Nations Economic Commission for Europe.

(28) In considering questions relating to cooperation in Europe covered by this mandate, the Committee will bear in mind the relationship which exists between such cooperation in Europe and in the Mediterranean area.

(29) The Committee in its final draft/drafts will formulate relevant proposals, based on full respect for the principles guiding relations among the participating States enumerated in the terms of reference for the Committee on item I of the agenda.

(30) The Committee, assisted by the appropriate Sub-Committees, will examine the following questions:

Commercial Exchanges

(31) The Committee/Sub-Committee will examine general provisions designed to promote trade and the exchange of services between participating States. It could discuss general problems relating to most favoured nation treatment. It could also examine measures aiming at the reduction or progressive elimination of all kinds of obstacles to the development of trade.

(32) The Committee/Sub-Committee will examine specific measures designed to facilitate commercial transactions and the exchange of services, such as measures aiming at the improvement of

– business contacts and facilities
– the exchange of information on commercial opportunities and specific trading
  conditions
– provisions for the settlement of commercial disputes including various forms
  of arbitration.

Industrial Cooperation and Projects of Common Interest

(33) The Committee/Sub-Committee will study the forms and modalities of industrial cooperation and will examine the various measures by which participating States could encourage the development of this cooperation using, as appropriate, the framework of bilateral or multilateral intergovernmental agreements.

(34) The Committee/Sub-Committee will examine, in particular, the measures which governments could take to create conditions favourable to this cooperation between competent organizations, firms and enterprises of participating States. It will bear in mind that the specific forms of such cooperation should be settled bilaterally unless otherwise agreed upon by the participants. This examination could bear on the various forms of cooperation, such as cooperation in production and sales, on the exchange of information concerning the possibilities of industrial co-operation, on the improvement of conditions for setting up projects, and on other measures which could develop and facilitate various forms of industrial cooperation.

(35) The Committee/Sub-Committee will also examine the possibilities of encouraging projects of common interest and of working out, where relevant, recommendations in this respect.

(36) This examination could bear on the possibilities of implementing projects

of common interest in the fields of energy resources, exploitation of raw materials and, when appropriate, of transport and communications.

3. Science and Technology

(37) The Committee/Sub-Committee shall consider proposals for the development of cooperation in the field of science and technology, taking into account already existing or planned cooperation in this field, with a view to facilitating, through such means as the improvement of contacts and information, access to new develop ments in science and technology, and to contributing to the most effective solution of problems of common interest and to the betterment of the conditions of human life.

(38) These proposals, in particular, shall be concerned with the areas where there are the most favourable prerequisites for such cooperation, the forms and methods for its implementation, as well as with the obstacles that hinder such cooperation and measures for their removal. In the consideration of these questions, the Committee/Sub-Committee will seek to build on existing practices and take int account the possibilities and capabilities of relevant existing international organizations.

4. Environment

(39) The Committee/Sub-Committee shall be responsible for discussing questions of environmental protection and improvement and in particular for determining the fields that are important for the participating States and can best lend themselves to the development of cooperation between them, such as: protection of the seas surrounding Europe, of the waters and of the atmosphere; improvement of environmental and living conditions, especially in towns; protection of nature and of its resources.

(40) The Committee/Sub-Committee shall examine and put forward the most appropriate bilateral and multilateral forms and methods of cooperation, including cooperation on a regional and subregional basis, for the various fields that have bee determined. In the consideration of these questions, the Committee/Sub-Committe will seek to build on existing practices and take into account the possibilities and capabilities of the relevant existing international organizations.

5. Cooperation in Other Areas

(41) The Committee/Sub-Committee could examine the following questions:
 — problems relating to the development of transport and communications betwe participating States;
 — promotion of tourism by the exchange of information, techniques and the results of practical experience and by the study of appropriate measures;
 — economic and social aspects of migrant labour;

— training of personnel in various fields of economic activity;
— such other questions as may be decided by common agreement.

III. Cooperation in Humanitarian and Other Fields

(42) With the aim of contributing to the strengthening of peace and understanding among the peoples of the participating States and to the spiritual enrichment of the human personality, without distinction as to race, sex, language or religion and irrespective of their political, economic and social systems, the Committee, assisted by the appropriate Sub-Committees, shall be charged with examining all possibilities of cooperation conducive to creating better conditions for increased cultural and educational exchanges, for broader dissemination of information, for contacts between people, and for the solution of humanitarian problems. In this connection, it shall not only draw upon existing forms of cooperation, but shall also work out new ways and means appropriate to these aims.

(43) The Committee in its final document will formulate relevant proposals, based on full respect for the principles guiding relations among the participating States enumerated in the terms of reference for the Committee on item I of the agenda.

(44) The Committee shall also consider to what extent existing institutions could be used to achieve these aims.

1. Human Contacts

(45) The Committee/Sub-Committee shall prepare proposals to facilitate freer movement and contacts, individually or collectively, privately or officially, among persons, institutions and organisations of the participating States.

(46) With a view to contributing to the favourable examination and settlement of relevant matters by the States concerned under mutually acceptable conditions, it shall pay particular attention to:

(a) contacts and regular meetings on a basis of family ties; reunification of families; marriage between nationals of different States;

(b) travel for personal or professional reasons; improvement of conditions for tourism, on an individual or collective basis;

(c) meetings among young people; expansion of contacts and competitions, particularly in the field of sport.

2. Information

(47) The Committee/Sub-Committee shall prepare proposals to facilitate the freer and wider dissemination of information of all kinds. In doing so it shall pay particular attention to:

(a) improving the circulation of, and access to, oral, printed, filmed and broadcast information and extending the exchange of information;

(*b*) encouraging cooperation in these fields of information on a basis of short or long term agreements;

(*c*) improving conditions under which journalists from one participating State exercise their profession in another participating State.

3. Cooperation and exchanges in the field of culture

(48) The Committee/Sub-Committee shall prepare proposals aimed at extending and improving cooperation and exchanges in the various fields of culture and shall indicate the components and objectives of a consistent long-term development of such exchanges. In its work, it shall bear in mind the results of the Intergovernmental Conference on Cultural Policies in Europe, Helsinki, June 1972 including the broader concept of culture outlined by that Conference.

(49) The Committee/Sub-Committee shall consider in particular:

(*a*) Extension of relations among competent government agencies and non-governmental bodies dealing with matters of culture;

(*b*) Promotion of fuller mutual knowledge of and access to achievements in literature, art and other fields of cultural activity;

(*c*) Improvement of facilities for contacts and exchanges in the above-mentioned spheres;

(*d*) Extension of contacts and cooperation among creative artists and people engaged in cultural activities;

(*e*) Common search for new fields and forms of cooperation; cooperation in the investigation of the social aspects of culture;

(*f*) Encouragement of such forms of cultural cooperation as: international events in the fields of art, film, theatre, music, folklore, etc.; book fairs and exhibitions; joint projects in the field of protection of monuments and sites; co-production and exchange of films and of radio and television programmes.

(50) The Committee/Sub-Committee while considering the role of States in co-operation in the field of culture will bear in mind the contribution that national minorities or regional cultures could make to it within the framework of respect for principles referred to above.

4. Cooperation and exchanges in the field of education

(51) The Committee/Sub-Committee shall prepare proposals aimed at broadening cooperation and exchanges in the fields of education and science on a short or long-term basis. These proposals shall be carried out bilaterally and multilaterally as appropriate, between participating States and non-governmental bodies. The Committee/Sub-Committee shall consider in particular:

(*a*) Expansion of links between State institutions and non-governmental bodies whose activities are concerned with questions of education and science.

(*b*) Improved access, under mutually acceptable conditions, for students, teachers and scholars from the participating States to each other's educational, cultural and scientific institutions, and a more exact assessment of the problems of comparison and equivalence between academic degrees and diplomas.

(*c*) Encouragement of the study of the languages and civilizations of other peoples for the purpose of creating favourable conditions for promoting wider acquaintance with the culture of each country.

(*d*) Exchange of experience in teaching methods in various fields including those used in adult education and exchanges in the field of teaching materials.

(52) The Committee/Sub-Committee while considering the role of States in co-operation in the field of education will bear in mind the contribution that national minorities or regional cultures could make to it within the framework of respect for principles referred to above.

IV. Follow-up to the Conference

(53) The Coordinating Committee shall consider, on the basis of the progress made at the Conference such measures as may be required to give effect to the decisions of the Conference and to further the process of improving security and developing cooperation in Europe. Having considered proposals to this effect, including proposals of an organizational nature, it shall make any recommendations which it deems necessary. In examining the follow-up of the Conference, the Committee shall also consider the contributions which it believes could be asked from existing international organizations.

3. PARTICIPATION, CONTRIBUTIONS, GUESTS

(*a*) Participation

(54) All European States, the United States and Canada shall be entitled to take part in the Conference on Security and Cooperation in Europe. If any of these States wishes to attend as an observer it may do so. In that case, its representatives may attend all stages of the Conference and of its working bodies, but shall not participate in the taking of decisions. Such a State may decide later to accept these decisions or some of them under the conditions defined by the Conference.

(55) States referred to in the first sentence of the paragraph above wishing to participate in the Conference or attend as observers must so inform the Finnish Government at the latest on 25 June 1973.

(*b*) Contributions

(56) The Conference and its working bodies will acquaint themselves, in such manner as they may determine, with the points of view held by non-participating States on the subject of the various agenda items.

(57) States situated in regions adjacent to Europe and to whom reference is made in the provisions of Chapter 2, and in particular those of the Mediterranean

States which have already expressed their interest in stating their views to the Conference, are especially envisaged by this Chapter.

(58) The Coordinating Committee may decide, by consensus, the means by which the working bodies of the Conference may consult appropriate international organizations, on the subject of the various agenda items.

(c) Guests

(59) The Secretary-General of the United Nations will be invited as guest of honour to the inaugural session of the Conference.

4. DATE

(60) 1. The Conference on Security and Cooperation in Europe shall be opened on 3 July 1973 at 11.30 a.m.

(61) 2. The date of the opening of the second stage shall be determined by the Ministers during the first stage.

(62) 3. The date of the opening of the third stage shall be decided during the second stage by agreement among the participating States on the basis of the recommendations of the Coordinating Committee.

5. PLACE OF THE CONFERENCE

(63) Taking into account with appreciation the invitation by the Government of Finland, having in view practical considerations and rotation, the first stage of the Conference on Security and Cooperation in Europe will be held in Helsinki; the second stage will be held in Geneva; the third stage will be held in Helsinki.

6. RULES OF PROCEDURE

(64) The States participating in the Conference on Security and Cooperation in Europe shall conduct their work as follows:

(65) 1. All States participating in the Conference shall do so as sovereign and independent States and in conditions of full equality. The Conference shall take place outside military alliances.

(66) 2. The representation of the participating States at each stage of the Conference shall be determined in accordance with the provisions laid down in Chapter 1 of these Final Recommendations.

(67) 3. The working bodies of the Conference shall be the Coordinating Committee the Committees and Sub-Committees. These working bodies will function during the second stage of the Conference. However, the Coordinating Committee will meet at the site of the second stage before opening the second stage in order to settle questions relating to the organization of that stage.

(68) The working bodies of the Conference may, if they so wish, set up such

working groups as they may consider useful. The working bodies and working groups of the Conference shall be open to all participating States.

(69) 4. Decisions of the Conference shall be taken by consensus. Consensus shall be understood to mean the absence of any objection expressed by a Representative and submitted by him as constituting an obstacle to the taking of the decision in question.

5. CHAIRMANSHIP

(70) A. The Chair at the inaugural and closing meetings of the first stage of the Conference shall be taken by the Minister for Foreign Affairs of the host country. The Chair at other meetings shall be taken on a basis of rotation, as follows:

(*a*) The Chair at each meeting shall be taken by the Minister for Foreign Affairs of a different participating State, in an order established in accordance with a list selected by lot country by country before the end of the Helsinki Consultations;

(*b*) If the Conference should meet both in the morning and in the afternoon of the same day, the two meetings shall be regarded as constituting two distinct meetings;

(*c*) In the interval between meetings of the Conference, the functions of the Chair shall be exercised by that Minister for Foreign Affairs who presided over the immediately preceding meeting of the Conference;

(*d*) Should a Minister for Foreign Affairs be prevented from taking the Chair, it shall be taken by the Minister for Foreign Affairs of the country next in the order established.

(71) B. The Chair at the inaugural meeting of the working bodies of the Conference shall be taken by the Representative of the host country. Thereafter, the office of Chairman shall be filled as follows:

(*a*) The Chairman of the Coordinating Committee and the Chairman of the Committees shall be designated on a basis of daily rotation, in French alphabetical order, starting from a letter drawn by lot;

(*b*) The Chairmen of Sub-Committees and of other subsidiary bodies of the Conference shall be designated on a basis of rotation in accordance with practical arrangements to be established at the appropriate time by the bodies in question.

(72) Where necessary, a rapporteur shall be designated by consensus.

(73) C. The provisions laid down for the meetings of the first stage shall be applicable *mutatis mutandis* to the meetings of the third stage of the Conference. They may be further defined by the Coordinating Committee.

(74) 6. The Executive Secretary for technical matters at each stage of the Conference shall be a national of the corresponding host country. He is designated by the host country subject to agreement by the participating States.

(75) In organizing the services, the Executive Secretary of each stage will be responsible for the recruitment of his staff and assured of the collaboration of the Secretariats of the other stages.

(76) The Executive Secretaries will work under the authority of the Conference

and report on their activities to the appropriate body of each stage of the Conferenc̊ especially on financial matters.

(77) 7. Official verbatim records shall be taken at the meetings of the first and third stages of the Conference.

(78) Proposals on matters of substance and amendments thereto shall be submitteʔ in writing to the Chairman and circulated to all participants. The proposals adopted shall be registered by the Executive Secretary and circulated among the participants.

(79) Representatives of States participating in the Conference may ask for their formal reservations or interpretative statements concerning given decisions to be duly registered by the Executive Secretary and circulated to the participating States. Such statements must be submitted in writing to the Executive Secretary.

(80) 8. The inaugural and closing sessions of the first stage of the Conference will be open. Other sessions of the first stage may be open if the Ministers so decide. The Coordinating Committee, the Committee and the Sub-Committee shall not, as a rule, meet in open sessions, unless the participants decide otherwise. Arrangements for the third stage will be similar to those for the first stage and may be further defined by the Coordinating Committee.

(81) 9. The working languages of the Conference and of its working bodies shall be: English, French, German, Italian, Russian and Spanish.

(82) Speeches made in any of the working languages shall be interpreted into the other working languages.

(83) 10. Any Representative may make a statement in a language other than the working languages. In this case, he shall himself provide for interpretation into one of the working languages.

(84) 11. Records and decisions of the Conference shall be issued and circulated to participants in the working languages.

(85) The participants shall decide by consensus whether it is desirable to make public, through the appropriate services of the Conference, certain documents or communiqués on the work of the Conference, and if they decide in the affirmative shall specify the contents.

(86) 12. During the discussion of any matter, a Representative may raise a point of order and the Chairman shall give him the floor immediately. A Representative raising a point of order may not speak on the substance of the matter under discussion.

(87) 13. During the meeting the Chairman shall keep a list of speakers and may declare it closed with the consent of the meeting. He shall, however, accord the right of reply to any Representative if a speech after he has declared the list closed makes this desirable.

(88) 14. These procedural arrangements shall be adopted by consensus. Once adopted, they can only be altered by consensus.

7. FINANCIAL ARRANGEMENTS
A. Distribution of Expenses

(89) The following scale of distribution has been agreed for the expenses of the

Conference, subject to the reservation that the distribution in question concerns the Conference only and shall not be considered as a precedent which could be relied on in other circumstances:

(90)

France	8.80 per cent	
Federal Republic of Germany	8.80	
Italy	8.80	
Union of Soviet Socialist Republics	8.80	
United Kingdom	8.80	
United States of America	8.80	52.80 per cent
Canada	5.52	5.52
Belgium	3.48	
German Democratic Republic	3.48	
Netherlands	3.48	
Poland	3.48	
Spain	3.48	
Sweden	3.48	20.88
Austria	2.00	
Czechoslovakia	2.00	
Denmark	2.00	
Finland	2.00	
Hungary	2.00	
Norway	2.00	
Switzerland	2.00	14.00
Greece	0.80	
Romania	0.80	
Turkey	0.80	
Yugoslavia	0.80	3.20
Bulgaria	0.60	
Ireland	0.60	
Luxembourg	0.60	
Portugal	0.60	2.40
Cyprus	0.20	
Holy See	0.20	
Iceland	0.20	
Liechtenstein	0.20	
Malta	0.20	
San Marino	0.20	1.20
	100 per cent	100 per cent

(91) Necessary alterations of the cost sharing scale due to any possible modification in the list of participating States above will be decided upon by consensus.

B. System of Financing

(92) 1. The monies needed to finance the Conference will be advanced by the host country of each stage subject to reimbursement out of the contributions of the participating States according to the agreed cost sharing scale.

(93) 2. Payment of contributions by participating States shall be made to a special account of the Conference.

(94) 3. Payment shall be made in the currency of the host country.

(95) 4. Accounts will be rendered in respect of each stage or at intervals of three (3) months, as appropriate.

(96) 5. Accounts shall be expressed in the currency of the host country and shall be rendered as soon as technically possible after the termination of a billing period. They shall be payable [within] sixty (60) days of presentation.

106. Communiqué of the Conference on Security and Cooperation in Europe, Helsinki, 7 July 1973[1]

The first stage of the Conference on Security and Cooperation in Europe took place in Helsinki from 3 to 7 July 1973. In accordance with the agreement reached earlier, this stage of the Conference was held at Foreign Minister level.

The following states are participating in the conference: Austria, Belgium, Bulgaria, Canada, Cyprus, Czechoslovakia, Denmark, Finland, France, German Democratic Republic, Federal Republic of Germany, Greece, Holy See, Hungary, Iceland, Ireland, Italy, Liechtenstein, Luxembourg, Malta, Monaco, Netherlands, Norway, Poland, Portugal, Romania, San Marino, Spain, Sweden, Switzerland, Turkey, Union of Soviet Socialist Republics, United Kingdom, United States of America, Yugoslavia.

At the Inaugural Session of the Conference Dr. Urho Kekkonen, President of the Republic of Finland, made a speech of welcome. Dr. Kurt Waldheim, Secretary-General of the United Nations, also addressed the Conference.

The Ministers adopted the Final Recommendations of the Helsinki Consultations which comprise the agenda and instructions of the working bodies of the Conference together with the rules of procedure and the other arrangements relating to the conduct of the Conference. The text of these final recommendations is available to the public.

The Ministers stated the views of their governments on essential problems relating to security and cooperation in Europe, and on the further work of the Conference.

The Foreign Ministers of several states submitted proposals on various questions relating to the agenda.[2] Others announced the intention to submit proposals during the second stage of the Conference.

The Ministers examined the manner in which the Conference would acquaint itself with points of view expressed by non-participating states on the subject of various agenda items. This matter was in particular considered in connection with the request of Malta and Spain in favor of Algeria and Tunisia. This matter was also considered in relation to other non-participating states bordering the Mediterranean. No consensus was reached for the time being.

The Ministers decided that the second stage of the Conference will meet in Geneva on September 18, 1973, in order to pursue the study of the questions on the agenda and in order to prepare drafts of declarations, recommendations, resolutions or any other final documents on the basis of the proposals submitted during the first stage as well as those to be submitted.

1 *DSB*, 30 July 1973, p. 181.
2 See the Draft General Declaration submitted by the Soviet Union, 3 July 1973, in *Soviet News*, 17 July 1973.

The coordinating committee made up of representatives of participating states will assemble for its first meeting in Geneva on August 29, 1973, in order to prepare the organization of the second stage.

The Ministers expressed the determination of their governments to contribute to the success of the further work of the Conference.

The participants in the Conference expressed their profound gratitude to the Government of Finland for its hospitality and for the important contribution made by Finland to the preparation of the Conference on Security and Cooperation in Europe and to the conduct of the first stage.

107. Final Act of the Conference on Security and Cooperation in Europe, Helsinki, 1 August 1975[1]

The Conference on Security and Cooperation in Europe, which opened at Helsinki on 3 July 1973 and continued at Geneva from 18 September 1973 to 21 July 1975, was concluded at Helsinki on 1 August 1975 by the High Representatives of Austria, Belgium, Bulgaria, Canada, Cyprus, Czechoslovakia, Denmark, Finland, France, the German Democratic Republic, the Federal Republic of Germany, Greece, the Holy See, Hungary, Iceland, Ireland, Italy, Liechtenstein, Luxembourg, Malta, Monaco, the Netherlands, Norway, Poland, Portugal, Romania, San Marino, Spain, Sweden, Switzerland, Turkey, the Union of Soviet Socialist Republics, the United Kingdom, the United States of America and Yugoslavia.

During the opening and closing stages of the Conference the participants were addressed by the Secretary-General of the United Nations as their guest of honour. The Director-General of UNESCO and the Executive Secretary of the United Nations Economic Commission for Europe addressed the Conference during its second stage.

During the meetings of the second stage of the Conference, contributions were received, and statements heard, from the following non-participating Mediterranean States on various agenda items: the Democratic and Popular Republic of Algeria, the Arab Republic of Egypt, Israel, the Kingdom of Morocco, the Syrian Arab Republic, Tunisia.

Motivated by the political will, in the interest of peoples, to improve and intensify their relations and to contribute in Europe to peace, security, justice and cooperation as well as to rapprochement among themselves and with the other States of the world.

Determined, in consequence, to give full effect to the results of the Conference and to assure, among their States and throughout Europe, the benefits deriving from those results and thus to broaden, deepen and make continuing and lasting the process of detente.

The High Representatives of the participating States have solemnly adopted the following:

1 Cmnd. 6198.

QUESTIONS RELATING TO SECURITY IN EUROPE

The States participating in the Conference on Security and Cooperation in Europe,

Reaffirming their objective of promoting better relations among themselves and ensuring conditions in which their people can live in true and lasting peace free from any threat to or attempt against their security;

Convinced of the need to exert efforts to make detente both a continuing and an increasingly viable and comprehensive process, universal in scope, and that the implementation of the results of the Conference on Security and Cooperation in Europe will be a major contribution to this process;

Considering that solidarity among peoples, as well as the common purpose of the participating States in achieving the aims as set forth by the Conference on Security and Cooperation in Europe, should lead to the development of better and closer relations among them in all fields and thus to overcoming the confrontation stemming from the character of their past relations, and to better mutual understanding;

Mindful of their common history and recognising that the existence of elements common to their traditions and values can assist them in developing their relations, and desiring to search, fully taking into account the individuality and diversity of their positions and views for possibilities of joining their efforts with a view to overcoming distrust and increasing confidence, solving the problems that separate them and cooperating in the interest of mankind;

Recognising the indivisibility of security in Europe as well as their common interest in the development of cooperation throughout Europe and among themselves and expressing their intentions to pursue efforts accordingly;

Recognising the close link between peace and security in Europe and in the world as a whole and conscious of the need for each of them to make its contribution to the strengthening of world peace and security and to the promotion of fundamental rights, economic and social progress and well-being for all peoples;

Have adopted the following:

1.

(a) Declaration on Principles Guiding Relations between Participating States

The participating States,

Reaffirming their commitment to peace, security and justice and the continuing development of friendly relations and cooperation;

Recognising that this commitment, which reflects the interest and aspirations of peoples, constitutes for each participating State a present and future responsibility, heightened by experience of the past;

Reaffirming, in conformity with their membership in the United Nations and in accordance with the purposes and principles of the United Nations, their full and active support for the United Nations and for the enhancement of its role and effectiveness in strengthening international peace, security and justice, and in

romoting the solution of international problems, as well as the development of
riendly relations and cooperation among States;

Expressing their common adherence to the principles which are set forth below
nd are in conformity with the Charter of the United Nations, as well as their
ommon will to act, in the application of these principles, in conformity with the
urposes and principles of the Charter of the United Nations;

Declare their determination to respect and put into practice, each of them in
s relations with all other participating States, irrespective of their political, economic
r social systems as well as of their size, geographical location or level of economic
evelopment, the following principles, which all are of primary significance, guiding
heir mutual relations:

Sovereign equality, respect for the rights inherent in sovereignty

he participating States will respect each other's sovereign equality and individuality
s well as all the rights inherent in and encompassed by its sovereignty, including
a particular the right of every State to juridical equality, to territorial integrity
nd to freedom and political independence. They will also respect each other's
ght freely to choose and develop its political, social, economic and cultural systems
s well as its right to determine its laws and regulations.

Within the framework of international law, all the participating States have equal
ights and duties. They will respect each other's right to define and conduct as it
vishes its relations with other States in accordance with international law and in
he spirit of the present Declaration. They consider that their frontiers can be
hanged, in accordance with international law, by peaceful means and by agreement.
hey also have the right to belong or not to belong to international organisations, to
e or not to be a party to bilateral or multilateral treaties including the right to be
r not to be a party to treaties of alliance; they also have the right to neutrality.

I. Refraining from the threat or use of force

he participating States will refrain in their mutual relations, as well as in their
aternational relations in general, from the threat or use of force against the territorial
ategrity or political independence of any State, or in any other manner inconsistent
vith the purposes of the United Nations and with the present Declaration. No con-
ideration may be invoked to serve to warrant resort to the threat or use of force
a contravention of this principle.

Accordingly, the participating States will refrain from any acts constituting a
hreat of force or direct or indirect use of force against another participating State.
ikewise they will refrain from any manifestation of force for the purpose of inducing
nother participating State to renounce the full exercise of its sovereign rights.
ikewise they will also refrain in their mutual relations from any act of reprisal by force.

No such threat or use of force will be employed as a means of settling disputes, or
uestions likely to give rise to disputes, between them.

296 The Diplomacy of Detente

III. Inviolability of frontiers

The participating States regard as inviolable all one another's frontiers as well as the frontiers of all States in Europe and therefore they will refrain now and in the future from assaulting these frontiers.

Accordingly, they will also refrain from any demand for, or act of, seizure and usurpation of part or all of the territory of any participating State.

IV. Territorial integrity of States

The participating States will respect the territorial integrity of each of the participal States.

Accordingly, they will refrain from any action inconsistent with the purposes and principles of the Charter of the United Nations against the territorial integrity, political independence or the unity of any participating State, and in particular from any such action constituting a threat or use of force.

The participating States will likewise refrain from making each other's territory the object of military occupation or other direct or indirect measures of force in contravention of international law, or the object of acquisition by means of such measures or the threat of them. No such occupation or acquisition will be recognised as legal.

V. Peaceful settlement of dispute:

The participating States will settle disputes among them by peaceful means in such a manner as not to endanger international peace and security, and justice.

They will endeavour in good faith and a spirit of cooperation to reach a rapid and equitable solution on the basis of international law.

For this purpose they will use such means as negotiation, enquiry, mediation, conciliation, arbitration, judicial settlement or other peaceful means of their own choice including any settlement procedure agreed to in advance of disputes to whic they are parties.

In the event of failure to reach a solution by any of the above peaceful means, the parties to a dispute will continue to seek a mutually agreed way to settle the dispute peacefully.

Participating States, parties to a dispute among them, as well as other participati States, will refrain from any action which might aggravate the situation to such a degree as to endanger the maintenance of international peace and security and there make a peaceful settlement of the dispute more difficult.

VI. Non-intervention in internal affairs

The participating States will refrain from any intervention, direct or indirect, individual or collective, in the internal or external affairs falling within the domestic jurisdiction of another participating State, regardless of their mutual relations.

They will accordingly refrain from any form of armed intervention or threat of such intervention against another participating State.

They will likewise in all circumstances refrain from any other act of military, or of political, economic or other coercion designed to subordinate to their own interest the exercise by another participating State of the rights inherent in its sovereignty and thus to secure advantages of any kind.

Accordingly, they will, *inter alia*, refrain from direct or indirect assistance to terrorist activities, or to subversive or other activities directed towards the violent overthrow of the regime of another participating State.

VII. Respect for human rights and fundamental freedoms, including the freedom of thought, conscience, religion or belief

The participating States will respect human rights and fundamental freedoms, including the freedom of thought, conscience, religion or belief, for all without distinction as to race, sex, language or religion.

They will promote and encourage the effective exercise of civil, political, economic, social, cultural and other rights and freedoms all of which derive from the inherent dignity of the human person and are essential for his free and full development.

Within this framework the participating States will recognise and respect the freedom of the individual to profess and practise, alone or in community with others, religion or belief acting in accordance with the dictates of his own conscience.

The participating States on whose territory national minorities exist will respect the right of persons belonging to such minorities to equality before the law, will afford them the full opportunity for the actual enjoyment of human rights and fundamental freedoms and will, in this manner, protect their legitimate interests in this sphere.

The participating States recognise the universal significance of human rights and fundamental freedoms, respect for which is an essential factor for the peace, justice and well-being necessary to ensure the development of friendly relations and co-operation among themselves as among all States.

They will constantly respect these rights and freedoms in their mutual relations and will endeavour jointly and separately, including in cooperation with the United Nations, to promote universal and effective respect for them.

They confirm the right of the individual to know and act upon his rights and duties in this field.

In the field of human rights and fundamental freedoms, the participating States will act in conformity with the purposes and principles of the Charter of the United Nations and with the Universal Declaration of Human Rights. They will also fulfil their obligations as set forth in the international declarations and agreements in this field, including *inter alia* the International Covenants on Human Rights, by which they may be bound.

VIII. Equal rights and self-determination of peoples

The participating States will respect the equal rights of peoples and their right to self-determination, acting at all times in conformity with the purposes and principle of the Charter of the United Nations and with the relevant norms of international law, including those relating to territorial integrity of States.

By virtue of the principle of equal rights and self-determination of peoples, all peoples always have the right, in full freedom, to determine, when and as they wish their internal and external political status, without external interference, and to pursue as they wish their political, economic, social and cultural development.

The participating States reaffirm the universal significance of respect for and effective exercise of equal rights and self-determination of peoples for the development of friendly relations among themselves as among all States; they also recall the importance of the elimination of any form of violation of this principle.

IX. Cooperation among States

The participating States will develop their cooperation with one another and with all States in all fields in accordance with the purposes and principles of the Charter of the United Nations. In developing their cooperation the participating States will place special emphasis on the fields as set forth within the framework of the Conference on Security and Cooperation in Europe, with each of them making its contribution in conditions of full equality.

They will endeavour, in developing their cooperation as equals, to promote mutual understanding and confidence, friendly and good-neighbourly relations among themselves, international peace, security and justice. They will equally endeavour, in developing their cooperation, to improve the well-being of peoples and contribute to the fulfilment of their aspirations through, *inter alia*, the benefits resulting from increased mutual knowledge and from progress and achievement in the economic, scientific, technological, social, cultural and humanitarian fields. They will take steps to promote conditions favourable to making these benefits available to all; they will take into account the interest of all in the narrowing of differences in the levels of economic development, and in particular the interest of developing countries throughout the world.

They confirm that governments, institutions, organisations and persons have a relevant and positive role to play in contributing toward the achievement of these aims of their cooperation.

They will strive, in increasing their cooperation as set forth above, to develop closer relations among themselves on an improved and more enduring basis for the benefit of peoples.

X. Fulfilment in good faith of obligations under international law

The participating States will fulfil in good faith their obligations under international

w, both those obligations arising from the generally recognised principles and
les of international law and those obligations arising from treaties or other
.reements, in conformity with international law, to which they are parties.

In exercising their sovereign rights, including the right to determine their laws
.d regulations, they will conform with their legal obligations under international
.w; they will furthermore pay due regard to and implement the provisions in the
.nal Act of the Conference on Security and Cooperation in Europe.

The participating States confirm that in the event of a conflict between the
.ligations of the members of the United Nations under the Charter of the United
.ations and their obligations under any treaty or other international agreement,
.eir obligations under the Charter will prevail, in accordance with Article 103 of
.e Charter of the United Nations.

All the principles set forth above are of primary significance and, accordingly,
.ey will be equally and unreservedly applied, each of them being interpreted
.king into account the others.

The participating States express their determination fully to respect and apply
.ese principles, as set forth in the present Declaration, in all aspects, to their mutual
.lations and cooperation in order to ensure to each participating State the benefits
.sulting from the respect and application of these principles by all.

The participating States, paying due regard to the principles above and, in par-
.cular, to the first sentence of the tenth principle, 'Fulfilment in good faith of
.ligations under international law', note that the present Declaration does not
.fect their rights and obligations, nor the corresponding treaties and other agree-
.ents and arrangements.

The participating States express the conviction that respect for these principles
.ill encourage the development of normal and friendly relations and the progress
. cooperation among them in all fields. They also express the conviction that
.spect for these principles will encourage the development of political contacts
.nong them which in turn would contribute to better mutual understanding of
.eir positions and views.

The participating States declare their intention to conduct their relations with
. other States in the spirit of the principles contained in the present Declaration.

●) Matters related to giving effect to certain of the above Principles

● The participating States,

.eaffirming that they will respect and give effect to refraining from the threat or
.e of force and convinced of the necessity to make it an effective norm of inter-
.tional life,

Declare that they are resolved to respect and carry out, in their relations with one
.other, *inter alia*, the following provisions which are in conformity with the Dec-
.ration on Principles Guiding Relations between Participating States;

To give effect and expression, by all the ways and forms which they consider appropriate, to the duty to refrain from the threat or use of force in their relations with one another.

To refrain from any use of armed forces inconsistent with the purposes and principles of the Charter of the United Nations and the provisions of the Declaration on Principles Guiding Relations between Participating States, against another participating State, in particular from invasion of or attack on its territory.

To refrain from any manifestation of force for the purpose of inducing anoth participating State to renounce the full exercise of its sovereign rights.

To refrain from any act of economic coercion designed to subordinate to their own interest the exercise by another participating State of the rights inherent in its sovereignty and thus to secure advantages of any kind.

To take effective measures which by their scope and by their nature constitu steps towards the ultimate achievement of general and complete disarmamen under strict and effective international control.

To promote, by all means which each of them considers appropriate, a climat of confidence and respect among peoples consonant with their duty to refrai from propaganda for wars of aggression or for any threat or use of force inconsistent with the purposes of the United Nations and with the Declaration on Principles Guiding Relations between Participating States, against another participating State.

To make every effort to settle exclusively by peaceful means any dispute between them, the continuance of which is likely to endanger the maintenan of international peace and security in Europe, and to seek, first of all, a solut through the peaceful means set forth in Article 33 of the United Nations Charter.

To refrain from any action which could hinder the peaceful settlement of disputes between the participating States.

(ii) The participating States,

Reaffirming their determination to settle their disputes as set forth in the Princi of Peaceful Settlement of Disputes;

Convinced that the peaceful settlement of disputes is a complement to refrainin from the threat or use of force, both being essential though not exclusive factors for the maintenance and consolidation of peace and security;

Desiring to reinforce and to improve the methods at their disposal for the peace settlement of disputes;

1. Are resolved to pursue the examination and elaboration of a generally accept method for the peaceful settlement of disputes aimed at complementing existing methods, and to continue to this end to work upon the 'Draft Convention on a European System for the Peaceful Settlement of Disputes' submitted by Switzerlan during the second stage of the Conference on Security and Cooperation in Europe, as well as other proposals relating to it and directed towards the elaboration of suc a method.

2. Decide that, on the invitation of Switzerland, a meeting of experts of all the

participating States will be convoked in order to fulfil the mandate described in paragraph 1 above within the framework and under the procedures of the follow-up to the Conference laid down in the chapter 'Follow-up to the Conference'.

3. This meeting of experts will take place after the meeting of the representatives appointed by the Ministers of Foreign Affairs of the participating States, scheduled according to the chapter 'Follow-up to the Conference' for 1977, the results of the work of this meeting of experts will be submitted to Governments.

2.

Document on confidence-building measures and certain aspects of security and disarmament

The participating States,

Desirous of eliminating the causes of tension that may exist among them and thus of contributing to the strengthening of peace and security in the world;

Determined to strengthen confidence among them and thus to contribute to increasing stability and security in Europe;

Determined further to refrain in their mutual relations, as well as in their international relations in general, from the threat or use of force against the territorial integrity or political independence of any State, or in any other manner inconsistent with the purposes of the United Nations and with the Declaration on Principles Guiding Relations between Participating States as adopted in this Final Act,

Recognising the need to contribute to reducing the dangers of armed conflict and of misunderstanding or miscalculation of military activities which could give rise to apprehension, particularly in a situation where the participating States lack clear and timely information about the nature of such activities:

Taking into account considerations relevant to efforts aimed at lessening tension and promoting disarmament;

Recognising that the exchange of observers by invitation at military manoeuvres will help to promote contacts and mutual understanding;

Having studied the question of prior notification of major military movements in the context of confidence-building;

Recognising that there are other ways in which individual States can contribute further to their common objectives;

Convinced of the political importance of prior notification of major military manoeuvres for the promotion of mutual understanding and the strengthening of confidence, stability and security;

Accepting the responsibility of each of them to promote these objectives and to implement this measure, in accordance with the accepted criteria and modalities, as essentials for the realisation of these objectives;

Recognising that this measure deriving from political decision rests upon a voluntary basis;

Have adopted the following:

I

Prior notification of major military manoeuvres

They will notify their major military manoeuvres to all other participating States through usual diplomatic channels in accordance with the following provisions:

Notification will be given of major military manoeuvres exceeding a total of 25,000 troops, independently or combined with any possible air or naval components (in this context the word 'troops' includes amphibious and airborne troops In the case of independent manoeuvres of amphibious or airborne troops, or of combined manoeuvres involving them, these troops will be included in this total. Furthermore, in the case of combined manoeuvres which do not reach the above total but which involve land forces together with significant numbers of either amphibious or airborne troops, or both, notification can also be given.

Notification will be given of major military manoeuvres which take place on the territory, in Europe, of any participating State as well as, if applicable, in the adjoining sea area and air space.

In the case of a participating State whose territory extends beyond Europe, prior notification need be given only of manoeuvres which take place in an area within 250 kilometres from its frontier facing or shared with any other European participating State; the participating State need not, however, give notification in cases in which that area is also contiguous to the participating State's frontier facing or shared with a non-European non-participating State.

Notification will be given 21 days or more in advance of the start of the manoeuv or in the case of a manoeuvre arranged at shorter notice at the earliest possible oppc tunity prior to its starting date.

Notification will contain information of the designation, if any, the general purpose of and the States involved in the manoeuvre, the type or types and numeric strength of the forces engaged, the area and estimated time-frame of its conduct. The participating States will also, if possible, provide additional relevant informatio₁ particularly that related to the components of the forces engaged and the period of involvement of these forces.

Prior notification of other military manoeuvres

The participating States recognise that they can contribute further to strengthening confidence and increasing security and stability, and to this end may also notify smaller-scale military manoeuvres to other participating States, with special regard for those near the area of such manoeuvres.

To the same end, the participating States also recognise that they may notify oth military manoeuvres conducted by them.

Exchange of observers

The participating States will invite other participating States, voluntarily and on a ateral basis, in a spirit of reciprocity and goodwill towards all participating States, send observers to attend military manoeuvres.

The inviting State will determine in each case the number of observers, the pro-dures and conditions of their participation, and give other information which it y consider useful. It will provide appropriate facilities and hospitality.

The invitation will be given as far ahead as is conveniently possible through usual lomatic channels.

or notification of major military movements

accordance with the Final Recommendations of the Helsinki Consultations the rticipating States studied the question of prior notification of major military vements as a measure to strengthen confidence.

Accordingly, the participating States recognise that they may, at their own dis-tion and with a view to contributing to confidence-building, notify their major litary movements.

In the same spirit, further consideration will be given by the States participating the Conference on Security and Cooperation in Europe to the question of prior tification of major military movements, bearing in mind, in particular, the ex-rience gained by the implementation of the measures which are set forth in this cument.

her confidence-building measures

e participating States recognise that there are other means by which their common jectives can be promoted.

In particular, they will, with due regard to reciprocity and with a view to better tual understanding, promote exchanges by invitation among their military rsonnel, including visits by military delegations.

order to make a fuller contribution to their common objective of confidence-ilding, the participating States, when conducting their military activities in the ea covered by the provisions for the prior notification of major military manoeuvres, ll duly take into account and respect this objective.

They also recognise that the experience gained by the implementation of the ovisions set forth above, together with further efforts, could lead to developing d enlarging measures aimed at strengthening confidence.

estions relating to disarmament

e participating States recognise the interest of all of them in efforts aimed at ssening military confrontation and promoting disarmament which are designed to mplement political detente in Europe and to strengthen their security. They are

convinced of the necessity to take effective measures in these fields which by thei
scope and by their nature constitute steps towards the ultimate achievement of
general and complete disarmament under strict and effective international control
and which should result in strengthening peace and security throughout the world

III

General considerations

Having considered the views expressed on various subjects related to the strengthe
of security in Europe through joint efforts aimed at promoting detente and disarmament, the participating States, when engaged in such efforts, will, in this con
proceed, in particular, from the following essential considerations:

The complementary nature of the political and military aspects of security;
The interrelation between the security of each participating State and securi
in Europe as a whole and the relationship which exists, in the broader conte
of world security, between security in Europe and security in the Mediterran
area;
Respect for the security interests of all States participating in the Conferenc
on Security and Cooperation in Europe inherent in their sovereign equality;
The importance that participants in negotiating fora see to it that informatic
above relevant developments, progress and results is provided on an appropri
basis to other States participating in the Conference on Security and Cooperation in Europe and, in return, the justified interest of any of those Stat
in having their views considered.

COOPERATION IN THE FIELD OF ECONOMICS, SCIENCE AND TECHNOLOGY AND OF THE ENVIRONMENT

The participating States,

Convinced that their efforts to develop cooperation in the fields of trade, indus
science and technology, the environment and other areas of economic activity
contribute to the reinforcement of peace and security in Europe and in the world
as a whole,

Recognising that cooperation in these fields would promote economic and socia
progress and the improvement of the conditions of life,

Aware of the diversity of their economic and social systems,

Reaffirming their will to intensify such cooperation between one another,
irrespective of their systems.

Recognising that such cooperation, with due regard for the different levels of
economic development, can be developed, on the basis of equality and mutual
satisfaction of the partners, and of reciprocity permitting, as a whole, an equitable
distribution of advantages and obligations of comparable scale, with respect for
bilateral and multilateral agreements,

Taking into account the interests of the developing countries throughout the world, including those among the participating countries as long as they are developing from the economic point of view; reaffirming their will to cooperate for the achievement of the aims and objectives established by the appropriate bodies of the United Nations in the pertinent documents concerning development, it being understood that each participating State maintains the positions it has taken on them; giving special attention to the least developed countries,

Convinced that the growing world-wide economic interdependence calls for increasing common and effective efforts towards the solution of major world economic problems such as food, energy, commodities, monetary and financial problems, and therefore emphasises the need for promoting stable and equitable international economic relations, thus contributing to the continuous and diversified economic development of all countries,

Having taken into account the work already undertaken by relevant international organisations and wishing to take advantage of the possibilities offered by these organisations, in particular by the United Nations Economic Commission for Europe, for giving effect to the provisions of the final documents of the Conference,

Considering that the guidelines and concrete recommendations contained in the following texts are aimed at promoting further development of their mutual economic relations, and convinced that their cooperation in this field should take place in full respect for the principles guiding relations among participating States as set forth in the relevant document,

Have adopted the following:

. Commercial Exchanges

General provisions

The participating States,

Conscious of the growing role of international trade as one of the most important factors in economic growth and social progress,

Recognising that trade represents an essential sector of their cooperation, and bearing in mind that the provisions contained in the above preamble apply in particular to this sector,

Considering that the volume and structure of trade among the participating States do not in all cases correspond to the possibilities created by the current level of their economic, scientific and technological development,

Are resolved to promote, on the basis of the modalities of their economic cooperation, the expansion of their mutual trade in goods and services, and to ensure conditions favourable to such development;

Recognise the beneficial effects which can result for the development of trade from the application of most favoured nation treatment,

Will encourage the expansion of trade on as broad a multilateral basis as possible, thereby endeavouring to utilise the various economic and commercial possibilities;

Recognise the importance of bilateral and multilateral intergovernmental and other agreements for the long-term development of trade,

Note the importance of monetary and financial questions for the development of international trade, and will endeavour to deal with them with a view to contributing to the continuous expansion of trade,

Will endeavour to reduce or progressively eliminate all kinds of obstacles to the development of trade;

Will foster a steady growth of trade while avoiding as far as possible abrupt fluctuations in their trade;

Consider that their trade in various products should be conducted in such a way as not to cause or threaten to cause serious injury — and should the situation arise, market disruption — in domestic markets for these products and in particular to the detriment of domestic producers of like or directly competitive products; as regards the concept of market disruption, it is understood that it should not be invoked in a way inconsistent with the relevant provisions of their international agreements; if they resort to safeguard measures, they will do so in conformity with their commitments in this field arising from international agreements to which they are parties and will take account of the interests of the parties directly concerned,

Will give due attention to measures for the promotion of trade and the diversification of its structure;

Note that the growth and diversification of trade would contribute to widening the possibilities of choice of products;

Consider it appropriate to create favourable conditions for the participation of firms, organisations and enterprises in the development of trade.

Business contacts and facilities

The participating States,

Conscious of the importance of the contribution which an improvement of business contacts, and the accompanying growth of confidence in business relationships, could make to the development of commercial and economic relations,

Will take measures further to improve conditions for the expansion of contacts between representatives of official bodies, of the different organisations, enterprises firms and banks concerned with foreign trade, in particular, where useful, between sellers and users of products and services, for the purpose of studying commercial possibilities, concluding contracts, ensuring their implementation and providing after-sales services,

Will encourage organisations, enterprises and firms concerned with foreign trade to take measures to accelerate the conduct of business negotiations;

Will further take measures aimed at improving working conditions of representa of foreign organisations, enterprises, firms and banks concerned with external trade particularly as follows,

by providing the necessary information, including information on legislation and procedures relating to the establishment and operation of permanent representation by the above mentioned bodies;

by examining as favourably as possible requests for the establishment of permanent representation and of offices for this purpose, including, where appropriate, the opening of joint offices by two or more firms;

by encouraging the provision, on conditions as favourable as possible and equal for all representatives of the above-mentioned bodies, of hotel accommodation, means of communication, and of other facilities normally required by them, as well as of suitable business and residential premises for purposes of permanent representation;

Recognise the importance of such measures to encourage greater participation by small and medium sized firms in trade between participating States.

Economic and commercial information

The participating States,

Conscious of the growing role of economic and commercial information in the development of international trade,

Considering that economic information should be of such a nature as to allow adequate market analysis and to permit the preparation of medium and long term forecasts, thus contributing to the establishment of a continuing flow of trade and better utilisation of commercial possibilities,

Expressing their readiness to improve the quality and increase the quantity and supply of economic and relevant administrative information,

Considering that the value of statistical information on the international level depends to a considerable extent on the possibility of its comparability,

Will promote the publication and dissemination of economic and commercial information at regular intervals and as quickly as possible, in particular:

statistics concerning production, national income, budget, consumption and productivity;

foreign trade statistics drawn up on the basis of comparable classification including breakdown by product with indication of volume and value, as well as country of origin or destination;

laws and regulations concerning foreign trade;

information allowing forecasts of development of the economy to assist in trade promotion, for example, information on the general orientation of national economic plans and programmes;

other information to help businessmen in commercial contacts, for example, periodic directories, lists, and where possible, organisational charts of firms and organisations concerned with foreign trade;

Will in addition to the above encourage the development of the exchange of economic and commercial information through, where appropriate, joint commissions for economic, scientific and technical cooperation, national and joint chambers of commerce, and other suitable bodies;

Will support a study, in the framework of the United Nations Economic Commission for Europe, of the possibilities of creating a multilateral system of notificatio of laws and regulations concerning foreign trade and changes therein,

Will encourage international work on the harmonisation of statistical nomenclatur notably in the United Nations Economic Commission for Europe.

Marketing

The participating States,

Recognising the importance of adapting production to the requirements of foreign markets in order to ensure the expansion of international trade,

Conscious of the need of exporters to be as fully familiar as possible with and take account of the requirements of potential users,

Will encourage organisations, enterprises and firms concerned with foreign trade to develop further the knowledge and techniques required for effective marketing;

Will encourage the improvement of conditions for the implementation of measure to promote trade and to satisfy the needs of users in respect of imported products, in particular through market research and advertising measures as well as, where useful, the establishment of supply facilities, the furnishing of spare parts, the functioning of after-sales services, and the training of the necessary local technical personnel;

Will encourage international cooperation in the field of trade promotion, includin marketing, and the work undertaken on these subjects within the international bodies, in particular the United Nations Economic Commission for Europe.

2. Industrial cooperation and projects of common interest

Industrial cooperation

The participating States,

Considering that industrial cooperation, being motivated by economic considerations, can

create lasting ties thus strengthening long-term overall economic cooperation, contribute to economic growth as well as to the expansion and diversification of international trade and to a wider utilisation of modern technology,

lead to the mutually advantageous utilisation of economic complementarities through better use of all factors of production, and

accelerate the industrial development of all those who take part in such cooperation,

Propose to encourage the development of industrial cooperation between the competent organisations, enterprises and firms of their countries;

Consider that industrial cooperation may be facilitated by means of intergovernmental and other bilateral and multilateral agreements between the interested parties;

Note that in promoting industrial cooperation they should bear in mind the
ᵒnomic structures and the development levels of their countries;
Note that industrial cooperation is implemented by means of contracts concluded
ᵂween competent organisations, enterprises and firms on the basis of economic
ᵃsiderations;
Express their willingness to promote measures designed to create favourable
ᵈditions for industrial cooperation;
Recognise that industrial cooperation covers a number of forms of economic
ᵃtions going beyond the framework of conventional trade, and that in concluding
ᵗtracts on industrial cooperation the partners will determine jointly the appropriate
ᵐs and conditions of cooperation, taking into account their mutual interests
ᵈ capabilities;
Recognise further that, if it is in their mutual interest, concrete forms such as
ᵉ following may be useful for the development of industrial cooperation: joint
ᵒduction and sale, specialisation in production and sale, construction, adaptation
ᵈ modernisation of industrial plants, cooperation for the setting up of complete
ᵈustrial installations with a view to thus obtaining part of the resultant products,
ˣed companies, exchanges of 'know-how', of technical information, of patents
ᵈ of licences, and joint industrial research within the framework of specific co-
ᵉration projects;
Recognise that new forms of industrial cooperation can be applied with a view
meeting specific needs;
Note the importance of economic, commercial, technical and administrative
ᶠormation such as to ensure the development of industrial cooperation;
Consider it desirable:
    to improve the quality and the quantity of information relevant to industrial
    cooperation, in particular the laws and regulations, including those relating to
    foreign exchange, general orientation of national economic plans and programmes
    as well as programme priorities and economic conditions of the market; and
    to disseminate as quickly as possible published documentation thereon;
Will encourage all forms of exchange of information and communication of
ᵖerience relevant to industrial cooperation, including through contacts between
ᵖtential partners and, where appropriate, through joint commissions for economic,
ᵈustrial, scientific and technical cooperation, national and joint chambers of com-
ᵉrce, and other suitable bodies;
Consider it desirable, with a view to expanding industrial cooperation, to encourage
ᵉ exploration of cooperation possibilities and the implementation of cooperation
ᵒjects and will take measures to this end, *inter alia*, by facilitating and increasing
. forms of business contacts between competent organisations, enterprises and firms
ᵗween their respective qualified personnel;
Note that the provisions adopted by the Conference relating to business contacts
the economic and commercial fields also apply to foreign organisations, enterprises
ᵈ firms engaged in industrial cooperation, taking into account specific conditions
this cooperation, and will endeavour to ensure, in particular, the existence of

appropriate working conditions for personnel engaged in the implementation of cooperation projects;

Consider it desirable that proposals for industrial cooperation projects should be sufficiently specific and should contain the necessary economic and technical data, in particular preliminary estimates of the cost of the project, information on the form of cooperation envisaged, and market possibilities, to enable potential partners to proceed with initial studies and to arrive at decisions in the shortest possible time,

Will encourage the parties concerned with industrial cooperation to take measures to accelerate the conduct of negotiations for the conclusion of cooperation contracts

Recommend further the continued examination – for example within the framework of the United Nations Economic Commission for Europe – of means of improving the provision of information to those concerned on general conditions of industrial cooperation and guidance on the preparation of contracts in this field;

Consider it desirable to further improve conditions for the implementation of industrial cooperation projects, in particular with respect to:

the protection of the interests of the partners in industrial cooperation projects, including the legal protection of the various kinds of property involved;

the consideration, in ways that are compatible with their economic systems, of the needs and possibilities of industrial cooperation within the framework of economic policy and particularly in national economic plans and programs

Consider it desirable that the partners, when concluding industrial cooperation contracts, should devote due attention to provisions concerning the extension of the necessary mutual assistance and the provision of the necessary information during the implementation of these contracts, in particular with a view to attaining the required technical level and quality of the products resulting from such cooperation

Recognise the usefulness of an increased participation of small and medium-sized firms in industrial cooperation projects.

Projects of common interest

The participating States,

Considering that their economic potential and their natural resources permit, through common efforts, long-term cooperation in the implementation, including at the regional or sub-regional level, of major projects of common interest, and that these may contribute to the speeding-up of the economic development of the countries participating therein,

Considering it desirable that the competent organisations, enterprises and firms of all countries should be given the possibility of indicating their interest in participating in such projects, and, in case of agreement, of taking part in their implementation,

Noting that the provisions adopted by the Conference relating to industrial cooperation are also applicable to projects of common interest,

Regard it as necessary to encourage, where appropriate, the investigation by competent and interested organisations, enterprises and firms of the possibilities for the carrying out of projects of common interest in the fields of energy resources and of the exploitation of raw materials, as well as of transport and communications;

Regard it as desirable that organisations, enterprises and firms exploring the possibilities of taking part in projects of common interest exchange with their potential partners, through the appropriate channels, the requisite economic, legal, financial and technical information pertaining to these projects;

Consider that the fields of energy resources, in particular, petroleum, natural gas and coal, and the extraction and processing of mineral raw materials, in particular, iron ore and bauxite, are suitable ones for strengthening long-term economic cooperation and for the development of trade which could result;

Consider that possibilities for projects of common interest with a view to long-term economic cooperation also exist in the following fields:

exchanges of electrical energy within Europe with a view to utilising the capacity of the electrical power stations as rationally as possible;

cooperation in research for new sources of energy and, in particular, in the field of nuclear energy;

development of road networks and cooperation aimed at establishing a coherent navigable network in Europe;

cooperation in research and the perfecting of equipment for multimodal transport operations and for the handling of containers;

Recommend that the States interested in projects of common interest should consider under what conditions it would be possible to establish them, and if they so desire, create the necessary conditions for their actual implementation.

3. Provisions concerning trade and industrial cooperation

Harmonisation of standards

The participating States,

Recognising the development of international harmonisation of standards and technical regulations and of international cooperation in the field of certification as an important means of eliminating technical obstacles to international trade and industrial cooperation, thereby facilitating their development and increasing productivity,

Reaffirm their interest to achieve the widest possible international harmonisation of standards and technical regulations;

Express their readiness to promote international agreements and other appropriate arrangements on acceptance of certificates of conformity with standards and technical regulations;

Consider it desirable to increase international cooperation on standardisation, in particular by supporting the activities of intergovernmental and other appropriate organisations in this field.

Arbitration

The participating States,

Considering that the prompt and equitable settlement of disputes which may aris
from commercial transactions relating to goods and services and contracts for industrial cooperation would contribute to expanding and facilitating trade and cooperation,

Considering that arbitration is an appropriate means of settling such disputes,

Recommend, where appropriate, to organisations, enterprises and firms in their
countries, to include arbitration clauses in commercial contracts and industrial
cooperation contracts, or in special agreements;

Recommend that the provisions on arbitration should provide for arbitration
under a mutually acceptable set of arbitration rules, and permit arbitration in a
third country, taking into account existing intergovernmental and other agreements
in this field.

Specific bilateral arrangements

The participating States,

Conscious of the need to facilitate trade and to promote the application of new
forms of industrial cooperation,

Will consider favourably the conclusion, in appropriate cases, of specific bilateral
agreements concerning various problems of mutual interest in the fields of commercial exchanges and industrial cooperation, in particular with a view to avoiding
double taxation and to facilitating the transfer of profits and the return of the value
of the assets invested.

4. Science and technology

The participating States,

Convinced that scientific and technological cooperation constitutes an important
contribution to the strengthening of security and cooperation among them, in that
it assists the effective solution of problems of common interest and the improvement of the conditions of human life,

Considering that in developing such cooperation, it is important to promote the
sharing of information and experience, facilitating the study and transfer of scientifi
and technological achievements, as well as the access to such achievements on a
mutually advantageous basis and in fields of cooperation agreed between interested
parties,

Considering that it is for the potential partners, i.e. the competent organisations,
institutions, enterprises, scientists and technologists of the participating States to
determine the opportunities for mutually beneficial cooperation and to develop
its details,

Affirming that such cooperation can be developed and implemented bilaterally and multilaterally at the governmental and non-governmental levels, for example, through intergovernmental and other agreements, international programmes, co-operative projects and commercial channels, while utilising also various forms of contacts, including direct and individual contacts,

Aware of the need to take measures further to improve scientific and technological cooperation between them,

Possibilities for improving cooperation

Recognise that possibilities exist for further improving scientific and technological cooperation, and to this end, express their intention to remove obstacles to such cooperation, in particular through:

the improvement of opportunities for the exchange and dissemination of scientific and technological information among the parties interested in scientific and technological research and cooperation including information related to the organisation and implementation of such cooperation;

the expeditious implementation and improvement in organisation, including programmes, of international visits of scientists and specialists in connection with exchanges, conferences and cooperation;

the wider use of commercial channels and activities for applied scientific and technological research and for the transfer of achievements obtained in this field while providing information on and protection of intellectual and industrial property rights;

Fields of cooperation

Consider that possibilities to expand cooperation exist within the areas given below as examples, noting that it is for potential partners in the participating countries to identify and develop projects and arrangements of mutual interest and benefit:

Agriculture. Research into new methods and technologies for increasing the productivity of crop cultivation and animal husbandry; the application of chemistry to agriculture; the design, construction and utilisation of agricultural machinery; technologies of irrigation and other agricultural land improvement works;

Energy. New technologies of production, transport and distribution of energy aimed at improving the use of existing fuels and sources of hydroenergy, as well as research in the field of new energy sources, including nuclear, solar and geo-thermal energy;

New technologies, rational use of resources. Research on new technologies and equipment designed in particular to reduce energy consumption and to minimise or eliminate waste;

Transport technology. Research on the means of transport and the technology applied to the development and operation of international, national and urban transport networks including container transport as well as transport safety;

Physics. Study of problems in high energy physics and plasma physics; research in the field of theoretical and experimental nuclear physics;

Chemistry. Research on problems in electrochemistry and the chemistry of polymers, of natural products, and of metals and alloys, as well as the development of improved chemical technology, especially materials processing; practical applicati of the latest achievements of chemistry to industry, construction and other sectors of the economy;

Meteorology and hydrology. Meteorological and hydrological research, including methods of collection, evaluation and transmission of data and their utilisation for weather forecasting and hydrology forecasting;

Oceanography. Oceanographic research, including the study of air/sea interaction

Seismological research. Study and forecasting of earthquakes and associated geological changes; development and research of technology of seism-resisting constructions;

Research on glaciology, permafrost and problems of life under conditions of cold Research on glaciology and permafrost; transportation and construction technologie human adaptation to climatic extremes and changes in the living conditions of indigenous populations;

Computer, communication and information technologies. Development of computers as well as of telecommunications and information systems; technology associated with computers and telecommunications, including their use for manage-ment systems, for production processes, for automation, for the study of economic problems, in scientific research and for the collection, processing and dissemination of information;

Space research. Space exploration and the study of the earth's natural resources and the natural environment by remote sensing in particular with the assistance of satellites and rocket-probes;

Medicine and public health. Research on cardiovascular, tumour and virus disease molecular biology, neurophysiology; development and testing of new drugs; study of contemporary problems of pediatrics, gerontology and the organisation and techniques of medical services;

Environmental research. Research on specific scientific and technological prob-lems related to human environment.

Forms and methods of cooperation

Express their view that scientific and technological cooperation should, in particular employ the following forms and methods:

exchange and circulation of books, periodicals and other scientific and tech-nological publications and papers among interested organisations, scientific and technological institutions, enterprises and scientists and technologists, as well as participation in international programmes for the abstracting and indexing of publications;

exchanges and visits as well as other direct contacts and communications among scientists and technologists, on the basis of mutual agreement and othei arrangements, for such purposes as consultations, lecturing and conducting research, including the use of laboratories, scientific libraries, and other documentation centres in connection therewith;

holding of international and national conferences, symposia, seminars, courses and other meetings of a scientific and technological character, which would include the participation of foreign scientists and technologists;

joint preparation and implementation of programmes and projects of mutual interest on the basis of consultation and agreement among all parties concerned, including, where possible and appropriate, exchanges of experience and research results, and correlation of research programmes, between scientific and technological research institutions and organisations;

use of commercial channels and methods for identifying and transferring technological and scientific developments, including the conclusion of mutually beneficial cooperation arrangements between firms and enterprises in fields agreed upon between them and for carrying out, where appropriate, joint research and development programmes and projects;

consider it desirable that periodic exchanges of views and information take place on scientific policy, in particular on general problems of orientation and administration of research and the question of a better use of large-scale scientific and experimental equipment on a cooperative basis;

recommend that, in developing cooperation in the field of science and technology, full use be made of existing practices of bilateral and multilateral cooperation, including that of a regional or sub-regional character, together with the forms and methods of cooperation described in this document;

recommend further that more effective utilisation be made of the possibilities and capabilities of existing international organisations, intergovernmental and non-governmental, concerned with science and technology, for improving exchanges of information and experience, as well as for developing other forms of cooperation in fields of common interest, for example:

in the United Nations Economic Commission for Europe, study of possibilities for expanding multilateral cooperation, taking into account models for projects and research used in various international organisations; and for sponsoring conferences, symposia, and study and working groups such as those which would bring together younger scientists and technologists with eminent specialists in their field;

through their participation in particular international scientific and technological cooperation programmes, including those of UNESCO and other international organisations, pursuit of continuing progress towards the objectives of such programmes, notably those of UNISIST with particular respect to information policy guidance, technical advice, information contributions and data processing.

Environment

the participating States,

Affirming that the protection and improvement of the environment, as well as the protection of nature and the rational utilisation of its resources in the interest of present and future generations, is one of the tasks of major importance to the well-being of peoples and the economic development of all countries and that many environmental problems, particularly in Europe, can be solved effectively only through close international cooperation,

Acknowledging that each of the participating States, in accordance with the principles of international law, ought to ensure, in a spirit of cooperation, that activities carried out on its territory do not cause degradation of the environment in another State or in areas lying beyond the limits of national jurisdiction,

Considering that the success of any environmental policy presupposes that all population groups and social forces, aware of their responsibilities, help to protect and improve the environment, which necessitates continued and thorough educative action, particularly with regard to youth,

Affirming that experience has shown that economic development and technological progress must be compatible with the protection of the environment and the preservation of historical and cultural values; that damage to the environment is best avoided by preventive measures; and that the ecological balance must be preserved in the exploitation and management of natural resources,

Aims of cooperation

Agree to the following aims of cooperation, in particular:

to study, with a view to their solution, those environmental problems which by their nature, are of a multilateral, bilateral, regional or sub-regional dime as well as to encourage the development of an interdisciplinary approach to environmental problems;

to increase the effectiveness of national and international measures for the protection of the environment, by the comparison and, if appropriate, the harmonisation of methods of gathering and analysing facts, by improving the knowledge of pollution phenomena and rational utilisation of natural resources, by the exchange of information, by the harmonisation of definiti and the adoption, as far as possible, of a common terminology in the field of the environment;

to take the necessary measures to bring environmental policies closer togeth and, where appropriate and possible, to harmonise them;

to encourage, where possible and appropriate, national and international efforts by their interested organisations, enterprises and firms in the develop ment, production and improvement of equipment designed for monitoring, protecting and enhancing the environment.

Fields of cooperation

To attain these aims, the participating States will make use of every suitable oppo tunity to cooperate in the field of environment and, in particular, within the areas described below as examples:

Control of Air Pollution. Desulphurisation of fossil fuels and exhaust gases; pollution control of heavy metals, particles, aerosols, nitrogen oxides, in particular those emitted by transport, power stations, and other industrial plants; systems and methods of observation and control of air pollution and its effects, including long-range transport of air pollutants;

Water Pollution Control and Fresh Water Utilisation. Prevention and control of water pollution, in particular of transboundary rivers and international lakes; techniques for the improvement of the quality of water and further development of ways and means for industrial and municipal sewage effluent purification; methods of assessment of fresh water resources and the improvement of their utilisation, in particular by developing methods of production which are less polluting and lead to less consumption of fresh water;

Protection of the Marine Environment. Protection of the marine environment of participating States, and especially the Mediterranean Sea, from pollutants emanating from land-based sources and those from ships and other vessels, notably the harmful substances listed in Annexes I and II to the London Convention on the Prevention of Marine Pollution by the Dumping of Wastes and Other Matters; problems of maintaining marine ecological balances and food chains, in particular such problems as may arise from the exploration and exploitation of biological and mineral resources of the seas and the sea-bed;

Land Utilisation and Soils. Problems associated with more effective use of lands, including land amelioration, reclamation and recultivation; control of soil pollution, water and air erosion, as well as other forms of soil degradation; maintaining and increasing the productivity of soils with due regard for the possible negative effects of the application of chemical fertilisers and pesticides;

Nature Conservation and Nature Reserves. Protection of nature and nature reserves; conservation and maintenance of existing genetic resources, especially rare animal and plant species; conservation of natural ecological systems; establishment of nature reserves and other protected landscapes and areas, including their use for research, tourism, recreation and other purposes;

Improvement of Environmental Conditions in Areas of Human Settlement. Environmental conditions associated with transport, housing, working areas, urban development and planning, water supply and sewage disposal systems; assessment of harmful effects of noise, and noise control methods; collection, treatment and utilisation of wastes, including the recovery and recycling of materials; research on substitutes for non-biodegradable substances;

Fundamental Research, Monitoring, Forecasting and Assessment of Environmental Changes. Study of changes in climate, landscapes and ecological balances under the impact of both natural factors and human activities; forecasting of possible genetic changes in flora and fauna as a result of environmental pollution; harmonisation of statistical data, development of scientific concepts and systems of monitoring networks, standardised method of observation, measurement and assessment of changes in the biosphere; assessment of the effects of environmental pollution levels and degradation of the environment upon human health; study and development of criteria and standards for various environmental pollutants and regulation regarding production and use of various products;

Legal and Administrative Measures. Legal and administrative measures for the protection of the environment including procedures for establishing environmental impact assessments.

Forms and methods of cooperation

The participating States declare that problems relating to the protection and improvement of the environment will be solved on both a bilateral and multilateral, including regional and sub-regional, basis, making full use of existing patterns and forms of cooperation. They will develop cooperation in the field of the environment in particular by taking into consideration the Stockholm Declaration on the Human Environment, relevant resolutions of the United Nations General Assembly and the United Nations Economic Commission for Europe Prague symposium on environmental problems.

The participating States are resolved that cooperation in the field of the environment will be implemented in particular through:

exchanges of scientific and technical information, documentation and research results, including information on the means of determining the possible effects on the environment of technical and economic activities;

organisation of conferences, symposia and meetings of experts;

exchanges of scientists, specialists and trainees;

joint preparation and implementation of programmes and projects for the study and solution of various problems of environmental protection;

harmonisation, where appropriate and necessary, of environmental protection standards and norms, in particular with the object of avoiding possible difficulties in trade which may arise from efforts to resolve ecological problems of production processes and which relate to the achievement of certain environmental qualities in manufactured products;

consultations on various aspects of environmental protection, as agreed upon among countries concerned, especially in connection with problems which could have international consequences.

The participating States will further develop such cooperation by:

promoting the progressive development, codification and implementation of international law as one means of preserving and enhancing the human environment, including principles and practices, as accepted by them, relating to pollution and other environmental damage caused by activities within the jurisdiction or control of their States affecting other countries and regions;

supporting and promoting the implementation of relevant international Conventions to which they are parties, in particular those designed to prevent

and combat marine and fresh water pollution, recommending States to
ratify Conventions which have already been signed, as well as considering
possibilities of accepting other appropriate Conventions to which they
are not parties at present;
advocating the inclusion, where appropriate and possible, of the various areas
of cooperation into the programmes of work of the United Nations Economic
Commission for Europe, supporting such cooperation within the framework
of the Commission and of the United Nations Environment Programme, and
taking into account the work of other competent international organisations
of which they are members;
making wider use, in all types of cooperation, of information already available from national and international sources, including internationally agreed
criteria, and utilising the possibilities and capabilities of various competent
international organisations.
    The participating States agree on the following recommendations on specific
measures:
to develop through international cooperation an extensive programme for the
monitoring and evaluation of the long-range transport of air pollutants, starting
with sulphur dioxide and with possible extension to other pollutants, and to
this end to take into account basic elements of a cooperation programme
which were identified by the experts who met in Oslo in December 1974
at the invitation of the Norwegian Institute of Air Research;
to advocate that within the framework of the United Nations Economic
Commission for Europe a study be carried out of procedures and relevant
experience relating to the activities of Governments in developing the capabilities
of their countries to predict adequately environmental consequences of economic activities and technological development.

5. Cooperation in other areas

Development of transport

The participating States,
    Considering that the improvement of the conditions of transport constitutes one
of the factors essential to the development of cooperation among them,
    Considering that it is necessary to encourage the development of transport and
the solution of existing problems by employing appropriate national and international means,
    Taking into account the work being carried out on these subjects by existing
international organisations, especially by the Inland Transport Committee of the
United Nations Economic Commission for Europe,
    note that the speed of technical progress in the various fields of transport makes
desirable a development of cooperation and an increase in exchanges of information
among them;

declare themselves in favour of a simplification and a harmonisation of administrative formalities in the field of international transport, in particular at frontiers;

consider it desirable to promote, while allowing for their particular national circumstances in this sector, the harmonisation of administrative and technical provisions concerning safety in road, rail, river, air and sea transport;

express their intention to encourage the development of international inland transport of passengers and goods as well as the possibilities of adequate participati‹ in such transport on the basis of reciprocal advantage;

declare themselves in favour, with due respect for their rights and international commitments, of the elimination of disparities arising from the legal provisions applied to traffic on inland waterways which are subject to international conventio‹ and, in particular, of the disparity in the application of those provisions; and to this end invite the member States of the Central Commission for the Navigation of the Rhine, of the Danube Commission and of other bodies to develop the work and studies now being carried out, in particular within the United Nations Economic Commission for Europe;

express their willingness, with a view to improving international rail transport and with due respect for their rights and international commitments, to work towa‹ the elimination of difficulties arising from disparities in existing international legal provisions governing the reciprocal railway transport of passengers and goods betwe‹ their territories;

express the desire for intensification of the work being carried out by existing international organisations in the field of transport, especially that of the Inland Transport Committee of the United Nations Economic Commission for Europe, and express their intention to contribute thereto by their efforts;

consider that examination by the participating States of the possibility of their accession to the different conventions or to membership of international organisati‹ specialising in transport matters, as well as their efforts to implement conventions when ratified, could contribute to the strengthening of their cooperation in this field.

Promotion of tourism

The participating States,

Aware of the contribution made by international tourism to the development of mutual understanding among peoples, to increased knowledge of other countries' achievements in various fields, as well as to economic, social and cultural progress,

Recognising the interrelationship between the development of tourism and measures taken in other areas of economic activity,

express their intention to encourage increased tourism on both an individual and group basis in particular by:

    encouraging the carrying out of joint tourist projects including technical co-
    operation, particularly where this is suggested by territorial proximity and
    the convergence of tourist interests;

encouraging the exchange of information, including relevant laws and regulations, studies, data and documentation relating to tourism, and by improving statistics with a view to facilitating their comparability;

dealing in a positive spirit with questions connected with the allocation of financial means for tourist travel abroad, having regard to their economic possibilities, as well as with those connected with the formalities required for such travel, taking into account other provisions on tourism adopted by the Conference;

facilitating the activities of foreign travel agencies and passenger transport companies in the promotion of international tourism;

encouraging tourism outside the high season;

examining the possibilities of exchanging specialists and students in the field of tourism, with a view to improving their qualifications;

promoting conferences and symposia on the planning and development of tourism;

consider it desirable to carry out in the appropriate international framework, and with the cooperation of the relevant national bodies, detailed studies on tourism, in particular:

a comparative study on the status and activities of travel agencies as well as on ways and means of achieving better cooperation among them;

a study of the problems raised by the seasonal concentration of vacations, with the ultimate objective of encouraging tourism outside peak periods;

studies of the problems arising in areas where tourism has injured the environment;

consider also that interested parties might wish to study the following questions:

uniformity of hotel classification; and

tourist routes comprising two or more countries;

Will endeavour, where possible, to ensure that the development of tourism does not injure the environment and the artistic, historic and cultural heritage in their respective countries;

Will pursue their cooperation in the field of tourism bilaterally and multilaterally with a view to attaining the above objectives.

Economic and social aspects of migrant labour

The participating States,

Considering that the movements of migrant workers in Europe have reached substantial proportions, and that they constitute an important economic, social and human factor for host countries as well as for countries of origin,

Recognising that workers' migrations have also given rise to a number of economic, social, human and other problems in both the receiving countries and the countries of origin,

Taking due account of the activities of the competent international organisations, more particularly the International Labour Organisation, in this area,

Are of the opinion that the problems arising bilaterally from the migration of workers in Europe as well as between the participating States should be dealt with by the parties directly concerned, in order to resolve these problems in their mutual interest, in the light of the concern of each State involved to take due account of the requirements resulting from its socio-economic situation, having regard to the obligation of each State to comply with the bilateral and multilateral agreements to which it is party, and with the following aims in view:

To encourage the efforts of the countries of origin directed towards increasing the possibilities of employment for their nationals in their own territories, in particular by developing economic cooperation appropriate for this purpose and suitable for the host countries and the countries of origin concerned;

To ensure, through collaboration between the host country and the country of origin, the conditions under which the orderly movement of workers might take place, while at the same time protecting their personal and social welfare and, if appropriate, to organise the recruitment of migrant workers and the provision of elementary language and vocational training;

To ensure equality of rights between migrant workers and nationals of the host countries with regard to conditions of employment and work and to social security, and to endeavour to ensure that migrant workers may enjoy satisfactory living conditions, especially housing conditions;

To endeavour to ensure, as far as possible, that migrant workers may enjoy the same opportunities as nationals of the host countries of finding other suitable employment in the event of unemployment;

To regard with favour the provision of vocational training to migrant workers and, as far as possible, free instruction in the language of the host country, in the framework of their employment;

To confirm the right of migrant workers to receive, as far as possible, regular information in their own language, covering both their country of origin and the host country;

To ensure that the children of migrant workers established in the host country have access to the education usually given there, under the same conditions as the children of that country and, furthermore, to permit them to receive supplementary education in their own language, national culture, history and geography;

To bear in mind that migrant workers, particularly those who have acquired qualifications, can by returning to their countries after a certain period of time help to remedy any deficiency of skilled labour in their country of origin;

To facilitate, as far as possible, the reuniting of migrant workers with their families;

To regard with favour the efforts of the countries of origin to attract the savings of migrant workers, with a view to increasing, within the framework of their economic development, appropriate opportunities for employment, thereby facilita the reintegration of these workers on their return home.

Training of personnel

The participating States,

Conscious of the importance of the training and advanced training of professional staff and technicians for the economic development of every country,

Declare themselves willing to encourage cooperation in this field notably by promoting exchange of information on the subject of institutions, programmes and methods of training and advanced training open to professional staff and technicians in the various sectors of economic activity and especially in those of management, public planning, agriculture and commercial and banking techniques;

Consider that it is desirable to develop, under mutually acceptable conditions, exchanges of professional staff and technicians, particularly through training activities, of which it would be left to the competent and interested bodies in the participating States to discuss the modalities — duration, financing, education and qualification levels of potential participants;

Declare themselves in favour of examining, through appropriate channels, the possibilities of cooperating on the organisation and carrying out of vocational training on the job, more particularly in professions involving modern techniques.

QUESTIONS RELATING TO SECURITY AND COOPERATION IN THE MEDITERRANEAN

The participating States,

Conscious of the geographical, historical, cultural, economic and political aspects of their relationship with the non-participating Mediterranean States,

Convinced that security in Europe is to be considered in the broader context of world security and is closely linked with security in the Mediterranean area as a whole, and that accordingly the process of improving security should not be confined to Europe but should extend to other parts of the world, and in particular to the Mediterranean area,

Believing that the strengthening of security and the intensification of cooperation in Europe would stimulate positive processes in the Mediterranean region, and expressing their intention to contribute towards peace, security and justice in the region, in which ends the participating States and the non-participating Mediterranean States have a common interest,

Recognising the importance of their mutual economic relations with the non-participating Mediterranean States, and conscious of their common interest in the further development of cooperation,

Noting with appreciation the interest expressed by the non-participating Mediterranean States in the Conference since its inception, and having duly taken their contributions into account,

Declare their intention:

to promote the development of good neighbourly relations with the non-participating Mediterranean States in conformity with the purposes and principles of the Charter of the United Nations, on which their relations are

based, and with the United Nations Declaration on Principles of International
Law concerning Friendly Relations and Cooperation among States and accordingly, in this context, to conduct their relations with the non-participating
Mediterranean States in the spirit of the principles set forth in the Declaration
on Principles Guiding Relations between Participating States;

to seek, by further improving their relations with the non-participating Mediterranean States, to increase mutual confidence, so as to promote security and
stability in the Mediterranean area as a whole;

to encourage with the non-participating Mediterranean States the development
of mutually beneficial cooperation in the various fields of economic activity,
especially by expanding commercial exchanges, on the basis of a common
awareness of the necessity for stability and progress in trade relations, of their
mutual economic interests, and of differences in the levels of economic development, thereby promoting their economic advancement and well-being;

to contribute to a diversified development of the economies of the non-
participating Mediterranean countries, whilst taking due account of their
national development objectives, and to cooperate with them, especially in
the sectors of industry, science and technology, in their efforts to achieve a
better utilisation of their resources, thus promoting a more harmonious
development of economic relations;

to intensify their efforts and their cooperation on a bilateral and multilateral
basis with the non-participating Mediterranean States directed towards the
improvement of the environment of the Mediterranean, especially the safeguarding of the biological resources and ecological balance of the sea, by
appropriate measures including the prevention and control of pollution; to
this end, and in view of the present situation, to cooperate through competent
international organisations and in particular within the United Nations Environment Programme (UNEP);

to promote further contacts and cooperation with the non-participating Mediter
ranean States in other relevant fields.

In order to advance the objectives set forth above, the participating States also
declare their intention of maintaining and amplifying the contacts and dialogue as
initiated by the CSCE with the non-participating Mediterranean States to include
all the States of the Mediterranean, with the purpose of contributing to peace,
reducing armed forces in the region, strengthening security, lessening tensions in
the region, and widening the scope of cooperation, ends in which all share a common
interest, as well as with the purpose of defining further common objectives.

The participating States would seek, in the framework of their multilateral efforts,
to encourage progress and appropriate initiatives and to proceed to an exchange of
views on the attainment of the above purposes.

COOPERATION IN HUMANITARIAN AND OTHER FIELDS

The participating States,

Desiring to contribute to the strengthening of peace and understanding among peoples and to the spiritual enrichment of the human personality without distinction as to race, sex, language or religion,

Conscious that increased cultural and educational exchanges, broader dissemination of information, contacts between people, and the solution of humanitarian problems will contribute to the attainment of these aims,

Determined therefore to cooperate among themselves, irrespective of their political, economic and social systems, in order to create better conditions in the above fields, to develop and strengthen existing forms of cooperation and to work out new ways and means appropriate to these aims,

Convinced that this cooperation should take place in full respect for the principles guiding relations among participating States as set forth in the relevant document,

Have adopted the following:

1. Human Contacts

The participating States,

Considering the development of contacts to be an important element in the strengthening of friendly relations and trust among peoples,

Affirming, in relation to their present effort to improve conditions in this area, the importance they attach to humanitarian considerations,

Desiring in this spirit to develop, with the continuance of detente, further efforts to achieve continuing progress in this field,

And conscious that the questions relevant hereto must be settled by the States concerned under mutually acceptable conditions,

Make it their aim to facilitate freer movement and contacts, individually and collectively, whether privately or officially, among persons, institutions and organisations of the participating States, and to contribute to the solution of the humanitarian problems that arise in that connection,

Declare their readiness to these ends to take measures which they consider appropriate and to conclude agreements or arrangements among themselves, as may be needed, and

Express their intention now to proceed to the implementation of the following:

a) Contacts and Regular Meetings on the Basis of Family Ties

In order to promote further development of contacts on the basis of family ties the participating States will favourably consider applications for travel with the purpose of allowing persons to enter or leave their territory temporarily, and on a regular basis if desired, in order to visit members of their families.

Applications for temporary visits to meet members of their families will be dealt with without distinction as to the country of origin or destination: existing requirements for travel documents and visas will be applied in this spirit. The preparation and issue of such documents and visas will be effected within reasonable time limits; cases of urgent necessity — such as serious illness or death will be given priority treatment. They will take such steps as may be necessary to ensure that the fees for official travel documents and visas are acceptable.

They confirm that the presentation of an application concerning contacts on the basis of family ties will not modify the rights and obligations of the applicant or of members of his family.

(b) Reunification of Families

The participating States will deal in a positive and humanitarian spirit with the applications of persons who wish to be reunited with members of their family, with special attention being given to requests of an urgent character — such as requests submitted by persons who are ill or old.

They will deal with applications in this field as expeditiously as possible.

They will lower where necessary the fees charged in connection with these applications to ensure that they are at a moderate level.

Applications for the purpose of family reunification which are not granted may be renewed at the appropriate level and will be reconsidered at reasonably short intervals by the authorities of the country of residence or destination, whichever is concerned; under such circumstances fees will be charged only when applications are granted.

Persons whose applications for family reunification are granted may bring with them or ship their household and personal effects; to this end the participating States will use all possibilities provided by existing regulations.

Until members of the same family are reunited meetings and contacts between them may take place in accordance with the modalities for contacts on the basis of family ties.

The participating States will support the efforts of Red Cross and Red Crescent Societies concerned with the problems of family reunification.

They confirm that the presentation of an application concerning family reunifica will not modify the rights and obligations of the applicant or of members of his family.

The receiving participating State will take appropriate care with regard to employ ment for persons from other participating States who take up permanent residence in that State in connection with family reunification with its citizens and see that they are afforded opportunities equal to those enjoyed by its own citizens for education, medical assistance and social security.

(c) Marriage between Citizens of Different States

The participating States will examine favourably and on the basis of humanitarian considerations requests for exit or entry permits from persons who have decided to marry a citizen from another participating State.

The processing and issuing of the documents required for the above purposes and for the marriage will be in accordance with the provisions accepted for family reunification.

In dealing with requests from couples from different participating States, once married, to enable them and the minor children of their marriage to transfer their permanent residence to a State in which either one is normally a resident, the participating States will also apply the provisions accepted for family reunification.

(d) Travel for Personal or Professional Reasons

The participating States intend to facilitate wider travel by their citizens for personal or professional reasons and to this end they intend in particular:

gradually to simplify and to administer flexibly the procedures for exit and entry;

to ease regulations concerning movement of citizens from the other participating States in their territory, with due regard to security requirements.

They will endeavour gradually to lower, where necessary, the fees for visas and official travel documents.

They intend to consider, as necessary, means — including, insofar as appropriate, the conclusion of multilateral or bilateral consular conventions or other relevant agreements or understandings — for the improvement of arrangements to provide consular services, including legal and consular assistance.

They confirm that religious faiths, institutions and organisations, practising within the constitutional framework of the participating States, and their representatives, can, in the field of their activities, have contacts and meetings among themselves and exchange information.

(e) Improvement of Conditions for Tourism on an Individual or Collective Basis

The participating States consider that tourism contributes to a fuller knowledge of the life, culture and history of other countries, to the growth of understanding among peoples, to the improvement of contacts and to the broader use of leisure. They intend to promote the development of tourism, on an individual or collective basis, and, in particular, they intend:

to promote visits to their respective countries by encouraging the provision of appropriate facilities and the simplification and expediting of necessary formalities relating to such visits;

to increase, on the basis of appropriate agreements or arrangements where necessary, cooperation in the development of tourism, in particular by considering bilaterally possible ways to increase information relating to travel to other countries and to the reception and service of tourists, and other related questions of mutual interest.

(f) Meetings among Young People

The participating States intend to further the development of contacts and exchanges among young people by encouraging:

increased exchanges and contacts on a short or long term basis among young people working, training or undergoing education through bilateral or multilateral agreements or regular programmes in all cases where it is possible;

study by their youth organisations of the question of possible agreements relating to frameworks of multilateral youth cooperation;

agreements or regular programmes relating to the organisation of exchanges of students, of international youth seminars, of courses of professional training and foreign language study;

the further development of youth tourism and the provision to this end of appropriate facilities;

the development, where possible, of exchanges, contacts and cooperation on a bilateral or multilateral basis between their organisations which represent wide circles of young people working, training or undergoing education;

awareness among youth of the importance of developing mutual understanding and of strengthening friendly relations and confidence among peoples.

(g) Sport

In order to expand existing links and cooperation in the field of sport the participating States will encourage contacts and exchanges of this kind, including sports meetings and competitions of all sorts, on the basis of the established international rules, regulations and practice.

(h) Expansion of Contacts

By way of further developing contacts among governmental institutions and nongovernmental organisations and associations, including women's organisations, the participating States will facilitate the convening of meetings as well as travel by delegations, groups and individuals.

2. Information

The participating States,

Conscious of the need for an ever wider knowledge and understanding of the various aspects of life in other participating States,

Acknowledging the contribution of this process to the growth of confidence between peoples,

Desiring, with the development of mutual understanding between the participating States and with the further improvements of their relations, to continue further efforts towards progress in this field,

Recognising the importance of the dissemination of information from the other participating States and of a better acquaintance with such information,

Emphasising therefore the essential and influential role of the press, radio, television, cinema and news agencies and of the journalists working in these fields,

Make it their aim to facilitate the freer and wider dissemination of information of all kinds, to encourage cooperation in the field of information and the exchange of information with other countries, and to improve the conditions under which journalists from one participating State exercise their profession in another participating State, and

Express their intention in particular:

(a) Improvement of the Circulation of, Access to, and Exchange of Information

(i) *Oral Information*

To facilitate the dissemination of oral information through the encouragement of lectures and lecture tours by personalities and specialists from the other participating States, as well as exchanges of opinions at round table meetings, seminars, symposia, summer schools, congresses and other bilateral and multilateral meetings.

(ii) *Printed Information*

To facilitate the improvement of the dissemination, on their territory, of newspapers and printed publications, periodical and non-periodical, from the other participating States. For this purpose:

they will encourage their competent firms and organisations to conclude agreements and contracts designed gradually to increase the quantities and the number of titles of newspapers and publications imported from the other participating States. These agreements and contracts should in particular mention the speediest conditions of delivery and the use of the normal channels existing in each country for the distribution of its own publications and newspapers, as well as forms and means of payment agreed between the parties making it possible to achieve the objectives aimed at by these agreements and contracts;

where necessary, they will take appropriate measures to achieve the above objectives and to implement the provisions contained in the agreements and contracts.

To contribute to the improvement of access by the public to periodical and non-periodical printed publications imported on the bases indicated above. In particular:

they will encourage an increase in the number of places where these publications are on sale;

they will facilitate the availability of these periodical publications during congresses, conferences, official visits and other international events and to tourists during the season;

they will develop the possibilities for taking out subscriptions according to
the modalities particular to each country;

they will improve the opportunities for reading and borrowing these publicatio:
in large public libraries and their reading rooms as well as in university libraries

They intend to improve the possibilities for acquaintance with bulletins of official
information issued by diplomatic missions and distributed by those missions on the
basis of arrangements acceptable to the interested parties.

(iii) *Filmed and Broadcast Information*

To promote the improvement of the dissemination of filmed and broadcast
information. To this end:

they will encourage the wider showing and broadcasting of a greater variety
of recorded and filmed information from the other participating States,
illustrating the various aspects of life in their countries and received on the
basis of such agreements or arrangements as may be necessary between the
organisations and firms directly concerned;

they will facilitate the import by competent organisations and firms of recorde:
audio-visual material from the other participating States.

The participating States note the expansion in the dissemination of information
broadcast by radio, and express the hope for the continuation of this process, so
as to meet the interest of mutual understanding among peoples and the aims set
forth by this Conference.

(b) Cooperation in the field of Information

To encourage cooperation in the field of information on the basis of short
or long term agreements or arrangements. In particular:

they will favour increased cooperation among mass media organisations, including press agencies, as well as among publishing houses and organisations;

they will favour cooperation among public or private, national or international radio and television organisations, in particular through the exchange
of both live and recorded radio and television programmes, and through the
joint production and the broadcasting and distribution of such programmes;

they will encourage meetings and contacts both between journalists' organisations and between journalists from the participating States;

they will view favourably the possibilities of arrangements between periodical
publications as well as between newspapers from the participating States, for
the purposes of exchanging and publishing articles;

they will encourage the exchange of technical information as well as the organi:
sation of joint research and meetings devoted to the exchange of experience
and views between experts in the field of the press, radio and television.

(c) Improvement of Working Conditions for Journalists

The participating States, desiring to improve the conditions under which journalists om one participating State exercise their profession in another participating State, tend in particular to:

examine in a favourable spirit and within a suitable and reasonable time scale requests from journalists for visas;

grant to permanently accredited journalists of the participating States, on the basis of arrangements, multiple entry and exit visas for specified periods;

facilitate the issue to accredited journalists of the participating States of permits for stay in their country of temporary residence and, if and when these are necessary, of other official papers which it is appropriate for them to have;

ease, on a basis of reciprocity, procedures for arranging travel by journalists of the participating States in the country where they are exercising their profession, and to provide progressively greater opportunities for such travel, subject to the observance of regulations relating to the existence of areas closed for security reasons;

ensure that requests by such journalists for such travel receive, in so far as possible, an expeditious response, taking into account the time scale of the request;

increase the opportunities for journalists of the participating States to communicate personally with their sources, including organisations and official institutions;

grant to journalists of the participating States the right to import, subject only to its being taken out again, the technical equipment (photographic, cinematographic, tape recorder, radio and television) necessary for the exercise of their profession;[1]

enable journalists of the other participating States, whether permanently or temporarily accredited, to transmit completely, normally and rapidly by means recognised by the participating States to the information organs which they represent, the results of their professional activity, including tape recordings and undeveloped film, for the purpose of publication or of broadcasting on the radio or television.

The participating States reaffirm that the legitimate pursuit of their professional tivity will neither render journalists liable to expulsion nor otherwise penalise em. If an accredited journalist is expelled, he will be informed of the reasons for is act and may submit an application for reexamination of his case.

Cooperation and Exchanges in the Field of Culture

he participating States,

Considering that cultural exchanges and cooperation contribute to a better com-

1 While recognising that appropriate local personnel are employed by foreign journalists in any instances, the participating States note that the above provisions would be applied, subject the observance of the appropriate rules, to persons from the other participating States, who e regularly and professionally engaged as technicians, photographers or cameramen of the ess, radio, television or cinema. [Footnote in the original.]

prehension among people and among peoples, and thus promote a lasting understa▮ among States,

Confirming the conclusions already formulated in this field at the multilateral level, particularly at the Intergovernmental Conference on Cultural Policies in Euro▮ organised by UNESCO in Helsinki in June 1972, where interest was manifested in the active participation of the broadest possible social groups in an increasingly diversified cultural life,

Desiring, with the development of mutual confidence and the further improvem▮ of relations between the participating States, to continue further efforts toward progress in this field,

Disposed in this spirit to increase substantially their cultural exchanges, with regard both to persons and to cultural works, and to develop among them an activ▮ cooperation, both at the bilateral and the multilateral level, in all the fields of culture,

Convinced that such a development of their mutual relations will contribute to the enrichment of the respective cultures, while respecting the originality of each, as well as to the reinforcement among them of a consciousness of common values, while continuing to develop cultural cooperation with other countries of the world,

Declare that they jointly set themselves the following objectives:

(a) to develop the mutual exchange of information with a view to a better knowledge of respective cultural achievements,

(b) to improve the facilities for the exchange and for the dissemination of cultural property,

(c) to promote access by all to respective cultural achievements,

(d) to develop contacts and cooperation among persons active in the field of culture,

(e) to seek new fields and forms of cultural cooperation,

Thus *give expression* to their common will to take progressive, coherent and lon▮ term action in order to achieve the objectives of the present declaration; and

Express their intention now to proceed to the implementation of the following▮

Extension of Relations

To expand and improve at the various levels cooperation and links in the field of culture, in particular by:

concluding, where appropriate, agreements on a bilateral or multilateral basis providing for the extension of relations among competent state institutions and non-governmental organisations in the field of culture, as well as among people engaged in cultural activities, taking into account the need both for flexibility and the fullest possible use of existing agreements, and bearing in mind that agreements and also other arrangements constitute important means of developing cultural cooperation and exchanges;

contributing to the development of direct communication and cooperation among relevant state institutions and non-governmental organisations, including, where necessary, such communication and cooperation carried out on the basis of special agreements and arrangements;

encouraging direct contacts and communications among persons engaged in cultural activities, including, where necessary, such contacts and communications carried out on the basis of special agreements and arrangements.

Mutual Knowledge

Within their competence to adopt, on a bilateral and multilateral level, appropriate measures which would give their peoples a more comprehensive and complete mutual knowledge of their achievements in the various fields of culture, and among them:

to examine jointly, if necessary with the assistance of appropriate international organisations, the possible creation in Europe and the structure of a bank of cultural data, which would collect information from the participating countries and make it available to its correspondents on their request, and to convene for this purpose a meeting of experts from interested States;

to consider, if necessary in conjunction with appropriate international organisations, ways of compiling in Europe an inventory of documentary films of a cultural or scientific nature from the participating States,

to encourage more frequent book exhibitions and to examine the possibility of organising periodically in Europe a large scale exhibition of books from the participating States;

to promote the systematic exchange, between the institutions concerned and publishing houses, of catalogues of available books as well as of pre-publication material which will include, as far as possible, all forthcoming publications; and also to promote the exchange of material between firms publishing encyclopaedias, with a view to improving the presentation of each country;

to examine jointly questions of expanding and improving exchanges of information in the various fields of culture, such as theatre, music library work as well as the conservation and restoration of cultural property.

Exchanges and Dissemination

To contribute to the improvement of facilities for exchanges and the dissemination of cultural property, by appropriate means, in particular by:

studying the possibilities for harmonising and reducing the charges relating to international commercial exchanges of books and other cultural materials, and also for new means of insuring works of art in foreign exhibitions and for reducing the risks of damage or loss to which these works are exposed by their movement;

facilitating the formalities of customs clearance, in good time for programmes of artistic events, of the works of art, materials and accessories appearing on lists agreed upon by the organisers of these events;

encouraging meetings among representatives of competent organisations and
relevant firms to examine measures within their field of activity — such as
the simplification of orders, time limits for sending supplies and modalities
of payment — which might facilitate international commercial exchanges
of books;
promoting the loan and exchange of films among their film institutes and film
libraries;
encouraging the exchange of information among interested parties concerning
events of a cultural character foreseen in the participating States, in fields
where this is most appropriate, such as music, theatre and the plastic and
graphic arts, with a view to contributing to the compilation and publication
of a calendar of such events, with the assistance, where necessary, of the
appropriate international organisations;
encouraging a study of the impact which the foreseeable development, and a
possible harmonisation among interested parties, of the technical means used
for the dissemination of culture might have on the development
of cultural cooperation and exchanges, while keeping in view the preservation
of the diversity and originality of their respective cultures;
encouraging, in the way they deem appropriate, within their cultural policies,
the further development of interest in the cultural heritage of the other
participating States, conscious of the merits and the value of each culture;
endeavouring to ensure the full and effective application of the international
agreements and conventions on copyrights and on circulation of cultural
property to which they are party or to which they may decide in the future
to become party.

Access

To promote fuller mutual access by all to the achievements — works, experiences an
performing arts — in the various fields of culture of their countries, and to that end
to make the best possible efforts, in accordance with their competence, more particularly:
to promote wider dissemination of books and artistic works, in particular by
such means as:
facilitating, while taking full account of the international copyright conventio
to which they are party, international contacts and communications between
authors and publishing houses as well as other cultural institutions, with a view
to a more complete mutual access to cultural achievements;
recommending that, in determining the size of editions, publishing houses take
into account also the demand from the other participating States, and that
rights of sale in other participating States be granted, where possible, to severa
sales organisations of the importing countries, by agreement between intereste
partners;
encouraging competent organisations and relevant firms to conclude agreemen

and contracts and contributing, by this means, to a gradual increase in the number and diversity of works by authors from the other participating States available in the original and in translation in their libraries and bookshops; promoting, where deemed appropriate, an increase in the number of sales outlets where books by authors from the other participating States, imported in the original on the basis of agreements and contracts, and in translation, are for sale;

promoting, on a wider scale, the translation of works in the sphere of literature and other fields of cultural activity, produced in the languages of the other participating States, especially from the less widely-spoken languages, and the publication and dissemination of the translated works by such measures as:

encouraging more regular contacts between interested publishing houses; developing their efforts in the basic and advanced training of translators;

encouraging, by appropriate means, the publishing houses of their countries to publish translations;

facilitating the exchange between publishers and interested institutions of lists of books which might be translated;

promoting between their countries the professional activity and co-operation of translators;

carrying out joint studies on ways of further promoting translations and their dissemination;

improving and expanding exchanges of books, bibliographies and catalogue cards between libraries;

to envisage other appropriate measures which would permit, where necessary by mutual agreement among interested parties, the facilitation of access to their respective cultural achievements, in particular in the field of books;

to contribute by appropriate means to the wider use of the mass media in order to improve mutual acquaintance with the cultural life of each;

to seek to develop the necessary conditions for migrant workers and their families to preserve their links with their national culture, and also to adapt themselves to their new cultural environment;

to encourage the competent bodies and enterprises to make a wider choice and effect wider distribution of full-length and documentary films from the other participating States, and to promote more frequent non-commercial showings, such as premieres, film weeks and festivals, giving due consideration to films from countries whose cinematographic works are less well known;

to promote, by appropriate means, the extension of opportunities for specialists from the other participating States to work with materials of a cultural character from film and audio-visual archives, within the framework of the existing rules for work on such archival materials;

to encourage a joint study by interested bodies, where appropriate with the assistance of the competent international organisations, of the expediency and the conditions for the establishment of a repertory of their recorded television programmes of a cultural nature, as well as of the means of viewing them rapidly in order to facilitate their selection and possible acquisition.

Contacts and Cooperation

To contribute, by appropriate means, to the development of contacts and co-operation in the various fields of culture, especially among creative artists and people engaged in cultural activities, in particular by making efforts to:
   promote for persons active in the field of culture, travel and meetings includi
   where necessary, those carried out on the basis of agreements, contracts or
   other special arrangements and which are relevant to their cultural cooperatic
   encourage in this way contacts among creative and performing artists and
   artistic groups with a view to their working together, making known their
   works in other participating States or exchanging views on topics relevant
   to their common activity;
   encourage, where necessary through appropriate arrangements, exchanges
   of trainees and specialists and the granting of scholarships for basic and
   advanced training in various fields of culture such as the arts and architecture
   museums and libraries, literary studies and translation, and contribute to the
   creation of favourable conditions of reception in their respective institutions;
   encourage the exchange of experience in the training of organisers of cultural
   activities as well as of teachers and specialists in fields such as theatre, opera,
   ballet, music and fine arts;
   continue to encourage the organisation of international meetings among
   creative artists, especially young creative artists, on current questions of
   artistic and literary creation which are of interest for joint study;
   study other possibilities for developing exchanges and cooperation among
   persons active in the field of culture, with a view to a better mutual knowled
   of the cultural life of the participating States.

Fields and Forms of Cooperation

To encourage the search for new fields and forms of cultural cooperation, to these ends contributing to the conclusion among interested parties, where necessary, of appropriate agreements and arrangements, and in this context to promote:
   joint studies regarding cultural policies, in particular in their social aspects,
   and as they relate to planning, town-planning, educational and environmental
   policies, and the cultural aspects of tourism;
   the exchange of knowledge in the realm of cultural diversity, with a view to
   contributing thus to a better understanding by interested parties of such
   diversity where it occurs;
   the exchange of information, and as may be appropriate, meetings of experts
   the elaboration and the execution of research programmes and projects, as
   well as their joint evaluation, and the dissemination of the results, on the
   subjects indicated above;

such forms of cultural cooperation and the development of such joint projects as:

> international events in the fields of the plastic and graphic arts cinema, theatre, ballet, music, folklore, etc.; book fairs and exhibitions, joint performances of operatic and dramatic works, as well as performances given by soloists, instrumental ensembles, orchestras, choirs and other artistic groups, including those composed of amateurs, paying due attention to the organisation of international cultural youth events and the exchange of young artists;
>
> the inclusion of works by writers and composers from the other participating States in the repertoires of soloists and artistic ensembles;
>
> the preparation, translation and publication of articles, studies and monographs, as well as of low-cost books and of artistic and literary collections, suited to making better known respective cultural achievements, envisaging for this purpose meetings among experts and representatives of publishing houses;
>
> the co-production and the exchange of films and of radio and television programmes, by promoting, in particular, meetings among producers, technicians and representatives of the public authorities with a view to working out favourable conditions for the execution of specific joint projects and by encouraging, in the field of co-production, the establishment of international filming teams;
>
> the organisation of competitions for architects and town-planners, bearing in mind the possible implementation of the best projects and the formation, where possible, of international teams;
>
> the implementation of joint projects for conserving, restoring and showing to advantage works of art, historical and archaeological monuments and sites of cultural interest, with the help, in appropriate cases, of international organisations of a governmental or non-governmental character as well as of private institutions – competent and active in these fields – envisaging for this purpose:
>
>> periodic meetings of experts of the interested parties to elaborate the necessary proposals, while bearing in mind the need to consider these questions in a wider social and economic context;
>>
>> the publication in appropriate periodicals of articles designed to make known and to compare, among the participating States, the most significant achievements and innovations;
>>
>> a joint study with a view to the improvement and possible harmonisation of the different systems used to inventory and catalogue the historical monuments and places of cultural interest in their countries;
>>
>> the study of the possibilities for organising international courses for the training of specialists in different disciplines relating to restoration.

National minorities or regional cultures. The participating States, recognising the contribution that national minorities or regional cultures can make to cooperation among them in various fields of culture, intend, when such minorities or cultures exist within their territory, to facilitate this contribution, taking into account the legitimate interests of their members.

4. Cooperation and Exchanges in the Field of Education

The participating States,

Conscious that the development of relations of an international character in the fields of education and science contributes to a better mutual understanding and is to the advantage of all peoples as well as to the benefit of future generations,

Prepared to facilitate, between organisations, institutions and persons engaged in education and science, the further development of exchanges of knowledge and experience as well as of contacts, on the basis of special arrangements where these are necessary,

Desiring to strengthen the links among educational and scientific establishments and also to encourage their cooperation in sectors of common interest, particularly where the levels of knowledge and resources require efforts to be concerted internationally, and

Convinced that progress in these fields should be accompanied and supported by a wider knowledge of foreign languages,

Express to these ends their intention in particular:

(a) Extension of Relations

To expand and improve at the various levels cooperation and links in the fields of education and science, in particular by:

concluding, where appropriate, bilateral or multilateral agreements providing for cooperation and exchanges among State institutions, non-governmental bodies and persons engaged in activities in education and science, bearing in mind the need both for flexibility and the fuller use of existing agreements and arrangements;

promoting the conclusion of direct arrangements between universities and other institutions of higher education and research, in the framework of agreements between governments where appropriate;

encouraging among persons engaged in education and science direct contacts and communications, including those based on special agreements or arrangements where these are appropriate.

(b) Access and Exchanges

To improve access, under mutually acceptable conditions, for students, teachers and scholars of the participating States to each other's educational, cultural and scientifi institutions, and to intensify exchanges among these institutions in all areas of common interest, in particular by:

increasing the exchange of information on facilities for study and courses open to foreign participants, as well as on the conditions under which they will be admitted and received;

facilitating travel between the participating States by scholars, teachers and students for purposes of study, teaching and research as well as for improving knowledge of each other's educational, cultural and scientific achievements;

encouraging the award of scholarships for study, teaching and research in their countries to scholars, teachers and students of other participating States;

establishing, developing or encouraging programmes providing for the broader exchange of scholars, teachers and students, including the organisation of symposia, seminars and collaborative projects, and the exchanges of educational and scholarly information such as university publications and materials from libraries;

promoting the efficient implementation of such arrangements and programmes by providing scholars, teachers and students in good time with more detailed information about their placing in universities and institutes and the programmes envisaged for them; by granting them the opportunity to use relevant scholarly, scientific and open archival materials; and by facilitating their travel within the receiving State for the purpose of study or research as well as in the form of vacation tours on the basis of the usual procedures;

promoting a more exact assessment of the problems of comparison and equivalence of academic degrees and diplomas by fostering the exchange of information on the organisation, duration and content of studies, the comparison of methods of assessing levels of knowledge and academic qualifications, and, where feasible, arriving at the mutual recognition of academic degrees and diplomas either through governmental agreements, where necessary, or direct arrangements between universities and other institutions of higher learning and research;

recommending, moreover, to the appropriate international organisations that they should intensify their efforts to reach a generally acceptable solution to the problems of comparison and equivalence between academic degrees and diplomas.

c) Science

Within their competence to broaden and improve cooperation and exchanges in the field of science, in particular:

To increase, on a bilateral or multilateral basis, the exchange and dissemination of scientific information and documentation by such means as:

making this information more widely available to scientists and research

workers of the other participating States through, for instance, participation
in international information-sharing programmes or through other appropriate
arrangements;
broadening and facilitating the exchange of samples and other scientific
materials used particularly for fundamental research in the fields of natural
sciences and medicine;
inviting scientific institutions and universities to keep each other more fully
and regularly informed about their current and contemplated research work
in fields of common interest.

To facilitate the extension of communications and direct contacts between
universities, scientific institutions and associations as well as among scientists and
research workers, including those based where necessary on special agreements or
arrangements, by such means as:
further developing exchanges of scientists and research workers and encouraging
the organisation of preparatory meetings or working groups on research topics
of common interest;
encouraging the creation of joint teams of scientists to pursue research projects
under arrangements made by the scientific institutions of several countries;
assisting the organisation and successful functioning of international conferences
and seminars and participation in them by their scientists and research workers
furthermore envisaging, in the near future, a 'Scientific Forum' in the form
of a meeting of leading personalities in science from the participating States
to discuss interrelated problems of common interest concerning current and
future developments in science, and to promote the expansion of contacts,
communications and the exchange of information between scientific institutions
and among scientists;
foreseeing, at an early date, a meeting of experts representing the participating
States and their national scientific institutions, in order to prepare such a
'Scientific Forum' in consultation with appropriate international organisations, such as UNESCO and ECE;
considering in due course what further steps might be taken with respect to
the 'Scientific Forum'.

To develop in the field of scientific research, on a bilateral or multilateral basis,
the coordination of programmes carried out in the participating States and the
organisation of joint programmes, especially in the areas mentioned below which
may involve the combined efforts of scientists and in certain cases the use of costly
or unique equipment. The list of subjects in these areas is illustrative; and specific
projects would have to be determined subsequently by the potential partners in the
participating States, taking account of the contributions which could be made by
appropriate international organisations and scientific institutions:
exact and natural sciences, in particular fundamental research in such fields
as mathematics, physics, theoretical physics, geophysics, chemistry, biology,
ecology and astronomy;
medicine, in particular basic research into cancer and cardiovascular diseases,

studies on the diseases endemic in the developing countries, as well as medico-social research with special emphasis on occupational diseases, the rehabilitation of the handicapped and the care of mothers, children and the elderly;

the humanities and social sciences, such as history, geography, philosophy, psychology, pedagogical research, linguistics, sociology, the legal, political and economic sciences; comparative studies on social, socio-economic and cultural phenomena which are of common interest to the participating States, especially the problems of human environment and urban development; and scientific studies on the methods of conserving and restoring monuments and works of art.

Foreign Languages and Civilisations

encourage the study of foreign languages and civilisations as an important ans of expanding communication among peoples for their better acquaintance h the culture of each country, as well as for the strengthening of international peration; to this end to stimulate, within their competence, the further develop-nt and improvement of foreign language teaching and the diversification of choice languages taught at various levels, paying due attention to less widely-spread or died languages, and in particular:

to intensify cooperation aimed at improving the teaching of foreign languages through exchanges of information and experience concerning the development and application of effective modern teaching methods and technical aids, adapted to the needs of different categories of students, including methods of accelerated teaching; and to consider the possibility of conducting, on a bilateral or multilateral basis, studies of new methods of foreign language teaching;

to encourage cooperation between institutions concerned, on a bilateral or multilateral basis, aimed at exploiting more fully the resources of modern educational technology in language teaching, for example through comparative studies by their specialists and, where agreed, through exchanges or transfers of audio-visual materials, of materials used for preparing textbooks, as well as of information about new types of technical equipment used for teaching languages;

to promote the exchange of information on the experience acquired in the training of language teachers and to intensify exchanges on a bilateral basis of language teachers and students as well as to facilitate their participation in summer courses in languages and civilisations, wherever these are organised; to encourage cooperation among experts in the field of lexicography with the aim of defining the necessary terminological equivalents, particularly in the scientific and technical disciplines, in order to facilitate relations among scientific institutions and specialists;

to promote the wider spread of foreign language study among the different types of secondary education establishments and greater possibilities of choice between an increased number of European languages; and in this context to consider, wherever appropriate, the possibilities for developing the recruitment and training of teachers as well as the organisation of the student groups required;

to favour, in higher education, a wider choice in the languages offered to language students and greater opportunities for other students to study vari foreign languages; also to facilitate, where desirable, the organisation of courses in languages and civilisations, on the basis of special arrangements as necessary, to be given by foreign lecturers, particularly from European countries having less widely-spread or studied languages;

to promote, within the framework of adult education, the further development of specialised programmes, adapted to various needs and interests, for teaching foreign languages to their own inhabitants and the languages of ho countries to interested adults from other countries; in this context to encourage interested institutions to cooperate, for example, in the elaboration of programmes for teaching by radio and television and by accelerated methods, and also, where desirable, in the definition of study objectives for such programmes, with a view to arriving at comparable levels of language proficiency;

to encourage the association, where appropriate, of the teaching of foreign languages with the study of the corresponding civilisations and also to make further efforts to stimulate interest in the study of foreign languages, includ relevant out-of-class activities.

(e) Teaching Methods

To promote the exchange of experience, on a bilateral or multilateral basis, in teaching methods at all levels of education, including those used in permanent and adult education, as well as the exchange of teaching materials, in particular by:

further developing various forms of contacts and cooperation in the differe fields of pedagogical science, for example through comparative or joint studies carried out by interested institutions or through exchanges of information on the results of teaching experiments;

intensifying exchanges of information on teaching methods used in various educational systems and on results of research into the processes by which pupils and students acquire knowledge, taking account of relevant experien in different types of specialised education;

facilitating exchanges of experience concerning the organisation and functioning of education intended for adults and recurrent education, the relatic ships between these and other forms and levels of education, as well as concerning the means of adapting education, including vocational and technica training, to the needs of economic and social development in their countries encouraging exchanges of experience in the education of youth and adults i international understanding, with particular reference to those major problems of mankind whose solution calls for a common approach and wider international cooperation;

encouraging exchanges of teaching materials — including school textbooks, having in mind the possibility of promoting mutual knowledge and facilitating the presentation of each country in such books — as well as exchanges of information on technical innovations in the field of education.

ational minorities or regional cultures. The participating States, recognising the ontribution that national minorities or regional cultures can make to cooperation nong them in various fields of education, intend, when such minorities or cultures :ist within their territory, to facilitate this contribution, taking into account the gitimate interests of their members.

OLLOW-UP TO THE CONFERENCE

he participating States,

Having considered and evaluated the progress made at the Conference on Security id Cooperation in Europe,

Considering further that, within the broader context of the world, the Conference an important part of the process of improving security and developing cooperation Europe and that its results will contribute significantly to this process,

Intending to implement the provisions of the Final Act of the Conference in :der to give full effect to its results and thus to further the process of improving curity and developing cooperation in Europe,

Convinced that, in order to achieve the aims sought by the Conference, they iould make further unilateral, bilateral and multilateral efforts and continue, in ie appropriate forms set forth below, the multilateral process initiated by the onference,

1. *Declare their resolve,* in the period following the Conference, to pay due regard to and implement the provisions of the Final Act of the Conference:
   (*a*) unilaterally, in all cases which lend themselves to such action;
   (*b*) bilaterally, by negotiations with other participating States;
   (*c*) multilaterally, by meetings of experts of the participating States, and also within the framework of existing international organisations, such as the United Nations Economic Commission for Europe and UNESCO, with regard to educational, scientific and cultural cooperation;

2. *Declare furthermore their resolve* to continue the multilateral process initiated by the Conference:
   (*a*) by proceeding to a thorough exchange of views both on the implementation of the provisions of the Final Act and of the tasks defined by the Conference, as well as, in the context of the questions dealt with by the latter, on the deepening of their mutual relations, the improvement of security and the development of cooperation in Europe, and the development of the process of detente in the future;

(*b*) by organising to these ends meetings among their representatives, beginning with a meeting at the level of representatives appointed by the Ministers of Foreign Affairs. This meeting will define the appropriate modalities for the holding of other meetings which could include further similar meetings and the possibility of a new Conference;

3. The first of the meetings indicated above will be held at Belgrade in 1977. A preparatory meeting to organise this meeting will be held at Belgrade on 15 June 1977. The preparatory meeting will decide on the date, duration, agenda and other modalities of the meeting of representatives appointed by the Ministers of Foreign Affairs;

4. The rules of procedure, the working methods and the scale of distribution fo the expenses of the Conference will, *mutatis mutandis*, be applied to the meetings envisaged in paragraphs 1 (c), 2 and 3 above. All the above-mention meetings will be held in the participating States in rotation. The services of a technical secretariat will be provided by the host country.

The original of this Final Act, drawn up in English, French, German, Italian, Russian and Spanish, will be transmitted to the Government of the Republic of Finland, which will retain it in its archives. Each of the participating States will receive from the Government of the Republic of Finland a true copy of this Final Act.

The text of this Final Act will be published in each participating State, which w: disseminate it and make it known as widely as possible.

The Government of the Republic of Finland is requested to transmit to the Secretary-General of the United Nations the text of this Final Act, which is not eligible for registration under Article 102 of the Charter of the United Nations, with a view to its circulation to all the members of the Organisation as an official document of the United Nations.

The Government of the Republic of Finland is also requested to transmit the te: of this Final Act to the Director-General of UNESCO and to the Executive Secreta of the United Nations Economic Commission for Europe.

II.   Changes in the Western Alliance

A. The North Atlantic Treaty Organization

**108. Communiqué of the NATO Council, Brussels,
16 November 1968[1]**

1. The North Atlantic Council met in Ministerial session in Brussels on 15th and
16th November. The meeting was attended by Foreign, Defence and Finance
Ministers. The Council had moved forward from mid-December its normal year-end
meeting so that Ministers might discuss at an earlier date the serious situation following the armed intervention in Czechoslovakia and the occupation of that country
by forces of the Soviet Union and four of its Warsaw Pact Allies.

2. Ministers reaffirmed the inviolability of the principle, which has been invoked
on numerous occasions by every country, including the USSR, that all nations are
independent and that consequently any intervention by one state in the affairs of
another is unlawful.

They noted that this principle has been deliberately violated by the Soviet
leaders with the backing of four of their allies. World opinion has been profoundly
shocked by this armed intervention carried out against the wishes of the Government and people of Czechoslovakia. All the members of the Alliance have denounced
this use of force which jeopardises peace and international order and strikes at the
principles of the United Nations Charter. Like all other peoples, the people of
Czechoslovakia must be free to shape their future without outside interference.
Agreements concluded under the pressure of occupying forces can provide no
justification for challenging this basic concept.

3. The contention of the Soviet leadership that there exists a right of intervention
in the affairs of other states deemed to be within a so-called 'Socialist Commonwealth' runs counter to the basic principles of the United Nations Charter, is
dangerous to European security and has inevitably aroused grave anxieties. It gives
rise to fears of a further use of force in other cases.

The use of force and the stationing in Czechoslovakia of Soviet forces not hitherto
deployed there have aroused grave uncertainty about the situation and about the
calculations and intentions of the USSR. This uncertainty demands great vigilance on
the part of the Allies.

4. Applied to Germany the policies which the USSR derives from its doctrine

1 *DSB*, 9 December 1968, pp. 595–7.

of a so-called 'Socialist Commonwealth' raise new obstacles to the rapprochement and ultimate unification of the two parts of Germany. Moreover, they would be contrary to the letter and spirit of the Four Power agreements relating to Germany as a whole.

In this situation, and bearing in mind the special responsibilities of the United States, the United Kingdom and France, the Ministers reaffirm the determination of the Alliance to persevere in its efforts to contribute to a peaceful solution of the German question based on the free decision of the German people and on the interests of European security. Their Governments do not recognize the 'GDR', and they reject all claims which would tend to perpetuate the division of Germany against the will of the German people.

Referring to their communiqué issued in Reykjavik on 25th June, 1968, the Ministers confirm the support of their Governments for the declared determination of the Three Powers to safeguard Berlin's security and to maintain freedom of acce to the city. They recall the declaration of the North Atlantic Council of December 16, 1958 on Berlin and the responsibilities which each Member State assumed with regard to the security and welfare of Berlin. They note with satisfaction the import measures taken by the Federal Republic of Germany in conformity with the status of Berlin for the purpose of maintaining the viability of the city. They associate themselves with the position of the Three Powers as regards the legitimate concern of the Federal Government for the welfare and viability of Berlin and as regards the resulting ties which exist between the two on the basis of the arrangements in force.

The Ministers associate themselves with the call made upon the Soviet Union by the Three Powers to respect the quadripartite agreements concerning Berlin and the decisions taken pursuant to these agreements by the United States, France and the United Kingdom.

5. The new uncertainties resulting from recent Soviet actions also extend to the Mediterranean basin. This situation requires that the Allies continue by every available means their efforts to promote stability and a just and equitable peace, as wel as mutual cooperation and understanding, in the area. The expansion of Soviet activity in the Mediterranean, including the increased presence of Soviet naval units requires vigilance to safeguard allied security.

6. The members of the Alliance urge the Soviet Union, in the interests of world peace, to refrain from using force and interfering in the affairs of other states.

Determined to safeguard the freedom and independence of their countries, they could not remain indifferent to any development which endangers their security.

Clearly any Soviet intervention directly or indirectly affecting the situation in Europe or in the Mediterranean would create an international crisis with grave consequences.

7. So long as the Soviet leaders adhere to a policy of force, these new uncertaint will remain. The Allies are convinced that their political solidarity remains indispensable to discourage aggression and other forms of oppression. Above all, they stand wholly determined to meet their common responsibilities and, in accordance

th the North Atlantic Treaty, to defend the members of the Alliance against any
ned attack.

8. The Allies participating in NATO's integrated defence programme have, there-
re, been obliged to reassess the state of their defences. They consider that the
uation arising from recent events calls for a collective response. The quality,
fectiveness, and deployment of NATO's forces will be improved in terms of both
anpower and equipment in order to provide a better capability for defence as
r forward as possible. The quality of reserve forces will also be improved and their
ility to mobilise rapidly will be directed to the provision of reinforcements for
e flanks and the strengthening of local forces there. The conventional capability
NATO's tactical air forces will be increased. Certain additional national units
ll be committed to the Major NATO Commanders. Specific measures have been
proved within these categories of action for improving the conventional capability
NATO's forces. Ministers agreed that the coordinated implementation of these
easures and the provision of additional budgetary resources to the extent necessary
support them would form part of the NATO Force Plan for 1969–1973 which
ll be submitted in January 1969. They also acknowledged that the solidarity of
e Alliance can be strengthened by cooperation between members to alleviate
rdens arising from balance of payments deficits resulting specifically from military
penditures for the collective defence.

9. A year ago Ministers affirmed in the Report on the Future Tasks of the Alliance
at, while maintaining adequate military strength and political solidarity to deter
y aggressor, the Alliance should work to promote a policy of detente. The Soviet
tervention in Czechoslovakia has seriously set back hopes of settling the out-
nding problems which still divide the European continent and Germany and of
tablishing peace and security in Europe, and threatens certain of the results already
hieved in the field of detente. Indeed, in view of the action of the five members
the Warsaw Pact, the scope and level of Allied contacts with them have had to
reduced.

10. More specifically, prospects for mutual balanced force reductions have suf-
red a severe setback. Nevertheless, the Allies in close consultation are continuing
eir studies and preparations for a time when the atmosphere for fruitful dis-
ssions is more favourable.

11. In any event, consistent with Western values the political goal remains that
secure, peaceful and mutually beneficial relations between East and West. The
lies are determined to pursue this goal, bearing in mind that the pursuit of
tente must not be allowed to split the Alliance. The search for peace requires
ogress, consistent with Western security, in the vital fields of disarmament and
ms control and continuing efforts to resolve the fundamental issues which divide
st and West.

12. The North Atlantic Alliance will continue to stand as the indispensable guarantor
security and the essential foundation for the pursuit of European reconciliation.
its constitution the Alliance is of indefinite duration. Recent events have further
monstrated that its continued existence is more than ever necessary. The Foreign

Minister of France recalled that, for its part, unless events in the years to come were to bring about a radical change in East–West relations, the French Government considers that the Alliance must continue as long as it appears to be necessary.

13. The next Ministerial Meeting of the Council will be held in Washington on the 10th and 11th April, 1969.

14. The Defence Planning Committee which met in Ministerial Session on 14th November will hold its next Ministerial Meeting in Brussels on 16th January, 1969

109. Communiqué of the NATO Council, Washington, 11 April 1969[1]

1. The North Atlantic Council met in Ministerial Session in Washington on 10th and 11th April, 1969. The Council commemorated the twentieth anniversary of the Treaty creating the Alliance and was addressed by the President of the United States. Ministers expressed their deep satisfaction at the decisive contribution the Alliance had made to the maintenance of peace in Europe and to the security of all its members.

2. The Alliance was established to safeguard the freedom, common heritage and civilisation of its peoples, founded on the principles of democracy, individual liberty and the rule of law, and in response to a common fear that without an effective security system, another war might erupt in a divided Europe. The Alliance continues as the expression of common purposes and aspirations.

3. In 1967 the Report on the Future Tasks of the Alliance emphasised the dual task of the latter: the defence of the West and the search for a stable peace with the East. In June 1968 Allied Ministers declared their readiness to seek, with the other States concerned, specific practical measures for disarmament and arms control, including possible measures for mutual and balanced force reductions[2] Notwithstanding the serious setback to hopes for improvement in East–West relations as a result of Soviet intervention in Czechoslovakia, Ministers in November 1968 stated that secure, peaceful and mutually beneficial relations between East and West remained the political goal of the Allies. They reaffirmed at this session that the intention of their Governments was to continue the search for real progress toward this objective by contacts and to explore all appropriate openings for negotiations.

4. Bearing especially in mind the situation in Eastern Europe, member governments recall that any lasting improvement in international relations presupposes full respect for the principles of the independence and territorial integrity of States, non-interference in their domestic affairs, the right of each people to shape its own future, and the obligations to refrain from the threat or use of force.

5. Ministers recalled that one of the essential aims of the Alliance is the establishment of a just and lasting peace in Europe, based on stability, security and mutual confidence. The Allies propose, while remaining in close consultation to

1 *DSB*, 28 April 1969, pp. 354–6.
2 Document No. 90.

explore with the Soviet Union and the other countries of Eastern Europe which concrete issues best lend themselves to fruitful negotiation and an early resolution. Consequently, they instructed the Council to draft a list of these issues and to study how a useful process of negotiation could best be initiated, in due course, and to draw up a report for the next meeting of Ministers. It is clear that any negotiations must be well prepared in advance and that all governments whose participation would be necessary to achieve a political settlement in Europe should take part.

6. The Allies will also pursue their efforts and studies in the field of disarmament and practical arms control, including balanced force reductions and the initiatives already undertaken for the renunciation of the use of force.

7. The political solidarity of the Alliance constitutes an essential element while approaching a period of expanding East—West contacts and possible negotiations. This solidarity can best be maintained by strict adherence to the principle of full consultation in the Council both before and during any negotiations that might affect the interests of the Alliance or any of its members. On this understanding, the Allied Governments welcome the intention of the United States to engage the USSR in discussion of limitations on offensive and defensive strategic arms.

8. The Allies participating in the NATO integrated defence programme agreed that it was extremely important that during an era of negotiation the defence posture of the Alliance should not be relaxed and that premature expectations of solutions to outstanding questions should not be generated. The maintenance of effective defence is a stabilising factor and a necessary condition for effective detente policies.

9. Accordingly these members of the Alliance reaffirmed their continuing determination to make appropriate contributions to joint efforts for defence and deterrence at all levels both nuclear and conventional. They accepted the continuing need for the current NATO strategy based on a forward defence and appropriate response to any aggression, and for a credible conventional and nuclear deterrent including adequate overall and local force levels. The necessary military posture of the Alliance consists of the strategic nuclear deterrent forces, the presence of sufficient substantial and effective North American and European conventional forces as well as supporting tactical nuclear forces in the European area and adequate ready reinforcements.

10. Defence Ministers will meet on 28th May, 1969 and will examine the more specific elements in the defence posture necessary to fulfill the above requirements. They will also examine the possibility of improving the efficiency of the defence effort by intensifying mutual and cooperative approaches to, for example, the problems of arms production and arms standardisation either among all Allied nations or between some of them.

11. Reviewing the situation in Berlin, the Ministers noted that obstacles have recently been placed on freedom of access to Berlin. Such obstructions cannot be accepted. The Ministers supported the determination of the Three Powers to maintain free access to the city, and recalled the declaration of the North Atlantic Council of 16th December 1958, and the responsibilities which each member State assumed with regard to the security and welfare of Berlin.

12. The Ministers consider that the achievement of a peaceful European settlement presupposes, among other things, progress towards eliminating existing sources of tension in the centre of Europe. They consider that concrete measures aimed at improving the situation in Berlin, safeguarding free access to the city, and removing restrictions which affect traffic and communications between the two parts of Germany would be a substantial contribution toward this objective. They expressed their support for continued efforts by the Three Powers to explore, in the framework of their special responsibilities for Berlin and Germany as a whole, possibilities for ordered and negotiated progress in these important questions.

13. A peaceful solution must be found for the German question based on the free decision of the German people and on the interests of European security.

14. The members of the Alliance are conscious that they share common environmental problems which, unless squarely faced, could imperil the welfare and progress of their societies. The Ministers recognise that important work on these problems is already being carried out within other international organizations. The Ministers instructed the Council in Permanent Session to examine how to improve, in every practical way, the exchange of views and experience among the Allied countries, whether by action in the appropriate international organizations or otherwise, in the task of creating a better environment for their societies.

15. While concerned with these problems, Ministers are also mindful that the Allied countries are entering an era in which scientific, technical and economic resources should contribute to the peaceful progress and development of all nations.

16. Apart from regular meetings at Ministerial level, Ministers agreed that the Council in Permanent Session should consider the proposal that high officials of their Foreign Ministries meet periodically for a review of major, long-range problems before the Alliance.

17. The next Ministerial Session of the North Atlantic Council will be held in Brussels in December 1969.

110. Statement by the NATO Council on the establishment of the Committee on the Challenges of Modern Society, Brussels, 6 November 1969[1]

The North Atlantic Council has established a Committee on the Challenges of Modern Society to consider problems of the human environment.

The Council based its work on Article II of the North Atlantic Treaty, in which the parties agreed that they would contribute towards further development of peaceful and friendly international relations by promoting conditions of stability and well-being.

The move towards this new endeavour began last April in Washington when NATO's Ministers stated that the members of the Alliance are convinced that they share common environmental problems which, unless squarely faced, could imperil

1 NATO Press Service.

the welfare and progress of their societies. The Ministers asked the Council to examine this question and the Council undertook a study of how the Alliance could engage in the task of dealing with these problems.

The Committee will examine how to improve, in every practical way, the exchange of views and experience among the allied countries in the task of creating a better environment for their societies. It will consider specific problems of the human environment with the deliberate objective of stimulating action by member governments. The Committee will collect information on and make assessments of selected activities of common interest, planned or pursued by member governments in their countries or in the international field.

The Committee itself will not take executive action and, in order to avoid duplication, will take due account of activities already under way in the environmental field in other international bodies. The Committee will make recommendations to the Council and will be subject to its direction and control.

The first meeting of this new NATO Committee is scheduled 8th, 9th and 10th December.

111. Message from President Nixon to the North Atlantic Council, 3 December 1970[1]

The meeting of the North Atlantic Alliance will be one of the most important conferences in the history of the Alliance. This past year has witnessed the completion of a comprehensive review of alliance defence that can serve as the basis for a common effort throughout this decade. This review testifies to the continuing value of candid consultations based on mutual respect and to the common recognition that the prospects for peace rest primarily on our ability and willingness to maintain an alliance sufficiently strong to deter those who might threaten war.

After the most searching consultations, together we have arrived at several fundamental conclusions which will help us maintain NATO's strength while the Alliance seeks to translate the promise of detente into the reality of a just and lasting peace.

We have reaffirmed flexibility of response as the proper strategy for a defensive alliance confronted by a formidable mix of a potentially hostile force, which is constantly improving.

We have agreed that NATO's conventional forces must not only be maintained, but in certain key areas, strengthened. Given a similar approach by our allies, the United States will maintain and improve its own forces in Europe and will not reduce them unless there is reciprocal action from our adversaries. We will continue to talk with our NATO allies with regard to how we can meet our responsibilities together.

The allies have agreed to move to transform the recommendations of the study into fact. This should provide NATO with an enhanced capability sufficient to make the strategy of flexible response a more credible factor in the equation of deterrence.

In the process of this review we were heartened by the efforts of several of the

1 *DSB*, 4 January 1971, pp. 1–2.

Alliance's members to create a new and more equitable sharing of the burdens of the Alliance through a greater effort by our allies to meet the challenges of NATO defence in the decade of the seventies. This European initiative gives concrete testimony to the vitality and spirit of the European allies. NATO has strong support among the American people. Successful efforts to improve European forces and absorb a greater share of the burden will ensure continued support.

I welcome the achievements of the Alliance. I am certain we can move from agreed goals to practical action with the same seriousness of purpose.

112. Communiqué of the NATO Council, Brussels, 4 December 1970, with Annex on Alliance Defence for the Seventies[1]

The North Atlantic Council met in Ministerial Session at Brussels on 3rd and 4th December, 1970. Foreign, Defence and Finance Ministers were present.

2. Ministers again stated that the political purpose of the Alliance is the common search for peace through initiatives aiming at the relaxation of tension and the establishment of a just and lasting peaceful order in Europe, accompanied by appropriate security guarantees.

3. The Council received a statement from President Nixon which pledged that, given a similar approach by the other Allies, the United States would maintain and improve its own forces in Europe and would not reduce them except in the context of reciprocal East—West action. Ministers expressed their profound satisfaction at the reaffirmation of Alliance solidarity expressed in this statement.

4. Ministers reviewed the international situation as it had developed since their last meeting in May in Rome. They noted that 1970 had been a year of extensive diplomatic activity by member governments of the Alliance to initiate or intensify contacts, discussions and negotiations with the members of the Warsaw Pact and wit. other European countries. Ministers paid particular attention to the Strategic Arms Limitations Talks, the Treaties negotiated by the Federal Republic of Germany with the Soviet Union and Poland, intra-German relations, Berlin and the situation in the Mediterranean.

5. Ministers welcomed the resumption at Helsinki in November of the negotiation between the United States and the USSR on Strategic Arms Limitations. They expressed the hope that the talks would lead, at an early date, to an agreement strengthening peace and security in Europe and in the world.

6. Ministers noted with satisfaction the signing of the Treaty between the Federal Republic of Germany and the USSR on 12th August, 1970, and the initialling of the Treaty between the Federal Republic of Germany and the Polish People's Republic on 18th November, 1970. They welcomed these Treaties as contributions toward reduction of tensions in Europe and as important elements of the *modus vivendi* which the Federal Republic of Germany wishes to establish with its Eastern neighbours. Ministers noted the clarifications made in the context of the Treaties,

1 NATO Press Service.

and reflected in the exchanges of notes between the Federal Republic of Germany and the Three Powers, to the effect that quadripartite rights and responsibilities for Berlin and Germany as a whole remain unaffected pending a peace settlement which would be based on the free decision of the German people and on the interests of European security.[1] Ministers welcomed the beginning of an exchange of views between the Federal Republic of Germany and the GDR and expressed the hope that this exchange will prepare the ground for genuine negotiations between the two. Ministers reviewed the development of the quadripartite talks in Berlin.

7. In considering the situation with regard to Berlin and Germany, Ministers recalled their statement in the Brussels Declaration of 5th December, 1969 (paragraph 10) to the effect that concrete progress in both these fields would constitute an important contribution to peace and would have great weight in their evaluation of the prospects for improving East–West relations in Europe. Indeed, these prospects would be put in question failing a satisfactory outcome to the current Berlin negotiations. With this in mind, Ministers stressed the importance of securing unhindered access to Berlin, improved circulation within Berlin and respect by all for the existing ties between the Western sectors of Berlin and the Federal Republic of Germany which have been established with the approval of the Three Powers. They underlined the need for an understanding between the Federal Republic of Germany and the GDR on a negotiated settlement of their mutual relations which would take account of the special features of the situation in Germany.

8. Ministers took note of a report on the situation in the Mediterranean prepared on their instructions by the Council in Permanent Session. They noted that the evolution of events in the area gives cause for concern and justifies careful vigilance on the part of the Allies. They recommended that consultations on this question should continue, and they invited the Council in Permanent Session to keep the situation under review and to report fully thereon at their next meeting.

9. As a result of their review of the international situation and its positive and negative aspects, Ministers emphasised that these developments in Europe and the Mediterranean all affect the Alliance directly or indirectly, and have a bearing on the possibilities of reducing tensions and promoting peace.

10. Ministers noted that the initiatives which had been taken by Allied Governments had already achieved certain results which constituted some progress in important fields of East–West relations. Nevertheless their hope had been that more substantial progress would have been recorded in bilateral exploratory contacts and in the on-going negotiations, so that active consideration could have been given to the institution of broad multilateral contacts which would deal with the substantial problems of security and cooperation in Europe. They affirmed the readiness of their governments, as soon as the talks on Berlin have reached a satisfactory conclusion and in so far as the other on-going talks are proceeding favourably, to enter into multilateral contacts with all interested governments to explore when it would be possible to convene a conference, or a series of conferences, on security

1 Documents Nos. 14, 16, 18.

and cooperation in Europe. In this event, the Council would give immediate attention to this question.

11. In the meantime, the Council in Permanent Session will continue its study of the results which might be achieved at any such conference or series of conference and of the appropriate exploratory and preparatory procedures, including the proposals that have already been advanced. The Allied Governments will also pursue energetically their bilateral exploratory conversations with all interested states on questions affecting security and cooperation.

12. Ministers recalled that any genuine and lasting improvement in East—West relations in Europe must be based on the respect of the following principles which should govern relations between states and which would be included among the points to be explored: sovereign equality, political independence and territorial integrity of each European state; non-interference and non-intervention in the internal affairs of any state, regardless of its political or social system; and the right of the people of each European state to shape their own destinies free of external constraint. A common understanding and application of these principles, without condition or reservation, would give full meaning to any agreement on mutual renunciation of the use or threat of force.

13. In the field of international cooperation, the contacts mentioned in paragraph 10 might provide an opportunity to consider ways and means of ensuring closer cooperation between interested countries on the cultural, economic, technical and scientific levels, and on the question of human environment. Ministers reaffirmed that the freer movement of people, ideas and information is an essential element for the development of such cooperation.

14. Ministers noted that Alliance studies on the various aspects of the mutual and balanced force reductions question have further progressed since the Rome Meeting and instructed the Council in Permanent Session to pursue studies in this field.

15. Ministers representing countries participating in NATO's integrated Defence Programme[1] reemphasised the importance they attach to mutual and balanced force reductions as a means of reducing tensions and lessening the military confrontation in Europe and recalled the Declarations on this question issued at Reykjavik in 1968 and at Rome earlier this year.[2] They noted that the Warsaw Pact Countries have not directly responded to these Declarations but have mentioned the possibility of a discussion at some future time of the question of reducing foreign armed forces on the territory of European states.

16. These Ministers renewed their invitation to interested states to hold exploratory talks on the basis of their Rome Declaration, and also indicated their readiness within this framework to examine different possibilities in the field of force reduction in the Central Region of Europe, including the possible mutual and balanced reduction of stationed forces as part of an integral programme for the reduction of both stationed and indigenous forces.

17. Ministers reaffirmed their profound interest in genuine disarmament and arms

1 All member states except France.
2 Documents Nos. 90, 95.

control measures. In this connection, they expressed their satisfaction with progress towards a ban on the emplacement of weapons of mass destruction on the sea bed. They further considered the pursuit of Allied efforts and studies in all fields related to disarmament to be essential, including those concerning biological and chemical weapons. They invited the Council in Permanent Session to continue to examine these matters.

18. Ministers endorsed the recent Council recommendation to Allied Governments to start work at once in order to achieve, by 1975 if possible but not later than the end of the decade, the elimination of intentional discharges of oil and oily wastes into the sea. This and the other accomplishments of the Committee on the Challenges of Modern Society during the past year were welcomed by Ministers as evidence that the Allies are effectively combining their resources to stimulate national and international action on environmental problems.

19. Ministers examined a report on the achievements of the Conference of National Armaments Directors and its subordinate bodies in the promotion of co-operation in research, development and production of military equipment during the four years of its existence. They noted that, in spite of the excellent progress that had been made in the exchange of information on defence equipment, it had proved possible to establish relatively few firm NATO projects for cooperative development and production of equipment. They recognised that more political support would be necessary to overcome the obstacles to greater cooperation. They agreed to the need for a more positive approach in order to achieve the financial and operational benefits of more widespread adoption of jointly developed and produced equipment.

20. Ministers of the countries participating in NATO's integrated defence programme met as the Defence Planning Committee on 2nd December, 1970.

21. Ministers concentrated their discussion on a comprehensive study, which has been in progress since last May, of the defence problems which the Alliance will face in the 1970s. They approved for public release the text at Annex.

22. Ministers confirmed that NATO's approach to security in the 1970s will continue to be based on the twin concepts of defence and detente. They reaffirmed the principle that the overall military capability of NATO should not be reduced except as part of a pattern of mutual force reductions balanced in scope and timing. They agreed that East—West negotiations can be expected to succeed only if NATO maintains an effective deterrent and defensive posture. Ministers confirmed the continued validity of the NATO strategy of flexibility in response, which includes forward defence, reinforcement of the flanks and capabilities for rapid mobilisation, and calls for the maintenance of military capabilities which are able to provide an appropriate counter to any aggression. They noted the continuous rise in Soviet defence and defence-related expenditure and the evidence that the USSR is continuing to strengthen still further its military establishment, including that in the maritime field where Soviet power and the range of its activity have markedly increased. They, therefore, emphasised the need for improvements in NATO's conventional deterrent, as well as the maintenance of a sufficient and modern tactical and strategic nuclear deterrent.

23. The security of NATO being indivisible, Ministers underlined the special military and political role of North American forces present in Europe as an irreplaceable contribution to the common defence. In parallel they welcomed the important decision of European member nations participating in NATO's integrated Defence Programme to make an increased common European effort to strengthen the defence capability of the Alliance.[1] The establishment of a special European Defence Improvement Programme of substantial additional measures will significantly strengthen NATO's capacity for defence and for crisis management in fields, including communications, which have been identified in the 'AD 70s' Study as having particular importance.

24. In respect of the above Study, Ministers invited the Defence Planning Committee in Permanent Session to draw up a suitable programme and to ensure that all possible progress is made.

25. Ministers noted the force commitments undertaken by member nations for the year 1971 and adopted the five-year NATO force plan covering the period 1971—1975. They gave directions for the development of a force plan for the next NATO planning period.

26. Ministers viewed with concern the evidence of continuing growth in Soviet military strength in the Mediterranean. Such developments, they felt, could constitute an increasingly significant threat to the security of the Alliance. Ministers commented with approval on steps which have been taken to improve the Alliance's defence posture in the Mediterranean. Referring to their Communiqué issued in Brussels on 11th June of this year, Ministers directed that urgent attention be given to the development and implementation of further appropriate measures.

27. Within the field of crisis management, Ministers reviewed communications facilities for high level political consultation and for command and control; they agreed to a number of important measures designed to improve and expand these vital facilities. They encouraged further efforts in the field of civil preparedness and civil emergency planning. They noted progress made on various defence studies. They also noted that the trend towards more sophisticated equipment at increasing cost may well continue, and they stressed that forthcoming modernisation programmes would offer an opportunity for increased cooperation.

28. The Ministerial Meeting also provided the Defence Ministers comprising the Nuclear Defence Affairs Committee (Belgium, Canada, Denmark, Germany, Greece, Italy, Netherlands, Norway, Portugal, Turkey, United Kingdom and United States) with the occasion to review work recently in progress in the Nuclear Planning Group and plans for the future. Acting on the recommendation of the Nuclear Defence Affairs Committee, the Defence Planning Committee adopted the policy documents elaborated by the Nuclear Planning Group at their meeting in Venice last Spring and finalised at Ottawa in October this year. These documents are in consonance with NATO's strategy of flexibility in response.

29. The next Ministerial Meeting of the Defence Planning Committee will take place in the Spring of 1971.

1 Document No. 122.

30. The Spring Ministerial Meeting of the Council will be held in Lisbon on 3rd and 4th June, 1971.

31. Ministers requested the Foreign Minister of Belgium to transmit this Communiqué on their behalf through diplomatic channels to all other interested parties including neutral and non-aligned governments.

ANNEX
Alliance Defence for the Seventies

The Allied countries participating in the integrated defence efforts decided at a meeting of the Defence Planning Committee in Permanent Session in May of this year to examine in depth NATO defence problems for the next decade.

2. The North Atlantic Alliance has made a practice over the years of periodically conducting major reviews and adapting its policies to accord with the changing circumstances of the times. A notable recent example was the study undertaken in 1967 which resulted in the Report on the Future Tasks of the Alliance establishing defence and detente as complementary pillars of its activities. That Report stated that 'collective defence is a stabilising factor in world politics. It is the necessary condition for effective policies directed towards a greater relaxation of tensions.' Against this background, governments earlier this year recognised the particular timeliness of a full and candid exchange of views among the Allies on their common defence over the next ten years. This examination of NATO's defence capability in the light of current and prospective military and political developments has now been completed.

3. NATO's approach to security in the 1970s will continue to be based on the twin concepts of defence and detente. Defence problems cannot be seen in isolation but must be viewed in the broader context of the Alliance's basic purpose of ensuring the security of its members. There is a close inter-relationship between the maintenance of adequate defensive strength and the negotiation of settlements affecting the security of the member states.

4. The 1970s could develop into an era of successful negotiations between members of the North Atlantic Alliance and those of the Warsaw Pact. On Western initiative, there are now negotiations under way between East and West which could lead to a real relaxation of tensions. It is hoped that there will be satisfactory progress in on-going talks on a limitation of strategic nuclear weapons and on an improvement of the situation in and around Berlin, and in other current negotiations between individual members of NATO and the Warsaw Pact. The Alliance will continue to seek improved East–West relations, and in the framework of this effort, one of its principal aims will be to engage the Soviet Union and its allies in meaningful talks on mutual and balanced force reductions and other disarmament measures. Progress in this field would facilitate dealing with the defence problems of the next decade. This period might also see convened one or more conferences on European security and cooperation.

5. On the other hand, the Allies cannot ignore certain disturbing features in the

international situation. The evidence thus far suggests that the USSR, intent on extending and strengthening its political power, conducts its international relations on the basis of concepts some of which are not conducive to detente. In particular, its concept of sovereignty is clearly inconsistent with United Nations principles. At the same time, Soviet military capabilities, besides guaranteeing the USSR's security, continue to increase and provide formidable backing for the wide-ranging assertion of Soviet influence and presence, persistently raising questions regarding their intentions. In real terms, there has been a continuous rise in Soviet defence and defence-related expenditures between 1965 and 1969 of about 5% to 6% per year on average and the evidence is that the USSR is continuing to strengthen its military establishments still further. The contrast between these figures and the corresponding information relating to the Alliance may be seen from paragraph 10 below. Whether East—West relations can in these circumstances be significantly improved will depend mainly on the actions of the USSR and its Warsaw Pact allies, and on the attitudes they bring to negotiations now in progress or in prospect

6. The position of the Alliance and its member countries during this period of exploration and negotiation, with special reference to European security and mutual force reductions, would be weakened if NATO were to reduce its forces unilaterally especially those in the European area, and in particular at a time when it is confronted with a steady growth in Soviet military power, which manifests itself above all in the strategic nuclear and maritime fields. NATO member states must, therefore, maintain a sufficient level of conventional and nuclear strength for defence as well as for deterrence, thus furnishing a sound basis from which to negotiate and underlining that negotiation is the only sensible road open. Progress towards a meaningful detente in an era of negotiations will, therefore, require the maintenance of a strong collective defence posture.

7. The present NATO defence strategy of deterrence and defence, with its constituent concepts of flexibility in response and forward defence, will remain valid. It will continue to require an appropriate mix of nuclear and conventional forces.

8. It is to be hoped that success in strategic arms limitation talks will be achieved Allied strategic nuclear capability will in any event remain a key element in the security of the West during the 1970s. At the present time, adequate nuclear forces exist and it will be essential to ensure that this capability, which includes the continued commitment of theatre nuclear forces, is maintained.

9. The situation in the field of conventional forces is less satisfactory in view of certain imbalances between NATO and Warsaw Pact capabilities. Careful attention needs to be paid to priorities in improving NATO's conventional strength in the 197 In the allocation of resources, priority will be given to measures most critical to a balanced Alliance defence posture in terms of deterrent effect, ability to resist external political pressure, and the prompt availability or rapid enhancement of the forward defensive capability in a developing crisis. In addition to a capability to deter and counter major deliberate aggression, Allied forces should be so structured and organized as to be capable of dealing also with aggressions and incursions with more limited objectives associated with intimidation or the creation of faits accomp

or with those aggressions which might be the result of accident or miscalculation. In short, Allied forces should be so structured and organized as to deter and counter any kind of aggression. Important areas in NATO's conventional defence posture to which attention should be paid in the next decade include: armour/anti-armour potential; the air situation including aircraft protection; overall maritime capabilities, with special reference to anti-submarine forces; the situation on NATO's flanks; the peacetime deployment of ground forces; further improvements in Allied mobilisation and reinforcement capabilities as well as in NATO communications, for crisis management purposes.

10. The Alliance possesses the basic resources for adequate conventional strength. However, member countries are confronted with diverging trends in the pattern of expenditures and costs. On the one hand the cost of personnel and equipment continues to mount and most NATO countries are faced with major reequipment programmes; on the other, in many member countries the share of GNP devoted to defence has declined and, even if outlays in money terms have risen, outlays in real terms have diminished owing to inflation. In marked contrast with the trend in Warsaw Pact countries' military expenditure, defence expenditures of the NATO European countries taken as a whole and calculated in real terms went down by 4% from 1964 to 1969.

11. It is of paramount importance that there be close collaboration among all member states to ensure the most effective collective defence posture. It is equally important that the burden of maintaining the necessary military strength should be borne cooperatively with each member making an appropriate contribution.

12. The commitment of substantial North American forces deployed in Europe is essential both politically and militarily for effective deterrence and defence and to demonstrate the solidarity of NATO. Their replacement by European forces would be no substitute. At the same time their significance is closely related to an effective and improved European defence effort. Ten of the European countries have therefore consulted among themselves to determine how it would be possible for them individually and collectively to make a more substantial contribution to the overall defence of the Treaty area.

13. As a result the ten countries have decided to adopt a special European Defence Improvement Programme going well beyond previously existing plans and designed to improve Alliance capability in specific fields identified as of particular importance in the current study. This Programme will comprise:

(a) an additional collective contribution, in the order of $420 million over five years, to NATO common infrastructure to accelerate work on the NATO integrated communications system and on aircraft survival measures;

(b) numerous important additions and improvements to national forces, costing at least $450–500 million over the next five years plus very substantial further amounts thereafter; the forces concerned will all be committed to NATO;

(c) other significant financial measures to improve collective defence capability, costing $79 million over the next two years.

The United States and Canada have welcomed this Programme, and have reaffirmed their intention to maintain their forces in Europe at substantially their current level

14. After careful review of the proposals emerging from the examination of defence problems in the Seventies, the Defence Planning Committee in Ministerial Session on 2nd December, 1970 adopted concrete proposals aimed at improving NATO's defence capabilities.

113. Message from President Nixon to the North Atlantic Council, 7 December 1972[1]

As we approach 1973 we stand on the threshold of negotiations that could bring us closer to the lasting peace that is the goal of the North Atlantic Alliance:
 — explorations have begun for a Conference on Security and Cooperation in Europe;
 — explorations will begin soon regarding Mutual and Balanced Force Reductions;
 — bilateral talks between individual Allies and members of the Warsaw Pact on issues of security and peace continue.
These prospects for peace, however, must rest on a foundation of continued military preparedness. Competing demands vie for the limited budgetary resources available to each Ally. Our peoples are increasingly sensitive to the just domestic needs of democratic and modern society, at the very time when the costs of modern and improved defense forces are increasing.

It will test the strength and vitality of this Alliance to maintain and improve our common defenses in these times. But this task must be accomplished.

For our part, the United States renews its pledge that given a similar approach by our Allies, we will maintain and improve our forces in Europe and will not reduce them unless there is reciprocal action from our adversaries.

We look to you — all of you — to continue the remarkable effort you have made in assuming a greater share of the burdens of common defense.

In our own way, each Ally must insure that its people understand the fundamental reasons that link a militarily strong NATO to successful negotiations. For without the understanding and the support of our peoples this Alliance cannot survive. With this in mind, I am confident that the statesmen and the free peoples of the North Atlantic Alliance will continue to support an undiminished defense effort by each member.

114. Speech by Dr Kissinger, Assistant to the President for National Security Affairs, to the Associated Press Editors, on the 'Year of Europe', New York, 23 April 1973[2]

This year has been called the year of Europe, but not because Europe was less

1 *DSB*, 1 January 1973, pp. 1–4.
2 *DSB*, 14 May 1973, pp. 593–8.

important in 1972 or in 1969. The alliance between the United States and Europe has been the cornerstone of all postwar foreign policy. It provided the political framework for American engagements in Europe, and marked the definitive end of US isolationism. It insured the sense of security that allowed Europe to recover from the devastation of the war. It reconciled former enemies. It was the stimulus for an unprecedented endeavor in European unity and the principal means to forge the common policies that safeguarded Western security in an era of prolonged tension and confrontation. Our values, our goals, and our basic interests are most closely identified with those of Europe.

Nineteen seventy-three is the year of Europe because the era that was shaped by decisions of a generation ago is ending. The success of those policies has produced new realities that require new approaches:
- The revival of western Europe is an established fact, as is the historic success of its movement toward economic unification.
- The East—West strategic military balance has shifted from American preponderance to near-equality, bringing with it the necessity for a new understanding of the requirements of our common security.
- Other areas of the world have grown in importance. Japan has emerged as a major power center. In many fields, 'Atlantic' solutions to be viable must include Japan.
- We are in a period of relaxation of tensions. But as the rigid divisions of the past two decades diminish, new assertions of national identity and national rivalry emerge.
- Problems have arisen, unforeseen a generation ago, which require new types of cooperative action. Insuring the supply of energy for industrialized nations is an example.

These factors have produced a dramatic transformation of the psychological climate in the West — a change which is the most profound current challenge to Western statesmanship. In Europe, a new generation to whom war and its dislocations are not personal experiences takes stability for granted. But it is less committed to the unity that made peace possible and to the effort required to maintain it. In the United States, decades of global burdens have fostered, and the frustrations of the war in Southeast Asia have accentuated a reluctance to sustain global involvements on the basis of preponderant American responsibility.

Inevitably this period of transition will have its strains. There have been complaints in America that Europe ignores its wider responsibilities in pursuing economic self-interest too one-sidedly and that Europe is not carrying its fair share of the burden of the common defense. There have been complaints in Europe that America is out to divide Europe economically, or to desert Europe militarily, or to bypass Europe diplomatically. Europeans appeal to the United States to accept their independence and their occasionally severe criticism of us in the name of Atlantic unity, while at the same time they ask for a veto on our independent policies — also in the name of Atlantic unity.

Our challenge is whether a unity forged by a common perception of danger can draw new purpose from shared positive aspirations.

If we permit the Atlantic partnership to atrophy, or to erode through neglect, carelessness, or mistrust, we risk what has been achieved and we shall miss our histor opportunity for even greater achievement.

In the forties and fifties the task was economic reconstruction and security agains the danger of attack; the West responded with courage and imagination. Today the need is to make the Atlantic relationship as dynamic a force in building a new struct of peace, less geared to crisis and more conscious of opportunities, drawing its inspirations from its goals rather than its fears. The Atlantic nations must join in a fresh act of creation equal to that undertaken by the postwar generation of leaders of Europe and America.

This is why the President is embarking on a personal and direct approach to the leaders of western Europe. In his discussions with the heads of government of Britain, Italy, the Federal Republic of Germany, and France, the Secretary General of NATO, and other European leaders, it is the President's purpose to lay the basis for a new era of creativity in the West.

His approach will be to deal with Atlantic problems comprehensively. The politic military, and economic issues in Atlantic relations are linked by reality, not by our choice nor for the tactical purpose of trading one off against the other. The solution will not be worthy of the opportunity if left to technicians. They must be addressed at the highest level.

In 1972 the President transformed relations with our adversaries to lighten the burdens of fear and suspicion.

In 1973 we can gain the same sense of historical achievement by reinvigorating shared ideals and common purposes with our friends.

The United States proposes to its Atlantic partners that by the time the President travels to Europe toward the end of the year we will have worked out a new Atlanti charter setting the goals for the future, a blueprint that:

— Builds on the past without becoming its prisoner.
— Deals with the problems our success has created.
— Creates for the Atlantic nations a new relationship in whose progress Japan can share.

We ask our friends in Europe, Canada, and ultimately Japan to join us in this effort.

This is what we mean by the year of Europe.

The problems in Atlantic relationships are real. They have arisen in part because during the fifties and sixties the Atlantic community organized itself in different ways in the many different dimensions of its common enterprise.

— In economic relations the European Community has increasingly stressed its regional personality; the United States at the same time must act as part of, and be responsible for, a wider international trade and monetary system. We must reconcile these two perspectives.
— In our collective defense we are still organized on the principle of unity and

integration, but in radically different strategic conditions. The full implications of this change have yet to be faced.

— Diplomacy is the subject of frequent consultations but is essentially being conducted by traditional nation-states. The United States has global interests and responsibilities. Our European allies have regional interests. These are not necessarily in conflict, but in the new era neither are they automatically identical.

In short, we deal with each other regionally and even competitively on an integrated basis in defense, and as nation-states in diplomacy. When the various collective institutions were rudimentary, the potential inconsistency in their modes of operation was not a problem. But after a generation of evolution and with the new weight and strength of our allies, the various parts of the construction are not always in harmony and sometimes obstruct each other.

If we want to foster unity we can no longer ignore these problems. The Atlantic nations must find a solution for the management of their diversity to serve the common objectives which underlie their unity. We can no longer afford to pursue national or regional self-interest without a unifying framework. We cannot hold together if each country or region asserts its autonomy whenever it is to its benefit and invokes unity to curtail the independence of others.

We must strike a new balance between self-interest and the common interest. We must identify interests and positive values beyond security in order to engage once again the commitment of peoples and parliaments. We need a shared view of the world we seek to build.

No element of American postwar policy has been more consistent than our support of European unity. We encouraged it at every turn. We knew that a united Europe would be a more independent partner. But we assumed, perhaps too uncritically, that our common interests would be assured by our long history of cooperation. We expected that political unity would follow economic integration and that a unified Europe working cooperatively with us in an Atlantic partnership would ease many of our international burdens.

It is clear that many of these expectations are not being fulfilled.

We and Europe have benefited from European economic integration. Increased trade within Europe has stimulated the growth of European economies and the expansion of trade in both directions across the Atlantic.

But we cannot ignore the fact that Europe's economic success and its transformation from a receipient of our aid to a strong competitor has produced a certain amount of friction. There have been turbulence and a sense of rivalry in international monetary relations.

In trade, the natural economic weight of a market of 250 million people has pressed other states to seek special arrangements to protect their access to it. The prospect of a closed trading system embracing the European Community and a growing number of other nations in Europe, the Mediterranean, and Africa appears to be at the expense of the United States and other nations which are excluded. In agriculture, where the United States has a comparative advantage, we are particular, concerned that Community protective policies may restrict access for our products

This divergence comes at a time when we are experiencing a chronic and growing deficit in our balance of payments and protectionist pressures of our own. European in turn question our investment policies and doubt our continued commitment to their economic unity.

The gradual accumulation of sometimes petty, sometimes major, economic disputes must be ended and be replaced by a determined commitment on both sides of the Atlantic to find cooperative solutions.

The United States will continue to support the unification of Europe. We have no intention of destroying what we worked so hard to help build. For us, European unity is what it has always been: not an end in itself but a means to the strengthening of the West. We shall continue to support European unity as a component of a larger Atlantic partnership.

This year we begin comprehensive trade negotiations with Europe as well as with Japan. We shall also continue to press the effort to reform the monetary system so that it promotes stability rather than constant disruptions. A new equilibrium must be achieved in trade and monetary relations.

We see these negotiations as a historic opportunity for positive achievement. They must engage the top political leaders, for they require above all a commitment of political will. If they are left solely to the experts the inevitable competitiveness of economic interests will dominate the debate. The influence of pressure groups and special interests will become pervasive. There will be no overriding sense of direction. There will be no framework for the generous solutions or mutual concess essential to preserve a vital Atlantic partnership.

It is the responsibility of national leaders to insure that economic negotiations serve larger political purposes. They must recognize that economic rivalry, if carried on without restraint, will in the end damage other relationships.

The United States intends to adopt a broad political approach that does justice to our overriding political interest in an open and balanced trading order with both Europe and Japan. This is the spirit of the President's trade bill and of his speech to the International Monetary Fund last year. It will guide our strategy in the trade and monetary talks. We see these negotiations not as a test of strength, but as a test of joint statesmanship.

Atlantic unity has always come most naturally in the field of defense. For many years the military threats to Europe were unambiguous, the requirements to meet them were generally agreed on both sides of the Atlantic, and America's responsibility was preeminent and obvious. Today we remain united on the objective of collective defense, but we face the new challenge of maintaining it under radically changed strategic conditions and with the new opportunity of enhancing our security through negotiated reductions of forces.

The West no longer holds the nuclear predominance that permitted it in the fties and sixties to rely almost solely on a strategy of massive nuclear retaliation. Because under conditions of nuclear parity such a strategy invites mutual suicide, the alliance must have other choices. The collective ability to resist attack in western Europe by means of flexible responses has become central to a rational strategy and crucial to the maintenance of peace. For this reason, the United States has maintained substantial conventional forces in Europe and our NATO allies have embarked on a significant effort to modernize and improve their own military establishments.

While the Atlantic alliance is committed to a strategy of flexible response in principle, the requirements of flexibility are complex and expensive. Flexibility by its nature requires sensitivity to new conditions and continual consultation among the allies to respond to changing circumstances. And we must give substance to the defense posture that our strategy defines. Flexible response cannot be simply a slogan wrapped around the defense structure that emerges from lowest-common-denominator compromises driven by domestic considerations. It must be seen by ourselves and by potential adversaries as a credible, substantial and rational posture of defense.

A great deal remains to be accomplished to give reality to the goal of flexible response:

— There are deficiencies in important areas of our conventional defense.
— There are still unresolved issues in our doctrine; for example, on the crucial question of the role of tactical nuclear weapons.
— There are anomalies in NATO deployments as well as in its logistics structure.

To maintain the military balance that has insured stability in Europe for 25 years, the alliance has no choice but to address these needs and to reach an agreement on our defense requirements. This task is all the more difficult because the lessening of tensions has given new impetus to arguments that it is safe to begin reducing forces unilaterally. And unbridled economic competition can sap the impulse for common defense. All governments of the Western alliance face a major challenge in educating their peoples to the realities of security in the 1970s.

The President has asked me to state that America remains committed to doing its fair share in Atlantic defense. He is adamantly opposed to unilateral withdrawals of US forces from Europe. But we owe to our peoples a rational defense posture, at the safest minimum size and cost with burdens equitably shared. This is what the President believes must result from the dialogue with our allies in 1973.

When this is achieved, the necessary American forces will be maintained in Europe, not simply as a hostage to trigger our nuclear weapons but as an essential contribution to an agreed and intelligible structure of Western defense. This, too, will enable us to engage our adversaries intelligently in negotiations for mutual balanced reductions.

In the next few weeks the United States will present to NATO the product of our own preparations for the negotiations on mutual balanced force reductions which will begin this year. We hope that it will be a contribution to a broader dialogue on security. Our approach is designed not from the point of view of special American interests, but of general alliance interests. Our position will reflect the President's view that these negotiations are not a subterfuge to withdraw US forces regardless of consequences. No formula for reductions is defensible, whateve its domestic appeal or political rationale, if it undermines security.

Our objective in the dialogue on defense is a new consensus on security, address to new conditions and to the hopeful new possibilities of effective arms limitations

We have entered a truly remarkable period of East–West diplomacy. The last two years have produced an agreement on Berlin, a treaty between West Germany and the USSR, a strategic arms limitation agreement, the beginning of negotiations on a European Security Conference and on mutual balanced force reductions, and a series of significant practical bilateral agreements between Western and Eastern countries, including a dramatic change in bilateral relations between the United States and the USSR. These were not isolated actions, but steps on a course charte in 1969 and carried forward as a collective effort. Our approach to detente stressed that negotiations had to be concrete, not atmospheric, and that concessions should be reciprocal. We expect to carry forward the policy of relaxation of tensions on this basis.

Yet this very success has created its own problems. There is an increasing uneasiness – all the more insidious for rarely being made explicit – that superpower diplomacy might sacrifice the interests of traditional allies and other friends. Where our allies' interests have been affected by our bilateral negotiations, as in the talks on the limitation of strategic arms, we have been scrupulous in consulting them; where our allies are directly involved, as in the negotiations on mutual balanced force reductions, our approach is to proceed jointly on the basis of agreed positions Yet some of our friends in Europe have seemed unwilling to accord America the same trust in our motives as they received from us or to grant us the same tactical flexibility that they employed in pursuit of their own policies. The United States is now often taken to task for flexibility where we used to be criticized for rigidity.

All of this underlines the necessity to articulate a clear set of common objectives together with our allies. Once that is accomplished, it will be quite feasible, indeed desirable, for the several allies to pursue these goals with considerable tactical flexibility. If we agree on common objectives it will become a technical question whether a particular measure is pursued in a particular forum or whether to procee bilaterally or multilaterally. Then those allies who seek reassurances of America's commitment will find it not in verbal reaffirmations of loyalty, but in an agreed framework of purpose.

We do not need to agree on all policies. In many areas of the world our approach will differ, especially outside of Europe. But we do require an understanding of wha should be done jointly and of the limits we should impose on the scope of our auto

We have no intention of buying an illusory tranquillity at the expense of our friends. The United States will never knowingly sacrifice the interests of others. But the perception of common interests is not automatic; it requires constant redefinitic The relaxation of tensions to which we are committed makes allied cohesion indispensable yet more difficult. We must insure that the momentum of detente maintained by common objectives rather than by drift, escapism, or complacency.

he agenda I have outlined here is not an American prescription, but an appeal
)r a joint effort of creativity. The historic opportunity for this generation is to
uild a new structure of international relations for the decades ahead. A revitalized
.tlantic partnership is indispensable for it. The United States is prepared to make
s contribution:

- — We will continue to support European unity. Based on the principles of partnership, we will make concessions to its further growth. We will expect to be met
  in a spirit of reciprocity.
- — We will not disengage from our solemn commitments to our allies. We will
  maintain our forces and not withdraw from Europe unilaterally. In turn, we
  expect from each ally a fair share of the common effort for the common
  defense.
- — We shall continue to pursue the relaxation of tensions with our adversaries
  on the basis of concrete negotiations in the common interest. We welcome the
  participation of our friends in a constructive East—West dialogue.
- — We will never consciously injure the interests of our friends in Europe or in
  Asia. We expect in return that their policies will take seriously our interests
  and our responsibilities.
- — We are prepared to work cooperatively on new common problems we face.
  Energy, for example, raises the challenging issues of assurance of supply,
  impact of oil revenues on international currency stability, the nature of
  common political and strategic interests, and long-range relations of oil-
  consuming to oil-producing countries. This could be an area of competition;
  it should be an area of collaboration.
- — Just as Europe's autonomy is not an end in itself, so the Atlantic community
  cannot be an exclusive club. Japan must be a principal partner in our common
  enterprise.

We hope that our friends in Europe will meet us in this spirit. We have before us
he example of the great accomplishments of the past decades and the opportunity
o match and dwarf them. This is the task ahead. This is how, in the 1970s, the
\tlantic nations can truly serve our peoples and the cause of peace.

15. Communiqué issued by the NATO Defence Planning Committee, Brussels, 2 May 1973[1]

n keeping with NATO's defensive concept, the Defence Planning Committee today
ipproved the formation of a standing naval force, Channel.

It will consist of nine counter-measure ships from Belgium, the Netherlands, and
he United Kingdom; other interested nations might participate on a temporary
)asis. Operational command of NATO's second standing naval force is vested in

1 NATO Press Service.

the Commander-in-Chief, Channel Command – at present Admiral Sir Edward Ashmore – with headquarters in Northwood, England.

The *Stanavforchan* will officially be commissioned on 11th May 1973.

116. Communiqué issued by the NATO Defence Planning Committee, Brussels, 7 December 1973[1]

1. The Defence Planning Committee of NATO met in Ministerial Session on 7th December 1973 in Brussels.

2. The Defence Ministers of countries represented in the Nuclear Defence Affairs Committee – Belgium, Canada, Denmark, Federal Republic of Germany, Greece, Italy, Netherlands, Norway, Portugal, Turkey, the United Kingdom and the United States – met first to review the Nuclear Planning Group's activities during 1973 and plans for future work.

3. All Ministers then met as the Defence Planning Committee. They first discusse the strategic situation as it affects the Alliance in the light of an appraisal by the Secretary-General and heard a statement by the Chairman of the Military Committe on current trends in the military situation of NATO and the Warsaw Pact.

4. Ministers took note of developments in the second phase of the United States Soviet talks on the limitation of strategic weapons. They discussed the security aspe of the conference on European security and cooperation now taking place in Geneva. They welcomed the opening of negotiations in Vienna on mutual and balanced force reductions in Central Europe; they also reiterated that the aim of negotiations in Vienna should be to achieve a more stable balance, consistent with the criterion of undiminished security for all members of the Alliance, at lower levels of forces; they confirmed that the overall military capability of NATO should not be reduced except in this context.

5. Ministers noted with concern that, despite these developments in the political field, the Soviet Union and her allies have continued to increase the scale of their military programme and to strengthen and improve their forces in every field. There is no indication that this trend will be reversed. The Soviet Union now possesses a capability for the worldwide use of military power well in excess of that needed to defend their own territory. Ministers emphasised that the planning of NATO defences must be directly related to the still growing power of the Warsaw Pact and the strategic situation created thereby. The Ministers recognised the responsibility of their governments to assure public understanding of the facts bearing on the military power of the Warsaw Pact and of the need for undiminished defence effort on the part of their nations.

6. Ministers discussed recent events in the Middle East and their implications for the security of the Alliance. Ministers took note of preliminary assessments of the lessons which NATO might learn from the conduct and outcome of this conflict, and resolved that the matter should be given further intensive study.

1 NATO Press Service.

the context of the discussion on the situation in the Middle East they noted with approval the steps which are being taken to ensure the sufficiency of military oil stocks essential for the defence of the Alliance.

7. Ministers discussed a report on some aspects of the possibility of specialisation of defence roles in the central region, prepared at their request following the initiative taken by the Defence Minister of the Netherlands at their spring meeting. They accepted the recommendations of this report and welcomed a statement by the Netherlands Minister with reference to the replacement of the F-104G aircraft. They moreover gave directions for the study to be extended into further fields of possible specialisation.

8. Ministers discussed an interim report on measures to improve the flexibility and effectiveness of the tactical air forces in the central region, through changes in organisation, command and control. As an initial measure, Ministers agreed in principle to the formation of a new headquarters under the title of Allied Air Forces Central Europe, and agreed that a Commander should be designated and a location determined in the near future.

9. With regard to MBFR, Ministers welcomed the position of the United States that, given a similar approach by their allies, their forces in Europe would be maintained and improved and would not be reduced unilaterally. They also recognised that the maintenance of United States forces in Europe at their present level calls for a common effort on the part of the allies to achieve a solution to the financial problems which the United States incurs thereby.

10. In this connection Ministers considered a report from a special study group on the budgetary and balance-of-payment problems arising from the stationing of United States forces in Europe and discussed a number of possible means of relieving them. They noted that study has been initiated on how a number of these measures might be implemented on a multilateral or bilateral basis. The United States has been assured that this examination will be conducted on a positive basis. They recognised the particular effort envisaged by the Federal Republic of Germany in the bilateral negotiations now in progress with the United States regarding arrangements for offsetting balance of payment deficits arising from the stationing of United States forces in Germany. Such arrangements will represent a major contribution towards a common solution. They emphasised the necessity for other countries of the Alliance to take active measures to this end. They declared the intention of their countries to participate in multilateral or bilateral arrangements towards providing a common solution to the United States problem, and directed their staffs to work actively and rapidly to this end. In this connection several countries pointed to the contribution which would be made to the United States balance of payments position by their prospective purchases of military equipment in the United States.

11. Ministers agreed to examine how the share of the United States in the civil and military budgets of NATO and in the infrastructure programme might be substantially reduced.

12. Ministers noted the stage reached in determining the size and cost of sharing of the new (1975–79) infrastructure programme. They also noted that consideration

was being given to widening the eligibility of projects for funding under the commo infrastructure programme.

13. Ministers received from the Chairman of the Eurogroup an account of the Group's continuing work. They welcomed the significant improvements in force capabilities planned for 1974 and the renewed emphasis being placed on closer practical cooperation, particularly in equipment procurement.[1]

14. Finally, Ministers gave directions for future military planning within the Alliance. They reaffirmed that the fundamental purpose of NATO forces is to dete aggression and to preserve all members of the Alliance from attack or threat of attack from outside. They stressed that fulfilment of this purpose depends on main taining a capability of conventional, as well as nuclear, forces balanced with the Warsaw Pact.

15. They recognised that the efforts made by member countries in recent years to maintain and improve their forces have provided NATO with the basis of a substantial conventional capability, but stressed that further improvement was still required bearing in mind the growing capability of the Warsaw Pact. In this connect they identified a number of key areas in which extra effort was required to correct current weaknesses in NATO defences, particularly in regard to the modernisation and readiness of forces and their ability to operate together. They pledged themselves to early action and decision to remedy these weaknesses and agreed that the resources required were well within the capability of the Alliance to provide. Specifically they agreed to give new impetus to the programmes to provide protecti for aircraft and airfields, to improve the anti-armour capability of NATO forces, and to raise the levels of war reserve stocks.

16. After reviewing the military contribution which each country plans to make towards the collective security of the Alliance over the years 1974–78, Ministers approved the NATO force plan for this period and designated the forces which thei countries undertake to commit to NATO over the coming twelve months.

117. Joint Announcement issued by the United States and the Federal Republic of Germany, 25 April 1974, with Explanatory Note[2]

The Governments of the Federal Republic of Germany and the United States of America represented by Ministerial Direktor Dr Peter Hermes and Ambassador Martin Hillenbrand, today signed an agreement which provides for offsetting the balance-of-payments costs of stationing US forces in the Federal Republic. The Agreement resulted from several months of negotiation and from informal talks held on March 19, 1974, between the Federal Minister of Finance, Herr Helmut Schmidt, and the Secretary of the Treasury of the United States of America, Mr George Shultz. Remaining details were subsequently agreed between the negotiating delegations.

1 Documents Nos. 124, 125.
2 *DSB*, 20 May 1974, p. 547. The text was issued in both Washington and Bonn.

The new agreement covers the period from July 1, 1973, to June 30, 1975.
t involves a total value of 5,920 million DM (about 2.2 billion dollars at a conversion
ate of $1 = 2.669 DM). As previously, military procurement is the largest element
2,750 million DM). Similar to the 1970/71 agreement the present agreement in-
ludes procurement of uranium separation work for civilian purposes and, for the
irst time, bilateral projects in the field of scientific and technological cooperation
300 million DM). The program for modernization of barracks and other facilities
sed by United States forces in Germany, included in the previous agreement, will
e continued (600 million DM). In addition, the United States forces will be exempt
rom landing charges in German civilian airfields and from certain real estate taxes
20 million DM). As previously, provision has been made for the acquisition of low-
nterest United States Treasury securities by the Deutsche Bundesbank (2,250
nillion DM).

The agreement is based on the strength of the United States forces in the Federal
Republic of Germany as of July 1, 1973. Both Governments are informing their
NATO Allies about this agreement, which will form an integral part of the NATO
urdensharing program currently under discussion.

Both sides welcome the agreement as a visible and convincing example of excellent
German—American cooperation within the Alliance.

Explanatory Note

n conjunction with the press release issued today by the Federal Republic of
Germany and the United States following signature of our new offset agreement,
he US Government wishes to add the following points:

The offset to be provided during fiscal years 1974—75 is larger in dollar terms and
contains more substantial economic benefits to us than was the case in previous offset
greements. Cognizant of the requirements of the Jackson—Nunn amendment,[1] the
American side views the agreement as a major component of the NATO-wide effort
o share more equitably the common burden of alliance defense. We anticipate
ufficient military procurement from our other European allies so that, together with
he German offset, we expect to meet the requirements of this amendment and to
naintain our forces in NATO Europe at present levels. We believe, therefore, that
vhat we have accomplished in this agreement, together with foreseeable action by
our other allies, responds to congressional intent and that our primary objective has
been achieved.

118. Declaration on Atlantic Relations issued by the NATO Council, Ottawa, 19 June 1974[2]

1. The members of the North Atlantic Alliance declare that the Treaty signed

---

1 To the United States Military Procurement Authorisation Bill for 1973, passed by a Legis-
ative Conference of Congress, 15 October 1973; for text see WEU, *Political Union*, 1963—73,
pp. 238—9.
    2 *DSB*, 8 July 1974, pp. 42—4.

25 years ago to protect their freedom and independence has confirmed their comm destiny. Under the shield of the Treaty, the Allies have maintained their security, permitting them to preserve the values which are the heritage of their civilization and enabling Western Europe to rebuild from its ruins and lay the foundations of its unity.

2. The members of the Alliance reaffirm their conviction that the North Atlanti Treaty provides the indispensable basis for their security, thus making possible the pursuit of detente. They welcome the progress that has been achieved on the road towards detente and harmony among nations, and the fact that a conference of 35 countries of Europe and North America is now seeking to lay down guidelines designed to increase security and cooperation in Europe. They believe that until circumstances permit the introduction of general, complete and controlled disarmament, which alone could provide genuine security for all, the ties uniting them must be maintained. The Allies share a common desire to reduce the burden of arms expenditure on their peoples. But states that wish to preserve peace have never achieved this aim by neglecting their own security.

3. The members of the Alliance reaffirm that their common defense is one and indivisible. An attack on one or more of them in the area of application of the Treaty shall be considered an attack against them all. The common aim is to preven any attempt by a foreign power to threaten the independence or integrity of a member of the Alliance. Such an attempt would not only put in jeopardy the secur of all members of the Alliance but also threaten the foundations of world peace.

4. At the same time they realize that the circumstances affecting their common defense have profoundly changed in the last ten years; the strategic relationship between the United States and the Soviet Union has reached a point of near equilibrium. Consequently, although all the countries of the Alliance remain vulnerable to attack, the nature of the danger to which they are exposed has changed. The Alliance's problems in the defense of Europe have thus assumed a different and mo distinct character.

5. However, the essential elements in the situation which gave rise to the Treaty have not changed. While the commitment of all the Allies to the common defense reduces the risk of external aggression, the contribution to the security of the entir Alliance provided by the nuclear forces of the United States based in the United States as well as in Europe and by the presence of North American forces in Europe remains indispensable.

6. Nevertheless, the Alliance must pay careful attention to the dangers to which it is exposed in the European region, and must adopt all measures necessary to aver them. The European members who provide three-quarters of the conventional strength of the Alliance in Europe, and two of whom possess nuclear forces capable of playing a deterrent role of their own contributing to the overall strengthening of the deterrence of the Alliance, undertake to make the necessary contribution to maintain the common defense at a level capable of deterring and if necessary repelling all actions directed against the independence and territorial integrity of th members of the Alliance.

7. The United States, for its part, reaffirms its determination not to accept any situation which would expose its Allies to external political or military pressure likely to deprive them of their freedom, and states its resolve, together with its Allies, to maintain forces in Europe at the level required to sustain the credibility of the strategy of deterrence and to maintain the capacity to defend the North Atlantic area should deterrence fail.

8. In this connection the member states of the Alliance affirm that as the ultimate purpose of any defense policy is to deny to a potential adversary the objectives he seeks to attain through an armed conflict, all necessary forces would be used for this purpose. Therefore, while reaffirming that a major aim of their policies is to seek agreements that will reduce the risk of war, they also state that such agreements will not limit their freedom to use all forces at their disposal for the common defense in case of attack. Indeed, they are convinced that their determination to do so continues to be the best assurance that war in all its forms will be prevented.

9. All members of the Alliance agree that the continued presence of Canadian and substantial US forces in Europe plays an irreplaceable role in the defense of North America as well as of Europe. Similarly the substantial forces of the European Allies serve to defend Europe and North America as well. It is also recognized that the further progress towards unity, which the member states of the European Community are determined to make, should in due course have a beneficial effect on the contribution to the common defense of the Alliance of those of them who belong to it. Moreover, the contributions made by members of the Alliance to the preservation of international security and world peace are recognized to be of great importance.

10. The members of the Alliance consider that the will to combine their efforts to ensure their common defense obliges them to maintain and improve the efficiency of their forces and that each should undertake, according to the role that it has assumed in the structure of the Alliance, its proper share of the burden of maintaining the security of all. Conversely, they take the view that in the course of current or future negotiations nothing must be accepted which could diminish this security.

11. The Allies are convinced that the fulfilment of their common aims requires the maintenance of close consultation, cooperation and mutual trust, thus fostering the conditions necessary for defense and favorable for detente, which are complementary. In the spirit of the friendship, equality and solidarity which characterize their relationships, they are firmly resolved to keep each other fully informed and to strengthen the practice of frank and timely consultations by all means which may be appropriate on matters relating to their common interests as members of the Alliance, bearing in mind that these interests can be affected by events in other areas of the world. They wish also to ensure that their essential security relationship is supported by harmonious political and economic relations. In particular they will work to remove sources of conflict between their economic policies and to encourage economic cooperation with one another.

12. They recall that they have proclaimed their dedication to the principles of

democracy, respect for human rights, justice and social progress, which are the fruit of their shared spiritual heritage and they declare their intention to develop and deepen the application of these principles in their countries. Since these principles, by their very nature, forbid any recourse to methods incompatible with the promot of world peace, they reaffirm that the efforts which they make to preserve their independence, to maintain their security and to improve the living standards of their peoples exclude all forms of aggression against anyone, are not directed against any other country, and are designed to bring about the general improvement of international relations. In Europe, their objective continues to be the pursuit of understanding and cooperation with every European country. In the world at large, each Allied country recognizes the duty to help the developing countries. It is in the interest of all that every country benefit from technical and economic progress in an open and equitable world system.

13. They recognise that the cohesion of the Alliance has found expression not only in cooperation among their governments, but also in the free exchange of view among the elected representatives of the peoples of the Alliance. Accordingly, they declare their support for the strengthening of links among Parliamentarians.

14. The members of the Alliance rededicate themselves to the aims and ideals of the North Atlantic Treaty during this year of the twenty-fifth anniversary of its signature. The member nations look to the future, confident that the vitality and creativity of their peoples are commensurate with the challenges which confront them. They declare their conviction that the North Atlantic Alliance continues to serve as an essential element in the lasting structure of peace they are determined to build.

119. Communiqué issued by the NATO Defence Planning Committee, Brussels, 11 December 1974[1]

1. The Defence Planning Committee of the North Atlantic Treaty Organisation met in Ministerial Session on 10th and 11th December, 1974, in Brussels.

2. During their meeting the Defence Planning Committee heard an appraisal of the overall situation from the Secretary-General and an assessment of the military situation from the Chairman of the Military Committee. In the light of these they discussed the implications for NATO of the continued strengthening and modernisation of Warsaw Pact forces on land and in the air, and the growing capability and world-wide deployment of the Soviet Navy. Ministers expressed their deep concern at the scale of resources which the Soviet Union is continuing to devote to military purposes, which indicates its determination to seek military superiority over the West, and noted that these resources already provide the Soviet Union and its Allies with a military power far in excess of that required for self-defence.

3. Ministers took note of the status of the current talks between the United States and the Soviet Union on the limitation of strategic armaments, and in

1 Foreign and Commonwealth Office, London.

particular of the important developments in this area represented by the agreements reached between President Ford and Mr Brezhnev at Vladivostok. Ministers also exchanged views on the state of negotiations in Vienna on Mutual and Balanced Force Reductions, in anticipation of the discussion which the North Atlantic Council will have on the subject in the next few days. In this connection, they confirmed their support for the agreed Alliance approach and, collectively and individually, they reaffirmed the importance they attach to the principle that NATO forces should not be reduced except in the context of a Mutual and Balanced Force Reduction agreement with the East.

4. Ministers heard with interest a report by the Chairman of the Eurogroup on the Group's discussions in Ministerial Session earlier in the week. They welcomed the announcement of substantial European force improvements planned for 1975 and expressed their appreciation of the Eurogroup's work in developing a strong and cohesive European contribution to the common defence. They also took note of a further report on the consultations between Belgium, Denmark, the Netherlands and Norway on the replacement programme for the F-104G and other aircraft.

5. After reviewing the national force contributions to Alliance defence for the current year, Ministers then turned their attention to plans for the next planning period. They discussed the extent to which national plans for the period up to 1979 provide for the implementation of the force goals adopted by them at their June meeting. They took note of certain proposed changes in national defence programmes on which Alliance consultation was proceeding. Subject to the outcome of these consultations they approved the NATO Force Plan for the period 1975–1979 and designated the forces which their countries undertook to commit to NATO over the coming twelve months.

6. Ministers took note with approval that substantial improvements had been made to the conventional capabilities of NATO forces during the past year; they also noted the programmes initiated in many countries for improving the quality of NATO forces in the important fields of anti-armour and low-level air defence, and the extra impetus being given to improvements in electronic warfare capabilities, the provision of modern aircraft munitions and the level of war reserve stocks. They noted the substantial aircraft modernisation programmes under way in some countries, and the need for early decision in others. They reviewed the plans for improving the survivability and anti-submarine warfare capabilities of the maritime forces. During this part of their discussion Ministers also identified areas of NATO defence where weaknesses seemed likely to persist, and agreed to redouble their efforts to correct them.

7. Ministers took note with special satisfaction of the intention of the United States to form the equivalent of two new brigades in Europe beginning in 1975 by the reallocation of personnel from supporting functions. They welcomed this practical recognition of the need for improving the capability of ready combat forces.

8. Ministers reviewed the present strategic situation in the Southern Region and the Mediterranean, and discussed measures needed to maintain the security of the

Alliance in this area. In particular they expressed concern at the scale of Soviet military activity in the Mediterranean area and the possible repercussions on the Alliance of the unstable situation in the Middle East.

9. Ministers next discussed the impact of inflation on defence budgets and the measures being taken by countries to maintain the current purchasing power of their defence expenditures. In so doing they reemphasised the need to make the optimum use of resources through cooperative efforts in defence.

10. In this connection Ministers received a report on current activities in the areas of rationalisation and specialisation selected for detailed examination. They agreed to give full support to those continuing activities and called for special efforts by countries to take advantage of these possible methods of improving the effectiveness of NATO forces.

11. Ministers received reports covering standardisation in certain areas of military equipment, with particular reference to the areas on which they had previously agreed to concentrate their efforts, namely airborne early warning, electronic warfare, the replacement for the F-104G aircraft, the standardisation of rifle ammunition and a new rifle for the 1980s. They welcomed in particular the prospect of standardising on two calibres only for the whole family of future portable infantry weapons. They agreed to give special attention to two further specific areas, interoperability and security of communications, and a second generation anti-ship missile. In so doing, they endorsed the urgent need for coordinated Alliance-wide action in the first of these and welcomed the promising initiative taken with respect to the second.

12. Ministers agreed to the level of funding for the next five-year Infrastructure programme covering the period up to 1979, subject to confirmation of the final cost-sharing arrangements and details of the programme by the Defence Planning Committee in Permanent Session.

13. Ministers then turned their attention to the Guidance that they will give next Spring to provide policy direction for defence planning activities in NATO for the period up to 1982. They decided that the new Ministerial Guidance should include a long range defence concept setting objectives for cooperative efforts within the framework of the NATO strategy of flexible response and forward defence, in order to obtain maximum efficiency from the force levels and resources which the Alliance can reasonably expect to have at its disposal. They instructed the Defence Planning Committee in Permanent Session to prepare a new Ministerial Guidance including such a planning concept, for consideration by Ministers at their Spring 1975 meeting.

120. Communiqué issued by the NATO Defence Planning Committee, Brussels, 23 May 1975, with Annex on Ministerial Guidance[1]

1. In the course of a general review of the strategic situation and the military relation-

1 NATO Press Service.

ship between East and West, Ministers were briefed on the latest developments in the growth of the military power of the Warsaw Pact. Against the background of the current economic situation, they reviewed the present state of NATO's defences; they emphasised the need for progress in the important fields of rationalisation of functions and standardisation of equipment and gave directions for further work in these areas. They also considered the military implications for the Alliance of the negotiations on MBFR currently in progress in Vienna.

2. They devoted special attention to the current strategic situation in the Mediterranean area in the light of recent political, economic and military developments, Soviet military and maritime activities in the area and the implications for the Alliance of the situation in adjoining regions.

3. Ministers heard with interest a statement by Mr Roy Mason, this year's Chairman of the Eurogroup Ministers, on current activities in the Eurogroup, and agreed to pursue within the appropriate machinery the establishment of a two-way street between Europe and North America in defence equipment procurement, in order to promote a more cost effective use of resources and increase standardisation of weapon systems.

4. Among the specific subjects discussed were the improvement of arrangements for crisis management in the Alliance and the financing of the common infrastructure programme up to 1979. Ministers also endorsed a proposed joint study of the possibilities of acquiring and operating an Airborne Early Warning and Control System on a cooperative basis to improve the effectiveness of NATO's air defences.

5. The United States Secretary of Defense informed his colleagues of the present state of the bilateral agreements on the use by the US forces of military facilities in Spain, it being understood that these arrangements remain outside the NATO context.

6. Finally Ministers laid down guidelines for defence planning in NATO. These guidelines restate the basic aims and strategy of the Alliance and place special emphasis on the adoption of a long-range defence concept. They also provide a fresh stimulus to the optimum use of resources through rationalisation, standardisation and greater cooperative efforts. This Ministerial Guidance will provide a directive and reference point for all defence planning activities in NATO up to 1982 and beyond. An abbreviated version is attached.

ANNEX
Ministerial Guidance 1975
Introduction

1. NATO procedures call for Ministers to give guidance for defence planning every two years. The guidance reflects the political, economic, technological and military factors which could affect the development of NATO forces during the next planning period. The guidance, being a major policy document endorsed by Ministers, provides a reference point and directive for all defence planning activities, at both the national and international level, in NATO.

Long-Range Defence Concept

2. Previous editions of Ministerial Guidance have covered the seven-year period of the NATO Defence Planning Cycle. However, lengthened timescales for the development and deployment of sophisticated weapon systems together with increased costs of military manpower and equipment now make it necessary to establish a more comprehensive framework for defence planning. To take account of these factors a Long-Range Defence Concept has been adopted, which places increased emphasis on cooperative measures within the Alliance and on the establishment of rigorous priorities.

3. The current international security situation and trends for the future underline the inescapable necessity for NATO to maintain a capability to deter aggression or the threat of it, and if deterrence fails, to restore and maintain the security of the North Atlantic area. The members of NATO are seeking improvements in relations with the East and the reduction of forces on a mutual and balanced basis, but negotiations are slow. Meanwhile the military capabilities of the Warsaw Pact nations continue to expand. Continued maintenance of NATO's defensive strength will furnish a secure basis from which to negotiate in addition to providing a bar to aggression or threats of aggression.

4. The long-range defence concept supports agreed NATO strategy by calling for a balanced force structure of interdependent strategic nuclear, theatre nuclear and conventional force capabilities. Each element of this Triad performs a unique role; in combination they provide mutual support and reinforcement. No single element of the Triad can substitute for another. The concept also calls for the modernisation of both strategic and theatre nuclear capabilities; however, major emphasis is placed on maintaining and improving Alliance conventional forces. NATO has already achieved a large measure of success in this regard. NATO has fielded the basic ingredients for a stalwart conventional defence. However, disparities between NATO and the Warsaw Pact conventional forces remain. The Allies must reduce these disparities and provide a stable, long-term basis for attaining and maintaining adequate conventional forces.

5. The essence of the long-range defence concept is that NATO can provide an adequate force structure for deterrence and defence if the Allies maintain the forces already in existence (or foreseen in plans currently declared to NATO) and continue to modernise and improve these forces and their supporting facilities. This will require some modest annual increase in real terms in defence expenditures; the actual increase for each country will vary in accordance with its current force contribution, its present efforts and its economic strength. It also requires the optimum use of resources available for defence through the rigorous setting of priorities and a greater degree of cooperation between national forces within the Alliance.

6. This long-range defence concept will help to provide a more comprehensive basis for NATO planning with both the flexibility to absorb effects of political, economic and technological changes, and with the stability in national defence programmes to prevent sudden and uneconomic fluctuations.

The need for Defence

7. The Allied governments have successfully engaged the Soviet Union and Warsaw Pact countries in discussions and negotiations on several issues of defence and security, e.g. on the limitation of strategic arms (SALT) and on Mutual and Balanced Force Reductions. But although the atmosphere in East–West relations has improved over the last decade, it remains a fact that the Warsaw Pact continues to maintain a military capability much greater than that needed for self-defence. In the strategic nuclear field the Soviet Union, having already attained rough parity with the United States, now seems to be seeking to attain a strategic advantage through the development of more sophisticated and powerful missiles. Improvements are also being made in the quality and quantity of Warsaw Pact conventional forces, particularly in the offensive capabilities of aircraft, tanks, artillery and missiles. At sea the expansion of Soviet maritime forces over the past decade and their world-wide deployment have added a new dimension to their capabilities which are now such that, independently of a land/air attack on NATO territory, Soviet maritime forces could be used against NATO forces at sea or against our maritime lines of communication in order to interfere with the economies and vital supplies of NATO nations.

8. The basis of the North Atlantic Treaty is that the common defence of the Alliance is one and indivisible. The Allies would consider an attack on one or more of them an attack against all. The essential solidarity of the Alliance depends upon the political resolve of individual nations and the scale of effort they are prepared to devote to the common defence. Should weaknesses in either cause the Warsaw Pact countries to doubt our readiness to withstand political pressure or our determination to defend ourselves by all the means at our disposal against aggression, they might come to believe that they could use their military power against us for political or military ends without undue risk; accordingly the defence posture of NATO should be so constructed as to take into account the deployment, capabilities and possible objectives of the Warsaw Pact forces.

NATO Strategy

9. The aim of NATO's strategy and military planning is to ensure security through deterrence. The primary aim is to deter an attack before it is launched, by making it clear to any aggressor that any attack on NATO would be met by a strong defence and might initiate a sequence of events which cannot be calculated in advance, involving risks to the aggressor out of all proportion to any advantages he might hope to gain. In an era of broad strategic nuclear parity deterrence to all forms of aggression cannot be based upon strategic nuclear forces alone, it must be provided by the overall capabilities of all NATO forces. The Alliance must be able to respond in an appropriate manner to aggression of any kind; the response must be effective in relation to the level of force used by the aggressor and must at the same time make him recognise the dangers of escalation to a higher level.

10. Should aggression occur, the military aim is to preserve or restore the integrity

and security of the NATO area by employing such forces as may be necessary within the concept of forward defence and flexibility in response. NATO forces must be prepared to use any capabilities at their disposal (including nuclear weapons) for this purpose. This determination must be evident to the aggressor.

NATO Forces

11. In order to implement this strategy of deterrence and defence NATO needs conventional land, sea and air forces, a capability for the effective use of nuclear weapons for tactical purposes, and strategic nuclear forces. These elements of NATO forces should each possess a credibility of their own, and should combine to produce an interlocking system of deterrence and defence. Specifically:

(a) the conventional forces should be strong enough to resist and repel a conventional attack on a limited scale, and to deter larger-scale conventional attacks through the prospect of an expansion of the area, scale and intensity of hostilities which could lead to the use of nuclear weapons. Nevertheless, should large-scale conventional aggression occur, these forces should be capable of sustaining a conventional defence in the forward areas sufficient to inflict serious losses on the aggressor and convince him of the risks of continuing his aggression;

(b) the purpose of the tactical nuclear capability is to enhance the deterrent and defensive effect of NATO's forces against large-scale conventional attack, and to provide a deterrent against the expansion of limited conventional attacks and the possible use of tactical nuclear weapons by the aggressor. Its aim is to convince the aggressor that any form of attack on NATO could result in very serious damage to his own forces, and to emphasise the dangers implicit in the continuance of a conflict by presenting him with the risk that such a situation could escalate beyond his control up to all-out nuclear war. Conversely, this capability should be of such a nature that control of the situation would remain in NATO hands;

(c) it is the function of the strategic nuclear forces to strengthen flexible response options, to provide the capability of extending deterrence across a wide range of contingencies, and to provide an ultimate sanction for the overall strategy.

These principles of deterrence and defence apply to aggression at sea as well as on land.

Resources

12. Until there is a downward trend in Warsaw Pact force levels, possibly as a result of MBFR negotiations, NATO's present force capabilities vis-à-vis the Warsaw Pact will at least have to be maintained. This implies the maintenance of the levels of forces already in existence (or foreseen in plans currently declared to NATO) and the regular replacement and modernisation of major equipments. This is the basic

principle which should determine the annual and long-term allocation of resources for defence purposes in all countries. Defence budgets should therefore compensate in full for necessary or unavoidable increases in operating and maintenance costs, including costs of personnel, e.g. those caused by inflation; moreover, in most countries the proportion of expenditure devoted to the provision of major new equipment needs to be substantially increased.

13. It is essential for the solidarity of the Alliance that each member nation should be seen to be making a contribution to the common defence which is commensurate with the role it has assumed in the structure of the Alliance and its economic strength.

Alliance Cooperation

14. NATO defence programmes are organized for the most part on a strictly national basis. The existence of sovereign governments and national systems of finance are bound to place limits on the degree to which integration of common programmes can be achieved; nevertheless there are a number of possibilities for cooperative effort where a more active approach is now urgently required, e.g.:

(a) Rationalisation. This means the adjustment of tasks and functions both within national force structures and as between nations; such adjustments must not involve any diminution of the overall capabilities of NATO forces or any reduction in national defence efforts.

(b) Flexibility. This requires the elimination of all obstacles to the optimum employment of all forces available.

(c) Standardisation. The standardisation (or interoperability) of equipment makes it easier for forces of different nations to operate effectively together. It simplifies training and logistic support.

(d) Cooperation in the development and production of military equipment is a particular form of standardisation which can exploit the benefits of scale and reduce unit costs. Cooperation between North America and Europe in this field should become a two-way street.

15. The fullest use should be made of existing civil assets in support of military plans. Detailed planning is also needed in the civil sector to prepare for a rapid transition of national economies to an emergency footing.

Guidance

16. In light of the above considerations, Ministers established guidance on the levels and characteristics of forces, the scale of resources, the nature of the cooperative efforts, and the criteria for the determination of priorities to be used in all defence planning in NATO both national and international, for the future.

B. The Eurogroup

121. Speech by Mr Healey, British Secretary of State for Defence, to the Association for Defence Studies, Munich, 1 February 1969[1] (extract)

What does seem to emerge strongly from a look at the possible developments of the next decade is the case for more military cooperation among the European members of NATO – the establishment of a European identity within the Atlantic Alliance. In the past many Europeans, myself among them, have been reluctant to move too far or fast in this direction for fear of encouraging a reduction in America's commitment to NATO. I believe that today the argument points in the opposite direction. As all American leaders have stressed, nothing would do more to encourage the United States to maintain its necessary commitment than the sight of the European countries working effectively together inside the Alliance.

In any case, once America and Russia begin discussions on the future of the nuclear balance between them issues of the most vital and direct importance to the countries of Western Europe will arise. Unless Europe is prepared to put a collective view on these issues, the chance of influencing the course of the discussions will be remote. I can conceive situations too in which movement towards solving some of the issues which separate the peoples of Eastern Europe from their West European brothers could be made easier to the extent that Western Europe is less totally dependent on the US for its security. Finally, if as seems certain, European defence budgets remain limited while defence costs rise, by exploiting the opportunities created by an interdependence which is inevitable the European countries may be able to get much better value for whatever money they can afford to spend on their defence.

The invasion of Czechoslovakia in August 1968 demonstrated the impressive capabili of Russia's forces in Eastern Europe and the readiness of the Soviet Government to use them for political gains when the risk of fighting is low. It also demonstrated NATO's ability to preserve the immunity of its members against such an attack providing it maintains the necessary political solidarity and military strength.

While NATO needs conventional forces at the existing level to police its frontiers,

1 *NATO Letter*, March 1969.

o suppress minor conflicts without the use of atomic weapons, and to make nuclear escalation credible if largescale attack is threatened, NATO's success in protecting ts members over the last twenty years argues against an attempt to match the Warsaw powers in every element of their military capability.

Possible developments in the world over the next decade emphasise the need or the European members of the alliance to cooperate more closely with one another within NATO and to be prepared to carry a larger share of the burden of common defence. Britain is ready to play a full part in such an effort.[1]

122. Communiqué issued by the Defence Ministers of the Eurogroup, Brussels, 1 December 1970[2]

Ministers of the Eurogroup agreed to implement together a special and wide-ranging European defence improvement programme, additional to existing plans and designed o improve alliance capability in specific fields identified as of particular importance n the AD 70 study. Their decision to carry out this programme was taken on the basis that the United States, whose forces in Europe are of critical political and military significance for the common security of the whole NATO area, would for ts part maintain those forces at substantially current levels.

The European defence improvement programme will comprise extra measures in three main categories of effort, as set out below.

There will be, on a collective basis, a special European scheme as an additional contribution to NATO common infrastructure, with the specific object of achieving a major acceleration and extension of work on two projects of high importance to the alliance's capability for deterrence and crisis management:

(*a*) The NATO Integrated Communications System (NICS) which would improve n particular alliance consultation and control in time of tension.

(*b*) Aircraft survival measures, to improve the ability of NATO air forces to survive enemy strikes on their bases.

The amount of this collective contribution would be in the order of $420 million over the next five years. Further definition of the composition and operation of the scheme will be worked out in the near future.

Parallel substantial additions and improvements, not previously planned, will be made to national forces in future years. All the forces concerned will be committed to NATO. The estimated capital and operating cost of the measures already identified will be between $450 and $500 million over the next five years. They will also give rise to very substantial further costs in subsequent years.

In addition one member country will make available within the alliance special financial aid to the value of $79 million.[3]

1 Negotiations to establish an informal consultative body for West European Defence Co-ordination had been started on a British initiative in November 1968.
2 *USIS*, 3 December 1970.
3 The Federal Republic to the Government of Turkey for the purchase of Transall tactical transport aircraft.

Ministers instructed permanent representatives to settle outstanding matters and to coordinate the final definition of the programme as soon as possible.

123. Communiqué issued by the Defence Ministers of the Eurogroup, Brussels, 7 December 1971, with Annex on AD 70: European Force Improvements[1]

1. The Defence Ministers of the Eurogroup met at NATO Headquarters on 7th December 1971 under the Chairmanship of the United Kingdom Secretary of State for Defence.

2. Ministers reviewed progress with the billion-dollar European defence improvement programme established in December 1970, comprising an extra contribution to NATO common infrastructure, additional national force improvements, and a special intra-Alliance aid programme.

3. As regards the infrastructure element, they noted with satisfaction that, in accordance with their desire for specially accelerated progress, over two-thirds of the total programme of aircraft survival measures was already the subject of definite NATO programming or implementation action. They noted also that the planned amount of $420 million was now fully covered by specific national pledges.

4. As regards the other EDIP[2] elements, Ministers noted that action on all special national force improvements was going ahead on time, and that aircraft deliveries to implement the intra-Alliance aid element were well advanced.

5. EDIP is only a small part of the European contribution to the Alliance; it is a special increment to the continuing efforts of all members, through their extensive normal defence programmes, to help remedy the known deficiencies in Alliance defence. In this context Ministers approved a summary statement (Annex) on current European force improvements. They welcomed the efforts being made and noted that in 1972, as in 1971, almost all member countries would be making significant increases in their defence budget provision. At current prices the total planned increase for 1972 is well over one billion dollars, without counting certain likely supplementary budget appropriations to meet further rises in costs. As a result, a substantial increase in Eurogroup defence effort is assured for 1972. Ministers reaffirmed the collective need to maintain such efforts so long as Warsaw Pact strength continued to grow, and to keep them closely geared to NATO's AD 70 follow-on work. They agreed to review progress together in 1972.

6. Ministers reviewed the development of various measures of practical cooperation. They welcomed the progress made, particularly in the field of training, where they gave instructions for additional joint courses to be implemented in 1972. They gave instructions for further work, and called for a report to be made at their next meeting.

1 WEU, *Political Year in Europe, 1971*, pp. 287–90.
2 European Defence Improvement Programme.

7. Minister Schmidt (Germany) accepted the invitation of his colleagues to take the Chair at their meetings in 1972.

ANNEX
AD 70: European force improvements

1. As the AD 70 report[1] underlined, NATO policy to ensure the security of its peoples rests on the twin pillars of defence and detente. Both are essential. NATO members are deeply committed to an active policy of negotiation to remove differences and to strengthen peace, but they cannot responsibly discount present realities purely on the basis of future hopes. They must take full account of developments in the military capabilities of the Warsaw Pact.

2. In practice, the NATO Alliance is confronted by Warsaw Pact forces whose power is being continuously augmented on a very large scale. In face of this growing military capability the Alliance forces constitute a defensive shield, though they are by no means equal to the Warsaw Pact's in conventional strength. Within the Alliance, the European members rightly provide forces which amount quantitatively to the great bulk of NATO's conventional strength in the European theatre. The United States forces deployed in the theatre, even though they are a minority in purely numerical terms, remain nevertheless of crucial importance. They are in general among the highest-quality elements available to the Alliance, and their capability is an indispensable part of the Alliance's ability to implement the strategy of forward defence and flexibility in response to aggression. They are moreover an earnest of the continuing United States determination to fulfil its role in the defence of the whole Alliance area, the security of which is indivisible. In particular, they represent a vital link with United States nuclear deterrent power. For all these reasons, United States forces in Europe cannot be replaced by European units. European members of the Alliance have therefore warmly welcomed the repeated undertaking of the United States Administration that United States force capability in the European theatre will not be reduced except in the context of mutual and balanced force reductions.

3. The Eurogroup members recognise that, in parallel, they have a special responsibility to maintain and improve — especially in quality — their own contribution to the common defence. Members have in recent years taken important steps to this end, as a part of the normal processes of modernising the structure and equipment of their forces. In addition, in December 1970 the ten members of the group announced, as a special extra effort on a collective basis, the billion-dollar European defence improvement programme. This is now being rapidly implemented.

4. At the same time, however, the major NATO study 'Alliance defence in the seventies' identified important areas where much still remained to be done to maintain the Alliance's defensive capability against the growing military power of the Warsaw Pact. For example the preponderant strength of Pact armoured forces and the added advantages that accrue from its more closely subordinated command

1 Document No. 112.

arrangements and greater logistic integration are obvious causes for concern. As a result of this report the Eurogroup countries are, in common with the other participants in the integrated defence planning of the Alliance, engaged in reexamining and where necessary reshaping their ongoing defence programmes.

5. In view of the above, members have thought it useful to set out in summary form a number of important measures which they will implement or initiate in 1971 and 1972. These programmes are in general already directly related to the priority areas identified in the AD 70 report. They will be paid for entirely by the Eurogroup countries, and will together constitute an important contribution to a more effective collective defence. Much more, however, remains to be done by individual and collective effort among all members of the Alliance before the Alliance defence posture can be regarded as fully satisfactory.

6. In the years 1971 and 1972 programmes will be implemented covering the provision of the following major items of modern equipment:

Army
  (*a*) over 1,100 main battle tanks;
  (*b*) over 300 self-propelled heavy artillery pieces;
  (*c*) approximately 700 medium-range anti-tank weapons;
  (*d*) over 600 combat vehicles, armoured cars and armoured personnel carriers.

Navy
  (*a*) 2 guided-missile destroyers;
  (*b*) 5 other destroyers and ocean escort frigates;
  (*c*) 3 nuclear fleet submarines;
  (*d*) 10 other submarines;
  (*e*) 27 maritime patrol aircraft;
  (*f*) 25 anti-submarine helicopters;
  (*g*) 8 tank landing craft;
  (*h*) 4 guided-missile fast patrol boats.

Air force
  (*a*) approximately 400 modern combat aircraft;
  (*b*) over 50 heavy tactical transport aircraft;
  (*c*) approximately 200 troop-lift and reconnaissance helicopters;
  (*d*) over 450 anti-aircraft guns.

7. Also in these years, in addition to the special programme to help forward the NATO aircraft shelter programme and the NATO integrated communications system, programmes will have been initiated or firm procurement commitments undertaken for the following further items;

Army
  (*a*) 600 main battle tanks;
  (*b*) some 8,500 anti-tank weapons;
  (*c*) over 3,500 combat vehicles, armoured cars and armoured personnel carriers.

Navy
  (*a*) 11 guided-missile destroyers;
  (*b*) 17 other destroyers and ocean escort frigates;

(*c*) 3 nuclear fleet submarines of improved design;
(*d*) 22 other submarines;
(*e*) 18 maritime patrol aircraft;
(*f*) 44 anti-submarine helicopters;
(*g*) 45 guided-missile fast patrol boats;
(*h*) 6 tank landing craft.

Air force

(*a*) approximately 500 modern combat aircraft;
(*b*) some 20 heavy tactical transport aircraft;
(*c*) over 130 heavy-lift helicopters;
(*d*) over 3,000 anti-aircraft guns.

8. The above lists are concerned with major equipment programmes lending themselves to broad aggregations. Many of the figures are only part of much larger programmes. That for tanks, for example, represents the current instalment of programmes involving the introduction of some 3,000 modern tanks since 1968. In the course of their renewal, modernisation and improvement programmes member countries have also carried out or undertaken as firm commitments a wide range of measures not so easily quantified but equally valuable in improving the effectiveness of their armed forces. Thus in the armour field, in addition to the major tank reequipment programmes that many members have recently completed, members have taken steps to improve their tank transportation and recovery systems and their bridging and barrier equipment. Extensive improvements are planned in tank fire control systems. Progress is being made by a number of countries towards improved levels for key items of war reserve stocks. A number of important additional base facilities have been provided and progress made in the planning of improved forward storage sites and supply depots. In the missile field several members are planning a joint improvement programme for Hawk and the introduction of a successor system to Honest John and Sergeant. A number of important improvements to radar installations and SAM systems are under way. At sea extensive projects exist to improve both the defensive and the offensive missile capability of allied naval forces, notably through the Exocet, Volcano and Penguin SSM programmes.

9. Force structures, and supporting facilities are being expanded and adjusted to provide for the efficient operation of the new equipment. In addition, although the efforts of member countries have properly been concentrated on the modernisation of existing forces, they have made a number of significant increases in the size of their forces. For example, two new armoured regiments and a second echelon armoured car regiment are being formed; four infantry companies are to be expanded to battalion strength; and a very significant increase is being made in the firepower of the brigade and divisional artillery of a number of units.

124. Communiqué issued by the Defence Ministers of the Eurogroup, Brussels, 23 May 1972,[1] with Annex on Principles of Equipment Collaboration

1. The Defence Ministers of the Eurogroup met at NATO headquarters in Brussels on 23 May 1972 under the chairmanship of Minister Helmut Schmidt (Germany). They held a thorough exchange of views on the work of the Eurogroup, which aims at strengthening the Alliance and rendering the defence efforts of the European partner more effective through increased practical cooperation.

2. Ministers reaffirmed the importance they attach to the continuing efforts of all member countries to improve Alliance defence capabilities in accordance with NATO's AD 70 following on work.

3. Ministers reviewed the special European defence improvement programme, and welcomed the progress made in implementing all its elements. As regards the additional infrastructure contribution, in which all member countries are taking part and which will provide aircraft shelters at nearly a hundred airfields, they noted that work was complete or in hand on some two-fifths of the total programme covered, and that a further two-fifths was covered by current programming or pre-financing. They noted that all the special national force improvements were going ahead as planned, and that, for example, the first of the additional C.130 transport aircraft would be delivered in June; work was well advanced on the new support facilities for strengthened local forces on the northern flank; funds were fully committed for the additional CH.53 heavy-lift helicopters; and a decision had been taken to station forward in Germany an increased proportion of the extra Jaguar close-support aircraft planned. They noted also that most of the C.160 tactical transport aircraft being brought into service as intra-Alliance aid had been delivered, and that the force should be complete within the next few months.

4. Ministers noted also the progress made in implementing local force improvements on the southern flank.

5. Ministers gave special attention to the need, within the Alliance framework, to strengthen cooperation in research, development, production and purchase of defence equipment. They endorsed a joint statement of principles which all member countries would follow in order to develop and intensify such cooperation. These principles cover extensive exchange of information, careful review of collaborative possibilities, maximum standardisation, and maximum cooperation in procurement and follow-on support. Ministers agreed that at their next meeting they would further consider what joint action might be taken to speed results in specific project areas, and in the field of long-term equipment cooperation in general.

6. Ministers received a report by a study group set up to examine improved interoperability and commonality in tactical area communications systems. Following this group's successful work, Ministers approved a common operational concept for the future, and endorsed an agreed decision whereby all member countries undertook

1 WEU, *Political Year in Europe, 1972*, pp. 89–90.

to introduce, as soon as practicable equipment conforming fully to detailed common technical parameters. They noted that, as a result, automatic inter-communication would in due course be possible throughout the tactical area.

7. Ministers reviewed work towards greater cooperation in training, logistic support and military medical services. They noted in particular that the first joint training courses deriving from the Eurogroup work had already taken place.

8. Ministers agreed to review progress on all these matters at their December meeting.

ANNEX
PRINCIPLES OF EQUIPMENT COLLABORATION[1]

I. Objectives

1. It is of the first importance to increase substantially the extent and depth of European collaboration in the procurement of defence equipment. (Throughout this paper the term 'procurement' is used in a comprehensive sense to cover research, development, production and purchase.) This importance derives from two main factors:

   a. The execution of numerous separate national projects on the scale common in the past causes wasteful duplication. This will be less and less tolerable in future, and the aim must be progressively to eliminate it.

   b. Standardisation of equipment characteristics brings major military as well as economic benefits.

Both these factors are aspects of the basic aim of getting the best possible collective defence output from the economic input which member countries individually make.

2. The concept of a special drive for closer equipment collaboration among European members of NATO is in no way exclusive. It is intended as a pragmatic step towards better rationalisation of effort within NATO as a whole. The Alliance needs to exploit the resources of all its members to the best collective advantage, and the European countries will continue to value, and indeed in many ways to depend on, closer cooperation among all members of the Alliance.

II. Principles

3. To further the objective systematically, guiding principles are needed in the following respects:

   a. The exchange of basic information.

   b. The review of possibilities.

   c. Maximum cooperation in procurement.

   d. Maximum standardisation.

1 NATO Information Service, *The Eurogroup*, 1975, pp. 39–42.

e. Maximum cooperation in logistic support.

f. Management and cost control considerations.

4. Paragraphs 5—10 below discuss what these guiding principles should be. We emphasise that in general they should be operated to the maximum possible extent through the machinery of NATO. It will be both unnecessary and highly undesirable that Eurogroup countries should seek to duplicate this machinery.

5. Exchange of Basic Information. There should be a regular and comprehensive exchange of information on the timing and content of plans for future military equipment. In addition to making full use of the extensive arrangements already existing within NATO for such exchange, the National Armaments Directors of European countries should arrange to maintain collectively a special watch, based on data kept regularly up-to-date, over areas where collaboration seems especially important or promising. They should meet at least annually to review the data on these areas, to promote the maximum harmonisation of concept and timescale, and to identify and exploit opportunities for joint action.

6. Review of Possibilities. When any Eurogroup country is preparing or drafting a military planning requirement for any item of equipment which could offer significant prospects for collaboration, it should ascertain from the other countries (either through existing NATO and other machinery, or else by special enquiry) whether they have the same or similar intentions, and whether they have already initiated a development on the basis of a relevant existing requirement. The member country should not finalise the planned characteristics of the equipment in question until it has satisfied itself that any substantial possibilities of harmonisation have been explored. It should whenever possible test or otherwise assess carefully any equipment developed or produced in another member country which might *prima facie* offer promise of meeting the requirement.

7. Maximum Cooperation in Procurement. Once the general possibility of a common need has been recognised, the effort should be made firstly to harmonise equipment characteristics, and secondly to agree how the equipment should be joint provided. As regards the former stage, the harmonisation of characteristics should be sought together through study and discussion of military, technological and economic factors (including cost-effectiveness), taking account of existing commitments, timescales and financial situations. As regards the latter stage, there can be no single optimum pattern for a coordinated procurement plan; the best solution will vary with circumstances — for example, whether or not one of the potential collaborators already has a relevant national development in progress. Depending on circumstances, the right course may be joint development, joint production, manufacture under licence, straight-forward purchase, or a combination of methods. One nation may take the lead in one or more phases of the project, or the work may be shared. Collaborative procurement may still be highly desirable even where the major development or initial production is undertaken outside the group of member countries. If it proves impracticable to achieve a joint plan for the procurement of a system as a whole the maximum collaboration should still be sought in respect of sub-systems and components. The prime aim should be to get the best value for

defence expenditure; but it will be important also that all participating countries
should have a fair share in the economic, technological and industrial advantages
of collaboration, not necessarily on a case-by-case basis but in the context of overall
efforts by means of some broadly-based equalising arrangements in defence procurement. It will be important to pursue this objective on the basis of fair opportunity
for all countries at each phase of the procurement process, in order to maintain the
willingness of all to cooperate.

8. Maximum Standardisation. In those areas where standardisation is militarily
essential, or where joint NATO or other agreed standards already exist, countries
should do their utmost to follow agreed standards. Even where, for valid reasons,
collaborative procurement proves impossible, nations should continue to attach
high importance to achieving and maintaining standardisation of characteristics and
components, especially where joint operation or joint support may be in question.
These considerations should continue to weigh heavily in the evaluation of any
modifications after equipment has entered service.

9. Maximum Joint Follow-On Support. The benefits of collaborative procurement and standardisation cannot be adequately realised unless they are followed
through into the field of post-design services and of logistic support – both production
logistics (the procurement of spares, support equipment and the like) and maintenance logistics (such as the storage and distribution of spares, and the provision
of servicing, repair and test facilities. The search for cooperation in these areas
on the widest possible basis of participation, should be pursued under the interdependent responsibilities both of National Armaments Directors and of military
logistic authorities. In particular, the attempt to evolve coordinated arrangements
for follow-on support should be an automatic accompaniment of any collaborative
procurement projects, making use to the utmost of existing NATO logistics organisations.

10. Management and Cost Control. The involvement of more than one country
in an equipment project often complicates the problem of effective management
control. Special attention will need to be paid to ensuring such control, particularly
as regards the cost of development, and appropriate measures will have to be considered. It is also important to keep close control of production costs. The aims of
collaboration would be defeated if cost escalation made it impossible for countries
(especially the smaller ones) to acquire the product, or damaged other fields of
defence effort. In addition, it is desirable that the product should be competitive
in the wider markets.

125. Communiqué issued by the Defence Ministers of the Eurogroup, Brussels, 6 June 1973,[1] with Annex on Principles of Cooperation in the Field of Training

1. The Defence Ministers of the Eurogroup met at NATO Headquarters in Brussels
on 6th June 1973 under the Chairmanship of Minister Mario Tanassi (Italy).

1 WEU, *Political Year in Europe, 1973*, pp. 147–8.

2. Ministers reviewed the special European defence improvement programme and welcomed the progress which has been made in implementing all its various elements As regards the special infrastructure contribution of 150 million IAU[1] (at current rates of exchange, approximately $495 million), which is being provided jointly by all members for the provision of aircraft shelters, work amounting to over 75% is completed or in hand. As regards the additional force improvements being undertaken, all the C430 transport aircraft and 25 of the extra CH-53 heavy-lift helicopters have been delivered; almost all the improved base facilities for local forces on the northern flank have been completed; plans for the extra Jaguar close support aircraft remain on schedule; and the additional second-echelon armoured reconnaiss regiment is now operationally available to SACEUR.[2] All the C-160 tactical transport aircraft being provided as intra-Alliance aid are in squadron service.

3. Ministers noted with satisfaction the continuing work being done by Eurogroup members within the framework of NATO's AD 70 efforts to develop their cooperation in support of the Alliance, for example by such measures as the recent formation of a NATO Standing Naval Force Channel.

4. Ministers continued to pay particular attention to equipment cooperation within the Eurogroup and examined progress in implementing the principles which they agreed in this field in 1972. They also reviewed the position reached in the various project areas previously designated for priority attention and they noted with satisfaction that:

(a) Belgium, the Federal Republic of Germany and the United Kingdom had either formally or conditionally accepted the United States letters of offer for a coordinated purchase of the Lance missile system, thereby achieving a more favourable and effective arrangement in terms of cost, delivery and logistic support;

(b) the Federal Republic of Germany, Italy and the United Kingdom had signed a memorandum of understanding for the joint research and development of a self-propelled 155 mm Howitzer (the SP-70);

(c) the Federal Republic of Germany and Norway had signed an agreement for collaboration on the development of the Viper air-to-air missile;

(d) substantial progress has been made in the field of future battlefield communications and in particular towards ensuring interoperability with non-Eurogroup allies.

5. Ministers received reports from the Belgian, German, Netherlands and United Kingdom Ministers on progress in the studies which their countries are leading into increased cooperation in, respectively, medical services, training, harmonising long-term equipment planning and logistic support. They confirmed the importance whic they attach to progress in these fields as a means to making better use of resources.

6. Ministers signed a declaration on principles of cooperation in the field of traini in order to underline their commitment and to give added impetus to activity in

---

1 Unit of account.
2 Supreme Allied Command, Europe.

this field, and so both improve cooperation and understanding between the forces of the member countries and make better use of training facilities.

7. Ministers took note of the report of a study carried out by Denmark and Germany into certain cost aspects of different force structures.

8. Ministers agreed to review progress on all these matters at their next meeting.

9. Ministers also held a wide-ranging exchange of views on general issues affecting Alliance defence and security, with particular reference to the collective role and interest of European members. They reaffirmed the importance they attach to the maintenance of the cohesion of the Alliance, and their collective determination to maintain and improve the effectiveness of the contribution made by European national forces to the overall Alliance defence effort, exploiting cooperation as fully as possible to achieve maximum defence value from the efforts made by countries.

ANNEX
EUROGROUP PRINCIPLES OF COOPERATION IN THE FIELD OF TRAINING[1]

I. Objectives

1. In accordance with the overall objective of the EUROGROUP 'to achieve savings and stimulate improvements in the defence posture by increased cooperation', the field of training seems particularly qualified for inclusion in such cooperative arrangements. (In this paper the term 'training' is used to cover training of individuals or groups of individuals at all levels in the acquisition of basic and applied skills. It does not cover training in an exercise environment.)

2. Training experts from the European countries in the Alliance established EUROGROUP TRAINING (EUROTRAINING) in September 1970, with their Defence Ministers' approval, in order to:

   a. improve and expand existing, and as appropriate initiate new, bilateral and multilateral training arrangements;

   b. develop these arrangements to a point where one nation might assume responsibility for training in specific areas on behalf of all or some of the European partners.

3. The second of the above aims offers the greater scope for savings, in both manpower and finance. In addition to saving personnel, training facilities and money, increased common training would promote better mutual understanding between personnel of different countries, favour standardization of equipment and lead to harmonization of operational and tactical doctrines.

II. Principles

4. The adoption of guiding principles is essential for future work on common training and to link the work of EURONAD and EUROTRAINING.[2] With this in view

1 NATO Information Service, *The Eurogroup*, 1975, pp. 42–5.
2 EURONAD: equipment collaboration. EUROTRAINING: joint training.

the following principles have been evolved to provide a suitable basis for cooperation in the field of common training:

  a. Exchange of information on training matters.

  b. Cooperation in planning and establishing new training facilities.

  c. Harmonization of training procedures and doctrines.

  d. Standardization, finance and cost control.

  e. Establishment of Expert Working Groups.

  f. Cooperation with NATO authorities and agencies.

Details of these principles are set out in paragraphs 5—10 below.

5. Exchange of Information on Training Matters. There should be regular and intensive exchange of information through the established EUROTRAINING Secretariat on:

  a. Training spaces offered or required;

  b. Experience gained from carrying out specific types of training.

For the purpose of a. above members of EUROTRAINING will list those existing military installations that offer substantial advantages for common training. The list will indicate training spaces that could be made available to other member nations and will be kept up-to-date regularly. For the purpose of b. above members will make available to each other reports of major developments in training matters and of any experience that might be of interest. The EUROTRAINING Secretariat will distribute information on training matters on the basis of data furnished by EUROGROUP members. National delegations should arrange to watch collectively over areas where cooperation in training seems especially important and promising to identify and explore possibilities for common training.

6. Cooperation in Planning and Establishing New Training Facilities. EURO-TRAINING will concentrate in the future on the investigation of new and extensive projects that lend themselves to common training on a centralised or regional basis, especially when new weapon systems are considered for procurement by two or more countries. Member nations agree to consult each other before planning and establishing new or expanding existing national training facilities in order to ascertain whether:

  a. any new or additional training requirement can be met by using the existing facilities in other countries, or expanding them at low cost, and,

  b. other countries have the same or similar requirement for training, so as to favour the establishment of a common European training facility.

7. Harmonization of Training Procedures and Doctrines. Member nations agree that it will be necessary to develop guidelines for common training and to investigate how far national training procedures can be harmonized. They realise the difficulties of implementing this principle owing to differing national characteristics and requirements, but it will be important to pursue this objective in order to maintain the willingness of all to cooperate. The closer members' doctrines come together the greater will be the scope for common training. For example, the common use of tactical trainers may well develop further the harmonization of tactical doctrines which exists already to a considerable degree amongst NATO countries.

8. Standardization, Finance and Cost Control. In those areas where standardization is essential, or where NATO or other agreed standards already exist, EUROGROUP countries should follow these agreed standards. The existing 'Guidelines for the Financing of Common EUROGROUP Training Projects' should continue on their present basis until they are incorporated in a STANAG[1] on Principles and Procedures for the Conduct and Financing of Common Training. The Guidelines should also provide a common basis for the determination of costs.

9. Establishment of Expert Working Groups. The involvement of two or more EUROGROUP nations in a given or planned training project will generally require the establishment of a Working Group of specialists to coordinate investigation, recommendations and follow-on action and to promote continuing cooperation in a particular field of training.

10. Cooperation with NATO Authorities and Agencies. Member nations further agree to continue to make available to the greatest possible extent their national or common training facilities to all armed forces of the North Atlantic Alliance in accordance with paragraph 5 above. They consider cooperation between EUROTRAINING and NATO authorities or agencies essential and important to avoid any unnecessary duplication of effort.

II. Conclusion

1. It must be stressed that principles in themselves cannot compel cooperation; they can only improve the conditions for it. Although in the final resort training functions are a national responsibility, decisions on the practical implementation of these principles will still require strong direction from EUROGROUP Ministers themselves and determination to accept flexibility in the assessment of national training requirements and constraints in order to achieve the long-term objectives of EUROTRAINING.

26. Communiqué issued by the Defence Ministers of the Eurogroup, London, 7 May 1975, with Declaration and Annex on Principles of Cooperation in Logistics[2]

The EUROGROUP met in Ministerial session in London on 7 May 1975 under the Chairmanship of Mr Roy Mason, United Kingdom Secretary of State for Defence.

2. Ministers discussed a general report submitted to them on the objectives and methods of work of the EUROGROUP sub-groups.[3] In this connection, they agreed that these groups are of great importance in furthering the role of the EUROGROUP

---

1 Standard Agreement.
2 Foreign and Commonwealth Office, London.
3 EUROCOM: battlefield communications. EUROLOG: logistic cooperation. EUROLONGTERM: long-term planning. EURONAD: equipment collaboration. EUROSTRUCTURE: force structures. EUROTRAINING: joint training.

in developing a strong and cohesive European contribution to the common defence of the whole Alliance; and they confirmed their determination to continue to play a personal role in directing and stimulating the work of the groups on individual issues.

3. Ministers also received oral reports from the Belgian, German, Netherlands and United Kingdom Defence Ministers on the recent work of each of the sub-groups chaired by their countries. They took note with great interest of the work in hand in the various fields under study; and proposed a number of ideas for further work. They welcomed in particular:

a. the agreement on operational requirements that has been achieved in EUROC which will ensure interoperability between future tactical communications systems of the land forces of the EUROGROUP nations; and

b. the progress made by EUROLONGTERM in developing agreed tactical concepts as a basis for drawing up the operational requirements of future weapon systems.

4. To complement the existing EUROGROUP principles of cooperation in equip ment and training, Ministers signed a declaration on principles of cooperation in logistics (text attached at Annex) and agreed to set in compliance with these princi in their future logistic planning. They stressed that closer collaboration in logistic support should enable member countries of the EUROGROUP to make more effect use of the resources available and to promote increased cooperation in this importal field of common concern. In this context, Ministers welcomed the signature by the Ministers of Defence of the Netherlands and the United Kingdom of a Memorandur of Understanding on a common project for marine gas turbine engines.

5. Ministers had a full and frank exchange of views on a wide range of questions concerning the research, development and production of defence equipment. They reviewed the work in hand to extend the information available on member countrie equipment plans and programmes; and they underlined the importance which they attach to maintaining a strong European technological and industrial base in the defence field and to increasing the degree of standardisation in defence equipment. Ministers also agreed on the need to develop a constructive dialogue between Europ and the United States on these matters; this dialogue will be prepared by very wide consultation between all the countries concerned.

6. Ministers took note with interest of a statement by the Norwegian Minister of Defence on the progress made in the collaboration between Belgium, Denmark, The Netherlands and Norway on the replacement programme for the F104G and other aircraft.

7. Ministers concluded with an exchange of views on the major issues currently affecting the defence of NATO Europe in preparation for the forthcoming NATO Ministerial meetings. They agreed that the EUROGROUP continues to provide a most important forum for developing cooperation and collaboration among its members in the Alliance framework; and they reaffirmed their personal support for the EUROGROUP and its work to this end.

Declaration on Eurogroup Principles of Cooperation in Logistics

The Ministers of Defence of Belgium, Denmark, the Federal Republic of Germany, Italy, Luxembourg, The Netherlands, Norway, Turkey and the United Kingdom:

> Desiring to achieve a greater measure of collaboration in logistic support among European member states of the North Atlantic Alliance:
>
> Anxious to make optimum use of their logistic resources:

on 7 May 1975 adopted the Principles of Cooperation in Logistics set out in the Annex herewith as a basis for common action.

Ministers confirm their understanding that each will:

— Act in compliance with these principles;

— Disseminate them within his national Defence Ministry;

— Instruct all those of his staffs who have responsibility for logistics to act in accordance with these principles.

ANNEX:
PRINCIPLES OF COOPERATION IN LOGISTICS

I. Objectives

1. One of the important overall objectives of the Eurogroup is to increase cooperation in defence among member nations. The field of logistics is one in which there is scope for improvements of this kind. Although the provision of logistic support for NATO-assigned forces is at present a national responsibility, closer collaboration in logistic support will enable member countries whose forces are deployed in the same area with similar or complementary operational responsibilities to make more efficient and economical use of their logistic resources.

2. The ultimate objective is to achieve the closest possible integration of logistics systems among Eurogroup members in respect of the forces they assign to NATO. This is, however, dependent on fundamental changes in the arrangements for financing those logistics systems and for the procurement of equipment; and also on the achievement of much greater standardisation of weapons and equipment than exists at present. In the meantime, worthwhile progress towards the objective can be made by developing cooperative logistic arrangements and coordinated procedures wherever the opportunity exists and greater efficiency and cost-effectiveness would result.

II. Principles

3. The following principles have been drawn up to provide a basis for cooperation in the field of logistic support:

> a. *New Collaborative Projects for Weapons Systems and Major Equipments.* Practical possibilities of collaboration in support of weapons systems and major equipments (e.g. maintenance, repair and spares provisioning) are

limited by the differences between weapons and equipments at present used by the member countries. A major effort is now being made by Eurogroup countries through the work of EURONAD to promote standardisation of new weapons and equipment by means of collaborative projects. Member countries have already agreed in the Principles of Equipment Collaboration that the requirement to attempt to evolve coordinated arrangements for follow-on support should be an automatic accompaniment of any collaborativ procurement project. EUROLOG will work with the relevant agencies to satisfy themselves that appropriate arrangements are being made in each case.

b. *Other New Equipment Projects.* Member countries agree that a similar effort to evolve coordinated arrangements for follow-on support should be made when any new weapon or equipment is under consideration or adopted by two or more countries, whether or not the particular item is categorized as a collaborative procurement project.

c. *Existing Weapons or Equipments.* Member countries agree that consideration should be given to the possibility of cooperation in the logistic support of existing weapons and equipments used by more than one country which are not already the subject of cooperative arrangements.

d. *Harmonization of Logistic Procedures.* Member countries agree that every effort will be made to harmonize/standardise logistic procedures with the object of achieving increased flexibility in logistic support.

e. *Future Logistic Planning.* Member countries agree that they should exchange information regularly about logistics, including information on planned logistic projects, with the general aim of enabling others to join in such projects if this would be of advantage. They agree also that there should be a regular exchange of information on the evaluation of national logistic concepts.

III. Method of Implementation

4. Responsibility for implementation of these principles lies with Eurogroup countr under the direction of Eurogroup Ministers. The sub-group established in the field of logistics (EUROLOG) has so far devoted its main efforts to examining the possibilities of logistic cooperation between the land forces in the Northern Army Group, between the air forces in the Second Allied Tactical Air Force and between the navies which operate in the Channel and the North Sea. The countries providing these forces are at present represented on EUROLOG. It is open to other Eurogrouµ countries to join EUROLOG when subjects of interest to them are under consideration.

127. Communiqué issued by the Defence Ministers of the Eurogroup, The Hague, 5 November 1975, with Annex[1]

1. At the invitation of Mr Henk Vredeling, Minister of Defence of the Netherlands,

1 Foreign and Commonwealth Office, London.

he Eurogroup met in special Ministerial session in the Hague on 5 November 1975 to consider ways of improving standardization and European armaments cooperation. The meeting was chaired by Mr Roy Mason, United Kingdom Secretary of State for Defence.

2. Ministers considered a report prepared for them by a working party of their Eurogroup National Armaments Directors (EURONAD). Ministers discussed the interrelated questions of standardization, European equipment collaboration and European—North American cooperation in defence procurement.

3. Ministers agreed that, in order to make better use of the limited defence resources available within the North Atlantic Alliance, it is of the greatest importance to increase the interoperability and standardization of military equipment within the Alliance, while maintaining an effective and viable European defence industry. Ministers accordingly recognized that it was important to study the means of reducing the constraints of narrow national markets and to encourage industry to increase the efficiency of its operations.

4. Ministers agreed that, as a means to this end, European nations should coordinate and harmonize their equipment planning more effectively than hitherto. Ministers reaffirmed the importance they attach to extending the information available on member countries' equipment plans and programmes so as to set the basis for future cooperative ventures. With a view to improving the technological capacity and the competitiveness of the European defence industry, Ministers determined to strengthen inter-European cooperation in the fields of research, development and production of weapons and military equipment through industrial cooperation and co-production. Ministers agreed that the effective participation in this process of countries with less well-developed defence industries should be encouraged. They therefore instructed their Armaments Directors to pursue with fresh emphasis the standardization both of complete major equipments and weapons systems and of assemblies and components.

5. Ministers discussed the organizational arrangements for furthering inter-European cooperation in defence procurement. They agreed that there was a need to improve and strengthen the machinery available in this field. They decided to explore further the potential for extending cooperation in European armaments collaboration in an independent forum open to all European members of the Alliance. They agreed in principle to establish a European defence procurement secretariat. With a view to the longer term, Ministers commissioned a study into the tasks which a European defence procurement organization might undertake.

6. As a further step towards increased standardization, Ministers agreed that there was a need to establish a more equitable balance of defence equipment procurement between the North American and European members of the North Atlantic Alliance. They agreed that such transatlantic cooperation, while promoting the maintenance of a highly developed technological and industrial base in participating countries in Europe and having a bearing on the growing unity developing in this continent; would also promote interdependence and cohesion within the Alliance as a whole; and would enable all its members to make more cost-effective use of the resources available for their common defence and of their research, development and pro-

duction capacities. Ministers accordingly agreed to propose to the United States and Canada that a dialogue should be opened in the near future with a view to developing specific proposals for increasing transatlantic cooperation and the reciprocal purchasing of defence equipment. Ministers confirmed that this dialogue called for a harmonized approach by the European members of the Alliance, in which full account should be taken of their economic and social interests.

7. On the basis of a note by their Permanent Representatives, Ministers concluded with an exchange of views on how best to harmonize future work on this subject with any work carried out in the Alliance as a whole. They agreed that their activities should be vigorously pursued and that, at the same time, consideration should be given to the means of developing a common European position within the framework of the Alliance.

ANNEX

The intention is to establish an independent programme group of senior officials open to all European members of the Alliance for the purposes of:

a. exploring the conditions for a European cooperation in defence procurement;
b. studying the possibility of a number of joint projects where a common require-ment appears to exist;
c. preparing the basis for the dialogue with the North Americans.

This programme group will be served by the European Defence Procurement Secretariat and will report to the Ministers of the countries taking part.

C. The European Community

128. Communiqué issued by the Conference of Heads of State or Government of the European Community, The Hague, 2 December 1969[1]

On the initiative of the Government of the French Republic and at the invitation of the Netherlands Government:

1. The Heads of State or Government and the Ministers for Foreign Affairs of the member States of the European Communities met at The Hague on 1st and 2nd December 1969. The Commission of the European Communities was invited to participate in the work of the Conference on the second day.

2. Now that the Common Market is about to enter upon its final stage, they considered that it was the duty of those who bear the highest political responsibility in each of the member States to draw up a balance sheet of the work already accomplished, to show their determination to continue it and to define the broad lines for the future.

3. Looking back on the road that has been traversed, and finding that never before have independent States pushed their cooperation further, they were unanimous in their opinion that by reason of the progress made the Community has now arrived at a turning point in its history. Over and above the technical and legal sides of the problems involved, the expiry of the transitional period at the end of the year has therefore acquired major political significance. Entry upon the final stage of the Common Market not only means confirming the irreversible nature of the work accomplished by the Communities, but also means paving the way for a united Europe capable of assuming its responsibilities in the world of tomorrow and of making a contribution commensurate with its traditions and its mission.

4. The Heads of State or Government therefore wish to reaffirm their belief in the political objectives which give the Community its meaning and purport, their determination to carry their undertaking through to the end, and their confidence in the final success of their efforts. Indeed, they have a common conviction that a Europe composed of States which, in spite of their different national characteristics, are united in their essential interests, assured of its internal cohesion, true to its friendly relations with outside countries, conscious of the role it has to play in

1 *The Times*, 3 December 1969.

promoting the relaxation of international tension and the rapprochement among all peoples, and first and foremost among those of the entire European continent, is indispensable if a mainspring of development, progress and culture, world equilibrium and peace is to be preserved.

The European Communities remain the original nucleus from which European unity has been developed and intensified. The entry of other countries of this continent to the Communities – in accordance with the provisions of the Treaties of Rome – would undoubtedly help the Communities to grow to dimensions more in conformity with the present state of world economy and technology.

The creation of a special relationship with other European States which have expressed a desire to that effect would also contribute to this end. A development such as this would enable Europe to remain faithful to its traditions of being open to the world and increase its efforts on behalf of developing countries.

5. As regards the completion of the Communities, the Heads of State or Government reaffirmed the will of their governments to pass from the transitional period to the final stage of the European Community and accordingly to lay down a definitive financial arrangement for the common agricultural policy by the end of 1969.

They agreed progressively to replace, within the framework of this financial arrangement, the contributions of member countries by their own resources, taking into account all the interests concerned, with the object of achieving in due course the integral financing of the Communities' budgets in accordance with the procedure provided for in Article 201 of the treaty establishing the EEC and of strengthening the budgetary powers of the European Parliament.

The problem of the method of direct elections is still being studied by the Council of Ministers.

6. They asked the governments to continue without delay within the Council the efforts already made to ensure a better control of the market by a policy of agricultural production making it possible to limit budgetary charges.

7. The acceptance of a financial arrangement for the final stage does not exclude its adaptation by unanimous vote, in particular in the light of an enlarged Community and on condition that the principles of this arrangement are not infringed.

8. They reaffirmed their readiness to further the more rapid progress of the later development needed to strengthen the Community and promote its development into an economic union. They are of the opinion that the integration process should result in a community of stability and growth. To this end they agreed that within the Council, on the basis of the memorandum presented by the Commission on 12th February 1969 and in close collaboration with the latter, a plan in stages should be worked out during 1970 with a view to the creation of an economic and monetary union. The development of monetary cooperation should depend on the harmonisation of economic policies.

They agreed to arrange for the investigation of the possibility of setting up a European reserve fund in which a joint economic and monetary policy would have to result.

9. As regards the technological activity of the Community, they reaffirmed their readiness to continue more intensively the activities of the Community with a view to coordinating and promoting industrial research and development in the principal sectors concerned, in particular by means of common programmes, and to supply the financial means for the purpose.

10. They further agreed on the necessity of making fresh efforts to work out in the near future a research programme for the European Atomic Energy Community designed in accordance with the exigencies of modern industrial management, and making it possible to ensure the most effective use of the common research centre.

11. They reaffirmed their interest in the establishment of a European university.

12. The Heads of State or Government acknowledged the desirability of reforming the social fund, within the framework of a closely concerted social policy.

13. They reaffirmed their agreement on the principle of the enlargement of the Community as provided by Article 237 of the Treaty of Rome.

Insofar as the applicant States accept the treaties and their political finality, the decisions taken since the entry into force of the treaties and the options made in the sphere of development, the Heads of State or Government have indicated their agreement to the opening of negotiations between the Community on the one hand and the applicant States on the other.

They agreed that the essential preparatory work could be undertaken as soon as practically and conveniently possible; by common consent, the preparations would take place in a most positive spirit.

14. As soon as negotiations with the applicant countries have been opened, discussions will be started with such other EFTA members as may request them on their position in relation to the EEC.

15. They agreed to instruct the Ministers for Foreign Affairs to study the best way of achieving progress in the matter of political unification, within the context of enlargement. The Ministers would be expected to report before the end of July 1970.

16. All the creative activities and the actions conducive to European growth decided upon here will be assured of a better future if the younger generation is closely associated with them; the governments are resolved to endorse this and the Communities will make provision for it.

129. Agreement of the Central Banks of the EEC, establishing a system of short-term monetary support, approved by the Council of Ministers, 26 January 1970[1]

THE CENTRAL BANKS OF THE MEMBER STATES IN THE EUROPEAN COMMUNITY,

1 *Europe, Documents*, No. 561, 17 February 1970

In view of the Commission's Memorandum to the Council on the coordination of economic policies and monetary cooperation within the Community;[1]

In view of the letter from the Chairman of the Board of Governors to the President of the Commission dated 10 July 1969, containing the Board's opinion on the above-mentioned Memorandum;

In view of the Council Decision of 17 July 1969 concerning the coordination of Member States' short-term economic policies;

In view of the procedure regarding the coordination of medium-term economic policies;

HAVE AGREED ON THE FOLLOWING PROVISIONS.

Article I: Establishment of the system

1. The central banks of the EEC Member States, in view of the greater solidarity between their countries, shall set up among themselves a system of short-term monetary support to which they may have recourse by priority.

2. The implementing of this system is closely linked to the permanent system of consultation and coordination regarding economic policy between the Member States of the Community.

3. The possibilities offered by other systems of international aid will be taken into consideration when recourse is had to this system.

4. The practical working of the system is determined by the present Agreement.

The decisions needed for its application shall be taken by common agreement of the Governors of participating central banks meeting within the Governors' Board of the central banks of the Member States of the European Economic Community, henceforth referred to as 'the Governors'. The chair is taken by the Chairman of the Governors' Board of the central banks of the Member States of the European Economic Community, henceforth referred to as 'the Chairman'. The Commission representative within this Board is henceforth referred to as 'the Commission representative'.

5. For the application of the present Agreement, the Governors call upon an Agent and confer on him the duties they determine, according to arrangements concluded with him.

Article II: Quotas and extensions

1. Each participating central bank is assigned a quota, the sum of which is determined in Appendix 1 to the present Agreement.[2]

2. The quotas determine, on the one hand, the amount of support from which

---

1 Drawn up for the Council of Ministers' session of 17 July 1969, it is commonly referred to as the 'Barre plan'. For the text, see *Europe, Documents*, No. 536, 16 July 1969.

2 Appendix 1 sets the quotas as: Germany, 30% (to the value $300 million); Belgium, 10% ($100 million); France, 30% ($300 million); Italy, 20% ($200 million); the Netherlands, 10% ($100 million).

ach central bank may benefit and, on the other hand, the amount of support it
ill guarantee to finance, under the conditions fixed by the present Agreement.

3. The Governors may modify the quotas. Every five years, they consider the
dvisability of revising them. They may, however, undertake this examination
efore the expiry of this period.

4. In special cases where circumstances justify such action, the Governors may
ecide, as an exception to paragraph 2, as concerning the amount, duration and
onditions they determine

(*a*) either to increase beyond its quota the amount of support from which a
central bank may benefit ('debit extension');

(*b*) or to increase beyond its quota the amount of support which a central bank
guarantees to finance ('credit extension').

The total of credit extensions, and the total of debit extensions thus granted,
1ay at most amount to the sum of all the quotas.

In order to assess the circumstances justifying extensions, the Governors will in
articular take into consideration the evolution of the balance of payments and the
tate of exchange reserves of the Member State to which each central bank involved
elongs, and the other facilities available to them because of other international
rrangements.

Article III: Request for support

. The participating central bank which wishes to use the monetary support provided
or in the present Agreement informs the Chairman that an unexpected need for
hort-term financing has arisen because of a temporary deficit in the balance of
ayments due to accidental difficulties or to short-term economic discrepancies,
otwithstanding the coordination of economic policies. It informs him of the amount
f support desired, and of the other sources of financing to which it envisages having
ecourse in order to solve its difficulties.

2. No request for support will be introduced by a central bank in debt to the
ystem following the non-execution of its obligations to repay.

Unless a contrary decision is reached by the Governors, a request for support
ill not be taken into consideration in the circumstances described in Article VI,
'ara. 3.

Article IV: Granting and financing of support

. The Chairman informs the participating central banks and the Commission represen-
ative of all requests for support introduced in conformity with Article III.

The Chairman convenes a meeting of the Governors on his own initiative or when
central bank expresses the desire.

2. The monetary support is financed by each participating central bank, other than
he receiving central bank, within the proportion and the limits of its quota.

3. The Governors may decide to distribute the burden of financing in a proportion

different from the quotas; in this case, the contributions determined in application of paragraph 2 of the present article are the subject of appropriate refinancing amo₪ the central banks taking part in the financing, unless the Governors decide otherwis₪

4. Any central bank which, during consultations following a request for support, informs the Chairman that its country is suffering balance of payments difficulties and/or an alarming drop in its currency reserves, has the right to obtain from the other participating central banks, and in principle in proportions to their quotas, refinancing, partial or total, for its contribution to the financing of the support.

5. When the monetary support requested cannot be financed within the quotas, the Governors may decide, to the extent they consider most fitting, and taking into account possibilities of recourse to other international aid systems, to establish one or several credit extensions, in conformity with the provisions of Article II of the present Agreement, or, in the lack of this, to reduce as far as is necessary the amount of support desired.

6. After consultation with the participating central banks, the Chairman informs the central banks and the Commission representative of the granting of support, the amount of this support, its distribution and the deadlines by which funds must be made available.

Article V: Mobilisation of the debt

Any central bank which is a creditor in the context of the present agreement and o₪ which the Member State should start to have balance of payments difficulties and/c₪ to suffer a sudden drop in its currency reserves may ask the Governors for early repayment or for its debt to be transferred. The Governors will take the measures they consider fitting to this end.

Article VI: Technique of transactions

1. The beneficiary central bank receives from its partners, directly or through the Agent, facilities in the form of swaps, deposits or any other form agreed among the parties.

The Agent may, on behalf of the participating central banks which so request, advance all or part of the contributions incumbent on them.

2. If they are not used within one month, the facilities made available in applica₪ of the present article will be annulled. They will be available for use for a period of three months and will be renewable once for a period of three months at the reques₪ of the beneficiary central bank.

3. The beneficiary central bank will refrain from applying for further monetary support during a period equivalent to the time during which it used the previous support.

4. The support facilities are expressed in the currency which is effectively delive₪ by the central bank agreeing to them; this may be its national currency or any othe₪ means of payment agreed with the beneficiary central bank.

5. The cost of the support facilities by the debitor central bank will be established according to the rules fixed by the Governors.

6. The Governors will take the provisions they consider useful so as to make as far as possible uniform the conditions governing the support transactions.

7. The Agent is notified of the practical details of each support transaction.

Article VII: Coordination of economic policies

1. The participating central banks take note of the fact that the granting of monetary support gives rise to the special consultation procedure provided for by the European Communities' Council Decision of 17 July, 1969; the application of this procedure is an integral part of the short-term monetary support system.

2. The Governors are regularly informed of the working of the Community procedures as regards the coordination of short- and medium-term economic policies.

Article VIII: Duration

The present Agreement will have a duration of five years. It will be extended every five years by tacit renewal, unless an objection is raised six months in advance.

Article IX: Liquidation

In the event of the support system being liquidated, the present Agreement will remain in force as regards the repayment of the credit granted in conformity with Article IV.

EDITOR'S NOTE: ECONOMIC AND MONETARY UNION

The negotiations on the establishment of a European Economic and Monetary Union stemmed from the commitment recorded in paragraph 8 of the Hague Summit Communiqué (128). Documents nos. 129, 130, 134, 135, 136, 185 and 186 are concerned with different aspects of these negotiations. The principal documents not reproduced in this volume are:

Commission of the European Communities, *A Plan for the Establishment by Stages of an Economic and Monetary Union*, (Supplement to *Bull. EC*, 3–1970).

Resolution of the Council of the Representatives of the Governments of the member states on the phased establishment of economic and monetary union in the Community, 22 March 1971. (*OJ*, No. C 28, 27 March 1971, p. 1).

Decision on the strengthening of coordination of short term economic policies of the member states, adopted by the Council of the European Communities, 22 March 1971. (*OJ*, No. L 73/12, 27 March 1971, pp. 174–5).

Resolution on the implementation of the first phase of the economic and monetary union adopted by the Council of the European Communities, Brussels, 21 March 1972 *Europe, Bulletins*, No. 1002, 9 March 1972).

Resolution on the implementation of the second stage of economic and monetar union in the Community, adopted by the Council of the European Communities, Brussels, 17 December 1973 (Council of the European Communities, press release 2479/73 (Presse 160)).

130. Decision on the replacement of financial contributions from Member States by the Communities' own resources, adopted by the Council of the European Communities, Luxembourg, 21 April 1970[1]

The Council of the European Communities,

Having regard to the Treaty establishing the European Economic Community, and in particular Article 201 thereof;

Having regard to the Treaty establishing the European Atomic Energy Community, and in particular Article 173 thereof;

Having regard to the proposal from the Commission;

Having regard to the Opinion of the Assembly;

Having regard to the Opinion of the Economic and Social Committee;

Whereas complete replacement of the financial contributions from member States by the Communities' own resources can only be achieved progressively;

Whereas Article 2 (1) of Regulation No. 25 on financing the common agricultura policy stipulates that at the single market stage revenue from agricultural levies shall be allocated to the Community and appropriated to Community expenditure;

Whereas Article 201 of the Treaty establishing the European Economic Community refers explicitly, among the Community's own resources which could replace financial contributions from member States, to revenue accruing from the common customs tariff when the latter has been finally introduced;

Whereas the effects on the budgets of the member States of the transfer to the Communities of revenue accruing from the common customs tariff should be mitigated; whereas a system should be provided which will make it possible to achie total transfer progressively and within a definite period of time;

Whereas revenue accruing from agricultural levies and customs duties is not sufficient to ensure that the budget of the Communities is in balance; whereas, therefore, it is advisable to allocate to the Communities, in addition, tax revenue, the most appropriate being that accruing from the application of a single rate to the basis for assessing the value added tax, determined in a uniform manner for the member States;

Has laid down these provisions, which it recommends to the member States for adoption:

Article 1

The Communities shall be allocated resources of their own in accordance with the following articles in order to ensure that their budget is in balance.

1 *OJ*, No. L 94, 28 April 1970 (unofficial translation).

Article 2

From 1st January 1971 revenue from:
(*a*) levies, premiums, additional or compensatory amounts, additional amounts or factors and other duties established or to be established by the institutions of the Communities in respect of trade with non-member countries within the framework of the common agricultural policy, and also contributions and other duties provided for within the framework of the organisation of the markets in sugar (hereinafter called 'agricultural levies');
(*b*) common customs tariff duties and other duties established or to be established by the institutions of the Communities in respect of trade with non-member countries (hereinafter called 'customs duties');
shall, in accordance with Article 3, constitute own resources to be entered in the budget of the Communities.

In addition, revenue accruing from other taxes introduced within the framework of a common policy in accordance with the provisions of the Treaty establishing the European Economic Community or the Treaty establishing the European Atomic Energy Community shall constitute own resources to be entered in the budget of the Communities, subject to the procedure laid down in Article 201 of the Treaty establishing the European Economic Community or in Article 173 of the Treaty establishing the European Atomic Energy Community having been followed.

Article 3

1. From 1st January 1971 the total revenue from agricultural levies shall be entered in the budget of the Communities.

From the same date, revenue from customs duties shall progressively be entered in the budget of the Communities.

The amount of the customs duties appropriated to the Communities each year by each member State shall be equal to the difference between a reference amount and the amount of the agricultural levies appropriated to the Communities pursuant to the first sub-paragraph. Where this difference is negative, there shall be no payment of customs duties by the member State concerned nor repayment of agricultural levies by the Communities.

The reference amount referred to in the third sub-paragraph shall be:
 − 50% in 1971
 − 62.5% in 1972
 − 75% in 1973
 − 87.5% in 1974
 − 100% from 1st January 1975 onwards
of the total amount of the agricultural levies and customs duties collected by each member State.

The Communities shall refund to each member State 10% of the amounts paid in accordance with the preceding sub-paragraphs in order to cover expenses incurred in collection.

2. During the period 1st January 1971 to 31st December 1974, the financial contributions from member States required in order to ensure that the budget of the Communities is in balance shall be apportioned on the following scale:

- Belgium   6.8
- Germany   32.9
- France   32.6
- Italy   20.2
- Luxembourg   0.2
- Netherlands   7.3

3. During the same period, however, the variation from year to year in the share of each member State in the aggregate of the amounts paid in accordance with paragraphs 1 and 2 may not exceed 1% upwards or 1.5% downwards, where these amounts are taken into consideration within the framework of the second sub-paragraph. For 1971, the financial contributions of each member State to the combined budgets for 1970 shall be taken as reference for the application of this rule, to the extent that these budgets are taken into consideration within the framework of the second sub-paragraph.

In the application of the first sub-paragraph, the following factors shall be taken into consideration for each financial year:

(*a*) expenditure relating to payment appropriations decided on for the financial year in question for the research and investment budget of the European Atomic Energy Community, with the exception of expenditure relating to supplementary programmes;

(*b*) expenditure relating to appropriations to the European social fund;

(*c*) for the European agricultural guidance and guarantee fund, expenditure relating to appropriations to the guarantee section and to the guidance section, with the exception of appropriations entered or reentered for accounting periods preceding the financial year concerned. For the reference year 1970 such expenditure shall be:

   - for the guarantee section, that referred to in Article 8 of Council Regulation (EEC) No. 723/70 of 21st April 1970 laying down additional provisions for financing the common agricultural policy;
   - for the guidance section, an amount of 285 million units of account apportioned on the basis of the scale laid down in Article 7 of that regulation it being understood that, for calculating the share of Germany, a percentage of 31.5 shall be taken as the reference scale;

(*d*) other expenditure relating to the appropriations entered in the Community budget.

Should the application of this paragraph to one or more member States result in a deficit in the budget of the Communities, the amount of that deficit shall be shared for the year in question between the other member States, within the limits laid down in the first sub-paragraph and according to the contribution scale fixed in paragraph 2. If necessary, the operation shall be repeated.

4. Financing from the Communities' own resources of the expenditure connected

with research programmes of the European Atomic Energy Community shall not exclude entry in the budget of the Communities of expenditure relating to supplementary programmes or the financing of such expenditure by means of financial contributions from member States determined according to a special scale fixed pursuant to a decision of the Council acting unanimously.

5. By way of derogation from this article, appropriations entered in a budget preceding that for the financial year 1971 and carried over or reentered in a later budget shall be financed by financial contributions from member States according to scales applicable at the time of their first entry.

Appropriations to the guidance section which, while being entered for the first time in the 1971 budget, refer to accounting periods of the European agricultural guidance and guarantee fund preceding 1st January 1971 shall be covered by the scale relating to those periods.

Article 4

1. From 1st January 1975 the budget of the Communities shall, irrespective of other revenue, be financed entirely from the Communities' own resources.

Such resources shall include those referred to in Article 2 and also those accruing from the value added tax and obtained by applying a rate not exceeding 1% to an assessment basis which is determined in a uniform manner for member States according to Community rules. The rate shall be fixed within the framework of the budgetary procedure. If at the beginning of a financial year the budget has not yet been adopted, the rate previously fixed shall remain applicable until the entry into force of a new rate.

During the period 1st January 1975 to 31st December 1977, however, the variation from year to year in the share of each member State in relation to the preceding year may not exceed 2%. Should this percentage be exceeded, the necessary adjustments shall be made, within that variation limit, by financial compensation between the member States concerned proportionate to the share borne by each of them in respect of revenue accruing from value added tax or from the financial contributions referred to in paragraphs 2 and 3.

2. By way of derogation from the second sub-paragraph of paragraph 1, if on 1st January 1975 the rules determining the uniform basis for assessing the value added tax have not yet been applied in all member States but have been applied in at least three of them, the financial contribution to the budget of the Communities to be made by each member State not yet applying the uniform basis for assessing the value added tax shall be determined according to the proportion of its gross national product to the sum total of the gross national products of the member States. The balance of the budget shall be covered by revenue accruing from the value added tax in accordance with the second sub-paragraph of paragraph 1, collected by the other member States. This derogation shall cease to be effective as soon as the conditions laid down in paragraph 1 are fulfilled.

3. By way of derogation from the second sub-paragraph of paragraph 1, if on

1st January 1975 the rules determining the uniform basis for assessing the value added tax have not yet been applied in three or more member States, the financial contribution of each member State to the budget of the Communities shall be determined according to the proportion of its gross national product to the sum total of the gross national products of the member States. This derogation shall cease to be effective as soon as the conditions laid down in paragraphs 1 or 2 are fulfilled.

4. For the purpose of paragraphs 2 and 3, 'gross national product' means the gross national product at market prices.

5. From the complete application of the second sub-paragraph of paragraph 1, any surplus of the Communities' own resources over and above the actual expenditure during a financial year shall be carried over to the following financial year.

6. Financing expenditure connected with research programmes of the European Atomic Energy Community from the Communities' own resources shall not exclude entry in the budget of the Communities of expenditure relating to supplementary programmes nor the financing of such expenditure by means of financial contribution from member States determined according to a special scale fixed pursuant to a decision of the Council acting unanimously.

Article 5

The revenue referred to in Article 2, Article 3 (1) and (2) and Article 4 (1) to (5) shall be used without distinction to finance all expenditure entered in the budget of the Communities in accordance with Article 20 of the Treaty establishing a single Council and a single Commission of the European Communities.

Article 6

1. The Community resources referred to in Articles 2, 3 and 4 shall be collected by member States in accordance with national provisions imposed by law, regulation or administrative action, which shall, where necessary, be amended for that purpose. Member States shall make these resources available to the Commission.

2. Without prejudice to the auditing of accounts provided for in Article 206 of the Treaty establishing the European Economic Community, or to the inspection arrangements made pursuant to Article 209 (*c*) of that Treaty, the Council shall, acting unanimously on a proposal from the Commission and after consulting the Assembly, adopt provisions relating to the supervision of collection, the making available to the Commission, and the payment of the revenue referred to in Articles 2, 3 and 4, and also the procedure for application of Article 3 (3) and Article 4.

Article 7

Member States shall be notified of this Decision by the Secretary-General of the Council of the European Communities. It shall be published in the *Official Journal of the European Communities.*

Member States shall notify the Secretary-General of the Council of the European Communities without delay of the completion of the procedures for the adoption of this Decision in accordance with their respective constitutional requirements.

This Decision shall enter into force on the first day of the month following receipt of the last of the notifications referred to in the second sub-paragraph. If, however, the instruments of ratification provided for in Article 12 of the Treaty amending certain budgetary provisions of the Treaties establishing the European Communities and the Treaty establishing a single Council and a single Commission of the European Communities, have not been deposited before that date by all the member States, this Decision shall enter into force on the first day of the month following the deposit of the last of those instruments of ratification.

131. Treaty amending certain budgetary provisions of the Treaties establishing the European Communities and of the Treaty establishing a single Council and a single Commission of the European Communities, Luxembourg, 22 April 1970[1]

CHAPTER I – PROVISIONS AMENDING THE TREATY ESTABLISHING THE EUROPEAN COAL AND STEEL COMMUNITY

Article 1

The following provisions shall be substituted for Article 78 of the Treaty establishing the European Coal and Steel Community:

Article 78

1. The financial year shall run from 1 January to 31 December.

The administrative expenditure of the Community shall comprise the expenditure of the High Authority, including that relating to the functioning of the Consultative Committee, and that of the Court, the Assembly and the Council.

2. Each institution of the Community shall, before 1 July, draw up estimates of its administrative expenditure. The High Authority shall consolidate these estimates in a preliminary draft administrative budget. It shall attach thereto an opinion which may contain different estimates.

The preliminary draft budget shall contain an estimate of revenue and an estimate of expenditure.

3. The High Authority shall place the preliminary draft administrative budget before the Council not later than 1 September of the year preceding that in which the budget is to be implemented.

The Council shall consult the High Authority and, where appropriate, the other institutions concerned whenever it intends to depart from the preliminary draft budget.

1 Cmnd. 5179–II.

The Council shall, acting by a qualified majority, establish the draft administrative budget and forward it to the Assembly.

4. The draft administrative budget shall be placed before the Assembly not later than 5 October of the year preceding that in which the budget is to be implemented.

The Assembly shall have the right to amend the draft administrative budget, acting by a majority of its members, and to propose to the Council, acting by an absolute majority of the votes cast, modifications to the draft budget relating to expenditure necessarily resulting from this Treaty or from acts adopted in accordance therewith.

If, within forty-five days of the draft administrative budget being placed before it, the Assembly has given its approval, the administrative budget shall stand as finally adopted. If within this period the Assembly has not amended the draft administrative budget nor proposed any modifications thereto, the administrative budget shall be deemed to be finally adopted.

If within this period the Assembly has adopted amendments or proposed modifications, the draft administrative budget together with the amendments or proposed modifications shall be forwarded to the Council.

5. After discussing the draft administrative budget with the High Authority and, where appropriate, with the other institutions concerned, the Council may, acting by a qualified majority, modify any of the amendments adopted by the Assembly and shall pronounce, also by a qualified majority, on the modifications proposed by the latter. The draft administrative budget shall be modified on the basis of the proposed modifications accepted by the Council.

If, within fifteen days of the draft administrative budget being placed before it, the Council has not modified any of the amendments adopted by the Assembly and has accepted the modifications proposed by the latter, the administrative budget shall be deemed to be finally adopted. The Council shall inform the Assembly that is has not modified any of the amendments and has accepted the proposed modifications.

If within this period the Council has modified one or more of the amendments adopted by the Assembly or has not accepted the modifications proposed by the latter, the draft administrative budget shall again be forwarded to the Assembly. The Council shall inform the Assembly of the results of its deliberations.

6. Within fifteen days of the draft administrative budget being placed before it, the Assembly, which shall have been notified of the action taken on its proposed modifications, shall act, by a majority of its members and three fifths of the votes cast, on the modifications to its amendments made by the Council, and shall adopt the administrative budget accordingly. If within this period the Assembly has not acted, the administrative budget shall be deemed to be finally adopted.

7. When the procedure provided for in this Article has been completed, the President of the Assembly shall declare that the administrative budget has been finally adopted.

8. A maximum rate of increase in relation to the expenditure of the same

type to be incurred during the current year shall be fixed annually for the total expenditure other than that necessarily resulting from this Treaty or from acts adopted in accordance therewith.

The High Authority shall, after consulting the Conjunctural Policy Committee and the Budgetary Policy Committee, declare what this maximum rate is as it results from:
- the trend, in terms of volume, of the gross national product within the Community;
- the average variation in the budgets of the Member States; and
- the trend of the cost of living during the preceding financial year.

The maximum rate shall be communicated, before 1 May, to all the institutions of the Community. The latter shall be required to conform to this during the budgetary procedure, subject to the provisions of the fourth and fifth subparagraphs of this paragraph.

If, in respect of expenditure other than that necessarily resulting from this Treaty or from acts adopted in accordance therewith, the actual rate of increase in the draft administrative budget established by the Council is over half of the maximum rate, the Assembly may, exercising its right of amendment, further increase the total amount of that expenditure to a limit not exceeding half the maximum rate.

Where, in exceptional cases, the Assembly, the Council or the High Authority considers that the activities of the Communities require that the rate determined according to the procedure laid down in this paragraph should be exceeded, another rate may be fixed by agreement between the Council, acting by a qualified majority, and the Assembly, acting by a majority of its members and three fifths of the votes cast.

9. Each institution shall exercise the powers conferred upon it by this Article, with due regard for the provisions of this Treaty and for acts adopted in accordance therewith, in particular those relating to the Communities' own resources and to the balance between revenue and expenditure.

10. Final adoption of the administrative budget shall have the effect of authorising and requiring the High Authority to collect the corresponding revenue in accordance with the provisions of Article 49.

Article 2

The following provisions shall be added to the Treaty establishing the European Coal and Steel Community:

Article 78a

By way of derogation from the provisions of Article 78, the following provisions shall apply to budgets for financial years preceding the financial year 1975:
1. The financial year shall run from 1 January to 31 December.

The administrative expenditure of the Community shall comprise the expendi
of the High Authority, including that relating to the functioning of the Consulta
Committee, and that of the Court, the Assembly and the Council.

2. Each institution of the Community shall before 1 July, draw up estimates
of its administrative expenditure. The High Authority shall consolidate these
estimates in a preliminary draft administrative budget. It shall attach thereto an
opinion which may contain different estimates.

The preliminary draft budget shall contain an estimate of revenue and an
estimate of expenditure.

3. The High Authority shall place the preliminary draft administrative budget
before the Council not later than 1 September of the year preceding that in whic
the budget is to be implemented.

The Council shall consult the High Authority and, where appropriate, the
other institutions concerned whenever it intends to depart from the preliminary
draft budget.

The Council shall, acting by a qualified majority, establish the draft administrative budget and forward it to the Assembly.

4. The draft administrative budget shall be placed before the Assembly not
later than 5 October of the year preceding that in which the budget is to be
implemented.

The Assembly shall have the right to propose to the Council modifications
to the draft administrative budget.

If, within forty-five days of the draft administrative budget being placed befor
it, the Assembly has given its approval or has not proposed any modifications to
the draft budget, the administrative budget shall be deemed to be finally adopted

If within this period the Assembly has proposed modifications, the draft
administrative budget together with the proposed modifications shall be forwarde
to the Council.

5. The Council shall, after discussing the draft administrative budget with
the High Authority and, where appropriate, with the other institutions concerned
adopt the administrative budget, within thirty days of the draft budget being
placed before it, under the following conditions.

Where a modification proposed by the Assembly does not have the effect of
increasing the total amount of the expenditure of an institution, owing in particular to the fact that the increase in expenditure which it would involve would
be expressly compensated by one or more proposed modifications corresponding
reducing expenditure, the Council may, acting by a qualified majority, reject the
proposed modification. In the absence of a decision to reject it, the proposed
modification shall stand as accepted.

Where a modification proposed by the Assembly has the effect of increasing
the total amount of the expenditure of an institution, the Council must act by
a qualified majority in accepting the proposed modification.

Where, in pursuance of the second or third subparagraph of this paragraph,
the Council has rejected or has not accepted a proposed modification, it may,

acting by a qualified majority, either retain the amount shown in the draft administrative budget or fix another amount.

6. When the procedure provided for in this Article has been completed, the President of the Council shall declare that the administrative budget has been finally adopted.

7. Each institution shall exercise the powers conferred upon it by this Article, wth due regard for the provisions of this Treaty and for acts adopted in accordance therewith, in particular those relating to the Communities' own resources and to the balance between revenue and expenditure.

8. Final adoption of the administrative budget shall have the effect of authorising and requiring the High Authority to collect the corresponding revenue in accordance with the provisions of Article 49.

Article 3

The following provisions shall be substituted for the last paragraph of Article 78d of the Treaty establishing the European Coal and Steel Community:

The Council and the Assembly shall give a discharge to the High Authority in respect of the implementation of the administrative budget. To this end, the report of the Audit Board shall be examined in turn by the Council, which shall act by a qualified majority, and by the Assembly. The High Authority shall stand discharged only after the Council and the Assembly have acted.

CHAPTER II – PROVISIONS AMENDING THE TREATY ESTABLISHING THE EUROPEAN ECONOMIC COMMUNITY

Article 4

The following provisions shall be substituted for Article 203 of the Treaty establishing the European Economic Community:

Article 203

1. The financial year shall run from 1 January to 31 December.

2. Each institution of the Community shall, before 1 July, draw up estimates of its expenditure. The Commission shall consolidate these estimates in a preliminary draft budget. It shall attach thereto an opinion which may contain different estimates.

The preliminary draft budget shall contain an estimate of revenue and an estimate of expenditure.

3. The Commission shall place the preliminary draft budget before the Council not later than 1 September of the year preceding that in which the budget is to be implemented.

The Council shall consult the Commission and, where appropriate, the other institutions concerned whenever it intends to depart from the preliminary draft budget.

The Council shall, acting by a qualified majority, establish the draft budget and forward it to the Assembly.

4. The draft budget shall be placed before the Assembly not later than 5 October of the year preceding that in which the budget is to be implemented.

The Assembly shall have the right to amend the draft budget, acting by a majority of its members, and to propose to the Council, acting by an absolute majority of the votes cast, modifications to the draft budget relating to expenditⱤ necessarily resulting from this Treaty or from acts adopted in accordance therewith.

If, within forty-five days of the draft budget being placed before it, the Assembly has given its approval, the budget shall stand as finally adopted. If within this period the Assembly has not amended the draft budget nor proposed any modifications thereto, the budget shall be deemed to be finally adopted.

If within this period the Assembly has adopted amendments or proposed modifications, the draft budget together with the amendments or proposed modifications shall be forwarded to the Council.

5. After discussing the draft budget with the Commission and, where appropriate, with the other institutions concerned, the Council may, acting by a qualified majority, modify any of the amendments adopted by the Assembly and shall pronounce, also by a qualified majority, on the modifications proposed by the latter. The draft budget shall be modified on the basis of the proposed modifications accepted by the Council.

If, within fifteen days of the draft budget being placed before it, the Council has not modified any of the amendments adopted by the Assembly and has accepted the modifications proposed by the latter, the budget shall be deemed to be finally adopted. The Council shall inform the Assembly that it has not modified any of the amendments and has accepted the proposed modifications.

If within this period the Council has modified one or more of the amendments adopted by the Assembly or has not accepted the modifications proposed by the latter, the draft budget shall again be forwarded to the Assembly. The Council shall inform the Assembly of the results of its deliberations.

6. Within fifteen days of the draft budget being placed before it, the Assembly which shall have been notified of the action taken on its proposed modifications, shall act, by a majority of its members and three fifths of the votes cast, on the modifications to its amendments made by the Council and shall adopt the budget accordingly. If within this period the Assembly has not acted, the budget shall be deemed to be finally adopted.

7. When the procedure provided for in this Article has been completed, the President of the Assembly shall declare that the budget has been finally adopted.

8. A maximum rate of increase in relation to the expenditure of the same type to be incurred during the current year shall be fixed annually for the total

expenditure other than that necessarily resulting from this Treaty or from acts adopted in accordance therewith.

The Commission shall, after consulting the Conjunctural Policy Committee and the Budgetary Policy Committee, declare what this maximum rate is as it results from:

- the trend in terms of volume, of the gross national product within the Community;
- the average variation in the budgets of the Member States; and
- the trend of the cost of living during the preceding financial year.

The maximum rate shall be communicated, before 1 May, to all the institutions of the Community. The latter shall be required to conform to this during the budgetary procedure, subject to the provisions of the fourth and fifth sub-paragraphs of this paragraph.

If, in respect of expenditure other than that necessarily resulting from this Treaty or from acts adopted in accordance therewith, the actual rate of increase in the draft budget established by the Council is over half of the maximum rate, the Assembly may, exercising its right of amendment, further increase the total amount of that expenditure to a limit not exceeding half of the maximum rate.

Where, in exceptional cases, the Assembly, the Council or the Commission considers that the activities of the Communities require that the rate determined according to the procedure laid down in this paragraph should be exceeded, another rate may be fixed by agreement between the Council, acting by a qualified majority, and the Assembly, acting by a majority of its members and three fifths of the votes cast.

9. Each institution shall exercise the powers conferred upon it by this Article, with due regard for the provisions of this Treaty and for acts adopted in accordance therewith, in particular those relating to the Communities' own resources and to the balance between revenue and expenditure.

Article 5

The following provisions shall be added to the Treaty establishing the European Economic Community.

Article 203a

By way of derogation from the provisions of Article 203, the following provisions shall apply to budgets for financial years preceding the financial year 1975:

1. The financial year shall run from 1 January to 31 December.

2. Each institution of the Community shall, before 1 July, draw up estimates of its expenditure. The Commission shall consolidate these estimates in a preliminary draft budget. It shall attach thereto an opinion which may contain different estimates.

The preliminary draft budget shall contain an estimate of revenue and an estimate of expenditure.

3. The Commission shall place the preliminary draft budget before the Council not later than 1 September of the year preceding that in which the budget is to be implemented.

The Council shall consult the Commission and, where appropriate, the other institutions concerned whenever it intends to depart from the preliminary draft budget.

The Council shall, acting by a qualified majority, establish the draft budget and forward it to the Assembly.

4. The draft budget shall be placed before the Assembly not later than 5 October of the year preceding that in which the budget is to be implemented.

The Assembly shall have the right to propose to the Council modifications to the draft budget.

If, within forty-five days of the draft budget being placed before it, the Assembly has given its approval or has not proposed any modifications to the draft budget, the budget shall be deemed to be finally adopted.

If within this period the Assembly has proposed modifications, the draft budget together with the proposed modifications shall be forwarded to the Council.

5. The Council shall, after discussing the draft budget with the Commission and, where appropriate, with the other institutions concerned, adopt the budget, within thirty days of the draft budget being placed before it, under the following conditions.

Where a modification proposed by the Assembly does not have the effect of increasing the total amount of the expenditure of an institution, owing in particular to the fact that the increase in expenditure which it would involve would be expressly compensated by one or more proposed modifications correspondingly reducing expenditure, the Council may, acting by a qualified majority, reject the proposed modification. In the absence of a decision to reject it, the proposed modification shall stand as accepted.

Where a modification proposed by the Assembly has the effect of increasing the total amount of the expenditure of an institution, the Council must act by a qualified majority in accepting the proposed modification.

Where, in pursuance of the second or third subparagraph of this paragraph, the Council has rejected or has not accepted a proposed modification, it may, acting by a qualified majority, either retain the amount shown in the draft budget or fix another amount.

6. When the procedure provided for in this Article has been completed, the President of the Council shall declare that the budget has been finally adopted.

7. Each institution shall exercise the powers conferred upon it by this Article, with due regard for the provisions of this Treaty and for acts adopted in accordance therewith, in particular those relating to the Communities' own resources and to the balance between revenue and expenditure.

Article 6

The following provisions shall be substituted for the last paragraph of Article 206 of the Treaty establishing the European Economic Community:

The Council and the Assembly shall give a discharge to the Commission in respect of the implementation of the budget. To this end, the report of the Audit Board shall be examined in turn by the Council, which shall act by a qualified majority and by the Assembly. The Commission shall stand discharged only after the Council and the Assembly have acted.

CHAPTER III – PROVISIONS AMENDING THE TREATY ESTABLISHING THE EUROPEAN ATOMIC ENERGY COMMUNITY

Article 7

The following provisions shall be substituted for Article 177 of the Treaty establishing the European Atomic Energy Community:

Article 177

1. **The financial year shall run from 1 January to 31 December.**
   Within the meaning of this Article, 'budget' shall include the operating budget and the research and investment budget.

2. Each institution of the Community shall, before 1 July, draw up estimates of its expenditure. The Commission shall consolidate these estimates in a preliminary draft budget. It shall attach thereto an opinion which may contain different estimates.

   The preliminary draft budget shall contain an estimate of revenue and an estimate of expenditure.

3. The Commission shall place the preliminary draft budget before the Council not later than 1 September of the year preceding that in which the budget is to be implemented.

   The Council shall consult the Commission and, where appropriate, the other institutions concerned whenever it intends to depart from the preliminary draft budget.

   The Council shall, acting by a qualified majority, establish the draft budget and forward it to the Assembly.

4. The draft budget shall be placed before the Assembly not later than 5 October of the year preceding that in which the budget is to be implemented.

   The Assembly shall have the right to amend the draft budget, acting by a majority of its members, and to propose to the Council, acting by an absolute majority of the votes cast, modifications to the draft budget relating to expenditure necessarily resulting from this Treaty or from acts adopted in accordance therewith.

If, within forty-five days of the draft budget being placed before it, the Assembly has given its approval, the budget shall stand as finally adopted. If within this period the Assembly has not amended the draft budget nor proposed any modifications thereto, the budget shall be deemed to be finally adopted.

If within this period the Assembly has adopted amendments or proposed modifications, the draft budget together with the amendments or proposed modifications shall be forwarded to the Council.

5. After discussing the draft budget with the Commission and, where appropri with the other institutions concerned, the Council may, acting by a qualified majority, modify any of the amendments adopted by the Assembly and shall pronounce, also by a qualified majority, on the modifications proposed by the latter. The draft budget shall be modified on the basis of the proposed modifications accepted by the Council.

If, within fifteen days of the draft budget being placed before it, the Council has not modified any of the amendments adopted by the Assembly and has accepted the modifications proposed by the latter, the budget shall be deemed to be finally adopted. The Council shall inform the Assembly that it has not modifi any of the amendments and has accepted the proposed modifications.

If within this period the Council has modified one or more of the amendment adopted by the Assembly or has not accepted the modifications proposed by the latter, the draft budget shall again be forwarded to the Assembly. The Council shall inform the Assembly of the results of its deliberations.

6. Within fifteen days of the draft budget being placed before it, the Assembly which shall have been notified of the action taken on its proposed modifications, shall act, by a majority of its members and three-fifths of the votes cast, on the modifications to its amendments made by the Council, and shall adopt the budge accordingly. If within this period the Assembly has not acted, the budget shall be deemed to be finally adopted.

7. When the procedure provided for in this Article has been completed, the President of the Assembly shall declare that the budget has been finally adopted.

8. A maximum rate of increase in relation to the expenditure of the same type to be incurred during the current year shall be fixed annually for the total expenditure other than that necessarily resulting from the Treaty or from acts adopted in accordance therewith.

The Commission shall, after consulting the Conjunctural Policy Committee and the Budgetary Policy Committee, declare what this maximum rate is as it results from:
— the trend, in terms of volume, of the gross national product within the Community;
— the average variation in the budgets of the Member States; and
— the trend of the cost of living during the preceding financial year.

The maximum rate shall be communicated, before 1 May, to all the institution of the Community. The latter shall be required to conform to this during the

budgetary procedure, subject to the provisions of the fourth and fifth sub-
paragraphs of this paragraph.

If, in respect of expenditure other than that necessarily resulting from this
Treaty or from acts adopted in accordance therewith, the actual rate of increase
in the draft budget established by the Council is over half of the maximum rate,
the Assembly may, exercising its right of amendment, further increase the total
amount of that expenditure to a limit not exceeding half the maximum rate.

Where, in exceptional cases, the Assembly, the Council or the Commission
considers that the activities of the Communities require that the rate determined
according to the procedure laid down in this paragraph should be exceeded,
another rate may be fixed by agreement between the Council, acting by a qualified
majority, and the Assembly, acting by a majority of its members and three
fifths of the votes cast.

9. Each institution shall exercise the powers conferred upon it by this Article,
with due regard for the provisions of this Treaty and for acts adopted in accordance
therewith, in particular those relating to the Communities' own resources and
to the balance between revenue and expenditure.

Article 8

The following provisions shall be added to the Treaty establishing the European
Atomic Energy Community.

Article 177a

By way of derogation from the provisions of Article 177, the following provisions
shall apply to budgets for financial years preceding the financial year 1975:

1. The financial year shall run from 1 January to 31 December.

Within the meaning of this Article, 'budget' shall include the operating budget
and the research and investment budget.

2. Each institution of the Community shall, before 1 July, draw up estimates
of its expenditure. The Commission shall consolidate these estimates in a preliminary
draft budget. It shall attach thereto an opinion which may contain different
estimates.

The preliminary draft budget shall contain an estimate of revenue and an
estimate of expenditure.

3. The Commission shall place the preliminary draft budget before the Council
not later than 1 September of the year preceding that in which the budget is to
be implemented.

The Council shall consult the Commission and, where appropriate, the other
institutions concerned whenever it intends to depart from the preliminary draft
budget.

The Council shall, acting by a qualified majority, establish the draft budget and forward it to the Assembly.

4. The draft budget shall be placed before the Assembly not later than 5 October of the year preceding that in which the budget is to be implemented.

The Assembly shall have the right to propose to the Council modifications to the draft budget.

If, within forty-five days of the draft budget being placed before it, the Assembly has given its approval or has not proposed any modifications to the draft budget, the budget shall be deemed to be finally adopted.

If within this period the Assembly has proposed modifications, the draft budget together with the proposed modifications shall be forwarded to the Council.

5. The Council shall, after discussing the draft budget with the Commission and, where appropriate, with the other institutions concerned, adopt the budget within thirty days of the draft budget being placed before it, under the following conditions.

Where a modification proposed by the Assembly does not have the effect of increasing the total amount of the expenditure of an institution, owing in particular to the fact that the increase in expenditure which it would involve would be expressly compensated by one or more proposed modifications corresponding reducing expenditure, the Council may, acting by a qualified majority, reject the proposed modification. In the absence of a decision to reject it, the proposed modification shall stand as accepted.

Where a modification proposed by the Assembly has the effect of increasing the total amount of the expenditure of an institution, the Council must act by a qualified majority in accepting the proposed modification.

Where, in pursuance of the second or third subparagraph of this paragraph, the Council has rejected or has not accepted a proposed modification, it may, acting by a qualified majority, either retain the amount shown in the draft budget or fix another amount.

6. When the procedure provided for in this Article has been completed the President of the Council shall declare that the budget has been finally adopted.

7. Each institution shall exercise the powers conferred upon it by this Article with due regard for the provisions of this Treaty and for acts adopted in accorda therewith, in particular those relating to the Communities' own resources and to the balance between revenue and expenditure.

Article 9

The following provisions shall be substituted for the last paragraph of Article 180 of the Treaty establishing the European Atomic Energy Community:

The Council and the Assembly shall give a discharge to the Commission in respec of the implementation of each budget. To this end, the report of the Audit Board shall be examined in turn by the Council, which shall act by a qualified majority, and by the Assembly. The Commission shall stand discharged only after the Council and the Assembly have acted.

CHAPTER IV – PROVISIONS AMENDING THE TREATY ESTABLISHING A SINGLE COUNCIL AND A SINGLE COMMISSION OF THE EUROPEAN COMMUNITIES

Article 10

The following provisions shall be substituted for Article 20(1) of the Treaty establishing a single Council and a single Commission of the European Communities:
1. The administrative expenditure of the European Coal and Steel Community and the revenue relating thereto, the revenue and expenditure of the European Economic Community, and the revenue and expenditure of the European Atomic Energy Community, with the exception of that of the Supply Agency and the Joint Undertakings, shall be shown in the budget of the European Communities in accordance with the appropriate provisions of the Treaties establishing the three Communities. This budget, which shall be in balance as to revenue and expenditure, shall take the place of the administrative budget of the European Coal and Steel Community, the budget of the European Economic Community and the operating budget and research and investment budget of the European Atomic Energy Community.

CHAPTER V – FINAL PROVISIONS

Article 11

This Treaty shall be ratified by the High Contracting Parties in accordance with their respective constitutional requirements. The instruments of ratification shall be deposited with the Government of the Italian Republic.

Article 12

This Treaty shall enter into force[1] on the first day of the month following the deposit of the instrument of ratification by the last signatory State to take this step.

If, however, the notification provided for in Article 7 of the Decision of 21 April 1970 on the replacement of financial contributions from Member States by the Communities' own resources has not been given before that date by all the signatory States, this Treaty shall enter into force on the first day of the month after the last notification has been given.

If this Treaty enters into force during the budgetary procedure, the Council shall, after consulting the Commission, lay down the measures required in order

1 The Treaty entered into force on 1 January 1971.

to facilitate the application of this Treaty to the remainder of the budgetary procedure.

Article 13

This Treaty, drawn up in a single original in the Dutch, French, German and Italian languages, all four texts being equally authentic, shall be deposited in the archives of the Government of the Italian Republic, which shall transmit a certified copy to each of the Governments of the other signatory States.

132. Report on European Political Unification, the 'Davignon Report', adopted by the Ministers of Foreign Affairs of the Member States of the EEC, 27 October 1970[1]

FIRST PART

1. The Ministers of Foreign Affairs of the Member States of the European Communi were instructed by the Chiefs of State and of Government who met at the Hague on December 1 and 2, 1969, 'to study the best way to bring about progress in the area of political unification, in the perspective of the enlargement' of the European Communities.

2. In carrying out this mandate, the Ministers took care to remain faithful to the spirit which covered the drafting of the Hague Communiqué. The Chiefs of State and Government in particular noted that the construction of Europe has arrived, with the beginning of the definitive phase of the Common Market, 'at a turning point in its history'; they affirmed that 'the European Communities remain the original basis on which European unity was developed and from which it has arisen' finally, they expressed their determination to 'prepare the way of a united Europe capable of assuming its responsibilities in the world of tomorrow, and of making a contribution which corresponds to its tradition and its mission'.

3. The Chiefs of State and Government were determined to express 'the commo conviction that a Europe – which groups together States which, in their national diversity, are united in their essential interests, assured of their own cohesion, faithful to their external friendships, aware of the role which they have to play to facilitate international detente and the rapprochement of all peoples and, above all, of those of the entire European continent – is indispensable for the preservation of an exceptional centre of development, of progress and of culture, for the stability of the world, and for the protection of peace'.

4. United Europe, aware of the responsibilities which it has by reason of its econ omic development, its industrial power and its standard of living, intends to increas

1 *Europe, Documents*, No. 593, 14 September 1970. The text of this report was released to the press on 21 July 1970.

s efforts with regard to developing countries in an effort to establish relations of onfidence among peoples.

5. United Europe must be founded on a common patrimony of respect for liberty nd for the rights of man, and must bring together democratic states endowed with freely-elected parliament. This united Europe remains the fundamental goal which 1ust be attained as soon as possible, thanks to the political will of the people and 1e decision of their governments.

6. The Ministers therefore considered that, in order to respect continuity and to e consistent with the political finality of the European design, as the Conference of 1e Hague so strongly emphasized, their proposals should be based on three premises.

7. The first is that it is desirable, in the spirit of the preambles of the Treaties f Paris and Rome, to give form to the desire for political union which has never eased to underlie the progress of the European Communities.

8. The second is that, as common policies — both those already established and 1ose that are being proposed — are put into effect, corresponding developments 1ould take place in the purely political domain, in order to bring nearer the moment hen Europe can express itself with a single voice. This is why it is important that 1e construction of Europe should be pursued in successive steps, and that the most ppropriate method and instruments for allowing common political action should evelop in a gradual manner.

9. The last, finally, is that Europe must prepare itself to carry out the responsi-1lities which, because of its greater cohesion and its growing role, it has the duty and ecessity to assume in the world.

10. The present developments in the European Communities impose on the member ates the need to increase their political cooperation and in a first stage, to give 1emselves the means to harmonize their points of view with regard to international olitics.

It thus appeared to the Ministers that it is in the area of the concertation of foreign olicy that it would be best to make the first concrete efforts to make clear to all 1at Europe has a political vocation. In effect, the Ministers are convinced that rogress in this area would benefit the development of the Communities and would ve to Europeans a more active awareness of their common responsibility.

ECOND PART

he Ministers propose the following:

Desirous of making progress in the area of political unification, the governments 2cide to cooperate on foreign policy matters.

Goals

he goals of this cooperation are the following:

— to assure, by information and regular consultation, better mutual comprehension on the major problems of international politics;

— to strengthen solidarity by promoting the harmonization of points of view, the concerting of attitudes and, when it seems possible and desirable, common actions.

II. Ministerial Meetings

1. On the initiative of the president pro tempore, the Ministers of Foreign Affairs shall meet at least every six months.
  — If they consider that the gravity of the circumstances or the importance of the subjects to be treated so justify, their meeting can be replaced by a conference of chiefs of state or of government.
  — In case of grave crisis or particular urgency, a special consultation will be organized by the governments of the member states. The president pro tempore will contact his colleagues to ensure this consultation.
2. The Minister of Foreign Affairs of the state which has the presidency of the Council of the European Communities will preside over the meetings.
3. The ministerial meetings shall be prepared by a committee made up of the Directors for Political Affairs.

III. Political Committee

1. A Committee made up of the Directors for Political Affairs shall meet at least four times per year in order to prepare the ministerial meetings and to carry out tasks which will be assigned to it by the Ministers.

Besides, the president pro tempore can, on an exceptional basis and after consulting his colleagues, convoke the Committee, either on his own initiative or at the request of one of the members.
2. The presidency of the Committee follows the same rules as those of the minis meetings.
3. The Committee can create working groups charged with particular tasks.

It can instruct a group of experts to assemble the facts relating to a given proble and to present the different possible options.
4. All other forms of consultation can be envisaged as the need arises.

IV. Subjects for Consultation

The governments shall consult on all important questions of foreign policy.

The member states will be able to propose any subjects they choose for political consultation.

V. The Commission of the European Communities

In cases where the work of the Ministers would have an effect on the activities of the European Communities, the Commission would be invited to make known its opinion.

VI. European Parliamentary Assembly

In order to give a democratic character to the building of political union, it is necessary to associate public opinion and its representatives with it.

A semi-yearly meeting will bring together the Ministers and the members of the Political Committee of the European Parliamentary Assembly in order to discuss the questions which will be the subject of the consultations in the framework of cooperation on foreign policy matters. This meeting will be held in an informal manner in order to permit the parliamentarians and ministers to express their opinions freely.

VII. General Provisions

1. Meetings will normally be held in the state whose representative is president pro tempore of the meeting.

2. The host government will make the necessary arrangements for the secretariat and the administrative details of the meetings.

3. Each state will designate within its Ministry of Foreign Affairs an official who will correspond with his counterparts in the other states.

THIRD PART

1. In order to ensure the continuity of the task undertaken, the Ministers plan to pursue their work on the best way to bring about progress in the area of political unification and to present a second report.

2. This work will involve both the improvement of cooperation on foreign policy matters and the search for new areas in which progress could be realized. They should take account of what will be undertaken in the framework of the European Communities, notably with a view to strengthening its structure, enabling the Communities, if it seems necessary, to respond in a satisfactory way to the growth and development of their tasks.

3. For this purpose, the Ministers instruct the Political Committee to organize its work in such a way as to accomplish this task and to submit status reports to them on the occasion of each of their semi-yearly meetings.

4. Once a year the President of the Council will make a report to the European Parliamentary Assembly on the evolution of this work.

5. Without prejudice to any interim report which they might consider it useful to make if the studies permit, the Ministers of Foreign Affairs will submit their second general report within two years of the establishment of consultation on foreign policy matters. This report should contain an evaluation of the results achieved by this consultation.

FOURTH PART

Proposals concerning the association of the candidate states with the work envisaged in parts II and III of this report.

1. The Ministers stress the correlation which exists between membership in the European Communities and participation in activities which should bring about progress in the area of political unification.

2. Given the fact that the candidate states should be consulted on the objectives and mechanisms described in this report and that they should take part in them when they become members of the European Communities, it is necessary to keep these states informed of the evolution of the work of the Six.

3. With these different objectives in view, the following procedures are proposed to ensure that the candidate states are informed:

(a) Ministerial Meetings

The Ministers will set at each of their semi-yearly meetings the date of their next meeting.

They will agree at the same time on a date to propose for a ministerial meeting of the Ten. This date ought to be set at a time as close as possible to the meeting of the Six, and normally after that meeting, taking account of occasions when the ten Ministers or certain of them already intend to meet.

After the ministerial meeting of the Six the president will inform the candidate states of the question which the Ministers intend to include on the agenda of the ministerial meeting of the Ten, and any other information likely to make the exchange of views of the Ten as fruitful as possible.

Taking account of the fact that this information and these exchanges of view should be characterized by a certain flexibility, it is understood that they will be made deeper when the agreements for the entry of the candidate states into the European Communities have been signed.

(b) Meetings of the Political Committee

This Committee will communicate to the candidate states the information that is likely to interest them. This information will be transmitted by the president pro tempore who will obtain their possible reactions. The president will inform the Political Committee of these reactions.

133. Treaty between the Kingdom of Belgium, the Federal Republic of Germany, the French Republic, the Italian Republic, the Grand Duchy of Luxembourg, the Kingdom of the Netherlands, Member States of the European Communities, the Kingdom of Denmark, Ireland, the Kingdom of Norway, and the United Kingdom of Great Britain and Northern Ireland concerning the accession of the Kingdom of Denmark, Ireland, the Kingdom of Norway and the United Kingdom of Great Britain and Northern Ireland to the European Economic Community and the European Atomic Energy Community, Burssels, 22 January 1972[1] (extract)

His Majesty the King of the Belgians, Her Majesty the Queen of Denmark, the
1 Cmnd. 4862–I.

President of the Federal Republic of Germany, the President of the French Republic, the President of Ireland, the President of the Italian Republic. His Royal Highness the Grand Duke of Luxembourg, Her Majesty the Queen of the Netherlands, His Majesty the King of Norway, Her Majesty the Queen of the United Kingdom of Great Britain and Northern Ireland
  United in their desire to pursue the attainment of the objectives of the Treaty establishing the European Economic Community and the Treaty establishing the European Atomic Energy Community,
  Determined in the spirit of those Treaties to construct an ever closer union among the peoples of Europe on the foundations already laid,
  Considering that Article 237 of the Treaty establishing the European Economic Community and Article 205 of the Treaty establishing the European Atomic Energy Community afford European States the opportunity of becoming members of these Communities,
  Considering that the Kingdom of Denmark, Ireland, the Kingdom of Norway and the United Kingdom of Great Britain and Northern Ireland have applied to become members of these Communities,
  Considering that the Council of the European Communities, after having obtained the Opinion of the Commission, has declared itself in favour of the admission of these States,
  Have decided to establish by common agreement the conditions of admission and the adjustments to be made to the Treaties establishing the European Economic Community and the European Atomic Energy Community and to this end have designated as their Plenipotentiaries: . . .[1]

Article I

1. The Kingdom of Denmark, Ireland, the Kingdom of Norway and the United Kingdom of Great Britain and Northern Ireland hereby become members of the European Economic Community and of the European Atomic Energy Community and Parties to the Treaties establishing these Communities as amended or supplemented.
  2. The conditions of admission and the adjustments to the Treaties establishing the European Economic Community and the European Atomic Energy Community necessitated thereby are set out in the Act annexed to this Treaty. The provisions of that Act concerning the European Economic Community and the European Atomic Energy Community shall form an integral part of this Treaty.
  3. The provisions concerning the rights and obligations of the Member States and the powers and jurisdiction of the institutions of the Communities as set out in the Treaties referred to in paragraph 1 shall apply in respect of this Treaty.

Article II

This Treaty will be ratified by the High Contracting Parties in accordance with their respective constitutional requirements. The instruments of ratification will be deposited with the Government of the Italian Republic by 31 December 1972 at the latest.

  1 There follows a list of plenipotentiaries.

This Treaty will enter into force on 1 January 1973, provided that all the instruments of ratification have been deposited before that date and that all the instrument of accession to the European Coal and Steel Community are deposited on that date.

If, however, the States, referred to in Article 1 (1) have not all deposited their instruments of ratification and accession in due time, the Treaty shall enter into force for those States which have deposited their instruments.[1] In this case, the Council of the European Communities, acting unanimously, shall decide immediatel upon such resulting adjustments as have become indispensable, to Article 3 of this Treaty, and to Articles 14, 16, 17, 19, 20, 23, 129, 142, 143, 155 and 160 of the Act concerning the Conditions of Accession and the Adjustments to the Treaties, to the provisions of Annex I to that Act concerning the composition and functionin of various committees, and to Articles 5 and 8 of the Protocol on the Statute of the European Investment Bank: acting unanimously, it may also declare that those provisions of the aforementioned Act which refer expressly to a State which has not deposited its instruments of ratification and accession have lapsed, or it may adjust them.

Article III

This Treaty, drawn up in a single original in the Danish, Dutch, English, French, German, Irish, Italian and Norwegian languages, all eight texts being equally authent will be deposited in the archives of the Government of the Italian Republic, which will transmit a certified copy to each of the Governments of the other signatory States.

In witness whereof, the undersigned Plenipotentiaries have affixed their signature below this Treaty.

Done at Brussels on this twenty-second day of January in the year one thousand nine hundred and seventy-two.

ACT CONCERNING THE CONDITIONS OF ACCESSIONS AND THE ADJUSTMENTS TO THE TREATIES
Part One — Principles

Article I

For the purposes of this Act:
the expression 'original Treaties' means the Treaty establishing the European Coal and Steel Community, the Treaty establishing the European Economic Community and the Treaty establishing the European Atomic Energy Community, as supplemented or amended by treaties or other acts which entered into force before accession; the expressions 'ECSC Treaty', 'EEC Treaty' and 'Euratom Treaty' mean the relevant original Treaties thus supplemented or amended:

1 Norway withdrew from the Treaty after the Norwegian people had rejected accession in a referendum on 26 September 1972.

the expression 'original Member States' means the Kingdom of Belgium, the Federal Republic of Germany, the French Republic, the Italian Republic, the Grand Duchy of Luxembourg and the Kingdom of the Netherlands;
the expression 'new Member States' means the Kingdom of Denmark, Ireland, the Kingdom of Norway and the United Kingdom of Great Britain and Northern Ireland,

Article II

From the date of accession, the provisions of the original Treaties and the acts adopted by the institutions of the Communities shall be binding on the new Member States and shall apply in those States under the conditions laid down in those Treaties and in this Act.

Article III

1. The new Member States accede by this Act to the decisions and agreements adopted by the Representatives of the Governments of the Member States meeting in Council. They undertake to accede from the date of accession to all other agreements concluded by the original Member States relating to the functioning of the Communities or connected with their activities.

2. The new Member States undertake to accede to the conventions provided for in Article 220 of the EEC Treaty, and to the protocols on the interpretation of those conventions by the Court of Justice, signed by the original Member States, and to this end they undertake to enter into negotiations with the original Member States in order to make the necessary adjustments thereto.

3. The new Member States are in the same situation as the original Member States in respect of declarations or resolutions of, or other positions taken up by, the Council and in respect of those concerning the European Communities adopted by common agreement of the Member States; they will accordingly observe the principles and guidelines deriving from those declarations, resolutions or other positions and will take such measures as may be necessary to ensure their implementation.

Article IV

1. The agreements or conventions entered into by any of the Communities with one or more third States, with an international organization or with a national of a third State, shall, under the conditions laid down in the original Treaties and in this Act, be binding on the new Member States.

2. The new Member States undertake to accede, under the conditions laid down in this Act, to agreements or conventions concluded by the original Member States and any of the Communities, acting jointly, and to agreements concluded by the original Member States which are related to those agreements or conventions. The Community and the original Member States shall assist the new Member States in this respect.

3. The new Member States accede by this Act and under the conditions laid down therein to the internal agreements concluded by the original Member States for the purpose of implementing the agreements or conventions referred to in paragraph 2.

4. The new Member States shall take appropriate measures, where necessary, to adjust their positions in relation to international organisations and international agreements to which one of the Communities or to which other Member States are also parties, to the rights and obligations arising from their accession to the Communities.

Article V

Article 234 of the EEC Treaty and Articles 105 and 106 of the Euratom Treaty shall apply, for the new Member States, to agreements or conventions concluded before accession.

Article VI

The provisions of this Act may not, unless otherwise provided herein, be suspended, amended or repealed other than by means of the procedure laid down in the original Treaties enabling those Treaties to be revised.

Article VII

Acts adopted by the institutions of the Communities to which the transitional provisions laid down in this Act relate shall retain their status in law: in particular, the procedures for amending those acts shall continue to apply.

Article VIII

Provisions of this Act the purpose or effect of which is to repeal or amend acts adopted by the institutions of the Communities, otherwise than as a transitional measure, shall have the same status in law as the provisions which they repeal or amend and shall be subject to the same rules as those provisions.

Article IX

1. In order to facilitate the adjustment of the new Member States to the rules in force within the Communities, the application of the original Treaties and acts adopted by the institutions shall, as a transitional measure, be subject to the derogations provided for in this Act.

2. Subject to the dates, time limits and special provisions provided for in this act, the application of the transitional measures shall terminate at the end of 1977.

Part Two — Adjustments to the Treaties[1]

34. Decision of Principle on the Economic and Monetary Union, adopted by the Ministers of Finance of the enlarged Community, Rome, 12 September 1972[2]

The Ministers of Finance and of Economic Affairs have decided to create, in the first phase of the economic and monetary union, a European monetary cooperation fund, whose administration will be carried out by the Committee of Central Bank Governors in the framework of the general economic policy guidelines decided on by the Council of Ministers, and which will have the following characteristics in the initial phase:

1. concentration between the central banks on the needs of the narrowing of the fluctuation margins of the Community currencies;

2. multilateralisation of the positions resulting from the financing in Community currencies and multilateralisation of intra-Community settlements;

3. use of a European unit of account for the settlements mentioned at the previous point;

4. management of the short-term monetary support between the central banks.

To meet with the new needs, the very short-term financing of the agreement on the narrowing of margins and the short-term monetary support will be grouped together in the fund by means of renovated machinery. For this purpose, the short-term support will be adapted at technical level, without changing its main characteristics and particularly the consultation procedures which it involves. The Ministers are calling upon the Governors to study the conditions for the gradual pooling of reserves during the further phases of the economic and monetary union, taking the suggestions of the Italian Government into account.

35. Final Declaration of the Paris summit conference, 21 October 1972,[3] with Annex

The Heads of State or of Government of the countries of the enlarged Community, meeting for the first time on 19 and 20 October 1972 in Paris, at the invitation of the President of the French Republic, solemnly declare:

— at the moment when enlargement, decided upon in accordance with the rules laid down in the Treaties and with due respect for what the six original

1 The remainder of the treaty consists of a series of detailed amendments to the texts of the original treaties.
2 *Europe, Bulletins*, 13 September 1972.
3 Ambassade de France, Service de Presse et d'Information.

member States have already achieved, is to become a reality and to give a
new dimension to the Community;
— at a time when world events are profoundly changing the international situation;
— now that there is a general desire for detente and cooperation in response to
the underlying interests and wishes of all peoples;
— now that serious monetary and trade problems require a search for lasting
solutions that will favour growth with stability;
— now that many developing countries see the gap widening between themselves and the industrial nations and are justifiably demanding more aid and a
fairer use of wealth;
— now that the tasks of the Community are growing, and fresh responsibilities
are being laid upon it, the time has come for Europe to recognize clearly the
unity of its interests, the extent of its capacities and the magnitude of its
duties; Europe must be able to make its voice heard in world affairs, and to
make an original contribution commensurate with its human, intellectual and
material resources. It must assert its own views in international relations, as
befits its outward-looking mission for progress, peace and cooperation.

To this end:

(i) The member States reaffirm their determination to base the development of
their Community on democracy, freedom of opinion, the free movement of people
and of ideas, and participation by their peoples through their freely-elected represer
tatives;

(ii) The member States are determined to strengthen the Community by establishing an economic and monetary union, the guarantee of stability and growth,
the foundation of their solidarity and the indispensable basis for social progress,
and by ending disparities between the regions;

(iii) Economic expansion is not an end in itself. Its first aim should be to reduce
disparities in living conditions. It must take place with the participation of all the
social partners. It should result in an improvement in the quality of life as well as
in standards of living. As befits the genius of Europe, particular attention will
be given to non-material values and to protecting the environment, so that progress
may really serve mankind:

(iv) The Community, fully aware of the problem presented by continuing underdevelopment in the world, affirms its determination, within the framework of a
world-wide policy towards the developing countries, to increase its effort of aid and
technical assistance to the least privileged peoples. It will take particular account
of the concerns of those countries towards which, in view of geographical and
historical reasons and of the commitments entered into by the Community, it has
specific responsibilities;

(v) The Community reaffirms its determination to encourage the development of
international trade. This determination applies to all countries without exception.

The Community is ready to participate as soon as possible in the open-minded
spirit that it has already shown, and according to the procedures laid down by the

MF and the GATT, in negotiations based on the principle of reciprocity. These
1ould make it possible to establish, in the monetary and commercial fields, stable
nd balanced economic relations in which the interests of the developing countries
1ust be taken fully into account;

(vi) The member States of the Community, in the interests of the good-neighbourly
elations which should exist among all European countries whatever their regime,
ffirm their determination, notably on the occasion of the Conference on Security
nd Cooperation in Europe, to pursue their policy of detente and peace with the
ountries of Eastern Europe and to establish with them wider economic and human
ooperation on lasting bases;

(vii) The construction of Europe will allow it, in conformity with its ultimate
olitical objectives, to assert its personality while remaining true to its traditional
riendships and to the alliances of the member States, and to establish its position
1 world affairs as a distinct entity determined to promote a better international
quilibrium, while respecting the principles of the United Nations Charter. The
1ember States of the Community, the driving force of European construction, affirm
heir intention to transform the whole complex of their relations into a European
Jnion before the end of the present decade.

Economic and monetary questions

. The Heads of State or of Government reaffirm the determination of the member
States of the enlarged European Communities irreversibly to achieve Economic and
Monetary Union, confirming all the elements of the instruments adopted by the
Council and by the representatives of member States on 22 March 1971 and 21 March
972.

The necessary decisions should be taken in the course of 1973 so as to allow the
ransition to the second stage of Economic and Monetary Union on 1 January 1974,
nd with a view to its completion not later than 31 December 1980.

The Heads of State or of Government reaffirmed the principle of parallel progress
n the different fields of Economic and Monetary Union.

2. They declared that fixed but adjustable parities between their currencies
onstitute an essential basis for the achievement of the Union and expressed their
1etermination to set up within the Community mechanisms for [currency] defence
nd mutual support which would enable member States to ensure that they are
espected.

They decided to institute before 1 April 1973 by a solemn instrument based on
he EEC Treaty, a European Monetary Cooperation Fund which will be administered
1y the Committee of Governors of Central Banks within the context of general
guidelines on economic policy laid down by the Council of Ministers. In an initial
1hase the Fund will operate on the following bases:

— concerted action among the Central Banks for the measures required to narrow
fluctuation margins between their currencies;

– the multilateralization of positions resulting from interventions in Community currencies and the multilateralization of intra-Community settlements;
– the use for this purpose of a European monetary unit of account;
– the administration of short-term monetary support among the Central Banks;
– the very short-term financing of the agreement on the narrowing of margins and short-term monetary support will be regrouped in the Fund under a renovated mechanism; to this end, short-term support will be adjusted on the technical plane without modifying its essential characteristics and in particular without modifying the consultation procedures they involve.

The competent bodies of the Community shall submit reports:
– not later than 30 September 1973 on the adjustment of short-term support;
– not later than 31 December 1973 on the conditions for the progressive pooling of reserves.

3. The Heads of State or of Government stressed the need to coordinate more closely the economic policies of the Community and for this purpose to introduce more effective Community procedures.

Under existing economic conditions they consider that priority should be given to the fight against inflation and to a return to price stability. They instructed their competent Ministers to adopt, on the occasion of the enlarged Council of 30 and 31 October 1972, precise measures in the various fields which lend themselves to effective and realistic short-term action towards those objectives, taking account of the respective situations of the countries of the enlarged Community.

4. The Heads of State or of Government express their determination that the member States of the enlarged Community should contribute by a common attitude to directing the reform of the international monetary system towards the establishment of a fair and lasting order.

They consider that this system should be based on the following principles:
– fixed but adjustable parities,
– the general convertibility of currencies,
– effective international regulation of the world supply of liquidity,
– a reduction of the role of national currencies as reserve instruments,
– the effective and equitable operation of the adjustment process,
– equal rights and duties for all participants in the system,
– the need to lessen the unstabilizing effects of short-term capital movements,
– the taking into account of the interests of the developing countries.

Such a system would be fully compatible with the achievement of Economic and Monetary Union.

Regional Policy

5. The Heads of State or of Government agreed that high priority should be given to the policy of correcting, in the Community, the structural and regional imbalances which might affect the implementation of Economic and Monetary Union.

The Heads of State or of Government invite the Commission to prepare without delay a report analyzing the regional problems which arise in the enlarged Community and to put forward appropriate proposals.

From now on they undertake to coordinate their regional policies. Desirous of directing their efforts towards finding a Community solution to regional problems, they invite the Community institutions to create a Regional Development Fund. This will be set up before 31 December 1973 and will be financed, from the beginning of the second phase of Economic and Monetary Union, out of the Community's own resources. The Fund's intervention, in coordination with national aids, should gradually make it possible, as Economic and Monetary Union progresses, to correct the main regional imbalances in the enlarged Community and particularly those resulting from the preponderance of agriculture and from industrial change and structural underemployment.

Social Policy

5. The Heads of State or of Government emphasized that they attached as much importance to vigorous action in the social field as to the achievement of Economic and Monetary Union. They considered it essential to bring about an increasing involvement of labour and management in the economic and social decisions of the Community. They invited the institutions, after consulting labour and management, to draw up by 1 January 1974 a programme of action providing for concrete measures and the corresponding resources, particularly in the framework of the Social Fund, based on the suggestions made at the Conference by Heads of State or of Government and by the Commission.

This programme should aim, in particular, to carry out a coordinated employment and vocational training policy, to improve working and living conditions, to achieve the cooperation of workers within company structures, to facilitate on the basis of the situation in the different countries the conclusion of collective bargains at European level in appropriate fields, and to strengthen and coordinate measures of consumer protection.

Industrial, Scientific and Technological Policy

7. The Heads of State or of Government consider it necessary to seek to establish a single industrial base for the whole Community.

This involves the elimination of technical barriers to trade as well as the elimination, particularly in the fiscal and legal fields, of barriers which hinder closer relations and mergers between firms, and rapid adoption of a European company statute, the progressive and effective opening up of public-sector purchases, the promotion on a European scale of competitive firms in the field of high technology, the transformation and conversion of declining industries under acceptable social conditions, the formulation of measures to ensure that mergers affecting firms established in the Community are in harmony with the latter's economic and social aims, and the maintenance of fair competition as much within the Common Market as in external markets in conformity with the rules laid down by the treaties.

Objectives will have to be defined and a common policy in the field of science and technology developed. This policy will require the coordination of national policies, within the Community institutions, and joint implementation of projects of interest to the Community.

To this end, a programme of action together with a precise timetable and approp provisions should be decided upon by the Community institutions before 1 January 1974.

Environment Policy

8. The Heads of State or of Government emphasized the importance of a Communi environmental policy. To this end they invited the Community institutions to establish, before 31 July 1973, a programme of action accompanied by a precise timetable.

Energy Policy

9. The Heads of State or of Government deem it necessary to invite the Community institutions to formulate as soon as possible an energy policy guaranteeing secure and lasting supplies under satisfactory economic conditions.

External relations

10. The Heads of State or of Government declare that their efforts to construct their Community attain their full meaning only insofar as the member States succee in acting together to cope with the growing world responsibilities incumbent on Europe.

11. The Heads of State or of Government are convinced that the Community must, without impairing the advantages enjoyed by countries with which it has special relations, respond even more than in the past to the expectations of all the developing countries.

With this in view, it attaches essential importance to the policy of association as confirmed in the Treaty of Accession and to the fulfilment of its commitments to the countries of the Mediterranean Basin with which agreements have been or will be concluded, agreements which should be the subject of an overall and balanced approach.

In the same perspective, in the light of the results of the UNCTAD[1] Conference and in the context of the Development Strategy adopted by the United Nations, the Community institutions and member States are invited progressively to adopt an overall policy of development cooperation on a world-wide scale, comprising, in particular, the following elements:

1 United Nations Conference on Trade and Development.

— the promotion in appropriate cases of agreements concerning the primary products of the developing countries with a view to arriving at market stabilization and an increase in their exports;

— the improvement of generalized preferences with the aim of achieving a steady increase in imports of manufactures from the developing countries.

In this connection the Community institutions will study from the beginning of 973 the conditions which will permit the achievement of a substantial growth arget.

— An increase in the volume of public financial aid.

— An improvement in the financial conditions of this aid, particularly in favour of the least-developed countries, bearing in mind the recommendations of the OECD[1] Development Assistance Committee.

These questions will be studied and decisions taken in due course during 1973.

12. With regard to the industrial countries, the Community is determined, in rder to ensure the harmonious development of world trade:

— to contribute, while respecting what has been achieved by the Community, to a gradual liberalization of international trade by measures based on reciprocity and relating to both tariffs and non-tariff barriers;

— to maintain a constructive dialogue with the United States, Japan, Canada and other industrialized trade partners in an outward-looking spirit, using the most appropriate methods.

In this context the Community attaches major importance to the multilateral egotiations in the context of GATT, in which it will participate in accordance with ts earlier statement.

To this end, the Community institutions are invited to decide not later than 1 July 973 on a global approach covering all aspects of trade.

The Community hopes that an effort on the part of all partners will allow these egotiations to be completed in 1975.

It confirms its desire for the full participation of the developing countries in he preparation and the negotiations themselves, which should take due account of he interests of those countries.

Furthermore, having regard to the agreements concluded with the EFTA countries vhich are not members, the Community declares its readiness to seek with Norway speedy solution to the trade problems facing that country in its relations with the nlarged Community.

13. In order to promote detente in Europe, the Conference reaffirmed its deternination to follow a common commercial policy towards the countries of Eastern Europe with effect from 1 January 1973; member States declared their determination o promote a policy of cooperation, founded on reciprocity, with these countries.

This policy of cooperation is, at the present stage, closely linked with the preparation nd holding of the Conference on Security and Cooperation in Europe to which the nlarged Community and its member States are called upon to make a concerted and constructive contribution in this field.

1 Organization for Economic Cooperation and Development.

Political cooperation

14. The Heads of State or of Government agreed that political cooperation between the member States of the Community on foreign policy matters had begun well and should be still further improved. They agreed that consultations should be intensified at all levels and that the Foreign Ministers should in future meet four times a year instead of twice for this purpose. They considered that the aim of this cooperation was to deal with problems of current interest and, where possible, to formulate common medium and long-term positions, keeping in mind, *inter alia*, the international political implications and effects of Community policies under elaboration. On matters which have a direct bearing on Community activities, close contact will be maintained with the institutions of the Community. They agreed that the Foreign Ministers should produce, not later than 30 June 1973, a second report on methods of improving political cooperation in accordance with the Luxembourg report.

Reinforcement of Institutions

15. The Heads of State or of Government recognized that the structures of the Community had proved themselves, though they felt that the decision-making procedures and the functioning of the institutions should be improved, in order to make them more effective.

The Community institutions and, where appropriate, the Representatives of the Governments of member States are invited to decide, before the end of the first stage in the achievement of Economic and Monetary Union, on the basis of the report which the Commission, pursuant to the resolution of 22 March 1971, is to submit before 1 May 1973, on the measures relating to the distribution of competences and responsibilities among the Community institutions and member States, which are necessary to the proper functioning of an Economic and Monetary Union.

They felt it desirable that the date on which meetings of national Cabinets were normally held should be the same, so that the Council of the Committees could organize itself with a more regular timetable.

Desiring to strengthen the powers of control of the European Parliamentary Assembly, independently of the date on which it will be elected by universal suffrage under Art. 138 of the Treaty of Rome, and to play their part in contributing toward improving its operating conditions, the Heads of State or of Government confirmed the decision of 22 April 1970 of the Council of the Communities, and invited the Council and the Commission to put into effect without delay the practical measures designed to achieve this reinforcement and to improve the relations both of the Council and of the Commission with the Assembly.

The Council will, before 30 June 1973, take practical steps to improve its decision-making procedures and the cohesion of Community action.

They invited the Community institutions to recognize the right of the Economic

nd Social Committee in future to advise on its own initiative on all questions
ffecting the Community.

They were agreed in thinking that, for the purpose in particular of carrying out
he tasks laid down in the different programmes of action, it was desirable to make
he widest possible use of all the provisions of the Treaties, including Art. 235 of
he EEC Treaty.

Luropean Union

6. The Heads of State or of Government, having set themselves the major objective
•f transforming, before the end of the present decade and with the fullest respect
or the Treaties already signed, the whole complex of the relations of member
'tates into a European Union, request the institutions of the Community to draw up
report on this subject before the end of 1975 for submission to a later Summit
'onference.

ANNEX
'IMETABLE FOR MEASURES DECIDED UPON BY THE PARIS SUMMIT 'ONFERENCE, 20 OCTOBER 1972

January 1973	A common commercial policy in regard to the countries of eastern Europe to be put in hand.
April 1973	Creation of the European Monetary Cooperation Fund.
May 1973	Measures relating to the distribution of powers and responsibilities between the Community institutions and the member States.
0 June 1973	Report on measures to improve political cooperation. Practical measures by the Council to improve its decision-making procedures and the cohesion of Community action.
July 1973	Definition of an overall concept on multilateral economic and monetary negotiations.
1 July 1973	Programme of action concerning the environment.
0 September 1973	Report on the Adjustment of short-term monetary support.
1 December 1973	Creation of the Regional Development Fund. Report on the terms of a gradual pooling of monetary reserves.
January 1974	Programme of action on common industrial, scientific and technological policy. Second stage of Economic and Monetary Union. Programme of action on social policy.
1 December 1975	Report on European Union for submission to a later Summit Conference.
1 December 1980	Completion of Economic and Monetary Union.

136. Regulation and Declaration of the Council of the European 'ommunities establishing a European Monetary Cooperation 'und, Luxembourg, 3 April 1973[1]

'HE COUNCIL OF THE EUROPEAN COMMUNITIES,

1 *Europe, Documents*, No. 730, 6 April 1973.

Having regard to the Treaty establishing the European Economic Community, and in particular Article 235 thereof;

Having regard to the proposal from the Commission;

Having regard to the Opinion of the European Parliament;

Having regard to the Opinion of the Economic and Social Committee;

Whereas the Resolution of the Council and the Representatives of the Governments of the Member States of 22 March 1971 on the progressive establishment of economic and monetary union in the Community provided for the establishment of a European Monetary Cooperation Fund to be integrated at a later stage into a Community organisation of central banks;

Whereas the Heads of State or of Government meeting in Paris on 19 and 20 October 1972 envisaged that the Fund should be established before 1 April 1973;

Whereas the Council has been informed of the Opinions requested on this subjec in the Resolution of the Council and the Representatives of the Member States, of 21 March 1972, from the Monetary Committee and from the Committee of Govern of the Central Banks;

Whereas the purpose of the Fund must be to contribute to the progressive establishment of an Economic and Monetary Union between the Member States of the European Economic Community, which, in its final stage as regards its monetary aspects will have the following characteristics:

- either the total and irreversible convertibility, at irrevocable parities, of Community currencies against each other,
- or the introduction of a common currency;

Whereas it is necessary to confer immediately on the Fund the responsibility for facilitating both the concertation necessary for the smooth operation of the exchan arrangements introduced in the Community and for the settlement of the positions resulting from interventions in Community currencies, for assuring thereby the mul lateralisation of intra-Community settlements, and for administering a financing mechanism which combines the mechanism for short-term monetary support contained in the Agreement of 9 February 1970 between the Central Banks of the Community with the mechanism for very short-term financing which was contained in the Agreement of 10 April 1972 between those same Central Banks;

Whereas the conference of these responsibilities constitutes merely a first stage in the progressive development of the Fund; whereas it is therefore important that the Statutes of the Fund should be drawn up in such a way as to permit the scope of its activities to be gradually extended;

Whereas it is necessary to establish the Fund if Community objectives are to be attained, in particular as regards the progressive harmonisation of the Member State economic policies, the proper functioning of the common market and the establishment of economic and monetary union; whereas the Treaty made no provision for the powers essential to the establishment of the Fund;

Whereas it is appropriate to specify that the general provisions of the Treaties concerning the European Communities as regards privileges and immunities, noncontractual liability and the obligation of professional secrecy are applicable to the Fund,

HAS ADOPTED THIS REGULATION:

Article 1

A European Monetary Cooperation Fund, Hereinafter referred to as 'the Fund', is hereby established. It shall have legal personality.

Article 2

Within the limits of its powers the Fund shall promote:
- the proper functioning of the progressive narrowing of the margins of fluctuation of the Community currencies against each other;
- interventions in Community currencies or the exchange markets;
- settlements between Central Banks leading to a concerted policy on reserves.

Article 3

In the first stage of its functions the Fund shall be responsible for:
- the concerted action necessary for the proper functioning of the Community exchange system;
- the multilateralisation of positions resulting from interventions by Central Banks in Community currencies and the multilateralisation of intra-Community settlements;
- the administration of the very short-term financing provided for by the Agreement between the Central Banks of the Enlarged Community of 10 April 1972 and of the short-term monetary support provided for in the Agreement between the Central Banks of the Community of 9 February 1970, to which the Central Banks of Denmark, Ireland and the United Kingdom acceded with effect from 8 January 1973, and the regroupment of these mechanisms in a renewed mechanism.

Article 4

The provisions contained in the Agreements referred to in the third indent of Article 3 shall become the administrative rules of the Fund. The necessary technical adaptations to these provisions shall be made by the Board of Governors of the Fund without however changing the basic nature of those provisions and in particular the consultation procedures contained therein.

Article 5

The Statutes of the Fund are set out in the Annex to this Regulation and form an integral part thereof.

Article 6

This Regulation shall enter into force on 6 April 1973.

This Regulation shall be binding in its entirety and directly applicable in all Member States.

ANNEX
STATUTES OF THE EUROPEAN MONETARY COOPERATION FUND

Article 1

The Fund shall be directed and managed by a Board of Governors. The members of the Board of Governors shall be the members of the Committee of Governors of the Central Banks of the Member States of the European Economic Community established by the Council Decision of 8 May 1964 on collaboration between the Central Banks of the Member States of the European Economic Community.

If unable to attend they may be represented by another member of the governing body of their Central Bank.

A member of the Luxembourg currency authorities shall sit on the Board of Governors. He shall take part in decisions whenever the rights and obligations of the Grand-Duchy of Luxembourg are not exercised by the National Bank of Belgium on behalf of the two Member States of the Belgo-Luxembourg Economic Union.

A member of the Commission shall take part in the proceedings of the Board of Governors. He may appoint an alternate.

Article 2

The Board of Governors shall, in order to achieve the aims of the Fund, act in accordance with the general economic policy guidelines drawn up under the Treaty by the Council and in accordance with such directives as the Council may adopt acting unanimously on a proposal from the Commission.

On 30 June and 31 December of each year, the Board of Governors shall draw up a report on its activities for submission to the Council and the Commission.

Article 3

The Board of Governors shall represent the Fund. It shall decide on the organisation of the Fund, the powers which will be delegated and who may commit the Fund vis-à-vis third parties.

The Board of Governors may delegate to an agent the responsibility for the execut of technical aspects of the Fund's operations.

Article 4

In the first stage of its functions, the expenditure incurred in the management of the

Fund which is not covered by income shall where necessary be made up by contributions from the Central Banks in accordance with the scale of contributions for short-term monetary support.

Article 5

The Fund's operations in the currencies of the Member States shall be expressed in a European monetary unit of account of a value of 0.88867088 grammes of fine gold.

When all the Member States alter the parity or the central rate of their currency simultaneously in the same direction, the value of the unit of account shall be changed automatically:

— where the parities change in the same proportion: in the same direction and by the same proportion as the changes in parities or in the central rates;

— where the parities change in different proportions: in the same direction as the change and in the same proportion as the smallest change in parity or central rate, unless the Council decides on a larger change. In such a case the Council shall act within three days from that of the official announcement by the first Member State to change the parity or central rate of its currency, and in accordance with the procedure laid down in the fourth paragraph of this Article.

Simultaneous changes mean changes in the parity or central rate of the currencies of the Member States made within the three-day period referred to above.

Any other changes in the value of the unit of account shall be decided on by the Council, acting unanimously on a proposal from the Commission after consulting the Monetary Committee and the Board of Governors of the Fund.

Article 6

In each of the Member States the Fund shall enjoy the most extensive legal capacity accorded to legal persons under their laws. It may in particular acquire or dispose of movable or immovable property, open accounts for and conclude agreements with the Central Banks of the Member States of the Community, receive and grant credit, invest the funds for whose management it is responsible, recruit personnel and may be a party to legal proceedings.

Article 7

The Protocol on the Privileges and Immunities of the European Communities shall apply to the Fund, the Board of Governors and the personnel of the Fund.

Article 8

The obligation of professional secrecy contained in Article 214 of the Treaty shall apply to the members of the Board of Governors, the member of the Commission sitting on the Board and his alternate, and any other person engaged in the activities of the Fund.

Article 9

In the case of non-contractual liability, the provisions of Article 215 of the Treaty shall apply to damage or loss caused by the Fund or by its servants in the performanc of their duties.

Article 10

The Board of Governors shall adopt the rules of procedure of the Fund. These rules of procedure shall require the unanimous approval of the Council, given after consulting the Commission.

DECLARATION CONCERNING THE EUROPEAN MONETARY COOPERATION FUND

I

1. The Ministers have instructed the Permanent Representatives together with the Commission to examine, in the light of the Commission's Opinion of 1 March 1973, what arrangements could be adopted in order to ensure the proper functioning of the European Monetary Cooperation Fund under the conditions laid down by the Decision of 8 April 1965, Article 10 which stipulates that:

'The Governments of the Member States are willing to locate in Luxembourg, or to transfer thereto, other Community bodies and departments, particularly those concerned with finance, provided that their proper functioning can be assured.

To this end, they request the Commission to present to them annually a report on the current situation concerning the location of Community bodies and departments and on the possibility of taking new steps to give effect to this provision, account being taken of the need to ensure the proper functioning of the Communities.'

2. In the light of the study by the Permanent Representatives, the Representatives of the Governments of the Member States will take a decision on the location of the Fund by 30 June 1973 at the latest.

3. Without prejudging the decision referred to in 2 above there should meanwhile be, to the extent that the Fund's task may require, appropriate administrative support in Luxembourg.

II

In the light of the above, the Council adopts the Regulation setting up a European Monetary Cooperation Fund.

137. Second report on European political cooperation on foreign policy, approved by the nine Foreign Ministers, Copenhagen, 23 July 1973,[1] with Annex

Part I

The Heads of State or of Government of the member States of the European Communities approved on 27th October 1970 the report of the Foreign Ministers drawn up in implementation of paragraph 15 of the communiqué of the Hague conference of 1st and 2nd December 1969. The document reflected the belief that progress towards concerted action in the field of foreign policy was likely to promote the development of the Communities and to help the Europeans to realise more fully their common responsibilities. The objectives of that cooperation are:
— to ensure, by means of regular consultations and exchanges of information, improved mutual understanding as regards the main problems of international relations;
— to strengthen solidarity between governments by promoting the harmonisation of their views and the alignment of their positions and, wherever it appears possible and desirable, joint action.

The report also proposed that the Foreign Ministers should submit a second general report which would, *inter alia*, contain an assessment of the results obtained from such consultation. At the time when the enlargement of the European Communities became a fact, paragraph 14 of the summit declaration in Paris on 21st October 1972 required the Foreign Ministers to produce by 30th June 1973 a second report on methods of improving political cooperation in accordance with the Luxembourg report.

The Heads of State or of Government, meeting in Paris, expressed their satisfaction at the results obtained since the political cooperation machinery was formally set up on the basis of the texts of 27th October 1970. In several fields, the member States have been able to consider and decide matters jointly so as to make common political action possible. This habit has also led to the 'reflex' of coordination among the member states which has profoundly affected the relations of the member States between each other and with third countries. This collegiate sense in Europe is becoming a real force in international relations.

The Ministers note that the characteristically pragmatic mechanisms set up by the Luxembourg report have shown their flexibility and effectiveness. What is involved in fact is a new procedure in international relations and an original European contribution to the technique of arriving at concerted action. The experience acquired so far has resulted in a strengthening of the belief in the usefulness of concerted action by means of direct contact between senior officials of Foreign Ministries and of a very thorough preparation of the matters under consideration as a basis for the decisions by Ministers.

1 Cmnd. 5432.

Such concerted action has also had a positive influence insofar as it has brought about a more conscious collaboration between representatives of member States of the Communities in third countries. They have been encouraged to meet and compare the information available to them. This habit of working together has enabled the procedure for concerted action to become more widespread wherever common action or common consideration seemed desirable.

In the Luxembourg report provision was made for the Commission to be invited to make known its views when the work of the Ministers affected the activities of the European Communities. The Foreign Ministers express satisfaction that these contacts have now become a reality and that a constructive and continuing dialogue is in course both at the level of experts and of the Political Committee, and at ministerial meetings.

The colloquy with Political Commissions of the European Parliament and the communication by the President of the Council to the European Parliament have put into effect the desire of the Foreign Ministers to make a contribution to the democratic character of the construction of political union.

The final declaration of the conference of Heads of State or of Government held on 19–21 October 1972 expressed, *inter alia*, the conviction that Europe must be able to make its voice heard in world affairs and to affirm its own views in international relations.

Europe now needs to establish its position in the world as a distinct entity, especially in international negotiations which are likely to have a decisive influence in the international equilibrium and on the future of the European Community.

In the light of this it is essential that, in the spirit of the conclusions of the Paris summit conference, cooperation among the Nine on foreign policy should be such as to enable Europe to make an original contribution to the international equilibrium. Europe has the will to do this, in accordance with its traditionally outward-looking mission and its interest in progress, peace and cooperation. It will do so, loyal to its traditional friends and to the alliances of its member States, in the spirit of good neighbourliness which must exist between all the countries of Europe both to the east and the west, and responding to the expectations of all the developing countries.

The results obtained by the procedure of political consultation since its inception, referred to in the preceding paragraphs, are the subject of a descriptive annex attached to this report.

Part II

In implementation of the task entrusted to them by paragraph 14 of the Paris summit declaration, and having regard to the objective which the Heads of State or of Government set themselves, namely to transform, before the end of the present decade, the whole complex of the relations between the member States of the European Communities into a European union, the Foreign Ministers propose that the Heads of State or of Government approve the following measures:

1. Ministerial meetings

Henceforth, the Foreign Ministers will meet four times a year. They may also, whenever they consider it necessary to consult each other on specific subjects between meetings, meet for that purpose when they happen to come together on other occasions.

2. The Political Committee of the member States of the European Communities

The Political Directors of the member States of the Community will meet in the Political Committee of the member States of the European Communities with a view to preparing ministerial meetings and carrying out tasks entrusted to them by the Ministers. In order to attain that objective, meetings of the committee will be held as frequently as the intensification of the work requires.

3. The Group of 'Correspondents'

A group consisting of European 'Correspondents' in the Foreign Ministry (called the Group of Correspondents) will be set up. That group will be entrusted with the task of following the implementation of political cooperation and of studying problems of organisation and problems of a general nature. Furthermore, for certain matters, the group will prepare the work of the Political Committee on the basis of instructions given by that committee.

4. Working parties

(*a*) In order to ensure more thorough consultation on individual questions, working parties will be set up to bring together senior officials of the Ministries for Foreign Affairs responsible for the subject under consideration. These working parties will cease to meet as soon as they have completed the task entrusted to them. Exceptionally, and especially in order to ensure continuity if the work can be completed in the near future, the chairman of a working party may be required to continue in office beyond the usual period.

(*b*) The chairman-in-office may approach the Political Committee about the need to bring together senior officials of the major ministerial departments who have not met during the preceding six-month period with a view to keeping them in contact with each other.

5. Medium- and long-term studies

In accordance with paragraph 14 of the declaration of the Paris summit conference, which set as an objective of political cooperation the formulation, where possible, of common medium- and long-term positions, several methods of work can be envisaged. According to circumstances, this will be done either by groups of experts in addition to the current matters which they normally deal with, or by entrusting the preparations of such studies to a special analysis and research group consisting normally of officials.

The Political Committee will propose to the Foreign Ministers specific subjects for study.

6. The role of the embassies of the Nine in the capitals of the member countries of the Community

The embassies of the Nine participate closely in the implementation of political cooperation. In particular, they receive information on a Community basis issued by the Foreign Ministry of their country of residence. Furthermore, they are occasionally entrusted with consultations on specific subjects:

— at the seat of the Presidency at the request of the Political Committee, the Presidency or another member State; or

— in another capital at the request of the Foreign Ministry.

They will appoint one of their diplomatic staff who will specifically be entrusted with ensuring the necessary contacts with the Foreign Ministry of their country of residence, within the framework of political cooperation.

7. Roles of the embassies in third countries and of the offices of permanent representatives to major international organisations

With the introduction of the political cooperation machinery, it proved useful to associate embassies and permanent representatives' offices with the work. In the light of the experience gained, better information on the work in progress in the field of political cooperation should be provided so as to enable them, where necessary, to put forward in an appropriate form those aspects which they consider of interest for this work, including considerations on joint action.

With this in mind, the Political Committee will notify the missions concerned when it considers it necessary to obtain a contribution on a specific item of its agenda. Where appropriate, it may require a common report to be prepared by them on specific questions.

In addition to the provisions contained in the texts in force governing reciprocal information on the occasion of important visits, the Ambassador concerned, accredited in the country where the visit takes place, should first provide information to his colleagues on the spot so as to enable any appropriate exchange of views. After the visit, such information as may interest them should be given to them in the most appropriate manner.

Finally, in application of the provisions governing the role of missions abroad, the permanent representatives of the member States to the major international organisations will regularly consider matters together and, on the basis of instructions received, will seek common positions in regard to important questions dealt with by those organisations.

8. The Presidency

As regards the internal organisation of the work of political cooperation, the Presidency:
— sees to it that the conclusions adopted at meetings of Ministers and of the Political Committee are implemented on a collegiate basis;
— proposes, on its own initiative or on that of another State, consultation at an appropriate level;
— may also, between meetings of the Political Committee, meet the Ambassadors of the member States in order to inform them of the progress of the work of political cooperation. The meeting may take place at the request of an Ambassador of a member State seeking consultation on a specific subject.

Experience has also shown that the Presidency's task presents a particularly heavy administrative burden. Administrative assistance may therefore be provided by other member States for specific tasks.

9. Improvement of contact between the Nine

The Foreign Ministers have agreed to establish a communications system with a view to facilitating direct contact between their departments.

10. Relations with the European Parliament

Having regard to the widening scope of the European Communities and the intensification of political cooperation at all levels, four colloquies will be held each year at which the Ministers will meet with members of the Political Committee of the European Parliament. For the purpose of preparing the colloquies, the Political Committee will draw to the attention of Ministers proposals adopted by the European Parliament on foreign policy questions.

In addition the Minister exercising the function of President will continue, as in the past, to submit to the European Parliament, once a year, a communication on progress made in the field of political cooperation.

11. Priorities to be set in respect of the matters to be dealt with within the framework of political cooperation

Governments will consult each other on all important foreign policy questions and will work out priorities, observing the following criteria:
— the purpose of the consultation is to seek common policies on practical problems;
— the subjects dealt with must concern European interests whether in Europe itself or elsewhere where the adoption of a common position is necessary or desirable.

On these questions each State undertakes as a general rule not to take up final positions without prior consultation with its partners within the framework of the political cooperation machinery.

The Political Committee will submit to the meetings of Foreign Ministers subjects among which the Ministers may select those to be given priority in the course of political cooperation. This is without prejudice to the examination of additional subjects either at the suggestion of a member State or as a result of recent developments.

12. Relationship between the work of the political cooperation machinery and that carried out within the framework of the European Communities

(*a*) The political cooperation machinery, which deals on the intergovernmental level with problems of international politics, is distinct from and additional to the activities of the institutions of the Community which are based on the juridical commitments undertaken by the member States in the Treaty of Rome. Both sets of machinery have the aim of contributing to the development of European unificati The relationship between them is discussed below.

(*b*) The political cooperation machinery, which is responsible for dealing with questions of current interest and where possible for formulating common medium- and long-term positions, must do this keeping in mind, *inter alia*, the implications for and the effects of, in the field of international politics, Community policies under construction.

For matters which have an incidence on Community activities close contact will be maintained with the institutions of the Community.

(*c*) The last section of the previous paragraph is implemented in the following way:

— the Commission is invited to make known its views in accordance with current practice;

— the Council, through the President of the Committee of Permanent Representatives, is informed by the Presidency of the agreed conclusions which result from the work of the political cooperation machinery, to the extent that these conclusions have an interest for the work of the Community;

— the Ministers will similarly be able, if it is so desired, to instruct the political cooperation machinery to prepare studies on certain political aspects of problems under examination in the framework of the Community. These reports will be transmitted to the Council through the President of the Committee of Permanent Representatives.

In drawing up this report, the Ministers have demonstrated their belief that even more important than the contents of their proposals is the spirit in which these are put into effect. That spirit is the one that emerges from the decisions taken at the Paris summit meeting.

The Ministers consider that cooperation on foreign policy must be placed in the perspective of European union.

From now on, it is of the greatest importance to seek common positions on major international problems.

ANNEX
Results obtained from European political cooperation on foreign policy

1. Ministerial meetings

(LUXEMBOURG REPORT – SECOND PART, II)

As from the second half of 1970, the Ministers for Foreign Affairs of member States of the European Communities have met regularly twice a year.

In pursuance of the decision taken by the conference of Heads of State or of Government in Paris on 19th–21st October 1972, the number of these meetings has, from 1973, been increased from two to four.

2. Political Committee

(LUXEMBOURG REPORT – SECOND PART, III)

(*a*) The Luxembourg report provided for at least four meetings a year. From the outset, the Political Committee met more often than had been foreseen; in fact, during the last twelve months, it has held nine meetings.

(*b*) The Political Committee has noted that the aims defined in the Luxembourg report could only be achieved by adequate preparation. To this effect and without thereby discarding other possible formulas, it has established, within the framework of its activities, working parties entrusted with particular tasks:

– a sub-committee was set up to study problems relating to the conference on security and cooperation in Europe (CSCE), and an *ad hoc* group, in which the Commission of the European Communities takes part, was set up to examine the economic aspects. In view of the need for such studies, it was decided that the sub-committee and the *ad hoc* group should meet on a permanent basis in Helsinki in order to work, on the spot, for agreed positions in response to developments in the negotiations;
– three working parties were set up with a view to following and studying problems relating, respectively, to the situation in the Middle East, the Mediterranean area and Asia; senior officials in the Foreign Ministries with responsibility for those questions usually participate in this work;
– there were also meetings of experts dealing with various questions as, for example, cooperation in the event of natural disasters;
– consultations also took place between the Presidency and the embassies of member States on the situation in the Indian sub-continent and in the Middle East.

(*c*) Furthermore, it was decided to place within the framework of political cooperation the consultations which used to take place within the WEU before sessions of the General Assembly of the United Nations, of the Economic and Social Council and of the FAO. For this purpose, alongside the coordination meetings of the permanent representatives, senior officials responsible for the different sectors within each of the national administrations get together to discuss certain items placed on the agendas of these sessions; they report to the Political Committee.

3. Group of 'Correspondents'

(LUXEMBOURG REPORT – SECOND PART, VII–3)

In order to facilitate the internal organisation of political cooperation, the Luxembourg report provided that each State should appoint from within its Ministry for Foreign Affairs an official who should act as the 'correspondent' of his opposite numbers in other States. These officials were established as a 'Group of Correspondents'; this group, in addition to the task of drafting summaries of the conclusions reached at ministerial meetings and meetings of the Political Committee, was entrusted with the duty of closely following the implementation of political cooperation and of studying the problems of organisation and those of a general nature, as well as particular problems which the Political Committee gave it to examine, in particular for the purpose of preparing their meetings.

4. Activities of embassies of the Nine in the capitals of member States of the Communities

The role of Ambassadors of the Nine in the capitals of member States has proved important for the implementation of political cooperation in particular with respect to the exchange of information. In order to facilitate contacts with the Ministries for Foreign Affairs in the countries of their residence with respect to matters of political cooperation, each of these embassies has appointed a diplomat on its staff whose special duty is to ensure contact with the Ministry for Foreign Affairs in its country of residence on matters of political cooperation.

Since the Ambassadors receive information concerning the Community from the Ministry for Foreign Affairs of their country of residence and, in particular, since they are expected by the Political Committee to engage in discussions from time to time, in the capital of the Presidency, it is important that they should be fully informed of the progress of political cooperation with the implementation of which their missions are associated.

5. Association of Ambassadors in third countries and of permanent representatives to international organisations with the political cooperation

It has been judged necessary and in line with the Luxembourg report to associate heads of the diplomatic missions of the Nine with political cooperation. For that purpose, it has been arranged that the Political Committee can ask Ambassadors accredited to a particular country to provide it with reports and thus to encourage cooperation among the diplomatic representatives of member States.

It had also been arranged that regular discussions can take place between Ambassadors accredited to countries other than those of the Community, on problems of common interest concerning the country to which they are accredited, in accordance with such procedures as the Ambassadors themselves would find appropriate.

These provisions were put into operation and developed during the first two years of political cooperation.

Heads of diplomatic missions in many posts, or their representatives, while taking account of local conditions, take part increasingly in political cooperation, especially through exchanges of view and in certain cases by means of joint reports.

5. Commission of the European Communities

'LUXEMBOURG REPORT – SECOND PART, V)

The Luxembourg report provides that:
'should the work of the Ministers affect the activities of the European Communities, the Commission will be invited to make known its views'.

In accordance with this the Commission of the Communities has been invited to participate in ministerial discussions and in sessions of the Political Committee and of groups of experts when the agenda of the meeting provides for the examination of questions affecting the activities of the Communities: for example, the examination of problems relating to the economic aspects of the CSCE and to the future role of the Council of Europe.

7. European Parliament

(LUXEMBOURG REPORT – SECOND PART, VI, and THIRD PART, 4)

In accordance with the Luxembourg report which provided for two methods of associating public opinion and its representatives with the development of political cooperation, Ministers for Foreign Affairs and members of the Political Commission of the European Parliament held a colloquy every six months and the President-in-Office of the Council reported every year to the Parliament on the progress of work concerning the best means of advancing towards political union.

At the last two colloquies, a new procedure consisting essentially of the notification in advance to the Political Commission of the European Parliament of the main subjects for discussion, was adopted in order to make the exchange of views more fruitful.

8. Participation of new members

Political cooperation was started when the European Communities consisted of only six members – the applicant States being associated with their activities in accordance with the procedure specified in the fourth part of the Luxembourg report. The procedure provided that the Ministers of the Six would meet their colleagues from acceding States at a time as near as possible to their meetings in order to ensure

necessary consultation for keeping those States informed of the progress of the
work of the Six.

Similarly, it was arranged for the President-in-Office of the Political Committee
to communicate to applicant States information likely to interest them and for him
to obtain any reactions they had. This rule was adopted to take account of the
essential connection between membership of the European Communities and
participation in activities enabling further progress to be made towards political
union.

After signature of the Act of Accession on 22nd January 1972 these States have
fully participated in meetings at every level.

138. Statement by President Pompidou, Paris, 31 October 1973[1]

I do not feel it is necessary to review France's position on the conflict in the Middle
East, or to reaffirm that we are ready to help as much as we can, under the authorit
of the Security Council, toward the establishment of a lasting and just peace,
guaranteeing the security of all the States in the area. On the other hand we are
forced to note, in the light of recent events, that the cessation of hostilities and
the attempts to open negotiations were prepared and carried out without Europe
participating in any capacity whatsoever. This manner of proceeding is dangerous,
experience having shown that the dialogue between the two super powers — the
United States and the USSR — might just as well serve detente as lead to a generalis
conflict. Nor does it correspond to the role which should be played by the Europea
countries directly interested as they are in the Middle East by virtue of their history
geography, through all sorts of links with the Mediterranean countries concerned,
and by basic economic interests.

For these reasons and for many others, and while reaffirming our loyalty to our
alliances and to our cooperation with the East, I feel that it is absolutely necessary
to prove and put to the test the soundness of European construction as well as
its ability to contribute to the settlement of international problems. Therefore
the French Government intends to propose to its partners:

1. In the political domain:

That regular meetings between Heads of State or Governments be agreed to in
principle in accordance with specific rules for the purpose of comparing and harmonising their attitudes within the framework of political cooperation. The first
of these meetings should take place before the end of 1973.

That during this first meeting a procedure should be established whereby, in
case of crisis, an emergency meeting could be convened of representatives from the
nine governments charged with defining and proposing insofar as possible a commo
attitude of these governments.

1 WEU, *Political Union, 1963–1973*, p. 114.

2. In the economic and monetary domain:

That at a future meeting the finance ministers propose to the nine governments the measures that are needed to ensure the stability of their currencies and enable them to resist speculative movements.

That the ministers of the economy should meet to draw up a concerted plan to fight inflation. This has been made even more necessary in view of the rising cost of energy. These two meetings would take place with the normal participation of the [EEC] Commission.

139. Declaration of the EEC Member States on 'the European identity', Copenhagen, 14 December 1973[1]

The Nine member countries of the European Communities have decided that the time has come to draw up a document on the European identity. This will enable them to achieve a better definition of their relations with other countries and of their responsibilities and the place which they occupy in world affairs.

They have decided to define the European identity with the dynamic nature of the Community in mind. They have the intention of carrying the work further in the future in the light of the progress made in the construction of a united Europe.

Defining the European identity involves reviewing the common heritage, interests and special obligations of the Nine, as well as the degree of unity so far achieved within the Community; assessing the extent to which the Nine are already acting together in relation to the rest of the world and the responsibilities which result from this; taking into consideration the dynamic nature of European unification.

The unity of the nine member countries of the Community

1. The nine European states might have been pushed towards disunity by their history and by selfishly defending misjudged interests. But they have overcome their past enmities and have decided that unity is a basic European necessity to ensure the survival of the civilization which they have in common.

The Nine wish to ensure that the cherished values of their legal, political and moral order are respected, and to preserve the rich variety of their national cultures. Sharing as they do the same attitudes to life based on a determination to build a society which measures up to the needs of the individual, they are determined to defend the principles of representative democracy, of the rule of law, of social justice — which is the ultimate goal of economic progress — and of respect for human rights.

All of these are fundamental elements of the European identity. The Nine believe that this enterprise corresponds to the deepest aspirations of their peoples, who should participate in its realization, particularly through their elected representatives.

1 *The Times*, 15 December 1973.

2. The Nine have the political will to succeed in the construction of a united Europe. On the basis of the Treaties of Paris and Rome setting up the European Communities, and of subsequent decisions, they have created a common market, based on a customs union, and have established institutions, common policies and machinery for cooperation. All these are an essential part of the European identity.

The Nine are determined to safeguard the elements which make up the unity they have achieved so far and the fundamental objectives laid down for future developments at the summit conferences in The Hague and Paris. On the basis of the Luxembourg and Copenhagen reports, the Nine Governments have established a system of political cooperation with a view to determining common attitudes and, where possible and desirable, common action. They propose to develop this further.

In accordance with the decision taken at the Paris conference, the Nine reaffirm their intention of transforming the whole complex of their relations into a European union before the end of the present decade.

3. The diversity of cultures within the framework of a common European civilization, the attachment to common values and principles, the increasing convergence of attitudes to life, the awareness of having specific interests in common and the determination to take part in the construction of a united Europe, all give the European identity its originality and its own dynamism.

4. The construction of a united Europe, which the nine member countries of the Community are undertaking, is open to other European nations who share the same ideals and objectives.

5. The European countries have, in the course of their history, developed close ties with many other parts of the world. These relationships, which will continue to evolve, constitute an assurance of progress and international equilibrium.

6. Although in the past the European countries were individually able to play a major role on the international scene, present international problems are difficult for any of the Nine to solve alone. International developments and the growing concentration of power and responsibility in the hands of a very small number of great powers mean that Europe must unite and speak increasingly with a single voice if it wants to make itself heard and play its proper role in the world.

7. The Community, the world's largest trading group, could not be a closed economic entity. It has close links with the rest of the world as regards its supplies and market outlets. For this reason the Community, while remaining in control of its own trading policies, intends to exert a positive influence on world economic relations with a view to the greater well-being of all.

8. The Nine, one of whose essential aims is to maintain peace, will never succeed in doing so if they neglect their own security. Those of them who are members of the Atlantic Alliance consider that in present circumstances there is no alternative to the security provided by the nuclear weapons of the United States and the presence of North American forces in Europe; and they agree that in the light of the relative military vulnerability of Europe, the Europeans should, if they wish to preserve their independence, hold to their commitments and make constant efforts to ensure that they have adequate means of defence at their disposal.

The European identity in relation to the world

9. The Europe of the Nine is aware that, as it unites, it takes on new international obligations. European unification is not directed against anyone, nor is it inspired by a desire for power. On the contrary, the Nine are convinced that their union will benefit the whole international community since it will constitute an element of equilibrium and a basis for cooperation with all countries, whatever their size, culture or social system.

The Nine intend to play an active role in world affairs and thus to contribute, in accordance with the purposes and principles of the United Nations Charter, to ensuring that international relations have a more just basis; that prosperity is more equitably shared, and that the security of each country is more effectively guaranteed. In pursuit of these objectives the Nine should progressively define common positions in the sphere of foreign policy.

10. As the Community progresses towards a common policy in relation to third countries, it will act in accordance with the following principles:

(a) The Nine, acting as a single entity, will strive to promote harmonious and constructive relations with these countries. This should not however jeopardize, hold back or affect the will of the Nine to progress towards European union within the time limits laid down.

(b) In future when the Nine negotiate collectively with other countries, the institutions and procedures chosen should enable the distinct character of the European entity to be respected.

(c) In bilateral contacts with other countries, the member states of the Community will increasingly act on the basis of agreed common positions.

11. The Nine intend to strengthen their links. In the present institutional framework, with the member countries of the Council of Europe, and with other European countries with whom they already have friendly relations and close cooperation.

12. The Nine attach essential importance to the Community's policy of association. Without diminishing the advantages enjoyed by the countries with which it has special relations, the Community intends progressively to put into operation a policy for development aid on a worldwide scale in accordance with the principles and aims set out in the Paris summit declaration.

13. The Community will implement its undertakings towards the Mediterranean and African countries in order to reinforce its long-standing links with these countries. The Nine intend to preserve their historic links with the countries of the Middle East and to cooperate over the establishment and maintenance of peace, stability and progress in the region.

14. The close ties between the United States and Europe of the Nine — who share values and aspirations based on a common heritage — are mutually beneficial and must be preserved. These ties do not conflict with the determination of the Nine to establish themselves as a distinct and original entity. The Nine intend to maintain their constructive dialogue and to develop their cooperation with the United States on the basis of equality and in a spirit of friendship.

15. The Nine also remain determined to engage in close cooperation and to pursue a constructive dialogue with the other industrialized countries, such as Japan and Canada, which have an essential role in maintaining an open and balanced world economic system. They appreciate the existing fruitful cooperation with these countries, particularly in OECD.

16. The Nine have contributed, both individually and collectively, to the first results of a policy of detente and cooperation with the Soviet Union and the East European countries. They are determined to carry this policy further forward on a reciprocal basis.

17. Conscious of the major role played by China in international affairs, the Nine intend to intensify their relations with the Chinese Government and to promote exchanges in various fields, as well as contacts between European and Chinese leaders.

18. The Nine are also aware of the important role played by other Asian countries. They are determined to develop their relations with these countries as is demonstrated as far as commercial relations are concerned, by the declaration of intent made by the Community at the time of its enlargement.

19. The Nine are traditionally bound to the Latin American countries by friendly links and many other contacts. They intend to develop these. In this context they attach great importance to the agreements concluded between the European Community and certain Latin American countries.

20. There can be no real peace if the developed countries do not pay more heed to the less favoured nations. Convinced of this fact and conscious of their responsibilities and particular obligations, the Nine attach very great importance to the struggle against underdevelopment. They are, therefore, resolved to intensify their efforts in the fields of trade and development aid and to strengthen international cooperation to these ends.

21. The Nine will participate in international negotiations in an outward-looking spirit, while preserving the fundamental elements of their unity and their basic aims. They are also resolved to contribute to international progress, both through their relations with Third countries and by adopting common positions wherever possible in international organizations, notably the United Nations and the specialized agencies.

The dynamic nature of the construction of a united Europe

22. The European identity will evolve as a function of the dynamic of the construction of a united Europe. In their external relations, the Nine propose progressively to undertake the definition of their identity in relation to other countries or groups of countries. They believe that in so doing they will strengthen their own cohesion and contribute to the framing of a genuinely European foreign policy.

They are convinced that building up this policy will help them to tackle with confidence and realism further stages in the constitution of a united Europe, thus making easier the proposed transformation of the whole complex of their relations into a European union.

140. Statement by the Heads of State or Government of the European Community, Copenhagen, 15 December 1973[1]

The heads of state or government of the member states of the European Community met in Copenhagen on December 14 and 15, 1973, at the invitation of the Prime Minister of Denmark. The President of the Commission participated actively in their work on Community questions. They agreed as follows:

1. The nine countries affirm their common will that Europe should speak with one voice in important world affairs. They adopted the declaration on the European identity, which defines, with the dynamic nature of the Community in mind, the principles which are to underlie their action.

2. They decided to speed up the work required to define the European union which they had set themselves as their major objective at the Paris summit. They asked the presidency to make the necessary proposals without delay.

3. They decided to meet more frequently. These meetings will be held whenever justified by the circumstances and when it appears necessary to provide a stimulus or to lay down further guidelines for the construction of a united Europe. They also agreed to meet whenever the international situation so requires.

It will be for the country providing the President to convene these meetings and to make detailed proposals concerning their preparation and organization.

The heads of state or government attach the greatest importance to the institutions of the Community playing their full role and to the necessary decisions being taken here in good time.

4. It was agreed that the foreign ministers of the member states should, at their next meeting, decide on the means by which a common position should be worked out quickly in times of crisis. The development of political cooperation will also enable them to make joint assessments of crisis situations, with the aim of foreseeing them and of taking the measures needed to deal with them.

5. They confirmed their support for the policy of international detente which respects the independence and security of each state and the rules laid down in the Charter of the United Nations for the prevention and settlement of conflicts.

6. They agreed that the growing unity of the Nine would strengthen the West as a whole and will be beneficial for the relationship between Europe and the United States.

7. The heads of state or government welcome the convening of a peace conference in Geneva and call on the participants to make every effort to achieve a just and lasting settlement at an early date. The nine governments are ready to assist in the search for peace and in the guaranteeing of a settlement.

The heads of state or government reaffirmed the united stand of their governments on the Middle East question embodied in the declaration issued on 6 November. Recent events have strengthened them in their view that the security of all states in the area, whether it be Israel, or her Arab neighbours, can only be based on the full

1 *The Times*, 17 December 1973.

implementation of Security Council Resolution 242 in all its parts taking into account also the legitimate rights of the Palestinians.

The heads of state or governments are convinced that the requirements of sovereignty and the requirements of security can be met by the conclusion of peace agreements including among other arrangements international guarantees and the establishment of demilitarized zones.

They will inform the Secretary-General of the United Nations thereof.

8. As regards the European Communities, the heads of state or government reaffirmed the importance they attach to what the Community has already achieved and their will to see it develop. After examining the progress already made in implementing earlier decisions they agreed:—

To invite the Community institutions to take measures to achieve more rapid progress towards the full establishment of economic and monetary union building on the decisions already taken;

To seek actively the definition of a common position on reform of the international monetary situation to increase the instruments at the disposal of the European monetary cooperation fund and to strengthen the coordination of their action to deal with destabilizing capital movements, in order to create an area of stability in Europe;

The heads of state and government agreed that the regional development fund should be established on 1 January, 1974. As an expression of their positive attitude to the establishment of the fund they agreed to recommend to their foreign ministers that the Council of the European Communities at its next session shall take the necessary decisions concerning the size and the distribution of the fund and the criteria for the fund's operations;

To make the functioning of the Community's institutions more effective by improving cooperation between the Council, the Commission and the Parliament, by a more rapid procedure for the settlement of questions submitted to the Community authorities and by reinforcing its financial control, involving *inter alia* the establishment of an independent Community audit board and the strengthening of the role of the European Parliament in budgetary matters;

That the foreign ministers at the next session of the Council of the European Communities find a solution to enable the Faroe Islands to postpone their decision concerning membership of the European Communities until the result of the conference on the law of the sea is known;

To implement a social action programme having as its aims the achievement of full and better employment in the Community, the improvement of living and working conditions in a way which makes possible their harmonization while the improvement is being maintained and growing participation by the social partners in the Community's economic and social decisions and by workers in the activities of enterprises;

The heads of state or government, mindful of the importance they attach to problems arising from international trade in primary products and raw materials, asked the Commission to prepare a detailed study and to put proposals to the Council;

To develop more actively between them a common policy on industrial, scientific and technological cooperation in all fields.

9. The heads of state or government have considered the question of energy in a separate paper attached to this declaration.[1]

10. The heads of state or government are convinced that a united Europe will be able to play a role consonant with its history and its abilities in the service of economic and social progress in the Community, of the growth and industrialization of developing countries and of peace between all nations.

141. Statement by Mr Callaghan, British Secretary of State for Foreign and Commonwealth Affairs, to the Council of the European Communities, Luxembourg, 1 April 1974[2]

1. Mr Chairman, with your permission I should like to make a statement about the policy of my Government towards the Community. It will come as no surprise to you that the Labour Government opposes membership of the Community on the terms that were negotiated at the time of our entry in January 1973. We do not consider that they provided for a fair balance of advantages in the Community and we are of the opinion that the terms should have been specifically put to the British people for their approval or otherwise. We wish to put these errors right and if we succeed there will then be a firm basis for continuing British membership of a strengthened Community.

2. We seek to raise with you a number of important questions on which my Government consider a successful renegotiation to be necessary. We shall negotiate in good faith and if we are successful in achieving the right terms we shall put them to our people for approval. But if we fail, we shall submit to the British people the reason why we find the terms unacceptable and consult them on the advisability of negotiating the withdrawal of the United Kingdom from the Community. I am confident that no one in the Community would wish to argue that it would be in the interests of the Community to seek to retain my country as a member against its will. But I stress that I do not hope for a negotiation about withdrawal. I would prefer successful renegotiation from which the right terms for continued membership will emerge. To some extent that will depend upon us – but it will also depend upon the attitude of the other partners in the negotiations.

3. For our part, we have made clear – in the Labour Party Manifesto for the recent election – that 'Britain is a European nation, and a Labour Britain would always seek a wider cooperation between the European peoples.' I would now like to quote a passage of fundamental importance to my Government from our Manifesto. In our view the terms of entry negotiated by the previous Government involved, as we have said: 'the imposition of food taxes on top of rising world prices, crippling fresh burdens on our balance of payments, and a draconian curtailment of the power of the British Parliament to settle questions affecting vital British interests.' This

---

1 Not published here; for text, see WEU, *Political Year in Europe, 1973*, p. 320.
2 *Bull. EC*, 3–1974, pp. 14–19.

is why we are immediately seeking a fundamental renegotiation of the terms of entry, for which we have spelled out our objectives in the following terms:

'The Labour Party *opposes* British membership of the European Communities on the terms negotiated by the Conservative Government.

We have said that we are ready to renegotiate.

In preparing to renegotiate the entry terms, our main objectives are these:

Major changes in the *Common Agricultural Policy*, so that it ceases to be a threat to world trade in food products, and so that low-cost producers outside Europe can continue to have access to the British food market.

New and fairer methods of financing the *Community Budget*. Neither the taxes that form the so-called "own resources" of the Communities, nor the purposes mainly agricultural support, on which the funds are mainly to be spent, are acceptab. to us. We would be ready to contribute to Community finances only such sums as were fair in relation to what is paid and what is received by other member countries.

As stated earlier, we would reject any kind of international agreement which compelled us to accept increased unemployment for the sake of maintaining a fixed parity, as is required by current proposals for a European *Economic and Monetary Union*. We believe that the monetary problems of the European countries can be resolved only in a world-wide framework.

The retention by *Parliament* of those powers over the British economy needed to pursue effective regional, industrial and fiscal policies. Equally we need an agreement on capital movements which protects our balance of payments and full employment policies. The economic interests of the *Commonwealth* and the *developing countries* must be better safeguarded. This involves securing continued access to the British market and, more generally, the adoption by an enlarged Community of trade and aid policies designed to benefit not just "associated oversea territories" in Africa, but developing countries throughout the world.

No harmonization of *Value Added Tax* which would require us to tax necessities.

If renegotiations are successful, it is the policy of the Labour Party that, in view of the unique importance of the decision, the people should have the right to decide the issue through a General Election or a Consultative Referendum. If these two tests are passed, a successful renegotiation and the expressed approval of the majority of the British people, then we shall be ready to play our full part in developing a new and wider Europe.

If renegotiations do not succeed, we shall not regard the Treaty obligations as binding upon us. We shall then put to the British people the reasons why we find the new terms unacceptable, and consult them on the advisability of negotiating our withdrawal from the Communities.

An incoming Labour Government will immediately set in train the procedures designed to achieve an early result and whilst the negotiations proceed and until the British people have voted, we shall stop further processes of integration, particularly as they affect food taxes. The Government will be free to take decisions, subject to the authority of Parliament, in cases where decisions of the Common Market prejudice the negotiations. Thus, the right to decide the final issue of British entry into the Market will be restored to the British people.'

4. My Government now proposes that we should consider together how these objectives can be met. In view of the great importance of the issue of membership of the Community, my Government is now engaged in a root and branch review of the effect of Community policies and will place before you in due course in detail the proposals which we would wish to see the Community adopt in order to remedy the situation. In particular, we are examining with great care the working of the Common Agricultural Policy; the estimates for future contributions to and receipts from the Community budget; the Community's trade and aid policies towards the Commonwealth and developing countries and how far in practice the existing rules, as they are interpreted, interfere with the powers over the British economy which we need to pursue effective regional, industrial and fiscal policies. As soon as this review is completed, we shall be ready to put forward proposals for the changes which will in our view be necessary if Britain is to remain a member of the Community and thus, as the Manifesto put it, 'to play our full part in developing a new and wider Europe'.

5. Why do my Government, and indeed the British people, question whether all is well in the Community as it is and why are we planning to seek changes?

6. First, we were deeply concerned by the Resolutions of March 1971 and 1972 which were confirmed at the Summit Meeting of October 1972. They seemed to lay down a rigid programme under which Economic and Monetary Union, including permanently fixed parities, would be achieved by 1980. This seemed to us to be dangerously over-ambitious: over-ambitious because the chances of achieving by 1980 the requisite degree of convergence of the rates of growth of productivity and wages rates, of investment and savings, seemed to us to be very small: dangerous because of the impossibility for any country, particularly a country with a relatively low growth rate, to manage its own economy efficiently and provide for full employment if it accepted permanently fixed parities without such convergence having been achieved. I understand that much new thinking is going on in the Community on the subject of Economic and Monetary Union and that the proposals now being considered for a second stage in it do not provide for automatic movement towards permanently fixed parities. You will find our objections very much lessened if we can all agree that there can be no question of trying to force the pace, of compelling member countries to accept permanently fixed parities if this means accepting massive unemployment or before their economies are ready.

7. Then we are concerned at another phrase from the Paris Summit Communiqué – at the intention there stated of transforming the whole complex of the relations of Member States into a European Union by 1980. What does this mean? Is it to be taken literally? It seems to us to imply a change which is quite unrealistic and not desired by our peoples, certainly not by the British people. I understand that work on clarifying this issue is about to begin within the Community. I shall watch carefully to see if this clarification will help to relieve our anxieties.

8. Then there is the Common Agricultural Policy. The position of the United Kingdom is different from that of the other Members of the Community in an important sense. We import a very much larger proportion of our food and if we have to pay a high price for these imports, this can impose a heavy burden on our

balance of payments. This is much more of a problem for us than for other Member
We are of course aware that the Community's prices are at present lower than they
were relative to other Community prices and that many of them are now below
world prices. But how long will this last? We are unable to agree to perpetuate
policies that would allow the butter mountains and the cheap butter sales to Russia
to recur. Are you sure that there will be no future mountain of beef in store? Have
the interests of the consumer been sufficiently safeguarded? Could overseas produc
have better access to Community markets? Is financial control sufficiently strict?
It is our view that more needs to be done to keep down the cost of the CAP which
accounts for 80% of the Community budget. At present the system does not take
sufficient account of the differing interests and circumstances of member countries
It confers privileges on some and imposes unfair burdens on others. That is why we
shall certainly be proposing major changes.

9. Then there is the question of the trade of Commonwealth and developing
countries, which is linked with the Common Agricultural Policy because of the nee
to offer a fair deal to the Community's consumers as well as to the suppliers overse
We are not satisfied that the arrangements made in the entry negotiations are as
good as they should have been, for the one or for the other. We have in mind not
only sugar and New Zealand butter, but the position of those Commonwealth
countries for whom the option of Association is not open. Apart from changes in
the field of the Common Agricultural Policy, no doubt the general position could b
improved if the Community's generalized preference scheme undergoes serious
improvement both in the industrial and agricultural sectors, if the Community whe
it comes to draw up its detailed mandate for the multilateral trade negotiations tak
a liberal attitude especially about agricultural trade and if the Protocol 22 negotiati
result in really generous terms for access to our markets of developing countries'
agricultural products, which is on the whole what they want to sell, as well as for
their industrial products. There is also the field of aid in which in our view the
Community should look wider than those countries eligible for association. We are
examining this whole field most carefully in the context of renegotiation in order
to see what should be done.

10. I turn next to the question whether existing rules interfere with the powers
over the British economy which we need to pursue effective regional, industrial,
fiscal and counter-inflationary policies. We want to be sure that, in cases where jobs
are in danger or where there is a need to sustain and develop valuable industrial
capacity, we can give aid quickly and effectively. To give another example, coordination of regional aids can usefully prevent over-bidding for internationally
available funds. But there is a major difference between those regional problems
which are mainly agricultural and those which are mainly industrial. We want to
make sure, in particular, that, against this background, we can continue to give our
own assisted areas the help which they need.

11. Finally, I come to the Community budget. Here fundamental changes are
required. Britain's income per head and her rate of growth is lower than in many of
your countries. I take it you would agree that the out-turn of the Community

udget should not in all justice result in massive subsidies across the exchanges from my country to yours. This is not acceptable.

12. We are not asking for charity. We seek a fair deal. In 1973, only paying 8.5% of the Community budget in accordance with the transitional key, we were already the second largest net contributors. At the end of our normal transitional period we shall be paying over 19%, well over the 16.5% which is our likely share of GNP at that time. If the full 'own resources' system were to be applied to us with no changes in 1980, we should find ourselves paying still more, perhaps several percentage points more, of the Community budget — in even sharper contrast with the relatively low share of GNP we can then expect to have. I am sure you will agree that something must be done about that. Britain cannot accept a permanent drain across the exchanges of several hundred million pounds sterling a year.

13. You will wish to know how we would propose that this renegotiation should proceed. I can assure the Council that we do not wish to disrupt the work of the Community more than is necessary during the period of renegotiation.

14. I shall come back to the Council at an early date with detailed proposals on the Common Agricultural Policy, the treatment of the Commonwealth and of developing countries, the Community budget and other areas of difficulty in the economic field. I hope you will agree then to have a general discussion; and to agree how certain of our requests for changes in the Community's arrangements should be handled.

15. Our initial approach will be to seek changes in the Community's policies and decisions which will meet our needs. We must see how we go and where we get. But we shall have to reserve the right to propose changes in the Treaties if it should turn out that essential interests cannot be met without them. I must also reserve the right to propose changes in the Treaties, if we find that in practice the existing rules, as they are interpreted, interfere with the powers over the British economy, which we need to pursue effective regional, industrial and fiscal policies.

16. I have spoken so far today about bread and butter issues, for these are very important to all our people. But we are also deeply concerned about the politics of the Community; about the broad direction which it is going to take both in its internal developments and in its relations with other countries or groups of countries.

17. The image of the Community in the United Kingdom is not good. My country wishes to remain a member of an effective Atlantic Alliance; and there is therefore concern about the degree of disagreement between the Community and the United States. Surely this is not inevitable. If the British people thought it was, it would adversely influence their attitude towards the development of the Community.

18. We shall not always be able to agree with the United States but the Community in devising its procedures and its common positions must always try to work with America whenever it can. Conversely America must try and work with us. Only if the Nine work harmoniously with the United States on both economic issues in the framework of the Community and on political issues in the framework of political cooperation, shall we surmount the difficulties to which President Nixon and Dr Kissinger have recently drawn attention.

19. We should also like to work with you to produce a stable, healthy and co-operative relationship with all those countries or groups of countries with whom Europe's life is intimately connected, for example with Japan, Canada and other industrialized countries; with the Commonwealth and the Community's Associates; with the Arab countries; and with the Soviet Union and Eastern Europe.

20. We are ready to intensify political consultation and cooperation. But before we can do so we need to agree on our broad aims. I should certainly like to see if we can do this together. The informal meeting to which our President has so kindly invited us later this month will provide an excellent opportunity.

21. So to conclude, we shall work for an early and successful result to what we in Britain have come to call renegotiation. Meanwhile we shall participate in the work of the Community and act in accordance with Community procedures, subject only to not proceeding with further processes of integration if these seem likely to prejudge the outcome of the negotiations. Our aim will be to get an agreement which can be regarded as providing a fair balance of advantage for each of our countries. If this can be achieved successfully, renegotiation will not damage the Community but will strengthen it.

142. Declaration by the President of the Council and the President of the Commission on the state of the Community, 2 April 1974[1]

I. After the discussion in the Council on 4 February the Presidents of the Council and the Commission were requested to draw up a joint report. Today, the point is not to add a further analysis to those already existing concerning the causes of the situation of the Community. The point is what we can do in order to overcome the stagnation which is threatening the Community. The guideline of our action in the coming months is to ensure the existence of the Community, to prevent any disintegration and to keep it moving, in particular, in all those fields in which important decisions have soon to be made.

This report is deliberately limited to the concrete questions which are of importance today. In this connection, the Decisions of the Summit Conferences of The Hague, Paris and Copenhagen remain our guides.

Energetic action is required because many fields of the Common Market are exposed to disruptions which jeopardize its very essence. This applies in particular to the payments-balances difficulties, whose type and extent may have permanent effects on everything which has so far been achieved by the Community.

The Presidents of the Council and of the Commission consider it necessary that the following proposals should be implemented as soon as possible, so that the Community's essential policies may be continued and the efficiency of the Institutions improved.

II. The most dangerous of the disruptive forces which threaten to undermine the

1 *Bull. EC*, 3–1974, pp. 9–11.

ommunity from inside is inflation. We must energetically combat this evil, which extending to ever more Community fields, by joint efforts. For this purpose we ust, as soon as possible, give concrete content to the major instruments of a ommunity policy, the stabilization guidelines and the converging decisions on which e Economics and Finance Ministers had agreed already in their February meeting. t the same time, we require immediate approval of the general resolution concerning e transition to a consolidation phase of the Economic and Monetary Union.

Any further loosening of the inter-Community currency association must be sisted with every force available. The Economics and Finance Ministers should e requested to seek means, on the basis of Commission proposals, on the one hand) ensure the continuation of the 'rump' serpent, and on the other to make possible e building of bridges to the Member States which are freely floating.

In order to further Economic and Monetary Union, we must now begin to alleviate e regional imbalances existing in the Community. For this, the Community needs e Regional Fund. The Council must as soon as possible arrive at an agreement on e main questions still outstanding; the capital endowment and the distribution y.

In the field of energy policy considerable demands are being made on the Com- unity, both from inside and outside. The Council must now rapidly agree the oposals submitted by the Commission. When the time comes, the Commission will bmit more demanding and comprehensive proposals of capital importance to which e Council will have to devote an initial examination in its meeting of May. These oposals are aimed at an effective Community energy-policy strategy, and they ill include problems of supply and of savings of energy and the proper functioning f the market. The definition of such a policy will give the Community the minimum f common action, solidarity and unity which it needs in order to be able to face s responsibility in the discussion of energy-policy problems in the different inter- ational bodies. In addition, such a policy will require the comprehensive cooperation hich is being sought with the oil-producing countries.

With a view to the entry into force of the Communities' 'own resources' system n 1 January 1975, the proposals for the strengthening of the budgetary powers of e European Parliament must be passed. In this way, the democratic element in e Community will be strengthened – and this also with an eye to further develop- ents.

In external relations also, decisions must finally be taken if a vacuum is not to ccur and common interests to suffer damage.

In relation to the Mediterranean countries with which negotiations are at present ing on, the Community is lagging behind as regards the fulfilment of its legal and olitical obligations. This being so, the Council must agree the supplementary egotiations mandate. Otherwise the claim that there exists a European Mediterranean olicy will cease to be credible.

In order that the negotiations with the African, Caribbean and Pacific developing untries may be concluded in good time, the Council must here also decide on e necessary additions to the guidelines for negotiations as soon as possible.

The equalization negotiations with the Community's leading trade partners under GATT Article XXIV Sec. 6 must be brought to a successful conclusion.

The endeavours to implement a Community development policy on a world-wide scale must be further pushed forward.

III. It will only be possible to make further progress with positive decisions and, in the long run, to ensure the efficiency of the Community, if we improve the decision-making process, as was already decided at the Paris Summit Conference. In this connection, the main elements are now the following practical proposals:

(*a*) In order to achieve an acceleration of the method of decision-making within a reasonable time, the members of the Council should make it their business – in particular when a clear majority has emerged in the Council – to enable a decision to be arrived at, *inter alia*, by refraining from voting.

(*b*) The political role of the Council as the European Executive should be reinfo For this purpose, we propose to begin each general Council meeting with a discussi in a limited framework, in which only Ministers, State Secretaries and the Presiden of the Commission are present. This would make it possible for the President to report on the progress of the work and offer the opportunity for a frank and free political discussion.

(*c*) In the week before each Council meeting there should be a working session of the Permanent Representatives Committee with the President of the Commissio at which the Agenda would be prepared and the most important political question on which the Council has to concentrate would be pinpointed.

(*d*) The Governments of all the Member States should, in their instructions, give more negotiating room to the Permanent Representatives, so that, as far as human possible, they may already agree at their level.

(*e*) More responsibility should be given to the Commission by applying Article 155, paragraph 4 of the Treaty establishing the European Economic Community, and in this way the cooperation between the Commission and the competent national authorities would be ensured by procedures which are based on those of the administrative or other existing committees in the Community.

IV. None of these decisions can be put off for long. They are required on politi and practical grounds. Nor may they be left to the Heads of State or Government. In order to guarantee the most important common interests, the Community must precisely at this time, prove its capacity to function and decide, and also its readin to advance, quite independently of whether the concepts of the future developme of the Community or of the form of its policy in all fields are already completely uniform. The outside world cares nothing about internal difficulties with which we have to struggle. The most important internal problems can only be overcome by us all acting together.

Naturally, there are differences of opinion which may not be simply glossed ov We will have to talk about these in the Council. However, they must not have the effect that every advance in internal policy which we have set ourselves as an aim, and the current negotiations, are inhibited and that the Community as a whole is crippled. Today, it is not a matter of discussing fundamental questions. But witho

a solid basis of Community agreement on the aims, there can in the long run be
no successful policy on the practical issues.

143. Regulation adopted by the Council of the European Communities concerning Community Loans, Brussels, 21 October 1974[1]

THE COUNCIL OF THE EUROPEAN COMMUNITIES,

Having regard to the Treaty establishing the European Economic Community,
and in particular Article 235 thereof;

Having regard to the proposal from the Commission;

Having regard to the Opinion of the European Parliament;

Whereas the considerable changes in the terms of international trade have produced
a deterioration in the balance of payments of the Member States of the Community;

Whereas the effects of this deterioration will vary from one Member State to
another and may thereby compromise the proper operation of the Common Market;

Whereas the Community should accordingly contribute to the financing required
by this situation, and to this end itself borrow funds to be put at the disposal of
Member States whose balance of payments is affected by the increase in the price
of petroleum products, in the form of loans having identical financial characteristics;

Whereas, moreover, intervention by the Community as such is likely to contribute to a stabilization of capital movements due to the increase in the price of
petroleum products, to the benefit of the whole international community;

Whereas each loan to a Member State must be conditional upon the adoption by
that Member State of economic policy measures designed to redress its balance of
payments;

Whereas it follows from the foregoing that transactions of this type are necessary
to attain the objectives of the Community as defined in the Treaty, and in particular
the harmonious development of economic activities throughout the Community;

Whereas the Treaty makes no provision for the powers of action required for this
purpose,

HAS ADOPTED THIS REGULATION:

Article 1

The Community may undertake a series of operations to raise funds, either directly
from third countries and financial institutions, or on the capital markets, with the
sole aim of re-lending those funds to one or more Member States in balance of payments difficulties caused by the increase in prices of petroleum products.

Article 2

The opening of the negotiations necessary for each loan transaction shall be authorized

1 *Europe, Documents*, No. 823, 24 October 1974.

by the Council on the initiative of one or more Member States. The decision to open negotiations shall also lay down the procedures for those negotiations.

In the light of the outcome of those negotiations, the Council shall decide on what terms each loan agreement is to be concluded. The average period for which funds are borrowed shall not be less than 5 years.

Article 3

The Council shall decide on the principle and the terms of loans to be granted to one or more Member States and on the economic policy conditions to be fulfilled by each beneficiary Member State in order to redress its balance of payments.

The funds shall be paid only into Central Banks and shall be used only for the purposes indicated in Article 1.

Article 4

The operations of borrowing and lending referred to in Article 1 shall be expressed in the same currency and carried out on the same terms with respect to repayment of the principal and payment of interest. The costs incurred by the Community in concluding and carrying out each operation shall be borne by the beneficiary Member State concerned.

Article 5

The loan operations authorized by this Regulation shall be limited to the equivalent in European monetary units of account of 3,000 million US dollars in principal and interest payments.

Article 6

The guarantees designed to ensure that the loans referred to in Article 1 are serviced and repaid in all circumstances shall not exceed the following percentages applied to the total amount of the loan in principal and interest:

	%
Germany	44.04
United Kingdom	44.04
France	44.04
Italy	29.36
Belgium/Luxembourg	14.68
Netherlands	14.68
Denmark	6.60
Ireland	2.56

Article 7

The Council shall lay down detailed rules for the implementation of this Regulation

Article 8

The measures referred to in Articles 2, 3 and 7 shall be adopted by the Council acting unanimously on a proposal from the Commission, which shall consult the Monetary Committee on the matter.

This Regulation shall be binding in its entirety and directly applicable in all Member States.

144. Communiqué issued following the Conference of the Heads of Government of the European Community, Paris, 10 December 1974[1]

1. The Heads of Government of the nine States of the Community, the Ministers of Foreign Affairs and the President of the Commission, meeting in Paris at the invitation of the French President, examined the various problems confronting Europe. They took note of the reports drawn up by the Ministers of Foreign Affairs and recorded the agreement reached by these Ministers on various points raised in the reports.

2. Recognizing the need for an overall approach to the internal problems involved in achieving European unity and the external problems facing Europe, the Heads of Government consider it essential to ensure progress and overall consistency in the activities of the Communities and in the work on political cooperation.

3. The Heads of Government have therefore decided to meet, accompanied by the Ministers of Foreign Affairs, three times a year and, whenever necessary, in the Council of the Communities and in the context of political cooperation.

The administrative Secretariat will be provided for in an appropriate manner with due regard for existing practices and procedures.

In order to ensure consistency in Community activities and continuity of work, the Ministers of Foreign Affairs, meeting in the Council of the Community, will act as initiators and coordinators. They may hold political cooperation meetings at the same time.

These arrangements do not in any way affect the rules and procedures laid down in the Treaties or the provisions on political cooperation in the Luxembourg and Copenhagen Reports. At the various meetings referred to in the preceding paragraphs the Commission will exercise the powers vested in it and play the part assigned to it by the above texts.

4. With a view to progress towards European unity, the Heads of Government reaffirm their determination gradually to adopt common positions and coordinate their diplomatic action in all areas of international affairs which affect the interests of the European Community. The President-in-office will be the spokesman for the Nine and will set out their views in international diplomacy. He will ensure that the necessary concertation always takes place in good time.

1 *Europe, Documents*, No. 831, 11 December 1974.

In view of the increasing role of political cooperation in the construction of Eur the European Assembly must be more closely associated with the work of the Presidency, for example through replies to questions on political cooperation put to him by its Members.

5. The Heads of Government consider it necessary to increase the solidarity of the Nine both by improving Community procedures and by developing new common policies in areas to be decided on and granting the necessary powers to the Institutions.

6. In order to improve the functioning of the Council of the Community, they consider that it is necessary to renounce the practice which consists of making agreement on all questions conditional on the unanimous consent of the Member States, whatever their respective positions may be regarding the conclusions reached in Luxembourg on 28 January 1966.

7. Greater latitude will be given to the Permanent Representatives so that only the most important problems need be discussed in the Council. To this end, each Member State will take the measures it considers necessary to strengthen the role of the Permanent Representatives and involve them in preparing the national positions on European affairs.

8. Moreover, they agree on the advantage of making use of the provisions of the Treaty of Rome whereby the powers of implementation and management arising out of the Community rules may be conferred on the Commission.

9. Cooperation between the Nine in areas outside the scope of the Treaty will be continued where it has already begun. It should be extended to other areas by bringing together the representatives of the Governments, meeting within the Coun whenever possible.

10. A working party will be set up to study the possibility of establishing a Passport Union and, in anticipation of this, the introduction of a uniform passport.

If possible, this draft should be submitted to the Governments of the Member States before 31 December 1976. It will, in particular, provide for stage-by-stage harmonization of legislation affecting aliens and for the abolition of passport contr within the Community.

11. Another working party will be instructed to study the conditions and the timing under which the citizens of the nine Member States could be given special rights as members of the Community.

12. The Heads of Government note that the election of the European Assembly by universal suffrage, one of the objectives laid down in the Treaty, should be achieved as soon as possible. In this connection, they await with interest the propos of the European Assembly, on which they wish the Council to act in 1976. On this assumption, elections by direct universal suffrage could take place at any time in or after 1978.

Since the European Assembly is composed of representatives of the peoples of the States united within the Community, each people must be represented in an appropriate manner.

The European Assembly will be associated with the achievement of European unity. The Heads of Government will not fail to take into consideration the points of view which, in October 1972, they asked it to express on this subject.

The competence of the European Assembly will be extended, in particular by granting it certain powers in the Communities' legislative process.

Statement by the United Kingdom delegation

The Prime Minister of the United Kingdom explained that Her Majesty's Government did not wish to prevent the Governments of the other eight Member States from making progress with the election of the European Assembly by universal suffrage.

Her Majesty's Government could not themselves take up a position on the proposal before the process of renegotiation had been completed and the results of renegotiation submitted to the British people.

Statement by the Danish delegation

The Danish delegation is unable at this stage to commit itself to introducing elections by universal suffrage in 1978.

13. The Heads of Government note that the process of transforming the whole complex of relations between the Member States, in accordance with the decision taken in Paris in October 1972, has already started. They are determined to make further progress in this direction. In this connection, they consider that the time has come for the Nine to agree as soon as possible on an overall concept of European Union. Consequently, in accordance with the requests made by the Paris meeting of Heads of State and of Government in October 1972, they confirm the importance which they attach to the reports to be made by the Community Institutions. They request the European Assembly, the Commission and the Court of Justice to bring the submission of their reports forward to before the end of June 1975. They agreed to invite Mr Tindemans, Prime Minister of the Kingdom of Belgium, to submit a comprehensive report to the Heads of Government before the end of 1975, on the basis of the reports received from the Institutions and the consultations which he is to have with the Governments and with a wide range of public opinion in the Community.

Economic and monetary union

14. The Heads of Government having noted that internal and international difficulties have prevented in 1973 and 1974 the accomplishment of expected progress on the road to EMU affirm that in this field their will has not weakened and that their objective has not changed since the Paris Conference.

Convergence of economic policies

15. The Heads of Government discussed the economic situation in the world and in the Community.

16. They noted that the increase in energy prices is adding to inflationary tendencies and balance of payments deficits and intensifying the threat of general recession. The resulting alterations in the terms of trade are forcing the Member States to re-direct their production structures.

17. The Heads of Government reaffirm that the aim of their economic policy continues to be to combat inflation and maintain employment. The cooperation of both sides of industry will be essential if this policy is to succeed. They emphasize that in the present circumstances high priority must be given to economic revival in conditions of stability i.e. action aimed both at preventing a general economic recession and restoring stability. This must not involve any recourse to protectionist measures which, by setting up a chain reaction, could jeopardize economic revival.

Member States which have a balance of payments surplus must implement an economic policy of stimulating domestic demand and maintaining a high level of employment, without creating new inflationary conditions. Such an attitude would make it easier for countries which have considerable balance of payments deficits to follow a policy which will ensure a satisfactory level of employment, stabilization of costs and an improvement in their external trade balance without resorting to protectionist measures.

18. In the context of the effort to be made by countries having a surplus, the Heads of Government greet the economic policy measures already adopted by the Netherlands Government as a step in the right direction. They also note with satisfaction the short-term economic programme which the Government of the Federal Republic of Germany intends to follow particularly as regards stimulating public and private investment, and the fact that the Belgian Government intends to follow suit.

They also express satisfaction at the efforts made by the countries having a balance of payments deficit to maintaining their competitive position so as to achieve a more satisfactory balance of payments and to improve the level of employment.

19. While acknowledging the special situation of each of the Member States of the Community – which makes a uniform policy inappropriate – the Heads of Government stress that it is absolutely necessary to agree on the policies to be adopted. This convergence will be meaningful only if it works towards Community solidarity and is based on effective permanent consultation machinery. The Ministers of Economic Affairs and Finance will be responsible, within the framework of Communi procedures, for implementing these guidelines.

20. It is obvious that all these policies will be really effective only insofar as the world's major industrialized countries succeed in arresting incipient recessionary tendencies.

In this connection, they note with satisfaction the account given by the Chancellor of the Federal Republic of Germany of his talks with the President of the United States.

They desire that, at his forthcoming meeting with President Ford, the President of the French Republic should, on behalf of the Community, stress the importance of convergence between the economic policies of all industrialized countries along the lines indicated above.

They also wish the Community and its Member States to do the same during the forthcoming international consultations and in the appropriate international bodies.

21. The Community will continue to contribute to the harmonious expansion of world trade, especially in relation to developing countries, and in order to do so will take a constructive part in the GATT trade negotiations which it hopes to see actively continued in the near future.

Regional policy

22. The Heads of Government decide that the European Regional Development Fund, designed to correct the principal regional imbalances in the Community resulting notably from agricultural predominance, industrial change and structural under-employment will be put into operation by the institutions of the Community with effect from 1 January 1975.

23. The Fund will be endowed with 300 mua in 1975, with 500 mua for each of the years 1976 and 1977, i.e. 1300 mua.[1]

24. This total sum of 1300 mua will be financed up to a level of 150 mua by credits not presently utilised from EAGGF[2] (Guidance Section).

The resources of the Fund will be divided along the lines envisaged by the Commission:

Belgium	1.5%
Denmark	1.3%
France	15%
Ireland	6%
Italy	40%
Luxembourg	0.1%
Netherlands	1.7%
Federal Republic of Germany	6.4%
United Kingdom	28%

Ireland will in addition be given another 6 mua which will come from a reduction in the shares of the other Member States with the exception of Italy.

Employment problems

25. The effort needed to combat inflation and the risks of recession and unemployment as described above must accord with the imperative of a progressive and equitable social policy if it is to receive support and cooperation from both sides of industry, both at national and Community level.

In this respect, the Heads of Government emphasize that the Economic and Social Committee can play an important role in associating both sides of industry in the definition of the Community's economic and social aims.

1 Units of account.
2 European Regional Development Fund.

Above all, vigorous and coordinated action must be taken at Community level to deal with the problem of employment. This will require the Member States, in conjunction with the organizations concerned, to coordinate their employment policies in an appropriate manner and to set priority targets.

26. When the time is ripe, the Council of the Community will consider, in the light of experience and with due regard to the problem of the regions and categories of workers most affected by employment difficulties, whether and to what extent it will be necessary to increase the resources of the Social Fund.

27. Being convinced that in this period of economic difficulty special emphasis should be placed on social measures, the Heads of Government reaffirm the importance which they attach to implementation of the measures listed in the Social Action Programme approved by the Council in its Resolution of 21 January 1974.

28. The Heads of Government make it their objective to harmonize the degree of social security afforded by the various Member States, while maintaining progress but without requiring that the social system obtaining in all Member States should be identical.

Energy

29. The Heads of Government discussed the energy problem and in this connection the related major financial problems created for the Community and for the wider world.

30. They further noted that the Ministers of Energy of the Community countries are due to meet on 17 December.

31. The Heads of Government, aware of the paramount importance which the energy problem has in world economy, have discussed the possibilities for cooperation between oil exporting and oil importing countries, on which subject they heard a report from the Federal Chancellor.

32. The Heads of Government attach very great importance to the forthcoming meeting between the President of the United States and the President of the French Republic.

33. The Heads of Government, referring to the Council Resolution of 17 September 1974, have invited the Community Institutions to work out and to implement a common energy policy in the shortest possible time.

Britain's membership of the Community

34. The Prime Minister of the United Kingdom indicated the basis on which Her Majesty's Government approached the negotiations regarding Britain's continued membership of the Community, and set out the particular issues to which the Government attached the highest importance.

35. The Heads of Government recall the statement made during the accession negotiations by the Community to the effect that 'if unacceptable situations were

to arise, the very life of the Community would make it imperative for the institutions to find equitable solutions'.

36. They confirm that the system of 'own resources' represents one of the fundamental elements of the economic integration of the Community.

37. They invite the institutions of the Community (the Council and the Commission) to set up as soon as possible a correcting mechanism of a general application which, in the framework of the system of 'own resources' and in harmony with its normal functioning, based on objective criteria and taking into consideration in particular the suggestions made to this effect by the British Government, could prevent during the period of convergence of the economies of the Member States, the possible development of situations unacceptable for a Member State and incompatible with the smooth working of the Community.

145. Resolution approved by the Council of the European Communities concerning Energy Policy, Brussels, 17 December 1974[1]

The Council of the European Communities,

Having noted the Commission's communication of 29 November 1974 'Community energy policy — Objectives for 1985';

Considering the Resolution it adopted on 17 September 1974;

Whereas, in accordance with point 10 of that Resolution, the Commission will record every six months and the Council will periodically discuss the progress made in the realization of the Community objectives, and in particular the measures taken at Community and national level;

Whereas, at their meeting in Paris on 9 and 10 December 1974 the Heads of Government of the Member States of the Community called upon the Community institutions to work out and implement a common energy policy as quickly as possible;

Whereas implementation of such a policy involves the drawing up of quantitative joint objectives representing guidelines for national policies and serving as a significant guide for energy producers and consumers in the Community;

Whereas the energy policy objectives of the Community show how much can be achieved by implementing a common policy;

Whereas each of the Member States should be able, according to its own resources and restraints, to contribute to the attainment of these objectives;

Whereas the continuation of a high degree of Community dependence on energy sources, especially oil, imported from third countries, would, under the present and foreseeable conditions on the world market, be such as to jeopardize the economic balance of the Community and economic and social progress; and whereas it is therefore necessary to reduce this dependence as much as possible;

1 *Bull. EC*, 12–1974, pp. 14–17.

Considering the prospects held out by the various sources of energy for the attainment of this objective, taking account of the time required to put them into use, of their potential long-term contribution, of the economic conditions for making them available and of the need to develop secure and competitive resources and to ensure the protection of the environment;

Whereas it should be possible to apply coherent guidelines to the various energy resources of the Community while complying with the Treaties;

PART I – GENERAL OBJECTIVES
Paragraph 1

Affirms that, on the basis of present prospects within the Member States, the Community's level of dependence on imported energy will reach 50% by 1985.

Paragraph 2

Approves the objectives of reducing Community dependence on imported energy to 50% and if possible to 40% by 1985 (63% in 1973).

Paragraph 3

— Takes note of the Commission's opinion that the more ambitious objective of 40% could be attained;
— Requests Community institutions to keep the means of achieving this objective under constant review.

Paragraph 4

Notes that, if these objectives are to be attained, the Community supply pattern should be as follows by 1985:

Total primary energy requirements* (in %)

	For the record		1985 Objectives (figures rounded off)	
	1973 Estimates	1985 Initial forecasts†	50% dependence	40% dependence
Solid fuels	22.6	10	17	17
Oil	61.4	64	49	41
Natural gas	11.6	15	18	23
Hydroelectric and geothermal power	3.0	2	3	3
Nuclear energy	1.4	9	13	16
Total requirements	100	100	100	100

* Internal consumption + exports + bunkers.
† Source. 'Prospects of primary energy demand in the Community (1975 – 1980 – 1985)', supplemented by an estimate made in January 1973 for the new Member States.

PART II – SPECIFIC OBJECTIVES
Paragraph 5

Decides to pursue the following specific objectives:

1. Energy demand

A. Reduce the rate of growth of energy consumption for the Community as a whole
in order to achieve by 1985 a level 15% below the January 1973 estimates, bearing
in mind that this percentage may be different for the various Member States and
without ruling out the possibility of setting specific objectives, depending on
circumstances, for saving energy in the shorter term.
B. Alter the pattern in energy consumption by progressively increasing the use of
reliable energy sources and relying more and more on electricity as nuclear energy
in particular is developed. The Commission feels that in this way electricity would
cover 35% of energy consumption by 1985.

2. Energy supply
2A. Solid fuels

- Maintain the level of the Community's coal production (180 Mtoe by 1985)
  under economically satisfactory conditions,
- Increase the possibilities of importing coal from third countries (40 Mtoe by
  1985),
- Raise brown coal and peat production to 30 Mtoe.

2B. Natural gas

- Step up Community research and production (land and underwater deposits)
  to obtain at least 175, and if possible 225 Mtoe by 1985;
- Secure imports of 95–115 Mtoe from third countries.

2C. Nuclear energy

Provide power stations with an installed capacity of at least 160 GWe and, if possible,
of 200 GWe by 1985.

2D. Hydroelectric and geothermal power

Establish and develop sites for the production of hydroelectric and geothermal
power to raise their contribution to energy supply to 45 Mtoe.

2E. Oil

- Restrict oil consumption where it can be economically replaced by other
  energy sources,

– Step up research and Community production (land and underwater deposits) to at least 180 Mtoe by 1985,

– Cut back imports from third countries to 550 Mtoe (640 in 1973) according to national prospects; the objective proposed by the Commission for other energy sources would enable this amount to be reduced to 420 Mtoe. The percentage of imported oil in the total energy requirements would be respectively 38 and 28% (61% in 1973) or 75 to 70% of oil consumption (98% in 1973).

2F. Other sources of energy

Ensure by a technological research and development policy that traditional forms of energy are better exploited and, in the long term, replaced by new sources of energy.

Paragraph 6

Requests Member States to take account of these Community objectives when framing their energy policies.

Paragraph 7

Requests the Commission to submit six-monthly reports to it, the first on 30 June 1975, on the progress made towards achieving the Community objectives, and in particular on the measures taken at Community and national level.

Paragraph 8

Requests the Commission to submit proposals for the implementation of this Resolution.

146. Joint declaration by the European Parliament, the Council and the Commission, 19 February 1975[1]

The European Parliament, the Council and the Commission,

Whereas from 1 January 1975, the Budget of the Communities will be financed entirely from the Communities' own resources;

Whereas in order to implement this system the Parliament will be given increased budgetary powers;

Whereas the increase in the budgetary powers of the European Parliament must

---

1 *Bull. EC*, 2–1975, p. 87. Approved by the Council in December 1974, the Parliament on 19 February 1975, and the Commission on 26 February 1975.

be accompanied by an effective participation by the latter in the procedure for preparing important decisions which give rise to expenditure charged to the budget of the Communities;

Have agreed as follows:

1. A conciliation procedure between the European Parliament and the Council with the active assistance of the Commission shall be instituted.

2. This procedure may be followed for Community acts of general application which have appreciable financial implications, and of which the adoption is not required by virtue of acts already in existence.

3. When submitting its proposal the Commission shall indicate whether the act in question is, in its opinion, capable of being the subject of the conciliation procedure. The European Parliament, when giving its Opinion, and the Council may request that this procedure be initiated.

4. The procedure shall be initiated if the criteria laid down in paragraph 2 are met and if the Council intends to depart from the Opinion adopted by the European Parliament.

5. The conciliation shall take place in a 'Conciliation Committee' consisting of the Council and representatives of the European Parliament. The Commission shall participate in the work of the Conciliation Committee.

6. The aim of the procedure shall be to seek an agreement between the European Parliament and the Council.

The procedure should normally take place during a period not exceeding three months, unless the act in question has to be adopted before a specific date or if the matter is urgent, in which case the Council may fix an appropriate time-limit.

7. When the positions of the two institutions are sufficiently close, the European Parliament may give a new Opinion, after which the Council shall take definitive action.

147. Convention signed by the Member States of the European Community and Forty-six African, Caribbean and Pacific States, Lomé, Republic of Togo, 28 February 1975[1]

TITLE 1
TRADE COOPERATION

Article 1

In the field of trade cooperation, the object of this Convention is to promote trade between the Contracting Parties, taking account of their respective levels of development, and, in particular, of the need to secure additional benefits for the trade of ACP States, in order to accelerate the rate of growth of their trade and improve

1 Commission of the European Communities, *The Courier*, 31, Special issue, March 1975, pp. 6–21. See also for the texts of the Five Protocols which are annexed to the Convention.

the conditions of access of their products to the market of the European Economic Community, (hereinafter called the 'Community') so as to ensure a better balance in the trade of the Contracting Parties.

To this end the Contracting Parties shall apply Chapters 1 and 2 of this Title.

Chapter 1
Trade arrangements

Article 2

1. Products originating in the ACP States shall be imported into the Community free of customs duties and charges having equivalent effect, but the treatment applied to these products may not be more favourable than that applied by the Member States among themselves.

For the purpose of the first subparagraph the transitional provisions in force relating to the residual customs duties and charges having equivalent effect resulting from the application of Articles 32 and 36 of the Act concerning the Conditions of Accession and the Adjustments to the Treaties shall have no application.

2 (a) Products originating in the ACP States:
– listed in Annex II to the Treaty when they come under a common organization of the market within the meaning of Article 40 of the Treaty, or
– subject, on importation into the Community, to specific rules introduced as a result of the implementation of the common agricultural policy; shall be imported into the Community notwithstanding the general arrangements applied in respect of third countries, in accordance with the following provisions:

(i) those products shall be imported free of customs duties for which Community provisions in force at the time of importation do not provide, apart from customs duties, for the application of any other measure relating to their importation;

(ii) for products other than those referred to under (i), the Community shall take the necessary measures to ensure, as a general rule, more favourable treatment than the general treatment applicable to the same products originating in third countries to which the most-favoured-nation clause applies.

(b) These arrangements shall enter into force at the same time as this Convention and shall remain applicable for its duration.

If, however, during the application of this Convention, the Community,
– subjects one or more products to common organization of the market or to specific rules introduced as a result of the implementation of the common agricultural policy, it reserves the right to adapt the import treatment for these products originating in the ACP States, following consultations within the Council of Ministers. In such cases, paragraph 2 (a) shall be applicable;
– modifies the common organization of the market in a particular product or the specific rules introduced as a result of the implementation of the common agricultural policy, it reserves the right to modify the arrangements laid down

for products originating in the ACP States, following consultations within the Council of Ministers. In such cases, the Community undertakes to ensure that products originating in the ACP States continue to enjoy an advantage comparable to that previously enjoyed in relation to products originating in third countries benefiting from the most-favoured-nation clause.

Article 3

. The Community shall not apply to imports of products originating in the ACP States any quantitative restrictions or measures having equivalent effect other than those which the Member States apply among themselves.

2. Paragraph 1, however, shall not prejudice the import treatment applied to the products referred to in the first indent of Article 2 (2) (a).

The Community shall inform the ACP States when residual quantitative restrictions are eliminated in respect of any of these products.

3. This Article shall not prejudice the treatment that the Community applies to certain products in implementation of world commodity agreements to which the Community and the ACP States concerned are signatory.

Article 4

Nothing in this Convention shall preclude prohibitions or restrictions on imports, exports or goods in transit justified on grounds of public morality, public policy or public security; the protection of health and life of humans, animals and plants; the protection of national treasures possessing artistic, historic or archaeological value or the protection of industrial and commercial property.

Such prohibitions or restrictions shall not, however, constitute a means of arbitrary discrimination or a disguised restriction on trade.

Article 5

Where new measures or measures stipulated in programmes adopted by the Community for the approximation of laws and regulations in order to facilitate the movement of goods are likely to affect the interests of one or more ACP States the Community shall, prior to adopting such measures, inform the ACP States thereof through the Council of Ministers.

In order to enable the Community to take into consideration the interests of the ACP States concerned, consultations shall be held upon the request of the latter with a view to reaching a satisfactory solution.

Article 6

Where existing rules or regulations of the Community adopted in order to facilitate the movement of goods or where the interpretation, application or administration thereof affect the interests of one or more ACP States, consultations shall be held at the request of the latter with a view to reaching a satisfactory solution.

With a view to finding a satisfactory solution, the ACP States may also bring up within the Council of Ministers any other problems relating to the movement of goods which might result from measures taken or to be taken by the Member States

The competent institutions of the Community shall to the greatest possible extent inform the Council of Ministers of such measures.

Article 7

1. In view of their present development needs, the ACP States shall not be required for the duration of this Convention, to assume, in respect of imports of produce originating in the Community, obligations corresponding to the commitments entered into by the Community in respect of imports of the products originating in the ACP States, under this Chapter.

2. (a) In their trade with the Community, the ACP States shall not discriminate among the Member States, and shall grant to the Community treatment no less favourable than the most-favoured-nation treatment.

(b) The most-favoured-nation treatment referred to in subparagraph (a) shall not apply in respect of trade or economic relations between ACP States or between one or more ACP States and other developing countries.

Article 8

Each Contracting Party shall communicate its customs tariff to the Council of Ministers within a period of three months following the entry into force of this Convention. It shall also communicate any subsequent amendments to that tariff as and when they occur.

Article 9

1. The concept of 'originating products' for the purposes of implementing this Chapter, and the methods of administrative cooperation relating thereto, are laid down in Protocol No. 1.

2. The Council of Ministers may adopt any amendment to Protocol No 1.

3. Where the concept of 'originating products' has not yet been declined for a given product in implementation of paragraphs 1 or 2, each Contracting Party shall continue to apply its own rules.

Article 10

1. If, as a result of applying the provisions of this Chapter, serious disturbances occur in a sector of the economy of the Community or of one or more of its Memb States, or jeopardize their external financial stability, or if difficulties arise which

may result in a deterioration in a sector of the economy of a region of the Community, the latter may take, or may authorize the Member State concerned to take, the necessary safeguard measures. These measures and the methods of applying them shall be notified immediately to the Council of Ministers.

2. For the purpose of implementing paragraph 1, priority shall be given to such measures as would least disturb the trade relations between the Contracting Parties and the attainment of the objectives of the Convention. These measures shall not exceed the limits of what is strictly necessary to remedy the difficulties that have arisen.

Article 11

In order to ensure effective implementation of the provisions of this Convention in the field of trade cooperation, the Contracting Parties agree to inform and consult each other.

Consultations shall take place, at the request of the Community or of the ACP States, in accordance with the conditions provided for in the rules of procedure in Article 74, particularly in the following cases:

1. Where Contracting Parties envisage taking any trade measures affecting the interest of one or more Contracting Parties under this Convention, they shall inform the Council of Ministers thereof. Consultations shall take place, where the Contracting Parties concerned so request, in order to take into account their respective interests.

2. Where the Community envisages concluding a preferential trade agreement it shall inform the ACP States thereof. Consultations shall take place, where the ACP States so request, in order to safeguard their interests.

3. Where the Community or the Member States take safeguard measures in accordance with Article 10, consultations on these measures may take place within the Council of Ministers, where the Contracting Parties concerned so request, notably with a view to ensuring compliance with Article 10 (2).

4. If, during the application of this Convention, the ACP States consider that agricultural products covered by Article 2 (2) (a), other than those subject to special treatment, call for special treatment, consultations may take place within the Council of Ministers.

Chapter 2
Trade promotion
Article 12

With a view to attaining the objectives they have set themselves as regards trade and industrial cooperation the Contracting Parties shall carry out trade promotion activities which will be aimed at helping the ACP States to derive maximum benefit from Title I. Chapter 1 and Title III and to participate under the most favourable conditions in the Community, regional and international markets.

Article 13

The trade promotion activities provided for in Article 12 shall include:

(*a*) improving the structure and working methods of organizations, departments or firms contributing to the development of the foreign trade of ACP States, or setting up such organizations, departments or firms;

(*b*) basic training or advanced vocational training of staff in trade promotion;

(*c*) participation by the ACP States in fairs, exhibitions, specialized international shows and the organization of trade events;

(*d*) improving cooperation between economic operators in the Member States and the ACP States and establishing links to promote such cooperation;

(*e*) carrying out and making use of market research and marketing studies;

(*f*) producing and distributing trade information in various forms within the Community and the ACP States with a view to developing trade.

Article 14

Applications for financing of trade promotion activities shall be presented to the Community by the ACP State or ACP States concerned under the conditions laid down in Title IV.

Article 15

The Community shall participate, under the conditions laid down in Title IV and in Protocol No. 2, in financing trade promotion activities for promoting the development of exports of ACP States.

TITLE II
EXPORT EARNINGS FROM COMMODITIES
Chapter 1
Stabilization of export earnings

Article 16

With the aim of remedying the harmful effects of the instability of export earnings and of thereby enabling the ACP States to achieve the stability, profitability and sustained growth of their economies, the Community shall implement a system for guaranteeing the stabilization of earnings from exports by the ACP States to the Community of certain products on which their economies are dependent and which are affected by fluctuations in price and/or quantity.

Article 17

1. Export earnings to which the stabilization system applies shall be those accruing

from the exportation by the ACP States to the Community of the products on the following list, drawn up taking account of factors such as employment, deterioration of the terms of trade between the Community and the ACP State concerned, the level of development of the State concerned and the particular difficulties of the least developed, landlocked or island ACP States listed in Article 24:

a. Groundnut products
(aa) groundnuts, shelled or not
(ab) groundnut oil
(ac) groundnut oilcake

b. Cocoa products
(ba) cocoa beans
(bb) cocoa paste
(bc) cocoa butter

c. Coffee products
(ca) raw or roasted coffee
(cb) extracts, essences or concentrates of coffee

d. Cotton products
(da) cotton, not carded or combed
(db) cotton linters

e. Coconut products
(ea) coconuts
(eb) copra
(ec) coconut oil
(ed) coconut oilcake

f. Palm, palm nut and kernel products
(fa) palm oil
(fb) palm nut and kernel oil
(fc) palm nut and kernel oilcake
(fd) palm nuts and kernels

g. Raw hides, skins and leather
(ga) raw hides and skins
(gb) bovine cattle leather
(gc) sheep and lamb skin leather
(gd) goat and kid skin leather

h. Wood products
(ha) wood in the rough
(hb) wood roughly squared or half-squared, but not further manufactured
(hc) wood sawn lengthwise, but not further prepared

i. Fresh bananas

k. Tea

l. Raw sisal

m. Iron ore
Iron ores and concentrates and roasted iron pyrites.
The statistics used for implementation of the system shall be those obtained by cross-

checking the statistics of the ACP States and of the Community, account being taken of the fob values.

The system shall be implemented in respect of the products listed above where they are:

(a) released for home use in the Community;

(b) brought under the inward processing arrangements there in order to be processed.

2. The system shall apply to an ACP State's export earnings from the products listed above if, during the year preceding the year of application, earnings from the export of the product or products to all destinations represented at least 7.5% of its total earnings from merchandise exports, for sisal, however, the percentage shall be 5%. For the least developed, landlocked or island ACP States listed in Article 24 the percentage shall be 2.5%.

3. Nonetheless if, not sooner than 12 months following the entry into force of this Convention, one or more products not contained in this list, but upon which the economies of one or more ACP States depend to a considerable extent, are affected by sharp fluctuations, the Council of Ministers may decide whether the product or products should be included in the list, without prejudice to Article 18 (1).

4. For certain special cases the system shall apply to exports of the products in question irrespective of destination.

5. The ACP States concerned shall certify that the products to which the stabiliz ation system applies have originated in their territory.

Article 18

1. For the purposes specified in Article 16 and for the duration of this Convention, the Community shall allocate to the stabilization system a total amount of 375 million units of account to cover all its commitments under the said system. This amount shall be managed by the Commission of the European Communities (hereinafter called the 'Commission').

2. This total amount shall be divided into five equal annual instalments. Every year except the last, the Council of Ministers may authorize, where required, the use in advance of a maximum of 20% of the following year's instalment.

3. Whatever balance remains at the end of each year of the first four years of the application of this Convention shall be carried forward automatically to the followi year.

4. On the basis of a report submitted to it by the Commission the Council of Ministers may reduce the amount of the transfers to be made under the stabilizatio system.

5. Before the expiry of this Convention, the Council of Ministers shall decide on the use to which any balance remaining from the total amount referred to in paragraph 1 is to be put and also on the terms to be laid down for the further use of amounts still to be paid by the ACP States, under Article 21, after the expiry of this Convention.

Article 19

1. In order to implement the stabilization system a reference level shall be calculated for each ACP State and for each product.

This reference level shall correspond to the component of export earnings during the four years preceding each year of application.

2. An ACP State shall be entitled to request a financial transfer if, on the basis of the results of a calendar year, its actual earnings, as defined in Article 17, from each of the products considered individually, are at least 7.5% below the reference level. For the least developed, landlocked or island ACP States listed in Article 24 the percentage shall be 2.5%.

3. The request from the ACP State concerned shall be addressed to the Commission, which shall examine it in the light of the volume of resources available.

The difference between the reference level and actual earnings shall constitute the basis of the transfer.

4. However,

(a) should examination of the request, to be undertaken by the Commission in conjunction with the ACP State concerned, show that the fall in earnings from exports to the Community of the products in question is the result of a trade policy measure of the ACP State concerned adversely affecting exports to the Community in particular, the request shall not be admissible;

(b) should examination of the total exports of the requesting ACP State show a significant change, consultations shall be held between the Commission and the requesting State to determine whether such changes are likely to have an effect on the amount of the transfer, and if so to what extent.

5. Except in the case referred to in paragraph 4 (a) the Commission shall, in conjunction with the requesting ACP State, draw up a draft decision to make a transfer.

6. All necessary steps shall be taken to ensure that transfers are made rapidly, for example by means of advances, normally six-monthly.

Article 20

The recipient ACP State shall decide how the resources will be used. It shall inform the Commission annually of the use to which it has put the resources transferred.

Article 21

1. The amounts transferred shall not bear interest.

2. The ACP States which have received transfers shall contribute, in the five years following the allocation of each transfer, towards the reconstitution of the resources made available for the system by the Community.

3. Each ACP State shall help reconstitute the resources when it is found that the trend of its export earnings will so permit.

To this effect, the Commission shall determine, for each year and for each product, and on the conditions specified in Article 17 (1), whether

— the unit value of the exports is higher than the reference unit value;
— the quantity actually exported to the Community is at least equal to the reference quantity.

If the two conditions are met at the same time, the recipient ACP State shall pay back into the system, within the limit of the transfers it has received, an amount equal to the reference quantity multiplied by the difference between the reference unit value and the actual unit value.

4. If, on expiry of the five-year period referred to in paragraph 2, the resources have not been fully reconstituted, the Council of Ministers, taking into consideration in particular the situation of and prospects for the balance of payments, exchange reserves and foreign indebtedness of the ACP States concerned, may decide that:

— the sums outstanding are to be reconstituted wholly or partially, in one or more instalments;
— rights to repayment are to be waived.

5. Paragraphs 2, 3 and 4 shall not apply to the ACP States listed in Article 48.

Article 22

For each transfer a 'transfer agreement' shall be drawn up and concluded between the Commission and the ACP State concerned.

Article 23

1. In order to ensure that the stabilization system functions efficiently and rapidly, statistical and customs cooperation shall be instituted between the Community and the ACP States. The detailed arrangements for such cooperation shall be established by the Council of Ministers.

2. The ACP States and the Commission shall adopt by mutual agreement any practical measures facilitating the exchange of necessary information and the submission of requests for transfers, for example by producing a form for requesting transfers.

Article 24

The least developed, landlocked or island ACP States referred to in Article 17 (1) and (2) and Article 19 (2) are as follows:

— the Bahamas	— Dahomey
— Barbados	— Equatorial Guinea
— Botswana	— Ethiopia
— Burundi	— Fiji
— Central African Republic	— the Gambia
— Chad	— Grenada

— Guinea	— Somalia
— Guinea-Bissau	— Sudan
— Jamaica	— Swaziland
— Lesotho	— Tanzania
— Madagascar	— Togo
— Malawi	— Tonga
— Mali	— Trinidad and Tobago
— Mauritania	— Uganda
— Mauritius	— Upper Volta
— Niger	— Western Samoa
— Rwanda	— Zambia

Chapter 2
Specific provisions concerning sugar

Article 25

1. Notwithstanding any other provisions of this Convention the Community undertakes for an indefinite period to purchase and import, at guaranteed prices, specific quantities of cane sugar, raw or white, which originate in the ACP States producing and exporting cane sugar and which those States undertake to deliver to it.

2. Protocol No 3 annexed to this Convention determines the conditions of implementation of this Article.

TITLE III
INDUSTRIAL COOPERATION

Article 26

The Community and the ACP States, acknowledging the pressing need for the industrial development of the latter, agree to take all measures necessary to bring about effective industrial cooperation.

Industrial cooperation between the Community and the ACP States shall have the following objectives:

(*a*) to promote the development and diversification of industry in the ACP States and to help bring about a better distribution of industry both within those States and between them;

(*b*) to promote new relations in the industrial field between the Community, its Member States and the ACP States, in particular the establishment of new industrial and trade links between the industries of the Member States and those of the ACP States;

(*c*) to increase the links between industry and the other sectors of the economy, in particular agriculture;

(*d*) to facilitate the transfer of technology to the ACP States and to promote the adaptation of such technology to their specific conditions and needs, for example by expanding the capacity of the ACP States for research, for adaptation of technology and for training in industrial skills at all levels in these States;

(*e*) to promote the marketing of industrial products of the ACP States in foreign markets in order to increase their share of international trade in those products;

(*f*) to encourage the participation of nationals of ACP States, in particular that of small and medium-sized industrial firms, in the industrial development of those States;

(*g*) to encourage Community firms to participate in the industrial development of the ACP States, where those States so desire and in accordance with their economic and social objectives.

Article 27

In order to attain the objectives set out in Article 26, the Community shall help to carry out, by all the means provided for in the Convention, programmes, projects and schemes submitted to it on the initiative or with the agreement of the ACP States in the fields of industrial infrastructures and ventures, training, technology and research, small and medium-sized firms, industrial information and promotion, and trade cooperation.

Article 28

The Community shall contribute to the setting up and the extension of the infrastructure necessary for industrial development, particularly in the fields of transport and communications, energy and industrial research and training.

Article 29

The Community shall contribute to the setting up and the extension in the ACP States of industries processing raw materials and industries manufacturing finished and semi-finished products.

Article 30

At the request of the ACP States and on the basis of the programmes submitted by the latter, the Community shall contribute to the organization and financing of the training, at all levels, of personnel of the ACP States in industries and institutions within the Community.

In addition, the Community shall contribute to the establishment and expansion of industrial training facilities in the ACP States.

Article 31

With a view to helping the ACP States to overcome obstacles encountered by them

n matters of access to and adaptation of technology, the Community is prepared
n particular to:

(a) keep the ACP States better informed on technological matters and assist
hem in selecting the technology best adapted to their needs;

(b) facilitate their contacts and relations with firms and institutions in possession
of the appropriate technological know-how;

(c) facilitate the acquisition, on favourable terms and conditions, of patents and
other industrial property, in particular through financing and/or through other
uitable arrangements with firms and institutions within the Community;

(d) contribute to the establishment and expansion of industrial research facilities
n the ACP States with particular reference to the adaptation of available technology
o the conditions and needs of those States.

Article 32

The Community shall contribute to the establishment and development of small
and medium-sized industrial firms in the ACP States through financial and technical
cooperation schemes adapted to the specific needs of such firms and covering inter
alia:

(a) the financing of firms,

(b) the creation of appropriate infrastructure and industrial estates,

(c) vocational and advanced training,

(d) the setting up of specialized advisory services and credit facilities.

The development of these firms shall, as far as possible, be conducive to the
strengthening of the complementary relationship between small and medium-sized
ndustrial firms and of their links with large industrial firms.

Article 33

Industrial information and promotion schemes shall be carried out in order to secure
and intensify regular information exchanges and the necessary contacts in the industrial field between the Community and the ACP States.

These schemes could have the following aims:

(a) to gather and disseminate all relevant information on the trends of industry
and trade in the Community and on the conditions and possibilities for industrial
development in the ACP States;

(b) to organize and facilitate contacts and meetings of all kinds between Community and ACP States' industrial policy-makers, promoters and firms;

(c) to carry out studies and appraisals aimed at pinpointing the practical opportunities for industrial cooperation with the Community in order to promote the
industrial development of the ACP States;

(d) to contribute, through appropriate technical cooperation schemes, to the
setting up, launching and running of the ACP States' industrial promotion bodies.

Article 34

In order to enable the ACP States to obtain full benefit from trade and other arrang
ments provided for in this Convention, trade promotion schemes shall be carried
out to encourage the marketing of industrial products of ACP States both in the
Community as well as in other external markets. Furthermore, programmes shall
be drawn up jointly between the Community and the ACP States in order to stimul
and develop the trade of industrial products among the said States.

Article 35

1. A Committee on Industrial Cooperation shall be established. It shall be supervised by the Committee of Ambassadors.
2. The Committee on Industrial Cooperation shall:
(*a*) see to the implementation of this Title;
(*b*) examine the problems in the field of industrial cooperation submitted to it
by the ACP States and/or by the Community, and suggest appropriate solutions;
(*c*) guide, supervise and control the activities of the Centre for Industrial Develop
ment referred to in Article 36 and report to the Committee of Ambassadors and,
through it, to the Council of Ministers;
(*d*) submit from time to time reports and recommendations which it considers
appropriate to the Committee of Ambassadors;
(*e*) perform such other functions as may be assigned to it by the Committee of
Ambassadors.
3. The composition of the Committee on Industrial Cooperation and the details
for its operation shall be determined by the Council of Ministers.

Article 36

A Centre for Industrial Development shall be set up. It shall have the following
functions:
(*a*) to gather and disseminate in the Community and the ACP States all relevant
information on the conditions of and opportunities for industrial cooperation;
(*b*) to have, at the request of the Community and the ACP States, studies carried
out on the possibilities and potential for industrial development of the ACP States,
bearing in mind the necessity for adaptation of technology to their needs and requir
ments, and to ensure their follow-up;
(*c*) to organize and facilitate contacts and meetings of all kinds between Community and ACP States' industrial policy-makers, promoters, and firms and financial
institutions;
(*d*) to provide specific industrial information and support services;
(*e*) help to identify, on the basis of needs indicated by ACP States, the opportuni
for industrial training and applied research in the Community and in the ACP States
and to provide relevant information and recommendations.

The Centre's Statutes and rules of operation shall be adopted by the Council of Ministers on a proposal from the Committee of Ambassadors upon the entry into force of this Convention.

Article 37

Programmes, projects or schemes undertaken in the field of industrial cooperation and involving Community financing shall be implemented in accordance with Title IV, taking into account the particular characteristics of interventions in the industrial sector.

Article 38

. Each ACP State shall endeavour to give as clear an indication as possible of its priority areas for industrial cooperation and the form it would like such cooperation to take. It will also take such steps as are necessary to promote effective cooperation within the framework of this Title with the Community and the Member States or with firms or nationals of Member States who comply with the development programmes and priorities of the host ACP State.

2. The Community and its Member States, for their part, shall endeavour to set up measures to attract the participation of their firms and nationals in the industrial development efforts of the ACP States concerned, and shall encourage such firms and nationals to adhere to the aspirations and development objectives of those ACP States.

Article 39

This Title shall not prevent any ACP State or groups of ACP States from entering into specific arrangements for the development in ACP States of agricultural, mineral, energy and other specific resources with a Member State or States of the Community, provided that these arrangements are compatible with this Convention. Such arrangements must be complementary to the efforts on industrialization and must not operate to the detriment of this Title.

TITLE IV
FINANCIAL AND TECHNICAL COOPERATION

Article 40

1. The purpose of economic, financial and technical cooperation is to correct the structural imbalances in the various sectors of the ACP States' economies. The cooperation shall relate to the execution of projects and programmes which contribute essentially to the economic and social development of the said States.

2. Such development shall consist in particular in the greater wellbeing of the

population, improvement of the economic situation of the State, local authorities and firms, and the introduction of structures and factors whereby such improvemen can be continued and extended by their own means.

3. This cooperation shall complement the efforts of the ACP States and shall be adapted to the characteristics of each of the said States.

Article 41

1. The Council of Ministers shall examine at least once a year whether the objectives referred to in Article 40 are being attained and shall also examine the general problems resulting from the implementation of financial and technical cooperation. It shall take stock, on the basis of information gathered both by the Community and the ACP States, of action undertaken in this context by the Community and by the ACP States. This stocktaking shall also cover regional cooperation and measures in favour of the least developed ACP States.

. As regards the Community, the Commission shall submit to the Council of Ministers an annual report on the management of Community financial and technica aid. This report shall be drawn up in collaboration with the European Investment Bank (hereinafter called the 'Bank') for the parts of the report which concern it. It shall in particular show the position as to the commitment, implementation and utilization of the aid, broken down by type of financing and by recipient State.

The ACP States for their part shall submit to the Council of Ministers any observations, information or proposals on the problems concerning the implementatio in their respective countries, of the economic, financial and technical cooperation, and also on the general problems of this cooperation.

The work on the annual stocktaking of financial and technical cooperation shall be prepared by the experts of the Community and of the ACP States who are responsible for the implementation of that cooperation.

2. On the basis of the information submitted by the Community and the ACP States and of the examination referred to in paragraph 1, the Council of Ministers shall define the policy and guidelines of financial and technical cooperation and shall formulate resolutions on the measures to be taken by the Community and the ACP States in order to ensure that the objectives of such cooperation are attained.

Article 42

For the duration of this Convention, the overall amount of the Community's aid shall be 3,390 million units of account.

This amount comprises:

1. 3,000 million units of account from the European Development Fund (hereinafter called the 'Fund'), allocated as follows:

(*a*) for the purposes set out in Article 40: 2,625 million units of account, consisting of:

− 2,100 million units of account in the form of grants,

— 430 million units of account in the form of special loans,
— 95 million units of account in the form of risk capital;
(b) for the purposes set out in Title II, up to 375 million units of account, like-
ise from the Fund, in the form of transfers for the stabilization of export earnings.

2. For the purposes set out in Article 40, up to 390 million units of account in
e form of loans from the Bank, made from its own resources on the terms and
nditions provided for in its Statute, and supplemented, as a general rule, by a 3%
terest rate subsidy, under the conditions laid down in Article 5 of Protocol No 2.

The total cost of the interest rate subsidies shall be charged against the amounts
aid provided for in 1 (a) above.

rticle 43

The method or methods of financing which may be contemplated for each project
r programme shall be selected jointly by the Community and the ACP State or
ates concerned with a view to the best possible use being made of the resources
ailable and by reference to the level of development and the economic and
nancial situation of the ACP State or ACP States concerned. Moreover, account
all be taken of the factors which ensure the servicing of repayable aid.

The definitive choice of methods of financing for projects and programmes shall
e made only at an appropriate stage in the appraisal of such projects and programmes.

2. Account shall also be taken of the nature of the project or programme, of its
rospects of economic and financial profitability and of its economic and social
npact.

In particular, productive capital projects in the industrial, tourism and mining
ectors shall be given priority financing by means of loans from the Bank and risk
apital.

rticle 44

. Where appropriate, a number of methods may be combined for financing a project
r programme.

2. With the agreement of the ACP State or ACP States concerned, financial aid
rom the Community may take the form of co-financing with participation by, in
articular, credit and development agencies and institutions, firms, Member States,
CP States, third countries or international finance organizations.

rticle 45

. Grants and special loans may be made available to or through the ACP State
oncerned.

2. Where these funds are on-lent through the ACP State concerned, the terms
nd procedure for the on-lending by the intermediate recipient to the final borrower
hall be laid down between the Community and the State concerned in an inter-
nediate financing agreement.

3. Any benefits accruing to the intermediate recipient, either because that recipi receives a grant or a loan for which the interest rate or the repayment period is more favourable than that of the final loan, shall be employed by the intermediate recipient for the purposes and on the terms set out in the intermediate financing agreement.

Article 46

1. The financing of projects and programmes comprises the means required for thei execution, such as:
  – capital projects in the fields of rural development, industrialization, energy, mining, tourism, and economic and social infrastructure;
  – schemes to improve the structure of agricultural production;
  – technical cooperation schemes, in particular in the fields of training and technological adaptation or innovation;
  – industrial information and promotion schemes;
  – marketing and sales promotion schemes;
  – specific schemes to help small and medium-sized national firms;
  – microprojects for grassroots development, in particular in rural areas.
  2. Financial and technical cooperation shall not cover current administrative, maintenance and operating expenses.
  3. Financial aid may cover import costs and local expenditure required for the execution of projects and programmes.

Article 47

1. In the implementation of financial and technical cooperation, the Community shall provide effective assistance for attaining the objectives which the ACP States set themselves in the context of regional and interregional cooperation. This assistar shall aim to:
  (*a*) accelerate economic cooperation and development both within and between the regions of the ACP States;
  (*b*) accelerate diversification of the economies of the ACP States;
  (*c*) reduce the economic dependence of the ACP States on imports by maximizir output of those products for which the ACP States in question have real potential;
  (*d*) create sufficiently wide markets within the ACP States and neighbouring States by removing the obstacles which hinder the development and integration of those markets in order to promote trade between the ACP States;
  (*e*) maximize the use of resources and services in the ACP States.
  2. To this end approximately 10% of the total financial resources provided for in Article 42 for the economic and social development of the ACP States shall be reserved for financing their regional projects.

Article 48

1. In the implementation of financial and technical cooperation, special attention

hall be paid to the needs of the least developed ACP States so as to reduce the
pecific obstacles which impede their development and prevent them from taking
ull advantage of the opportunities offered by financial and technical cooperation.

2. The following ACP States shall be eligible, according to their particular needs,
or the special measures established under this Article:

Botswana	Mauritania
Burundi	Niger
Central African Republic	Rwanda
Chad	Somalia
Dahomey	Sudan
Ethiopia	Swaziland
the Gambia	Tanzania
Guinea	Togo
Guinea-Bissau	Tonga
Lesotho	Uganda
Malawi	Upper Volta
Mali	Western Samoa.

3. The list of ACP States in paragraph 2 may be amended by decision of the
Council of Ministers:

— where a third State in a comparable economic situation accedes to this Convention;
— where the economic situation of an ACP State undergoes a radical and lasting
change either so as to necessitate the application of special measures or so
that this treatment is no longer warranted.

Article 49

1. The following shall be eligible for financial and technical cooperation:

(*a*) the ACP States;

(*b*) the regional or interstate bodies to which the ACP States belong and which
are authorized by the said States;

(*c*) the joint bodies set up by the Community and the ACP States and authorized
by the latter to attain certain specific objectives, notably in the field of industrial
and trade cooperation.

2. Subject to the agreement of the ACP State or ACP States concerned, the
following shall be eligible for such cooperation in respect of projects or programmes
approved by the latter:

(*a*) local authorities and public or semi-public development agencies of the ACP
States, in particular their development banks;

(*b*) private bodies working in the countries concerned for the economic and social
development of the population of those ACP States;

(*c*) firms carrying out their activities, in accordance with industrial and business
management methods, which are set up as companies or firms of an ACP State
within the meaning of Article 63.

(*d*) groups of producers that are nationals of the ACP States or like bodies, and, where no such groups or bodies exist, the producers themselves;

(*e*) for training purposes, scholarship holders and trainees.

Article 50

1. There shall be close cooperation between the Community and the ACP States in implementing aid measures financed by the former. This cooperation shall be achieved through active participation by the ACP State or group of ACP States concerned in each of the various stages of a project; the aid programming, the submission and appraisal of projects, the preparation of financing decisions, execution of projects and final evaluation of the results, in accordance with the various procedures laid down in Articles 51 to 57.

2. As regards project financing for which the Bank is responsible, application of the principles defined in Article 51 to 58 may be adapted, in concert with the ACP State or ACP States concerned, to take account of the nature of the operations financed and of the Bank's procedures under its Statute.

Article 51

1. Community aid, which is complementary to the ACP States' own efforts, shall be integrated in the economic and social development plans and programmes of the said States so that projects undertaken with the financial support of the Community dovetail with the objectives and priorities set up by those States.

2. At the beginning of the period covered by this Convention, Community aid shall be programmed, in conjunction with each recipient State, in such a way that the latter can obtain as clear an idea as possible of the aid, in particular as regards the amount and terms, it can expect during that period and especially of specific objectives which this aid may meet. This programme shall be drawn up on the basis of proposals made by each ACP State, in which it has fixed its objectives and priorit. Projects or programmes already identified on an indicative basis may be the subject of a provisional timetable as regards preparation.

3. The Community indicative aid programme for each ACP State shall be drawn up by mutual agreement by the competent bodies of the Community and those of the ACP State concerned. It shall then be the subject of an exchange of views, at the beginning of the period covered by this Convention, between the representatives of the Community and those of the ACP State concerned.

This exchange of views shall enable the ACP State to set out its development policy and priorities.

4. The aid programmes shall be sufficiently flexible to enable account to be taken of changes occurring in the economic situation of the various ACP States, and any modifications of their initial priorities. Therefore, each programme may be reviewed whenever necessary during the period covered by this Convention.

5. These programmes shall not cover the exceptional aid referred to in Article 59 or the measures for stabilizing export earnings referred to in Title II.

Article 52

1. Preparation of the projects and programmes which come within the framework of the Community aid programme drawn up by mutual agreement shall be the responsibility of the ACP States concerned or of other beneficiaries approved by them. The Community may, where those States so request, provide technical assistance for drawing up the dossiers of projects or programmes.

2. Such dossiers shall be submitted to the Community as and when they are ready by the beneficiaries specified in Article 49 (1), or, with the express agreement of the ACP State or ACP States concerned, by those specified in Article 49 (2).

Article 53

1. The Community shall appraise projects and programmes in close collaboration with the ACP States and any other beneficiaries. The technical, social, economic, trade, financial, organizational and management aspects of such projects or programmes shall be reviewed systematically.

2. The aim of appraisal is:

(*a*) to ensure that the projects and programmes stem from economic or social development plans or programmes of the ACP States;

(*b*) to assess, as far as possible by means of an economic evaluation, the effectiveness of each project or programme by setting the effects it is expected to produce against the resources to be invested in it. In each project the expected effects shall be the practical expression of a number of specific development objectives of the ACP State or ACP States concerned.

On this basis, appraisal shall ensure that, as far as possible, the measures selected constitute the most effective and profitable method of attaining these objectives, taking into account the various constraints on each ACP State;

(*c*) to verify that the conditions guaranteeing the successful conclusion and the viability of the projects or programmes are met, which involves:

— verifying that the projects as conceived are suitable for bringing about the effects sought and that the means to be used commensurate with the circumstances and resources of the ACP State or region concerned;

— and furthermore guaranteeing that the staff and other means, particularly financial, necessary for operating and maintaining the investments and for covering incidental project costs are actually available. Particular attention shall be paid here to the possibility of the project being managed by national personnel.

Article 54

1. Financing proposals, which summarize the conclusions of the appraisal and are

submitted to the Community's decision-making body, shall be drawn up in close collaboration between the competent departments of the Community and those of the ACP State or ACP States concerned.

The final version of each financing proposal shall be transmitted by the competent departments of the Community simultaneously to the Community and to the ACP States concerned.

2. All projects or programmes put forward officially in accordance with Article 52 by an ACP State or ACP States, whether or not selected by the competent departments of the Community, shall be brought to the attention of the Community body responsible for taking financing decisions.

3. Where the Community body responsible for delivering an opinion on projects fails to deliver a favourable opinion, the competent departments of the Community shall consult the representatives of the ACP State or ACP States concerned on further action to be taken, in particular on the advisability of submitting the dossier afresh, possibly in a modified form, to the relevant Community body.

Before that body gives its final opinion, the representatives of the ACP State or ACP States concerned may request a hearing by the representatives of the Community in order to be able to state their grounds for the project.

Should the final opinion delivered by that body not be favourable, the competent departments of the Community shall consult afresh with the representatives of the ACP State or ACP States concerned before deciding whether the project should be submitted as it stands to the Community's decision-making bodies or whether it should be withdrawn or modified.

Article 55

The ACP States, or the other beneficiaries authorized by them, shall be responsible for the execution of projects financed by the Community.

Accordingly, they shall be responsible for negotiating and concluding works and supply contracts and technical cooperation contracts.

Article 56

1. As regards operations financed by the Community, participation in tendering procedures and other procedures for the award of contracts shall be open on equal terms to all natural and legal persons of the Member States and ACP States.

2. Paragraph 1 shall be without prejudice to measures intended to assist construction firms or manufacturing firms of the ACP States concerned, or of another ACP State, to take part in the execution of works contracts or supply contracts.

3. Paragraph 1 does not mean that the funds paid over by the Community must be used exclusively for the purchase of goods or for the remuneration of services in the Member States and in the ACP States.

Any participation by certain third countries in contracts financed by the Community must, however, be of an exceptional nature and be authorized case-by-case

y the competent body of the Community, account being taken in particular of a
esire to avoid excessive increases in the cost of projects attributable either to the
istances involved and transport difficulties or to the delivery dates.

Participation by third countries may also be authorized where the Community
articipates in the financing of regional or interregional cooperation schemes
involving third countries and in the joint financing of projects with other providers
f funds.

Article 57

. The effects and results of completed projects, and the physical state of the work
arried out, shall be evaluated regularly and jointly by the competent departments
of the Community and of the ACP State or ACP States concerned in order to ensure
hat the objectives set are attained under the best conditions.

Evaluations may also be made of projects in progress where this is warranted
y their nature, importance or difficulty of execution.

2. The competent institutions of the Community and of the ACP States concerned
hall, each for their respective parts, take the measures which evaluation shows to
e necessary. The Council of Ministers shall be kept informed of such measures
y the Commission and each ACP State for the purposes of Article 41.

Article 58

. The management and maintenance of work carried out within the context of
inancial and technical cooperation shall be the responsibility of the ACP States or
other beneficiaries.

2. Exceptionally, and by way of derogation from Article 46 (2), in particular
under the circumstances specified in Article 10 of Protocol No 2, supplementary
id may be provided temporarily and on a diminishing scale in order to ensure that
ull use is made of investments which are of special importance for the economic
nd social development of the ACP State concerned and the running of which
emporarily constitutes a truly excessive burden for the ACP State or other benefici-
ries.

Article 59

.. Exceptional aid may be accorded to ACP States faced with serious difficulties
esulting from natural disasters or comparable extraordinary circumstances.

2. For the purposes of financing the exceptional aid referred to in paragraph 1,
a special appropriation shall be constituted within the Fund.

3. The special appropriation shall initially be fixed at 50 million units of account.
At the end of each year of application of this Convention this appropriation shall be
estored to its initial level.

The total amount of monies transferred from the Fund to the special appropriation during the period of application of the Convention may not exceed 150 million units of account.

Upon expiry of the Convention any monies transferred to the special appropriat which have not been committed for exceptional aid shall be returned to the Fund proper for financing other schemes falling within the field of application of financi and technical cooperation, unless the Council of Ministers decides otherwise.

In the event of the special appropriation being exchausted before the expiry of this convention, the Community and the ACP States shall adopt, within the relevant joint bodies, appropriate measures to deal with the situations described in paragraph 1.

4. Exceptional aid shall be non-reimbursable. It shall be allocated on a case-by-case basis.

5. Exceptional aid shall help finance the most suitable means of remedying the serious difficulties referred to in paragraph 1.

These means may take the form of works, supplies or provision of services, or cash payments.

6. Exceptional aid shall not be used for dealing with the harmful effects of the instability of export earnings, which are the subject of Title II.

7. The arrangements for allocating exceptional aid, for payments and for implementing the programmes shall be worked out under an emergency procedure, with account being taken of the provisions of Article 54.

Article 60

The fiscal and customs arrangements applicable in the ACP States to contracts financed by the Community shall be adopted by a decision of the Council of Ministers at its first meeting following the date of entry into force of this Conventi

Article 61

In the event of failure of an ACP State to ratify this Convention pursuant to Title \ or denunciation of this Convention in accordance with that Title, the Contracting Parties shall be obliged to adjust the amounts of the financial aid provided for in this Convention.

TITLE V
PROVISIONS RELATING TO ESTABLISHMENT, SERVICES, PAYMENTS AND CAPITAL MOVEMENTS

Chapter 1
Provisions relating to establishment and services

Article 62

As regards the arrangements that may be applied in matters of establishment and provision of services, the ACP States on the one hand and the Member States on the other shall treat nationals and companies or firms of Member States and nationals and companies or firms of the ACP States respectively on a non-discriminatory basis. However, if, for a given activity, an ACP State or a Member State is unable to provide such treatment, the Member States or the ACP States, as the case may be, shall not be bound to accord such treatment for this activity to the nationals and companies or firms of the State concerned.

Article 63

For the purpose of this Convention 'companies or firms' means companies or firms constituted under civil or commercial law, including cooperative societies and other legal persons governed by public or private law, save for those which are non-profit-making.

'Companies or firms of a Member State or of an ACP State' means companies or firms formed in accordance with the law of a Member State or ACP State and whose registered office, central administration or principal place of business is a Member State or ACP State; however, a company or firm having only its registered office in a Member State or ACP State must be engaged in an activity which has an effective and continuous link with the economy of that Member State or ACP State.

Article 64

At the request of the Community or of the ACP States, the Council of Ministers shall examine any problems raised by the application of Articles 62 and 63. It shall also formulate any relevant recommendations.

Chapter 2
Provisions relating to current payments and capital movements

Article 65

With regard to capital movements linked with investments and to current payments, the Contracting Parties shall refrain from taking action in the field of foreign exchange transactions which would be incompatible with their obligations under this Convention resulting from the provisions relating to trade in goods, to services, establishment and industrial cooperation. These obligations shall not, however, prevent the Contracting Parties from adopting the necessary protective measures, should this be justified by reasons relating to serious economic difficulties or severe balance of payments problems.

Article 66

In respect of foreign exchange transactions linked with investments and current payments, the ACP States on the one hand and the Member States on the other shall avoid, as far as possible, taking discriminatory measures vis-à-vis each other or according more favourable treatment to third States, taking full account of the evolving nature of the international monetary system, the existence of specific monetary arrangements and balance of payments problems.

To the extent that such measures or treatment are unavoidable they will be maintained or introduced in accordance with international monetary rules and every effort will be made to minimize any adverse effects on the Parties concerned.

Article 67

Throughout the duration of the loans and risk capital operations provided for in Article 42, each of the ACP States undertakes:
- to place at the disposal of the beneficiaries referred to in Article 49 the currency necessary for the payment of interest and commission on and amortization of loans and quasi-capital aid granted for the implementation of aid measures on their territory;
- to make available to the Bank the foreign exchange necessary for the transfer of all sums received by it in national currency which represent the net revenue and proceeds from transactions involving the acquisition by the Community of holdings in the capital of firms.

Article 68

At the request of the Community or of the ACP States, the Council of Ministers shall examine any problems raised by the application of Articles 65 to 67. It shall also formulate any relevant recommendations.

TITLE VI
INSTITUTIONS

Article 69

The Institutions of this Convention are the Council of Ministers, assisted by the Committee of Ambassadors, and the Consultative Assembly.

Article 70

1. The Council of Ministers shall be composed, on the one hand, of the members of the Council of the European Communities and of members of the Commission of the European Communities and, on the other hand, of a member of the Government of each of the ACP States.

2. Any member of the Council of Ministers unable to attend may be represented. The representative shall exercise all the rights of the accredited member.

3. The proceedings of the Council of Ministers shall be valid only if half the members of the Council of the European Communities, one member of the Commission and two thirds of the accredited members representing the Governments of the ACP States are present.

4. The Council of Ministers shall lay down its rules of procedure.

Article 71

The office of President of the Council of Ministers shall be held alternately by a member of the Council of the European Communities and a member of the Government of an ACP State, the latter to be designated by the ACP States.

Article 72

1. Meetings of the Council of Ministers shall be called once a year by its President.

2. The Council of Ministers shall, in addition, meet whenever necessary, in accordance with the conditions laid down in its rules of procedure.

Article 73

1. The Council of Ministers shall act by mutual agreement between the Community on the one hand and the ACP States on the other.

2. The Community on the one hand and the ACP States on the other shall each, by means of an internal protocol, determine the procedure for arriving at their respective positions.

Article 74

1. The Council of Ministers shall define the broad outlines of the work to be undertaken in the context of the application of this Convention.

2. The Council of Ministers shall periodically review the results of the arrangements under this Convention and shall take such measures as may be necessary for the attainment of the objectives of this Convention.

3. Where provided for in this Convention, the Council of Ministers shall have the power to take decisions; such decisions shall be binding on the Contracting Parties, which must take such measures as are required to implement these decisions.

4. The Council of Ministers may likewise formulate such resolutions, recommendations or opinions as it may deem necessary to attain the common objectives and to ensure the smooth functioning of the arrangements of this Convention.

5. The Council of Ministers shall publish an annual report and such other information as it considers appropriate.

6. The Council of Ministers may make all the arrangements that are appropriate for ensuring the maintenance of effective contacts, consultations and cooperation between the economic and social sectors of the Member States and of the ACP States.

7. The Community or the ACP States may raise in the Council of Ministers any problems arising from the application of this Convention.

8. Where provided for in this Convention, consultations shall take place, at the request of the Community or of the ACP States, within the Council of Ministers, in accordance with the conditions laid down in the rules of procedure.

9. The Council of Ministers may set up committees or groups and ad hoc working groups, to undertake such activities as it may determine.

10. At the request of one of the Contracting Parties, exchanges of view may take place on questions having direct repercussions on the matters covered by this Convention.

11. By agreement among the parties, exchanges of views may take place on other economic or technical questions which are of mutual interest.

Article 75

The Council of Ministers may, where necessary, delegate to the Committee of Ambassadors any of its powers. In this event, the Committee of Ambassadors shall give its decisions in accordance with the conditions laid down in Article 73.

Article 76

The Committee of Ambassadors shall be composed, on the one hand, of one represen tative of each Member State and one representative of the Commission and, on the other, of one representative of each ACP State.

Article 77

1. The Committee of Ambassadors shall assist in the performance of its functions the Council of Ministers and shall carry out any mandate entrusted to it by the Council of Ministers.

2. The Committee of Ambassadors shall exercise such other powers and perform such other duties as are assigned to it by the Council of Ministers.

3. The Committee of Ambassadors shall keep under review the functioning of this Convention and the development of the objectives as defined by the Council of Ministers.

4. The Committee of Ambassadors shall account for its actions to the Council of Ministers particularly in matters which have been the subject of delegation of powers. It shall also submit to the Council of Ministers any pertinent proposal and such resolutions, recommendations or opinions as it may deem necessary or consider appropriate.

5. The Committee of Ambassadors shall supervise the work of all the committees and all other bodies or working groups, whether standing or ad hoc, established or provided for by or under this Convention and submit periodical reports to the Council of Ministers.

Article 78

The office of Chairman of the Committee of Ambassadors shall be held alternately by a representative of a Member State designated by the Community and a representative of an ACP State designated by the ACP States.

The Committee of Ambassadors shall lay down its rules of procedure which shall be submitted to the Council of Ministers for approval.

Article 79

The secretariat duties and other work necessary for the functioning of the Council of Ministers and the Committee of Ambassadors or other joint bodies shall be carried out on a basis of parity and in accordance with the conditions laid down in the rules of procedure of the Council of Ministers.

Article 80

1. The Consultative Assembly shall be composed on a basis of parity of members of the Assembly on the side of the Community and of the representatives designated by the ACP States on the other.

2. The Consultative Assembly shall appoint its Bureau and shall adopt its own rules of procedure.

3. The Consultative Assembly shall meet at least once a year.

4. Each year, the Council of Ministers shall submit a report on its activities to the Consultative Assembly.

5. The Consultative Assembly may set up ad hoc consultative committees to undertake such specific activities as it may determine.

6. The Consultative Assembly may adopt resolutions on matters concerning or covered by this Convention.

Article 81

1. Any dispute which arises between one or more Member States or the Community on the one hand, and one or more ACP States on the other, concerning the interpretation or the application of this Convention may be placed before the Council of Ministers.

2. Where circumstances permit, and subject to the Council of Ministers being informed, so that any parties concerned may assert their rights, the Contracting Parties may have recourse to a good offices procedure.

3. If the Council of Ministers fails to settle the dispute at its next meeting, either Party may notify the other of the appointment of an arbitrator; the other Party must then appoint a second arbitrator within two months. For the application of this procedure, the Community and the Member States shall be deemed to be one Party to the dispute.

The Council of Ministers shall appoint a third arbitrator.

The decisions of the arbitrators shall be taken by majority vote.

Each Party to the dispute must take the measures required for the implementation of the arbitrators' decision.

Article 82

The operating expenses of the Institutions under this Convention shall be defrayed in accordance with the terms set out in Protocol No 4 to this Convention.

Article 83

The privileges and immunities for the purpose of this Convention shall be as laid down in Protocol No 5 to this Convention.

TITLE VII
GENERAL AND FINAL PROVISIONS

Article 84

No treaty, convention, agreement or arrangement of any kind between one or more Member States and one or more ACP States may impede the implementation of this Convention.

Article 85

1. This Convention shall apply to the European territories to which the Treaty establishing the European Economic Community applies, in accordance with the conditions set out in that Treaty, on the one hand, and to the territories of the ACP States on the other.

2. Title I of this Convention shall also apply to the relations between the French Overseas Departments and the ACP States.

Article 86

1. As regards the Community, this Convention shall be validly concluded by a decision of the Council of the European Communities taken in accordance with the provisions of the Treaty and notified to the Parties.

It will be ratified by the Signatory States in conformity with their respective constitutional requirements.

2. The instruments of ratification and the act of notification of the conclusion of the Convention shall be deposited, as concerns the ACP States, with the Secretariat of the Council of the European Communities and as concerns the Community and its Member States, with the Secretariat of the ACP States. The Secretariats shall forthwith give notice thereof to the Signatory States and the Community.

Article 87

1. This Convention shall enter into force on the first day of the second month following the date of deposit of the instruments of ratification of the Member States and of at least two thirds of the ACP States, and of the act of notification of the conclusion of the Convention by the Community.

2. Any ACP State which has not completed the procedures set out in Article 86 by the date of the entry into force of this Convention as specified in paragraph 1 may do so only within the twelve months following such entry into force and shall be able to proceed with these procedures only during the twelve months following such entry into force, unless before the expiry of this period it gives notice to the Council of Ministers of its intention to complete these procedures not later than six months after this period and on condition that it undertakes the deposit of its instrument of ratification within the same time-limit.

3. As regards those ACP States which have not completed the procedures set out in Article 86 by the date of entry into force of this Convention as specified in paragraph 1, this Convention shall become applicable on the first day of the second month following the completion of the said procedures.

4. Signatory ACP States which ratify this Convention in accordance with the conditions laid down in paragraph 2 shall recognize the validity of all measures taken in implementation of this Convention between the date of its entry into force and the date when its provisions became applicable to them. Subject to any extension which may be granted to them by the Council of Ministers they shall, not later than six months following the completion of the procedures referred to in Article 86, carry out all the obligations which devolve upon them under the terms of this Convention or of implementing decisions adopted by the Council of Ministers.

5. The rules of procedure of the Institutions set up under this Convention shall lay down whether and under what conditions the representatives of Signatory States which, on the date of entry into force of this Convention have not yet completed the procedures referred to in Article 86, shall sit in those Institutions as observers. The arrangements thus adopted shall be effective only until the date on which this Convention becomes applicable to these States; such arrangements shall in any case cease to apply on the date on which, pursuant to paragraph 2, the State concerned may no longer ratify the Convention.

Article 88

1. The Council of Ministers shall be informed of any request by any State for membership of, or association with, the Community.

2. The Council of Ministers shall be informed of any request made by any State wishing to become a member of an economic grouping composed of ACP States.

Article 89

1. Any request for accession to this Convention by a country or territory to which

Part Four of the Treaty applies, and which becomes independent, shall be referred to the Council of Ministers.

With the approval of the Council of Ministers, the country in question shall accede to this Convention by depositing an instrument of accession with the Secretariat of the Council of the European Communities which shall transmit a certified copy to the Secretariat of the ACP States and shall give notice thereof to the Signatory States.

2. That State shall then enjoy the same rights and be subject to the same obligation as the ACP States. Such accession shall not adversely affect the advantages accruing to the ACP States signatory to this Convention from the provisions on financial and technical cooperation and on the stabilization of export earnings.

Article 90

Any request for accession to this Convention submitted by a State whose economic structure and production are comparable with those of the ACP States shall require approval by the Council of Ministers. The State concerned may accede to this Convention by concluding an agreement with the Community.

That State shall then enjoy the same rights and be subject to the same obligations as the ACP States.

The Agreement may however stipulate the date on which certain of these rights and obligations shall become applicable to that State.

Such accession shall not, however, adversely affect the advantages accruing to the ACP States signatory to this Convention from the provisions on financial and technical cooperation, the stabilization of export earnings and industrial cooperation.

Article 91

This Convention shall expire after a period of five years from the date of its signature, namely 1 March 1980.

Eighteen months before the end of this period the Contracting Parties shall enter into negotiations in order to examine what provisions shall subsequently govern relations between the Community and its Member States and the ACP States.

The Council of Ministers shall adopt any transitional measures that may be required until the new Convention comes into force.

Article 92

This Convention may be denounced by the Community in respect of each ACP State and by each ACP State in respect of the Community, upon six months' notice.

Article 93

The Protocols annexed to this Convention shall form an integral part thereof.

Article 94

This Convention, drawn up in two copies in the Danish, Dutch, English, French, German and Italian languages, all texts being equally authentic, shall be deposited in the archives of the General Secretariat of the Council of the European Communities and the Secretariat of the ACP States which shall both transmit a certified copy to the Government of each of the Signatory States.

148. Decision and Statement by the European Council, Dublin, 11 March 1975[1]

Budgetary correcting mechanism

The Heads of Government meeting in Council agreed on the correcting mechanism described in the Commission Communication entitled 'Unacceptable situation and correcting mechanism'[2] subject to the following provisions:

1. The criterion concerning the balance of payments deficit and the two-thirds ceiling are dropped.

2. The following provisions will be incorporated into the agreed mechanism:

(*a*) The correcting mechanism shall be subject to a ceiling of 250 million u.a. However, as soon as the amount of the Community budget exceeds 8,000 million u.a., the ceiling shall be fixed at an amount representing 3% of total budget expenditure.

(*b*) When a moving average drawn up over 3 years indicates that the balance of payments on current accounts of the country in question is in surplus, the correction shall only affect any difference between the amount of its VAT payments and the figure which would result from its relative share in the Community GNP.

New Zealand

The Heads of Government, meeting in Council at Dublin on 10 March, underline the importance which they attach to Protocol 18 of the Act of Accession, as regards the relations of the Community with New Zealand, a traditional supplier of dairy products to a substantial part of the enlarged Community.

They invite the Commission to present a report in order to prepare the review provided for in Article 5 of the Protocol and to submit as soon as practicable a proposal for the maintenance after 31 December 1977 of special import arrangements as referred to in that Article. They observe that the institutions of the Community have already carried out certain price adjustments in the framework of the Protocol. In the same spirit, the Community, which remains attached to a fair implementation of the Protocol is ready to review periodically and as necessary to

1 *Bull. EC*, 3–1975, pp. 6–7.
2 *Bull. EC*, 1–1975, points 2504 to 2510.

adjust the prices having regard to the supply and demand developments in the major producing and consuming countries of the world and also to the level and evolution of prices in the Community – including intervention prices – and in New Zealand, taking moreover into account cost developments in New Zealand and trends in freight charges.

As regards the annual quantities to be established by the Community institutions in the framework of the special arrangements after 1977, these should not deprive New Zealand of outlets which are essential for it. Thus for the period up to 1980, these annual quantities depending upon future market developments, could remain close to effective deliveries under Protocol 18 in 1974 and the quantities currently envisaged by New Zealand for 1975.

They note that Protocol 18 provides that the exceptional arrangements for the import of cheese cannot be maintained after 31 December 1977, and that this situation and the problems which may arise from it will be given due attention with appropriate urgency, taking into account also the considerations in the following paragraph.

The Heads of Government note, moreover, that New Zealand and the Community together provide the major part of world exports of dairy products. They, therefore, express the wish that, in the same spirit with which the Community approaches the application of Protocol 18, an ever closer cooperation be developed between the institutions of the Community and the New Zealand authorities with the objective of promoting in their mutual interest an orderly operation of world markets. Such cooperation, apart from its intrinsic value, should provide a basis from which to achieve, in a wider framework, the conclusion of an effective world agreement such as is envisaged in Protocol 18.

149. Summary of conclusions drawn up by the European Council, Rome, 3 December 1975[1]

The economic and social situation

The European Council discussed the development of the economic and social situation in the Community and again stressed the need for close coordination to be maintained between the economic policies of the Member States in order to consolidate the economic recovery which seems to have begun and to improve the present level of employment.

The European Council confirms the broad lines which emerged at the July meeting in Brussels and which were echoed in the declaration issued after the Rambouillet Summit,[2] concerning the desirability of closer international cooperation and of a constructive dialogue among all the countries concerned to overcome current economic problems.

1 *Bull. EC*, 11–1975, pp. 7–9.
2 Document No. 206.

The European Council has noted with satisfaction the follow-up to the Tripartite Conference[1] held in Brussels on 18 November and the decision to instruct the Commission of the European Communities, in contact with both sides of industry, to study the main problems discussed and to prepare a report with a view to a future meeting of that Conference.

Community budget and financing

The European Council carried out a thorough examination of the problems connected with the supervision of Community expenditure and the Community's budget policy.

The Council agreed on the need for more effective financial control over Community expenditure and stated that it was in favour of the suggestions made by the Heads of Government of the United Kingdom, the Federal Republic of Germany and Ireland, and the proposals of the Commission, being examined expeditiously.

The President of the Council and the President of the Commission were invited to make contact with the President of the European Parliament with a view to examining the role which that Institution might play in controlling Community expenditure by means of a Committee or Sub-Committee.

The Heads of Government agreed to make every effort to ensure the early completion of the procedure for the ratification of the Treaty setting up a European Court of Auditors signed on 22 July last in Brussels, with a view to enabling the Court to commence activities during 1976.

The European Council noted with satisfaction the information communicated by the President of the Commission regarding the strengthening which had taken place to date in the powers of the Member of the Commission responsible for the budget, without prejudice, however, to the principle of the collective responsibility of the Commission as laid down in the Treaties.

With reference to the agreement reached at Villa Marlia and formally adopted by the Council meeting in Brussels on 5 and 6 November regarding the annual joint meeting of Ministers for Foreign Affairs and Ministers for Finance to carry out an overall assessment of Community budget problems, the European Council considers that discussions at such meetings should concentrate on general Community policy, ensure greater consistency as regards policies to be followed and budget decisions and allow better distribution of Community resources to be achieved by means of the gradual introduction of multiannual expenditure forecasts. The discussion relating to next year should take place, on the basis of a Commission communication, before the end of April.

The European Council noted the Commission's intention to submit to the Council proposals concerning the use of the European unit of account in the Community budget.

---

1 Between Finance and Labour Ministers from the member states of the European Communities, representatives of the Commission and of both sides of industry.

Elections to the European Parliament

The European Council is agreed that elections to the European Parliament shall take place on a single date in May or June 1978.

Any country which at that date is unable to hold direct elections shall be allowed to appoint its representatives from amongst the elected members of its national parliament.

The European Council noted Mr Wilson's statement that the United Kingdom Government required a further period for internal consultations before adopting a final position regarding the date fixed, and the conditions set by Mr Jorgensen for direct elections to the European Parliament in Denmark.

The European Council instructed the Council of Ministers to continue examination of the problems encountered and to submit a report which will enable the text of the Convention on elections to the European Parliament to be finalized at the next European Council.

Passport Union

The European Council is agreed on the introduction of a uniform passport which may be issued as from 1978.

To that end, the European Council asks the Council (Ministers for Foreign Affairs) to resolve all outstanding questions in this area.

The European Council also asks the Council (Ministers for Foreign Affairs) to continue work on the abolition of frontier controls and on the harmonization of conditions of entry into and abode in the Member States.

Communication from Mr Tindemans on the accomplishment of his mission

The European Council heard a statement by Mr Tindemans, Prime Minister of Belgium, on the accomplishment of his mission of preparing a report on European Union. As agreed, a copy of this report will be sent to all Governments before the end of the year.

Conference on international economic cooperation

I. *Basic problems*

The Commission will submit proposals and the Council decide as soon as possible on appropriate mechanisms to protect existing sources and ensure the development of alternative sources of Community energy, on reasonable economic conditions and also to encourage conservation in the use of energy.

II. *Procedure*

(*a*) The Community will be represented by a single delegation at the conference on international economic cooperation.[1]

1 Mr Callaghan had announced, in a speech in the House of Commons on 10 November, that Britain would seek a separate seat at the Conference. Paragraph II represents a compromise.

(*b*) The Presidents of the Council and the Commission will act as spokesman for the Community.

During the ministerial conference, the Chairman of the Community delegation will be able to invite the representatives of two Member States to submit further comments in the light of their experience and in accordance with the mandate adopted.

(*c*) In each commission, the spokesmen for the Community shall be assisted by a Community delegation comprising representatives of the Member States.

(*d*) It may be agreed in the framework of the Community coordination procedure that a member of the Communities' delegation be invited by the Chair to comment on specific questions in the context of the mandate. These statements shall not conflict with the agreed Community position.

(*e*) As the dialogue proceeds, the mandate will be further developed in accordance with the Community procedure.

Other business

The European Council adopted a proposal by the Prime Minister of the United Kingdom that Community Ministers for the Interior (or Ministers with similar responsibilities) should meet to discuss matters coming within their competence, in particular with regard to law and order.

The European Council also discussed the problems posed by the shortage of oil and steps to be taken in that connection. It also considered the compilation of the list of industrialized countries who should be invited to attend the North–South Conference.

IV.   The Warsaw Treaty Organisation

150. Speech by Mr Brezhnev at the Fifth Congress of the Polish United Workers' Party, the 'Brezhnev doctrine', Warsaw, 12 November 1968[1] (extract)

The socialist states stand for strict respect for the sovereignty of all countries. We emphatically oppose interference in the affairs of any states and violations of their sovereignty.

At the same time the establishment and defence of the sovereignty of states which have set out on the road of building socialism is of particular importance for us communists. The forces of imperialism and reaction are seeking to deprive the people now of this, now of that socialist country of the sovereign right they have won to ensure the prosperity of their country and the wellbeing and the happiness of the broad masses of the working people by building a society free from all oppression or exploitation. And when attacks on this right meet with a united rebuff from the socialist camp, bourgeois propagandists raise a clamour around 'defence of sovereignty' and 'non-interference'. It is clear that this is a complete fraud and utter demagogy on their part. In reality those who shout in that way are not concerned with preserving socialist sovereignty but with destroying it.

It is common knowledge that the Soviet Union has done much for the real strengthening of the sovereignty and independence of the socialist countries. The Communist Party of the Soviet Union has always advocated that each socialist country should determine the specific forms of its development along the road of socialism, taking into consideration its own specific national conditions. However, as we know, comrades, there are also common laws governing socialist construction, departure from which might lead to a departure from socialism as such.

And when internal and external forces that are hostile to socialism seek to reverse the development of any socialist country in the direction of restoring the capitalist system, when a threat to the cause of socialism in that country appears, and a threat to the security of the socialist community as a whole, that is no longer only a problem for the people of that country but also a common problem, a matter of concern for all socialist countries.

It goes without saying that such an action as military aid to a fraternal country

1 *Soviet News*, 19 November 1968.

to put an end to a threat to the socialist system is an extraordinary, an enforced step, which can be sparked off only by direct actions on the part of enemies of socialism inside the country and beyond its frontiers — actions creating a threat to the common interests of the socialist camp.

Experience shows us that in present conditions the victory of the socialist system in this or that country can be regarded as final and the restoration of capitalism can be regarded as being precluded, only if the Communist Party, as the leading force of society, firmly carries through a Marxist—Leninist policy in the development of all spheres of public life; only if the party tirelessly strengthens the defences of the country and the defence of its revolutionary gains, if the party itself maintains and propagates among the people vigilance with regard to the class enemy and an irreconcilable attitude towards bourgeois ideology; only if the principle of socialist internationalism is observed as something sacred, and unity and fraternal solidarity with other socialist countries are strengthened. . .

151. Final Document of the International Conference of Communist and Workers' Parties, Moscow, 12 June 1969[1] (extracts)

II

The world socialist system is the decisive force in the anti-imperialist struggle. Each liberation struggle receives indispensable aid from the world socialist system, above all from the Soviet Union.

The Great October Socialist Revolution, the building of socialism in the Soviet Union, the victory over German fascism and Japanese militarism in the Second World War, the triumph of the revolution in China and in several other countries — in Europe and Asia — the emergence of the first socialist state in America, the Republic of Cuba, the rise and development of the world socialist system, comprising fourteen states, and the inspiring influence of socialism on the entire world have created the prerequisite for accelerating historical progress and opened new prospects for the advance and triumph of socialism throughout the world. . .

The contribution of the world socialist system to the common cause of the anti-imperialist forces is determined primarily by its growing economic potential. The swift economic development of the countries belonging to the socialist system at rates outpacing the economic growth of the capitalist countries, the advance of socialism to leading positions in a number of fields of scientific and technological progress, and the blazing of a trail into outer space by the Soviet Union — all these tangible results, produced by the creative endeavours of the peoples of the socialist countries, decisively contribute to the preponderance of the forces of peace, democracy and socialism over imperialism.

The socialist world has now entered a stage of its development when the possibili-

1 *Information Bulletin*, No. 12, 1969, pp. 6—37.

arises of utilising on a scale far greater than ever before the tremendous potentialities inherent in the new system. This is furthered by evolving and applying better economic and political forms corresponding to the requirements of mature socialist society, which already rests on the new social structure. . .

Practice has shown that socialist transformations and the building of the new society are a long and complex process, and that the utilisation of the tremendous possibilities opened up by the new system depends on the Communist Parties in the leadership of the state, on their ability to resolve the problems of socialist development the Marxist—Leninist way. . .

The formation of the socialist world constitutes an integral part of the class struggle being waged in the international arena. The enemies of socialism are keeping up their attempts to undermine the foundations of the socialist state power, thwart the socialist transformation of society and restore their own rule. To give a firm rebuff to these attempts is an essential function of the socialist state, which relies on the broad masses led by the working class and its Communist vanguard.

The defence of socialism is an internationalist duty of Communists.

The development and strengthening of each socialist country is a vital condition of the progress of the world socialist system as a whole. Successful development of the national economy, improvement of social relations and the all-round progress of each socialist country conform both to the interests of each people separately and the common cause of socialism.

One of the most important tasks before the Communist and Workers' Parties of the socialist countries is to develop all-embracing cooperation between their countries and ensure fresh successes in the decisive areas of the economic competition between the two systems, in the advance of science and technology. As the struggle between the two world systems grows sharper, this competition demands that on the basis of the socialist countries' fundamental interests and aims and of the Marxist—Leninist principles underlying their policy, the socialist system should place greater reliance on the international socialist division of labour and voluntary cooperation between them, which rules out any infringement of national interests, and ensures the advance of each country and consolidates the might of the world socialist system as a whole.

Relying on its steadily growing economic and defence potential, the world socialist system fetters imperialism, reduces its possibilities of exporting counter-revolution, and in fulfilment of its internationalist duty, furnishes increasing aid to the peoples fighting for freedom and independence, and promotes peace and international security. So long as the aggressive NATO bloc exists, the Warsaw Treaty Organisation has an important role to play in safeguarding the security of the socialist countries against armed attack by the imperialist powers and in ensuring peace.

The successes of socialism, its impact on the course of world events and the effectiveness of its struggle against imperialist aggression largely depend on the cohesion of the socialist countries. Unity of action of the socialist countries is an important factor in bringing together all anti-imperialist forces.

The establishment of international relations of a new type and the development of the fraternal alliance of the socialist countries is a complex historical process. Following the victory of the socialist revolution in many countries, the building of socialism on the basis of general laws is proceeding in various forms, which take into account concrete historical conditions and national distinctions. Successful development of this process implies strict adherence to the principles of proletarian internationalism, mutual assistance and support, equality, sovereignty and non-interference in each other's internal affairs.

Socialism is not afflicted with the contradictions inherent in capitalism. When divergences between socialist countries do arise owing to differences in the level of economic development, in social structure or international position or because of national distinctions, they can and must be successfully settled on the basis of proletarian internationalism, through comradely discussion and voluntary fraternal cooperation. They need not disrupt the united front of socialist countries against imperialism.

Communists are aware of the difficulties in the development of the world socialist system. But this system is based on the identity of the socio-economic structure of its member-countries and on the identity of their fundamental interests and objectives. This identity is an earnest that the existing difficulties will be overcome and that the unity of the socialist system will be further strengthened on the basis of the principles of Marxism–Leninism and proletarian internationalism. . .

IV

The participants in the Meeting consider that the most important prerequisite for increasing the Communist and Workers' Parties' contribution to the solution of the problems facing the peoples is to raise the unity of the communist movement to a higher level in conformity with present-day requirements. This demands determined and persistent effort by all the Parties. *The cohesion of the Communist and Workers' Parties is the most important factor in rallying together all the anti-imperialist forces.*

The participants in the Meeting reaffirm their common view that relations between the fraternal Parties are based on the principles of proletarian internationalism, solidarity, and mutual support, respect for independence and equality, and non-interference in each other's internal affairs. Strict adherence to these principles is an indispensable condition for developing comradely cooperation between the fraternal Parties and strengthening the unity of the communist movement. Bilateral consultations, regional meetings and international conferences are natural forms of such cooperation and are conducted on the basis of the principles accepted in the communist movement. These principles and these forms give the Communist and Workers' Parties every possibility to unite their efforts in the struggle for their common aims, under conditions of the growing diversity of the world revolutionary process. All Parties have equal rights. As there is no leading centre of the international communist movement, voluntary coordination of the actions of Parties in order effectively to carry out the tasks before them acquires increased importance.

United action by Communist and Workers' Parties will promote cohesion of the communist movement on Marxist–Leninist principles. Joint actions aimed at solving vital practical problems of the revolutionary and general democratic movements of our time promote a necessary exchange of experience between the various contingents of the communist movement. They help to enrich and creatively develop Marxist–Leninist theory, to strengthen internationalist revolutionary positions on urgent political problems.

The participants in the Meeting proclaim their Parties' firm resolve to do their utmost for the working people and for social progress, with a view to advancing towards complete victory over international capital. They regard joint action against imperialism and for general democratic demands as a component and a stage of the struggle for socialist revolution and the abolition of the system of exploitation of man by man.

The participants in the Meeting are convinced that the effectiveness of each Communist Party's policy depends on its successes in its own country, on the successes of other fraternal Parties and on the extent of their cooperation. Each Communist Party is responsible for its activity to its own working class and people and, at the same time, to the international working class. The national and international responsibilities of each Communist and Workers' Party are indivisible. Marxists–Leninists are both patriots and internationalists; they reject both national narrow-mindedness and the negation or underestimation of national interests, and the striving for hegemony. At the same time, the Communist Parties – the Parties of the working class and all working people – are the standard bearers of genuine national interests unlike the reactionary classes, which betray these interests. The winning of power by the working class and its allies is the greatest contribution which a Communist Party fighting under capitalist conditions can make to the cause of socialism and proletarian internationalism.

The Communist and Workers' Parties are conducting their activity in diverse, specific conditions, requiring an appropriate approach to the solution of concrete problems. Each Party, guided by the principles of Marxism–Leninism and in keeping with concrete national conditions, fully independently elaborates its own policy, determines the directions, forms and methods of struggle, and, depending on the circumstances, chooses the peaceful or non-peaceful way of transition to socialism, and also the forms and methods of building socialism in its own country. At the same time, the diverse conditions in which the Communist Parties operate, the different approaches to practical tasks and even differences on certain questions must not hinder concerted international action by fraternal Parties, particularly on the basic problems of the anti-imperialist struggle. The greater the strength and the unity of each Communist Party, the better can it fulfil its role both inside the country and in the international communist movement.

Communists are aware that our movement, while scoring great historical victories in the course of its development, has recently encountered serious difficulties. Communists are convinced, however, that these difficulties will be overcome. This belief is based on the fact that the international working class has common long-term objectives and interests, on the striving of each Party to find a solution to existing problems which would meet both national and international interests and the Communists' revolutionary mission; it is based on the will of Communists for cohesion on an international scale.

The Communist and Workers' Parties, regardless of some difference of opinion, reaffirm their determination to present a united front in the struggle against imperialism.

Some of the divergences which have arisen are eliminated through an exchange of opinion or disappear as the development of events clarifies the essence of the outstanding issues. Other divergences may last long. The Meeting is confident that the outstanding issues can and must be resolved correctly by strengthening all forms of cooperation among the Communist Parties, by extending inter-Party ties, mutual exchange of experience, comradely discussion and consultation and unity of action in the international arena. It is an internationalist duty of each Party to do everything it can to help improve relations and promote trust between all Parties and to undertake further efforts to strengthen the unity of the international communist movement. This unity is strengthened by a collective analysis of concrete reality...

152. Comprehensive Programme for the Further Extension and Improvement of Cooperation and the Development of Socialist Economic Integration, adopted by the member countries of the Council for Mutual Economic Assistance, Bucharest, 29 July 1971[1] (extracts)

This Programme has been drawn up on the basis of the fundamental principles of the CMEA Charter and in pursuance of the decisions of the 23rd (Special) and 24th Council Sessions, and has been endorsed by the 25th Session of the Council of Mutual Economic Assistance.

CHAPTER I
Section 1

A brief formulation of successful achievements, fundamental principles, aims, ways and means for the further extension and improvement of economic, scientific and technological cooperation and the development of Socialist Economic Integration by the CMEA member countries.

1. The CMEA member countries, under the guidance of the Communist and Workers' Parties, thanks to the creative labour of their people, as a result of the mobilization of each country's resources, and also of the development and extension of all-round cooperation and mutual assistance, have achieved major successes in the construction of Socialism and Communism and the development of Economics, Science and Technology.

1 *Politizdat*, Moscow, 1972, pp. 5–12 and 116–18 (unofficial translation). A complete English translation is published by the CMEA Secretariat, Moscow, 1971.

The friendship and collaboration which exists between socialist states rests on the fact that in each country an identical economic basis has been set up – public ownership of the means of production with a uniform state system – power in the hands of the people headed by the working class, on a single common ideology – Marxism–Leninism.

The all-round development and strengthening of each separate Socialist country is a decisive factor in the progressive movement of the Socialist World System as a whole. The successful development of the national economy and the improvement of social relations, the overall progress of each Socialist country, further the common interests of Socialism.

The productive forces in the CMEA member countries have attained a high level of development, a diversified industrial structure has been created in the national economies of these countries, the technical standard of production has risen.

For those people within the CMEA member countries the material and cultural levels of life have grown significantly as a result of the rapidly increasing national income.

Foreign trade links within CMEA member countries have widened considerably. The solid, all-round cooperation between member countries of CMEA has been an important factor in the rapid growth of the national economies of these countries, in the preservation of their independence and the strengthening of Socialist collaborative potentiality as a whole.

The new higher rate of economic growth in those countries which had lagged behind industrially as compared with the average growth rate of CMEA countries as a whole, is gradually leading to a rapprochement and equalization of their economic levels of development.

The superiority of economic growth rates within CMEA member countries over the capitalist developed countries strengthens their position in the world economy.

2. CMEA member countries consider that, as a result of their high level of development in productive forces, the large-scale structural changes in the fields of production and consumption, present-day tasks directed at implementing the scientific and technological revolution, the overall acceleration of technological progress, the increase of effectiveness of social production and the rise in standard of the peoples' welfare together with the nature of social relations of production and the demands of the class struggle against imperialism, it is vitally necessary to extend and improve constantly the economic, scientific and technological cooperation between CMEA member countries and to develop Socialist Economic Integration and economic, scientific and technological relations with other Socialist countries.

The further extension and improvement of cooperation and the development of Socialist Economic Integration promote the growth of economic potential within the Socialist world system, strengthen each country's national economy, and are important factors in consolidating unity and superiority over Capitalism in all spheres of social life and of ensuring its victory in the competition between Socialism and Capitalism.

The extension and improvement of economic, scientific and technological cooperation and the development of Socialist Economic Integration among member countries of CMEA is regarded as a consciously and systematically controlled proce of the International Division of Labour by way of the Communist and Working Parties and the governments of CMEA member countries; a process of rapprocheme in their economies, of the formation of modern, highly effective national economic structures, of the gradual rapprochement and equalization of their levels of econom development, of the formation of deep and persistent ties in the fundamental spheres of economics, science and technology, the expansion and consolidation of the international market within these countries and the improvement of money— commodity relations.

This process creates favourable conditions for more effective use of a country's resources and the broad development of the scientific and technological revolution, which last has become one of the main areas of historical competition between Capitalism and Socialism and an important condition for the development of Socialist Society.

The further extension and improvement of cooperation and the development of Socialist Economic Integration are, and shall continue to be, implemented accordin to the principles of Socialist Internationalism on the basis of respect for State Sovereignty, independence and national interests, non-interference in the internal affairs of countries, full equality of rights, mutual advantage and friendly mutual assistance. History fully confirms the vital force of these Marxist—Leninist principle concerning inter-state relations of a new type, which are in accordance with the objective demands of strengthening Socialist construction in every country and with the conditions for development within the world Socialist system and will enable the creation of a firm basis for extensive and fruitful international cooperation.

Socialist Economic Integration is completely voluntary and does not involve the creation of supranational bodies; it does not affect questions of internal plannin nor the financial or management activities of organizations.

3. CMEA member countries, in accordance with their policy of peaceful co-existence and in the interests of social progress as well as the fact that the Inter-national Socialist Division of Labour is structured with regard to the World Division of Labour, shall continue to develop their economic, scientific and technological links with other countries irrespective of their social or state structure on the principles of equal rights, mutual advantage and respect for sovereignty. On this bas they shall attach particular significance to the further extension of trade, and of economic, scientific and technological cooperation with the developing countries.

The CMEA member countries shall undertake, jointly or separately, measures guaranteeing cooperation and equal membership for those Socialist states still discriminated against in international economic, scientific and technological organiz ations.

With these aims in view the CMEA member countries shall coordinate their foreign economic policies in the interests of standardizing international economic-trade relations and primarily in order to eliminate discrimination in this field.

4. The CMEA member countries act on the principle that the system of economi scientific and technological cooperation between the CMEA member countries is

based on the general laws governing Socialist construction and the basic principles for the direction of Socialist economics, the integral combination of coordinated plans as well as fundamental methods for organizing cooperation with a more extensive application of money–commodity relations.

Guided by the working class and its parties in CMEA member countries economic functions within Socialist states are being further developed on the basis of Democratic Centralism and planned management of the national economy.

5. The CMEA member countries shall extend and improve economic, scientific and technological cooperation and develop Socialist Economic Integration with the aim of promoting the following:

— a more rapid development of the productive forces in all member countries of CMEA, the highest possible achievement on the scientific and technological level and the maximum increase in the economic effectiveness of social production and also maximum growth in the productivity of social labour;

— improvement in the structure, and growth in the scale of production together with a systematic rise in the level of technical equipment for different branches and the introduction of advanced technology in accordance with the demands of the scientific and technological revolution;

— provision, on a long-term basis, for the growing demands in the different countries' national economies for fuel, energy and raw materials, modern equipment, agricultural and food-consumption commodities and other national consumer goods mainly concerned with the production and rational utilization of resources in CMEA member countries;

— a rise in the material and cultural standards of life among peoples of the CMEA member countries;

— the gradual rapprochement and equalization of economic development levels among CMEA member countries;

— growth in the capacity and stability of the world Socialist market;

— a strengthening of the positions of CMEA member countries in the world economy and ultimately securing victory in the economic competition with Capitalism;

— strengthening the defence capability of the CMEA member countries.

6. The fundamental ways and means for the further extension and improvement of economic, scientific and technological cooperation and the development of Socialist Economic Integration are as follows:

— the holding of multilateral and bilateral consultations on basic questions of economic policy;

— the extension of multilateral and bilateral cooperation in the planning activities of countries, including cooperation in the field of forecasting, the coordination of five-year and long-term plans in the most important spheres of the national economy and along production lines, joint planning by interested countries with regard to certain agreed branches of industry and individual works or factories, as well as the exchange of methods designed to improve planning and directional systems within the national economy;

— the systematic extension of international specialization and cooperation in the fields of production, science and technology, combined efforts by the countries concerned in the prospecting and mining of useful minerals, the construction of industrial units and carrying out scientific research work;

— the systematic extension and increase in effectivity of mutual trade, improvement in its organizational forms on the basis of State monopolies, the development of mutual trade connections in coordination with financial exchange relations and foreign trade marketing systems;

— the extension of direct links between ministries, departments and other State bodies, management, scientific research, design and planning organizations within the CMEA member countries;

— the development of existing international economic organizations and the creation of new ones by interested countries;

— improvement in the legal basis of economic, scientific and technological cooperation with particular reference to an increase in the material responsibil of the sides concerned for the non-execution or inappropriate execution of their mutual obligations.

7. In accordance with the decisions of the 23rd (Special) Session of the Council of Mutual Economic Assistance, the CMEA member countries consider it necessary to carry out, on the basis of the firm and stable international Socialist Division of Labour, a combined series of measures both economic and organizational for extending and improving cooperation and for the development of Socialist Economic Integration. With these aims in view, the CMEA member countries have worked out a Comprehensive Programme for the Further Extension and Improvement of Cooperation and the Development of Socialist Economic Integration between CME member countries, henceforth referred to as the Comprehensive Programme. The present Comprehensive Programme is designed for a 15 to 20-year period and contains the necessary economic and organizational measures which are to be implemen by stages and periods as laid down by the Comprehensive Programme with regard to the interests of each country and their collaboration as a whole.

In the course of carrying out the envisaged measures of the Comprehensive Programme, consideration will be taken of the need to help and promote the more rapid and effective development of economics, science and technology in the less developed of the industrialized CMEA member countries with maximum mobilizati and effective utilization of their own efforts and resources.

8. In the extension and improvement of economic, scientific and technological cooperation and the development of Socialist Economic Integration between CMEA member countries an ever increasing role will be taken by the Council of Mutual Economic Assistance, which in its practical activities shall undertake all requisite measures for carrying out the present Comprehensive Programme.

The procedure and time limits for carrying out the proposals and recommendatic as scheduled in the Composite Programme shall be determined by negotiations between the CMEA member countries and as designated in the working plans of the appropriate Council bodies.

The CMEA agencies shall organize multilateral cooperation between the CMEA member countries, give assistance to countries in the implementation of this end, analyse and inform on the results of collaborative work and prepare recommendations or further improving cooperation.

CHAPTER IV
Section 17
Final Propositions

On Forms of Participation among the CMEA member countries in separate measures of the Comprehensive Programme.

1. All activities in implementing the Comprehensive Programme shall be conducted in conformity with the principles of the Charter of the Council for Mutual Economic Assistance and the Resolution of the 23rd (Special) Session of CMEA.

The working out of measures to implement the Comprehensive Programme shall be conducted by the interested countries as well as within the framework of bilateral inter-governmental Committees on economic, scientific and technological cooperation, by way of direct links between competent State bodies, economic, scientific research and other organizations, in international economic organizations as created by the CMEA member countries interested and through the utilization of other organizational forms which countries may recognize as expedient.

2. The CMEA member countries have agreed that in implementing the present Programme, they shall seek out such forms, ways and means of economic, scientific and technological cooperation as would permit the participation of all CMEA member countries, and promote each country's interest in the most extensive participation in cooperation. Each CMEA member country participating in the implementation of the Comprehensive Programme on the basis of complete voluntariness, shall undertake the responsibility and create the conditions for guaranteeing the fulfilment of its accepted obligations.

3. Any CMEA member country has the right at any time to declare its interest in participating in any measure of the Composite Programme, in which previously it may not have wished to participate for one reason or another, on conditions which shall be agreed upon between the country in question and the other interested countries.

4. Non-participation by one or several CMEA member countries in separate measures of the Comprehensive Programme shall not preclude the interested countries from fulfilling their joint cooperation. Non-participation by certain countries in particular measures shall not influence their collaboration or cooperation in other spheres of activity.

5. With the aim of creating possibilities (for those member countries of CMEA who are not participating in some specific measures of the Comprehensive Programme) for full or partial adherence to certain measures, the interested CMEA member countries shall, by request of the member country who is not participating in the

implementation of the given measure, inform on the principal results of its activitie in an order agreed between them. This procedure may envisage invitations to representatives of CMEA member countries not participating in the inter-State economic organizations created by the interested countries, to meetings of the leading bodies of these organizations specially convened for examination of the problems connected with implementing specific measures of the Comprehensive Programme, at a time when these measures are being carried out within the said organizations.

On the full or partial participation of non-CMEA member countries in implementing the Comprehensive Programme.

6. Any country who is not a CMEA member may participate fully or partially in the implementation of the comprehensive Programme. A non-CMEA member country who shares the aims and principles of the Programme may participate fully

A non-CMEA member country wishing to participate fully or partially in the implementation of the Comprehensive Programme, shall submit the relevant application to the Secretary of CMEA. On the agreement by all CMEA member countrie: to a non-member country's participation, the conditions for participation by this country in the work of CMEA agencies examining questions relating to the impleme tation of the Comprehensive Programme, or those of its propositions in which the said country is taking part, are determined by agreement between CMEA and the country in question. In such an agreement, where necessary, the conditions for participation in the implementation of specific measures outlined in the Compreheni Programme, may be determined.

7. Participation by a non-member country of CMEA or its economic organizatioi in implementing specific measures of the Comprehensive Programme outside the CMEA framework, shall be effected on the basis of negotiations between that count or its economic organizations, and those countries, or their economic organizations, taking part in such measures.

Procedure for Supplementing and Clarifying the Comprehensive Programme.

8. According to how the measures envisaged by the Comprehensive Programme are carried out, the accumulation of experience or as new demands or possibilities arise relating to the process of extending and improving economic, scientific and technological cooperation and the Development of Socialist Economic Integration, the Comprehensive Programme shall be supplemented and further clarified in accordanc with resolutions of the Council Session.

V. The Great Powers and the Middle East War of October 1973

153. Statement by the Soviet Union on the situation in the Middle East, Moscow, 7 October 1973[1]

The absence of a political settlement in the Middle East has resulted in military operations flaring up there again, involving loss of life, calamities and destruction.

The peoples of the world, who responded with feelings of relief to the process of international detente which had started recently, are again faced with a dangerous development of events.

It is no secret from anyone that the cause of this situation in the Middle East is the expansionist policy of Israel's ruling circles.

Enjoying the support and patronage of imperialist circles, Israel, for a number of years now, has been constantly heating up the situation in the Middle East by its senseless aggressive actions. Ignoring the demands of world public opinion and of most of the world's States and trampling on the Charter and resolutions of the United Nations and the generally-accepted standards of international law, the Israeli ruling circles have raised violence and piracy to the level of their State policy.

Frustrating all the efforts aimed at establishing a just peace in the Middle East and committing constant provocations against neighbouring Arab States, the Israeli military have gone on fanning in every way the smouldering embers of the military conflict in that area unleashed by Tel Aviv in 1967.

The endless armed provocations of the Israeli military against Egypt, Syria and Lebanon have repeatedly created critical situations in the area. In recent days Israel had concentrated considerable armed forces on the cease-fire lines with Syria and Egypt, had called up reservists and, having thereby heated up the situation to the limit, unleashed military operations.

The responsibility for the present development of events in the Middle East and for the consequences of those events rests wholly and entirely with Israel and with those external reactionary circles which have constantly encouraged Israel in its aggressive ambitions.

It is well known that the Arab States have shown quite a lot of restraint and readiness to seek a political settlement of the conflict on a just basis. The justice of

1 *Soviet News*, 9 October 1973.

the Arab States' demands for the withdrawal of the aggressor's troops from all the Arab territories occupied in 1967 is recognized by all. These demands fully accord with the principle of the inadmissibility of acquiring territories by war, laid down in the well-known resolutions of the United Nations Security Council and General Assembly on the Middle East.

However, the efforts of the Arab countries, like those of the United Nations and all the peace-loving forces, to attain a just and lasting peace in the Middle East, have invariably come up against the obstructionist position of Tel Aviv. The present events in the Middle East are a direct outcome of Israel's continuing aggression.

What is taking place now in the Middle East strongly confirms the immutable truth that it is impossible to eliminate the hotbed of constant tension and establish reliable and guaranteed peace for all the States and peoples of the area without the complete liberation of all the Arab territories occupied by Israel and without ensuring the legitimate rights of the Arab people of Palestine.

True to its principled policy of support for the peoples striving for freedom and independence, the Soviet Union consistently comes out as a reliable friend of the Arab States.

Condemning the expansionist policy of Israel, the Soviet Union resolutely supports the legitimate demands of the Arab States for the relinquishing of all the Arab territories occupied by Israel in 1967.

If, obsessed by its expansionist ambitions, the Israeli Government remains deaf to the voice of reason and goes on, as before, pursuing its annexationist policy by retaining the occupied Arab territories, ignoring the decisions of the Security Council and of the United Nations General Assembly and challenging world public opinion, this may cost the people of Israel dear. The responsibility for the consequences of such an unreasonable course will be entirely borne by the leaders of the State of Israel.

154. Joint statement on the Middle East issued by the nine Governments of the European Community, 13 October 1973[1]

The nine governments of the European Community, extremely concerned by the resumption of hostilities in the Middle East, appeal to the parties to agree to stop the hostilities. The cease-fire will not only spare the population afflicted by the war new and tragic sufferings, but ought to open the way to a meaningful negotiation, in a framework to be defined allowing for a settlement of the conflict in conformity with all the provisions of Resolution 242 adopted by the Security Council on 22 November 1967.[2] Those of them who are members of the Security Council will work in this direction.

1 WEU, *Political year in Europe, 1973*, p. 237.
2 Resolution 242 (1967):
The Security Council,
Expressing its continuing concern with the grave situation in the Middle East,

155. Statement by Sir Alec Douglas-Home, British Secretary of State for Foreign and Commonwealth Affairs, in the House of Commons, 16 October 1973[3] (extract)

. . . When the hostilities broke out, Her Majesty's Government called for an immediate cease-fire, and suspended all shipments of arms to the battlefield. We did this because we considered it inconsistent to call for an immediate end to the fighting and yet to continue to send arms to the conflict. This seems to me to be the best posture from which to make an effective contribution to a constructive settlement. As regards the effect of the embargo, we have supplied a limited number of arms to both sides in recent years. Whereas in 1967 an embargo would have discriminated against Israel it is now even-handed. I would like to add here that British military facilities overseas have not been and are not being used for the transit of military supplies to the battlefield.

We also sought to bring the Security Council into action at once but neither side was willing to contemplate a cease-fire, except on terms totally unacceptable to the other. The Security Council has met several times but has been unable to find a consensus on any action.

Her Majesty's Government have therefore been engaged in consultation with other governments with the twin objectives of bringing about an end to the fighting and ensuring that urgent steps are at last taken to implement in full Security Council Resolution 242. The nine countries of the European Community joined in issuing

Emphasizing the inadmissibility of the acquisition of territory by war and the need to work for a just and lasting peace in the area in which every State in the area can live in security,

Emphasizing further that all Member States in their acceptance of the Charter of the United Nations have undertaken a commitment to act in accordance with Article 2 of the Charter,

1. *Affirms* that the fulfilment of Charter principles requires the establishment of a just and lasting peace in the Middle East which should include the application of both the following principles:

   (i)   Withdrawal of Israel armed forces from territories occupied in the recent conflict;

   (ii) Termination of all claims or states of belligerency and respect for and acknowledgement of the sovereignty, territorial integrity and political independence of every State in the area and their right to live in peace within secure and recognized boundaries free from threats or acts of force;

2. *Affirms further* the necessity

   (*a*) for guaranteeing freedom of navigation through international waterways in the area;

   (*b*) For achieving a just settlement of the refugee problem;

   (*c*) For guaranteeing the territorial inviolability and political independence of every State in the area, through measures including the establishment of demilitarized zones;

3. *Requests* the Secretary-General to designate a Special Representative to proceed to the Middle East to establish and maintain contacts with the States concerned in order to promote agreement and assist efforts to achieve a peaceful and accepted settlement in accordance with the provisions and principles in this resolution;

4. *Requests* the Secretary-General to report to the Security Council on the progress of the efforts of the Special Representative as soon as possible.

3 HC Deb., vol. 861, cols. 30–3.

an appeal to this effect on 13 October. Resolution 242 still offers the best chance of a settlement because to it and it alone both the Arabs and Israelis subscribe.

Three years ago at Harrogate I put forward our suggestions about how Resolution 242 might be put into effect. I outlined how a permanent settlement of the boundary question might be reached which could satisfy both the demand of the Arab States for Israeli withdrawal and the equally legitimate demand of Israel, which we all support, for recognition within secure boundaries.

Clearly no settlement can be imposed. But unless the future is merely to be a repetition of the futile and dangerous confrontation of the past a new effort at conciliation must be made.

I feel that the ingredients of a settlement will have to include action by the Secretary-General of the United Nations and the introduction of an international force first to police a cease-fire and then to guarantee the terms of a settlement. It will be necessary too, I believe, to establish demilitarised zones.

The success of any initiative must depend on the state of the battle. Timing will therefore be all important. We are ready to play our part in the making of peace and the keeping of it, so vital is it to the whole world that peace should be re-established in this area.

We will do our best to turn what appears to be a disaster now into an opportunity for securing a permanent settlement in the Middle East. I will of course keep the House regularly informed of developments. . .

156. Message to Congress from President Nixon, 19 October 1973[1]

I am today requesting that the Congress authorize emergency security assistance of $2.2 billion for Israel and $200 million for Cambodia. This request is necessary to permit the United States to follow a responsible course of action in two areas where stability is vital if we are to build a global structure of peace.

For more than a quarter of a century, as strategic interests of the major powers have converged there, the Middle East has been a flashpoint for potential world conflict. Since war broke out again on 6 October, bringing tragedy to the people of Israel and the Arab nations alike, the United States has been actively engaged in efforts to contribute to a settlement. Our actions there have reflected my belief that we must take these steps which are necessary for maintaining a balance of military capabilities and achieving stability in the area. The request I am submitting today would give us the essential flexibility to continue meeting those responsibilities

To maintain a balance of forces and thus achieve stability, the United States Government is currently providing military material to Israel to replace combat losses. This is necessary to prevent the emergence of a substantial imbalance resulting from a large-scale resupply of Syria and Egypt by the Soviet Union.

The costs of replacing consumables and lost equipment for the Israeli Armed Forces have been extremely high. Combat activity has been intense, and losses on

1 *DSB*, 12 November 1973, pp. 596–7.

oth sides have been large. During the first 12 days of the conflict, the United States as authorized shipments to Israel of material costing $825 million, including ransportation.

Major items now being furnished by the United States to the Israeli forces include onventional munitions of many types, air-to-air and air-to-ground missiles, artillery, rew-served and individual weapons, and a standard range of fighter aircraft ordnance. dditionally, the United States is providing replacements for tanks, aircraft, radios, nd other military equipment which have been lost in action.

Thus far, Israel has attempted to obtain the necessary equipment through the use f cash and credit purchases. However, the magnitude of the current conflict oupled with the scale of Soviet supply activities has created needs which exceed srael's capacity to continue with cash and credit purchases. The alternative to ash and credit sales of United States military materials is for us to provide Israel ith grant military assistance as well.

The United States is making every effort to bring this conflict to a very swift and onorable conclusion, measured in days not weeks. But prudent planning also equires us to prepare for a longer struggle. I am therefore requesting that the ongress approve emergency assistance to Israel in the amount of $2.2 billion. f the conflict moderates, or as we fervently hope, is brought to an end very quickly, unds not absolutely required would of course not be expended.

I am also requesting $200 million emergency assistance for Cambodia. As in the ase of Israel, additional funds are urgently needed for ammunition and consumable ilitary supplies. The increased requirement results from the larger scale of hostilities nd the higher levels of ordnance required by the Cambodian Army and Air Force o defend themselves without American air support.

The end of United States bombing on August 15 was followed by increased com- unist activity in Cambodia. In the ensuing fight, the Cambodian forces acquitted emselves well. They successfully defended the capital of Phnom Penh and the rovincial center of Kampong Cham, as well as the principal supply routes. Although is more intense level of fighting has tapered off somewhat during the current rainy eason, it is virtually certain to resume when the dry season begins about the end f the year.

During the period of heaviest fighting in August and September, ammunition osts for the Cambodian forces were running at almost $1 million per day. We antici- ate similar average costs for the remainder of this fiscal year. These ammunition re- uirements, plus minimum equipment replacement, will result in a total funding equirement of $380 million for the current fiscal year, rather than the $180 million reviously requested. To fail to provide the $200 million for additional ammunition ould deny the Cambodian Armed Forces the ability to defend themselves and their ountry.

We remain hopeful that the conflict in Cambodia be resolved by a negotiated ettlement. A communist military victory and the installation of a government in hnom Penh which is controlled by Hanoi would gravely threaten the fragile structure f peace established in the Paris agreements.

I am confident that the Congress and the American people will support this request for emergency assistance for these two beleaguered friends. To do less wou[ld] not only create a dangerous imbalance in these particular arenas but would also endanger the entire structure of peace in the world.

157. Security Council Resolution 338, 22 October 1973[1]

The Security Council

1. *Calls upon* all parties to the present fighting to cease all firing and terminate all military activity immediately, no later than 12 hours after the moment of the adoption of this decision, in the positions they now occupy;

2. *Calls upon* the parties concerned to start immediately after the cease-fire the implementation of Security Council resolution 242 (1967) in all of its parts;

3. *Decides* that, immediately and concurrently with the cease-fire, negotiations start between the parties concerned under appropriate auspices aimed at establishing a just and durable peace in the Middle East.

158. Security Council Resolution 339, 23 October 1973[2]

The Security Council,

Referring to its decision on an immediate cessation of all kinds of firing and of all military action, and urges that the forces of the two sides be returned to the positions they occupied at the moment the cease-fire became effective;

2. *Requests* the Secretary-General to take measures for immediate dispatch of United Nations observers to supervise the observance of the cease-fire between the forces of Israel and the Arab Republic of Egypt, using for this purpose the personn[el] of the United Nations now in the Middle East and first of all the personnel now in Cairo.

159. Security Council Resolution 340, 25 October 1973[3]

The Security Council,

Recalling its resolutions 338 (1973) of 22 October and 339 (1973) of 23 Octob[er] 1973,

Noting with regret the reported repeated violations of the cease-fire in non-compliance with resolutions 338 (1973) and 339 (1973),

1 UN Doc. S/RES/338 (1973); adopted by a vote of 14 to 0 (the People's Republic of China did not participate in the vote).
2 UN Doc. S/RES/339 (1973); adopted by a vote of 14 to 0 (the People's Republic of China did not participate in the vote).
3 UN Doc. S/RES/340 (1973): adopted by a vote of 14 to 0 (the People's Republic of China did not participate in the vote).

Noting with concern from the Secretary-General's report that the United Nations military observers have not yet been enabled to place themselves on both sides of the cease-fire line,

1. *Demands* that immediate and complete cease-fire be observed and that the parties return to the positions occupied by them at 1650 hours GMT on 22 October 1973;

2. *Requests* the Secretary-General, as an immediate step, to increase the number of United Nations military observers on both sides;

3. *Decides* to set up immediately under its authority a United Nations Emergency Force to be composed of personnel drawn from States Members of the United Nations except the permanent members of the Security Council, and requests the Secretary General to report within 24 hours on the steps taken to this effect;

4. *Requests* the Secretary-General to report to the Council on an urgent and continuing basis on the state of implementation of the present resolution,[1] as well as resolutions 338 (1973) and 339 (1973);

5. *Requests* all Member States to extend their full cooperation to the United Nations in the implementation of the present resolution, as well as resolutions 338 (1973) and 339 (1973).

160. Statement by President Nixon to the press, Washington, 26 October 1973[2] (extract)

Ladies and gentlemen, before going to your questions, I have a statement with regard to the Mideast which I think will anticipate some of the questions, because this will update the information which is breaking rather fast in that area, as you know, for the past two days.

The cease-fire is holding. There have been some violations, but generally speaking it can be said that it is holding at this time. As you know, as a result of the UN Resolution which was agreed to yesterday by a vote of 14 to 0, a peace-keeping force will go to the Mideast, and this force, however, will not include any forces from the major powers, including, of course, the United States and the Soviet Union.

The question, however, has arisen as to whether observers from major powers could go to the Mideast. My up-to-the-minute report on that, and I just talked to Dr Kissinger five minutes before coming down, is this: we will send observers to the Mideast if requested by the Secretary-General of the United Nations, and we have reason to expect that we will receive such a request.

With regard to the peacekeeping force, I think it is important for all of you ladies and gentlemen, and particularly for those listening on radio and television to know why the United States has insisted that major powers not be part of the peacekeeping

1 For text see UN Doc. S/11052/Rev.1. This report was approved and a force established for an initial period of six months by SC Res. 341, 27 October 1973.
2 *DSB*, 12 November 1973, pp. 581–4.

force, and that major powers not introduce military forces into the Mideast. A very significant and potentially explosive crisis developed on Wednesday of this week. We obtained information which led us to believe that the Soviet Union was planning to send a very substantial force into the Mideast, a military force.

When I received that information, I ordered, shortly after midnight on Thursday morning, an alert for all American forces around the world. This was a precautionary alert. The purpose of that was to indicate to the Soviet Union that we could not accept any unilateral move on their part to move military forces into the Mideast. At the same time, in the early morning hours, I also proceeded on the diplomatic front. In a message to Mr Brezhnev, an urgent message, I indicated to him our reasoning and I urged that we not proceed along that course, and that, instead, that we join in the United Nations in supporting a resolution which would exclude any major powers from participating in a peacekeeping force.

As a result of that communication, and the return that I received from Mr Brezhnev — we had several exchanges, I should say — we reached the conclusion that we would jointly support the resolution which was adopted in the United Nations.

We now come, of course, to the critical time in terms of the future of the Mideast. And here, the outlook is far more hopeful than what we have been through this past week. I think I could safely say that the changes for not just a cease-fire, which we presently have and which, of course, we have had in the Mideast for some time, but the outlook for a permanent peace is the best that it has been in 20 years.

The reason for this is that the two major powers, the Soviet Union and the United States, have agreed — this was one of the results of Dr Kissinger's trip to Moscow — have agreed that we would participate in trying to expedite the talks between the parties involved. That does not mean that the two major powers will impose a settlement. It does mean, however, that we will use our influence with the nations in the area to expedite a settlement.

The reason we feel this is important is that first, from the standpoint of the nations in the Mideast, none of them, Israel, Egypt, Syria, none of them can or should go through the agony of another war.

The losses in this war on both sides have been very, very high. And the tragedy must not occur again. There have been four of these wars, as you ladies and gentlemen know, over the past 20 years. But beyond that, it is vitally important to the peace of the world that this potential troublespot, which is really one of the most potentially explosive areas in the world, that it not become an area in which the major powers come together in confrontation.

What the developments of this week should indicate to all of us is that the United States and the Soviet Union, who admittedly have very different objectives in the Mideast, have now agreed that it is not in their interest to have a confrontation there, a confrontation which might lead to a nuclear confrontation and neither of the two major powers wants that.

We have agreed, also, that if we are to avoid that, it is necessary for us to use our influence more than we have in the past, to get the negotiating track moving again, but this time, moving to a conclusion. Not simply a temporary truce, but a permanent peace.

I do not mean to suggest that it is going to come quickly because the parties involved are still rather far apart. But I do say that now there are greater incentives within the area to find a peaceful solution and there are enormous incentives as far as the United States is concerned, and the Soviet Union and other major powers, to find such a solution. . .

161. Security Council Resolution 341, 27 October 1973[1]

The Security Council,

1. *Approves* the report of the Secretary-General on the implementation of Security Council resolution 340 (1973) contained in document S/11052/ Rev. 1 dated 27 October 1973:

2. *Decides* that the Force shall be established in accordance with the above-mentioned report for an initial period of six months, and that it shall continue in operation thereafter, if required, provided the Security Council so decides.[2]

162. Joint statement adopted by the nine Governments of the European Community, Brussels, 6 November 1973[3]

The nine governments of the European Community have continued their exchange of views on the situation in the Middle East. While emphasising that the views set out below are only a first contribution on their part to the search for a comprehensive solution to the problem, they have agreed on the following:

I. They strongly urge that the forces of both sides in the Middle East conflict should return immediately to the positions they occupied on 22nd October in accordance with Resolutions 339 and 340 of the Security Council. They believe that a return to these positions will facilitate a solution to other pressing problems concerning the prisoners of war and the Egyptian Third Army.

II. They have the firm hope that following the adoption by the Security Council of Resolution 338 of 22nd October, negotiations will at last begin for the restoration in the Middle East of a just and lasting peace through the application of Security Council Resolution 242 in all of its parts. They declare themselves ready to do all in their power to contribute to that peace. They believe that those negotiations must take place in the framework of the United Nations. They recall that the Charter has entrusted to the Security Council the principal responsibility for international peace and security. The Council and the Secretary-General have a special

1 UN Doc. S/RES/341 (1973); adopted by a vote of 14 to 0 (the People's Republic of China did not participate in the vote).
2 See UN Doc. S/RES/346 of 8 April 1974.
3 WEU, *Political Year in Europe, 1973*, pp. 254–5.

role to play in the making and keeping of peace through the application of Council Resolutions 242 and 338.

III. They consider that a peace settlement should be based particularly on the following points:

(1) The inadmissibility of the acquisition of territory by force.

(2) The need for Israel to end the territorial occupation which it has maintained since the conflict of 1967.

(3) Respect for the sovereignty, territorial integrity and independence of every State in the area and their right to live in peace within secure and recognised boundaries.

(4) Recognition that, in the establishment of a just and lasting peace, account must be taken of the legitimate rights of the Palestinians.

IV. They recall that according to Resolution 242, the peace settlement must be the object of international guarantees. They consider that such guarantees must be reinforced among other means by the dispatch of peace-keeping forces to the demilitarised zones envisaged in Article 2 (*c*) of Resolution 242. They are agreed that such guarantees are of primary importance in settling the overall situation in the Middle East in conformity with Resolution 242 to which the Council refers in Resolution 338. They reserve the right to make proposals in this connection.

V. They recall on this occasion the ties of all kinds which have long linked them to the littoral States of the South and East of the Mediterranean. In this connection they reaffirm the terms of the declaration of the Paris summit of 21 October 1972[1] and recall that the Community has decided in the framework of a global and balance approach to negotiate agreements with those countries.

163. Agreement between Egypt and Israel in implementation of Article 1 of Security Council Resolutions 338 and 339, 9 November 1973[2]

1. Egypt and Israel agree to observe scrupulously the cease-fire called for by the United Nations Security Council.

2. Both sides agree that discussions between them will begin immediately to settle the question of the return to the 22 October positions in the framework of agreement on the disengagement and separation of forces under the auspices of the United Nations.

3. The town of Suez will receive daily supplies of food, water and medicine. All wounded civilians in the town of Suez will be evacuated.

4. There shall be no impediment to the movement of non-military supplies to the east bank.

5. The Israeli checkpoints on the Cairo—Suez road will be replaced by United Nations checkpoints. At the Suez end of the road, Israeli officers can participate

1 Document No. 135.
2 WEU, *Political Year in Europe, 1973*, p. 262.

with the United Nations to supervise the non-military nature of the cargo at the bank of the canal.

6. As soon as the United Nations checkpoints are established on the Cairo—Suez road, there will be an exchange of prisoners of war, including wounded.

164. Announcement by President Nixon, issued simultaneously in Washington, Cairo and Jerusalem, 17 January 1974[1]

In accordance with the decision of the Geneva Conference, the Governments of Egypt and Israel, with the assistance of the Government of the United States, have reached agreement on the disengagement and separation of their military forces. The agreement is scheduled to be signed by the Chiefs of Staff of Egypt and Israel at noon Egypt—Israel time, Friday, 18 January at Kilometer 101 on the Cairo—Suez Road. The Commander of the United Nations Emergency Force, General Siilasvuo, has been asked by the parties to witness the signing.

165. Joint statement by the Soviet Union and the Syrian Arab Republic, Moscow, 13 April 1974[2] (extract)

From April 11 to April 16, 1974, a Syrian party and government delegation was in the Soviet Union on an official friendly visit. The delegation was led by Hafez Assad, general secretary of the Arab Socialist Renaissance Party and President of the Syrian Arab Republic. During the visit, the President of Syria and the delegation he headed had talks with Leonid Brezhnev, general secretary of the central committee of the Communist Party of the Soviet Union, Nikolai Podgorny, member of the political bureau of the CPSU central committee and President of the Presidium of the USSR Supreme Soviet, Alexei Kosygin, member of the political bureau of the CPSU central committee and Chairman of the USSR Council of Ministers, and other leaders of the Communist Party of the Soviet Union and the Soviet state.

A thorough and constructive exchange of views, which was held in an atmosphere of frankness and mutual understanding, once again clearly confirmed the desire of both sides for the further development and all-out strengthening of the friendship and mutual trust that have taken shape between the Soviet Union and Syria and between the CPSU and the Arab Socialist Renaissance Party. The fact that both sides take a common stand on the most important problems of present-day international life, and their solidarity in the struggle for the freedom, independence and social progress of the peoples and for lasting peace were reaffirmed.

Soviet—Syrian cooperation has assumed a wide and comprehensive character over recent years. It is developing along state, party and public lines, encompassing

1 *DSB*, 11 February 1974, p. 145.
2 *Soviet News*, 23 April 1974.

the political, economic and cultural fields. It also extends to the sphere of defence, the importance of which for Syria, because of the continued Israeli aggression, is generally known.

The Soviet Union and the Syrian Arab Republic are convinced that the unbreakable friendship and fraternal cooperation between the Soviet and Syrian peoples accord with the vital interests of both countries and serve the cause of strengthening peace and security.

The two sides point out with satisfaction that extensive Soviet—Syrian cooperatio; in the construction of large industrial enterprises and projects and particularly in the field of energetics, oil extraction, railway transport and irrigation is of great importance for the successful implementation of plans of the Syrian Arab Republic aimed at developing and strengthening economic independence and increasing the prosperity of the Syrian people. The Euphrates hydro-electric complex is an importai project of Soviet—Syrian cooperation.

Attaching great importance to the high level of Soviet—Syrian cooperation, the parties to the talks went on record in favour of improving forms of this cooperation which have already proved their value and also of exploring fresh avenues for the further development of cooperation. With this aim in view, the sides agreed to sign a new agreement on the further development of economic and technical cooperation and also a protocol on trade in 1974. The two sides discussed and outlined steps for further strengthening the defence capacity of the Syrian Arab Republic.

Confidence was also expressed that the further development of Soviet—Syrian contacts in culture, science, education, art, sound radio, television, tourist travel and sport would be facilitated by the programme for cultural and scientific cooperati; between the two countries for 1974—5, which was signed during the visit in Moscow.

While striving for the creation of favourable conditions enabling both countries to become acquainted with each other's achievements in various fields, the two sides will promote the extension of cooperation between the Communist Party of the Soviet Union and the Arab Socialist Renaissance Party, and between state agencies and also trade union, youth, women's and other mass organisations. In this context the parties to the talks note with satisfaction the programme for inter-party contacts between the Communist Party of the Soviet Union and the Arab Socialist Renaissanci Party, signed for 1974.

Bearing in mind the great significance of close political cooperation and the coordination of the actions of the Soviet Union and Syria in the international field, both sides are fully determined to continue regular consultations with each other at various levels on topical international problems and on questions concerning the further development of Soviet—Syrian relations. Of particular importance are the traditional personal contacts between leaders of the two countries, especially in conditions in which tension is being maintained in the Middle East as a result of the continuing Israeli aggression.

The two sides paid particular attention to recent developments in the Middle East.

President Hafez Assad told the Soviet leaders what has been done by the Syrian Arab Republic and its armed forces at the time of the military operations last October.

The Soviet side expressed great appreciation of the staunchness of the Syrian armed forces, of the courage of the Syrian people and of their unity behind their leadership which largely facilitated the strengthening of the positions of the Syrian Arab Republic in the Arab world and in the international arena and its struggle for the recovery of the occupied Arab territories.

The Syrian side expressed great appreciation of the all-round support from the Soviet Union, which helped the Syrian Arab Republic to hold out in the face of Israeli aggression.

Steps which are being taken to achieve a lasting and just peace in the Middle East were considered. The sides laid emphasis on the tense situation on the Syrian front, which is a result of the unceasing aggressive actions of Israel, who, defying United Nations resolutions and world opinion as a whole, is seeking to perpetuate the occupation of Arab territories.

The two sides again emphasised with the utmost determination that peace and tranquility in the Middle East could be achieved only if the Israeli armed forces were withdrawn from all the occupied Arab territories and the lawful national rights of the Arab people of Palestine safeguarded.

When the ways to settle the conflict in the Middle East were being discussed, it was stressed that partial steps which are now being taken do not cover the main, key elements of a settlement and that any agreement on the disengagement of armed forces must be part and parcel of an overall settlement of the Middle East problem, a step on the way to a radical and all-embracing settlement which must be based on the withdrawal of the Israeli armed forces from all the occupied Arab lands and on the ensuring of the rights of the Arab people of Palestine.

The two sides again stressed the importance of the Soviet Union's participation in all the stages and spheres of a settlement aimed at establishing a just and lasting peace in the Middle East.

The two sides pointed out that the explosive situation which has now taken shape on the Syrian front confirms more strongly than ever the fact that the ignoring of the aforementioned principles can lead to a further deterioration of the dangerous situation in the area.

In the conditions of continued Israeli aggression, the sides reaffirmed the importance of strengthening the defence potential of the Syrian Arab Republic and its lawful, inalienable right to use all effective means for the liberation of its occupied territories.

The general secretary of the CPSU central committee, on behalf of the Communist Party of the Soviet Union, the Soviet state and the entire Soviet people, confirmed that the Soviet Union would continue to render all-round support to the just cause of the Arab peoples. . .

166. Announcement by President Nixon issued simultaneously in Washington, Jerusalem and Damascus, 29 May 1974[1]

The discussions conducted by United States Secretary of State Dr Henry Kissinger

1 *DSB*, 24 June 1974, p. 679.

with Syria and Israel have led to an agreement on the disengagement of Syrian and Israeli forces. The agreement will be signed by Syrian and Israeli military representatives in the Egyptian—Israeli Military Working Group of the Geneva Conference on Friday (this Friday) May 31.

167. Joint announcement by the United States and Egypt, 31 May 1974[1]

The Governments of the United States and Egypt agreed today to the formation of a joint cooperation commission which will be designed to promote intensified cooperation in the economic, scientific and cultural fields between the two countries. Both Governments are convinced that such a joint commission will enable the United States and Egypt to develop far-reaching programs to their mutual benefit. Today's agreement is a result of a series of discussions between President Anwar Sadat and Secretary of State Henry A. Kissinger and reflects the deep desire of the two countries to strengthen their overall relationships. In agreeing to establish this joint commission, both Governments are further reaffirming their hope that a lasting and just peace in the Middle East will be realized thus helping the people of the area enjoy the rewards of stability and development. The commission will be chaired by the Foreign Ministers of each country. It will establish working groups. Its first meeting will take place in the near future.

168. Security Council Resolution 350, concerning the United Nations Disengagement Observer Force, 31 May 1974[2]

The Security Council,
    Having considered the report of the Secretary-General contained in document S/11302 and Add.1, and having heard his statement made at the 173rd meeting of the Security Council,
    1. *Welcomes* the Agreement on Disengagement between Israeli and Syrian Forces, negotiated in implementation of Security Council resolution 338 (1973) of 22 October 1973;
    2. *Takes note* of the Secretary-General's report and its annexes and his statement;
    3. *Decides* to set up immediately under its authority a United Nations Disengagement Observer Force, and requests the Secretary-General to take the necessary steps to this effect in accordance with his above-mentioned report and the annexes thereto. The Force shall be established for an initial period of six months, subject to renewal by further resolution of the Security Council;[3]

1 *DSB*, 24 June 1974, p. 698.
2 UN Doc. S/RES/350 (1974); adopted by a vote of 13 to 0 (the People's Republic of China and Iraq did not participate in the vote).
3 See UN Doc. S/RES/363 of 29 November 1974.

4. *Requests* the Secretary-General to keep the Security Council fully informed of further developments.

169. Agreement between the United States and Egypt on Principles of Relations and Cooperation, Cairo, 14 June 1974[1]

The President of the Arab Republic of Egypt, Muhammed Anwar el-Sadat, and the President of the United States of America, Richard Nixon,
— Having held wide-ranging discussions on matters of mutual interest to their two countries,
— Being acutely aware of the continuing need to build a structure of peace in the world and to that end and to promote a just and durable peace in the Middle East, and,
— Being guided by a desire to seize the historic opportunity before them to strengthen relations between their countries on the broadest basis in ways that will contribute to the well-being of the area as a whole and will not be directed against any of its states or peoples or against any other state,
Have agreed that the following principles should govern relations between Egypt and the United States.

I. General Principles of Bilateral Relations

Relations between nations, whatever their economic or political systems, should be based on the purposes and principles of the United Nations Charter, including the right of each state to existence, independence, and sovereignty; the right of each state freely to choose and develop its political, social, economic and cultural systems; non-intervention in each other's internal affairs; and respect for territorial integrity and political independence.

Nations should approach each other in the spirit of equality respecting their national life and the pursuit of happiness.

The United States and Egypt consider that their relationship reflects these convictions.

Peace and progress in the Middle East are essential if global peace is to be assured. A just and durable peace based on full implementation of UN Security Council Resolution 242 of November 22, 1967, should take into due account the legitimate interest of all the peoples in the Mid East, including the Palestinian people, and the right to existence of all states in the area. Peace can be achieved only through a process of continuing negotiation as called for by United Nations Security Council Resolution 338 of October 22, 1973, within the framework of the Geneva Middle East Peace Conference.

In recognition of these principles, the Governments of the Arab Republic of Egypt and the United States of America set themselves to these tasks:

1 *DSB*, 15 July 1974, pp. 92–3.

They will intensify consultations at all levels, including further consultations between their Presidents, and they will strengthen their bilateral cooperation whenever a common or parallel effort will enhance the cause of peace in the world.

They will continue their active cooperation and their energetic pursuit of peace in the Middle East.

They will encourage increased contacts between members of all branches of their two governments — executive, legislative and judicial — for the purpose of promoting better mutual understanding of each other's institutions, purposes and objectives.

They are determined to develop their bilateral relations in a spirit of esteem, respect and mutual advantage. In the past year, they have moved from estrangement to a constructive working relationship. This year, from that base, they are moving to a relationship of friendship and broad cooperation.

They view economic development and commercial relations as an essential element in the strengthening of their bilateral relations and will actively promote them. To this end, they will facilitate cooperative and joint ventures among appropriate governmental and private institutions and will encourage increased trade between the two countries.

They consider encouragement of exchanges and joint research in the scientific and technical field as an important mutual aim and will take appropriate concrete steps for this purpose.

They will deepen cultural ties through exchanges of scholars, students, and other representatives of the cultures of both countries.

They will make special efforts to increase tourism in both directions, and to amplify person-to-person contact among their citizens.

They will take measures to improve air and maritime communications between them.

They will seek to establish a broad range of working relationships and will look particularly to their respective Foreign Ministers and Ambassadors and to the Joint Commission on Cooperation, as well as to other officials and organizations, and private individuals and groups as appropriate, to implement the various aspects of the above principles.

II. Joint Cooperation Commission

The two governments have agreed that the intensive review of the areas of economic cooperation held by President el-Sadat and President Nixon on June 12 constituted the first meeting of the Joint Cooperation Commission, announced May 31, 1974. This Commission will be headed by the Secretary of State of the United States and the Minister of Foreign Affairs of Egypt. To this end, they have decided to move ahead rapidly on consultations and coordination to identify and implement programs agreed to be mutually beneficial in the economic, scientific and cultural fields.

The United States has agreed to help strengthen the financial structure of Egypt. To initiate this process, United States Secretary of the Treasury William Simon will visit Egypt in the near future for high level discussions.

III. Nuclear Energy

Since the atomic age began, nuclear energy has been viewed by all nations as a double-edged sword — offering opportunities for peaceful applications, but raising the risk of nuclear destruction. In its international programs of cooperation, the United States Government has made its nuclear technology available to other nations under safeguard conditions. In this context, the two governments will begin negotiation of an Agreement for Cooperation in the field of nuclear energy under agreed safeguards. Upon conclusion of such an agreement, the United States is prepared to sell nuclear reactors and fuel to Egypt, which will make it possible for Egypt by the early 1980s to generate substantial additional quantities of electric power to support its rapidly growing development needs. Pending conclusion of this Agreement, the United States Atomic Energy Commission and the Egyptian Ministry of Electricity will this month conclude a provisional agreement for the sale of nuclear fuel to Egypt.

IV. Working Groups

The two governments have agreed to set up Joint Working Groups to meet in the near future to prepare concrete projects and proposals for review by the Joint Commission at a meeting to be held later this year in Washington, D.C. These Joint Working Groups will be composed of governmental representatives from each country and will include the following:

(1) A Joint Working Group on Suez Canal Reconstruction and Development to consider and review plans for reopening the Suez Canal and reconstruction of the cities along the Canal, and the United States role in this endeavor.

(2) A Joint Working Group to investigate and recommend measures designed to open the way for United States private investment in joint ventures in Egypt and to promote trade between the two countries. Investment opportunities would be guided by Egypt's needs for financial, technical, and material support to increase Egypt's economic growth. The United States regards with favor and supports the ventures of American enterprises in Egypt. It is noted that such ventures, currently being negotiated, are in the field of petrochemicals, transportation, food and agricultural machinery, land development, power, tourism, banking, and a host of other economic sectors. The estimated value of projects under serious consideration exceeds two billion dollars. American technology and capital combined with Egypt's absorptive capacity, skilled manpower and productive investment opportunities can contribute effectively to the strengthening and development of the Egyptian economy. The United States and Egypt will therefore negotiate immediately a new Investment Guarantee Agreement between them.

(3) A Joint Working Group on Agriculture to study and recommend actions designed to increase Egypt's agricultural production through the use of the latest agricultural technology.

(4) A Joint Working Group on Technology, Research and Development in scientific fields, including space, with special emphasis on exchanges of scientists.

(5) A Joint Working Group on Medical Cooperation to assist the Government of Egypt to develop and strengthen its medical research, treatment and training facilities. These efforts will supplement cooperation in certain forms of medical research already conducted through the Naval Medical Research Unit (NAMRU), whose mutually beneficial work will continue.

(6) A Joint Working Group on Cultural Exchanges to encourage and facilitate exhibitions, visits, and other cultural endeavors to encourage a better understanding of both cultures on the part of the peoples of the United States and Egypt.

The two governments have agreed to encourage the formation of a Joint Economic Council to include representatives from the private economic sector of both countries to coordinate and promote mutually beneficial cooperative economic arrangements.

In support of their economic cooperation, the United States will make the maximum feasible contribution, in accordance with Congressional authorization, to Egypt's economic development, including clearing the Suez Canal, reconstruction projects, and restoring Egyptian trade. In addition, the United States is prepared to give special priority attention to Egypt's needs for agricultural commodities.

Consistent with the spirit of cultural cooperation, the United States Government has agreed to consider how it might assist the Egyptian Government in the reconstruction of Cairo's Opera House. The Egyptian Government for its part intends to place the 'Treasures of Tutankhamen' on exhibit in the United States.

Both governments, in conclusion, reiterate their intention to do everything possible to broaden the ties of friendship and cooperation consistent with their mutual interests in peace and security and with the principles set forth in this statement.

In thanking President el-Sadat for the hospitality shown to him and the members of his party, President Nixon extended an invitation to President el-Sadat, which President el-Sadat has accepted, to visit the United States during 1974.

170. Joint statement by Israel and the United States following the visit of President Nixon to Jerusalem, 17 June 1974[1]

The President of the United States, Richard Nixon, visited Israel June 16–17 1974. This is the first visit ever to have been paid by an American President to the State of Israel. It symbolizes the unique relationship, the common heritage and the close and historic ties that have long existed between the United States and Israel.

President Nixon and Prime Minister Rabin held extensive and cordial talks on matters of mutual interest to the United States and Israel and reviewed the excellent relations between their two countries. They discussed in a spirit of mutual understanding the efforts of both countries to achieve a just and lasting peace which will provide security for all States in the area and the need to build a structure of peace

1 *DSB*, 15 July 1974, pp. 110–12.

in the world. United States Secretary of State Henry Kissinger and members of the Israeli Cabinet participated in these talks.

Prime Minister Rabin expressed Israel's appreciation for the outstanding and effective role of the United States in the quest for peace under the leadership of President Nixon assisted by the tireless efforts of Secretary Kissinger and indicated Israel's intention to participate in further negotiations with a view to achieving peace treaties with its neighbors which will permit each State to pursue its legitimate rights in dignity and security.

President Nixon and Prime Minister Rabin agreed that peace and progress in the Middle East are essential if global peace is to be assured. Peace will be achieved through a process of continuing negotiations between the parties concerned as called for by UN Security Council Resolution 338 of October 22, 1973.

The President and the Prime Minister agreed on the necessity to work energetically to promote peace between Israel and the Arab States. They agreed that States living in peace should conduct their relationship in accordance with the purposes and principles of the United Nations Charter, and the UN Declaration on Principles of International Law concerning Friendly Relations and Cooperation among States which provides that every State has the duty to refrain from organizing or encouraging the organization of irregular forces or armed bands including mercenaries for incursion into the territory of another State. They condemned acts of violence and terror causing the loss of innocent human lives.

The President and the Prime Minister expressed their great pleasure in the intimate cooperation which characterizes the warm relationship between their two countries and peoples. They agreed to do everything possible to broaden and deepen still further that relationship in order to serve the interests of both countries and to further the cause of peace.

President Nixon reiterated the commitment of the United States to the long-term security of Israel and to the principle that each State has the right to exist within secure borders and pursue its own legitimate interests in peace.

Prime Minister Rabin expressed his appreciation for the US military supplies to Israel during the October War and thereafter. The President affirmed the continuing and long-term nature of the military supply relationship between the two countries, and reiterated his view that the strengthening of Israel's ability to defend itself is essential in order to prevent further hostilities and to maintain conditions conducive to progress towards peace. An Israeli Defense Ministry delegation will soon come to Washington in order to work out the concrete details relating to long-term military supplies.

President Nixon affirmed the strong continuing support of the United States for Israel's economic development. Prime Minister Rabin expressed the gratitude of Israel for the substantial help which the United States has provided particularly in recent years. The President and Prime Minister agreed that future economic assistance from the United States would continue and would be the subject of long-range planning between their governments. The President affirmed that the United States, in accordance with Congressional authorization, will continue to provide substantial economic assistance for Israel at levels needed to assist Israel to offset the heavy additional costs inherent in assuring Israel's military capability for the maintenance of peace.

In the economic field, the President and the Prime Minister noted with satisfaction the effective working relationship between their governments at all levels and the depth of the relationship between the economies of the two nations. They agreed to strengthen and develop the framework of their bilateral relations. The primary goal will be to establish a firmer and more clearly defined structure of consultation and cooperation. Where appropriate, they will set up special bi-national committees. Both sides recognize the importance of investments in Israel by American companies, the transmission of general know-how and marketing assistance, and cooperation of American companies with Israeli counterparts on research and development. The United States Government will encourage ventures by American enterprises and private investment in Israel designed to increase Israel's economic growth, including in the fields of industry, power, and tourism. They agreed to begin immediately negotiations for concrete arrangements to implement such policy including in the area of avoidance of double taxation.

The President and Prime Minister announce that their two governments will negotiate an agreement on cooperation in the field of nuclear energy, technology and the supply of fuel from the United States under agreed safeguards. This agreement will in particular take account of the intention of the Government of Israel to purchase power-reactors from the United States. These will secure additional and alternative sources of electricity for the rapidly developing Israel economy. As an immediate step, Israel and the United States will in the current month reach provisional agreement on the further sale of nuclear fuel to Israel.

Prime Minister Rabin particularly expressed the view that the supply of oil and other essential raw materials to Israel must be assured on a continuous basis. President Nixon proposed that United States and Israeli representatives meet soon in order to devise ways of meeting this problem.

The President and the Prime Minister stressed as an important mutual aim the further encouragement of the fruitful links already existing between the two countries in the scientific and technical field, including space research. Special emphasis will be put on exchanges of scientists and the sponsorship of joint projects. With this end in view they will explore means to widen the scope and substance of existing agreements and activities including those pertaining to the Bi-National Science Foundation.

In the area of water desalination the two countries will expand their joint projects.

The President and the Prime Minister agreed to develop further the cultural ties between the two countries through exchanges of scholars, students, artists, exhibitions, mutual visits and musical and other cultural events. In the near future, Israel will send to the United States an archaeological exhibition depicting the Land of the Bible. The Israel Philharmonic Orchestra will visit the United States on the occasion of the American bicentennial celebrations.

The President and the Prime Minister noted with gratification the large number of

ourists from their respective countries visiting both the United States and Israel
and affirmed that they would continue their efforts to foster this movement. To
this end, the two governments will resume negotiations on an agreement granting
landing rights to the Israel national carrier in additional major cities in the continental United States.

The President and the Prime Minister discussed the plight of Jewish minorities
in various countries in the spirit of the Universal Declaration of Human Rights. The
Prime Minister thanked the President for his efforts in support of the right of free
emigration for all peoples without harassment, including members of Jewish minorities.
The President affirmed that the United States would continue to give active support
to these principles in all feasible ways.

The President was particularly pleased at the opportunity to meet with former
Prime Minister Golda Meir, whose courage, statesmanship, patience and wisdom he
greatly admires. The President expressed his satisfaction at the constructive cooperation between Israel and the United States under Prime Minister Meir's leadership which had led to the conclusion of the agreements between Egypt and Israel and
between Israel and Syria respectively on the disengagement of their military forces.

In departing, President and Mrs Nixon expressed their deep appreciation of the
warm reception accorded to them in Israel and their admiration for the achievements
of the Israeli people. They were deeply impressed by the manner in which the overwhelming problems of integrating many hundreds of thousands of immigrants of
many various backgrounds and cultures were being successfully overcome. Convinced
of the determination of this valiant people to live in peace, the President gave them
renewed assurance of the support of the people of the United States.

The Prime Minister and the President agreed that the cordiality of Israel's reception
of the President reflected the long friendship between Israel and the United States
and pledged their continued energies to nurture and strengthen that friendship.
To this end, the President invited Prime Minister Rabin to pay an early visit to
Washington.

171. Joint statement by Jordan and the United States following the visit of President Nixon to Amman, 18 June 1974[1]

On the invitation of His Majesty King Hussein, President Richard Nixon paid the
first visit of a President of the United States of America to the Hashemite Kingdom
of Jordan on June 17 and 18, 1974.

During this visit President Nixon and His Majesty King Hussein discussed the full
range of common interests which have long bound Jordan and the United States in
continued close friendship and cooperation.

The United States reaffirmed its continued active support for the strength and
progress of Jordan. The President explained to His Majesty in detail the proposal
he has submitted to the Congress of the United States for a substantial increase in

1 *DSB*, 15 July 1974, pp. 118–19.

American military and economic assistance for Jordan in the coming 12 months. The President expressed his gratification over the efforts which Jordan is making under its development plan to expand the Jordanian economy, to give significant new impetus to the development of Jordan's mineral and other resources and production, and to raise the standard of living for all its people.

The President expressed admiration for His Majesty's wise leadership and stated his view that effective and steady development would make a substantial contributi to peace and stability in the Middle East. The President promised a special effort by the United States Government to provide support in a variety of ways for Jordan development efforts and in this regard welcomed the recent visit to Washington of His Royal Highness Crown Prince Hassan.

His Majesty emphasized the importance of maintaining Jordan's military strength if economic progress and development are to be assured.

His Majesty expressed the view that resources invested in maintaining the security and stability of the Kingdom are related to its economic growth, for without order and peace it is unrealistic to expect to marshal the energies and investment needed for economic progress. The President agreed with His Majesty and promised, in cooperation with the Congress, to play a strong role in maintaining Jordan's military strength.

His Majesty and the President agreed that they will continue to give US–Jordania relations their personal attention. In this context, it was agreed that a joint Jordania US Commission will be established at a high level to oversee and review on a regular basis the various areas of cooperation between Jordan and the United States in the fields of economic development, trade and investment, military assistance and suppl and scientific, social and cultural affairs.

His Majesty and the President have long agreed on the importance of moving toward peace in the Middle East. The President discussed the steps which have been taken in this regard since His Majesty's visit to Washington in March of this year. His Majesty expressed Jordan's support for the very significant diplomatic efforts which the United States has made to help bring peace to the Middle East. His Majesty and the President discussed the strategy of future efforts to achieve peace, and the President promised the active support of the United States for agreement between Jordan and Israel on concrete steps toward the just and durable peace called for in United Nations Security Council Resolution 338 of October 22, 1973.

The President has invited His Majesty to pay a visit to Washington at an early date. The purpose of the visit will be to hold further talks on the strategy of future efforts to achieve peace in accord with the objectives of United Nations Security Council Resolution 338. Further discussions of the details of the establishment of the Joint Commission will also be held. His Majesty has accepted the invitation and the date of the visit will be announced shortly.

The President expressed his gratitude and that of Mrs Nixon for the warm hospitality extended by His Majesty, by Her Majesty Queen Alia and by the Jordanian people.

172. Resolution of the Conference of Arab Heads of State, Rabat, 28 October 1974[1]

The seventh Arab summit has decided:
1. To affirm the rights of the Palestinian people to return to their homeland and to self-determination.
2. To affirm the rights of the Palestinian people to establish an independent national authority, under Palestine Liberation Organization leadership, as the sole legitimate representative of the Palestinian people on any liberated Palestinian territory. The Arab states must support this authority when set up in all fields and at all levels.
3. To support the Palestine Liberation Organization in the exercise of its responsibilities in the national and international fields in the framework of Arab commitments.
4. To invite Jordan, Egypt, Syria and the Palestine Liberation Organization to work out a formula governing their relations in the light of these decisions and in order to implement them.
5. To affirm the undertaking of all Arab states to safeguard Palestinian national unity and not to interfere in internal affairs regarding Palestinian action.

173. Joint communiqué issued by Egypt and the Soviet Union, following the visit of Mr Gromyko to Cairo, 5 February 1975 (extracts)[2]

[Both sides] reaffirmed their unswerving and principled position that a real lasting peace in the Middle East cannot be achieved without the total withdrawal of Israeli forces from all the Arab lands occupied in 1967 and without ensuring the national rights of the Arab people of Palestine, including their right to self-determination and to their own national home. . .

A Middle East settlement should be comprehensive in character: it should encompass all the sides involved in the conflict and should solve all the questions engendered by this conflict. . .

[Both sides] reaffirmed their belief that the Geneva Peace Conference on the Middle East is the most suitable forum for discussing all aspects of a settlement. . .

[Both sides] are in favour of an immediate resumption of this conference with the participation of all the sides concerned, including representatives of the Palestinian Liberation Organization. . .

The Egyptian side reaffirmed its opinion concerning the importance and need for Soviet participation in all fields and at all stages of a Middle East settlement,

1 *New York Times*, 30 October 1974.
2 *Soviet News*, 11 February 1975.

including its participation in all the working bodies that may be set up at the Geneva Conference. . .

The Soviet Union declared its determination to continue to give all-round aid and support to the just cause of the Arab peoples in their struggle for the elimination of the aftermaths of the Israeli aggression and for the establishment of a just and stable peace in the Middle East. . .

Both countries stressed their determination to follow the policy of expanding and deepening Soviet–Egyptian cooperation and friendship which are an achievement of historic significance attained at the cost of great efforts by the Soviet and Egyptian peoples. . .

174. Agreement between the Governments of Egypt and Israel, signed Geneva, 4 September 1975,[1] with Annex and United States Proposal

The Government of the Arab Republic of Egypt and the Government of Israel have agreed that:

Article I

The conflict between them and in the Middle East shall not be resolved by military force but by peaceful means.

The Agreement concluded by the Parties January 18, 1974, within the framework of the Geneva Peace Conference, constituted a first step towards a just and durable peace according to the provisions of Security Council Resolution 338 of October 22, 1973.

They are determined to reach a final and just peace settlement by means of negotiations called for by Security Council Resolution 338, this Agreement being a significant step towards that end.

Article II

The Parties hereby undertake not to resort to the threat or use of force or military blockade against each other.

Article III

The Parties shall continue scrupulously to observe the ceasefire on land, sea and air and to refrain from all military or para-military actions against each other.

The Parties also confirm that the obligations contained in the Annex and, when concluded, the Protocol shall be an integral part of this Agreement.

1 *DSB*, 29 September 1975, pp. 466–70.

Article IV

A. The military forces of the Parties shall be deployed in accordance with the following principles:

(1) All Israeli forces shall be deployed east of the lines designated as Lines J and M on the attached map.

(2) All Egyptian forces shall be deployed west of the line designated as Line E on the attached map.

(3) The area between the lines designated on the attached map as Lines E and F and the area between the lines designated on the attached map as Lines J and K shall be limited in armament and forces.

(4) The limitations on armament and forces in the areas described by paragraph (3) above shall be agreed as described in the attached Annex.

(5) The zone between the lines designated on the attached map as Lines E and J, will be a buffer zone. In this zone the United Nations Emergency Force will continue to perform its functions as under the Egyptian–Israeli Agreement of January 18, 1974.

(6) In the area south from Line E and west from Line M, as defined on the attached map, there will be no military forces, as specified in the attached Annex.

B. The details concerning the new lines, the redeployment of the forces and its timing, the limitation on armaments and forces, aerial reconnaissance, the operation of the early warning and surveillance installations and the use of the roads, the United Nations functions and other arrangements will all be in accordance with the provisions of the Annex and map[1] which are an integral part of this Agreement and of the Protocol which is to result from negotiations pursuant to the Annex and which, when concluded, shall become an integral part of this Agreement.

Article V

The United Nations Emergency Force is essential and shall continue its functions and its mandate shall be extended annually.

Article VI

The Parties hereby establish a Joint Commission for the duration of this Agreement. It will function under the aegis of the Chief Coordinator of the United Nations Peacekeeping Missions in the Middle East in order to consider any problem arising from this Agreement and to assist the United Nations Emergency Force in the execution of its mandate. The Joint Commission shall function in accordance with procedures established in the Protocol.

1 Not reproduced here; see *DSB*, 29 September 1975, p. 467.

Article VII

Non-military cargoes destined for or coming from Israel shall be permitted through the Suez Canal.

Article VIII

This Agreement is regarded by the Parties as a significant step toward a just and lasting peace. It is not a final peace agreement.

The Parties shall continue their efforts to negotiate a final peace arrangement within the framework of the Geneva Peace Conference in accordance with Security Council Resolution 338.

Article IX

This Agreement shall enter into force upon signature of the Protocol and remain in force until superseded by a new agreement.

ANNEX

Within 5 days after the signature of the Egypt—Israel Agreement, representatives of the two Parties shall meet in the Military Working Group of the Middle East Peace Conference at Geneva to begin preparation of a detailed Protocol for the implementation of the Agreement. The Working Group will complete the Protocol within 2 weeks. In order to facilitate preparation of the Protocol and implementatio of the Agreement, and to assist in maintaining the scrupulous observance of the ceasefire and other elements of the Agreement, the two Parties have agreed on the following principles, which are an integral part of the Agreement, as guidelines for the Working Group.

1. Definitions of Lines and Areas

The deployment lines, areas of limited forces and armaments, Buffer Zones, the area south from Line E and west from Line M, other designated areas, road sections for common use and other features referred to in Article IV of the Agreement shall be as indicated on the attached map (1:100,000 — US Edition).

2. Buffer Zones

(*a*) Access to the Buffer Zones will be controlled by the United Nations Emergency Force, according to procedures to be worked out by the Working Group and the United Nations Emergency Force.

(*b*) Aircraft of either Party will be permitted to fly freely up to the forward line of that Party. Reconnaissance aircraft of either Party may fly up to the middle line of the Buffer Zone between E and J on an agreed schedule.

(c) In the Buffer Zone, between line E and J there will be established under Article IV of the Agreement an Early Warning System entrusted to United States civilian personnel as detailed in a separate proposal, which is part of this Agreement.

(d) Authorized personnel shall have access to the Buffer Zone for transit to and from the Early Warning System; the manner in which this is carried out shall be worked out by the Working Group and the United Nations Emergency Force.

3. Area South of Line E and West of Line M

(a) In this area, the United Nations Emergency Force will assure that there are no military or para-military forces of any kind, military fortifications and military installations; it will establish checkpoints and have the freedom of movement necessary to perform this function.

(b) Egyptian civilians and third country civilian oil field personnel shall have the right to enter, exit from, work, and live in the above indicated area, except for Buffer Zones 2A, 2B and the United Nations Posts. Egyptian civilian police shall be allowed in the area to perform normal civil police functions among the civilian population in such numbers and with such weapons and equipment as shall be provided for in the Protocol.

(c) Entry to and exit from the area, by land, by air or by sea, shall be only through United Nations Emergency Force checkpoints. The United Nations Emergency Force shall also establish checkpoints along the road, the dividing line and at other points, with the precise locations and number to be included in the Protocol.

(d) Access to the airspace and the coastal area shall be limited to unarmed Egyptian civilian vessels and unarmed civilian helicopters and transport planes involved in the civilian activities of the area as agreed by the Working Group.

(e) Israel undertakes to leave intact all currently existing civilian installations and infrastructures.

(f) Procedures for use of the common sections of the coastal road along the Gulf of Suez shall be determined by the Working Group and detailed in the Protocol.

4. Aerial Surveillance

There shall be a continuation of aerial reconnaissance missions by the United States over the areas covered by the Agreement (the area between lines F and K), following the same procedures already in practice. The missions will ordinarily be carried out at a frequency of one mission every 7—10 days, with either Party or the United Nations Emergency Force empowered to request an earlier mission. The United States Government will make the mission results available expeditiously to Israel, Egypt and the Chief Coordinator of the United Nations Peace-keeping Missions in the Middle East.

5. Limitation of Forces and Armaments

(*a*) Within the Areas of Limited Forces and Armaments (the areas between lines J and K and lines E and F) the major limitations shall be as follows:

(1) Eight (8) standard infantry battalions

(2) Seventy-five (75) tanks

(3) Seventy-two (72) artillery pieces, including heavy mortars (i.e. with caliber larger than 120 mm), whose range shall not exceed twelve (12) km.

(4) The total number of personnel shall not exceed eight thousand (8,000).

(5) Both Parties agree not to station or locate in the area weapons which can reach the line of the other side.

(6) Both Parties agree that in the areas between lines J and K and between line A (of the Disengagement Agreement of January 18, 1974) and line E, they will construct no new fortifications or installations for forces of a size greater than that agreed herein.

(*b*) The major limitations beyond the Areas of Limited Forces and Armament will be:

(1) Neither side will station nor locate any weapon in areas from which they can reach the other line.

(2) The Parties will not place antiaircraft missiles within an area of ten (10) kilometres east of Line K and west of Line F, respectively.

(*c*) The United Nations Emergency Force will conduct inspections in order to ensure the maintenance of the agreed limitations within these areas.

6. Process of Implementation

The detailed implementation and timing of the redeployment of forces, turnover of oil fields, and other arrangements called for by the Agreement, Annex and Protocol shall be determined by the Working Group, which will agree on the stages of this process, including the phased movement of Egyptian troops to line E and Israeli troops to line J. The first phase will be the transfer of the oil fields and installations to Egypt. This process will begin within two weeks from the signature of the Protocol with the introduction of the necessary technicians, and it will be completed no later than eight weeks after it begins. The details of the phasing will be worked out in the Military Working Group.

Implementation of the redeployment shall be completed within 5 months after signature of the Protocol.

PROPOSAL

In connection with the Early Warning System referred to in Article IV of the Agreement between Egypt and Israel concluded on this date and as an integral part of that Agreement, (hereafter referred to as the Basic Agreement), the United States proposes the following:

1. The Early Warning System to be established in accordance with Article IV in the area shown on the map attached to the Basic Agreement will be entrusted to the United States. It shall have the following elements:

   a. There shall be two surveillance stations to provide strategic early warning, one operated by Egyptian and one operated by Israeli personnel. Their locations are shown on the map attached to the Basic Agreement. Each station shall be manned by not more than 250 technical and administrative personnel. They shall perform the functions of visual and electronic surveillance only within their stations.

   b. In support of these stations, to provide tactical early warning and to verify access to them, three watch stations shall be established by the United States in the Mitla and Giddi Passes as will be shown on the map attached to the Basic Agreement. These stations shall be operated by United States civilian personnel. In support of these stations, there shall be established three unmanned electronic sensor fields at both ends of each Pass and in the general vicinity of each station and the roads leading to and from those stations.

2. The United States civilian personnel shall perform the following duties in connection with the operation and maintenance of these stations.

   a. At the two surveillance stations described in paragraph 1 a. above, the United States civilian personnel will verify the nature of the operations of the stations and all movement into and out of each station and will immediately report any detected divergency from its authorized role of visual and electronic surveillance to the Parties to the Basic Agreement and to the United Nations Emergency Force.

   b. At each watch station described in paragraph 1 b. above, the United States civilian personnel will immediately report to the Parties to the Basic Agreement and to the United Nations Emergency Force any movement of armed forces, other than the United Nations Emergency Force, into either Pass and any observed preparations for such movement.

   c. The total number of United States civilian personnel assigned to functions under this Proposal shall not exceed 200. Only civilian personnel shall be assigned to functions under this Proposal.

3. No arms shall be maintained at the stations and other facilities covered by this Proposal, except for small arms required for their protection.

4. The United States personnel serving the Early Warning System shall be allowed to move freely within the area of the System.

5. The United States and its personnel shall be entitled to have such support facilities as are reasonably necessary to perform their functions.

6. The United States personnel shall be immune from local criminal, civil, tax and customs jurisdiction and may be accorded any other specific privileges and immunities provided for in the United Nations Emergency Force agreement of February 13, 1957.

7. The United States affirms that it will continue to perform the functions described above for the duration of the Basic Agreement.

8. Notwithstanding any other provision of this Proposal, the United States may withdraw its personnel only if it concludes that their safety is jeopardized or that

continuation of their role is no longer necessary. In the latter case the Parties to the Basic Agreement will be informed in advance in order to give them the opportunity to make alternative arrangements. If both Parties to the Basic Agreement request the United States to conclude its role under this Proposal, the United States will consider such requests conclusive.

9. Technical problems including the location of the watch stations will be worked out through consultation with the United States.

VI.   The crisis of
the International Economic Order

A. The International Monetary System

175. Communiqué issued following the meeting of the Governors of the Central Bank of the seven 'Gold Pool' nations, Washington, 17 March 1968[1]

The Governors of the Central Banks of Belgium, Germany, Italy, the Netherlands, Switzerland, the United Kingdom, and the United States met in Washington on March 16 and 17, 1968 to examine operations of the gold pool, to which they are active contributors. The Managing Director of the International Monetary Fund and the General Manager of the Bank for International Settlements also attended the meeting.

The Governors noted that it is the determined policy of the United States Government to defend the value of the dollar through appropriate fiscal and monetary measures and that substantial improvement of the US balance of payments is a high priority objective.

They also noted that legislation approved by Congress makes the whole of the gold stock of the nation available for defending the value of the dollar.

They noted that the US Government will continue to buy and sell gold at the existing price of $35 an ounce in transactions with monetary authorities. The Governors support this policy, and believe it contributes to the maintenance of exchange stability.

The Governors noted the determination of the UK authorities to do all that is necessary to eliminate the deficit in the UK balance of payments as soon as possible and to move to a position of large and sustained surplus.

Finally, they noted that the Governments of most European countries intend to pursue monetary and fiscal policies that encourage domestic expansion consistent with economic stability, avoid as far as possible increases in interest rates or a tightening of money markets, and thus contribute to conditions that will help all countries move toward payments equilibrium.

The Governors agreed to cooperate fully to maintain the existing parities as well as orderly conditions in their exchange markets in accordance with their obligations under the Articles of Agreement of the International Monetary Fund. The Governors believe that henceforth officially-held gold should be used only to

1 *DSB*, 8 April 1968, p. 464.

effect transfers among monetary authorities and, therefore, they decided no longer to supply gold to the London gold market or any other gold market. Moreover, as the existing stock of monetary gold is sufficient in view of the prospective establishment of the facility for Special Drawing Rights, they no longer feel it necessary to buy gold from the market. Finally, they agreed that henceforth they will not sell gold to monetary authorities to replace gold sold in private markets.

The Governors agreed to cooperate even more closely than in the past to minimize flows of funds contributing to instability in the exchange markets, and to offset as necessary any such flows that may arise.

In view of the importance of the pound sterling in the international monetary system, the Governors have agreed to provide further facilities which will bring the total of credits immediately available to the UK authorities (including the IMF standby) to $4 billion.

The Governors invite the cooperation of other central banks in the policies set forth above.

176. Resolution adopted by the Board of Governors of the IMF, 9 February 1970,[1] with Annex

WHEREAS the Executive Directors have considered the adjustment of the quotas of members in accordance with the Resolution of the Board of Governors of the International Monetary Fund at its 1969 Annual Meeting:

That the Executive Directors proceed promptly with the consideration of the adjustment of the quotas of members of the Fund and submit an appropriate proposal to the Board of Governors not later than December 31, 1969;

WHEREAS the Executive Directors have submitted to the Board of Governors a Report entitled 'Increases in Quotas of Members – Fifth General Review'; and

WHEREAS the Executive Directors have recommended the adoption of the following Resolution of the Board of Governors, which Resolution proposes increases in the quotas of members of the Fund as a result of the fifth general review of quotas and deals with certain related matters, by vote without meeting pursuant to Section 13 of the By-Laws of the Fund;

NOW, THEREFORE, the Board of Governors, noting the said Report of the Executive Directors, hereby resolves that:

1. The International Monetary Fund proposes that, subject to the provisions of this Resolution, the quotas of members of the Fund shall be increased to the amounts shown against their names in the Annex to this Resolution, provided that any member (a) may consent to an increase in its quota which is smaller than that shown in the said Annex and (b) may consent thereafter to further increases up to the said amount.

2. An increase in a member's quota under this Resolution shall become effective when the member has notified the Fund that it consents to the increase and has paid in full the increase in the quota, provided, however, that no increase

1 IMF, *Annual Report, 1970*, pp. 181–4, Resolution No. 25–3.

in quota shall become effective before October 30, 1970. The increase in the quota of a member which has notified the Fund of its consent and has completed payment of the increase at any time prior to October 30, 1970, shall become effective on that date.

3. Notices in accordance with paragraph 2 shall be executed by a duly authorized official of the member.

4. Notices in accordance with paragraph 2 shall be received in the Fund not later than November 15, 1971, provided that the Executive Directors may extend this period as they may determine.

5. Subject to paragraph 6 (b), each member shall pay to the Fund the increase in its quota within 30 days after the date on which it notified the Fund of its consent or October 30, 1970, whichever is later. Twenty-five per cent of the increase shall be paid in gold and the balance in the member's currency, provided, however, that, if on the date when a member consents to any increase under paragraph 1 or paragraph 6 its monetary reserves are less than the new quota to which it has consented, the member may pay in gold that proportion of 25 per cent of the increase in quota which the member's monetary reserves on the date of consent bear to the quota to which the member has consented and the balance of the increase in quota shall be paid in currency. A member which, in accordance with this paragraph, pays more than 75 per cent of the increase in currency, shall undertake to repurchase the currency paid in excess of 75 per cent of the increase. Unless the Fund's holdings resulting from such payment are otherwise reduced, repurchase shall be completed in five equal annual installments commencing one year after the date on which the increase becomes effective.

6. (*a*) In giving notice in accordance with paragraph 2, any member consenting to the increase in its quota to the full amount shown against its name in the Annex to this Resolution may consent to that increase as increases by installments.

   (*b*) Notwithstanding paragraph 2, a member increasing its quota by installments shall pay not less than one fifth of the increase in gold and currency in accordance with paragraph 5 within 30 days after the date on which it notified the Fund of its consent or October 30, 1970, whichever is later, and shall pay further installments of gold and currency of not less than one fifth of the increase in each twelve months after the first payment until the full amount has been paid. For the purpose of determining under paragraph 5 the gold and currency portions of an installment subsequent to the initial installment, a member shall be deemed to have consented to the increase in its quota equivalent to the installment 30 days before it pays the installment.

   (*c*) Subject to paragraph 2, on the completion of the payment of each installment of the increase, the member's quota shall be increased by an amount equal to the installment.

7. The Fund shall replenish its holdings of the currencies of members which sell gold to other members to enable the latter members to pay the increases in

their quotas under this Resolution. Replenishment under this paragraph shall be by the sale of gold in accordance with the provisions of Article VII, Section 2 and shall not exceed an amount equivalent to US$700 million.

ANNEX TO RESOLUTION

	Proposed Maximum Quota *(In millions of US dollars)*		Proposed Maximum Quota *(In millions of US dollars)*
1. Afghanistan	37	43. Iceland	23
2. Algeria	130	44. India	940
3. Argentina	440	45. Indonesia	260
4. Australia	665	46. Iran	192
5. Austria	270	47. Iraq	109
6. Belgium	650	48. Ireland	121
7. Bolivia	37	49. Israel	130
8. Botswana	5	50. Italy	1,000
9. Brazil	440	51. Ivory Coast	52
10. Burma	60	52. Jamaica	53
11. Burundi	19	53. Japan	1,200
12. Cameroon	35	54. Jordan	23
13. Canada	1,100	55. Kenya	48
14. Central African Republic	13	56. Korea	80
15. Ceylon	98	57. Kuwait	114
16. Chad	13	58. Laos	13
17. Chile	158	59. Lebanon	56
18. China	550	60. Lesotho	5
19. Colombia	157	61. Liberia	29
20. Congo (Brazzaville)	13	62. Libya	67
21. Congo, Democratic Republic of	113	63. Luxembourg	24
22. Costa Rica	32	64. Malagasy Republic	26
23. Cyprus	26	65. Malawi	15
24. Dahomey	13	66. Malaysia	186
25. Denmark	260	67. Mali	22
26. Dominican Republic	43	68. Malta	16
27. Ecuador	33	69. Mauritania	13
28. El Salvador	35	70. Mauritius	22
29. Ethiopia	27	71. Mexico	370
30. Equatorial Guinea	8	72. Morocco	113
31. Finland	190	73. Nepal	14
32. France	1,500	74. Netherlands	700
33. Gabon	15	75. New Zealand	202
34. Gambia, The	7	76. Nicaragua	27
35. Germany, Federal Republic of	1,600	77. Niger	13
36. Ghana	87	78. Nigeria	135
37. Greece	138	79. Norway	240
38. Guatemala	36	80. Pakistan	235
39. Guinea	24	81. Panama	36
40. Guyana	20	82. Paraguay	19
41. Haiti	19	83. Peru	123
42. Honduras	25	84. Philippines	155

	Proposed Maximum Quota			Proposed Maximum Quota
	(In millions of US dollars)			*(In millions of US dollars)*
85. Portugal	117	101. Togo		15
86. Rwanda	19	102. Trinidad and Tobago		63
87. Saudi Arabia	134	103. Tunisia		48
88. Senegal	34	104. Turkey		151
89. Sierra Leone	25	105. Uganda		40
90. Singapore	62	106. United Arab Republic		188
91. Somalia	19	107. United Kingdom		2,800
92. South Africa	320	108. United States		6,700
93. Southern Yemen	29	109. Upper Volta		13
94. Spain	395	110. Uruguay		69
95. Sudan	72	111. Venezuela		330
96. Swaziland	8	112. Vietnam		62
97. Sweden	325	113. Yugoslavia		207
98. Syrian Arab Republic	50	114. Zambia		76
99. Tanzania	42	*115. Cambodia		25
100. Thailand	134			

*Cambodia was added by Board of Governors' Resolution No. 25–4, adopted June 15, 1970 which amended Resolution No. 25–3. The amendment allows Cambodia, which became a member of the Fund on December 31, 1969 after the Executive Directors' report and proposed Resolution had already been submitted to the Governors, the same opportunity as other members to increase its quota in accordance with Resolution No. 25–3.

177. Address by President Nixon on American radio and television, 15 August 1971[1] (extracts)

Good evening. I have addressed the Nation a number of times over the past 2 years on the problems of ending a war. Because of the progress we have made toward achieving that goal, this Sunday evening is an appropriate time for us to turn our attention to the challenges of peace.

America today has the best opportunity in this century to achieve two of its greatest ideals: to bring about a full generation of peace and to create a new prosperity without war.

This not only requires bold leadership ready to take bold action; it calls forth the greatness in a great people.

Prosperity without war requires action on three fronts: We must create more and better jobs; we must stop the rise in the cost of living; we must protect the dollar from the attacks of international money speculators.

We are going to take that action — not timidly, not halfheartedly, and not in piecemeal fashion. We are going to move forward to the new prosperity without war as befits a great people — all together and along a broad front.

1 *DSB*, 6 September 1971, pp. 253–5.

The time has come for a new economic policy for the United States. Its targets are unemployment, inflation, and international speculation. And this is how we are going to attack these targets. . .

First, on the subject of jobs: We all know why we have an unemployment problem. Two million workers have been released from the Armed Forces and defense plants because of our success in winding down the war in Vietnam. Putting those people back to work is one of the challenges of peace, and we have begun to make progress. Our unemployment rate today is below the average of the 4 peacetime years of the 1960s.

But we can and we must do better than that.

The time has come for American industry, which has produced more jobs at higher real wages than any other industrial system in history, to embark on a bold program of new investment in production for peace.

To give that system a powerful new stimulus, I shall ask the Congress when it reconvenes after its summer recess to consider as its first priority the enactment of the Job Development Act of 1971.

I will propose to provide the strongest short-term incentive in our history to invest in new machinery and equipment that will create new jobs for Americans: a 10-percent Job Development Credit for 1 year, effective as of today, with a 5-percent credit after August 15, 1972. This tax credit for investment in new equipment will not only generate new jobs; it will raise productivity; it will make our goods more competitive in the years ahead. . .

The third indispensable element in building the new prosperity is closely related to creating new jobs and halting inflation. We must protect the position of the American dollar as a pillar of monetary stability around the world.

In the past 7 years, there has been an average of one international monetary crisis every year. Now, who gains from these crises? Not the workingman; not the investor; not the real producers of wealth. The gainers are the international money speculators. Because they thrive on crises, they help to create them.

In recent weeks, the speculators have been waging an all-out war on the American dollar. The strength of a nation's currency is based on the strength of that nation's economy — and the American economy is by far the strongest in the world. According I have directed the Secretary of the Treasury to take the action necessary to defend the dollar against the speculators.

I have directed Secretary Connally to suspend temporarily the convertibility of the dollar into gold or other reserve assets, except in amounts and conditions determined to be in the interest of monetary stability and in the best interests of the United States.

Now what is this action — which is very technical — what does it mean for you?

Let me lay to rest the bugaboo of what is called devaluation.

If you want to buy a foreign car or take a trip abroad, market conditions may cause your dollar to buy slightly less. But if you are among the overwhelming majority of Americans who buy American-made products in America, your dollar will be worth just as much tomorrow as it is today.

The effect of this action, in other words, will be to stabilize the dollar.

Now, this action will not win us any friends among the international money traders. But our primary concern is with the American workers, and with fair competition around the world.

To our friends abroad, including the many responsible members of the international banking community who are dedicated to stability and the flow of trade, I give this assurance: The United States has always been, and will continue to be, a forward-looking and trustworthy trading partner. In full cooperation with the International Monetary Fund and those who trade with us, we will press for the necessary reforms to set up an urgently needed new international monetary system. Stability and equal treatment is in everybody's best interest. I am determined that the American dollar must never again be a hostage in the hands of international speculators.

I am taking one further step to protect the dollar, to improve our balance of payments, and to increase jobs for Americans. As a temporary measure, I am today imposing an additional tax of 10 percent on goods imported into the United States.[1] This is a better solution for international trade than direct controls on the amount of imports.

This import tax is a temporary action. It isn't directed against any other country. It is an action to make certain that American products will not be at a disadvantage because of unfair exchange rates. When the unfair treatment is ended, the import tax will end as well.

As a result of these actions, the product of American labor will be more competitive, and the unfair edge that some of our foreign competition has will be removed. This is a major reason why our trade balance has eroded over the past 15 years.

At the end of World War II the economies of the major industrial nations of Europe and Asia were shattered. To help them get on their feet and to protect their freedom, the United States has provided over the past 25 years $143 billion in foreign aid. That was the right thing for us to do.

Today, largely with our help, they have regained their vitality. They have become our strong competitors, and we welcome their success. But now that other nations are economically strong, the time has come for them to bear their fair share of the burden of defending freedom around the world. The time has come for exchange rates to be set straight and for the major nations to compete as equals. There is no longer any need for the United States to compete with one hand tied behind her back.

The range of actions I have taken and proposed tonight — on the job front, on the inflation front, on the monetary front — is the most comprehensive new economic policy to be undertaken in this Nation in four decades. . .

---

1 For text of the official proclamation, see *DSB*, 6 September 1971, pp. 256–7.

178. Communiqué issued following the meeting of the Commission of the European Communities, Brussels, 17 August 1971[1]

The Commission of the European Communities has made a preliminary examination of the implications for the Community and the world economy of the economic, monetary and commercial measures that have just been taken by the Government of the United States.

It notes that the principles on which the international monetary system has so far been based and which have been conducive to an expansion of trade are being called in question.

The Commission is also concerned about certain measures which will have a negative impact on international trade and may in fact nullify the progress achieved in the Kennedy round. In this connection it does not consider that the policies pursued within the Community have created situations of 'unfair competition' in dealings with the United States and other non-member countries.

The Commission is convinced that the member countries of the Community will adopt common solutions enabling them to maintain their cohesion, strengthen their solidarity and contribute to further progress in international economic relations It will do everything in its power to help them implement these solutions.

The Commission hopes it will be possible for the countries which have applied for membership to concert their action with that taken by the Community, and that the United States and the Community will succeed in overcoming the present difficulties in a spirit of cooperation and friendship.

179. Communiqué issued by the French Government on the international monetary situation, 18 August 1971[2]

The French Government sees in the decisions announced by President Nixon the proof that the American authorities henceforth appreciate the gravity of the monetan situation due to the balance of payments of the United States.

While taking note of the desire for the recovery stand by the Government of the United States, the French Government notes that the decisions taken on external affairs are not in accordance with the rules which govern the International Monetary Fund and the General Agreement on Tariffs and Trade or with the agreement on the use of special drawing rights.

The French Government believes that the current disturbance of the international monetary system hinders the development of trade and, in consequence, the economic and social progress of all nations. It thus believes it indispensable that, within a reasonable time, a complete reexamination of the international monetary system should be undertaken.

1 WEU, *Political Year in Europe, 1971*, p. 227.
2 WEU, *Political Year in Europe, 1971*, pp. 227–8.

The French Government remains attached to the principle of fixed parities based on the definition in gold of the value of currencies, as was chosen in 1944 by the Bretton Woods negotiators, clearly informed of the crises of protectionism and unemployment engendered by the prewar monetary competitions. Experience is confirming its diagnosis, formulated a long time ago, according to which the world system of fixed parities is incompatible with the exclusive usage, as a reserve instrument, of a currency which is linked to the uncertainty of a national economic situation and not bound by the disciplines of equilibrium and balanced payments. As far as it is concerned, the French Government confirms that it will maintain the franc at its parity of 160 milligrammes of fine gold.

As a first step, the French Government believes that the six member countries of the European Economic Community should define a common policy, both to ensure the regular development of their internal trade in accordance with the terms of the Rome Treaty and with Community regulations and to coordinate their attitude vis-à-vis the new situation created by floating the dollar.

This coordination is all the more necessary since the countries of the European Community and those preparing to join it constitute the most significant trading unit in the world.

Therefore, during the EEC Council of Ministers meeting to be held in Brussels on 19th August, the French Delegation will propose the following measures to its partners: in order to prevent currency values from being fixed by the uncertain laws of supply and demand in a world fraught with speculative movement, access to exchange markets operating in accordance with the rules of the International Monetary Fund could be reserved for trade transactions; at the same time, markets could be organised to deal with currencies destined for other transactions abroad; the intervention of central banks on these markets could be concerted among Community members.

Concerned by the need for effective international cooperation, particularly on a European level, the President of the Republic will, when the time comes, propose to the Community countries and those preparing to join it that preliminary consultations be organised for a meeting at the level of Chiefs of State and Heads of Government.

By its decisions and its proposals the French Government is deliberately taking into account both the exigencies of international cooperation and the need to preserve France's chances for stability, expansion and full employment.

In addition, the necessary procedures for concertation with the United States and the franc zone are being put into motion.

180. Statement by Mr Mikio Mizuta, the Japanese Finance Minister, Tokyo, 27 August 1971[1]

In view of the recent international monetary situation, it has been decided to suspend

1 *The Times*, 28 August 1971.

temporarily the existing fluctuation margin for buying and selling quotations of foreign exchange, while maintaining the present parity of the yen.

Since Japan's accession to the International Monetary Fund in August 1952, Japan has been consistently observing, under the present parity, the 1 per cent margin either side of the parity as stipulated in the agreement governing IMF.

Recently, however, the international monetary situation has become extremely fluid and most of the currencies of Western nations are being quoted in excess of the margins stipulated in the agreement.

Meanwhile, the real strength of the yen has steadily increased reflecting the efforts of the Japanese people during the past 20 years or so, so that the smooth execution of export, import and other external transactions have come to be impeded, under the present shaky international monetary situation, by the fluctuation margin stipulated by the IMF agreement.

I am hoping that through the present measures we can proceed to establish a new international monetary system.

To compensate for a decline in exports and stagnation of domestic demand, that might arise from the present measures as well as other factors including the imposition of the United States import surcharge, and to create new domestic demand and promote improvement of the people's standard of living and modernization of social overhead capital, it is planned to actively utilize the national bond policy and present a supplementary budget to the national Diet, expand fiscal loan and investment programmes and take other constructive monetary and taxation measures.

181. Joint statement by President Nixon and President Pompidou, The Azores, 14 December 1971[1]

President Nixon and President Pompidou reached a broad area of agreement on measures necessary to achieve a settlement at the earliest possible date of the immediate problems of the international monetary system. In cooperation with other nations concerned, they agree to work toward a prompt realignment of exchange rates through a devaluation of the dollar and revaluation of some other currencies. This realignment could, in their view, under present circumstances, be accompanied by broader permissible margins of fluctuation around the newly established exchange rates.

Aware of the interest of measures involving trade for a lasting equilibrium of the balance of payments, President Pompidou confirmed that France, together with the governments of the other countries which are members of the European Economic Community, was preparing the mandate which would permit the imminent opening of negotiations with the United States in order to settle the short-term problems currently pending and to establish the agenda for the examination of fundamental questions in the area of trade.

1 *DSB*, 10 January 1972, pp. 30–1.

President Nixon underscored the contribution that vigorous implementation by the United States of measures to restore domestic wage—price stability and productivity would make toward international equilibrium and the defense of the new dollar exchange rate.

The Presidents agreed that discussion should be undertaken promptly in appropriate forums to resolve fundamental and interrelated issues of monetary reform.

182. Communiqué issued following the ministerial meeting of the Group of Ten, Washington, 18 December 1971,[1] the 'Smithsonian Agreement'

1. The Ministers and Central Bank Governors of the ten countries participating in the General Arrangements to Borrow met at the Smithsonian Institution in Washington on 17th—18th December, 1971, in executive session under the Chairmanship of Mr J. B. Connally, Secretary of the Treasury of the United States. Mr P.-P. Schweitzer, the Managing Director of the International Monetary Fund, took part in the meeting, which was also attended by the President of the Swiss National Bank, Mr E. Stopper, and in part by the Secretary-General of the OECD [Organization for Economic Cooperation and Development], Jonkheer E. van Lennep, the General Manager of the Bank for International Settlements, Mr R. Larre, and the Vice-President of the Commission of the EEC [European Economic Community], Mr R. Barre. The Ministers and Governors welcomed a report from the Managing Director of the Fund on a meeting held between their Deputies and the Executive Directors of the Fund.

2. The Ministers and Governors agreed to an inter-related set of measures designed to restore stability to international monetary arrangements and to provide for expanding international trade. These measures will be communicated promptly to other governments. It is the hope of the Ministers and Governors that all governments will cooperate through the International Monetary Fund to permit implementation of these measures in an orderly fashion.

3. The Ministers and Governors reached agreement on a pattern of exchange rate relationships among their currencies. These decisions will be announced by individual governments, in the form of par values or central rates as they desire. Most of the countries plan to close their exchange markets on Monday. The Canadian Minister informed the Group that Canada intends temporarily to maintain a floating exchange rate and intends to permit fundamental market forces to establish the exchange rate without intervention except as required to maintain orderly conditions.

4. It was also agreed that, pending agreement on longer-term monetary reforms, provision will be made for 2¼ percent margins of exchange rate fluctuation above and below the new exchange rates. The Ministers and Governors recognized that all members of the International Monetary Fund not attending the present discussions will need urgently to reach decisions, in consultation with the International Monetary Fund, with respect to their own exchange rates. It was the view of the Ministers and

1 *DSB*, 10 January 1972, pp. 32—4.

Governors that it is particularly important at this time that no country seek improper competitive advantage through its exchange rate policies. Changes in parities can only be justified by an objective appraisal which establishes a position of disequilibrium.

5. Questions of trade arrangements were recognized by the Ministers and Governor as a relevant factor in assuring a new and lasting equilibrium in the international economy. Urgent negotiations are now under way between the United States and the Commission of the European Community, Japan, and Canada to resolve pending short-term issues at the earliest possible date and with the European Community to establish an appropriate agenda for considering more basic issues in a framework of mutual cooperation in the course of 1972 and beyond. The United States agreed to propose to Congress a suitable means for devaluing the dollar in terms of gold to $38.00 per ounce as soon as the related set of short-term measures is available for Congressional scrutiny. Upon passage of required legislative authority in this framework, the United States will propose the corresponding new par value of the dollar to the International Monetary Fund.

6. In consideration of the agreed immediate realignment of exchange rates, the United States agreed that it will immediately suppress the recently imposed 10 percent import surcharge and related provisions of the Job Development Credit.

7. The Ministers and Governors agreed that discussions should be promptly undertaken, particularly in the framework of the IMF, to consider reform of the international monetary system over the longer term. It was agreed that attention should be directed to the appropriate monetary means and division of responsibilities for defending stable exchange rates and for insuring a proper degree of convertibility of the system; to the proper role of gold, of reserve currencies, and of Special Drawing Rights in the operation of the system; to the appropriate volume of liquidity; to reexamination of the permissible margins of fluctuation around established exchange rates and other means of establishing a suitable degree of flexibility; and to other measures dealing with movements of liquid capital. It is recognized that decisions in each of these areas are closely linked.

183. Statement on foreign economic policy by Mr Shultz, United States Secretary of the Treasury, Washington, 12 February 1973[1] (extract)

Progress in the work of the Committee of Twenty has been too slow and should move with a greater sense of urgency. The time has come to give renewed impetus to our efforts on behalf of a stronger international economic order.

To that end, in consultation with our trading partners and in keeping with the basic principles of our proposals for monetary reform, we are taking a series of actions designed to achieve three interrelated purposes:

1 WEU, *Political Year in Europe, 1973*, pp. 51–3.

(*a*) to speed improvement of our trade and payments position in a manner that will support our effort to achieve constructive reform of the monetary system;

(*b*) to lay the legislative groundwork for broad and outward-looking trade negotiations, parallelling our efforts to strengthen the monetary system; and

(*c*) to assure that American workers and American businessmen are treated equitably in our trading relationships.

For these purposes:

First, the President is requesting that the Congress authorise a further realignment of exchange rates. This objective will be sought by a formal 10% reduction in the par value of the dollar from 0.92106 SDR to the dollar to 0.82895 SDR to the dollar.

Although this action will, under the existing articles of agreement of the International Monetary Fund, result in a change in the official relationship of the dollar to gold, I should like to stress that this technical change has no practical significance. The market price of gold in recent years has diverged widely from the official price, and under these conditions gold has not been transferred to any significant degree among international monetary authorities. We remain strongly of the opinion that orderly arrangements must be negotiated to facilitate the continuing reduction of the role of gold in international monetary affairs.

Consultations with our leading trading partners in Europe assure me that the proposed change in the par value of the dollar is acceptable to them, and will therefore be effective immediately in exchange rates for the dollar in international markets. The dollar will decline in value by about 10% in terms of those currencies for which there is an effective par value, for example the Deutschmark and the French franc.

Japanese authorities have indicated that the yen will be permitted to float. Our firm expectation is that the yen will float into a relationship vis-à-vis other currencies consistent with achieving a balance of payments equilibrium not dependent upon significant government intervention.

These changes are intended to supplement and work in the same direction as the changes accomplished in the Smithsonian agreement of December 1971. They take into account recent developments and are designed to speed improvement in our trade and payments position. In particular, they are designed, together with appropriate trade liberalisation, to correct the major payments imbalance between Japan and the United States which has persisted in the past year.

Other countries may also propose changes in their par values or central rates to the International Monetary Fund. We will support all changes that seem warranted on the basis of current and prospective payments imbalances, but plan to vote against any changes that are inappropriate.

We have learned that time must pass before new exchange relationships modify established patterns of trade and capital flows. However, there can be no doubt we have achieved a major improvement in the competitive position of American workers and American business.

The new exchange rates being established at this time represent a reasonable estimate of the relationships which — taken together with appropriate measures for the removal of existing trade and investment restraints — will in time move international economic relationships into sustainable equilibrium. We have, however, undertaken no obligations for the United States Government to intervene in foreign exchange markets.

Second, the President has decided to send shortly to the Congress proposals for comprehensive trade legislation. Prior to submitting that legislation, intensive consultations will be held with members of Congress, labour, agriculture, and business to assure that the legislation reflects our needs as fully as possible.

This legislation, among other things, should furnish the tools we need to:

(i) provide for lowering tariff and non-tariff barriers to trade, assuming our trading partners are willing to participate fully with us in that process;

(ii) provide for raising tariffs when such would contribute to arrangements assuring that American exports have fair access to foreign markets;

(iii) provide safeguards against the disruption of particular markets and production from rapid changes in foreign trade; and

(iv) protect our external position from large and persistent deficits.

In preparing this legislation, the President is particularly concerned that, however efficient our workers and businesses, and however exchange rates might be altered, American producers be treated fairly and that they have equitable access to foreign markets. Too often we have been shut out by a web of administrative barriers and controls. Moreover, the rules governing trading relationships have, in many instances, become obsolete and, like our international monetary rules, need extensive reform.

We cannot be faced with insuperable barriers to our exports and yet simultaneousl be expected to end our deficit.

At the same time, we must recognise that in some areas the United States, too, can be cited for its barriers to trade. The best way to deal with these barriers on both sides is to remove them. We shall bargain hard to that end. I am convinced the American workers and the American consumer will be the beneficiaries.

In proposing this legislation, the President recognises that the choice we face will not lie between greater freedom and the *status quo*. Our trade position must be improved. If we cannot accomplish that objective in a framework of freer and fairer trade, the pressures to retreat inward will be intense.

We must avoid that risk, for it is the road to international recrimination, isolation, and autarky.

Third, in coordination with the Secretary of Commerce, we shall phase out the interest equalisation tax and the controls of the Office of Foreign Direct Investment. Both controls will be terminated at the latest by 31 December 1974.

I am advised that the Federal Reserve Board will consider comparable steps for their voluntary foreign credit restraint programme.

The phasing out of these restraints is appropriate in view of the improvement which will be brought to our underlying payments position by the cumulative effect of the exchange rate changes, by continued success in curbing inflationary tendencies, and by the attractiveness of the United States economy for investors from abroad. The termination of the restraints on capital flows is appropriate in the light of our broad objective of reducing governmental controls on private transactions.

The measures I have announced today — the realignment of currency values, the proposed new trade legislation, and the termination of United States controls on capital movements — will serve to move our economy and the world economy closer to conditions of international equilibrium in a context of competitive freedom. They will accelerate the pace of successful monetary and trade reform.

They are not intended to, and cannot, substitute for effective management of our domestic economy. The discipline of budgetary and monetary restraint and effective wage-price stabilisation must and will be pursued with full vigour. We have proposed a budget which will avoid a revival of inflationary pressure in the United States. We again call upon the Congress, because of our international financial requirement as well as for the sake of economic stability at home, to assist in keeping federal expenditures within the limits of the President's budget. We are continuing a strong system of price and wage controls. Recent international economic developments reemphasise the need to administer these controls in a way that will further reduce the rate of inflation. We are determined to do that. . .

184. Press release issued by the IMF concerning the Japanese decision to float the yen, 13 February 1973[1]

The Fund has been advised by the Government of Japan that for the time being the market rate for the Japanese yen will not necessarily be confined within the margins observed hitherto. The Government of Japan has also expressed the intention to return as soon as conditions permit to the maintenance of normal IMF margins around parity in accordance with the decisions of the Fund.

The Fund notes the circumstances that led the Japanese Government to take the temporary action described and expects that it will assist in the establishment of an appropriate par value. The Fund welcomes the intention of the Japanese authorities to collaborate with it in accordance with the Articles of Agreement and to resume as soon as conditions permit the observance of margins around parity consistent with the decisions of the Fund. The Fund, and in particular the Managing Director, will remain in close consultation with the Japanese authorities on their policies and on their resumption of the maintenance of margins around parity, and the Managing Director will take appropriate initiatives for these consultations.

1 IMF, press release, 14 February 1973.

185. Communiqué issued by the Council of the European Communities, 12 March 1973[1]

The Council met on 11 and 12 March 1973 to review measures to be taken to deal with the international monetary crisis and with special reference to the meeting of the enlarged Group of Ten, held in Paris on 9 March 1973.

The Council officially records the following decisions:

(i) to keep the maximum spot variance between the DM, the Danish crown, the florin, the Belgian franc, the Luxembourg franc and the French franc at 2.25%. For Member States keeping a two-tier system of exchange this commitment applies only to the regulated market;

(ii) to release the Central Banks from having to intervene in the fluctuation margins of the US dollar;

(iii) to apply more strictly the Directive of 21 March 1972 and set up whatever additional monitoring devices may be necessary so as to shelter the system from disruptive capital movements.

The British, Irish and Italian members said that their Governments intended to back as soon as possible the decision to keep the Community fluctuation margins.

Therefore when the Commission submits within the scheduled deadline, that is by 30 June 1973, its Report on the development of short-term monetary support and the terms for progressive pooling of reserves it will at the same time put forward the suggestions it finds appropriate.

The Council agreed that meanwhile a close and perpetual concertation over monetary matters will be kept up between the competent Member States authorities.

The representative of the West German Government indicated his Government's intention of making a limited adjustment to the central rate of the DM before the exchange markets opened again so as to help towards an orderly development of exchange relationships.

The technical details involved in the above-mentioned questions will be finalized shortly, considering the forthcoming meeting of the enlarged Group of Ten to be held in Paris on 16 March, and in order to become applicable for 19 March 1973 when the exchange markets are scheduled to reopen.

186. Communiqué issued following the meeting of the Finance Ministers and Central Bank Governors of major trading nations, Paris, 16 March 1973[2]

1. The Ministers and Central Bank Governors of the ten countries participating in the General Arrangements to Borrow and the member countries of the European

1 *Bull. EC*, 3–1973, pp. 22–3.
1 *DSB*, 16 April 1973, pp. 454–5.

Economic Community met in Paris on 16th March, 1973 under the Chairmanship of Mr Valéry Giscard d'Estaing, Minister of the Economy and of Finance of France. Mr P.-P. Schweitzer, Managing Director of the International Monetary Fund, took part in the meeting, which was also attended by Mr Nello Celio, head of the Federal Department of Finance of the Swiss Confederation, Mr E. Stopper, President of the Swiss National Bank, Mr W. Haferkamp, Vice-President of the Commission of the European Economic Community, Mr E. van Lennep, Secretary General of the Organisation for Economic Cooperation and Development, Mr René Larre, General Manager of the Bank for International Settlements, and Mr Jeremy Morse, Chairman of the Deputies of the Committee of Twenty of the IMF.

2. The Ministers and Governors heard a report by the Chairman of their Deputies, Mr Rinaldo Ossola, on the results of the technical study which the Deputies have carried out in accordance with the instructions given to them.

3. The Ministers and Governors took note of the decisions of the members of the EEC announced on Monday. Six members of the EEC and certain other European countries, including Sweden, will maintain 2¼ per cent margins between their currencies. The currencies of certain countries, such as Italy, the United Kingdom, Ireland, Japan and Canada remain, for the time being, floating. However, Italy, the United Kingdom and Ireland have expressed the intention of associating themselves as soon as possible with the decision to maintain EEC exchange rates within margins of 2¼ per cent and meanwhile of remaining in consultation with their EEC partners.

4. The Ministers and Governors reiterated their determination to ensure jointly an orderly exchange rate system. To this end, they agreed on the basis for an operational approach towards the exchange markets in the near future and on certain further studies to be completed as a matter of urgency.

5. They agreed in principle that official intervention in exchange markets may be useful at appropriate times to facilitate the maintenance of orderly conditions, keeping in mind also the desirability of encouraging reflows of speculative movements of funds. Each nation stated that it will be prepared to intervene at its initiative in its own market, when necessary and desirable, acting in a flexible manner in the light of market conditions and in close consultation with the authorities of the nation whose currency may be bought or sold. The countries which have decided to maintain 2¼ per cent margins between their currencies have made known their intention of concerting among themselves the application of these provisions. Such intervention will be financed, when necessary, through use of mutual credit facilities. To ensure fully adequate resources for such operations, it is envisaged that some of the existing 'swap' facilities will be enlarged.

6. Some countries have announced additional measures to restrain capital inflows. The United States authorities emphasized that the phasing out of their controls on longer-term capital outflows by the end of 1974 was intended to coincide with strong improvement in the US balance-of-payments position. Any steps taken during the interim period toward the elimination of these controls would take due account of exchange market conditions and the balance-of-payments

trends. The US authorities are also reviewing actions that may be appropriate to remove inhibitions on the inflow of capital into the United States. Countries in a strong payments position will review the possibility of removing or relaxing any restrictions on capital outflows, particularly long-term.

7. Ministers and Governors noted the importance of dampening speculative capital movements. They stated their intention to seek more complete understanding of the sources and nature of the large capital flows which have recently taken place. With respect to Euro-currency markets, they agreed that methods of reducing the volatility of these markets will be studied intensively, taking into account the implications for the longer run operation of the international monetary system. These studies will address themselves, among other factors, to limitations on placement of official reserves in that market by member nations of the IMF and to the possible need for reserve requirements comparable to those in national banking markets. With respect to the former, the Ministers and Governors confirmed that their authorities would be prepared to take the lead by implementing certain undertakings that their own placements would be gradually and prudently withdrawn. The United States will review possible action to encourage a flow of Euro-currency funds to the United States as market conditions permit.

8. In the context of discussions of monetary reform, the Ministers and Governors agreed that proposals for funding or consolidation of official currency balances deserved thorough and urgent attention. This matter is already on the agenda of the Committee of Twenty of the IMF.

9. Ministers and Governors reaffirmed their attachment to the basic principles which have governed international economic relations since the last war — the greatest possible freedom for international trade and investment and the avoidance of competitive changes of exchange rates. They stated their determination to continue to use the existing organisations of international economic cooperation to maintain these principles for the benefit of all their members.

10. Ministers and Governors expressed their unanimous conviction that international monetary stability rests, in the last analysis, on the success of national efforts to contain inflation. They are resolved to pursue fully appropriate policies to this end.

11. Ministers and Governors are confident that, taken together, these moves will launch an internationally responsible programme for dealing with the speculative pressures that have recently emerged and for maintaining orderly international monetary arrangements, while the work of reform of the international monetary system is pressed ahead. They reiterated their concern that this work be expedited and brought to an early conclusion in the framework of the Committee of Twenty of the IMF.

187. Communiqué issued by the Interim Committee of the Board of Governors of the IMF, Washington, 31 August 1975[1] (extract)

6. The Committee discussed the problem of gold, including the disposition of the

1 *DSB*, 22 September 1975, pp. 451–2.

gold holdings of the Fund. The elements of the consensus reached are described in this paragraph.

At the meeting of the Interim Committee on January 16, 1975, it was decided to move 'toward a complete set of agreed amendments on gold, including the abolition of the official price and freedom for national monetary authorities to enter into gold transactions under certain specific arrangements, outside the Articles of the Fund, entered into between national monetary authorities in order to ensure that the role of gold in the international monetary system would be gradually reduced'.

To implement this general undertaking, provision should be made for:

1. Abolition of an official price for gold.

2. Elimination of the obligation to use gold in transactions with the Fund, and elimination of the Fund's authority to accept gold in transactions unless the Fund so decides by an 85 per cent majority. This understanding would be without prejudice to the study of a Gold Substitution Account.

3. Sale of 1/6 of the Fund's gold (25 million ounces) for the benefit of developing countries without resulting in a reduction of other resources for their benefit, and restitution of 1/6 of the Fund's gold to members. The proportion of any profits or surplus value of the gold sold for the benefit of developing countries that would correspond to the share of quotas of these countries would be transferred directly to each developing country in proportion to its quota. The rest of the Fund's gold would be subject to provisions in an amendment of the Articles that would create enabling powers exercisable by an 85 per cent majority of the total voting power.

The Committee noted that, in order to give effect to the understandings arrived at in this Committee, the countries in the Group of Ten have agreed to observe during the period referred to below the following arrangements, which could be subscribed to by any other member country of the Fund that wishes to do so. Other members might adhere to these arrangements, and on such occasions the necessary modifications in them would be made:

1. That there be no action to peg the price of gold.

2. That the total stock of gold now in the hands of the Fund and the monetary authorities of the Group of Ten will not be increased.

3. That the parties to these arrangements agree that they will respect any further condition governing gold trading that may be agreed to by their central bank representatives at regular meetings.

4. That each party to these arrangements will report semi-annually to the Fund and to the BIS the total amount of gold that has been bought or sold.

5. That each party agree that these arrangements will be reviewed by the participants at the end of two years and then continued, modified or terminated. Any party to these arrangements may terminate adherence to them after the initial two-year period.

Many members from developing countries expressed concern that the proposed arrangements for gold would give rise to a highly arbitrary distribution of new liquidity, with the bulk of gains accruing to developed countries. This would greatly reduce the chances of further allocations of SDRs, thereby detracting from the agreed objective of making the SDR the principal reserve asset and phasing out the monetary role of gold. This aspect should be studied and measures explored to avoid these distortions.

7. The Committee noted the work done so far by the Executive Directors on the subject of the establishment of a trust fund and the possible sources of its financing in response to the request of the Development Committee. It was agreed to ask the Executive Directors to pursue their work with a view to completing it at an early date, taking into account the understandings reached in the Committee with regard to the use of profits from the sale of part of the Fund's gold for the benefit of developing countries, without neglecting the consideration of other possible sources of financing.

8. It was agreed that acceptable solutions must be found on the subject of the exchange rate system under the amended Articles, so that these agreed solutions can be combined with those on quotas and gold. The Executive Directors were requested to continue their work in order to arrive at acceptable solutions and to prepare for submission to the Board of Governors, after examination by the Committee at its next meeting, appropriate proposals for amendment of the Fund's Articles on all aspects that have been under consideration.

9. The Committee noted that the Executive Directors are in the process of conducting a review of the Fund's facility on compensatory financing with a view to improving a number of its aspects. It was agreed to urge the Executive Directors to complete their work on this subject as soon as possible, taking into account the variou proposals that have been made by members of the Committee.

B. The Framework of International Trade

188. European Community offer on trade relations with the United States, 11 June 1971[1]

In the second round of the consultations between the European Community and the United States, Professor Dahrendorf, the European Commissioner for external relations and trade, has put forward an offer on the Community's behalf for a settlement of relations with the United States in the sensitive sector of agricultural produce. The offer, a unilateral and unconditional one, is designed to ease relations in four hitherto very much argued-over fields, namely poultry, lard, tobacco and oranges.

The offer concerns a number of agricultural products, and primarily citrus fruits, on which the Community rate of duty will be reduced from 15% to 8% for certain important months; the great bulk of American exports will be thereby favoured. Then again, binding assurances are provided on tobacco, to obviate alleged potential injury to the United States, and in addition there are to be arrangements which will enhance the United States' competitive position in non-Community markets with regard to poultry.

Professor Dahrendorf said that the offer which was the outcome of intensive and protracted negotiations within the Community, was made in token of the declared political intention to break the long log-jam in the sectors concerned. The intra-Community negotiations had been opened and conducted by the Commission acting through its Director-General for external trade, Mr. Hijzen. Professor Dahrendorf emphasised that the offer was so framed as to ensure that its operation would not be at the expense of the associated Mediterranean countries: the Community accepted that any sacrifices involved should be made by itself.

No negotiations will follow the offer, since it has been made without request for counter-concessions. A statement from the American side may be expected.

189. Joint statement by the United States and Japan on International Economic Relations, Washington, 9 February 1972[2]

Japan and the United States today made the following declaration and agreed to

1 WEU, *Political Year in Europe, 1971*, p. 196.
2 GATT press release.

communicate the declaration to the Director General of the GATT for transmittal to the contracting parties. Other contracting parties are invited to associate themselves with this declaration to the extent and at the time which they would deem appropriate.

Japan and the United States recognize the need for proceeding with a comprehensive review of international economic relations with a view to negotiating improvements in it in the light of structural changes which have taken place in recent years. The review shall cover *inter alia* all elements of trade, including measures which impede or distort agricultural, raw material and industrial trade. Special attention shall be given to the problems of developing countries.

Japan and the United States will seek to utilize every opportunity in the GATT for the settlement of trade problems, the removal of which would lessen current trade distortions, and will strive for further progress with respect to those matters now being discussed in the GATT Committee on Trade in Industrial Products and the GATT Agricultural Committee. Japan and the United States agree that progress in GATT in solving some problems in 1972 could facilitate the way in the GATT for a new major initiative for dealing with longer term trade problems. To this end, they also agree in 1972 to analyze and evaluate in the GATT alternative techniques and modalities for multilateral negotiation of long term problems affecting all elements of world trade.

Japan and the United States undertake to initiate and actively support multilateral and comprehensive negotiations in the framework of GATT beginning in 1973 (subject to such internal authorization as may be required) with a view to the expansion and liberalization of world trade, improvement in the international framework for the conduct of commercial relations, and improvements in the standard of living of the people of the world. These multilateral negotiations shall be conducted on the basis of mutual advantage and mutual commitment with overall reciprocity, and shall cover agricultural as well as industrial trade. The negotiations should involve active participation of as many countries as possible.

190. Joint statement by the European Community and the United States, transmitted to the GATT, 11 February 1972[1]

Within the framework of their negotiations, the United States and the European Community have agreed to communicate the following declaration to the Director-General of the GATT for transmittal to the contracting parties. Other contracting parties are invited to associate themselves with the declaration to the extent and at the moment they would deem appropriate.

The United States and the Community recognize the need for proceeding with a comprehensive review of international-economic relations with a view to negotiating improvements in the light of structural changes which have taken place in recent years. The review shall cover *inter alia* all elements of trade, including

1 GATT press release.

measures which impede or distort agricultural, raw material and industrial trade. Special attention shall be given to the problems of developing countries.

The United States and the Community undertake to initiate and actively support multilateral and comprehensive negotiations in the framework of GATT with a view to the expansion and the ever greater liberalization of world trade and improvement in the standard of living of the people of the world, aims which can be achieved *inter alia* through the progressive dismantling of obstacles to trade and the improvement of the international framework for the conduct of world trade. The Community states that in appropriate cases the conclusion of international commodity agreements is also one of the means to achieve these aims. The United States states that such agreements do not offer a useful approach to the achievement of these aims.

The negotiations shall be conducted on the basis of mutual advantage and mutual commitment with overall reciprocity, and shall cover agricultural as well as industrial trade. The negotiations should involve active participation of as many countries as possible.

The United States and the Community agree to initiate and support in 1972 an analysis and evaluation in the GATT of alternative techniques and modalities for multilateral negotiation of long term problems affecting all elements of world trade.

The United States and the Community will seek to utilize every opportunity in the GATT for the settlement of particular trade problems, the removal of which would lessen current frictions, and will strive for further progress with respect to those matters now being discussed in the GATT Committee on Trade in Industrial Products and the GATT Agricultural Committee. They agree that progress in GATT in solving specific problems in 1972 could facilitate the way in the GATT for a new major initiative for dealing with longer term trade problems.

191. Message from President Nixon to Congress on his proposed Trade Reform Bill, 10 April 1973[1]

The Trade Reform Act of 1973, which I am today proposing to the Congress, calls for the most important changes in more than a decade in America's approach to world trade.

This legislation can mean more and better jobs for American workers.

It can help American consumers get more for their money.

It can mean expanding trade and expanding prosperity, for the United States and for our trading partners alike.

Most importantly, these proposals can help us reduce international tensions and strengthen the structure of peace.

The need for trade reform is urgent. The task of trade reform requires an effective, working partnership between the executive and legislative branches. The legislation I submit today has been developed in close consultation with the Congress and it

1 *USIS*, 11 April 1973.

envisions continuing cooperation after it is enacted. I urge the Congress to examine these proposals in a spirit of constructive partnership and to give them prompt and favourable consideration.

This legislation would help us to:

— Negotiate for a more open and equitable world trading system;
— Deal effectively with rapid increases in imports that disrupt domestic markets and displace American workers;
— Strengthen our ability to meet unfair competitive practices;
— Manage our trade policy more efficiently and use it more effectively to deal with special needs such as our balance of payments and inflation problems; and
— Take advantage of new trade opportunities while enhancing the contribution trade can make to the development of poorer countries.

The world is embarked today on a profound and historic movement away from confrontation and toward negotiation in resolving international differences.

Increasingly in recent years, countries have come to see that the best way of advancing their own interests is by expanding peaceful contacts with other peoples. We have thus begun to erect a durable structure of peace in the world from which all nations can benefit and in which all nations have a stake.

This structure of peace cannot be strong, however, unless it encompasses international economic affairs. Our progress toward world peace and stability can be significantly undermined by economic conflicts which breed political tensions and weaken security ties. It is imperative, therefore, that we promptly turn our negotiati efforts to the task of resolving problems in the economic arena.

My trade reform proposals would equip us to meet this challenge. They would help us in creating a new economic order which both reflects and reinforces the progress we have made in political affairs. As I said to the Governors of the International Monetary Fund last September, our common goal should be to 'set in force an economic structure that will help and not hinder the world's historical movement toward peace'.

The principal institutions which now govern the world economy date from the close of World War Two. At that time, the United States enjoyed a dominant position. Ou industrial and agricultural systems had emerged from the war virtually intact. Our substantial reserves enabled us to finance a major share of international reconstructi We gave generously of our resources and our leadership in helping the world econom get back on track.

The result has been a quarter century of remarkable economic achievement — and profound economic change. In place of a splintered and shattered Europe stand a new and vibrant European Community. In place of a prostrate Japan stands one o the free world's strongest economies. In all parts of the world new economic pattern have developed and new economic energies have been released.

These successes have now brought the world into a very different period. Americ is no longer the sole, dominating economic power. The new era is one of growing economic interdependence, shared economic leadership, and dramatic economic change.

These sweeping transformations, however, have not been matched by sufficient change in our trading and monetary systems. The approaches which served us so well in the years following World War Two have become outmoded; they are simply no longer equal to the challenges of our time.

The result has been a growing sense of strain and stress in the international economy and even a resurgence of economic isolationism as some have sought to insulate themselves from change. If we are to make our new economic era a time of progress and prosperity for all the world's peoples, we must resist the impulse to turn inward and instead to do all we can to see that our international economic arrangements are substantially improved.

The United States has already taken a number of actions to help build a new international economic order and to advance our interests within it.
- Our new economic policy, announced on August 15, 1971, has helped to improve the performance of our domestic economy, reducing unemployment and inflation and thereby enhancing our competitive position.
- The realignment of currencies achieved under the Smithsonian Agreement of December 18, 1971, and by the adjustments of recent weeks have also made American goods more competitive with foreign products in markets at home and abroad.
- Building on the Smithsonian Agreement we have advanced far-reaching proposals for lasting reform in the world's monetary system.
- We have concluded a trade agreement with the Soviet Union that promises to strengthen the fabric of prosperity and peace.
- Opportunities for mutually beneficial trade are developing with the People's Republic of China.
- We have opened negotiations with the enlarged European Community and several of the countries with which it has concluded special trading agreements concerning compensation due us as a result of their new arrangements.

But despite all these efforts, underlying problems remain. We need basic trade reform, and we need it now. Our efforts to improve the world's monetary system, for example, will never meet with lasting success unless basic improvements are also achieved in the field of international trade.

A wide variety of barriers to trade still distort the world's economic relations, harming our own interests and those of other countries.
- Quantitative barriers hamper trade in many commodities, including some of our potentially most profitable exports.
- Agricultural barriers limit and distort trade in farm products, with special damage to the American economy because of our comparative advantage in the agricultural field.

— Preferential trading arrangements have spread to include most of Western Europe, Africa and other countries bordering on the Mediterranean Sea.
— Non-tariff barriers have greatly proliferated as tariffs have declined.

These barriers to trade, in other countries and in ours, presently cost the United States several billion dollars a year in the form of higher consumer prices and the inefficient use of our resources. Even an economy as strong as ours can ill afford such losses.

Fortunately, our major trading partners have joined us in a commitment to broad, multilateral trade negotiations beginning this fall. These negotiations will provide a unique opportunity for reducing trading barriers and expanding world trade.

It is in the best interest of every nation to sell to others the goods it produces more efficiently and to purchase the goods which other nations produce more efficiently. If we can operate on this basis, then both the earnings of our workers and the buying power of our dollars can be significantly increased.

But while trade should be more open, it should also be more fair. This means, first, that the rules and practices of trade should be fair to all nations. Secondly, it means that the benefits of trade should be fairly distributed among American workers, farmers, businessmen and consumers alike and that trade should create no undue burdens for any of these groups.

I am confident that our free and vigorous American economy can more than hold its own in open world competition. But we must always insist that such competition takes place under equitable rules.

The key to success in our coming trade negotiations will be the negotiating authority the United States brings to the bargaining table. Unless our negotiations can speak for this country with sufficient authority, other nations will undoubtedly be cautious and non-committal — and the opportunity for change will be lost.

We must move promptly to provide our negotiators with the authority their task requires. Delay can only aggravate the strains we have already experienced. Disruptions in world financial markets, deficits in our trading balance, inflation in the international marketplace, and tensions in the diplomatic arena all argue for prompt and decisive action. So does the plight of those American workers and busines who are damaged by rapidly rising imports of whose products face barriers in foreign markets.

For all of these reasons, I urge the Congress to act on my recommendations as expeditiously as possible. We face pressing problems here and now. We cannot wait until tomorrow to solve them.

Negotiators from other countries will bring to the coming round of trade discussions broad authority to alter their barriers to trade. Such authority makes them more effective bargainers; without such authority the hands of any negotiator would be severely tied.

Unfortunately, the President of the United States and those who negotiate at his direction do not now possess authorities comparable to those which other countries will bring to these bargaining sessions. Unless these authorities are provided, we will be badly hampered in our efforts to advance American interests and improve our trading system.

My proposed legislation therefore calls upon the Congress to delegate significant new negotiating authorities to the Executive branch. For several decades now, both the Congress and the President have recognized that trade policy is one field in which such delegations are indispensable. This concept is clearly established; the questions which remain concern the degree of delegation which is appropriate and the conditions under which it should be carried out.

The legislation I submit today spells out only that degree of delegation which I believe is necessary and proper to advance the national interest. And just as we have consulted closely with the Congress in shaping this legislation, so the Executive branch will consult closely with the Congress in exercising any negotiating authorities it receives. I invite the Congress to set up whatever mechanism it deems best for closer consultation and cooperation to ensure that its views are properly represented as trade negotiations go forward.

It is important that America speak authoritatively and with a single voice at the international bargaining table. But it is also important that many voices contribute as the American position is being shaped.

The proposed Trade Reform Act of 1973 would provide for the following new authorities:

First, I request authority to eliminate, reduce, or increase customs duties in the context of negotiated agreements. Although this authority is requested for a period of five years, it is my intention and my expectation that agreements can be concluded in a much shorter time. Last October, the member governments of the European Community expressed their hope that the coming round of trade negotiations will be concluded by 1975. I endorse this timetable and our negotiators will cooperate fully in striving to meet it.

Secondly, I request a Congressional declaration favouring negotiations and agreements on non-tariff barriers. I am also asking that a new, optional procedure be created for obtaining the approval of the Congress for such agreements when that is appropriate. Currently, both houses of the Congress must take positive action before any such agreement requiring changes in domestic law becomes effective — a process which makes it difficult to achieve agreements since our trading partners know it is subject to much uncertainty and delay. Under the new arrangement, the President would give notice to the Congress of his intention to use the procedure at least 90 days in advance of concluding an agreement in order to provide time for appropriate House and Senate committees to consider the issues involved and to make their views known. After an agreement was negotiated, the President would submit that agreement and proposed implementing orders to the Congress. If neither House rejected them by a majority vote of all members within a period of 90 days, the agreement and implementing orders would then enter into effect.

Thirdly, I request advance authority to carry out mutually beneficial agreements concerning specific customs matters primarily involving valuation and the marking of goods by country of origin.

The authorities I outline in my proposed legislation would give our negotiators the leverage and the flexibility they need to reduce or eliminate foreign barriers to American products. These proposals would significantly strengthen America's bargaining position in the coming trade negotiations.

I am not requesting specific negotiating authority relating to agricultural trade. Barriers to such trade are either tariff or non-tariff in nature and can be dealt with under the general authorities I am requesting.

One of our major objectives in the coming negotiations is to provide for expansion in agricultural trade. The strength of American agriculture depends on the continued expansion of our world markets — especially for the major bulk commodities our farmers produce so efficiently. Even as we have been moving toward a great reliance on free market forces here at home under the Agricultural Act of 1970, so we seek to braoden the role of market forces on the international level by reducing and removing barriers to trade in farm products.

I am convinced that the concerns which all nations have for their farmers and consumers can be met most effectively if the home market plays a far greater role in determining patterns of agricultural production and consumption. Movement in this direction can do much to help ensure adequate supplies and relief of pressure on consumer prices.

As other countries agree to reduce their trading barriers, we expect to reduce ours. The result will be expanding trade, creating more and better jobs for the American people and providing them with greater access to a wider variety of products from other countries.

It is true, of course, that reducing import barriers has on some occasions led to sudden surges in imports which have had disruptive effects on the domestic economy. It is important to note, however, that most severe problems caused by surging import have not been related to the reduction of import barriers. Steps toward a more open trading order generally have a favourable rather than an unfavourable impact on domestic jobs.

Nevertheless, damaging import surges, whatever their cause, should be a matter of great concern to our people and our government. I believe we should have effective instruments readily available to help avoid serious injury from imports and give American industries and workers time to adjust to increased imports in an orderly way. My proposed legislation outlines new measures for achieving these goals.

To begin with, I recommend a less restrictive test for invoking import restraints. Today, restraints are authorized only when the Tariff Commission finds that imports are the 'major cause' of serious injury or threat thereof to a domestic industry, meaning that their impact must be larger than that of all other causes combined. Under my proposal, restraints would be authorized when import competition was the 'primary cause' of such injury, meaning that it must only be the largest single cause. In addition, the present requirement that injury must result from a previous tariff concession would be dropped.

I also recommend a new method for determining whether imports actually are the primary cause of serious injury to domestic producers. Under my proposal, a finding of 'market disruption' would constitute *prima facie* evidence of that fact. Market disruption would be defined as occurring when imports are substantial, are rising rapidly both absolutely and as a percentage of total domestic consumption, and are offered at prices substantially below those of competing domestic products.

My proposed legislation would give the President greater flexibility in providing appropriate relief from import problems — including orderly marketing agreements or higher tariffs or quotas. Restraints could be imposed for an initial period of five years and, at the discretion of the President, could be extended for an additional period of two years. In exceptional cases, restrictions could be extended even further after a two-year period and following a new investigation by the Tariff Commission.

Our responsibilities for easing the problems of displaced workers are not limited to those whose unemployment can be traced to imports. All displaced workers are entitled to adequate assistance while they seek new employment. Only if all workers believe they are getting a fair break can our economy adjust effectively to change.

I will therefore propose in a separate message to the Congress new legislation to improve our systems of unemployment insurance and compensation. My proposals would set minimum Federal standards for benefit levels in State programmes, ensuring that all workers covered by such programmes are treated equitably, whatever the cause of their involuntary unemployment. In the meantime, until these standards become effective, I am recommending as a part of my trade reform proposals that we immediately establish benefit levels which meet these proposed general standards for workers displaced because of imports.

I further propose that until the new standards for unemployment insurance are in place, we make assistance for workers more readily available by dropping the present requirement that their unemployment must have been caused by prior tariff concessions and that imports must have been the 'major cause' of injury. Instead, such assistance would be authorized if the Secretary of Labor determined that unemployment was substantially due to import-related causes. Workers unemployed because of imports would also have job training, job search allowances, employment services and relocation assistance available to them as permanent features of trade adjustment assistance.

In addition, I will submit to the Congress comprehensive pension reform legislation which would help protect workers who lose their jobs against loss of pension benefits. This legislation will contain a mandatory vesting requirement which has been developed with older workers particularly in mind.

The proposed Trade Reform Act of 1973 would terminate the present programme of adjustment assistance to individual firms. I recommend this action because I believe this programme has been largely ineffective, discriminates among firms within a given industry and has needlessly subsidized some firms at the taxpayer's expense. Changing competitive conditions, after all, typically act not upon particular firms but upon an industry as a whole and I have provided for entire industries under my import relief proposals.

The President of the United States possesses a variety of authorities to deal with unfair trade practices. Many of these authorities must now be modernized if we are to respond effectively and even-handedly to unfair import competition at home and to practices which unfairly prejudice our export opportunities abroad.

To cope with unfair competitive practices in our own markets, my proposed legislation would amend our antidumping and countervailing duty laws to provide for more expeditious investigations and decisions. It would make a number of procedural and other changes in these laws to guarantee their effective operation. The Bill would also amend the current statute concerning patent infringement by subjecting cases involving imports to judicial proceedings similar to those which involve domestic infringement, and by providing for fair processes and effective action in the event of court delays. I also propose that the Federal Trade Commission Act be amended to strengthen our ability to deal with the foreign producer whose cartel or monopoly practices raise prices in our market or otherwise harm our interest by restraining trade.

In addition, I ask for a revision and extension of my authority to raise barriers against countries which unreasonably or unjustifiably restrict our exports. Existing law provides such authority only under a complex array of conditions which vary according to the practices or exports involved. My proposed Bill would simplify the authority and its use. I would prefer, of course, that other countries agree to remove such restrictions on their own, so that we should not have to use this authority. But I will consider using it whenever it becomes clear that our trading partners are unwilling to remove unreasonable or unjustifiable restrictions against our exports.

Most-Favoured-Nation authority. My proposed legislation would grant the President authority to extend Most-Favoured-Nation treatment to any country when he deemed it in the national interest to do so. Under my proposal, however, any such extension to countries not now receiving Most-Favoured-Nation treatment could be vetoed by a majority vote of either the House or the Senate within a three-month period.

This new authority would enable us to carry out the trade agreement we have negotiated with the Soviet Union and thereby ensure that country's repayment of its lend-lease debt. It would also enable us to fulfill our commitment to Romania and to take advantage of opportunities to conclude beneficial agreements with other countries which do not now receive Most-Favoured-Nation treatment.

In the case of the Soviet Union, I recognize the deep concern which many in the Congress have expressed over the tax levied on Soviet citizens wishing to emigrate to new countries. However, I do not believe that a policy of denying Most-Favoured-

Nation treatment to Soviet exports is a proper or even an effective way of dealing with this problem.

One of the most important elements of our trade agreement with the Soviet Union is the clause which calls upon each party to reduce exports of products which cause market disruptions in the other country. While I have no reason to doubt that the Soviet Union will meet its obligations under this clause if the need arises, we should still have authority to take unilateral action to prevent disruption if such action is warranted.

Because of the special way in which State-trading countries market their products abroad, I would recommend two modifications in the way we take such action. First, the Tariff Commission should only have to find 'material injury' rather than 'serious injury' from imports in order to impose appropriate restraints. Secondly, such restraints should apply only to exports from the offending country. These recommendations can simplify our laws relating to dumping actions by State-trading countries, eliminating the difficult and time-consuming problems associated with trying to reach a constructed value for their exports.

Balance of payments authority. Though it should only be used in exceptional circumstances, trade policy can sometimes be an effective supplementary tool for dealing with our international payments imbalances. I therefore request more flexible authority to raise or lower import restrictions on a temporary basis to help correct deficits or surpluses in our payments position. Such restraints could be applied to imports from all countries across the board or only to those countries which fail to correct a persistent and excessive surplus in their global payments position.

Anti-inflation authority. My trade recommendations also include a proposal I made on March 30th as part of this Administration's effort to curb the rising cost of living. I asked the Congress at that time to give the President new, permanent authority to reduce certain import barriers temporarily and to a limited extent when he determined that such action was necessary to relieve inflationary pressures within the United States. I again urge prompt approval for this important weapon in our war against inflation.

Generalized tariff preferences. Another significant provision of my proposed Bill would permit the United States to join with other developed countries, including Japan and the members of the European Community, in helping to improve the access of poorer nations to the markets of developed countries. Under this arrangement, certain products of developing nations would benefit from preferential treatment for a ten-year period, creating new export opportunities for such countries, raising their foreign exchange earnings, and permitting them to finance those higher levels of imports that are essential for more rapid economic growth.

This legislation would allow duty-free treatment for a broad range of manufactured and semi-manufactured products and for a selected list of agricultural and primary products which are now regulated only by tariffs. It is our intention to exclude certain import-sensitive products such as textile products, footwear, watches and certain steel products from such preferential treatment, along with products which are now subject to outstanding orders restricting imports. As is the case for the multilateral negotiations authority, public hearing procedures would be held before such preferences were granted and preferential imports would be subject to the import relief provisions which I have recommended above. Once a particular product from a given country became fully competitive, however, it would no longer qualify for special treatment.

The United States would grant such tariff preferences on the basis of international fair play. We would take into account the actions of other preference-granting countri and we would not grant preferences to countries which discriminate against our products in favour of goods from other industrialized nations unless those countries agreed to end such discrimination.

Permanent management authorities. To permit more efficient and more flexible management of American trade policy, I request permanent authority to make limited reductions in our tariffs as a form of compensation to other countries. Such compensation could be necessary in cases where we have raised certain barriers under the new import restraints discussed above and would provide an alternative in such cases to increased barriers against our exports.

I also request permanent authority to offer reductions in particular United States barriers as a means of obtaining significant advantages for American exports. These reductions would be strictly limited; they would involve tariff cuts of no more than 20 per cent covering no more than two per cent of total United States imports in any one year.

The coming multilateral trade negotiations will give us an excellent opportunity to reform and update the rules of international trade. There are several areas where we will seek such changes.

One important need concerns the use of trade policy in promoting equilibrium in the international payments system. We will seek rule changes to permit nations, in those exceptional cases where such measures are necessary, to increase or decrease trade barriers across the board as one means of helping to correct their payments imbalances. We will also seek a new rule allowing nations to impose import restriction: against individual countries which fail to take effective action to correct an excessive surplus in their balance of payments. This rule would parallel the authority I have requested to use American import restrictions to meet our own balance of payments problem.

A second area of concern is the need for a multilateral system for limiting imports to protect against disruptions caused by rapidly changing patterns of international trade. As I emphasized earlier, we need a more effective domestic procedure to meet such problems. But it is also important that new arrangements be developed at the international level to cope with disruptions caused by the accelerating pace of change in world trade.

We will therefore seek new international rules which would allow countries to gain time for adjustment by imposing import restrictions, without having to compensa their trading partners by simultaneously reducing barriers to other products. At the same time, the interests of exporting countries should be protected by providing that such safeguards will be phased out over a reasonable period of time.

As trade barriers are reduced around the world, American exports will increase substantially, enhancing the health of our entire economy.

Already our efforts to expand American exports have moved forward on many fronts. We have made our exports more competitive by realigning exchange rates. Since 1971, our new law permitting the establishment of domestic international sales corporations has been helping American companies organize their export activities more effectively. The lending, guaranty and insurance authorities of the Export—Import Bank have been increased and operations have been extended to include a short-term discount loan facility. The Department of Commerce has reorganized its facilities for promoting exports and has expanded its services for exporters. The Department of State, in cooperation with the Department of Commerce, is giving increased emphasis to commercial service programs in our missions abroad.

In addition, I am today submitting separate legislation which would amend the Export Trade Act in order to clarify the legal framework in which associations of exporters can function. One amendment would make it clear that the Act applies not only to the export of goods but also to certain kinds of services — architecture, construction, engineering, training and management consulting, for example. Another amendment would clarify the exemption of export associations from our domestic anti-trust laws, while setting up clear information, disclosure and regulatory requirements to ensure that the public interest is fully protected.

In an era when more countries are seeking foreign contracts for entire industrial projects — including steps ranging from engineering studies through the supply of equipment and the construction of plants — it is essential that our laws concerning joint export activities allow us to meet our foreign competition on a fair and equal basis.

The rapid growth of international investment in recent years has raised new questions and new challenges for businesses and governments. In our own country, for example, some people have feared that American investment abroad will result in a loss of American jobs. Our studies show, however, that such investment on balance has meant more and better jobs for American workers, has improved our balance of trade and our overall balance of payments, and has generally strengthened our economy. Moreover, I strongly believe that an open system for international investment, one which eliminates artificial incentives or impediments here and abroad, offers great promise for improved prosperity throughout the world.

It may well be that new rules and new mechanisms will be needed for international investment activities. It will take time, however, to develop them. And it is important that they be developed as much as possible on an international scale. If we restrict the ability of American firms to take advantage of investment opportunities abroad, we can only expect that foreign firms will seize these opportunities and prosper at our expense.

I therefore urge the Congress to refrain from enacting broad new changes in our laws governing direct foreign investment until we see what possibilities for multilateral agreements emerge.

It is in this context that we must also shape our system for taxing the foreign profits of American business. Our existing system permits American-controlled businesses in foreign countries to operate under the same tax burdens which apply to its foreign competitors in that country. I believe that system is fundamentally sound. We should not penalize American business by placing it at a disadvantage with respect to its foreign competitors.

American enterprises abroad now pay substantial foreign income taxes. In most cases, in fact, Americans do not invest abroad because of an attractive tax situation but because of attractive business opportunities. Our income taxes are not the cause of our trade problems and tax changes will not solve them.

The Congress exhaustively reviewed this entire matter in 1962 and the conclusion it reached then is still fundamentally sound: there is no reason that our tax credit and deferral provisions relating to overseas investment should be subjected to drastic surgery.

On the other hand, ten years of experience have demonstrated that in certain specialized cases American investment abroad can be subject to abuse. Some artificial incentives for such investment still exist, distoring the flow of capital and producing unnecessary hardship. In those cases where unusual tax advantages are offered to induce investment that might not otherwise occur, we should move to eliminate that inducement.

A number of foreign countries presently grant major tax inducements such as extended 'holidays' from local taxes in order to attract investment from outside their borders. To curb such practices, I will ask the Congress to amend our tax laws so that earnings from new American investments which take advantage of such incentives will be taxed by the United States at the time they are earned — even though the earnings are not returned to this country. The only exception to this provision would come in cases where a bilateral tax treaty provided for such an exception under mutually advantageous conditions.

American companies sometimes make foreign investments specifically for the purpose of reexporting products to the United States. This is the classic 'runaway plant' situation. In cases where foreign subsidiaries of American companies have receipts from exports to the United States which exceed 25 per cent of the subsidiaries' total receipts, I recommend that the earnings of those subsidiaries also be taxed at current American rates. This new rule would only apply, however, to new investments and to situations where lower taxes in the foreign country are a factor in the decision to invest.

The rule would also provide for exceptions in those unusual cases where our national interest required a different result.

There are other situations in which American companies so design their foreign operations that the United States Treasury bears the burden when they lose money and deduct it from their taxes. Yet when that same company makes money, a foreign treasury receives the benefit of taxes on its profits.

I will ask the Congress to make appropriate changes in the rules which now allow this inequity to occur.

We have also found that taxing of mineral imports by United States companies from their foreign affiliates is subject to lengthy delays. I am therefore instructing the Department of the Treasury, in consultation with the Department of Justice and the companies concerned, to institute a procedure for determining inter-company prices and tax payments in advance. If a compliance program cannot be developed voluntarily, I shall ask for legislative authority to create one.

Over the past year, this Administration has repeatedly emphasized the importance of bringing about a more equitable and open world trading system. We have encouraged other nations to join in negotiations to achieve this goal. The declaration of European leaders at their summit meeting last October demonstrates their dedication to the success of this effort. Japan, Canada and other nations share this dedication.

The momentum is there. Now we — in this country — must seize the moment if that momentum is to be sustained.

When the history of our time is written, this era will surely be described as one of profound change. That change has been particularly dramatic in the international economic arena.

The magnitude and pace of economic change confronts us today with policy questions of immense and immediate significance. Change can mean increased disruption and suffering, or it can mean increased well-being. It can bring new forms of deprivation and discrimination, or it can bring wider sharing of the benefits of progress. It can mean conflict between men and nations, or it can mean growing opportunities for fair and peaceful competition in which all parties can ultimately gain.

My proposed Trade Reform Act of 1973 is designed to ensure that the inevitable changes of time are beneficial changes — for our people and for people everywhere.

I urge the Congress to enact these proposals, so that we can help move our country and our world away from trade confrontation and toward trade negotiation, away from a period in which trade has been a source of international and domestic friction and into a new era in which trade among nations helps us to build a peaceful, more prosperous world.

192. Declaration adopted at the GATT ministerial meeting, Tokyo, 14 September 1973[1]

1. The Ministers, having considered the report of the Preparatory Committee for the Trade Negotiations and having noted that a number of governments have decided

1 WEU, *Political Year in Europe, 1973*, pp. 217–19.

to enter into comprehensive multilateral trade negotiations in the framework of GATT and that other governments have indicated their intention to make a decision as soon as possible, declare the negotiations officially open. Those governments whic. have decided to negotiate have notified the Director-General of GATT to this effect, and the Ministers agree that it will be open to any other government, through a notification to the Director-General, to participate in the negotiations. The Ministers hope that the negotiations will involve the active participation of as many countries as possible. They expect the negotiations to be engaged effectively as rapidly as possible, and that, to that end, the governments concerned will have such authority as may be required.

2. The negotiations shall aim to:

— achieve the expansion and ever-greater liberalisation of world trade and improve ment in the standard of living and welfare of the people of the world, objective which can be achieved, *inter alia*, through the progressive dismantling of obstacles to trade and the improvement of the international framework for the conduct of world trade;

— secure additional benefits for the international trade of developing countries so as to achieve a substantial increase in their foreign exchange earnings, the diversification of their exports, the acceleration of the rate of growth of their trade, taking into account their development needs, an improvement in the possibilities for these countries to participate in the expansion of world trade and a better balance as between developed and developing countries in the sharing of the advantages resulting from this expansion, through, in the largest possible measure, a substantial improvement in the conditions of access for the products of interest to the developing countries and, wherever appropriate, measures designed to attain stable, equitable and remunerative prices for primary products.

To this end, coordinated efforts shall be made to solve in an equitable way the trade problems of all participating countries, taking into account the specific trade problems of the developing countries.

3. To this end the negotiations should aim, *inter alia*, to:

(*a*) conduct negotiations on tariffs by employment of appropriate formulae of as general application as possible;

(*b*) reduce or eliminate non-tariff measures or, where this is not appropriate, to reduce or eliminate their trade restricting or distorting effects, and to bring such measures under more effective international discipline;

(*c*) include an examination of the possibilities for the coordinated reduction or elimination of all barriers to trade in selected sectors as a complementary technique;

(*d*) include an examination of the adequacy of the multilateral safeguard system, considering particularly the modalities of application of Article XIX, with a view to furthering trade liberalisation and preserving its results;

(*e*) include, as regards agriculture, an approach to negotiations which, while in line with the general objectives of the negotiations, should take account of the special characteristics and problems in this sector;

(f) treat tropical products as a special and priority sector.

4. The negotiations shall cover tariffs, non-tariff barriers and other measures which impede or distort international trade in both industrial and agricultural products, including tropical products and raw materials, whether in primary form or at any stage of processing including in particular products of export interest to developing countries and measures affecting their exports.

5. The negotiations shall be conducted on the basis of the principles of mutual advantage, mutual commitment and overall reciprocity, while observing the most-favoured-nation clause, and consistently with the provisions of the General Agreement relating to such negotiations. Participants shall jointly endeavour in the negotiations to achieve, by appropriate methods, an overall balance of advantage at the highest possible level. The developed countries do not expect reciprocity for commitments made by them in the negotiations to reduce or remove tariff and other barriers to the trade of developing countries, i.e. the developed countries do not expect the developing countries, in the course of the trade negotiations, to make contributions which are inconsistent with their individual development, financial and trade needs. The Ministers recognise the need for special measures to be taken in the negotiations to assist the developing countries in their efforts to increase their export earnings and promote their economic development and, where appropriate, for priority attention to be given to products or areas of interest to developing countries. They also recognise the importance of maintaining and improving the generalised system of preferences. They further recognise the importance of the application of differential measures to developing countries in ways which will provide special and more favourable treatment for them in areas of the negotiation where this is feasible and appropriate.

6. The Ministers recognise that the particular situation and problems of the least developed among the developing countries shall be given special attention, and stress the need to ensure that these countries receive special treatment in the context of any general or specific measures taken in favour of the developing countries during the negotiations.

7. The policy of liberalising world trade cannot be carried out successfully in the absence of parallel efforts to set up a monetary system which shields the world economy from the shocks and imbalances which have previously occurred. The Ministers will not lose sight of the fact that the efforts which are to be made in the trade field imply continuing efforts to maintain orderly conditions and to establish a durable and equitable monetary system.

The Ministers recognise equally that the new phase in the liberalisation of trade which it is their intention to undertake should facilitate the orderly functioning of the monetary system.

The Ministers recognise that they should bear these considerations in mind both at the opening of and throughout the negotiations. Efforts in these two fields will thus be able to contribute effectively to an improvement of international economic relations taking into account the special characteristics of the economies of the developing countries and their problems.

8. The negotiations shall be considered as one undertaking, the various elements of which shall move forward together.

9. Support is reaffirmed for the principles, rules and disciplines provided for under the General Agreement.[1] Consideration shall be given to improvements in the international framework for the conduct of world trade which might be desirable in the light of progress in the negotiations and, in this endeavour, care shall be taken to ensure that any measures introduced as a result are consistent with the overall objectives and principles of the trade negotiations and particularly of trade liberalisation.

10. A Trade Negotiations Committee is established with authority, taking into account the present declaration, *inter alia*:

   (*a*) to elaborate and put into effect detailed trade negotiating plans and to establish appropriate negotiating procedures, including special procedures for the negotiations between developed and developing countries;

   (*b*) to supervise the progress of the negotiations.

The Trade Negotiations Committee shall be open to participating governments.[2] The Trade Negotiations Committee shall hold its opening meeting not later than 1st November 1973.

11. The Ministers intend that the trade negotiations be concluded in 1975.

---

1 This does not necessarily represent the views of representatives of countries not now parties to the General Agreement. [Footnote in original.]
2 Including the European Communities. [Footnote in original.]

C. The Question of Energy and Raw Materials

193. Communiqué issued following the meeting of the Organisation of Arab Petroleum Exporting Countries (OAPEC), Kuwait, 17 October 1973[1]

Arab countries with their oil exports participate in world prosperity and economic development and in spite of the fact that the production has passed the limit which is required by the local economic situation and the prospective needs, these countries carried on increasing their production, sacrificing their local interest for the sake of world cooperation and of the consumers' interests.

It is a well-known fact that vast areas in the Arab countries were occupied by Israel by the force of arms in June, 1967. Israel carried on with its occupation, ignoring United Nations resolutions, defying all calls for peace whether from Arab countries or from other peace-loving countries.

In spite of another fact that the world community has commitments to implement the United Nations resolutions and not to allow the aggressor to get the fruit of his aggression or to occupy other countries by force, most big industrialised countries which consume mainly Arab oil did not adopt any procedure which demonstrated their awareness of their commitment.

On the contrary, some of these countries have backed the occupation and the US in particular, has been very active before and during the present war in supporting Israel with all available resources, a situation which increased the Israeli arrogance and enabled it to go on defying the legal rights and the basic rules of international law.

In 1967 Israel caused the closure of the Suez Canal and the European economy suffered as a result. During this war, Israel bombed the terminals in the Eastern Mediterranean and Europe suffered another shortage in its oil supplies.

As a result of this defiance of our legal rights and because it is backed and supported by the US, Israel is pushing the Arabs to take a decision not to carry on with their economic sacrifice by producing quantities of oil far in excess of their economic needs.

Unless the world community corrects the situation by forcing Israel to withdraw

1 *Financial Times*, 18 October 1973 (unofficial translation). The ten OAPEC countries are: Abu Dhabi, Algeria, Bahrain, Egypt, Iraq, Kuwait, Libya, Qatar, Saudi Arabia and Syria.

from our occupied territories and by making the US realise the high price, European industrialised countries will pay as a result of the unlimited American support to Israel.

Because of all this, the Arab Oil Ministers met in Kuwait on 17 October and decided to start immediately reducing oil production by not less than 5 per cent per month from September production.

The same percentage will be supplied in each month compared with the previous one until the Israeli withdrawal is completed from the whole Arab territories occupie in June 1967, and the legal rights of the Palestinian people are restored.

The conferees are aware that this reduction should not harm any friendly state who assisted or will assist the Arabs actively and materially. Such countries would receive their shares as they did before the reduction.

This exceptional treatment will be extended also to any other countries which might take active steps against Israel in a way to force Israel to end its occupation.

The Arab Ministers appeal to the peoples of the world and the American people in particular to help us in our struggle against imperialism and Israeli occupation.

The Arab Ministers confirm the Arab nations' sincere will for cooperation with all other peoples and our readiness to supply the world with its oil needs in spite of all sacrifices on our side provided that the world sympathises with us and condem the aggression.

194. Communiqué issued following the meeting of Oil Ministers of the six Gulf member countries of the Organisation of Petroleum Exporting Countries (OPEC), Tehran, 23 December 1973[1]

The ministers of the six Gulf member countries met in Tehran on Dec. 22 and 23, 1973. The meeting was also attended by other [Organization of Petroleum Exporting Countries] delegations, Algeria, Indonesia, Libya and Nigeria, and Venezuela as an observer.

The ministers reviewed the report prepared by the Economic Commission Board held in Vienna between Dec. 17 and 20, 1973. Although the findings of the Econonomic Commission Board as well as direct sales realized by some of the member countries indicated a price in excess of $17 per barrel, the ministerial committee decided to set government take of $7 per barrel for the marker crude, Arabian light 34-degree API.

The relevant posted price for this crude will therefore be $11.651 per barrel. The effective date for this posted price shall be Jan. 1, 1974. This posted price has already taken into consideration the effect of Geneva II agreement.

It was also decided to hold an extraordinary meeting of the conference on Jan. 7, 1974, to discuss the bases of a long-term pricing policy and to review the possibility of establishing a dialogue between oil-producing and consuming countries in order

1 *New York Times*, 24 December 1973.

to avoid entering into a spiral increase in prices and to protect the real value of their oil.

Considering that the government take $7 per barrel is moderate, the ministers hope that the consuming countries will refrain from further increase of their export prices.

195. President Nixon to the Heads of Government of the major industrial oil-consuming countries, 9 January 1974[1]

Developments in the international energy situation have brought consumer and producer nations to an historic crossroad. The world's nations face a fundamental choice that can profoundly affect the structure of international political and economic relations for the remainder of this century.

Today the energy situation threatens to unleash political and economic forces that could cause severe and irreparable damage to the prosperity and stability of the world. Two roads lie before us. We can go our own separate ways, with the prospect of progressive division, the erosion of vital interdependence, and increasing political and economic conflict, or we can work in concert, developing enlightened unity and cooperation, for the benefit of all mankind — producer and consumer countries alike.

It was with these thoughts in mind that I asked Secretary of State Kissinger in his December speech to the Society of Pilgrims in London[2] to propose establishment of an Energy Action Group and to urge a concerted action program among consumers and producers to meet the world's energy needs in a manner which would satisfy the legitimate interests of both the consuming and producing countries.

As a first step to carry out this concept, I invite (name of country) to a meeting of major industrial consumer nations to be held at the Foreign Minister level on 11 February 1974, or any other convenient date that week. I would like to take this opportunity to invite you to send your representative to such a meeting here in Washington. After I know your views, I plan to send a Special Representative to discuss with your Government the specifics of this meeting, including suggestions on agenda and substance.[3]

1 *DSB*, 4 February 1974, pp. 123–4; the countries were Canada, France, the Federal Republic of Germany, Italy, Japan, the Netherlands, Norway, and the United Kingdom; the Secretary-General of the Organization for Economic Cooperation and Development was also invited to attend.

2 For text, see *DSB*, 31 December 1973, pp. 777–82.

3 The following paragraph was added between paragraphs 4 and 5 of President Nixon's letter to Chancellor Willy Brandt of the Federal Republic of Germany:

'As was pointed out in the original proposal we would wish to leave it to the European Community to decide whether and how it may wish to participate in the meeting in Washington. I am bringing this point to your attention in your capacity as head of the government now in the presidency of the Community and will be very pleased to extend an invitation to a representative of the Community. I shall appreciate it if you would inform me of the Community's decision.' [Footnote in original.]

Our concept is that the Foreign Ministers' meeting would agree on an analysis of the situation and the work to be done. It would establish a task force drawn from the consuming countries which would formulate a consumer action program. Part of this program would be concerned with new cooperative measures designed to deal with the explosive growth of global energy demand and to accelerate the co-ordinated development of new energy sources. Another task would be to develop a concerted consumer position for a new era of petroleum consumer–producer relations which would meet the legitimate interests of oil producing countries while assuring the consumer countries adequate supplies at fair and reasonable prices.

In calling for a meeting of the major industrial consumer countries, we are fully conscious that the energy problem is one of vital importance to all consuming countries, particularly those of the developing world whose hope for a better life critically depends on access to energy on reasonable terms. Whereas our immediate concern is to get preparations underway as promptly and effectively as possible, clearly the interests of all consumers, including the developing countries, will have to be represented in an appropriate manner.

A concerted effort of this kind is but a first and essential step toward the establishment of new arrangements for international energy and related economic matters. To this end, a meeting of consumer and producer representatives would be held within 90 days. I am sending personal messages to the heads of government of the OPEC states to assure that they understand the purpose of the proposed meeting of consumer states.

We face a profound challenge to turn this period of crisis into one of opportunity for constructive and creative cooperation which will be of benefit to all the peoples of the world. I look forward to hearing your reply and comments.

196. President Nixon to the Heads of Government of the Member States of OPEC, 9 January 1974[1]

Today I have invited governments of the major oil consuming countries to send representatives to a meeting in Washington on February eleventh. The purpose of this meeting will be to seek a consensus among the participants, looking toward a meeting of consumers and producers, which would establish new mutually beneficial arrangements for international energy and related economic matters.

Recent developments have emphasized the critical importance of energy to the prosperity and stability of the international economy. Severe disruptions of economic activity and of the world monetary system, whether caused by insufficiency of energy supplies or abrupt price movements could prove disastrous for consumers and producers alike.

Oil importing nations are vitally concerned with mechanisms which will assure adequate supplies at reasonable prices. Oil producing states, in turn, are concerned

1 *DSB*, 4 February 1974, p. 124; Abu Dhabi, Algeria, Ecuador, Gabon, Indonesia, Iran, Iraq, Kuwait, Libya, Nigeria, Qatar, Saudi Arabia, and Venezuela.

with arrangements that will assure fair payment for and rational use of their non-renewable resources.

Accordingly, as suggested by Secretary of State Kissinger in his speech in London in December, the United States believes it is necessary to deal with these matters urgently.

The United States is undertaking this initiative as a constructive and positive step, consistent with the publicly stated views of a number of oil producing nations which have called for a consultative relationship between producers and consumers. It is my hope that the results of the forthcoming meeting will lead to an early joint conference of consumer and producer nations.

197. Communiqué issued following the Energy Conference, Washington, 13 February 1974[1]

1. Foreign Ministers of Belgium, Canada, Denmark, France, the Federal Republic of Germany, Ireland, Italy, Japan, Luxembourg, The Netherlands, Norway, the United Kingdom, the United States met in Washington from February 11 to 13, 1974. The European Community was represented as such by the President of the Council and the President of the Commission. Finance Ministers, Ministers with responsibility for Energy Affairs, Economic Affairs and Science and Technology Affairs also took part in the meeting. The Secretary General of the OECD also participated in the meeting. The Ministers examined the international energy situation and its implications and charted a course of actions to meet this challenge which requires constructive and comprehensive solutions. To this end they agreed on specific steps to provide for effective international cooperation. The Ministers affirmed that solutions to the world's energy problem should be sought in consultation with producer countries and other consumers.

Analysis of the Situation

2. They noted that during the past three decades progress in improving productivity and standards of living was greatly facilitated by the ready availability of increasing supplies of energy at fairly stable prices. They recognized that the problem of meeting growing demand existed before the current situation and that the needs of the world economy for increased energy supplies require positive long-term solutions.

3. They concluded that the current energy situation results from an intensification of these underlying factors and from political developments.

4. They reviewed the problems created by the large rise in oil prices and agreed with the serious concern expressed by the International Monetary Fund's Committee of Twenty at its recent Rome meeting over the abrupt and significant changes in prospect for the world balance of payments structure.

5. They agreed that present petroleum prices presented the structure of world

1 *DSB*, 4 March 1974, pp. 220–2.

trade and finance with an unprecedented situation. They recognized that none of the consuming countries could hope to insulate itself from these developments, or expect to deal with the payments impact of oil prices by the adoption of monetary or trade measures alone. In their view the present situation, if continued, could lead to a serious deterioration in income and employment, intensify inflationary pressures, and endanger the welfare of nations. They believed that financial measures by themselves will not be able to deal with the strains of the current situation.

6. They expressed their particular concern about the consequences of the situation for the developing countries and recognized the need for efforts by the entire international community to resolve this problem. At current oil prices the additional energy costs for developing countries will cause a serious setback to the prospect for economic development of these countries.

7. *General Conclusions.* They affirmed, that in the pursuit of national policies, whether in trade, monetary or energy fields, efforts should be made to harmonize the interests of each country on the one hand and the maintenance of the world economic system on the other. Concerted international cooperation between all the countries concerned including oil producing countries could help to accelerate an improvement in the supply and demand situation, ameliorate the adverse economic consequences of the existing situation and lay the groundwork for a more equitable and stable international energy relationship.

8. They felt that these considerations taken as a whole made it essential that there should be a substantial increase of international cooperation in all fields. Each participant in the Conference stated its firm intention to do its utmost to contribute to such an aim, in close cooperation both with the other consumer countries and with the producer countries.

9. They concurred in the need for a comprehensive action program to deal with all facets of the world energy situation by cooperative measures. In so doing they will build on the work of the OECD. They recognized that they may wish to invite, as appropriate, other countries to join with them in these efforts. Such an action program of international cooperation would include, as appropriate, the sharing of means and efforts, while concerting national policies, in such areas as:

— The conservation of energy and restraint of demand.
— A system of allocating oil supplies in times of emergency and severe shortages.
— The acceleration of development of additional energy sources so as to diversify energy supplies.
— The acceleration of energy research and development programs through international cooperative efforts.[1]

10. With respect to monetary and economic questions, they decided to intensify their cooperation and to give impetus to the work being undertaken in the IMF, the World Bank and the OECD on the economic and monetary consequences of the current energy situation, in particular to deal with balance of payments disequilibria. They agreed that:

1 France does not accept point 9. [Footnote in original.]

— In dealing with the balance of payments impact of oil prices they stressed the importance of avoiding competitive depreciation and the escalation of restrictions on trade and payments or disruptive actions in external borrowing.*[1]

— While financial cooperation can only partially alleviate the problems which have recently arisen for the international economic system, they will intensify work on short-term financial measures and possible longer-term mechanisms to reinforce existing official and market credit facilities.*

— They will pursue domestic economic policies which will reduce as much as possible the difficulties resulting from the current energy cost levels.*

— They will make strenuous efforts to maintain and enlarge the flow of development aid bilaterally and through multilateral institutions, on the basis of international solidarity embracing all countries with appropriate resources.

11. Further, they have agreed to accelerate wherever practicable their own national programs of new energy sources and technology which will help the overall world-wide supply and demand situation.

12. They agreed to examine in detail the role of international oil companies.

13. They stressed the continued importance of maintaining and improving the natural environment as part of developing energy sources and agreed to make this an important goal of their activity.

14. They further agreed that there was need to develop a cooperative multilateral relationship with producing countries, and other consuming countries that takes into account the long-term interests of all. They are ready to exchange technical information with these countries on the problem of stabilizing energy supplies with regard to quantity and prices.

15. They welcomed the initiatives in the UN to deal with the larger issues of energy and primary products at a world-wide level and in particular for a special session of the UN General Assembly.

Establishment of Follow-on Machinery

16. They agreed to establish a coordinating group headed by senior officials to direct and to coordinate the development of the actions referred to above. The coordinating group shall decide how best to organize its work. It should:

— Monitor and give focus to the tasks that might be addressed in existing organizations;

— Establish such *ad hoc* working groups as may be necessary to undertake tasks for which there are presently no suitable bodies;

— Direct preparations of a conference of consumer and producer countries which will be held at the earliest possible opportunity and which, if necessary, will be preceded by a further meeting of consumer countries.

17. They agreed that the preparations for such meeting should involve consultations with developing countries and other consumer and producer countries.[2]

1 In point 10, France does not accept paragraphs cited with asterisks. [Footnote in original.]
2 France does not accept points 16 and 17. [Footnote in original.]

198. Declaration on the establishment of a New International Economic Order, adopted by the Sixth Special Session of the United Nations General Assembly, 1 May 1974[1]

We, the Members of the United Nations,

Having convened a special session of the General Assembly to study for the first time the problems of raw materials and development, devoted to the consideration of the most important economic problems facing the world community,

Bearing in mind the spirit, purposes and principles of the Charter of the United Nations to promote the economic advancement and social progress of all peoples,

Solemnly proclaim our united determination to work urgently for THE ESTABLISHMENT OF A NEW INTERNATIONAL ECONOMIC ORDER based on equity, sovereign equality, interdependence, common interest and cooperation among all States, irrespective of their economic and social systems which shall correct inequalities and redress existing injustices, make it possible to eliminate the widening gap between the developed and the developing countries and ensure steadily accelerating economic and social development and peace and justice for present and future generations, and, to that end, declare:

1. The greatest and most significant achievement during the last decades has been the independence from colonial and alien domination of a large number of peoples and nations which has enabled them to become members of the community of free peoples. Technological progress has also been made in all spheres of economic activities in the last three decades, thus providing a solid potential for improving the well-being of all peoples. However, the remaining vestiges of alien and colonial domination, foreign occupation, racial discrimination, *apartheid* and neo-colonialism in all its forms continue to be among the greatest obstacles to the full emancipation and progress of the developing countries and all the peoples involved. The benefits of technological progress are not shared equitably by all members of the international community. The developing countries, which constitute 70 per cent of the world's population, account for only 30 per cent of the world's income. It has proved impossible to achieve an even and balanced development of the international community under the existing international economic order. The gap between the developed and the developing countries continues to widen in a system which was established at a time when most of the developing countries did not even exist as independent States and which perpetuates inequality.

2. The present international economic order is in direct conflict with current developments in international political and economic relations. Since 1970, the world economy has experienced a series of grave crises which have had severe repercussions, especially on the developing countries because of their generally greater vulnerability to external economic impulses. The developing world has become a powerful factor that makes its influence felt in all fields of international activity. These irreversible changes in the relationship of forces in the world necessitate

1 GA Res. No. 3201 (S–VI).

the active, full and equal participation of the developing countries in the formulation and application of all decisions that concern the international community.

3. All these changes have thrust into prominence the reality of interdependence of all the members of the world community. Current events have brought into sharp focus the realization that the interests of the developed countries and those of the developing countries can no longer be isolated from each other, that there is a close interrelationship between the prosperity of the developed countries and the growth and development of the developing countries, and that the prosperity of the international community as a whole depends upon the prosperity of its constituent parts. International cooperation for development is the shared goal and common duty of all countries. Thus the political, economic and social well-being of present and future generations depends more than ever on cooperation between all the members of the international community on the basis of sovereign equality and the removal of the disequilibrium that exists between them.

4. The new international economic order should be founded on full respect for the following principles:

(*a*) Sovereign equality of States, self-determination of all peoples, inadmissibility of the acquisition of territories by force, territorial integrity and non-interference in the internal affairs of other States;

(*b*The broadest cooperation of all the States members of the international community, based on equity, whereby the prevailing disparities in the world may be banished and prosperity secured for all;

(*c*) Full and effective participation on the basis of equality of all countries in the solving of world economic problems in the common interest of all countries, bearing in mind the necessity to ensure the accelerated development of all the developing countries, while devoting particular attention to the adoption of special measures in favour of the least developed, land-locked and island developing countries as well as those developing countries most seriously affected by economic crises and natural calamities, without losing sight of the interests of other developing countries;

(*d*) The right of every country to adopt the economic and social system that it deems the most appropriate for its own development and not to be subjected to discrimination of any kind as a result;

(*e*) Full permanent sovereignty of every State over its natural resources and all economic activities. In order to safeguard these resources, each State is entitled to exercise effective control over them and their exploitation with means suitable to its own situation, including the right to nationalization or transfer of ownership to its nationals, this right being an expression of the full permanent sovereignty of the State. No State may be subjected to economic, political or any other type of coercion to prevent the free and full exercise of this inalienable right;

(*f*) The right of all States, territories and peoples under foreign occupation, alien and colonial domination or *apartheid* to restitution and full compensation for the exploitation and depletion of, and damages to, the natural resources and all other resources of those States, territories and peoples;

(*g*) Regulation and supervision of the activities of transnational corporations by taking measures in the interest of the national economies of the countries where such transnational corporations operate on the basis of the full sovereignty of those countries;

(*h*) The right of the developing countries and the peoples of territories under colonial and racial domination and foreign occupation to achieve their liberation and to regain effective control over their natural resources and economic activities;

(*i*) The extending of assistance to developing countries, peoples and territories which are under colonial and alien domination, foreign occupation, racial discrimination or *apartheid* or are subjected to economic, political or any other type of coercive measures to obtain from them the subordination of the exercise of their sovereign rights and to secure from them advantages of any kind, and to neo-colonialism in all its forms, and which have established or are endeavouring to establish effective control over their natural resources and economic activities that have been or are still under foreign control;

(*j*) Just and equitable relationship between the prices of raw materials, primary commodities, manufactured and semi-manufactured goods exported by developing countries and the price of raw materials, primary commodities, manufactures, capital goods and equipment imported by them with the aim of bringing about sustained improvement in their unsatisfactory terms of trade and the expansion of the world economy;

(*k*) Extension of active assistance to developing countries by the whole international community, free of any political or military conditions;

(*l*) Ensuring that one of the main aims of the reformed international monetary system shall be the promotion of the development of the developing countries and the adequate flow of real resources to them;

(*m*) Improving the competitiveness of natural materials facing competition from synthetic substitutes;

(*n*) Preferential and non-reciprocal treatment for developing countries, wherever feasible, in all fields of international economic cooperation whenever possible;

(*o*) Securing favourable conditions for the transfer of financial resources to developing countries;

(*p*) Giving to the developing countries access to the achievements of modern science and technology, and promoting the transfer of technology and the creation of indigenous technology for the benefit of the developing countries in forms and in accordance with procedures which are suited to their economies;

(*q*) The need for all States to put an end to the waste of natural resources, including food products;

(*r*) The need for developing countries to concentrate all their resources for the cause of development;

(*s*) The strengthening, through individual and collective actions, of mutual economic, trade, financial and technical cooperation among the developing countries, mainly on a preferential basis;

(*t*) Facilitating the role which producers' associations may play within the framework of international cooperation and, in pursuance of their aims, *inter alia* assisting in the promotion of sustained growth of the world economy and accelerating the development of developing countries.

5. The unanimous adoption of the International Development Strategy for the Second United Nations Development Decade was an important step in the promotion of international economic cooperation on a just and equitable basis. The accelerated implementation of obligations and commitments assumed by the international community within the framework of the Strategy, particularly those concerning imperative development needs of developing countries, would contribute significantly to the fulfilment of the aims and objectives of the present Declaration.

6. The United Nations as a universal organization should be capable of dealing with problems of international economic cooperation in a comprehensive manner and ensuring equally the interests of all countries. It must have an even greater role in the establishment of a new international economic order. The Charter of Economic Rights and Duties of States, for the preparation of which the present Declaration will provide an additional source of inspiration, will constitute a significant contribution in this respect. All the States Members of the United Nations are therefore called upon to exert maximum efforts with a view to securing the implementation of the present Declaration, which is one of the principal guarantees for the creation of better conditions for all peoples to reach a life worthy of human dignity.

7. The present Declaration on the Establishment of a New International Economic Order shall be one of the most important bases of economic relations between all peoples and all nations.

199. Press conference by President Giscard d'Estaing, Paris, 24 October 1974 (extract)[1]

I myself believe that a conference convening a restricted number of countries, and when I say restricted I mean a figure approaching 10 or 12, meeting early in 1975 and bringing together an equal number of representatives from the principal oil-exporting countries, the industrialised oil-importing and the non-industrialised oil-importing countries — such a conference could be of immense value if it attempts to deal with the following two problems; the first problem is the nature of the guarantee which should be offered to oil-producing countries regarding protection of their revenue, in other words the question of oil price-indexing on certain recommended items. Set off against agreement on this point, there should be an examination of the conditions under which the present phase of adjustment of the world economy might operate; because an adjustment is necessary and the guarantee of revenue cannot be assured from any level, still less of course, from a continual re-fixing of prices or inflation. An adjustment is necessary to set the general level on which the guarantee can operate and, as from today, we shall be in touch with the principal industrialised

1 *La Politique étrangère de la France* (Paris, La Documentation Française) Textes, 2e Semestre, 24 October 1974, pp. 137–8 (unofficial translation).

and non-industrialised partners, consumers and producers, in order to discuss with them how such a conference might take place early in 1975. This idea was not just our own; it was expressed several times by representatives from Saudi Arabia, for example.

Q.   Mr President, does this mean that France definitely refuses to be part of the Group of Twelve[1] and its project and if so, what will happen if our European partners prefer the policy initiated with the United States, rather than any common policy on European energy?

A.   First I shall deal with the energy problem and then I'll reply to your two questions. As regards energy, first and foremost it is essential that a common attitude is adopted by the Nine, for as you know the basis for this attitude was decided on last month, but up to now, it has to be admitted, the Nine have not evolved a common attitude; they haven't evolved one amongst the Twelve, let alone amongst themselves. I myself should like, if possible, an Energy conference of restricted numbers to be held early in 1975 which would deal with the two problems I mentioned earlier. Europe would be represented as it is – that is to say as one of the participating countries speaking in the name of the Nine. Naturally, this makes it even more essential that the Nine are in agreement on a certain number of common principles concerning Energy policy. They are not in agreement within the Nine, consequently there is a different attitude vis-à-vis the Twelve. We are not against our partners taking part in other organisations, but I strongly believe that, in studying the oil problem in today's world, we should keep open every possibility for concerted action. I have had many talks on this subject, I have received many visitors in Paris and I believe amongst some of those with whom I talked there is the desire for such cooperation. Now, it is obvious that any attitude adopted by us at the present moment in favour of a highly organised structure and which is felt by the oil-producing countries to be a structure of confrontation and not concerted effort as far as it concerns them, will weaken the chances of concerted effort. And so, I repeat, since I should like this point to be clearly understood, that our present policy is not aimed at securing bilateral advantages for France. This is not our aim. Our aim is to keep open any chance of concerted action regarding the solution of the world's oil problem. I believe this concerted action is possible at the moment and certainly desirable. And it is with this in mind we shall adhere to our attitude over the coming months.

Q.   Another question follows from this: What will France's position be on 12 November at the next OECD meeting, particularly with regard to joining the Twelve and its agreement or not?

A.   France will certainly not be a party to the Treaty of the Twelve on 12 November. She has clearly indicated this. Neither shall she object to an energy agency being set up in connection with the OECD; she will let those who have undertaken to set up this organisation go ahead without putting any obstacle in the way, but

1 The Energy Coordinating Group, established by the Washington Energy Conference, comprises: The European Community (minus France), Norway, Japan, the United States and Canada. They met in Brussels on 19–20 September 1974.

rather than participating in this organisation, she believes she should maintain her role of research, dialogue and concerted effort with the oil-producing countries. And so, she will not take part in this organisation, she will not impede its birth, but she will maintain her attitude of concerted action even within the framework of the OECD. . .

200. Decision of the OECD Council establishing an International Energy Agency of the Organisation, 15 November 1974[1]

The Council,

Having regard to the Convention on the Organisation for Economic Cooperation and Development of 14th December, 1960[2] (hereinafter called the 'Convention') and, in particular, Articles 5 (*a*), 6, 9, 12, 13 and 20 of the Convention;

Having regard to the Financial Regulations of the Organisation and, in particular, to Articles 5, 10, 14 (*b*) and 16 (*b*) thereof:

Having regard to the regulations, Rules and Instructions for Council Experts and Consultants of the Organisation;

Noting that the Governments of certain Member countries have declared their intention to enter into a separate Agreement on an International Energy Program hereinafter referred to as the 'Agreement';

Having regard to the Recommendation of the Council of 29th June, 1971 on Oil Stockpiling;

Having regard to the Decision of the Council of 14th November, 1972 on Emergency Plans and Measures and Apportionment of Oil Supplies in an Emergency in the OECD European Area;

Having regard to the Recommendation of the Council of 10th January, 1974 on the Supply of Bunker Fuels for Shipping and Fishing;

Having regard to the Recommendation of the Council of 10th January, 1974 on the Supply of Fuel for Civil Aircraft;

Having regard to the Note by the Secretary-General of 6th November, 1974 concerning the International Energy Program;

Decides:[3]

Article 1

An International Energy Agency (hereinafter called the 'Agency') is hereby established as an autonomous body within the framework of the Organisation.

Article 2

Participating Countries of the Agency are:

1 Cmnd. 5826.
2 For text, see Cmnd. 1646.
3 Finland, France and Greece abstained.

(*a*) Austria, Belgium, Canada, Denmark, Germany, Ireland, Italy, Japan, Luxembourg, the Netherlands, Spain, Sweden, Switzerland, Turkey, the United Kingdom and the United States.

(*b*) other Member countries of the Organisation which accede to this Decision and to the Agreement in accordance with its terms.

Article 3

This Decision will be open for accession by the European Communities upon their accession to the Agreement in accordance with its terms.

Article 4

A Governing Board composed of all the Participating Countries of the Agency shall be the body from which all acts of the Agency derive, and shall have the power to make recommendations and to take decisions which shall, except as otherwise provided, be binding upon Participating Countries, and to delegate its powers to other organs of the Agency. The Governing Board shall adopt its own rules of procedure and voting rules.

Article 5

The Governing Board shall establish such organs and procedures as may be required for the proper functioning of the Agency.

Article 6

(*a*) The Governing Board shall decide upon and carry out an International Energy Program for cooperation in the field of energy, the aims of which are:

(i) development of a common level of emergency self-sufficiency in oil supplies;

(ii) establishment of common demand restraint measures in an emergency;

(iii) establishment and implementation of measures for the allocation of available oil in time of emergency;

(iv) development of a system of information on the international oil market and a framework for consultation with international oil companies;

(v) development and implementation of a long-term cooperation programme to reduce dependence on imported oil, including: conservation of energy, development of alternative sources of energy, energy research and development, and supply of natural and enriched uranium;

(vi) promotion of cooperative relations with oil producing countries and with other oil consuming countries, particularly those of the developing world.

The Governing Board may adopt other measures of cooperation in the energy field which it may deem necessary and otherwise amend the Program by unanimity, taking into account the constitutional procedures of the Participating Countries.

(*b*) Upon the proposal of the Governing Board of the Agency, the Council may confer additional responsibilities upon the Agency.

Article 7

(*a*) The organs of the Agency shall be assisted by an Executive Director and such staff as is necessary who shall form part of the Secretariat of the Organisation and who shall, in performing their duties under the International Energy Program, be responsible to and report to the organs of the Agency.

(*b*) The Executive Director shall be appointed by the Governing Board on the proposal or with concurrence of the Secretary-General.

(*c*) Consultants to the Agency may be appointed for a period exceeding that provided in Regulation 2 (*b*) of the Regulations and Rules for Council Experts and Consultants of the Organisation.

Article 8

The Governing Board shall report annually to the Council on the activities of the Agency. The Governing Board shall submit, upon the request of the Council or upon its own initiative, other communications to the Council.

Article 9

The Agency shall cooperate with other competent bodies of the Organisation in areas of common interest. These bodies and the Agency shall consult with one another regarding their respective activities.

Article 10

(*a*) The budget of the Agency shall form part of the Budget of the Organisation and expenditure of the Agency shall be charged against the appropriations authorised for it under Part II of the Budget which shall include appropriate Budget estimates and provisions for all expenditure necessary for the operation of the Agency. Each Participating Country's share in financing such expenditure shall be fixed by the Governing Board. Special expenses incurred by the Agency in connection with activities referred to in Article 11 shall be shared by the Participating Countries in such proportions as shall be determined by unanimous agreement of those countries. The Governing Board shall designate an organ of the Agency to advise the Governing Board as required on the financial administration of the Agency and to give its opinion on the annual and other budget proposals submitted to the Governing Board.

(*b*) The Governing Board shall submit the annual and other budget proposals of the Agency to the Council for adoption by agreement of those Participating Countries of the Agency which voted in the Governing Board to submit the proposals to the Council.

(*c*) Notwithstanding the provisions of Article 14 (*b*) of the Financial Regulations, the Governing Board may accept voluntary contributions and grants as well as payments for services rendered by the Agency.

(*d*) Notwithstanding the provisions of Article 16 (*b*) of the Financial Regulations of the Organisation, appropriations in respect of the special activities referred to in Article 11 of this Decision, for which no commitment has been entered into before the end of the Financial Year for which they were appropriated, shall be automatically carried forward to the budget for the ensuing year.

Article 11

Any two or more Participating Countries may decide to carry out within the scope of the Program special activities, other than activities which are required to be carried out by all Participating Countries under the Agreement. Participating Countries who do not wish to take part in such activities shall abstain from taking part in such decisions and shall not be bound by them. Participating Countries carrying out such activities shall keep the Governing Board informed thereof.

Article 12

In order to achieve the objectives of the Program, the Agency may establish appropriate relationships with countries which are not Participating Countries, international organisations whether Governmental or non-Governmental, other entities and individuals.

Article 13

(*a*) A Participating Country for which the Agreement shall have ceased to be in force or to apply provisionally shall be deemed to have withdrawn from the Agency. (*b*) Notwithstanding the provisions of paragraph (*a*), a Country whose Government shall have signed the Agreement may, upon written notice to the Governing Board and to the Government of Belgium to the effect that the adoption of the Program by the Governing Board is binding on it pursuant to this Decision, remain a Participating Country of the Agency after the Agreement shall have ceased to apply for it, unless the Governing Board decides otherwise. Such a Country shall have the same obligations and the same rights as a Participating Country of the Agency for which the Agreement shall have entered definitively into force.

Article 14

The present Decision shall enter into force on 15th November, 1974.

EDITOR'S NOTE: THE AGREEMENT ON AN INTERNATIONAL ENERGY PROGRAMME

Following the decision to establish an International Energy Agency, the same members of the OECD signed the Agreement on an International Energy Programme on 18 November 1974. This Agreement establishes the detailed objectives and procedures of the Agency. For text, see Cmnd. 6697.

201. Communiqué issued following the meeting between President Ford and President Giscard d'Estaing, Martinique, 16 December 1971[1] (extract)

The President of the United States, Gerald R. Ford, and the President of the French Republic, Valéry Giscard d'Estaing, met in Martinique December 14–16, 1974, to discuss current issues of mutual concern. They were joined in their discussions by the Secretary of State and Assistant to the President for National Security Affairs Henry A. Kissinger and Minister of Foreign Affairs Jean Sauvagnarguez, and by Secretary of the Treasury William Simon and Minister of Finance Jean-Pierre Fourcade. The Ministers also held complementary side talks.

The meeting took place in an atmosphere of cordiality and mutual confidence. President Ford and President Giscard d'Estaing welcomed the opportunity to conduct detailed substantive discussions on the whole range of subjects of mutual concern. As traditional friends and allies, the two nations share common values and goals and the two Presidents expressed their determination to cooperate on this basis in efforts to solve common problems.

They reviewed the international situation in the economic, financial and monetary fields.

The two Presidents agreed that the Governments of the United States and of the European Community, in the name of which the French President spoke on this subject, must adopt consistent economic policies in order to be effective in avoiding unemployment while fighting inflation. In particular, they agreed on the importance of avoiding measures of a protectionist nature. And they decided to take the initiative in calling additional intergovernmental meetings should they prove necessary for achievement of the desired consistency of basic economic policies among industrial nations.

In the light of the rapid pace of change in international financial positions in the world today, the Presidents were in full agreement on the desirability of maintaining the momentum of consideration of closer financial cooperation both within the International Monetary Fund and through supplementary measures. As one specific measure to strengthen the existing financial framework the Presidents agreed that it would be appropriate for any Government which wished to do so to adopt current market prices as the basis of valuation for its gold holdings.

The two Presidents considered in depth the energy problem and its serious and disturbing effects on the world economy. They recognized the importance for the USA, the EEC and other industrialized nations of implementing policies for the conservation of energy, the development of existing and alternative sources of energy, and the setting up of new mechanisms of financial solidarity. They stressed the importance of solidarity among oil importing nations on these issues.

The two Presidents also exchanged views on the desirability of a dialogue between consumers and producers and in that connection discussed the proposal of the President of the French Republic of October 24 for a conference of oil exporting and importing countries. They agreed that it would be desirable to convene such a meeting at the earliest possible date. They regard it as important that all parties concerned should be better informed of their respective interests and concerns and that harmonious relations should be established among them in order to promote a healthy development of the world economy.

The two Presidents noted that their views on these matters are complementary and, in this context, they agreed that the following interrelated steps should be taken in sequence:

— They agreed that additional steps should be taken, within the framework of existing institutions and agreements to which they are a party, and in consultation with other interested consumers, to strengthen their cooperation. In particular, such cooperation should include programs of energy conservation, for the development of existing and alternative sources of energy and for financial solidarity.

— Based on substantial progress in the foregoing areas, the two Presidents agreed that it will be desirable to propose holding a preparatory meeting between consumers and producers to develop an agenda and procedures for a consumer/ producer conference. The target date for such a preparatory meeting should be March 1975.

— The preparatory discussions will be followed by intensive consultations among consumer countries in order to prepare positions for the conference.

The two Presidents agreed that the actions enumerated above will be carried out in the most expeditious manner possible and in full awareness of the common interest in meeting this critical situation shared by the United States and France and all other countries involved.

President Ford and President Giscard d'Estaing reviewed current developments in East—West relations. They discussed their respective meetings with General Secretary Brezhnev, and Secretary Kissinger reported on his discussions with leaders of the People's Republic of China. They exchanged views on developments in East— West negotiations, including the Conference on Security and Cooperation in Europe. They expressed their conviction that progress in easing tensions was being made.

The two Presidents exchanged views on the present situation in the Middle East. They agreed on the importance of early progress toward a just and lasting peace in that area.

President Giscard d'Estaing described current efforts by France and other members of the European Community to further the process of European unity. President Ford reaffirmed the continuing support of the United States for efforts to achieve European unity.

The two Presidents discussed the situation in Indochina. They noted that progress in Laos toward reconciliation and reunification was encouraging.

The two Presidents agreed on the need for all parties to support fully the Paris Peace Agreements on Vietnam. Regarding Cambodia, they expressed the hope that the contending parties would enter into negotiations in the near future rather than continuing the military struggle. They expressed the hope that following Laos, Cambodia and Vietnam might also find their political way towards civil peace.

The two Presidents renewed the pledges of both Governments to continue close relations in the field of defense as members of the Atlantic Alliance. They agreed that the cooperation between France and NATO is a significant factor in the security of Europe.

They noted with satisfaction that the positive steps in negotiations on SALT taken during the Soviet–American meeting at Vladivostok have reduced the threat of a nuclear arms race. The two Presidents explored how, as exporters of nuclear materials and technology, their two countries could coordinate their efforts to assure improved safeguards of nuclear materials.

The President of France indicated that his Government was prepared to reach a final settlement in connection with the relocation of American forces and bases committed to NATO from France to other countries in 1967. The French offer of $100 million in full settlement was formally accepted by President Ford.

The two Presidents concluded that the personal contact and discussion in this meeting had demonstrated accord on many questions and expressed their determination to maintain close contact for the purpose of broad cooperation in areas of common concern to the two countries.

202. Invitation from President Giscard d'Estaing to nine states and the EEC to participate in a preparatory meeting for an International Conference on Energy Problems, 1 March 1975[1]

On 24 October last I proposed that a Conference be convened to examine energy problems with which numerous aspects of international economic relations are linked. This proposal has been the subject of much discussion highlighting the urgent need for opening of a dialogue. This favourable reaction encourages us to go ahead with a project in keeping with the interests of all parties concerned.

It seems to us that this dialogue could be organized in two stages: firstly, a preparatory meeting to fix the date, membership and agenda of a Conference and, secondly, the Conference itself.

In order to ensure that the proceedings of the preparatory meeting are conducted with efficiency and dispatch, we have adopted the list of countries which the Government of the Kingdom of Saudi Arabia suggested last year for such a meeting.

1 *Bull. EC*, 4–1975, p. 19; invitations went to the following countries: Algeria, Saudi Arabia, Iran, Venezuela, Brazil, India, Zaire, the United States and the European Economic Community.

As you know, this list of participants includes the European Economic Community whose views will be stated, as decided by the Council of the European Communities on 10 February 1975, by the delegate of the country holding the office of President of the Council.

We propose that the preparatory meeting should open in Paris on 7 April.

I have no doubt that the representation of the European Economic Community at this meeting will make a valuable contribution towards the success of its proceedings which is essential if the international community is to find a concerted remedy for the difficulties facing it.

203. Joint communiqué issued following the meeting between Euro-Arab experts, Cairo, 14 June 1975[1]

1. Two delegations of experts, one Arab and one European, met at the Headquarters of the Arab League in Cairo from 10 to 14 June in order to elaborate principles and objectives relating to cooperation between Europe and the Arab world through the Euro-Arab Dialogue.

2. Both sides agreed that the Euro-Arab Dialogue is the product of a joint political will that emerged at the highest level with a view to establishing a special relationship between the two sides.

3. They set out the objectives of the Dialogue in the following areas of cooperation:
   (i) Agriculture and rural development
   (ii) Industrialization
   (iii) Basic infrastructure
   (iv) Financial cooperation
   (v) Trade
   (vi) Scientific and technological cooperation, cultural and labour and social questions.

4. In order to set in train the task of implementing these objectives, both sides agreed that the present meeting of experts will be resumed periodically in the form of a Steering Committee of Experts; the first meeting of the Steering Committee of Experts will be in July in a European city. On that occasion groups of experts of both sides will consider together in greater depth the areas of cooperation set out above.

5. Throughout their discussions, the Arab and European experts were conscious of the significance to be attached to this meeting within the framework of the Euro-Arab dialogue. Consequently, they exerted all efforts in order to bring it to a successful conclusion.

1 *Bull. EC*, 6–1975, pp. 109–10.

204. Joint communiqué issued following the meeting between Euro-Arab experts, Rome, 24 July 1975[1]

In accordance with the decision taken in Cairo on 14 June 1975, the meeting of Arab and European experts was resumed in Rome from 22 to 24 July.

Both sides reemphasized that the Euro-Arab dialogue is the product of a joint political will that emerged at the highest level with a view to establishing a special relationship between the two sides.

After a general exchange of views, working groups were set up to consider and report in greater depth on the areas of cooperation agreed: industrialization, basic infrastructure, agriculture and rural development, financial cooperation, cultural and labour and social questions.

Both sides recalled the agreement reached in Cairo on 14 June 1975 to the effect that the present meeting of experts will be resumed periodically in the form of a steering committee of experts.

Both sides recommend that a meeting of Arab and European experts should take place in an Arab city in November 1975 and decided to maintain whatever appropriate contacts are needed to prepare adequately for the forthcoming meeting of experts and initiate action along the lines agreed.

Both sides noted that the Rome meeting marked the beginning of a more detailed examination of the possibilities of Euro-Arab cooperation and of the exploration of effective channels to advance the dialogue towards its objectives in all fields and to pursue all its purposes. They reaffirmed their common determination to achieve tangible results in the interest of the Arab and European peoples.

205. Resolution on development and international economic cooperation, adopted by the Seventh Special Session of the United Nations General Assembly, 16 September 1975[2]

The General Assembly,

Determined to eliminate injustice and inequality which afflict vast sections of humanity and to accelerate the development of developing countries,

Recalling the Declaration and the Programme of Action on the Establishment of a New International Economic Order, as well as the Charter of Economic Rights and Duties of States,[3] which lay down the foundations of the new international economic order.

Reaffirming the fundamental purposes of the above-mentioned documents and duties of all States to seek and participate in the solutions of the problems afflicting

1 *Bull. EC*, 7/8–1975, p. 111.
2 GA Res. 3362 (S–VII).
3 GA Res. 3281 (XXIX).

the world, in particular the imperative need of redressing the economic imbalance between developed and developing countries,

Recalling further the International Development Strategy for the Second United Nations Development Decade, which should be reviewed in the light of the Programme of Action on the Establishment of a New International Economic Order, and determined to implement the targets and policy measures contained in the International Development Strategy.

Conscious that the accelerated development of developing countries would be a decisive element for the promotion of world peace and security,

Recognizing that greater cooperation among States in the fields of trade, industry, science and technology as well as in other fields of economic activities, based on the principles of the Declaration and the Programme of Action on the Establishment of a New International Economic Order and of the Charter of Economic Rights and Duties of States, would also contribute to strengthening peace and security in the world,

Believing that the over-all objective of the new international economic order is to increase the capacity of developing countries, individually and collectively, to pursue their development,

Decides, to this end and in the context of the foregoing, to set in motion the following measures as the basis and framework for the work of the competent bodies and organizations of the United Nations system:

I. International Trade

1. Concerted efforts should be made in favour of the developing countries towards expanding and diversifying their trade, improving and diversifying their productive capacity, improving their productivity and increasing their export earnings, with a view to counteracting the adverse effects of inflation — thereby sustaining real incomes — and with a view to improving the terms of trade of the developing countries and in order to eliminate the economic imbalance between developed and developing countries.

2. Concerted action should be taken to accelerate the growth and diversification of the export trade of developing countries in manufactures and semi-manufactures and in processed and semi-processed products in order to increase their share in world industrial output and world trade within the framework of an expanding world economy.

3. An important aim of the fourth session of the United Nations Conference on Trade and Development, in addition to work in progress elsewhere, should be to reach decisions on the improvement of market structures in the field of raw materials and commodities of export interest to the developing countries, including decisions with respect to an integrated programme and the applicability of elements thereof. In this connexion, taking into account the distinctive features of individual raw materials and commodities, the decisions should bear on the following:

(*a*) Appropriate international stocking and other forms of market arrangements for securing stable, remunerative and equitable prices for commodities of export interest to developing countries and promoting equilibrium between supply and demand, including, where possible, long-term multilateral commitments;

(*b*) Adequate international financing facilities for such stocking and market arrangements;

(*c*) Where possible, promotion of long-term and medium-term contracts;

(*d*) Substantial improvement of facilities for compensatory financing of export revenue fluctuations through the widening and enlarging of the existing facilities. Note has been taken of the various proposals regarding a comprehensive scheme for the stabilization of export earnings of developing countries and for a development security facility as well as specific measures for the benefit of the developing countries most in need;

(*e*) Promotion of processing of raw materials in producing developing countries and expansion and diversification of their exports, particularly to developed countries;

(*f*) Effective opportunities to improve the share of developing countries in transport, marketing and distribution of their primary commodities and to encourage measures of world significance for the evolution of the infrastructure and secondary capacity of developing countries from the production of primary commodities to processing, transport and marketing, and to the production of finished manufactured goods, their transport, distribution and exchange, including advanced financial and exchange institutions for the remunerative management of trade transactions.

4. The Secretary-General of the United Nations Conference on Trade and Development should present a report to the Conference at its fourth session on the impact of an integrated programme on the imports of developing countries which are net importers of raw materials and commodities, including those lacking in natural resources, and recommend any remedial measures that may be necessary.

5. A number of options are open to the international community to preserve the purchasing power of developing countries. These need to be further studied on a priority basis. The Secretary-General of the United Nations Conference on Trade and Development should continue to study direct and indirect indexation schemes and other options with a view to making concrete proposals before the Conference at its fourth session.

6. The Secretary-General of the United Nations Conference on Trade and Development should prepare a preliminary study on the proportion between prices of raw materials and commodities exported by developing countries and the final consumer price, particularly in developed countries, and submit it, if possible, to the Conference at its fourth session.

7. Developed countries should fully implement agreed provisions on the principle of Standstill as regards imports from developing countries, and any departure should be subjected to such measures as consultations and multilateral surveillance and compensation, in accordance with internationally agreed criteria and procedures.

8. Developed countries should take effective steps within the framework of multilateral trade negotiations for the reduction or removal, where feasible and appropriate, of non-tariff barriers affecting the products of export interest to developing countries

on a differential and more favourable basis for developing countries. The generalized scheme of preferences should not terminate at the end of the period of ten years originally envisaged and should be continuously improved through wider coverage, deeper cuts and other measures, bearing in mind the interests of those developing countries which enjoy special advantages and the need for finding ways and means for protecting their interests.

9. Countervailing duties should be applied only in conformity with internationally agreed obligations. Developed countries should exercise maximum restraint within the framework of international obligations in the imposition of countervailing duties on the imports of products from developing countries. The multilateral trade negotiations under way should take fully into account the particular interests of developing countries with a view to providing them differential and more favourable treatment in appropriate cases.

10. Restrictive business practices adversely affecting international trade, particularly that of developing countries, should be eliminated and efforts should be made at the national and international levels with the objective of negotiating a set of equitable principles and rules.

11. Special measures should be undertaken by developed countries and by developing countries in a position to do so to assist in the structural transformation of the economy of the least developed and land-locked and island developing countries.

12. Emergency measures as spelled out in section X of General Assembly resolution 3202 (S–VI) should be undertaken on a temporary basis to meet the specific problems of the most seriously affected countries as defined in Assembly resolutions 3201 (S–VI) and 3202 (S–VI) of 1 May 1974, without any detriment to the interests of the developing countries as a whole.

13. Further expansion of trade between the socialist countries of Eastern Europe and the developing countries should be intensified as is provided for in resolutions 15 (II) of 25 March 1968 and 53 (III) of 19 May 1972 of the United Nations Conference on Trade and Development. Additional measures and appropriate orientation to achieve this end are necessary.

II. Transfer of Real Resources for financing the development of Developing Countries and International Monetary Reforms

1. Concessional financial resources to developing countries need to be increased substantially, their terms and conditions ameliorated and their flow made predictable, continuous and increasingly assured so as to facilitate the implementation by developing countries of long-term programmes for economic and social development. Financial assistance should, as a general rule, be untied.

2. Developed countries confirm their continued commitment in respect of the targets relating to the transfer of resources, in particular the official development assistance target of 0.7 per cent of gross national product, as agreed in the International Development Strategy for the Second United Nations Development Decade,

and adopt as their common aim an effective increase in official development assistance with a view to achieving these targets by the end of the decade. Developed countries which have not yet made a commitment in respect of these targets undertake to make their best efforts to reach these targets in the remaining part of this decade.

3. The establishment of a link between the special drawing rights and development assistance should form part of the consideration by the International Monetary Fund of the creation of new special drawing rights as and when they are created according to the needs of international liquidity. Agreement should be reached at an early date on the establishment of a trust fund, to be financed partly through the International Monetary Fund gold sales and partly through voluntary contributions and to be governed by an appropriate body, for the benefit of developing countries. Consideration of other means of transfer of real resources which are predictable, assured and continuous should be expedited in appropriate bodies.

4. Developed countries and international organizations should enhance the real value and volume of assistance to developing countries and ensure that the developing countries obtain the largest possible share in the procurement of equipment, consultants and consultancy services. Such assistance should be on softer terms and, as a general rule, untied.

5. In order to enlarge the pool of resources available for financing development, there is an urgent need to increase substantially the capital of the World Bank Group, in particular the resources of the International Development Association, to enable it to make additional capital available to the poorest countries on highly concessional terms.

6. The resources of the development institutions of the United Nations system, in particular the United Nations Development Programme, should also be increased. The funds at the disposal of the regional development banks should be augmented. These increases should be without prejudice to bilateral development assistance flows.

7. To the extent desirable, the World Bank Group is invited to consider new ways of supplementing its financing with private management, skills, technology and capital and also new approaches to increase financing of development in developing countries, in accordance with their national plans and priorities.

8. The burden of debt on developing countries is increasing to a point where the import capacity as well as reserves have come under serious strain. At its fourth session the United Nations Conference on Trade and Development shall consider the need for, and the possibility of, convening as soon as possible a conference of major donor, creditor and debtor countries to devise ways and means to mitigate this burden, taking into account the development needs of developing countries, with special attention to the plight of the most seriously affected countries as defined in General Assembly resolutions 3201 (S–VI) and 3202 (S–VI).

9. Developing countries should be granted increased access on favourable terms to the capital markets of developed countries. To this end, the joint Development Committee of the International Monetary Fund and the International Bank for

Reconstruction and Development should progress as rapidly as possible in its work. Appropriate United Nations bodies and other related intergovernmental agencies should be invited to examine ways and means of increasing the flow of public and private resources to developing countries, including proposals made at the current session to provide investment in private and public enterprises in the developing countries. Consideration should be given to the examination of an international investment trust and to the expansion of the International Finance Corporation capital without prejudice to the increase in resources of other intergovernmental financial and development institutions and bilateral assistance flows.

10. Developed and developing countries should further cooperate through investment of financial resources and supply of technology and equipment to developing countries by developed countries and by developing countries in a position to do so.

11. Developed countries, and developing countries in a position to do so, are urged to make adequate contributions to the United Nations Special Fund with a view to an early implementation of a programme of lending, preferably in 1976.

12. Developed countries should improve terms and conditions of their assistance so as to include a preponderant grant element for the least developed, land-locked and island developing countries.

13. In providing additional resources for assisting the most seriously affected countries in helping them to meet their serious balance-of-payments deficits, all developed countries, and developing countries in a position to do so, and international organizations such as the International Bank for Reconstruction and Development and the International Monetary Fund, should undertake specific measures in their favour, including those provided in General Assembly resolutions 3201 (S–VI) and 3202 (S–VI).

14. Special attention should be given by the international community to the phenomena of natural disasters which frequently afflict many parts of the world, with far-reaching devastating economic, social and structural consequences, particularly in the least developed countries. To this end, the General Assembly at its thirtieth session, in considering this problem, should examine and adopt appropriate measures.

15. The role of national reserve currencies should be reduced and the special drawing rights should become the central reserve asset of the international monetary system in order to provide for greater international control over the creation and equitable distribution of liquidity and in order to limit potential losses as a consequence of exchange rate fluctuations. Arrangements for gold should be consistent with the agreed objective of reducing the role of gold in the system and with equitable distribution of new international liquidity and should in particular take into consideration the needs of developing countries for increased liquidity.

16. The process of decision-making should be fair and responsive to change and should be most specially responsive to the emergence of a new economic influence on the part of developing countries. The participation of developing countries in

the decision-making process in the competent organs of international finance and development institutions should be adequately increased and made more effective without adversely affecting the broad geographic representation of developing countries and in accordance with the existing and evolving rules.

17. The compensatory financing facility now available through the International Monetary Fund should be expanded and liberalized. In this connexion, early consideration should be given by the Fund and other appropriate United Nations bodies to various proposals made at the current session — including the examination of a new development security facility — which would mitigate export earnings shortfalls of developing countries, with special regard to the poorest countries, and thus provide greater assistance to their continued economic development. Early consideration should also be given by the International Monetary Fund to proposals to expand and liberalize its coverage of current transactions to include manufactures and services, to ensure that, whenever possible, compensation for export shortfalls takes place at the same time they occur, to take into account, in determining the quantum of compensation, movements in import prices and to lengthen the repayment period.

18. Drawing under the buffer stock financing facility of the International Monetary Fund should be accorded treatment with respect to floating alongside the gold tranche, similar to that under the compensatory financing facility, and the Fund should expedite its study of the possibility of an amendment of the Articles of Agreement, to be presented to the Interim Committee, if possible at its next meeting, that would permit the Fund to provide assistance directly to international buffer stocks of primary products.

III. Science and Technology

1. Developed and developing countries should cooperate in the establishment, strengthening and development of the scientific and technological infrastructure of developing countries. Developed countries should also take appropriate measures, such as contribution to the establishment of an industrial technological information bank and consideration of the possibility of regional and sectoral banks, in order to make available a greater flow to developing countries of information permitting the selection of technologies, in particular advanced technologies. Consideration should also be given to the establishment of an international centre for the exchange of technological information for the sharing of research findings relevant to developing countries. For the above purposes institutional arrangements within the United Nations system should be examined by the General Assembly at its thirtieth session.

2. Developed countries should significantly expand their assistance to developing countries for direct support to their science and technology programmes, as well as increase substantially the proportion of their research and development devoted to specific problems of primary interest to developing countries, and in the creation of suitable indigenous technology, in accordance with feasible targets to be agreed upon. The General Assembly invites the Secretary-General to carry out a preliminary

study and to report to the Assembly at its thirty-first session on the possibility of establishing, within the framework of the United Nations system, an international energy institute to assist all developing countries in energy resources research and development.

3. All States should cooperate in evolving an international code of conduct for the transfer of technology, corresponding, in particular, to the special needs of the developing countries. Work on such a code should therefore be continued within the United Nations Conference on Trade and Development and concluded in time for decisions to be reached at the fourth session of the Conference, including a decision on the legal character of such a code with the objective of the adoption of a code of conduct prior to the end of 1977. International conventions on patents and trade marks should be reviewed and revised to meet, in particular, the special needs of the developing countries, in order that these conventions may become more satisfactory instruments for aiding developing countries in the transfer and development of technology. National patents systems should, without delay, be brought into line with the international patent system in its revised form.

4. Developed countries should facilitate the access of developing countries on favourable terms and conditions, and on an urgent basis, to relevant information on advanced and other technologies suited to their specific needs as well as on new uses of existing technology, new developments and possibilities of adapting them to local needs. Inasmuch as in market economies advanced technologies with respect to industrial production are most frequently developed by private institutions, developed countries should facilitate and encourage these institutions in providing effective technologies in support of the priorities of developing countries.

5. Developed countries should give developing countries the freest and fullest possible access to technologies whose transfer is not subject to private decision.

6. Developed countries should improve the transparency of the industrial property market in order to facilitate the technological choices of developing countries. In this respect, relevant organizations of the United Nations system, with the collaboration of developed countries, should undertake projects in the fields of information, consultancy and training for the benefit of developing countries.

7. A United Nations Conference on Science and Technology for Development should be held in 1978 or 1979 with the main objectives of strengthening the technological capacity of developing countries to enable them to apply science and technology to their own development; adopting effective means for the utilization of scientific and technological potentials in the solution of development problems of regional and global significance, especially for the benefit of developing countries; and providing instruments of cooperation to developing countries in the utilization of science and technology for solving socio-economic problems that cannot be solved by individual action, in accordance with national priorities, taking into account the recommendations made by the Intergovernmental Working Group of the Committee on Science and Technology for Development.

8. The United Nations system should play a major role, with appropriate financing,

in achieving the above-stated objectives and in developing scientific and technological cooperation between all States in order to ensure the application of science and technology to development. The work of the relevant United Nations bodies, in particular that of the United Nations Conference on Trade and Development, the United Nations Industrial Development Organization, the International Labour Organisation, the United Nations Educational, Scientific and Cultural Organization, the Food and Agriculture Organization of the United Nations, the World Intellectual Property Organization and the United Nations Development Programme, to facilitate the transfer and diffusion of technology should be given urgent priority. The Secretary-General of the United Nations should take steps to ensure that the technology and experience available within the United Nations system is widely disseminated and readily available to the developing countries in need of it.

9. The World Health Organization and the competent organs of the United Nations system, in particular the United Nations Children's Fund, should intensify the international effort aimed at improving health conditions in developing countries by giving priority to prevention of disease and malnutrition and by providing primary health services to the communities, including maternal and child health and family welfare.

10. Since the outflow of qualified personnel from developing to developed countries seriously hampers the development of the former, there is an urgent need to formulate national and international policies to avoid the 'brain drain' and to obviate its adverse effects.

IV. Industrialization

1. The General Assembly endorses the Lima Declaration and Plan of Action on Industrial Development Cooperation and requests all Governments to take individually and/or collectively the necessary measures and decisions required to implement effectively their undertakings in terms of the Lima Declaration and Plan of Action.

2. Developed countries should facilitate the development of new policies and strengthen existing policies, including labour market policies, which would encourage the redeployment of their industries which are less competitive internationally to developing countries, thus leading to structural adjustments in the former and a higher degree of utilization of natural and human resources in the latter. Such policies may take into account the economic structure and the economic, social and security objectives of the developed countries concerned and the need for such industries to move into more viable lines of production or into other sectors of the economy.

3. A system of consultations as provided for by the Lima Plan of Action should be established at the global, regional, interregional and sectoral levels within the United Nations Industrial Development Organization and within other appropriate international bodies, between developed and developing countries and among developing countries themselves, in order to facilitate the achievement of the goals

set forth in the field of industrialization, including the redeployment of certain productive capacities existing in developed countries and the creation of new industrial facilities in developing countries. In this context, the United Nations Industrial Development Organization should serve as a forum for negotiation of agreements in the field of industry between developed and developing countries and among developing countries themselves, at the request of the countries concerned.

4. The Executive Director of the United Nations Industrial Development Organization should take immediate action to ensure the readiness of that organization to serve as a forum for consultations and negotiation of agreements in the field of industry. In reporting to the next session of the Industrial Development Board on actions taken in this respect, the Executive Director should also include proposals for the establishment of a system of consultations. The Industrial Development Board is invited to draw up, at an early date, the rules of procedure according to which this system would operate.

5. To promote cooperation between developed and developing countries, both should endeavour to disseminate appropriate information about their priority areas for industrial cooperation and the form they would like such cooperation to take. The efforts undertaken by the United Nations Conference on Trade and Development on tripartite cooperation between countries having different economic and social systems could lead to constructive proposals for the industrialization of developing countries.

6. Developed countries should, whenever possible, encourage their enterprises to participate in investment projects within the framework of the development plans and programmes of the developing countries which so desire; such participation should be carried out in accordance with the laws and regulations of the developing countries concerned.

7. A joint study should be undertaken by all Governments under the auspices of the United Nations Industrial Development Organization, in consultation with the Secretary-General of the United Nations Conference on Trade and Development, making full use of the knowledge, experience and capacity existing in the United Nations system of methods and mechanisms for diversified financial and technical cooperation which are geared to the special and changing requirements of international industrial cooperation, as well as of a general set of guidelines for bilateral industrial cooperation. A progress report on this study should be submitted to the General Assembly at its thirty-first session.

8. Special attention should be given to the particular problems in the industrialization of the least developed, land-locked and island developing countries – in order to put at their disposal those technical and financial resources as well as critical goods which need to be provided to them to enable them to overcome their specific problems and to play their due role in the world economy, warranted by their human and material resources.

9. The General Assembly endorses the recommendation of the Second General Conference of the United Nations Industrial Development Organization to convert

that organization into a specialized agency and decides to establish a Committee on the Drafting of a Constitution for the United Nations Industrial Development Organization, which shall be an intergovernmental committee of the whole, including States which participated in the Second General Conference, to meet in Vienna to draw up a constitution for the United Nations Industrial Development Organization as a specialized agency, to be submitted to a conference of plenipotentiaries to be convened by the Secretary-General in the last quarter of 1976.

10. In view of the importance of the forthcoming Tripartite World Conference on Employment, Income Distribution, Social Progress and the International Division of Labour, Governments should undertake adequate preparations and consultations.

V. Food and Agriculture

1. The solution to world food problems lies primarily in rapidly increasing food production in the developing countries. To this end, urgent and necessary changes in the pattern of world food production should be introduced and trade policy measures should be implemented, in order to obtain a notable increase in agricultural production and the export earnings of developing countries.

2. To achieve these objectives, it is essential that developed countries, and developing countries in a position to do so, should substantially increase the volume of assistance to developing countries for agriculture and food production, and that developed countries should effectively facilitate access to their markets for food and agricultural products of export interest to developing countries, both in raw and processed form, and adopt adjustment measures, where necessary.

3. Developing countries should accord high priority to agricultural and fisheries development, increase investment accordingly and adopt policies which give adequate incentives to agricultural producers. It is a responsibility of each State concerned, in accordance with its sovereign judgement and development plans and policies, to promote interaction between expansion of food production and socio-economic reforms with a view to achieving an integrated rural development. The further reduction of post-harvest food losses in developing countries should be undertaken as a matter of priority, with a view to reaching at least a 50 per cent reduction by 1985. All countries and competent international organizations should cooperate financially and technically in the effort to achieve this objective. Particular attention should be given to improvement in the systems of distribution of food-stuffs.

4. The Consultative Group on Food Production and Investment in Developing Countries should quickly identify developing countries having the potential for most rapid and efficient increase of food production, as well as the potential for rapid agricultural expansion in other developing countries, especially the countries with food deficits. Such an assessment would assist developed countries and the competent international organizations to concentrate resources for the rapid increase of agricultural production in the developing countries.

5. Developed countries should adopt policies aimed at ensuring a stable supply and sufficient quantity of fertilizers and other production inputs to developing

countries at reasonable prices. They should also provide assistance to, and promote investments in, developing countries to improve the efficiency of their fertilizer and other agricultural input industries. Advantage should be taken of the mechanism provided by the International Fertilizer Supply Scheme.

6. In order to make additional resources available on concessional terms for agricultural development in developing countries, developed countries and developing countries in a position to do so should pledge, on a voluntary basis, substantial contributions to the proposed International Fund for Agricultural Development so as to enable it to come into being by the end of 1975, with initial resources of SDR 1,000 million. Thereafter, additional resources should be provided to the Fund on a continuing basis.

7. In view of the significant impact of basic and applied agricultural research on increasing the quantity and quality of food production, developed countries should support the expansion of the work of the existing international agricultural research centres. Through their bilateral programmes they should strengthen their links with these international research centres and with the national agricultural research centres in developing countries. With respect to the improvement of the productivity and competitiveness with synthetics of non-food agricultural and forestry products, research and technological assistance should be coordinated and financed through an appropriate mechanism.

8. In view of the importance of food aid as a transitional measure, all countries should accept both the principle of a minimum food aid target and the concept of forward planning of food aid. The target for the 1975–1976 session should be 10 million tons of food grains. They should also accept the principle that food aid should be channelled on the basis of objective assessment of requirements in the recipient countries. In this respect all countries are urged to participate in the Global Information and Early Warning System on Food and Agriculture.

9. Developed countries should increase the grant component of food aid, where food is not at present provided as grants, and should accept multilateral channelling of these resources at an expanding rate. In providing food grains and financing on soft terms to developing countries in need of such assistance, developed countries and the World Food Programme should take due account of the interests of the food-exporting developing countries and should ensure that such assistance includes, wherever possible, purchases of food from the food-exporting developing countries.

10. Developed countries, and developing countries in a position to do so, should provide food grains and financial assistance on most favourable terms to the most seriously affected countries, to enable them to meet their food and agricultural development requirements within the constraints of their balance-of-payments position. Donor countries should also provide aid on soft terms, in cash and in kind, through bilateral and multilateral channels, to enable the most seriously affected countries to obtain their estimated requirements of about 1 million tons of plant nutrients during 1975–1976.

11. Developed countries should carry out both their bilateral and multilateral food aid channelling in accordance with the procedures of the Principles of Surplus

Disposal of the Food and Agriculture Organization of the United Nations so as to avoid causing undue fluctuations in market prices or the disruption of commercial markets for exports of interest to exporting developing countries.

12. All countries should subscribe to the International Undertaking on World Food Security. They should build up and maintain world food-grain reserves, to be held nationally or regionally and strategically located in developed and developing, importing and exporting countries, large enough to cover foreseeable major production shortfalls. Intensive work should be continued on a priority basis in the World Food Council and other appropriate forums in order to determine, *inter alia*, the size of the required reserve, taking into account among other things the proposal made at the current session that the components of wheat and rice in the total reserve should be 30 million tons. The World Food Council should report to the General Assembly on this matter at its thirty-first session. Developed countries should assist developing countries in their efforts to build up and maintain their agreed shares of such reserves. Pending the establishment of the world food-grain reserve, developed countries and developing countries in a position to do so should earmark stocks and/or funds to be placed at the disposal of the World Food Programme as an emergency reserve to strengthen the capacity of the Programme to deal with crisis situations in developing countries. The aim should be a target of not less than 500,000 tons.

13. Members of the General Assembly reaffirm their full support for the resolutions of the World Food Conference and call upon the World Food Council to monitor the implementation of the provisions under section V of the present resolution and to report to the General Assembly at its thirty-first session.

VI. Cooperation among Developing Countries

1. Developed countries and the United Nations system are urged to provide, as and when requested, support and assistance to developing countries in strengthening and enlarging their mutual cooperation at subregional, regional and interregional levels. In this regard, suitable institutional arrangements within the United Nations development system should be made and, when appropriate, strengthened, such as those within the United Nations Conference on Trade and Development, the United Nations Industrial Development Organization and the United Nations Development Programme.

2. The Secretary-General, together with the relevant organizations of the United Nations system, is requested to continue to provide support to ongoing projects and activities, and to commission further studies through institutions in developing countries, which would take into account the material already available within the United Nations system, including in particular the regional commissions and the United Nations Conference on Trade and Development, and in accordance with existing subregional and regional arrangements. These further studies, which should be submitted to the General Assembly at its thirty-first session, should, as a first step, cover:

(*a*) Utilization of know-how, skills, natural resources, technology and funds available within developing countries for promotion of investments in industry, agriculture, transport and communications;

(*b*) Trade liberalization measures including payments and clearing arrangements, covering primary commodities, manufactured goods and services, such as banking, shipping, insurance and reinsurance;

(*c*) Transfer of technology.

3. These studies on cooperation among developing countries, together with other initiatives, would contribute to the evolution towards a system for the economic development of developing countries.

VII. Restructuring of the Economic and Social sectors of the United Nations System

1. With a view to initiating the process of restructuring the United Nations system so as to make it more fully capable of dealing with problems of international economic cooperation and development in a comprehensive and effective manner, in pursuance of General Assembly resolutions 3172 (XXVIII) of 17 December 1973 and 3343 (XXIX) of 17 December 1974, and to make it more responsive to the requirements of the provisions of the Declaration and the Programme of Action on the Establishment of a New International Economic Order as well as those of the Charter of Economic Rights and Duties of States, an *Ad Hoc* Committee on the Restructuring of the Economic and Social Sectors of the United Nations System, which shall be a committee of the whole of the General Assembly open to the participation of all States[1] is hereby established to prepare detailed action proposals. The *Ad Hoc* Committee should start its work immediately and inform the General Assembly at its thirtieth session on the progress made, and submit its report to the Assembly at its thirty-first session, through the Economic and Social Council at its resumed session. The *Ad Hoc* Committee should take into account in its work, *inter alia*, the relevant proposals and documentation submitted in preparation for the seventh special session of the General Assembly pursuant to Assembly resolution 3343 (XXIX) and other relevant decisions, including the report of the Group of Experts on the Structure of the United Nations System entitled *A New United Nations Structure for Global Economic Cooperation*, the records of the relevant deliberations of the Economic and Social Council, the Trade and Development Board, the Governing Council of the United Nations Development Programme and the seventh special session of the General Assembly, as well as the results of the forthcoming deliberations on institutional arrangements of the United Nations Conference on Trade and Development at its fourth session and of the Governing Council of the United Nations Environment Programme at its fourth session. All United Nations organs, including the regional commissions as well as the specialized agencies and the International

1 It is the understanding of the General Assembly that the 'all States' formula will be applied in accordance with the established practice of the General Assembly. [Footnote in original.]

Atomic Energy Agency, are invited to participate at the executive level in the work of the *Ad Hoc* Committee and to respond to requests that the Committee may make to them for information, data or views.

2. The Economic and Social Council should meanwhile continue the process of rationalization and reform which it has undertaken in accordance with Council resolution 1768 (LIV) of 18 May 1973 and General Assembly resolution 3341 (XXIX) of 17 December 1974, and should take into full consideration those recommendations of the *Ad Hoc* Committee that fall within the scope of these resolutions, at the latest at its resumed sixty-first session.

206. Statement issued following the meeting of the Heads of State or Government of France, the Federal Republic of Germany, Japan, Italy, Great Britain and the United States, Rambouillet, 17 November 1975[1]

The heads of states and governments of France, Federal Republic of Germany, Italy, Japan, the United Kingdom of Great Britain and Northern Ireland and the United States of America met in the Chateau de Rambouillet from 15 to 17 of November 1975, and agreed to declare as follows:

[1]

In these three days we held a searching and productive exchange of views on the world economic situation, on economic problems common to our countries, on their human, social and political implications and on plans for resolving them.

[2]

We came together because of shared beliefs and shared responsibilities. We are each responsible for the government of an open, democratic society dedicated to individual liberty and social advancement. Our success will strengthen, indeed is essential to, democratic societies everywhere. We are each responsible for assuring the prosperity of a major industrial economy. The growth and stability of our economies will help the entire industrial world and developing countries to prosper.

[3]

To assure in a world of growing interdependence the success of the objective set out in this declaration, we intend to play our own full part and strengthen our efforts for closer international cooperation and constructive dialogue among all countries, transcending differences in stages of economic development, degrees of resource endowment and political and social systems.

1 *New York Times*, 18 November 1975.

[4]

The industrial democracies are determined to overcome high unemployment, continuing inflation and serious energy problems. The purpose of our meeting was to review our progress, identify more clearly the problems that we must overcome in the future, and to set a course that we will follow in the period ahead.

[5]

The most urgent task is to assure the recovery of our economies and to reduce the waste of human resources involved in unemployment. In consolidating the recovery it is essential to avoid unleashing additional inflationary forces which would threaten its success. The objective must be growth that is steady and lasting. In this way consumer and business confidence will be restored.

[6]

We are confident that our present policies are compatible and complementary and that recovery is under way. Nevertheless, we recognize the need for vigilance and adaptability in our policies. We will not allow the recovery to falter. We will not accept another outburst of inflation.

[7]

We also concentrated on the need for new efforts in the areas of world trade, monetary matters and raw materials, including energy.

[8]

As domestic recovery and economic expansion proceed, we must seek to restore growth in the volume of world trade. Growth and price stability will be fostered by maintenance of an open trading system. In a period where pressures are developing for a return to protectionism, it is essential for the main trading nations to confirm their commitment to the principles of the OECD pledge and to avoid resorting to measures by which they could try to solve their problems at the expense of others, with damaging consequences in the economic, social and political fields. There is a responsibility on all countries, especially those with strong balance of payments positions and on those with current deficits, to pursue policies which will permit the expansion of world trade to their mutual advantage.

[9]

We believe that the multilateral trade negotiations should be accelerated. In accordance with the principles agreed in the Tokyo declaration, they should aim at achieving substantial tariff cuts, even eliminating tariffs in some areas, at significantly expanding agricultural trade and at reducing non-tariff measures. They should seek to achieve the maximum possible level of trade liberalization therefrom. We propose as our goal completion of the negotiations in 1977.

[10]

We look to an orderly and fruitful increase in our economic relations with socialist countries as an important element in progress in detente and in world economic growth.

[11]

We will also intensify our efforts to achieve a prompt conclusion of the negotiations concerning export credits.

[12]

With regard to monetary problems, we affirm our intention to work for greater stability. This involves efforts to restore greater stability in underlying economic and financial conditions in the world economy. At the same time, our monetary authorities will act to counter disorderly market conditions, or erratic fluctuations, in exchange rates. We welcome the rapprochement, reached at the request of many other countries, between the views of the US and France on the need for stability that the reform of the international monetary system must promote. This rapprochement will facilitate agreement through the IMF at the next session of the interim committee in Jamaica on the outstanding issues of international monetary reform.

[13]

A cooperative relationship and improved understanding between the developing nations and the industrial world is fundamental to the prosperity of each. Sustained growth in our economies is necessary to growth in developing countries: and their growth contributes significantly to health in our own economies.

[14]

The present large deficits in the current accounts of the developing countries represent a critical problem for them and also for the rest of the world. This must be dealt with in a number of complementary ways. Recent proposals in several international meetings have already improved the atmosphere of the discussion between developed and developing countries. But early practical action is needed to assist the developing countries. Accordingly, we will play our part, through the IMF and other appropriate international fora, in making urgent improvements in international arrangements for the stabilization of the export earnings of developing countries and in measures to assist them in financing their deficits. In this context, priority should be given to the poorest developing countries.

[15]

World economic growth is clearly linked to the increasing availability of energy sources. We are determined to secure for our economies the energy sources needed for their growth. Our common interests require that we continue to cooperate in order to reduce our dependence on imported energy through conservation and the development of alternative sources. Through these measures as well as international cooperation between producer and consumer countries, responding to the long-term interests of both, we shall spare no effort in order to insure more balanced conditions and a harmonious and steady development in the world energy market.

[16]

We welcome the convening of the conference on international economic cooperation scheduled for Dec. 16. We will conduct this dialogue in a positive spirit to assure that the interests of all concerned are protected and advanced. We believe that industrialized and developing countries alike have a critical stake in the future success of the world economy and in the cooperative political relationship on which it must be based.

[17]

We intend to intensify our cooperation on all these problems in the framework of existing institutions as well as in all the relevant international organizations.

207. Communiqué issued following the Conference on International Economic Cooperation, the 'North—South Conference', Paris, 19 December 1975[1]

1. The Conference on International Economic Cooperation met in Paris at ministerial level, from December 16 to December 19. Representatives of the following 27 members of the Conference took part: Algeria, Argentina, Australia, Brazil, Cameroon, Canada, EEC [European Economic Community], Egypt, India, Indonesia, Iran, Iraq, Jamaica, Japan, Mexico, Nigeria, Pakistan, Peru, Saudi Arabia, Spain, Sweden, Switzerland, United States, Venezuela, Yugoslavia, Zaire, Zambia. The ministerial representatives who attended the conference welcomed the presence of the Secretary-General of the United Nations.

2. The work of the Conference was opened by H. E. the President of the French Republic, Mr Valéry Giscard d'Estaing.

1 *DSB*, 12 January 1976, pp. 48–9.

3. The Hon. Allan J. MacEachen, Secretary of State for External Affairs of Canada, and Dr Manuel Perez-Guerrero, Minister of State for International Economic Affairs of Venezuela, co-chairmen of the Conference on International Economic Cooperation, presided at the ministerial meeting.

4. The ministerial representatives at the Conference expressed their views with regard to the international economic situation. They made suggestions as to how the problems which they had identified might be resolved. Attention was drawn to the plight of the most seriously affected countries. They recognized that the Conference on International Economic Cooperation provides a unique opportunity to address these problems and to further international economic cooperation for the benefit of all countries and peoples.

5. The Conference decided to initiate an intensified international dialogue. To this end, it established four Commissions (on energy, raw materials, development and financial affairs) which will meet periodically through the coming year. It was agreed that each of the four Commissions would consist of fifteen members, ten of them representing developing countries, five of them representing industrialized countries.

6. The Commissions shall start their work on February 11, 1976. Preparation for the work of the four commissions shall be reviewed at a meeting of the co-chairmen of the Conference and of the four Commissions after consultation with the other participants in the Conference. This meeting will take place on January 26, 1976 within the framework of the general guidelines contained in paragraphs 10—14 of the final declaration of the Second Preparatory Meeting which are approved by the Conference.

7. The Conference agreed that the following participants should serve on the Commissions:
 — Energy: Algeria, Brazil, Canada, Egypt, EEC, India, Iran, Iraq, Jamaica, Japan, Saudi Arabia, Switzerland, United States, Venezuela, Zaire.
 — Raw materials: Argentina, Australia, Cameroon, EEC, Indonesia, Japan, Mexico, Nigeria, Peru, Spain, United States, Venezuela, Yugoslavia, Zaire, Zambia.
 — Development: Algeria, Argentina, Cameroon, Canada, EEC, India, Jamaica, Japan, Nigeria, Pakistan, Peru, Sweden, United States, Yugoslavia, Zaire.
 — Finance: Brazil, EEC, Egypt, India, Indonesia, Iran, Iraq, Japan, Mexico, Pakistan, Saudi Arabia, Sweden, Switzerland, United States, Zambia.
The co-chairmen of the Commissions will be:
 — Energy: Saudi Arabia and United States.
 — Raw materials: Japan and Peru.
 — Development: Algeria and EEC.
 — Finance: EEC and Iran.
Joint meetings of the co-chairmen of the Conference and of the Commissions may be held if the need arises.

8. It was agreed that members of the Conference who wish to follow the work of a Commission to which they do not belong should be entitled to appoint a representative in the capacity of auditor without the right to speak.

9. The Conference decided that a number of inter-governmental functional organizations which are directly concerned with the problems to be considered would be able to make a useful contribution to their consideration. It therefore invited these organizations (United Nations Secretariat, OPEC, IEA, UNCTAD, OECD, FAO, GATT, UNDP, UNIDO, IMF, IBRD, SELA) to be represented on a permanent basis in the relevant commissions. Their observers will have the right to speak but not the right to vote and hence will not participate in the formation of a consensus. Each commission may, in addition, invite appropriate intergovernmental functional organizations to participate as observers *ad hoc* in the examination of specific questions.

10. The Conference decided to establish an international secretariat with an exclusively administrative and technical function on the basis of proposals put forward by the two co-chairmen. It named Mr Bernard Guitton [of France] as head of the secretariat and approved plans for its organization and operational procedures. The financial costs arising from the establishment of the secretariat and from future meetings of the Conference will be borne by members of the Conference on the basis of a formula agreed by the Conference.

11. It was agreed that the four Commissions should meet in Paris. Subsequent meetings of the Commissions will be convened by their co-chairmen.

12. One or several meetings of the Conference at the level of government officials may be held at least six months after this ministerial meeting. The Ministerial Conference agreed to meet again at ministerial level in about twelve months time.

13. The Conference adopted the rules of procedure recommended by the Preparatoy Meeting which are based on the principle of consensus, according to which decisions and recommendations are adopted when the chair has established that no member delegation has made any objection. English, Arabic, Spanish and French are the official and working languages of the Conference. The rules of procedure apply to all the bodies of the Conference.

14. The Conference took note of the resolution of the General Assembly entitled 'Conference on International Economic Cooperation' (Resolution 3515 (XXX)) and agreed to make reports available to the 31st session of the UN General Assembly.

15. The members of the Conference paid special tribute to President Giscard d'Estaing for the action he had taken to bring about the dialogue which is now engaged and expressed their warm appreciation to the Government of France for its hospitality and for the efforts and obligations it had undertaken in order to make the Ministerial Conference a success.